OXFORD EC LAW LIBRARY

General Editor: F. G. Jacobs
Advocate General, The Court of Justice
of the European Communities

EC COMPANY LAW

OXFORD EC LAW LIBRARY

The aim of this series is to publish important and original studies of the various branches of European Community Law. Each work will provide a clear, concise, and critical exposition of the law in its social, economic, and political context, at a level which will interest the advanced student, the practitioner, the academic, and government and Community officials.

Other Titles in the Library

EC Sex Equality Law
second edition
Evelyn Ellis

European Community Law of State Aid
Andrew Evans

External Relations of the European Communities
I. MacLeod, I. D. Hendry and Stephen Hyett

Directives in European Community Law
Sacha Prechal

EC Tax Law
Paul Farmer and Richard Lyal

EC Competition Law
third edition
D. G. Goyder

The European Internal Market and International Trade
Piet Eeckhout

The Law of Money and Financial Services in the European Community
J. A. Usher

Legal Aspects of Agriculture in the European Community
J. A. Usher

Trade and Environmental Law in the European Community
Andreas R. Ziegler

EC Company Law

VANESSA EDWARDS

CLARENDON PRESS · OXFORD
1999

Oxford University Press, Great Clarendon Street, Oxford OX2 6DP

Oxford New York

Athens Auckland Bangkok Bogotá Buenos Aires Calcutta
Cape Town Chennai Dar es Salaam Delhi Florence Hong Kong Istanbul
Karachi Kuala Lumpur Madrid Melbourne Mexico City Mumbai
Nairobi Paris São Paulo Singapore Taipei Tokyo Toronto Warsaw

and associated companies in
Berlin Ibadan

Oxford is a registered trade mark of Oxford University Press

Published in the United States
by Oxford University Press Inc., New York

British Library Cataloguing in Publication Data
Data available

Library of Congress Cataloging in Publication Data
Edwards, Vanessa.
EC company law / Vanessa Edwards
p. cm.—(Oxford European Community law series)
Includes bibliographical references and index.
1. Corporation Law—European Union countries. I. Series.
KJE2448.E39 1999 341.7'53—dc21 98–49312
ISBN 0–19–825993–X

1 3 5 7 9 10 8 6 4 2

Typeset in Bembo
by Hope Services (Abingdon) Ltd.
Printed in Great Britain
on acid-free paper by
Bookcraft Ltd., Midsomer Norton, Somerset

Outline Table of Contents

Detailed Table of Contents

General Editor's Foreword

Freedom of establishment and the freedom to provide services are cornerstones of the European single market. Companies and other commercial undertakings must be enabled to enjoy these freedoms if this market is to yield its benefits, or indeed to work at all. Community law has aims in this field which are extremely easy to formulate but less easy to achieve. Its aims are essentially on the one hand to enable companies to operate throughout the European Union as effectively as they can within a single Member State and to provide, for certain purposes, for the formation of transnational European bodies such as the European Economic Interest Grouping and the European Company, and on the other hand to ensure adequate protection for shareholders and others on the basis of uniform standards.

These aims have proved difficult to achieve because company law has special features. The company laws, the underlying theories of incorporation, the link between company and State of incorporation, and the structures of companies and other commercial undertakings differed greatly even among the original six Member States and still differ greatly among the fifteen Member States of today's European Union. Common European rules had to be superimposed on to differing national infrastructures.

Notwithstanding these difficulties, a substantial measure of harmonization has been achieved. There is an impressive framework of company law and securities directives. EC company law now constitutes a basic part of the equipment of the practitioner in this field.

The subject is also of wider interest. Precisely because of the special features of company law, it provides one of the best examples—perhaps indeed the best example —of the process of Community legislation by means of the directive. While regulations are directly applicable, upon enactment, in all Member States, directives are binding as to the result to be achieved but must be transposed by Member States to be accommodated into the national legal framework. For the reasons set out above company law could be harmonized only by directives, and the subject illustrates exceptionally well the process of legal harmonization. For that reason it appealed from the earliest days to scholars with an interest in transnational law.

Although the subject is now of great—and growing—practical importance, its significance is still not always fully appreciated. As the author points out, many practitioners do not yet seem to have grasped the impact of Community law in this field—a situation which contrasts strikingly with other fields of Community law. The publication of this book provides the practitioner and scholar with a comprehensive and authoritative treatment of the subject and will greatly increase the understanding of, and interest in, EC company law.

Francis G. Jacobs

But as to listening to what one lawyer says without asking another—
I wonder at a man o' your cleverness, Mr Dill. It's well known there's
always two sides, if no more; else who'd go to law, I should like to
know?

Middlemarch
George Eliot

Preface

This book seeks to explore in some depth the two major aspects of European Community company law: the Treaty provisions concerning the right of establishment of companies and the company law and securities law harmonization programme. The case-law of the European Court of Justice on Article 52 of the EC Treaty in so far as it applies to corporate entities is reviewed in full and all the adopted company law and securities directives are analysed in detail, with emphasis in particular on their historical context, legislative history, scope, substantive effect, interpretation by the Court of Justice, and implementation in the United Kingdom.

It is hoped that the book will be of interest to both company law practitioners and academics in the United Kingdom and further afield. Although I have frequently referred to issues arising out of the United Kingdom's implementation of the company law and securities directives, the book is intended for a wider audience: such bias as there is reflects my own background and my consequent awareness of a somewhat parochial attitude to company and securities law which is apparent in the United Kingdom. Weatherill and Beaumont make the point in their comprehensive work *EC Law* that the impact of the company law directives is such that no company lawyer can operate without a secure knowledge of the Community dimension.[1] Unfortunately this is not a view widely held in either the City or the Temple, notwithstanding the fact that much of the companies and securities legislation enacted since the United Kingdom's accession to the EC, including the Companies Acts 1980, 1981 and 1989, implements EC legislation. The result is that the bulk of United Kingdom legislation on ultra vires, pre-incorporation contracts, maintenance and alteration of capital, annual and consolidated accounts, qualification of auditors, Stock Exchange listing conditions and public offers of listed and unlisted securities, acquisitions and disposals of major shareholdings, and insider dealing derives from EC Directives. To the extent that this book prompts company lawyers to take account of the European roots of domestic legislation, the effort will have been worthwhile.

I have for this first edition used the numbering of the Treaty articles in the Treaty on European Union before the forthcoming amendment by the Treaty of Amsterdam; the index of legislation shows equivalents. The law is in general stated as at 31 July 1998; developments up to 30 September 1998 have however been briefly footnoted. Inevitably there have been developments since then, the most important of which is a further compromise on the European Company Statute put forward by the Austrian Presidency at the end of October. The draft Takeovers

---

[1] 2nd edn (1995), 601.

Directive, on the other hand, suffered a further setback in October after a meeting of delegates from Member States collapsed in serious disagreement.

I have been extremely fortunate in writing the book while working at the European Court of Justice, where I have had ready access both to colleagues who have been prepared to spare me much valued time and to the excellent library resources. I have also been able to use the results of research undertaken in the context of a doctoral thesis. I would like to extend particular thanks to the following: Francis Jacobs, who both gave me the opportunity to write this book and provided much encouragement while I was doing so; Paul Farmer, who has nobly read and commented on each chapter as it was written; Angus Mackay, who agreed to my working half time for four months to enable me to make a start on the book; Mads Andenas, Mary Arden, David Edward, Piet Eeckhout, Peter King, Barry Rider, Jackie Suter, Takis Tridimas and Jan Wouters, who have read and commented on various chapters; Giovanni Mendola at DGXV, who provided me with information about recent legislative developments; Julie Mackeonis (as she then was), Caroline Morgan and Shelagh Taylor, who took time to track down obscure documents for me, and Linklaters & Paines, who provided me with much useful information; Hilary Thompson, who made my manuscript look like a manuscript, and Posy Gosling, who turned it into a document fit for the printers; Dominique Till, who created a coherent bibliography out of a mountain of books and scraps of paper; and Douglas Green, who spent a summer in Luxembourg checking references. Finally, I would mention the late Jim Gower, without whose immensely readable book I would never have developed an interest in company law, and Steven Turnbull, without whose guidance I would never have continued it.

Vanessa Edwards
November 1998

Table of Cases

EUROPEAN COURT OF JUSTICE: ALPHABETICAL LIST OF CASES

EUROPEAN COURT OF JUSTICE: NUMERICAL LIST OF CASES

UNITED KINGDOM CASES

Table of Legislation

Decisions

Directives

Draft Legislation

Directives

Statutory Instruments (in alphabetical order)

I

Introduction and Overview of the Company Law Harmonization Programme

In 1973, the first year of the United Kingdom's membership of the European Community, Professor Schmitthoff[1] wrote: 'Company law will be the first branch of law which will emerge as a truly European law.'[2] A quarter of a century later, the prediction of a truly European company law (even if it is not necessarily the first branch) may be described as significantly realized: Community legislation now regulates companies' disclosure and publicity requirements,[3] the legality of pre-incorporation and ultra vires transactions,[4] the nullity of companies,[5] the formation of public companies and the maintenance and alteration of their capital,[6] mergers and divisions of public companies,[7] companies' annual and consolidated accounts,[8] the qualification of company auditors,[9] disclosure by cross-frontier branches of companies,[10] single-member companies,[11] admission to Stock Exchange listing,[12] public offers of listed and unlisted securities,[13] acquisitions and disposals of major shareholdings,[14] and insider dealing.[15] Draft legislation is on the table and, after in some cases many decades of delay, seems increasingly likely to be adopted by the millennium, providing a statute for a European Company[16] and regulating cross-border mergers of public companies,[17] takeovers[18] and the cross-border transfer of a company's seat or registered office.[19] The draft Fifth Directive on the structure of public companies and the powers and obligations of their organs, even though it has now been pronounced clinically dead, may yet lead to a future code on corporate governance.[20] Moreover the right of companies established in the European Community to create secondary establishments in other Member States by

---

[1] At that time Visiting Professor in International Business Law at the City University, London, and the University of Kent at Canterbury and Hon Professor of Law at the Ruhr-Universität Bochum.

[2] 'Company and Commercial Law in Europe' in Cheng, C-J (ed), *Clive M. Schmitthoff's Select Essays on International Trade Law* (1988) 74, 78.

[3] 1st Directive: see ch II.   [4] 1st Directive.   [5] 1st Directive.

[6] 2nd Directive: see ch III.   [7] 3rd and 6th Directives: see ch IV.

[8] 4th and 7th Directives: see chs V and VI.   [9] 8th Directive: see ch VII.

[10] 11th Directive: see ch VIII.   [11] 12th Directive: see ch IX.

[12] The Admissions and Listing Particulars Directives: see ch XI.

[13] The Public Offers Prospectus Directive: see ch XII.

[14] The Major Shareholdings Directive: see ch XIV.

[15] The Insider Dealing Directive: see ch XV.

[16] See ch XIX.   [17] Draft 10th Directive: see ch XIX.

[18] Draft 13th Directive: see ch XIX.   [19] Draft 14th Directive: see ch XVIII.

[20] See chs XVIII and XIX.

branches, agencies or subsidiaries, conferred by Articles 52 and 58 of the Treaty,[21] has been developed and strengthened by a series of cases before the European Court of Justice (generally referred to in this book as the Court of Justice). It is undeniable that there is now a substantial corpus of legislative and judge-made European Community company law; this body of law forms the subject-matter of this book.

The adopted directives (the First, Second, Third, Fourth, Sixth, Seventh, Eighth, Eleventh and Twelfth company law directives and the securities directives) and the case-law of the Court of Justice on companies' freedom of establishment are dealt with in detail; the way in which the directives have been implemented in the United Kingdom is also discussed where it is of particular interest. The draft directives which look increasingly likely to be adopted in the near future, together with the draft Fifth Directive and the draft Ninth Directive on groups of companies, which are unlikely to be revived, are discussed briefly in the conclusion (chapter XX); it is hoped to include in a subsequent edition full chapters on the pending legislation once adopted. Article 220 of the Treaty, which requires Member States, so far as necessary, to enter into negotiations with each other with a view to securing for the benefit of their nationals, inter alia, the mutual recognition of companies and firms, and the draft Fourteenth Directive are discussed in chapter XVIII.

The adoption of regulations providing for the creation of supra-national business entities is a parallel approach to harmonization for the facilitation of the cross-border conduct of business by companies. The Regulation on the European Economic Interest Grouping (EEIG)[22] and the proposed Regulation for a European Company[23] are both based on Article 235 of the Treaty, which provides for the Council, acting unanimously on a Proposal from the Commission, to take 'the appropriate measures' if Community action proves 'necessary to attain, in the course of the operation of the common market, one of the objectives of the Community' and the Treaty has not provided the necessary powers. The EEIG is a legal vehicle with legal personality which shares some of the features of a company and some of an unincorporated association, intended to enable natural persons, companies and firms to cooperate in the conduct of business across borders without losing their independence. It is fiscally transparent, so that only its members are taxed. Certain aspects of the EEIG are governed by the EEIG Regulation, others by the law of the Member State where it has its official address. The EEIG is the subject of extensive literature,[24] and is not further considered in this book.

---

[21] Used throughout this book to mean the Treaty establishing the European Community, originally the Treaty of Rome signed on 25 March 1957, subsequently amended by the Single European Act 1986 and the Treaty on European Union 1992 (the Maastricht Treaty). The Treaty of Amsterdam 1997 makes no substantive change to Arts 52 and 58 but renumbers them as Arts 43 and 48.

[22] Council Reg (EEC) 2137/85 on the European Economic Interest Grouping (EEIG) [1985] OJ L199/1.

[23] Amended Proposal for a Council Reg (EEC) on the Statute for a European Company COM (91) 174 final, 6 May 1991; [1991] OJ C176/1.

[24] For recent examples see Anderson, M, *European Economic Interest Groupings* (1990); Van Gerven, D and Aalders, C A V, *European Economic Interest Groupings: The EEC Regulation and its Application in the*

The Proposal for a regulation for the European Company, which in 1998 looks likely to be adopted within the next couple of years after a long and difficult gestation period, is considered briefly in the conclusion to this book (chapter XX); again, it is hoped that a future edition will give full coverage to this important instrument in full detail once adopted.

This Introduction will consider the history and effectiveness of the company law harmonization programme. There is a separate introduction to the securities directives in chapter X and a separate introduction to the chapters on companies' freedom of establishment in chapter XVI.

The Treaty framework

The cornerstone of the Treaty[25] is the establishment of a common market.[26] For that purpose inter alia the activities of the Community are to include the abolition, as between Member States, of obstacles to the free movement of goods, persons, services and capital[27] and the approximation of the laws of Member States to the extent required for the functioning of the common market.[28] There are a number of reasons why divergences in national company laws are likely to frustrate the goal of an optimally functioning internal market. Such divergences are liable primarily to distort competition: if national company laws governing important areas of creditor and shareholder protection and company management are fundamentally different, this may be expected to create a European 'Delaware effect', encouraging the establishment of new companies in the Member State with the laxest laws. Corporate decisions to expand across frontiers, which in a perfect internal market should be taken solely on economic grounds, may be significantly influenced by the relative burden of domestic regulation. Differing laws will impose administrative burdens on companies with subsidiaries in several Member States. Equivalent creditor and shareholder protection should encourage cross-border credit and investment, and, once companies are free to move their seat or registered office to another Member State, should ensure that members and creditors are not prejudiced by the relocation.

Member States of the European Community (1990); Prime, T, Gale, S and Scanlan, G, *The Law and Practice of Joint Ventures* (1997); Abell, M, 'The European Economic Interest Grouping' (1990) 12 Comparative Law Yearbook of International Business 169; Murphy, D T, 'The European Economic Interest Group (EEIG): A New European Business Entity' (1990) 23 Vanderbilt Journal of Transnational Law 65; Keegan, S, 'The European Economic Interest Grouping' [1991] JBL 457; Dine, J, 'The European Economic Interest Grouping and the European Company Statute: New Models for Company Law Harmonisation' in Andenas, M and Kenyon-Slade, S (eds), *EC Financial Market Regulation and Company Law* (1993); Mackay, R, 'The European Economic Interest Grouping' in *Corporate Law—The European Dimension* (1991); and the relevant chapter in Wooldridge, F, *Company Law in the United Kingdom and the European Community* (1991).

[25] See n 20 above.   [26] See Art 2.
[27] Art 3(c).   [28] Art 3(h).

Community legislation must be based on a specific Treaty provision empowering the Community legislature to adopt the measure in question. There are several such provisions, and the choice of the appropriate legal basis for a particular measure will determine the legislative procedure to be followed. It may also be relevant in order to identify the objectives of the legislation. A Community legislative measure may be challenged before the European Court of Justice on the basis that its express legal basis is not the correct basis for the measure: the power of the Court to annul incorrectly adopted legislation explains the intensity of some of the debate about legal basis and illustrates the importance of choosing the correct basis.

The Treaty basis for the company law harmonization programme is Article 54(3)(g). Articles 100 and, in the case of the Insider Dealing Directive, 100a have been used in some cases as an additional or alternative legal basis for the securities directives. Since investor protection is a clear objective of all the securities directives and since it is clear from the preamble to all these directives that market integration is a direct and specific aim, there is little room for doubt as to the appropriateness of their legal basis. There has accordingly been relatively little debate about the legal basis of the securities directives, except a brief skirmish in the case of the Insider Dealing Directive: see further chapter XV. The same cannot be said for the company law directives, at least in the early days.

Article 54(3)(g), set in Chapter 2, 'Right of establishment', in Title III, 'Free movement of persons, services and capital', provides:

The Council[29] and the Commission shall carry out the duties devolving upon them under the preceding provisions,[30] in particular:

. . .

(g) by coordinating to the necessary extent the safeguards which, for the protection of the interests of members and others, are required by Member States of companies or firms within the meaning of the second paragraph of Article 58[31] with a view to making such safeguards equivalent throughout the Community.

Article 100, set in the chapter on the approximation of laws (Chapter 3 of Title V, 'Common rules on competition, taxation and approximation of laws'), requires the Council, acting unanimously, to issue directives for the approximation of such legislative and administrative provisions 'as directly affect the establishment or functioning of the common market'. Article 100a introduced a different procedure for the adoption of measures having as their object the establishment and functioning of the internal market: a qualified majority in the Council suffices.

Since all the numbered company law directives are based on Article 54(3)(g),[32]

---

[29] Acting by qualified majority: see Art 148(2) of the Treaty for details of the operation of the qualified majority.

[30] Arts 52 and 53 requiring the abolition, and prohibiting the introduction, of restrictions on the freedom of establishment of nationals of a Member State in the territory of another Member State. See chs XVI to XVIII on the scope of the Treaty right of establishment for companies.

[31] See ch XVI for a discussion of the scope of Art 58.

[32] Although the formula is frequently the more cautious 'having regard to the Treaty . . ., in particular Article 54(3)(g) thereof . . .'.

it is the scope of that provision which will provide the focus for discussion of the harmonization programme.

The scope of Article 54(3)(g)

Early history

The proper scope of harmonization of company law under Article 54(3)(g) was the topic of a particularly lively debate in the early stages of the programme. Stein[33] relates how in the early days of the Community two rival camps, each claiming jurisdiction over certain aspects of company law, rapidly developed within the Commission. Initially, the Treaty chapter dealing with freedom of establishment, including Article 54(3)(g), was allocated to the Directorate General for the Internal Market, DG III, while the chapter on the approximation of laws, including Article 100, was allocated to the Directorate General of Competition, DG IV. DG IV established a separate 'directorate' for harmonization of law, which was to include company law.

DG III argued that Article 54(3)(g), as a *lex specialis* in the field of coordination of company law, prevailed over the *lex generalis* enshrined in Article 100. Since there was, in the view of DG III, virtually no provision in company law which would not concern the protection of either third parties or shareholders, it concluded that practically the whole of company law was covered by Article 54(3)(g). DG III moreover invoked in support of its view the different voting procedures laid down by the two provisions: Article 54(3)(g) required only a qualified majority in the Council, whereas Article 100 required unanimity. It was argued that unanimity would be particularly difficult to achieve in the area of company law, where the laws of one of the original six Member States (the Netherlands, the others being Belgium, France, Germany, Italy and Luxembourg) differed significantly from those of the other, legally more homogenous, five. Subsuming part of company law under Article 100 would seriously jeopardize any prospect of effective harmonization of the area.

DG IV also focused on the wording of Article 54(3)(g), but argued that the provision was restricted to a limited number of basic 'guarantees' such as the publication of the company's statutes and accounts and the maintenance of capital. The argument based on voting procedures was countered with the view that the difference in the voting requirement between the two provisions must reflect a distinction between important and less important areas and that unanimity would encourage more fruitful cooperation, since Member States would not fear being outvoted.

Professor Stein describes this controversy as 'without doubt a major cause of the initial delay in the Commission's work'.[34] It gradually waned in intensity and was resolved in 1967 with the merger of the executive bodies of the three

---

[33] Stein, E, *Harmonization of European Company Laws* (1971), ch 5.   [34] Ibid 178.

Communities (the European Coal and Steel Community, the European Economic Community and the European Atomic Energy Community). In the ensuing reorganization, all commercial and company law harmonization work was allocated to a single new Directorate General for the Internal Market and the Approximation of Legislation. However, although the internal divisions which had been responsible for delaying progress in company law harmonization were now healed, they cast a long shadow. In 1965, DG III had appointed five academics as permanent special consultants on company law to assist it in developing a comparative analytical study of national company law. These included Professor Houin of the Paris law faculty. DG IV, unambiguously responsible for progressing negotiations for conventions as required by Article 220,[35] had established working groups to prepare legal conventions on several topics within the scope of the Article, including the company law issues there mentioned (the mutual recognition of companies, the maintenance of their legal personality in case of a seat transfer, and merger of companies subject to the laws of different Member States). The advisers to that group included Professor Rodière, also of the Paris law faculty. Professors Houin and Rodière took different views of the scope of Article 54(3)(g), each in line with the general approach of the Directorate General which they advised, and in 1965 they each published a strong exposé of their arguments in the *Revue trimestrielle de droit européen*.[36]

The debate having thus moved into the public domain, it gathered momentum, doubtless helped by the Commission's Proposals issued in 1964 and 1966 (see chapter II) for a first company law directive based on Article 54(3)(g) which gave practical flesh to an argument hitherto theoretical. Other writers took up the torch[37] and the issue was still being hotly debated in the 1970s.

The broad and the narrow view

In outline, the advocates of a restrictive interpretation of Article 54(3)(g) argued that, given its place in the Treaty, the provision authorizes legislative intervention only where that is necessary to cure a specific discriminatory national rule or practice which prevents companies established in other Member States exercising their right of establishment and where the Community 'cure' also renders equivalent

---

[35] See further ch XVIII, pp 384–5.

[36] Houin, R, 'Le régime juridique des sociétés dans la Communauté Economique Européenne' [1965] Revue trimestrielle de droit européen 11; Rodière, R, 'L'harmonisation des législations européennes dans le cadre de la C.E.E.' [1965] Revue trimestrielle de droit européen 336.

[37] For writings in English, see Ault, H J, 'Harmonization of Company Law in the European Economic Community' (1968) 20 Hastings Law Journal 77; Scholten, Y, 'Company Law in Europe' (1967) 4 CMLR 377; Sanders, P, 'Review of Recent Literature on Corporation Law' (196–7) 4 CMLR 113, 119–20 and, some years later, Ficker, H C, 'The EEC Directives on Company Law Harmonisation' in Schmitthoff, C M (ed), *The Harmonisation of European Company Law* (1973), 66. For French and German sources see the articles cited by Stein, E, *Harmonization of European Company Laws* (1971), 192–3, n 45, 67–8, and sources cited in n 4. For a comprehensive review of the various arguments see Van Ommeslaghe, P, 'La première directive du conseil du 9 mars 1968 en matière de sociétés' [1969] Cahiers de droit européen 495, 502–16 and for further sources see the articles cited in nn 15, 16 and 18 of his article.

specific safeguards for the protection of the interests of members and/or others. Such a view would exclude from the scope of the Article directives seeking in more general terms to assimilate throughout the Community the legislative framework governing a particular area. The proponents of a broader view argued that the architects of the Treaty considered company law sufficiently important to require a specific article. Article 54(3)(g) seeks rather to ensure that, for the reasons suggested above,[38] once a company from another Member State has exercised its right of establishment in a Member State, its members and creditors are treated in a broadly comparable manner to members and creditors of a company originally established in the latter State. Seen from this perspective, virtually all areas of company law come within the scope of the provision. In between these two extremes was a spectrum of more or less tempered versions of one or other view.

The arguments in favour of a restrictive interpretation of Article 54(3)(g), however compelling they may have seemed thirty years ago when the company law harmonization programme was still embryonic, can no longer be regarded as convincing. Nine directives covering very diverse areas of company law have now been adopted and implemented on the basis of Article 54(3)(g) without legal challenge. While company law harmonization is not an end in itself, so that Article 54(3)(g) undoubtedly requires a link between the legislation adopted thereunder and the facilitation of companies' right of establishment,[39] that goal calls for a generous construction in accordance with the general approach developed by the Court of Justice over the last three decades to the interpretation of Treaty provisions. Harmonization measures which prima facie have little immediate impact on cross-border establishment will in any event normally be found on closer scrutiny indirectly to smooth the path of cross-border establishment. Even the Third and Sixth Directives on domestic mergers and divisions of public companies, which appear to focus purely on domestic matters, have on examination of their historical context a wider role, namely preparing the ground for a parallel instrument regulating cross-border mergers: it is obviously in the interests of companies that domestic and cross-border mergers should be regulated along the same lines rather than be subject to differing rules with consequential expense.[40] Similarly, directives with narrow ambits and specific, apparently protective, goals, such as the Eleventh Directive on branch disclosure[41] and the Twelfth Directive[42] on single-member companies, in fact facilitate cross-border establishment: the former is designed to reduce administrative burdens on branches of companies established in other

---

[38] See p 3.

[39] See, e g, Case C–122/96 *Saldanha and MTS Securities Corporation v Hiross Holding* [1997] ECR I–5325, where the Court of Justice stated that Art 54(3)(g) 'empowers the Council and the Commission, for the purpose of giving effect to the freedom of establishment, to coordinate to the necessary extent the safeguards . . .' (para 23).

[40] The 3rd Directive was in that sense premature, since the Convention on cross-border mergers which it was intended to mirror became enmired in the familiar ground of employee protection: see further ch XIX. The 6th Directive, although not directly relevant to the harmonization of domestic and cross-border mergers, was intimately linked to the 3rd Directive: see further ch IV.

[41] See ch VIII.   [42] See ch IX.

Member States, the latter to ensure equivalent protection for creditors of single-member companies. Finally, in the area of secondary establishment at least, Article 54(3)(g) would be redundant in the present state of Community law if it solely authorized measures invalidating specific national obstacles, since the Court of Justice has appropriated that role in its case-law.[43]

The terms of Article 54(3)(g)

Article 54(3)(g) refers to 'coordinating' certain areas of company law. Other terms used elsewhere in the Treaty are 'approximation' and 'harmonization' of laws. Scrutiny of the Treaty supports the common sense view that there is no significant distinction to be drawn between these three terms. Through accidents of translation, moreover, the pattern of use of the three terms is not faithfully reflected in the other official language versions of the Treaty. The most that can usefully be said, which again accords with common sense and a natural use of language, is that all three processes fall short of unification. That conclusion is confirmed by the end result spelled out in Article 54(3)(g): 'with a view to making such safeguards equivalent' rather than identical or uniform.[44] There are however areas where in practice only unification will bring about equivalence: for example, if it is sought to protect third parties by mandatory disclosure of the company's constitution then, since either a document requires disclosure or it does not, harmonization in this area will amount to the imposition of a uniform rule.

Article 54(3)(g) requires coordination 'to the necessary extent [of] the safeguards which, for the protection of the interests of members and others, are required by Member States of companies or firms'.[45] The Article leaves open the scope of 'safeguards . . . for the protection of the interests of members and others' and the question which persons are covered by 'others'. There is obvious scope for debate as to what is necessary, and why: the spectrum ranges from the view that only a minimum level throughout the Community is necessary to the view that all members, creditors and employees of companies established throughout the Community should benefit from uniform rights.

The Treaty is of course not static. A cursory glance at the directives adopted to date reveals the shift of emphasis that has taken place in the harmonization programme: the early measures focused on coordinating specific safeguards (for example, disclosure, validating corporate transactions, restricting the circumstances in which the nullity of a company could be declared,[46] setting a minimum capital

---

[43] See further ch XVII.

[44] See generally Ficker, H C, 'The EEC Directives on Company Law Harmonisation' in Schmitthoff, C M (ed), *The Harmonisation of European Company Law* (1973) 66, 67–8, and sources cited in Ault, H J, 'Harmonization of Company Law in the European Economic Community' (1968) 20 Hastings Law Journal 77, n 4, and Van Ommeslaghe, P, 'La première directive du conseil du 9 mars 1968 en matière de sociétés' [1969] Cahiers de droit européen 495, 513–16.

[45] To date, the harmonization programme has been restricted to companies, with some directives limited to public companies. See ch II for a list of the types of company subject to the 1st Directive, applicable also *mutatis mutandis* to subsequent directives.

[46] 1st Directive.

requirement and ensuring it could not be circumvented[47]). In the historical context, in which it was sought to bridge the gaps between, very broadly, the divergent approaches of the Netherlands on the one hand and those of the other original Member States on the other,[48] it was natural and necessary to concentrate on one piece of the legislative jigsaw at a time. More recently, the stress has been on removing obstacles and barriers: see, for example, the Eleventh Directive on disclosure by branches. This latter approach is particularly apparent in the legislation which finally looks likely to move after years, sometimes decades, of deadlock: the Thirteenth Directive on takeovers and the European Company Statute are primarily instruments to facilitate cross-border corporate transactions (as is the proposed Fourteenth Directive), although they include extremely important (albeit much watered down in the case of the European Company Statute) safeguards for shareholders and employees respectively.

The suitability of directives as the instrument of harmonization

Article 54 requires the Council to act in the fields which that Article covers by way of directives. Directives are initially proposed by the Commission and ultimately adopted by the Council, once approved by the requisite majority. In between the preliminary and final stage there is, since the Single European Act 1986, in the case of directives adopted under Articles 54 and 100a, a complex and lengthy procedure involving the European Parliament.[49] In addition, both Articles 54 and 100a require the Council to obtain the opinion of the Economic and Social Committee.

Article 189 of the Treaty defines the function of a directive: it shall be binding, as to the result to be achieved, upon each Member State to which it is addressed, but shall leave to the national authorities the choice of form and methods. It is questionable whether the former limb of that definition can be regarded as definitive, given the existence of directives[50] containing numerous highly specific and prescriptive provisions which are difficult to reconcile with the notion of a directive as expressed in Article 189. The second limb, however, remains essential to the concept of a directive: it requires transposition at national level.[51]

---

[47] 2nd Directive.

[48] Historically, the company law of the original six Member States developed in parallel, culminating in France with the five codes created by Napoleon I between 1804 and 1811. Thereafter, differences developed in particular in relation to the public company, which became closely regulated in the five Member States other than the Netherlands, which all had a private company form subject to simpler rules. The Netherlands on the other hand had no private company form until 1971 (see ch II); public companies, which were vehicles for both small and large undertakings, were subject to more flexible and less onerous rules.

[49] See Art 189b.

[50] This tendency is well illustrated in the company law field: see, e g, some of the detailed requirements of the 2nd, 4th and 7th Directives.

[51] Although in certain circumstances some provisions may have direct effect: see further below.

The use of options and alternatives

There has been much criticism of the efficacy of directives as an instrument of harmonization. Notwithstanding the above-noted tendency for directives to be more detailed and prescriptive than the architects of the Treaty may have envisaged, many of the company law directives contain numerous alternatives and options,[52] so that their contribution to harmonization is perceived by some as illusory. Similar consequences flow from the frequently used technique[53] by which a directive lays down 'minimum standards' which, though mandatory, may be bolstered by Member States' imposing more stringent or additional rules, although at least in this case a central core of uniform norms should result. In practice however even those directives which most resort to these various techniques are widely recognized as having made a significant contribution to the establishment of improved equivalent norms in important areas such as disclosure of information to investors.[54]

It must also be remembered that the use of alternatives, options and minimum standards frequently reflects national differences which could not be bridged otherwise than by compromise, so that the alternative to a less than perfect harmonizing directive may well have been no Community legislation in that area. That this is a real risk is shown in the field of worker participation, where divergences between national laws are particularly wide: those differences have 'held hostage'[55] progress on the draft Fifth, Tenth and Thirteenth Directives and the European Company Statute for, in some cases, several decades.[56]

The requirement of implementation

The requirement that a directive be implemented in order to have effect in national law is a further weakness of this type of instrument, although increasingly tempered by the readiness of the Court of Justice to accord vertical[57] direct effect to unconditional and sufficiently precise provisions of a directive which have not been adequately implemented by the prescribed deadline. For examples in company law, see the Greek cases on Articles 25 and 29 of the Second Directive discussed in chapter III. Although the Commission has the role of monitoring national implementation

---

[52] See in particular the 4th and 7th Directives, discussed in chs V and VI respectively, the rules on the acquisition by a company of its own shares in the 2nd Directive, discussed in ch III, and the 6th Directive, wholly optional for Member States which do not already permit division of public companies, discussed in ch IV. See also the worker participation provisions in the European Company Statute and the draft 5th Directive, discussed in ch XIX.

[53] See, e g, the securities directives discussed in chs X–XIII.

[54] In particular, the accounting and securities directives.

[55] Gordon, M W, 'European Community Company Law' in Folsom, R H, Lake, R B and Nanda, V P (eds), *European Community Law After 1992* (1993) 531, 556.

[56] See ch XIX.

[57] i e, the directive may be invoked only against the Member State concerned, not against individuals.

and pursuing defaulting Member States before the Court of Justice, its ability to do so is circumscribed by practical limitations.[58]

Petrification

Some commentators have expressed concern about the so-called danger of petrification inherent in legislation by directives, namely the risk that, because of the cumbersome legislative process involved, the provisions of a directive will prove resistant to evolution. Although that argument is superficially persuasive, experience does not appear to bear it out, at least in the company law field. The Second and Fourth Directives and the Listing Particulars Directives have, for example, been amended with little trouble to shape them to changing needs. Moreover, since the Single European Act 1986 the Commission's 'powers of implementation' under Article 145 of the Treaty enable it to make technical changes to the details of harmonizing directives by way of secondary legislation, without the need to consult the European Parliament; this procedure should make more flexible the procedure for amending legislation in matters other than those of substance.[59]

Evaluation of the harmonization process

Certain criticisms of the company law harmonization programme have been touched upon above, in the context of the suitability of directives as the instrument of harmonization. Assessing the success or failure of harmonization also raises more general issues.

Problems where legal notions are not coterminous

A particular problem in seeking to harmonize the laws of numerous Member States with disparate legal traditions is the difficulty in dovetailing legal concepts. A

---

[58] Wolff, G, Head of Unit for Company Law, Industrial Democracy and Accounting Standards in DG XV, recounted in 1992 how, when the Community comprised twelve Member States and there were nine official languages, there were only three lawyers and three accountants whose role was to check more than 100 national laws implementing adopted directives in addition to drafting new proposals or negotiating proposals already made: 'The Commission's Programme for Company Law Harmonisation: The Winding Road to a Uniform European Company Law?' in Andenas, M and Kenyon-Slade, S, *EC Financial Market Regulation and Company Law* (1993) 19, 24. Similarly in relation to investor protection and securities regulation, Professor Gower reports how the relevant Directorates and the Secretariat 'expressed particular gratitude for [Gower's initial Discussion Document reviewing the UK system of securities regulation and advising on new legislation, subsequently enacted as the Financial Services Act 1986] which, they said, had enabled them for the first time to understand what the regulatory position was in the United Kingdom and they lamented that they lacked similar reviews of the position in other Member States. But when I suggested that they might commission such studies, they replied that they could not afford it: "Do you not realize that our budget is less than that of the Hampshire County Council?"': Buxbaum, R M, Hertig G, Hirsch, A and Hopt, K J (eds), *European Business Law* (1991) 314, n 26.

[59] For general discussion of the arguments for and against the risk of petrification, see Buxbaum, R M and Hopt, K J, *Legal Harmonization and the Business Enterprise* (1988) 235–6, 242–3, 265, and the contributions of Fitchew, G, Timmermans, C, Tunc, A and Gower, L C B, in *European Business Law* (n 58 above).

directive may purport to regulate an area in which specific concepts are essential to one State's application and understanding of the law but alien and difficult to comprehend in another legal culture. An example is the introduction into Community company law of the concept of the company organ in the law relating to ultra vires transactions: a notion borrowed from German law which is familiar to the States whose legislation is derived from the Napoleonic code but which lies uneasily with the United Kingdom's analysis of company transactions within the framework of agency.[60] Similar problems arise—at least pending definitive interpretation by the Court of Justice—from the use of terms which may not be sufficiently proximate in the different language versions of a directive and in the Member States' implementing legislation. An analogous difficulty, albeit an extreme example, is provided by the Community legislature's abandonment of any attempt to impose a uniform meaning in the despairing admission in the Public Offers Prospectus Directive that it proved impossible to 'furnish a common definition of the term "public offer" and its constituent parts', a notion fundamental to the whole structure of the directive.[61]

The fields harmonized

More generally, criticisms of the harmonization process are directed at the Commission's priorities as illustrated by the topics which are the subject of adopted directives or the undertakings which are subject to them. Thus, for example, the wisdom of restricting the Second Directive to public companies is frequently questioned (although equal vigour has been deployed against the Commission's recent suggestion of extending the Second Directive to private companies). There is a significant disparity between the pattern of incorporation as public and private companies in the different Member States, which distorts the harmonizing effect of measures applying only to one category of companies. The United Kingdom and Germany, for example, have relatively small numbers of public compared to private companies, whereas in France and Italy, in contrast, many small undertakings use the form of a public company.[62] A similar point arises concerning the use of the corporate form generally: because incorporating a company in the United Kingdom is simple and swift, many very small businesses operate as companies which on the continent would be more likely to choose to conduct business as a sole trader or small partnership. Legislation directed at companies therefore affects a higher proportion of commercial businesses in the United Kingdom than in many other Member States.

Particular criticism has been levelled at the failure to promote any harmonization of the law relating to groups of companies: this topic is considered in Chapter XIX. An associated problem is that a directive will have to leave to domestic law areas linked with the topic which it seeks to harmonize, thus further undermining

---

[60] See further ch II.   [61] See further ch XII.
[62] The accounting directives resolve this problem by using size criteria rather than corporate form for certain exemptions and concessions.

its harmonizing effect: the Third Directive, for example, leaves much to national law.[63] All these problems however are perhaps inevitable consequences of the practical constraints fettering an ambitious programme: in the context of an ever growing number of Member States whose company law diverges widely in certain areas, the alternative to 'salami tactic' harmonization would almost certainly have been less rather than more effective legislation.

Moreover, and particularly in the early days of the harmonization programme, the Commission's steps towards company law harmonization had a significant indirect effect on the national company laws of several Member States: in a process graphically described by Professor Schmitthoff as the 'radiation effect of Community thinking', various domestic company law reforms were considerably influenced by the Community's harmonization endeavours which 'operated as a leaven on the otherwise rigid company laws of the Member States' and 'fertilised the national companies legislations'.[64] More recently, a similar effect arises from the implementation throughout the Community of directives which marry principles and techniques derived from the legal traditions of different Member States: for example, the United Kingdom concept of the true and fair view in company accounts[65] and of legal control as a criterion for the preparation of consolidated accounts[66] have now, thanks to national implementation of the Fourth and Seventh Directives, found their way into continental law and practice.

Timescale

The Council's General Programme for the abolition of restrictions on the freedom of establishment,[67] drawn up at the end of 1961, expressly envisaged completion of the coordination of company laws in accordance with Article 54(3)(g) by the end of 1963.[68] In 1965, the Commission, replying to a questionnaire sent by the *Commission du marché intérieur*, indicated that its company law harmonization programme undertaken on the basis of Article 54(3)(g) of the Treaty would enable it to draw up, before the end of 1966, draft legislation regulating public and private limited companies.[69] Over thirty years later, although considerable progress has been made, agreement has still not been reached on several important items of legislation the origin of which may be traced back almost as far: the seeds of the European Company Statute were first sown in 1959, the preliminary draft of the Convention on international mergers, now the draft Tenth Directive, was prepared in 1967 and the original Proposal for the Fifth Directive dates back to 1972.[70] Why has it taken so long?

[63] See further ch IV.
[64] 'The Success of the Harmonisation of European Company Law' (1976) 1 ELR 100, 100–1, 107.
[65] See further ch V.   [66] See ch VI.
[67] 18 December 1961, OJ Spec Ed IX, Resolutions of the Council and of the Representatives of the Member States, 7.
[68] Title VI of the General Programme.
[69] Berkhouwer, M M C, 'Rapport fait au nom de la Commission du marché intérieur' [1966] Revue trimestrielle de droit européen 434.
[70] See further ch XIX.

Reasons for delays in the early days of the harmonization programme have already been discussed.[71] Progress in finalizing certain directives, such as the Fourth Directive on annual accounts and the Seventh Directive on consolidated accounts, was substantially hindered by difficulties experienced in bridging major differences between national attitudes and practices.[72] There are moreover understandable practical reasons which have so delayed the adoption of, specifically, the Fifth and Tenth Directives, the Thirteenth Directive on Takeovers and the Regulation for a European Company Statute, closely linked to the Fifth Directive, and the complementary directive on worker participation in European Companies. These will be examined in the conclusion to this book (chapter XX), where the history and scope of these items of legislation, most of which look in 1998 as though they may after all be adopted by the millennium, are briefly reviewed.

More generally, perhaps it is misconceived to deduce from the Commission's original aims, which, however laudable, appear with the benefit of hindsight to be ambitious to the point of naivety, that the harmonization programme has proved unjustifiably long-winded. The issue in the 1960s was the harmonization of the company laws of six Member States which, even allowing for differences of approach between, for example, the Netherlands and the other five, or between Germany and France, had many common points of origin and many similarities (although even in that context it must not be overlooked that differences in national laws often reflect divergences of policy which may be harder to bridge). A more measured response to the timescale of company law harmonization which has seen the Community grown from six to fifteen Member States, embracing many more divergent legal orders, was expressed by the late Professor Gower:

although progress has indeed been slow, what is surprising to me is that it has not been slower. Any form of law reform is painfully slow and that which involves harmonization of the laws of States with different legal roots is slowest of all. Considering the inevitable dislocations caused where new Member States have been admitted, I find it remarkable that so much progress has been made.[73]

---

[71] See pp 5–6 above.

[72] See in relation to the history of the 4th and 7th Directives chs V and VI respectively.

[73] Buxbaum, Hertig, Hirsch, Hopt (eds), *European Business Law* (1991) 311. Although Professor Gower was speaking of harmonization generally, he referred in a footnote to the text cited to company law as an example of an area where much progress had been made. For a more humorous slant, see Lempereur, C, 'Myth and Reality in the European Harmonization Process' in Wymeersch, E (ed), *Further Perspectives in Financial Integration in Europe* (1994) 241, 247: 'the [company law, accounting and securities regulation] harmonization process, as it now is, could also be compared to a bottle of wine looked at, at the same time, by a pessimist and by an optimist. The pessimist would say: my bottle of wine is already half empty. The optimist would say: my bottle of wine is still half full.'

II

The First Directive

Background

The first company law directive[1] (the First Directive) seeks to harmonize publicity requirements applying to companies, the circumstances in which company transactions will be valid and the rules relating to the nullity of companies. Since it was the first directive to be issued under the legislative power conferred on the Council and the Commission by Article 54(3)(g) of the Treaty, the scope of which was already the subject of intense academic debate, it is perhaps unsurprising that much of the voluminous comment on the Directive focused more on its legal basis than on its content.[2] Now that thirty years have elapsed since adoption of the Directive, it seems less relevant to debate the precise scope of Article 54(3)(g)—as Prentice[3] points out, with refreshing common sense, it is 'hard to imagine any matter of significance in the field of company law that could not be subsumed, with ease, within the rubric of the protection of shareholder or creditor interests'.

This pragmatic approach is reflected in the range of topics put forward by the different national delegations during the preliminary discussions. In addition to the topics eventually dealt with in the First Directive, the suggestions included capital thresholds, availability and maintenance of capital and the protection of minority shareholders.[4] The three topics eventually chosen—regarded as

---

[1] First Council Directive (EEC) 68/151 of 9 March 1968 on coordination of safeguards which, for the protection of the interests of members and others, are required by Member States of companies within the meaning of the second paragraph of Art 58 of the Treaty, with a view to making such safeguards equivalent throughout the Community; [1968] OJ Spec Ed (I) 41. Van Ommeslaghe, P, 'La première directive du conseil du 9 mars 1968 en matière de sociétés' [1969] Cahiers de droit européen 495 contains a detailed review of the provisions of the 1st Directive and their implications.

[2] See Houin, R, 'Le régime juridique des sociétés dans la Communauté Economique Européenne' [1965] Revue trimestrielle de droit européen 11; Rodière, R, 'L'harmonisation des législations européennes dans le cadre de la C.E.E.' [1965] Revue trimestrielle de droit européen 336; Scholten, Y, 'Company Law in Europe' (1966–67) 4 CML Rev 377, and Van Ommeslaghe, 'La première directive du conseil' (n 1 above). The latter cites further articles examining the competence of the Commission and the Council in footnotes 15, 16 and 18 (as does Stein, E, *Harmonization of European Company Laws* (1971), in n 45, 192–3), and helpfully summarizes the positions of the conflicting camps (before contributing to the debate himself) at 502–8. There is also a useful—and rather less impassioned—summary of the issue in Prentice, D D, 'Section 9 of the European Communities Act' (1973) 89 LQR 518, 518–21.

[3] Ibid, 522. This view is echoed in the *Exposé des motifs* of the original Proposal for the 2nd Directive, which states that almost all the provisions of company law have the aim of protecting third parties or members: see the second paragraph of the introduction, [1970] JO C48/8.

[4] See résumé in Stein (n 2 above) 199–201.

particularly important for the protection of third parties[5]—had the advantage of being discrete. They could therefore be treated separately from other aspects of company law and, it was hoped, relatively quickly, leaving the remaining topics which had been suggested to be dealt with in the second company law directive.

The original Proposal for the Directive was approved by the Commission and transmitted to the Council in February 1964.[6] In March 1964 the Council referred it to the Economic and Social Committee and the European Parliament; the former commented in October 1964 and the latter in May 1966.[7] The amended Proposal,[8] which was transmitted to the Council of Ministers in October 1966, incorporated some of the suggestions of the Committee and the Parliament. The final version was adopted on 9 March 1968.

It should be borne in mind that, since the Directive was drafted, negotiated and finalized before the accession of the United Kingdom to the European Economic Community, the United Kingdom was wholly uninvolved in the process.[9] This partly explains the difficulty which the United Kingdom has experienced in implementing the provisions relating to the validity of obligations entered into by a company, which involve certain concepts alien to United Kingdom company law (although the changes required by the provisions 'are all changes which reformers in [the United Kingdom] have been demanding for years. There is nothing doctrinaire, exotic or "foreign" about them').[10] It will be seen in later chapters that, from the Second Directive onwards, the United Kingdom has been closely involved in the legislative process; although this has had the positive result that implementation has been on the whole less traumatic, it has also frustrated adoption of directives involving other controversial and alien concepts.[11]

---

[5] See the second recital in the preamble to the Directive.

[6] [1964] JO 3245. For a full account of the background and legislative history see Stein (n 2 above), ch 6, and Ault, H J, 'Harmonization of Company Law in the European Economic Community' (1968) 20 Hastings Law Journal 77.

[7] [1966] JO 1519. The report of the Parliament's Internal Market Committee, prepared by Berkhouwer, M M C, is published in [1966] Revue trimestrielle de droit européen 434. This report contains a useful outline of the relevant contemporaneous company law provisions applying in the six original Member States.

[8] COM (66) 366 final, 22 September 1966.

[9] The United Kingdom was of course party to the negotiations leading up to its accession to the EEC, which included negotiations to decide what amendments were necessary to existing directives including the 1st Directive. There is however an obvious difference in relative bargaining power between the two processes.

[10] Emlyn Davies, J A, 'Company Law and the Common Market: The First Step' in *An Introduction to the Law of the European Economic Community* (1972) 32.

[11] For example, the 5th Directive on the structure of public companies and the powers and obligations of their organs, the regulation and directive on the European Company and, to a lesser extent, the 13th Directive on takeovers.

Structure

The First Directive is divided into four sections dealing with different topics, all subject to Article 1 which precedes Section I and which sets out the types of company to which the Directive applies. Section I (Articles 2 to 6) makes provision for compulsory disclosure by companies of certain documents and particulars. Section II (Articles 7 to 9) concerns the effect of pre-incorporation and ultra vires transactions and those entered into by irregularly appointed or insufficiently authorized representatives. Section III (Articles 10 to 12) concerns nullity of companies. Section IV, headed 'General provisions', simply consists of Article 13, requiring implementation of the Directive within eighteen months of notification (subject to specified exceptions) and communication of the implementing legislation to the Commission, and Article 14, stating that the Directive is addressed to the Member States.

Scope

Company law coordination directives made under Article 54(3)(g) can extend to 'companies or firms within the meaning of the second paragraph of Article 58', where they are defined as 'companies or firms constituted under civil or commercial law, including co-operative societies, and other legal persons governed by public or private law, save for those which are non-profit-making'. The scope of the First Directive however is restricted to 'companies limited by shares or otherwise having limited liability, since the activities of such companies often extend beyond the frontiers of national territories . . . [and] since the only safeguards they offer to third parties are their assets'.[12] Article 1 lists the specific corporate vehicles covered in the various Member States:[13]

* Germany: *die Aktiengesellschaft*, die Kommanditgesellschaft auf Aktien**, die Gesellschaft mit beschränkter Haftung****;
* Belgium: *de naamloze vennootschap/la société anonyme*, de commanditaire vennootschap op aandelen/la société en commandite par actions**, de personenvennootschap met beperkte aansprakelijkheid/la société à responsabilité limitée****;
* France: *la société anonyme*, la société en commandite par actions**, la société à responsabilité limitée****;
* Italy: *società per azioni*, società in accomandita per azioni**, società a responsabilità limitata****;

[12] 1st and 3rd recitals in the preamble.
[13] See Pennington, R R and Wooldridge, F, *Company Law in the European Communities* (1982), for descriptions of these various types of company in the Member States up to and including the accession of Greece.

- Luxembourg: *la société anonyme**, *la société en commandite par actions***, *la société à responsabilité limitée****;
- the Netherlands: *de naamloze vennootschap, de commanditaire vennootschap op aandelen***.

To these were added by the First Act of Accession:[14]

- United Kingdom: companies incorporated with limited liability;
- Ireland: companies incorporated with limited liability;
- Denmark: *aktieselskab**, *kommandet-aktieselskab*** and *anpartsselskab****;

by the Second Act of Accession:[15]

- Greece: *anonymos etairia**, *heterorrythmos kata metoxes etairia*** and *etairia periosmenis efthynis****;

by the Third Act of Accession:[16]

- Spain: *la sociedad anonima**, *la socieded comaditaria por acciones*** and *la sociedad de responsabilidad limitada****;
- Portugal: *a sociedade anonima de responsabilidade limitada**, *a sociedade em comandita por accoes*** and *a sociedade por quotas de responsibilidade limitada****;

and by the Fourth Act of Accession:[17]

- Austria: *die Aktiengesellschaft**, *die Gesellschaft mit beschränkter Haftung****;
- Finland: *osakeyhtiö, aktiebolag*;
- Sweden: *aktiebolag*.[18]

Partnerships and limited partnerships (for example, *sociétés en nom collectif* and *sociétés en commandite simple* in France), and 'foundations' (*fondations, Stiftungen*) and co-operatives are thus excluded.

The types of company indicated with one asterisk are broadly equivalent to a public company in the United Kingdom. Those indicated with two asterisks are a form of public company whose directors are personally liable for their debts. Those indicated with three asterisks are broadly equivalent to a private company limited by shares in the United Kingdom.[19] It will be noted that in all the original Member States except the Netherlands there were at the time of implementation of the Directive three types of company. In the Netherlands the *naamloze vennootschap*

---

[14] [1972] JO L73/14.
[15] [1979] OJ L291/17.
[16] [1985] OJ L302/23.
[17] [1994] OJ C241/21.

[18] In Finland and Sweden, as in the UK, there was at the time of accession only one form of limited company, which could be either private or public. The two terms used in relation to Finland merely reflect the fact that it has two official languages, Finnish and Swedish.

[19] In this chapter, the terms 'private company' and 'public company' used of Member States other than the UK and Ireland refer to these equivalents. See Schmitthoff, C M, 'New Concepts in Company Law' [1973] JBL 312 for an interesting analysis of the conceptual differences between the continental types of private company and the British private company limited by shares.

was[20] used for large and small companies and there was no distinction between public and private companies as such: see below, pages 23 to 24, for an outline of the problem which this posed in relation to the requirement in the Directive for the publication of accounts, and the solution adopted.

Section I—Disclosure

Methods of publicity

The laws of the six original Member States all imposed certain requirements as to the publicity of documents and information relating to companies, so that—with the exception of the proposed accounting disclosure—the principle was uncontroversial. The existing systems in the various Member States were however widely divergent,[21] not only as to the specific items to be disclosed but also as to whether disclosure should be by depositing documents with a court or administrative bureau, entering details in a commercial or company register and/or publication in a journal, and this plurality of practice is reflected by the options for method of disclosure afforded by the Directive. Complete harmonization of national legislations has thus not been achieved in the matter of disclosure.

The Commission and governmental experts considered the advantages and disadvantages of the various systems and decided that they offered equivalent guarantees to third parties and shareholders; thought was also given to creating a central Euro-register, but the idea was rejected as too problematic.[22]

The original Proposal offered Member States the option of using all or any of the existing methods (Article 3(1)). This freedom of choice was however somewhat illusory, since Article 4 required that in any event for each company a file should be opened in a register, where an up-to-date record (whether by deposit of documents or entry of details) of all information subject to disclosure would be kept. The Economic and Social Committee and the European Parliament both pointed out this anomaly, and the Commission accepted the Parliament's amendment to Article 3(1) so that the final version required information to be accumulated in a

---

[20] The *besloten vennootschap*, private or closed company with limited liability, was introduced into Dutch company law in 1971: see Pennington, R R and Wooldridge, F, *Company Law in the European Communities* (1982) 124–7, for an outline of the relevant provisions. See also Sanders, P, 'The Reform of Dutch Company Law', in Schmitthoff, C M (ed), *The Harmonisation of European Company Law* (1973) 133.

[21] See Van Ommeslaghe, P, 'La première directive du conseil du 9 mars 1968 en matière de sociétés' [1969] Cahiers du droit européen 495, 525–43, for an exhaustive review of the different requirements, and Stein, E, *Harmonization of European Company Laws* (1971), 238–9, n 4, for a summary. Ault, H J, 'Harmonization of Company Law in the European Economic Community' (1968) Hastings Law Journal 77, 92–6 isolates Belgium and Germany as examples of the diversity of existing requirements. Schmitthoff, C M, gives an interesting insight into the historical background to commercial registration in 'Company and Commercial Law in Europe' in Cheng, C-J (ed), *Clive M Schmitthoff's Select Essays on International Trade Law* (1988) 74, 77.

[22] See Van Ommeslaghe, ibid, 544.

single register, whether central or decentralized and whether by deposit of documents or filing of details, to be supplemented in any event by publication in a 'national gazette appointed for that purpose by the Member State' of the full or partial text filed or of a notice of the deposit of a document (Article 3(4)). Article 5 leaves it to each Member State to determine by which person the disclosure formalities are to be carried out.[23]

Article 3(6) requires Member States to 'take the necessary measures to avoid any discrepancy between what is disclosed by publication in the press and what appears in the register or file', and provides that if there is such discrepancy 'the text published in the press may not be relied on as against third parties; the latter may nevertheless rely thereon, unless the company proves that they had knowledge[24] of the texts' filed or registered.[25]

Finally, the Directive gives the public the right to obtain copies of all documents or particulars filed for no more than the administrative cost of providing the copies (Article 3(3)).

What must be disclosed

The expressed rationale of the publicity requirements in the First Directive is that 'the basic documents of the company should be disclosed in order that third parties may be able to ascertain their contents and other information concerning the company, especially particulars of the persons who are authorised to bind the company'.[26] Article 2(1) requires disclosure of at least the following items relating to a company's legal and financial status:

(1)   The instrument of constitution and the statutes[27] if separate, together with any amendments thereto and a consolidation of each document as amended (Article 2(1)(a)(b)(c)).[28]

(2)   The appointment, termination of office and particulars of the persons who are 'authorised to represent the company' or who 'take part in the administration, supervision or control of the company' (Article 2(1)(d)). The disclosed details must show 'whether the persons authorised to represent the company may do so alone or must act jointly'.

---

[23] In the UK, the relevant provisions of the Companies Act 1985 require the company to submit the document or information to the Registrar of Companies and the Registrar to arrange for publication in the Gazette.

[24] See pp 29–30 below as to the extent of knowledge required.

[25] See Perret, F, 'Etude des dispositions spécifiques de la directive en matière de publicité' (1970) 3 Schweizerische Beitrage zum Europarecht 36–8, for an outline and refutation of the view that, by way of corollary, where there is such a discrepancy third parties may rely as against the company on an incorrect entry in the register or file.

[26] 4th recital in the preamble.

[27] Note that the 1st Directive does not prescribe the contents of these documents, but merely requires that they be published. Their contents are laid down by the 2nd Directive: see ch III.

[28] Implemented in the UK by the Companies Act 1985, ss 10, 18 and 711.

(3)   At least annually, 'the amount of the capital subscribed, where the instrument of constitution or the statutes mention an authorised capital,[29] unless any increase in the capital subscribed necessitates an amendment of the statutes' (Article 2(1)(e)).[30]

(4)   The balance sheet and profit and loss account for each financial year (Article 2(1)(f)).[31]

(5)   Any transfer of the company's seat (Article 2(1)(g)).[32]

(6)   Any declaration of nullity of the company by the courts; details of any liquidators,[33] liquidation, winding up and striking off (Article 2(1)(h)(i)(j)(k)).[34]

According to Van Ommeslaghe,[35] the reference to those who take part in the 'control of the company' (see (2) above) is to the auditors where they are also an organ of the company; this is not the case in the United Kingdom where auditors are in principle independent of the company, although their details must in any event be disclosed under Article 2(1)(f)—see (4) above. Van Ommeslaghe's view must however be regarded as questionable in the light of the Council's statement, incorporated in the minutes of the relevant session, seeking to clarify the intended meaning of 'the bodies responsible for . . . supervision or control of the company' in Article 2(d) of the Second Directive. The Council stated that those terms referred to the relevant organ in a public company which has adopted a two-tier management structure,[36] namely the French *conseil de surveillance*, the German *Aufsichtsrat* and the Dutch *raad van commissarissen* (essentially, in each case, a supervisory board). It was expressly stated that auditors under any name[37] were not among the above-mentioned bodies.[38]

The requirement to show whether the persons authorized to represent the company may do so alone ((2) above) was added at the amended Proposal stage to take account of those systems of law under which, although the company may be bound only by the board as a whole, it may be represented by certain members of the board.[39] The Court of Justice held in *Friedrich Haaga GmbH*[40] that Article 2(1)(d) must be interpreted as meaning that, where the body authorized to represent a

---

[29]   This is now required of public companies by the 2nd Directive: see ch III.

[30]   Implemented in the UK by the Companies Act 1985, ss 363, 364A and 711.

[31]   Implemented in the UK by the Companies Act 1985, ss 242 and 711.

[32]   Implemented in the UK by the Companies Act 1985, ss 287(3) and 711.

[33]   Including their appointment and powers, 'unless such powers are expressly and exclusively derived from law or from the statutes of the company'. This is the case in the UK where liquidators' powers derive from the Insolvency Act 1986.

[34]   Implemented in the UK by the Insolvency Act 1986, ss 109, 201 and 202 and the Companies Act 1985, ss 652 and 711.

[35]   'La première directive du conseil du 9 mars 1968 en matière de sociétés' [1969] Cahiers de droit européen 495, 554–5.

[36]   Of the sort pioneered in Germany and the subject-matter of the ill-fated 5th Directive.

[37]   *Abschlussprüfer, expert comptable, commissaire, commissaire-reviseur, commissaire aux comptes, auditor, revisor.*

[38]   See Keutgen, G, 'La deuxième directive en matière de sociétés' (1977) 5925 Revue pratique des sociétés 1, 4, n 11.

[39]   *Exposé des motifs* for amended Proposal, 25.   [40]   Case 32/74 [1974] ECR 1201.

company may consist of one or of several members, disclosure must be made not only of the scope of the authority to represent where there are several directors, but also, where there is only one director, of the fact that the latter represents the company alone, even if his authority to do so clearly flows from national law. See below, pages 25 to 26, for a discussion of the United Kingdom's inadequate implementation of this provision.

The proposal to require publicity of accounts (see (4) above) excited an impassioned debate in which some of the more extreme positions taken seem remarkable to lawyers from common law jurisdictions where this requirement has been a cornerstone of limited liability for a considerable time. Commentators pleaded that it was pointless to require publication of individual company accounts before publication of consolidated group accounts was compulsory, that accounts were of interest only to shareholders and not to third parties, and that disclosure would weaken a company's competitive position.[41] It should however be borne in mind that some of those views were expressed before the amendment postponing application of this provision for private companies until implementation of the Fourth Directive, so that they must be seen against the very different requirements as to content of accounts in the various Member States at the time.[42]

More specifically, there was fierce resistance from Germany to the proposed imposition of financial disclosure requirements on limited liability companies. In Germany in the 1960s no accounting disclosure was required of private limited companies (other than, after 1965, controlled subsidiaries of public companies), of which there were 58,000 in 1966 as against 2,400 public companies.[43] There was also strong opposition from France (which required disclosure only by listed companies whose balance sheet exceeded FFr10 million) to compulsory disclosure in general and to disclosure by private companies in particular.

The compromise on disclosure of accounts which was ultimately reached reflects the extreme divergence of the laws of the original Member States, from relative glasnost (for example Italy, where results of all companies limited by shares were required to be published) to secrecy (for example France and Germany). It also satisfied the German insistence on delay in extending the disclosure requirement to

---

[41] See articles cited by Van Ommeslaghe, P, 'La première directive du conseil du 9 mars 1968 en matière de sociétés' [1969] Cahiers de droit européen 495, 556, nn 98 and 99. See also n 44 below.

[42] See Stein, E, *Harmonization of European Company Laws* (1971), 244–69, for a review of the accounting disclosure requirements in the various Member States before the 1st Directive.

[43] The arguments adduced against disclosure are summarized in Stein, ibid, 252–4. Ault, H J, 'Harmonization of Company Law in the European Economic Community' (1968) 20 Hastings Law Journal 77, 97–8, n 79, recounts how a series of articles in a German publication asserted that the proposal for financial disclosure exceeded the competence of the Commission and violated the German constitutional privilege of privacy, implied that its adoption 'would lead to economic chaos throughout the Market' and culminated with a telegram to the Council, the Parliament and the Economic and Social Committee summarizing the objections and demanding 'that the provision be stricken from the Directive'.

private companies[44] and the Commission's opposition to a fixed floor for an exemption. The balance sheet threshold of one million units of account (US$1 million) which had been included in the original Proposal was dropped, and application of the provision to private companies[45] was postponed until 'implementation of a Directive concerning co-ordination of the contents of balance sheets and of profit and loss accounts and concerning exemption of such of those companies whose balance sheet total is less than that specified in the Directive from the obligation to make disclosure, in full or in part, of the said documents'.[46] That Directive, which was already in the course of preparation when the First Directive was being negotiated, was to be adopted by the Council within two years following the adoption of the First Directive, and was eventually adopted on 25 July 1978 as the Fourth Council Directive (EEC) 78/660 based on Article 54(3)(g) of the Treaty on the annual accounts of certain types of companies.[47]

An additional problem had been posed by company structures in the Netherlands. As mentioned above, in the Netherlands one type of company, the *naamloze vennootschap*, was used for large and small companies alike and there was no fundamental distinction between public and private companies as such, although Dutch law used the criterion of whether the company was 'open'[48] or 'closed' to determine whether it should publish its accounts. This raised the question of how to ensure that the requirement to disclose accounts was not imposed on small and, for practical purposes, private Netherlands companies before it applied to their equivalents in other Member States. It was not possible merely to reflect the Dutch law definition of a 'closed' company in the Directive, since the effect would have been to catch a number of public companies in other Member States and thus exempt them from the disclosure requirement intended to apply to them.[49] The European Parliament proposed adding to the original balance sheet

---

[44] Note however that in 1969 a German law was enacted requiring disclosure by all undertakings of a certain size, regardless of their legal form. This provision itself triggered a further round of critical comment: it was argued that the only relevant criterion should be whether or not shares were held by the public, that disclosure of accounts was wholly irrelevant to creditor protection, that the measure would provoke a flight of capital from Germany to Member States with more relaxed disclosure provisions, and that in practice disclosure of accounts had proved to be ineffective in preventing insolvency and indeed could even accelerate the process by causing the public to panic: see Perret, F, 'Etude des dispositions spécifiques de la directive en matière de publicité' (1970) 3 Schweizerische Beitrage zum Europarecht, 22–3, where the rather more predictable arguments in favour of disclosure are also summarized.

[45] Other than private limited companies incorporated in England, Wales or Scotland which became subject to the requirement on accession. Although this did not involve a change, since the Companies Act 1967 already required private companies to publish full accounts, it is not clear why, as a matter of principle, 'British' private companies should be treated as public companies for this purpose while private companies in all other Member States, including Northern Ireland and the Republic of Ireland, were treated more favourably. See Welch, J, 'The English Private Company—A Crisis of Classification' [1974] JBL 277, and see further in connection with the scope of the 2nd Directive ch III below.

[46] Art 2(1)(f).   [47] See ch V.

[48] Broadly, insurance and banking companies and companies with bearer or quoted shares.

[49] See Van Ommeslaghe, P, 'La première directive du conseil du 9 mars 1968 en matière de sociétés' [1969] Cahiers du droit européen 495, 560–1.

threshold of one million units of account a general distinction between public and private companies, the dividing line being whether the company sought to raise funds on public capital markets. The Commission felt that this definition was too wide, since it would free from disclosure 'too many stock companies whose financial situation is of interest to third parties'.[50] The final outcome was Article 2(2), which sets out five criteria[51] which a *naamloze vennootschap* must satisfy in order to be regarded as a *besloten naamloze vennootschap* for the purposes of disclosure of accounts.[52]

Article 4 requires letters and order forms[53] to give details of the register in which the company's file is kept pursuant to Article 3, the company's number in that register, the legal form of the company, the location of its seat and, where appropriate, the fact that it is being wound up. The original Proposal required that information to be given on *les factures et les autres documents émanant de la société* (invoices and other documents issued by the company) rather than just letters and order forms; this was subsequently narrowed as it was thought to be too wide and too vague. The first draft also required capital to be mentioned on the relevant documents, but failed to specify whether by this was meant issued, paid-up, or authorized capital. The Economic and Social Committee pointed out this imprecision, and the European Parliament suggested that the reference to capital be dropped altogether; ultimately, the final version was amended to read 'Where in these documents mention is made of the capital of the company, the reference shall be to the capital subscribed and paid up.'[54]

Implementation in the United Kingdom

For the United Kingdom, the policy of disclosure behind the publicity requirements of the First Directive was already substantially reflected in English company law, although the additional layer of disclosure by publication in a national journal required incorporation in the legislation[55] and the results of failing to make the

---

[50] Amended proposal, *Exposé des motifs*, 2.

[51] (a) It cannot issue bearer shares; (b) no bearer certificate in respect of its shares can be issued [the bearer certificate, or *certificaat*, is a peculiarity of Dutch company law: it is issued by an *administratiekantoor*, usually a subsidiary of a bank or an associated company of the *naamloze vennootschap* in question, which is the legal owner of the shares represented and which acts as trustee for the certificate holders, to whom it pays dividends which it receives on the shares]; (c) its shares cannot be quoted on a stock exchange; (d) its statutes require the company's approval for transfers of shares other than on death or (broadly) within the family; blank transfers are not permitted; and (e) its statutes specify that the company is a *besloten naamloze vennootschap* and its name includes those words or the initials *BNV*.

[52] There is now a Dutch equivalent of the private limited company, introduced in 1971 to provide a form of company for the purposes of, inter alia, the 1st Directive: see n 20 above.

[53] As to the meaning of 'order forms' see Bennett Miller, J, 'Harmonisation of Company Law: The second [sic] EEC directive' (1977) 22 Journal of the Law Society of Scotland 370, and Wooldridge, F, *Company Law in the United Kingdom and the European Community* (1991), 18.

[54] Implemented in the UK by the Companies Act 1985, s 351. Prentice, D D, 'Section 9 of the European Communities Act' (1973) 89 LQR 518, 535, complains that no definition of paid-up capital is given in the original implementing legislation (the European Communities Act 1972, s 9(7)), and suggests that it includes amounts unpaid on partly paid shares.

[55] The Companies Act 1985, s 711, originally the European Communities Act 1972, s 9(3).

required notification were novel.[56] There were however—and still are—specific problems relating to the disclosure of information about directors.

First, Article 2(1)(d) (details of persons authorized to represent the company, including specifically whether they 'may do so alone or must act jointly') is purportedly implemented by s 288 of the Companies Act 1985 (formerly s 200(1) of the Companies Act 1948, which was presumably thought to be an adequate reflection of Article 2(1)(d) as it stood, since the draftsman of the main implementing legislation, the European Communities Act 1972, apparently did not see the need to make separate provision). Section 288 merely requires that 'Every company shall keep at its registered office a register of its directors and secretaries', the register to contain the particulars specified in ss 289 and 290. These include fascinating details about, for example, whether the name by which a director who is a peer was known previous to the adoption of or succession to the title should be included,[57] but wholly fail to mention the question of whether the director may represent the company individually or must do so jointly. In 1977 the Commission was asked whether it considered that Article 2(1)(d) was given full effect by s 200, and replied in the negative.[58]

The second part of the written question to the Commission stated that in the United Kingdom Table A[59] 'provides that the business of the company shall be managed by the directors; . . . provides for entrusting the powers of the directors to a managing director or directors; and . . . provides that one director, along with either the company secretary or another director, may sign to authenticate the acts of the company'. The Commission was asked whether it considered that Article 2(1)(d) required the registration of the board of directors, or any director or directors so authorized to act for the board, or any director or directors so authorized to authenticate acts of the company. It replied that, in the light of the judgment of the Court of Justice in *Friedrich Haaga GmbH*[60], Article 2(1)(d):

requires that the appointment, termination of office and particulars of all the members of the board of directors and, separately, of each member of the board authorized to represent the company in dealings with third parties and in legal proceedings, must be disclosed. [It] must appear from the disclosure whether the persons authorized to represent the company may do so alone or must act jointly. [Disclosure] is required even where the system of representation stems *ipso jure* from national law. Under the law applicable in the United Kingdom, the board of directors as a whole is empowered to represent the company unless otherwise stated in the articles of association. Where the articles [provide for the appointment of a managing director] the arrangements regarding [his] powers are also subject to the disclosure requirement referred to above.

---

[56] See pp 26–30 below.   [57] The Companies Act 1985, 289(2)(b)(i): it isn't.
[58] Written Question No 23/77 of 16 March 1977: [1977] OJ C289/1. See also Wyatt, D (who originally raised the question, although it was eventually put by Sir Derek Walker-Smith), 'The First Directive and Company Law' (1978) 94 LQR 182.
[59] The statutory paradigm articles of association which a company limited by shares may adopt.
[60] Case 32/74 [1974] ECR 1201.

The Commission considered however that the provision in Table A relating to the signatures required to authenticate the seal were procedural and evidential in nature, and that 'since that article does not confer power equivalent in nature to the powers referred to in Article 2(1)(d) . . . the particulars of persons authorized to authenticate the seal do not have to be disclosed separately'.

It has been suggested[61] that the Commission's reply means that 'authority gained by operation of law is covered by the Directive, which will include both usual and apparent/ostensible authority.' This is presumably on the basis of the statement that disclosure is required even where the system of representation stems *ipso jure* from national law. It is submitted that this is a misinterpretation of the reply and hence of the dictum in the *Haaga* case which it repeats. Article 2(1)(d) requires disclosure of details of persons 'authorized to represent the company'. As a matter of construction this must refer to persons authorized by the company to represent it: apart from anything else, it is the company which is required to make the disclosure. *Ex hypothesi*, reliance on usual or apparent/ostensible authority presupposes a lack of actual authority and it would be unreasonable to expect the company to make such disclosure. The *Haaga* case concerned disclosure of actual authority flowing from the law, and it is unsound to extrapolate the decision to the conceptually different issue of usual and apparent/ostensible authority.

Effect of non-compliance

Article 6 requires Member States to provide for appropriate penalties for failure to disclose accounts and for the omission of prescribed details from commercial documents. This provision has been criticized as an unusually intrusive intervention by Community law in national law.[62] The Economic and Social Committee, on the other hand, apparently considered that it had not gone far enough, and complained that, since no indication was given as to the type of liability to be penalized (strict or with intent) or the type or degree of penalty, the measure did not establish any real harmonization.

Some guidance as to the type of penalty required by Article 6 has, however, now been provided by the Court of Justice in *Verband deutscher Daihatsu-Händler eV v Daihatsu Deutschland GmbH*.[63] Under German law the penalty for failure to disclose the accounts of a *GmbH* was a fine which may be imposed on application only by a member or creditor of the company, the central works council or the company's works council. On a preliminary reference from the *Oberlandsgericht* (Higher Regional Court) Düsseldorf, the Court of Justice ruled that Article 6 precluded a

---

[61] Morse, G, 'The First Directive and United Kingdom Company Law' (1978) 3 ELR 60.

[62] See Scholten, Y, 'Company Law in Europe' (1966–67) 4 CML Rev 377, 396: 'Article 189 provides that States are bound by directives in respect of the result to be achieved, while the national authorities are left free to decide the form and manner of enforcing them. Article 7 of the directive provides penal sanctions for a failure to publish balance sheets. The purpose of the directive, however, is publication and not how municipal law penalises those who fail to do so.'

[63] Case C–97/96 [1997] ECR I–6843.

Member State from so restricting the right to apply for imposition of the penalty for failure to disclose accounts.

The German Government had argued that the coordination of national systems of company law was designed[64] to safeguard the interests of members 'and others' and submitted that the latter comprised solely persons who had a legal relationship with the company. The Court of Justice took a broader view, stating that Article 54(3)(g) must be read in the light not only of Articles 52 and 54 of the Treaty, which clearly showed that the coordination of company law formed part of the general programme for the abolition of restrictions on freedom of establishment, but also of Article 3(h), which provided that the activities of the Community were to include the approximation of national laws to the extent required for the functioning of the common market. Furthermore, Article 54(3)(g) expressly referred to the need to protect the interests of 'others' generally: consequently, the term could not be limited to creditors of the company. Moreover, the objective of abolishing restrictions on freedom of establishment, assigned in very broad terms to the Council and the Commission by Article 54(1) and (2), could not be circumscribed by the provisions of Article 54(3), which merely set out a non-exhaustive list of measures to be taken in order to attain that objective.[65]

As regards Article 6, disclosure of accounts was primarily designed to provide information for third parties who did not know or could not obtain sufficient knowledge of the company's accounting and financial situation.[66] That was confirmed by Article 3, which provided that certain documents and particulars must be entered in a public register and be obtainable by any person upon application, and the preamble to the Fourth Directive,[67] which referred to the need to establish minimum equivalent requirements as regards the extent of the financial information to be made available to the public by companies in competition with one another.[68]

Article 6 was accordingly not properly implemented by national legislation such as that before the Court of Justice. However, as the Court noted, a directive may not of itself impose obligations on an individual and may therefore not be relied upon as such against such a person,[69] without prejudice to the possible applicability of the principle that Community law required Member States to make good loss

---

[64] In accordance with Art 54(3)(g) of the Treaty.

[65] See also to the same effect the Opinion of Advocate General Cosmas delivered on 3 July 1997, paras 13–17.

[66] See the 4th recital in the preamble to the 1st Directive.　　　　[67] In particular the 3rd recital.

[68] The Court of Justice unsurprisingly rejected the German Government's preliminary submission that the obligation to provide for appropriate penalties was not yet applicable to the *GmbH* since the Article provided that in respect of private limited companies, including the *GmbH*, its application was 'postponed until the date of implementation of a Directive concerning co-ordination of the contents of balance sheets and of profit and loss accounts' and no such directive had yet been adopted: the Court noted that the legislative lacuna left by the 1st Directive had been filled by the 4th Directive (para 14 of the judgment).

[69] See, in particular, Case 152/84 *Marshall I* [1986] ECR 723, para 48, Case C–91/92 *Faccini Dori v Recreb* [1994] ECR I–3325, para 20, and Case C–192/94 *El Corte Inglés v Blázquez Rivero* [1996] ECR I–1281, para 15.

and damage caused to individuals by reason of their failure to transpose a directive or their failure to do so correctly.[70]

The question in the *Daihatsu* case was referred to the Court of Justice in March 1996. In June 1995, the Commission had brought proceedings against Germany under Article 169 of the Treaty on the same issue, namely the compatibility with Community law of the German system of sanctions for breach of the obligation to publish company accounts. The Court repeated that, as it had ruled in the *Daihatsu* case, national legislation such as that at issue did not properly implement the Directive. Dismissing an argument advanced by the German Government, it stated further that the lack of appropriate penalties could not be justified by the fact that, because of the large numbers involved, application of such penalties to all companies that did not publish their accounts would create considerable difficulties for the German administrative authorities.[71]

Probably of greater deterrent effect than Article 6, however, are the provisions limiting a company's ability to rely as against third parties on items which have not been disclosed as required.[72]

Article 3(5) provides that documents and particulars subject to the disclosure requirement may be relied on by the company as against third parties only if they have been published in the relevant newspaper, unless the company proves that the third party 'had knowledge thereof'. Even after publication, for the first sixteen days the company cannot rely on any such item as against third parties who prove that it was 'impossible' for them to have had knowledge. As noted above, Member States are required to take the necessary measures to avoid discrepancies between the item published and that registered or filed, but should this occur, the company is bound by the filed or registered item, although the third party may choose to rely on the published item unless the company proves that he had knowledge of the text as filed or registered.[73]

Article 3(7) provides that third parties may 'always rely on any documents and particulars in respect of which the disclosure formalities have not yet been completed, save where non-disclosure causes them not to have effect.' Whether this is so or not depends on the relevant national law. In Germany, Italy and France at the time of implementation of the Directive, a company became a legal person when entered on the register: publicity in that context was accordingly constitutive. In the Benelux countries, the effect of registration was to record a legal development which had already occurred, and was hence declaratory. Where the effect of disclosure in particular circumstances is merely declaratory, then the effect of Article 3(7) is that third parties may rely on 'documents and particulars' which have not,

---

[70] Joined Cases C 46 and 48/93 *Brasserie du Pêcheur and Factortame* [1996] ECR I–1029, para 51, and Case C–392/93 *The Queen v HM Treasury, ex p British Telecommunications* [1996] ECR I–1631, para 39.

[71] Case C–191/95 *Commission v Germany*, judgment of 29 September 1998.

[72] Although this will obviously not be the case in relation to the objects of the company and limitations on the powers of those authorized to represent it, since disclosure of this information is in principle not effective against third parties: see pp 37–41 below.

[73] Art 3(6).

but should have, been disclosed. When the effect is constitutive, then clearly the failure to disclose will mean that the transaction is null and void and there will be nothing for the third party to rely on.

Whether knowledge by third parties for the purposes of Article 3(5) and 3(6) encompasses circumstances where the third party, although unaware, should or could have been is unclear. There are other provisions in the Directive in which a third party's 'knowledge' determines whether the company can rely on a particular transaction or document as against him. Guidance as to the intended meaning of the term may sometimes, but not always, be found in earlier drafts of the provision. Thus the original version of Article 3(7)[74] referred to 'third parties in good faith'. Although the 'good faith' rider was later dropped, 'apparently because it was not uniformly understood in the national laws',[75] it sheds light on the criteria to be satisfied before a third party is protected by the provision. However, neither Article 3(5) nor Article 3(6) featured in the original Proposal.[76]

Commentators have noted the difference in the wording of these provisions on the one hand and Article 9(1), which refers to proof that the 'third party knew . . . or could not in view of the circumstances have been unaware', on the other, and have drawn divergent conclusions. Van Ommeslaghe, for example, argues strongly that the difference is fortuitous and due to the different circumstances in which the provisions were drafted, and is sufficiently sure of his view to state unequivocally that 'it is certain that [the drafters of the Directive] intended to cover "third parties in good faith"' in Article 3(5) and 3(6).[77] Prentice[78] however considers that actual knowledge is required. He compares the wording of the United Kingdom legislation[79] implementing Article 3(5),[80] which uses the criterion of 'being known to the person concerned', with that implementing Article 9(1),[81] which uses the criterion of 'good faith', and argues that the difference manifests a legislative intention to draw a distinction. He concludes that to give effect to that differentiation the concept of 'knowledge' in the section implementing Article 3(5)

---

[74] Which was a mirror image of the final version, providing that, in Member States where publication was merely declaratory, failure to publish should entail as a minimum that the information could not be relied on against third parties in good faith: Art 9 of the original Proposal.

[75] Stein, E, *Harmonization of European Company Laws* (1971), 277, no source given.

[76] The only items which, if undisclosed, could not be relied on as against third parties in the first draft were alterations to the instruments of constitution or statutes in countries where non-publication of such alterations was merely declaratory (Art 9, which eventually, much changed, became Art 3(7)) and details of appointments of the company's representative organs (Art 10, subsequently Art 8).

[77] Van Ommeslaghe, P, 'La première directive du conseil du 9 mars 1968 en matière de sociétés' [1969] Cahiers de droit européen 495, 552. Wooldridge, F, who takes the same view, notes that 'in many member states constructive notice is enough': 'The Harmonization of Company Law: The First and Second Directives of the Council of Ministers of the European Economic Community' [1978] Acta Juridica 327, 330.

[78] n 54 above, 536–7.

[79] It should be borne in mind that Prentice barely considers the wording of the Directive, and that when he does he refers to a translation which differs from the official English version. See further n 125 below.

[80] The European Communities Act 1972, s 9(4); now the Companies Act 1985, s 42(1).

[81] The European Communities Act 1972, s 9(1); now the Companies Act 1985, s 35A.

should be construed as meaning actual knowledge.[82] Whichever view is correct, it can however safely be assumed that the Court of Justice would not lightly impute knowledge to a third party without actual knowledge unless there were some element of bad faith involved, since to do so would run counter to the principle of protection of third parties which is one of the aims of the Directive.[83]

Implementation of Article 3(5) in the United Kingdom

Article 3(5) is implemented in the United Kingdom by s 42 of the Companies Act 1985. The introduction of a civil sanction as opposed to a penalty for failure to register marked a significant change in UK company law. The original implementing legislation, s 9(4) of the European Communities Act 1972, was considered by the Court of Appeal in England in *Official Custodian for Charities v Parway Estates Ltd*.[84] That section provided that a company was 'not entitled to rely against other persons on the happening of . . . the making of a winding-up order . . . if the event had not been officially notified at the material time and is not shown by the company to have been known at that time to the person concerned . . .' It was argued on behalf of a company in respect of which such an order had been made and published in the Gazette in accordance with the United Kingdom's system of official notification that the company's landlord, by accepting rent after such publication, had done so in knowledge of the order and thus waived its right to forfeit the lease in the event of liquidation. The argument was that a corollary of the express terms of s 9(4) was that 'after an official notification of an event has become fully effective, all persons must be treated as having constructive knowledge of that event' and that the company could therefore rely on publication in the Gazette as against third parties even where they did not have actual knowledge. The Court of Appeal rejected that argument. It held that the sub-section 'was primarily intended for the protection of persons dealing with a company rather than for the protection of the company', and found support for this view in the relevant recital in the Directive, which stated that 'the basic documents of the company should be disclosed in order that third parties may be able to ascertain their contents and other information concerning the company . . .'.[85] The Court of Appeal agreed with the judge at first instance that s 9(4) 'did not impute knowledge to anyone and did not impute notice to anyone. It was essentially negative in its impact', and added that the link in s 9(4) between official notification and actual knowledge of an event not so notified did not require that

notification should be treated as importing notice of the event to everyone. The object of the legislation is that persons dealing with a company should be officially given an opportunity of finding out important information concerning the company but there is no sense in

---

[82] This interpretation has been confirmed by the Court of Appeal in a case considering a slightly different aspect of s 9(4): see *Official Custodian for Charities v Parway Estates Ltd* [1985] Ch 151 considered below.

[83] This view seems borne out by the tenor of the judgment in Case C–104/96 *Coöperatieve Rabobank 'Vecht en Plassengebied' BA v Erik Aarnoud Minderhoud (liquidator of Mediasafe BV)* [1997] ECR I–7211: see pp 38–9 below for further discussion of this case.

[84] [1985] Ch 151.   [85] 4th recital in the preamble.

hampering the company vis-à-vis those who have actual knowledge of the relevant event. Hence the qualification of the restriction imposed by the subsection on the company.

Some commentators[86] have speculated as to the exact meaning of 'unavoidably prevented from knowing' of the event in question (the wording used in s 42 of the Companies Act 1985 to reflect the concept of 'impossibility' of knowing used in Article 3(5)), but Pennington's more robust dismissal of the provision as 'unlikely to be of importance'[87] since the required combination of circumstances will rarely arise in practice has much to recommend it: there are many more pressing problems with the legislation.

Section II—Validity of Obligations Entered into by a Company

Pre-incorporation contracts

Article 7 provides as follows:

If, before a company being formed has acquired legal personality, action has been carried out in its name and the company does not assume the obligations arising from such action, the persons who acted shall, without limit, be jointly and severally liable therefor, unless otherwise agreed.

The law of the original Member States on pre-incorporation contracts before implementation of the Directive is summarized by Van Ommeslaghe.[88] Article 7 is inspired by German and Italian law. Its drafting and passage were uncontroversial: the only ripple was caused by the European Parliament, which sought, unsuccessfully, to amend the provision so that the liability of the persons who acted for the company would continue indefinitely, even after the company had assumed the obligations.

The United Kingdom in implementing Article 7 unfortunately failed to take the opportunity to bring national law fully into line with the spirit of the Article, which clearly envisages the company's having the option of easily assuming the relevant obligations.[89] This is not the case in English law, where a company cannot ratify a

---

[86] For example, Prentice, D D, 'Section 9 of the European Communities Act' (1973) 89 LQR 518, 537 ff, and Schmitthoff, there quoted. Prentice exhaustively analyses various perceived problems with s 42's predecessor: in an interesting historical cameo he attributes many of the deficiencies in the European Communities Act 1972, s 9, generally to 'the emotionally charged atmosphere surrounding the introduction of this piece of legislation' (544).

[87] Pennington, R R, *Company Law* (7th edn, 1995) 74, n 4.

[88] Van Ommeslaghe, P, 'La première directive du conseil du 9 mars 1968 en matière de sociétés' [1969] Cahiers de droit européen 495, 635–9. See generally for a comparison of the English and the German approach Reith, T, 'The Effect of Pre-incorporation Contracts in German and English Company Law' (1988) 37 ICLQ 109.

[89] Perret, however, considers that the *rédaction très souple* (very flexible terms) of the Article suggests that the intention was to leave Member States completely free to determine the way in which the obligations should be assumed: Perret, F, 'Etude des dispositions spécifiques de la directive en matière de publicité' (1970) 3 Schweizerische Beitrage zum Europarecht, 45.

pre-incorporation contract but has to enter into a fresh contract with the other parties by the process of novation; even that fresh contract will not release those who
acted on behalf of the proposed company if they were personally liable,[90] unless
this is expressly provided for. However, since the principal aim of the provision is
to protect third parties by ensuring that they have rights at least against those who
acted on behalf of the putative company, and this is achieved by the implementing
legislation,[91] this is not a serious flaw.

The Court of Justice briefly considered Article 7 in *Ubbink Isolatie v Dak- en
Wandtechniek*,[92] a case concerning acts performed in the name of a company not
yet incorporated. The Court held that the rules on the nullity of companies in
Section III of the Directive did not apply where acts had been performed in the
name of a company whose existence was not confirmed by the public register
because the formalities for incorporation required by national law had not been
completed, and stated that:

in so far as acts performed in the name of a limited liability company not yet incorporated
are regarded by the applicable national law as having been performed in the name of a company being formed within the meaning of Article 7 . . . it is for the national law in question
to provide, in accordance with that provision, that the persons who perform them are to be
jointly and severally liable.'[93]

A further point as to the scope of Article 7 was made by Advocate General Cruz
Vilaça, in whose view:

when the existence of a partnership is equivalent, under an express disposition of national
law or in accordance with the interpretation given of it by legal doctrine or the courts, to a
company in formation . . . Article 7 . . . must apply. Were it otherwise, its aim of safeguarding the interests of third parties could be frustrated by the legal expedient of regarding
such an organization as a partnership.[94]

---

[90] Which in UK law until recently depended on subtle nuances of intention and drafting; however
the Companies Act 1985, s 36C (inserted by the Companies Act 1989 to replace s 36(4) of the 1985
Act which re-enacted the original implementing provision, the European Communities Act 1972,
s 9(2)), has thankfully abolished this distinction, so that those who purport to act for or on behalf of the
company will in any event be personally liable.

[91] The Companies Act 1985, s 36C, which provides: 'A contract which purports to be made by or
on behalf of a company at a time when the company has not been formed has effect, subject to any
agreement to the contrary, as one made with the person purporting to act for the company or as agent
for it, and he is personally liable on the contract accordingly.' The English Court of Appeal has held that
that section applied even where the proposed company was never ultimately formed, and that the words
'subject to any agreement to the contrary' require 'a clear exclusion of personal liability': *Phonogram Ltd
v Lane* [1982] QB 938.

[92] Case 136/87 [1988] ECR 4665; see further pp 47–8 below.

[93] Para 18 of the judgment.   [94] Para 42 of the Opinion.

Irregular appointments of directors

Article 8 provides:

Completion of the formalities of disclosure of the particulars concerning the persons who, as an organ of the company, are authorised to represent it shall constitute a bar to any irregularity in their appointment being relied upon as against third parties unless the company proves that such third parties had knowledge thereof.

Again, this was an uncontroversial provision and has attracted little comment. It may be noted that the first draft of Article 8 referred to 'third parties in good faith'. The Article has not been specifically implemented in the United Kingdom, presumably because it was thought to be already adequately reflected by the Companies Act 1985, s 285[95] and the common law rules protecting outsiders against irregularities in the internal management of the company.[96]

Ultra vires and directors' authority

The first two paragraphs of Article 9 are concerned with the circumstances in which a company will be bound by acts in excess of (1) its objects or (2) the authority of those purporting to act on its behalf. They read as follows:

(1)   Acts done by the organs of the company shall be binding upon it even if those acts are not within the objects of the company, unless such acts exceed the powers that the law confers or allows to be conferred on those organs.

However, Member States may provide that the company shall not be bound where such acts are outside the objects of the company, if it proves that the third party knew that the act was outside those objects or could not in view of the circumstances have been unaware of it; disclosure of the statutes shall not of itself be sufficient proof thereof.

(2)   The limits on the powers of the organs of the company, arising under the statutes or from a decision of the competent organs, may never be relied on as against third parties, even if they have been disclosed.

This part of Article 9 represents something of a compromise between two incompatible theories of corporate acts. The difficulties which the United Kingdom has experienced in satisfactory implementation[97] are perhaps attributable to the fact that the provision draws heavily on two concepts which are relatively

---

[95] 'The acts of a director or manager are valid notwithstanding any defect that may afterwards be discovered in his appointment or qualification . . .'.

[96] The so-called 'rule in *Turquand's* case' (*Royal British Bank v Turquand* (1855) 5 E&B 248).

[97] See below, pp 42–4. Article 9 is not however wholly without difficulties itself (notwithstanding the beguilingly dismissive statement in Buxbaum, R M and Hopt, K J, *Legal Harmonization and the Business Enterprise* (1988) 251, that as well as providing for uniform disclosure of certain information it 'also settles a few technical questions of company law (validity of commitments made by company organs . . .)').

alien to English lawyers: the continental concept of a company 'organ' and the German theory of corporate representation, the *Organtheorie*. The matter is further confused by the fact that the word 'organ'—unfamiliar as it already is—is used in two different senses for these two purposes. It is helpful to an understanding of the Article to have some awareness of the two concepts. It is also helpful to separate the issues of acts beyond the objects of the company and acts beyond the authority of those purporting to represent the company.

A company's organs and division of powers

The term 'organ' is not a familiar one in UK company law,[98] but the concept is easily recognizable if described in more familiar terms. Companies, being artificial persons, of necessity have to be run by and act through individuals. There is no general term in English denoting the bodies which exercise the functions and powers of a company, in the United Kingdom the shareholders in general meeting and the board of directors; French, Dutch and German, however, have the useful term 'organ' (*orgaan*[99] in Dutch; *organe*[100] in French; *Organ* in German) which is used to cover bodies exercising such powers and functions. A distinction is drawn between the 'organs of decision and deliberation'[101] or internal administration and management—usually shared between the board of directors and the shareholders in general meeting—and the 'organs of representation', whose role is to effect relations between the company and third parties, and in particular to execute the decisions taken in exercise of the power of management. National law determines which organs have the power to commit the company *vis-à-vis* third parties and defines the scope of their power, whether directly by legislating or—as in the United Kingdom—indirectly by leaving it to be prescribed in the company's statutes.[102]

---

[98] Prentice, D D, goes so far as to assert that 'the First Directive does not fit neatly into the framework of English company law because of the absence of the concept of "organ" as being generally accepted within that system': 'Some Reflections on the Harmonisation of Company Law: An English Perspective' in De Witte, B and Forder, C (eds), *The Common Law of Europe and the Future of Legal Education* (1992) 349, 350–1.

[99] 'A (natural) person or board of persons, who pursuant to the law or statutes is competent to execute and express the will of the legal person. The legal person participates in legal matters by means of the organ. The organs of private law legal persons are: 1 the general meeting (of members and shareholders) . . . 2 the board of directors . . . 3 supervisors of the board of directors' [this refers to members of any supervisory board appointed: see the discussion of the draft 5th Directive in ch XIX]: *Fockema Andreae's Rechtsgeleerd Handwoordenboek* (1977), author's translation.

[100] 'An individual or a group of individuals, endowed with the power to carry out, with or without representation, the operation of a legal person. For example, the president [chairman], the board of directors, the general meeting . . .': Cornu, G, *Vocabulaire juridique* (1987), author's translation.

[101] Houin, R, 'Les pouvois des dirigeants des sociétés et la coordination des législations nationales' [1966] Revue trimestrielle de droit européen 307, 313.

[102] Although the continued existence of national differences will inevitably undermine the coordinating effect of the Directive, the alternative of a wholesale harmonization of the basic structure of the various types of corporate vehicle throughout the Community would be a major undertaking. See further Ault, H J, 'Harmonization of Company Law in the European Economic Community' (1968) 20 Hastings Law Journal 77, 108–9.

Theories of corporate representation

There are two conflicting theories of how a company's organs of representation may act for it. First, the mandate theory, which is derived from Roman law and reflected in the Napoleonic codes and the pre-implementation laws of the original Member States except Germany. The mandate theory is based on the view that the company acts through an agent the scope of whose authority, in accordance with the normal relationship between principal and agent, depends on his mandate from his principal, and hence may be more or less limited; it will be familiar to UK company lawyers since it is also the basis of the law of corporate representation in the United Kingdom. This may be contrasted[103] with the German *Organtheorie* of corporate acts, which views a company as itself acting through its 'organs', which express its will and whose powers so to act may be limited only by the law. Since the organ representing the company does so *as* the company, its powers to represent cannot be fettered by decisions of another organ of that company. The mandate theory unquestionably dominates UK company law, where the *Organtheorie* is only marginally recognized.[104]

It is useful to look further at the structure of corporate management and representation in Germany because Article 9 largely reflects the German approach, albeit tailored to meet the concerns of the other five original Member States. As a matter of German law, the *Vorstand* or executive board is the company's organ of representation; it is also, together with the general meeting, the organ of management. Its powers of management may be limited within legal parameters by the *Aufsichtsrat* (supervisory board), the statutes, the shareholders in general meeting or resolutions emanating from itself, but any such limitations are wholly ineffective as against third parties[105] except where the third party knows that the representative

---

[103] The distinction is more apparent in theory than relevant in practice: see Stein, E, *Harmonization of European Company Laws* (1971), 287–9, for a summary of 'the not-so-different legal reality', Van Ommeslaghe, P, 'La première directive du conseil du 9 mars 1968 en matière de sociétés [1969] Cahiers de droit européen 495, 619–27, for details of the situation in each of the original six Member States before implementation of the 1st Directive and Ault, ibid, 101–6 for an instructive comparison of German and French law and (at n 106) an outline of the reasons for the development of the different theories.

[104] See however Gower, L C B, *Principles of Modern Company Law* (5th edn, 1992), 193–7, for examples of judicial recognition of the organic theory in UK law. There is a more developed analysis of this in the 4th edition (1979) of Gower, 205–12; unfortunately the discussion has been much reduced in the 6th edition. Gower considers that the legislation by which the UK has implemented Art 9(2) (Companies Act 1985, s 35A) 'has, in effect, recognised that the board of directors is not a mere agent of the company but an organic part of it so that third parties can treat acts of the board as acts of the company itself' (5th edn, 197). It is arguable however that the wording of s 35A, which refers to 'the power of the board of directors to bind the company', is more in line with the mandate theory, and that it is s 35, which refers to the 'validity of an act *done by a company*' (emphasis added), which represents a more significant legislative acceptance of the *Organtheorie*. In any event the *Organtheorie* has at best a tenuous foothold in UK company law.

[105] The theory is heavily influenced by the German theory of *Prokura*, by virtue of which the powers of a commercial agent (*Prokurist*) are defined directly by the law and limitations on his powers set out in the agency contract are ineffective as against third parties. The effect of this is that such an agent

in exceeding them is abusing his power, or *a fortiori* colludes with him in so doing; mere knowledge that the limits are being exceeded does not operate against the third party. Such limitations however are effective internally, so that if the *Vorstand* disregards them its members will be in breach of their duty to the company.

Ultra vires

With the exception of Germany, the original Member States all subscribed to the principle of *spécialité statutaire* or ultra vires—the doctrine that acts beyond a company's stated capacity are void even when underpinned by the unanimous consent of its members. Although German law had originally encompassed a similar principle, by the time the Directive came to be negotiated it had been replaced by the principle that the validity of a corporate transaction was unaffected by whether the transaction fell within the company's objects and depended only on the scope of the representative power of the organ acting on its behalf; the extent to which that power could be fettered as against third parties by other organs, for example shareholders, was, as discussed above, strictly circumscribed by law. The corollary was that the law set the parameters of the representative power, and the company would not be bound by acts which the representative could not have as a matter of law.

Article 9(1) attempts to bridge the gap between Germany on the one hand and the remaining five original Member States on the other. It does this by drawing the basic principle—that ultra vires transactions bind the company—from one system of law, and the major qualification—that they may not bind the company as against certain third parties—from another. As outlined above, in Germany third parties will not fall outside the protection afforded by the German system unless there has been active collusion or fraud on their part. Less sufficed in the other systems, where a third party who merely knew or, even less, ought to have known was not protected. The qualification in the second sentence of Article 9(1) is couched in neutral terms to reflect the latter, and Member States are not required to provide for fraud or bad faith if they wish to make use of the option.[106]

The original Proposal for the Directive provided that transactions would bind a company unless they exceeded either the limits which the law imposed on the powers of the relevant organs or the company's objects; an ultra vires transaction would however be binding if the third party had good reasons (*justes motifs*) to believe that it fell within the scope of the objects (Article 11(1)). This clearly reflected a significant erosion of the German position, and was amended to deal with German fears that as drafted it required Germany to reintroduce the ultra vires

may carry out any transaction connected with any type of business: to use the example given by Heenen, J, in 'Le projet de première directive en matière de sociétés. Validité des engagements de la société' [1968] Europees Vennootschapsrecht 109, at 111: '*Le Prokurist d'un négoce de vin peut acheter des bas de soie*' (the commercial agent of a wine merchant may buy silk stockings).

[106] See La Villa, G, 'The Validity of Company Undertakings and the Limits of the E.E.C. Harmonization' (1974) 3 Anglo-American Law Review 346 for a well-argued analysis of this point.

doctrine and that the reasonable belief proviso would have undesirable repercussions in practice—for example, third parties would feel impelled to protect their position by requiring a legal opinion that proposed transactions were intra vires. The European Parliament suggested an amended Article 11 which provided that the company was bound as against third parties unless the transaction exceeded the limits laid down by the law on the powers of the representative organ, with the qualification that where national law recognized the ultra vires doctrine, the company could avoid a transaction on the ground that it was ultra vires only where it proved that the third party *savait ou devait savoir* (knew or should have/must have known) that the transaction was beyond the company's objects, thus reversing the burden of proof (Article 11(1)). The final version explicitly conferred an option on Member States to retain the principle that in certain circumstances a company was not bound by ultra vires transactions[107] and at the same time reinforced the qualification by expanding the elements to be proved by a company wishing to avoid such a transaction: the final version of Article 9(1) reads as follows:

Acts done by the organs of the company shall be binding upon it even if those acts are not within the objects of the company, unless such acts exceed the powers that the law confers or allows to be conferred on those organs.

However, Member States may provide that the company shall not be bound where such acts are outside the objects of the company, if it proves that the third party knew that the act was outside those objects or could not in view of the circumstances have been unaware of it; disclosure of the statutes shall not of itself be sufficient proof thereof.

Authority of a company's organs

Article 9(2), which restricts the circumstances in which a company may avoid a transaction on the ground that its organs exceeded their powers in purporting to effect it on behalf of the company, was also a compromise between Germany and the other five Member States. The latter all espoused the principle of constructive notice, by virtue of which third parties were deemed to have knowledge of publication of limitations on such powers and the company was able to avoid such a transaction. In Germany, as outlined above,[108] limitations on the powers of the representative organ, the *Vorstand*, other than mandatory limitations imposed by the law, were ineffective as against third parties. As in the case of ultra vires transactions, however, the courts had qualified the doctrine so as to narrow the difference for practical purposes.

Although it is Article 9(2) that focuses specifically on the powers of company organs, the starting point is the proviso to the first subparagraph of Article 9(1):

---

[107] Ficker, H C, notes in 'The EEC Directives on Company Law Harmonisation' in Schmitthoff, C M (ed), *The Harmonisation of European Company Law* (1973) 75 that the European Company Statute 'went a step further by resolving this question in the sense that even this last exception, restricting that power with external effect, would be abolished.' See ch XIX for a brief discussion of the European Company Statute, not yet adopted.

[108] See pp 35–6.

'Acts done by the organs of the company shall be binding upon it . . . unless such acts exceed the powers that the law confers or allows to be conferred on those organs.' This reflects the German principle that mandatory limits imposed by the law on the powers which may be conferred on the *Vorstand* may be relied on by the company against third parties. The effect is that:

the mere possibility at law of granting a power of decision or of representation to a given organ of the company is equivalent to granting that power, whether the possibility is exercised or not. As against third parties, acts carried out within the limits of this legal power are valid and bind the company.[109]

Article 9(1) was considered by the Court of Justice in the context of the power of directors to bind the company in *Rabobank v Minderhoud*,[110] which concerned the validity of an agreement entered into between a holding company HDG and various subsidiaries including Mediasafe on the one hand and Rabobank, the group's bank, on the other. The agreement dealt with, inter alia, the offsetting of debit and credit balances and under it the companies were to be jointly and severally liable to Rabobank. When it entered into the agreement Mediasafe was represented by HDG, its sole director. The Netherlands Civil Code provides that, where there is a conflict of interests between a company and the directors authorized to represent it, a legal instrument may be concluded only by the company's supervisory directors (*commissarrissen*). In proceedings as to the validity of the agreement, the Hoge Raad (Supreme Court) questioned whether it was compatible with Article 9 of the First Directive for a company to rely on that provision as against a third party and whether it was relevant that the third party knew or ought to have known of the conflict.

The Court of Justice stated that the purpose of the First Directive was to coordinate the safeguards required by Member States of limited companies for the purpose of protecting the interests of, inter alia, third parties. To that end, the Directive restricted to the greatest possible extent the grounds on which obligations entered into in the name of the company were not valid. It was clear from both the wording and the subject-matter of Article 9(1) that it concerned the limits on the powers[111] allocated by law to the various organs of the company and was not intended to coordinate the law applicable where there was a conflict of interest between a member of an organ and the company he represented because of the former's personal circumstances. Moreover, Article 9(1) related to the powers which the law, to which third parties could refer, granted or allowed to be granted to the company organ, and not to the question whether a third party was aware, or could not in the circumstances have been unaware, of a conflict of interests. The rules on the enforceability of acts done by members of company organs in such situations

---

[109] *Per* Advocate General Mayras in *Friedrich Haaga GmbH*, cited at n 60 above, at 1214.
[110] Case C–104/96 [1997] ECR I–7211.
[111] Although the English reads 'a company's powers', it is clear from the French that that is an error of translation.

accordingly fell outside the the First Directive and were matters for the national legislature.

Although the result is unobjectionable in the *Rabobank* case, it is submitted that the Court's statement that Article 9(1) relates only to the allocation of powers between the various organs is too narrow. The first phrase in Article 9(1) is, as discussed above, broader than that, laying down a general rule that transactions entered into on behalf of a company are binding. The proviso, as has been seen, reflects the position in those Member States with a two-tier board system, where mandatory limits imposed by the law on the powers which may be conferred on the executive (as opposed to the supervisory) board may be relied on by the company against third parties. The Court's ruling that the third party's actual or constructive knowledge is irrelevant to the type of situation at issue is, however, to be welcomed.

Article 9(2) continues: 'The limits on the powers of the organs of the company, arising under the statutes or from a decision of the competent organs, may never be relied on as against third parties, even if they have been disclosed.' The principle of constructive notice cannot therefore apply to such limits, and third parties are freed from the need to interpret the scope of limits which have been disclosed.

Where such limits have been imposed on the powers of an organ, Article 9(2) does not of course relieve that organ from its duty to observe the limits. Thus where a company's directors exceed limitations placed on their power by the statutes or by, for example, the general meeting, Article 9(2) will apply so as to protect third parties but will not relieve the directors from liability to the company for breach of duty. This was spelt out in the original Proposal, Article 11(2) of which provided that such limitations had effect only in the company's internal relations, but was dropped because this part of the Directive solely concerns the protection of third parties.[112]

What of the situation where the third party is aware that the organs have exceeded their powers? Article 9(1) gives Member States the option to derogate from the general protection of third parties to ultra vires transactions where the company 'proves that the third party knew that the act was outside [the] objects or could not in view of the circumstances have been unaware of it'. The question of incorporating a 'good faith' or analogous requirement in Article 9(2) was debated by the Council of Ministers after the European Parliament had proposed an amendment to the effect that limits in the statutes may never be relied on as against third parties in good faith. It was thought preferable however not to make specific provision but to leave it to national law to deal with the matter, although this is not made explicit in the Article. The Commission stated that

the 'good faith' qualification would introduce an ambiguity where security of transactions must prevail: 'How, for example, would one determine the good faith of a third party which questioned a limitation that was duly published? The adopted solution, in moving away from

---

[112] See the 5th recital in the preamble.

the ultra vires principle, constitutes a marked progress in the direction of the German system, recognized as offering maximum security of transactions in this matter'.[113]

The Council of Ministers agreed that it was preferable not to legislate specifically on this point, since each system of law would bring its own counterbalancing principle to bear, the legal nature of which would vary between the Member States,[114] and made it clear in a declaration incorporated in the minutes of the relevant session that Article 9(2) was intended to exclude fraud. The intention was presumably to reflect the position in Germany, where, as stated above, mere knowledge by a third party of limits on the representative's powers will not operate against him, but awareness of abuse or participation in fraud by the representative will defeat his claim.[115]

Conflict with the disclosure requirements

Stein[116] relates how the Italian deputy who cast the only negative vote in the European Parliament against the Directive gave as his reason that:

he could not conceive how [it] could provide in one article that the company may rely on properly published information against third parties, and at the same time in another article exclude such reliance with respect to properly published limitations on the powers of company officials. He called the approved text 'a beast with a Latin head and a German body and tail'.

Is there a conflict between Article 3(5), which provides that the 'documents [including the company's instrument of constitution and statutes] and particulars [including amendments thereto] may be relied on by the company as against third parties only after they have been published', and Article 9(1) and 9(2)? Certainly Prentice[117] considered that there was such a conflict between the relevant provisions of the United Kingdom implementing legislation. It seems clear however from the wording of the Directive that Article 9(1) and 9(2) are intended to prevail: 'disclosure of the statutes *shall not* of itself be sufficient proof [of knowledge by a third party]'; 'The limits . . . *may never* be relied on . . . even if they have been disclosed' (emphasis added). The Economic and Social Committee seems to have assumed that the intention behind at least the first draft was that any limitation on

---

[113] *Exposé des motifs* for the amended Proposal, 31, translation from Stein, E, *Harmonization of European Company Laws* (1971) 293, n 175.

[114] Van Ommeslaghe gives as examples '*responsibilité aquilienne, agissement en contravention avec les "Gute Sitten", complicité dans la violation d'une obligation contractuelle*' (tortious liability, acts contrary to good practice, complicity in breaching a contractual obligation): 'La première directive du conseil du 9 mars 1968 en matière de sociétés' [1969] Cahiers de droit Européen 495, 632, n 140.

[115] See Stein (n 113 above) 294, and Van Ommeslaghe (n 114 above) 632. In relation to the current UK implementing legislation, the Companies Act 1985, s 35A (inserted by the Companies Act 1989, s 108), it seems that it was the UK Government's intention that bad faith 'should mean participating knowingly in an act of the directors which constitutes a breach of their fiduciary duties and not merely an act in excess of their authority': Davies, P L, *Gower's Principles of Modern Company Law* (6th edn, 1997) 228, n 33.

[116] See n 113 above, 295–6.

[117] 'Section 9 of the European Communities Act' (1973) 89 LQR 518, 538–43.

the powers could not be relied on as against third parties, even if published, and rather plaintively stated that on that assumption it could not understand the requirement for publishing the statutes.[118]

This view appears to run counter to the dictum of the Court of Justice in *Ubbink Isolatie BV v Dak- en Wandtechniek BV*[119] that 'The purpose of the [First] directive is not therefore to permit third parties to rely on appearances created by the company's organs or representatives if those appearances do not conform to the information contained in the public register', but it is submitted that that dictum cannot have been intended to apply generally: the Court was there considering whether the rules on the nullity of companies in Section III of the Directive applied where the putative company had not been constituted in national law by reason of the failure to complete the requisite formalities required by that law, and was formulating the principle that the rules on nullity applied only where third parties had been led to believe by information published in accordance with Section I that a company existed. The case is considered in more detail at pages 47 to 48 below. The rather startling statement by Advocate General Mayras in *Friedrich Haaga GmbH*[120] that 'Where third parties are informed by such disclosure [of nominations, resignations or revocations concerning the organs of the company, and . . . of the clauses in the basic documents setting out the latters' precise powers], to which they generally have access, the company is entitled to rely on statements published' is somewhat harder to reconcile with the express terms of the Directive, but is fortunately contradicted by the subsequent statement that 'restrictions imposed upon the power to represent the company, even if disclosed, may not be relied on as against third parties, pursuant to . . . Article 9(2) of the Directive'.[121]

The point was considered, albeit obiter and by way of analogy only, by the Court of Appeal in England in *Official Custodian for Charities v Parway Estates Ltd*.[122] The case concerned the United Kingdom legislation originally implementing Article 3(5), s 9(4) of the European Communities Act 1972,[123] and in so far as relevant to Article 3(5) is considered above.[124] In addition, however, the court specifically considered the effect of the requirement in the sub-section to notify changes in the objects clause and among the company's directors. Dillon LJ stated:

it is plain to my mind from section 9(1) [purporting to implement Article 9(1)] that a person dealing in good faith with a company is not to be treated as having constructive notice . . . of the terms of the company's objects clause, whether in its original form or from time to time altered, and is not to be treated as having constructive notice of the composition from time to time of the board of directors of the company. The tenor of the section is thus against imputing constructive notice of relevant events to persons dealing with a company, while ensuring that they have an opportunity to find out information about those events.

---

[118] [1964] JO 3254.
[120] Case 32/74 [1974] ECR 1201, at 1210.
[122] [1985] Ch 151.
[124] See pp 30–31.

[119] Case 136/87 [1988] ECR 4665, at para 13.
[121] ibid, at 1214.
[123] Now the Companies Act 1985, s 42.

Implementation of Articles 9(1) and (2) in the United Kingdom

The problems arising from the United Kingdom's attempts to implement Article 9(1) and (2) are legion, and will be discussed here only to the extent that they may cast light on the Directive itself or, conversely, be resolved by recourse to the Directive.[125] Much of the difficulty, as suggested above, doubtless stems from the unfamiliar concepts; much however must also be attributed to the 'obscurities and inadequacies' and 'unhappy wording'[126] of the original implementing legislation, s 9(1) of the European Communities Act 1972. In relation to Article 9(1), many of the problems arising from s 9(1) have been resolved by its second re-enactment (by the Companies Act 1989) as s 35 of the Companies Act 1985: in particular, the problems caused by limiting the operation of the section to the third party,[127] the references to 'dealing with a company' and 'transaction', the incorporation of a requirement of good faith (still however retained in the provision implementing Article 9(2); see below) and the reference to 'decided on by the directors' have been resolved by drafting which is both clearer and closer to the Directive.

In relation to Article 9(2) however numerous problems remain, notwithstanding the extensive changes to the implementing legislation effected by the Companies Act 1989. The original s 35 of the Companies Act 1985 has been replaced, in so far as it purported to implement Article 9(2), by a new and relatively long s 35A dealing specifically with the power of directors to bind the company. Section 35A(1) reads: 'In favour of a person dealing with a company in good faith, the power of the board of directors to bind the company, or authorise others to do so, shall be deemed to be free of any limitation under the company's constitution.'

As indicated above, 'organ' is not a term of art in United Kingdom company law[128]

---

[125] It is a striking feature of UK commentators on EC-derived legislation that, despite the grave assurance by Farrar, J H and Powles, D G, that the Directive is 'admissible as evidence in construing' implementing legislation ('The Effect of Section 9 of the European Communities Act 1972 on English Company Law' (1973) 36 MLR 270, n 7), very few consider the source text. Unfortunately the tendency continues: Pennington, for example, makes no mention of the 1st Directive at all, let alone its wording, in his chapters on pre-incorporation contracts, the doctrine of ultra vires and transactions in excess of directors' authority (*Company Law* (1995) Chs 4 and 5), and indeed none of the company law or any other directives feature in his Table of Statutes, although two US Acts are included. Fortunately the judicature has been more prepared to refer to the Directive: Lawson J in *International Sales and Agencies Ltd v Marcus* [1982] 3 All ER 551, at 559, in construing the European Communities Act 1972, s 9(1), took into account the recitals in the Directive, the heading of s II and the words of Art 9 (which he described as 'the ancestor of s 9(1)') and Browne-Wilkinson VC in *TCB Ltd v Gray* [1986] Ch 621 took into account the 'manifest purpose' of the Directive in construing the section.

[126] Gower, L C B, *Principles of Modern Company Law* (4th edn, 1979) 179, 184.

[127] As Gower points out, the Directive 'does not specifically deal with this point, presumably because prior to the entry of the common law countries it did not occur to anyone concerned with the Directive that any legal system could be so asinine as to allow a third party to invoke ultra vires against the company': ibid (5th edn, 1992) 172, n 28.

[128] Although the Irish European Communities (Companies) Regulations 1973 (SI 1973/163) make use of the concept, defining the organs of the company as the board of directors and any other person registered under the regulations as authorized to bind the company. Companies may so register persons by delivering to the Registrar of Companies a notice of who these persons are. As at 1984, however, no Irish company had ever registered such a person, so that for practical purposes 'organ' meant board of

and there has been much confusion over its meaning[129] and therefore over the extent to which United Kingdom legislation fully implements Article 9(1) and (2). It is helpful to look at Article 9(2) in the context of the wording and purpose of the Directive as a whole, and to consider the combined effect of that provision and Article 2(1)(d), which it will be recalled requires disclosure of the 'appointment, termination of office and particulars of the persons who either as a body constituted pursuant to law or as members of any such body: (i) are authorised to represent the company in dealings with third parties and in legal proceedings . . .' Since the object of the latter is that 'third parties may be able to ascertain . . . particulars of the persons who are authorised to bind the company', and the object of the former is to ensure 'the protection of third parties . . . by provisions which restrict to the greatest possible extent the grounds on which obligations entered into in the name of the company are not valid',[130] it seems sensible to interpret acts of the 'organs' of the company under Article 9 by reference to Article 2(1)(d). The connection between these two aims was explored in *Friedrich Haaga GmbH* by Advocate General Mayras, who stated 'Third parties must be able to trust appearances while having the guarantee that, if they deal with one or more persons purporting to be the legal representatives of the company, a contract concluded with such person or persons will be binding upon the company itself.'[131] 'Organs' thus includes the board and those members of it authorized to represent the company alone or jointly. It seems clear therefore that in UK terms it includes both managing directors and chief executives with the normal powers attaching to such an office and secretaries within the relatively restricted scope of their authority. On that basis, the current implementing legislation, s 35A of the Companies Act 1985, is still defective in that it is restricted to 'the power of the board of directors to bind the company, or authorise others to do so'.

Article 9(2) refers to 'limits on the powers of the organs of the company, arising under the statutes or from a decision of the competent organs . . .': This is not fully reflected by s 35A, which specifies that the references in sub-s (1) to 'limitations on the directors' powers under the company's constitution include limitations deriving—(a) from a resolution of the company in general meeting or a meeting of any

---

directors alone: see Forde, M, 'The First Directive and Transactions with Outsiders' (1984) 7 Journal of the Irish Society of European Law 8, 15–16.

[129] Wooldridge, for example, considers that it excludes managing directors (*Company Law in the United Kingdom and the European Community* (1991) 20), as do Farrar and Powles ('The Effect of Section 9 of the European Communities Act 1972 on English Company Law' (1973) 36 MLR 270, 274–5), whose conclusion that *organe* 'probably means organ' is both unhelpful and, to the extent that it obscures the distinction between organs of representation and of management, misleading. Gower's statement that 'the members in general meeting . . . must be an "organ" of the company within the meaning of the First Directive' (*Principles of Modern Company Law* (4th edn, 1979) 187) surprisingly seems to reflect the same failure to distinguish between the two types of organ.

[130] See the 4th and 5th recitals in the preamble.

[131] Case 32/74 [1974] ECR 1201, at 1210. See Wyatt, D, 'The First Directive and Company Law' (1978) 94 LQR 182, for a lucid and cogent review of the issue, helpfully illustrated by reference to the relevant German law.

class of shareholders, or (b) from any agreement between the members of the company or of any class of shareholders.' This is fine as far as it goes, but does not go far enough. One of the major uncertainties raised by s 35A is whether it applies to limitations deriving from board resolutions; clearly Article 9(2) requires that it should. This problem is significant in practice, since delegated authority, for example to a managing director or chief executive, is often contained in board minutes, and if such authority is subject to specified limitations, s 35A will be of no assistance (although if power to delegate, rather than the authority delegated, is subject to limitations, then s 35A will apply).

The question of what is meant by 'good faith' in the implementing legislation has excited extensive comment. The issue seems less of a problem, however, in the light of the background to and drafting history of the Directive[132] than many United Kingdom commentators have assumed. Farrar and Powles observe that 'It seems strange that the United Kingdom Parliament should adopt a term rejected by the Commission';[133] this may not in fact be as strange as it seems, since it is clear that the Council deliberately left national law free to limit the operation of Article 9(2) in certain circumstances and within reasonably ascertainable parameters (this is not however to say that it would not have been helpful to have this explicitly stated in the Article). Furthermore, there is now sound authority on the construction of the former 'good faith' requirement in s 9(1) of the European Communities Act 1972 to be found in the judgments of Lawson J in *International Sales and Agencies Ltd v Marcus*[134] and Nourse J in *Barclays Bank Ltd v TOSG Trust Fund Ltd*:[135] it is interesting to note that the former referred to the purpose and wording of the Directive for guidance on the limits of 'good faith', while the latter felt that it was unnecessary to do so since the meaning of the term was clear.[136]

---

[132] See above, pp 36–7.   [133] See n 129 above, 273, n 30.

[134] [1982] 3 All ER 551, 559: '. . . the test of lack of good faith in somebody entering into obligations with a company will be found either in proof of his actual knowledge that the transaction was ultra vires the company or where it can be shown that such a person could not, in view of all the circumstances, have been unaware that he was party to a transaction ultra vires.'

[135] [1984] BCLC 1, 17: 'In my judgment the expression "in good faith" is one whose meaning is well established and understood in our law. It does not admit of any ambiguity or doubt . . . Notice and good faith, although two separate beings, are often inseparable . . . a person who deals with a company in circumstances where he ought anyway to know that the company has no power to enter into the transaction will not necessarily act in good faith . . . I emphatically refute the suggestion . . . that reasonableness is a necessary ingredient of good faith . . . a person acts in good faith if he acts genuinely and honestly in the circumstances of the case.'

[136] The term is apparently also a 'legislative stalwart' with an accepted meaning in Ireland: see Ussher, P, 'Questions of Capacity: The Implementation in the Republic of Ireland and in the United Kingdom of the First EEC Companies Directive' (1975) 10 Irish Jurist 39, who gives as an example 'the "bona fide" traveller of the liquor licensing legislation . . . who, it appears, was required to be genuinely travelling for a purpose other than drinking': 44, n 28.

Conferring authority on one or more persons

Article 9(3) provides:

If the national law provides that authority to represent a company may, in derogation from the legal rules governing the subject, be conferred by the statutes on a single person or on several persons acting jointly, that law may provide that such a provision in the statutes may be relied on as against third parties on condition that it relates to the general power of representation; the question whether such a provision in the statutes can be relied on as against third parties shall be governed by Article 3.

This clause is another compromise between Germany and the other original Member States. In Germany, where the authority of the *Vorstand* is prima facie collective, a company's statutes may provide that the power of representation may be exercised by one or more of the members of the *Vorstand*. Such a clause is regarded as extending rather than limiting the power of representation of the *Vorstand*. Since it is not a limitation, it is not caught by Article 9(2) which would not therefore prevent the company from relying on it as against third parties. In France, by contrast, the president of a company has by law sole power of representation *vis-à-vis* third parties, so that an analogous provision in a company's statutes to the effect that the power of representation was to be exercised by the president and another member of the board would conceptually be a limitation rather than an extension of powers. It would therefore fall within the scope of Article 9(2) and the company could not rely on it as against third parties. The intention behind Article 9(3) is to prevent the question whether such clauses in a company's constitution conferring representative power on one or several persons amount to limitations or extensions of the powers of the organs, and hence whether Article 9(2) precludes the company from relying on them as against third parties, from being determined by the somewhat arbitrary criterion of which country is involved.

Article 9(3) has not been implemented in the United Kingdom, although national law[137] satisfies the initial proviso so that implementation is possible in principle.

Section III—Nullity of the Company

Articles 10 to 12 concern the circumstances in which a company may be declared invalidly constituted and hence a nullity from its inception, with grave implications

---

[137] The common law rule that the board of directors can act on behalf of the company only by collective decision, and may not delegate its powers to one or more persons, unless the company's articles so permit. See cases cited in Pennington, R R, *Company Law* (7th edn, 1995) 153, nn 16 and 18. Cf Emlyn Davies, J A, 'Company Law and the Common Market: The First Step' in *An Introduction to the Law of the European Economic Community* (1972) 48, where the view is expressed in effect that Art 9(3) is already reflected in UK law: 'a registered company may provide for [the board's collective] power to be vested in an individual director or directors or in a committee of directors to the exclusion of the board. This is clearly a situation to which Art 9(3) applies'.

for shareholders, creditors and employees. The policy behind this section of the Directive is 'to limit the cases in which nullity can arise and the retroactive effect of a declaration of nullity, and to fix a short time limit within which third parties may enter objections to any such declaration.'[138] A declaration of nullity was a rare occurrence even in those original Member States which recognized the concept, so that these provisions are relatively unimportant. In the United Kingdom, the concept is unrecognized[139] and hence this section has not been implemented.

Before implementation of the Directive, Germany, Italy and the Netherlands all had a system of administrative or judicial supervision of compliance with the legal requirements for forming a company, intended to ensure that companies were validly incorporated. Any irregularity or defect in formation could be the basis of an action for a declaration of nullity, although the persons entitled to bring such an action and the effects of a declaration of nullity varied between those States. France was moving towards a similar system at the time the First Directive was being negotiated.[140] There was no analogous regime in Belgium or Luxembourg, where companies could be formed easily and without formal supervision, although a notary was required to draw up the constitutive documents as a notarial act; a declaration of nullity could be obtained in specified circumstances.[141]

Article 10 seeks to prevent the defective constitution of companies. It provides that in those Member States which do not have 'preventive control, administrative or judicial, at the time of formation of a company, the instrument of constitution, the company statutes and any amendments to those documents shall be drawn up and certified in due legal form.'

Article 11 provides that nullity may only be ordered by decision of a court of law and on the following grounds:[142]

(1)   failure to execute an instrument of constitution or comply with the rules of preventive control or the requisite legal formalities;

(2)   unlawfulness or conflict with public policy of company's objects;

(3)   failure to state in the instrument of constitution or the statutes the company's name or objects or the amount of the individual and total capital subscriptions;

(4)   failure to comply with national law requirements for minimum paid-up capital;

(5)   incapacity of all the founder members;

[138] 6th recital in the preamble.

[139] This flows from the conclusiveness of the certificate of incorporation issued by the Registrar of Companies: see the Companies Act 1985, s 13(7)(a).

[140] See Ault, H J, 'Harmonization of Company Law in the European Economic Community' (1968) 20 Hastings Law Journal 77, 110–11, for an outline of the position in French law.

[141] See Van Ommeslaghe, P, 'La première directive du conseil du 9 mars 1968 en matière de sociétés' [1969] Cahiers de droit européen 495, 640–53, for details of the relevant laws.

[142] See Stein, E, *Harmonization of European Company Laws* (1971) 304–9, for an account of the trade-offs between the various original Member States which led to the list of grounds in the final version. It is clear from the wording of the article that the grounds listed are exhaustive; this has been confirmed by the Court of Justice in Case C–106/89 *Marleasing v La Comercial Internacional de Alimentación* considered below.

(6)   reduction of the number of founder members to less than two, contrary to the national law governing the company.[143]

Article 12 provides that the question whether a declaration of nullity may be relied on as against third parties shall be governed by Article 3,[144] and that where national law entitles a third party to challenge the decision he may do so only within six months of public notice thereof. Nullity shall, and dissolution may, entail the winding up of the company; it shall not of itself affect the validity of existing commitments involving the company. National law may provide for the consequences of nullity as between members; holders of unpaid or partly paid shares shall remain obliged to pay the unpaid balance to the extent that debts are owed by the company.

The Court of Justice has considered the provisions of the Directive relating to nullity in two cases. The first, *Ubbink Isolatie BV v Dak- en Wandtechniek BV*,[145] concerned a partnership, Ubbink Isolatie, which was registered in the Dutch commercial register as a private company in the course of being formed, under the name 'Ubbink Isolatie BV, i.o.';[146] there was no mention in that register of a company 'Ubbink Isolatie BV'. Ubbink did not satisfy either of the two Dutch law requirements for the constitution of a private company, namely an authentic instrument of constitution and ministerial authorization. It entered into an agreement with Dak- en Wandtechniek under the name 'Ubbink Isolatie BV' and proceedings were brought against it under that name in connection with the agreement. Ubbink's defence was that no company of that name lawfully existed and that actions undertaken in that name had therefore been carried out unlawfully. The *Arrondissementsrechtbank* (District Court) ruled that even if Ubbink Isolatie BV had never been constituted, or the instrument of constitution was defective, a company of that name nonetheless existed until it was wound up or a declaration of nullity was made in accordance with Dutch legislation. The latter provided that where business had been carried on in the name of a private company which had not been registered in the commercial register and before an instrument forming the company had been duly drawn up, or without ministerial authorization, a declaration of nullity could be obtained. Ubbink appealed unsuccessfully to the *Gerechtshof* (Regional Court of Appeal), and on an application to review that decision, the Hoge Raad (Supreme Court) ruled that that legislation must be interpreted in the light of Section III of the Directive, which was its source. It accordingly sought a preliminary ruling from the Court of Justice on the question whether, where business is carried on in the name of a company which has not been constituted under national law, the rules in Section III 'mean that in proceedings brought against it

---

[143] Art 11(2)(a)–(f). In so far as concerns private companies, Art 11(2)(f) must now be regarded as otiose in the light of the Twelfth Directive on Single-member Companies, Art 1 of which provides: 'A company may have a sole member when it is formed . . .'; see ch IX.

[144] See pp 19–20 above.   [145] Case 136/87 [1988] ECR 4665.

[146] *In oprichting* (in formation).

"the company" must be treated as being in existence so long as its nullity has not been declared in separate proceedings for a declaration of nullity'.

The Court of Justice looked at the purpose of the Directive as a whole: to protect in particular the interests of third parties. Section I imposes disclosure requirements

to provide third parties with prior information on the essential features of companies . . . Consequently, third parties may legitimately rely on . . . information . . . the subject of disclosure . . . Consequently, the rules concerning . . . nullity . . . apply only where third parties have been led to believe by information published in accordance with Section I that a company . . . exists.

Since third parties cannot be in that position when

the formalities required by national law for incorporation . . . have not been completed and for that reason the company appears in the public register as a company in the course of formation . . . [the rules on nullity in the Directive] do not apply where the acts involved were performed in the name of a . . . company whose existence is not confirmed by the public register because the formalities for incorporation required by national law have not been completed.[147]

In *Marleasing v La Comercial Internacional de Alimentación*,[148] the Court was asked to rule on whether Article 11 of the Directive, which had not been implemented by Spain, was 'directly applicable so as to preclude a declaration of nullity of a public limited company on a ground other than those set out in [that] article'. Marleasing had sought, inter alia, annulment of La Comercial's instrument of incorporation for lack of cause, relying on provisions of the Spanish Civil Code. La Comercial argued that the application for annulment should be dismissed on the ground that 'the First Directive, Article 11 of which sets out the exhaustive list of cases in which a . . . company may be declared void, does not include lack of cause.'[149] At the relevant time, the First Directive had not, but should have, been implemented by Spain.[150] It was settled case-law that 'a directive may not of itself impose obligations on an individual and, consequently, a provision of a directive may not be relied upon as against such a person'.[151]

---

[147] Paras 12–16 of the judgment. For a commentary on the case, see Benoit-Moury, A, 'Droit européen des sociétés et interprétations des juridictions communautaires' (1993) Revue de droit international et de droit comparé vol LXX 105, 118–21.

[148] Case C–106/89 [1990] ECR I–4135. The case has been described by Judge David Edward of the Court of Justice as 'of particular significance for British company lawyers who are used to looking at the Companies Acts without regard to the underlying Community directives': 'Corporations and the Court' in *Corporate Law: The European Dimension* (1991) 149, 155.

[149] See the Report for the Hearing, [1990] ECR I–4135, 4139.

[150] It was subsequently implemented by Law No 19/1989 of 25 July 1989 on the partial reforming and adjustment of commercial legislation in order to comply with the directives of the EEC on companies.

[151] Para 6 of the judgment, citing Case 152/84 *Marshall v Southampton and South-West Hampshire Area Health Authority* [1986] ECR 723.

The Court however went on to hold that:

in applying national law, whether the provisions in question were adopted before or after the directive, the national court called upon to interpret it is required to do so, as far as possible, in the light of the wording and the purpose of the directive in order to achieve the result pursued by the latter . . . It follows that the requirement that national law must be interpreted in conformity with Article 11 . . . precludes the interpretation of provisions of national law relating to public limited companies in such a manner that the nullity of a public limited company may be ordered on grounds other than those exhaustively listed in Article 11 . . .[152]

The Court also confirmed the Commission's view that the expression 'objects of the company' in Article 11(2)(b) 'must be understood as referring to the objects of the company as described in the instrument of incorporation or the articles of association'[153] rather than to the company's actual activities or the purpose of incorporating it (in that case, allegedly fraud). Advocate General Van Gerven had pointed out the divergence between the phrase in the Dutch[154] and German[155] versions of the Directive on the one hand and in the French, Italian and Spanish[156] versions on the other, and concluded that in the light of the Directive's objective of 'protecting the interests of third parties', each ground of nullity must be given a narrow interpretation, and that accordingly:

the phrase 'the objects of the company' in Article 11(2)(b) . . . must be understood as meaning the company's objects as described and disclosed in the instrument of incorporation or the statutes . . . *Only where the objects, in that sense, 'are unlawful or contrary to public policy' can a declaration of nullity of the company be made.* An aim for which the company was incorporated but which is not stated in the instrument of incorporation or the statutes . . . cannot have that consequence: such illegality or conflict with public policy . . . must be dealt with otherwise than by a declaration of nullity [emphasis added].[157]

Confusingly, however, this is contradicted in the next paragraph: 'if the company's real activity . . . is unlawful or contrary to public policy, the ground of nullity provided for in Article 11(2)(b) can be relied upon, even though that activity is not in accordance with the company's presumably lawful objects as described in the instrument of incorporation or the statutes.' It is difficult to reconcile these two statements, but it seems that the second is intended to qualify the first, notwithstanding the unequivocal terms in which the first is expressed.

It is interesting to note that all the language versions except English, Danish[158] and Greek[159] distinguish between the objects of the company referred to in Article

---

[152] Paras 8 and 9.   [153] Para 12 of the judgment.
[154] [Het] *werkelijke doel van de vennootschap* (the actual objects of the company).
[155] [Der] *tatsächlich[er] Gegenstand des Unternehmens* (the actual objects of the company).
[156] Respectively *l'objet de la société*, [il] *oggetto della società* and [el] *objeto de la sociedad*. All language versions are of course equally authentic.
[157] Para 16 of the Opinion.
[158] Which uses the same word, *formål*, which like the English 'objects' covers both concepts.
[159] Which also uses the same word, *skopos*, which covers both concepts.

11(2)(b) and those referred to in Article 11(2)(c),[160] which does seem to support the view that a distinction was intended and that Article 11(2)(b) should be construed as referring to the actual objects. No help can be gleaned from the earlier drafts, since the forerunner of Article 11(2)(b) is in identical terms and Article 11(2)(c) was added, in its final terms, at a later stage. Both major commentators on the Directive, however, seem to consider that Article 11(2)(b) is intended to refer to the objects as set out in the instrument of constitution or statutes.[161]

Whatever the validity of Advocate General Van Gerven's argument as to the proper scope of Article 11(2)(b), it is submitted that there is nothing in the Directive to support the distinction he draws between an unlawful activity carried on from the outset, which he believes to be a ground of nullity, and unlawful activity subsequently carried on, which he considers 'cannot give rise to the nullity of the company'.[162]

---

[160] The French, Italian, Spanish and Portuguese texts refer to the 'object of the company' in Art 11(2)(b)—the French, Italian and Spanish terms are set out in n 156 above and the Portuguese is *do objecto da sociedade*—and the 'social object', respectively *l'objet social, l'oggetto sociale, [el] objeto social* and *[o] objecto social*, in Art 11(2)(c). The Dutch and German texts distinguish between the 'actual objects' in Art 11(2)(b) and the 'objects', unqualified, in Art 11(2)(c).

[161] Stein, E, *Harmonization of European Company Laws* (1971) 305; Van Ommeslaghe, P, 'La première directive du conseil du 9 mars 1968 en matière de sociétés' [1969] Cahiers de droit européen 495, 660. Van Ommeslaghe explicitly states that the Directive does not cover 'illegal purpose' (*cause illicite*) as distinct from unlawful stated objects. For further comment on the *Marleasing* case, see Benoit-Moury, A, 'Droit européen des sociétés et interprétations des jurisdictions communautaires' (1993) Revue de droit internatonal et de droit comparé vol LXX 105, 121–5 and Tridimas, T, 'The Case-Law of the European Court of Justice on Corporate Entities' (1993) 13 Yearbook of European Law 335, 348–51.

[162] Para 17 of the Opinion.

III

The Second Directive

Background

The second company law directive deals with the formation of public limited companies and the maintenance and alteration of their capital. In tenor and approach it differs from the First Directive: many of the provisions lay down detailed procedural requirements rather than simply directing the Member States to legislate to a certain end, and it has been criticized by some commentators for that reason.[1] In terms of its substance[2] however the Second Directive is undeniably of major importance, constituting a significant step towards company law harmonization in the European Community, and it has been welcomed by others as a heartening illustration of harmonization at its best.[3]

The drafting of the Second Directive, in contrast to that of the First Directive, was significantly influenced by British and Irish company lawyers and accountants, and the provisions relating to financial assistance for the purchase by a company of its own shares and to redemption of shares (Articles 23 and 39) are modelled on the existing United Kingdom legislation.[4] Certain of the other provisions relating to the maintenance of capital reflect at least in part the pre-existing United Kingdom law[5] and to that extent were uncontroversial. None the less, many of the provisions in the Directive derive from continental legal systems with different approaches to capital and to shareholder and creditor protection and its reception in the United Kingdom was mixed.[6] Its implementation involved a number of

---

[1] See for example Rodière, R, 'L'harmonisation des législations européennes dans le cadre de la C.E.E.' [1965] Revue trimestrielle de droit européen 336, 352.

[2] There are useful summaries from the UK perspective by Morse, G, 'The Second Directive: Raising and Maintenance of Capital' [1977] ELR 126 and by Schmitthoff, C M, 'The Second EEC Directive on Company Law' (1978) 15 CML Rev 43, and from the Irish perspective by Temple Lang, J, 'The Second EEC Company Law Directive, on Maintenance and Alteration of Capital, and its Implementation in Irish Law' (1976) 9 Irish Jurist 37. There is also a comprehensive analysis in French by Keutgen, G, 'La deuxième directive en matière de sociétés' (1977) 5925 Revue pratique des sociétés 1.

[3] See for example Schmitthoff's concluding comments, ibid, 54: 'With admirable skill, the best features of national company laws have been welded together.'

[4] Companies Act 1948, ss 54 and 58. See further, as to s 54, pp 73–5 below.

[5] For example, the statutory restriction on reduction of capital (Companies Act 1948, ss 66–8, now Companies Act 1985, ss 135–7) and the case-law prohibiting the acquisition by a company of shares in itself (*Trevor v Whitworth* (1887) 12 App Cas 409) and the issue of shares at a discount (*Ooregum Gold Mining Co v Roper* [1892] AC 125).

[6] Manifestations of resistance range from the palpable suspicion of 'the Civil Law' which runs through the 24th Report from the Select Committee of the House of Lords on the European

significant changes to United Kingdom company law (described by Gower as 'probably [amounting] to the most funadamental adoption so far by English company law of civil law practices'[7]) in particular in relation to minimum subscribed capital, the distinction between public and private companies, distributions, consideration for shares generally and in particular the valuation of non-cash consideration, pre-emptive rights, authorization for new issues and the requirement to hold a meeting in the event of a serious loss of capital.

The original Proposal for the Directive was approved by the Commission and transmitted to the Council in March 1970.[8] The Economic and Social Committee gave its Opinion on the text in May 1971[9] and the European Parliament in October 1971.[10] The Proposal was then amended to take account of the accession of the United Kingdom, Ireland and Denmark[11] and finally adopted as the Second Council Directive (EEC) 77/91 of 13 December 1976 on coordination of safeguards which, for the protection of interests of members and others, are required by Member States of companies within the meaning of the second paragraph of Article 58 of the Treaty, in respect of the formation of public limited liability companies and the maintenance and alteration of their capital, with a view to making such safeguards equivalent.[12]

Scope

Article 1(1) provides that 'the coordination measures prescribed by this Directive shall apply' to public limited companies and equivalent forms, and that the name of any such company 'shall comprise or be accompanied by a description which is distinct from the description required of other types of companies'.[13] The first recital in the preamble states that coordination is especially important in relation to such companies 'because their activities predominate in the economy of the Member States and frequently extend beyond their national boundaries'. The *Exposé des motifs* of the original Proposal added that such companies were legally the most sophisticated, and that their coordination would pave the way for coordination of other types of company. In this chapter, the term 'company' used in relation to the provisions of the Directive means a public limited company.[14]

Communities (Session 1974–75, HL Paper 239) to the colourful xenophobia of Bennett Miller, J, in 'Harmonisation of Company Law: The Second EEC Directive' (1977) 22 Journal of the Law Society of Scotland 370, who describes the Directive as 'obscure' (Art 6); 'orotund and rather futile' (Art 7); and 'luckless' (Art 25). Morse (n 2 above) concludes with the Delphic description of the Directive as 'a gauntlet, at least of cardboard'.

  [7] Davies, P L, *Gower's Principles of Modern Company Law* (6th edn, 1997) 239.
  [8] COM (70) 232 final, 5 March 1970; [1970] JO C48/8.   [9] [1971] JO C88/1.
  [10] [1971] JO C114/18.   [11] COM (72) 1310 final, 30 October 1972.
  [12] [1977] OJ L26/1.
  [13] In the UK, 'public limited company' or 'plc' or the Welsh equivalent: Companies Act 1985, s 25.
  [14] Note however that Art 24a, inserted by Directive (EEC) 92/101 [1992] OJ L347/64, covers the subscription, acquisition or holding of shares in a public company by another company within the meaning of Art 1 of the 1st Directive which is controlled by a public company: see pp 76–7 below.

The Commission's amended Proposal included in the list of companies to which it was to apply private companies incorporated in the United Kingdom and Ireland, the Commission having taken the view that those private companies did not have the same status as private companies in the other Member States. This may have been by analogy with the First Directive, where for the specific purpose of disclosure of accounts (and in the only provision to distinguish between private and public companies) British—though not Northern Irish or Irish—private companies were assimilated to public companies.[15] There were however sound reasons for assimilating British companies to continental public companies for the purpose of Article 2(1)(f) of the First Directive, since the former, like the latter and in general unlike continental private companies, were already subject to the requirement to publish their accounts.[16] Alternatively, the Commission's view may have reflected the continental view that public and private companies were two wholly distinct types of corporate vehicle,[17] whereas in the United Kingdom and Ireland before implementation of the Second Directive there was only one recognized type of company and public companies were the residual class of companies which did not satisfy the specific requirements of a private company.[18] As a compromise, the Commission initially suggested in response to resistance from the United Kingdom[19] and Ireland that private companies which satisfied specified conditions[20] should be required to have a minimum capital of only 10,000 units of

[15] See Art 2(1)(f) of the 1st Directive, discussed in ch II. For further discussion of this provision as the possible source of the Commission's initial view, see Welch, J, 'The English Private Company—A Crisis of Classification' [1974] JBL 277.

[16] Wooldridge however attributes the denial of the exemption from the requirement to disclose accounts to 'English private companies' to the fact that the requirements of the Companies Act 1948, s 28 (definition of private company) 'are merely regulatory requirements, specifying what must be contained in the articles of association, and are not statutory requirements as on the Continent': 'The Harmonization of Company Law: The First and Second Directives of the Council of Ministers of the European Economic Community' [1978] Acta Juridica 327, 329. For an interesting account of the policy reasons behind the Companies Act 1967 disclosure requirement, see Freedman, J, 'Small Businesses and the Corporate Form: Burden or Privilege?' (1994) 57 MLR 555.

[17] German law was the first to recognize the private limited liability company as a separate entity from public companies. For a brief history, see Großfeld, B, and Erlinghagen, S, 'European Company and Economic Law' in De Witte, B and Forder, C (eds), The Common Law of Europe and the Future of Legal Education (1992) 298.

[18] For further development of the theory that this underlay the Commission's initial view, see Schmitthoff, C M, 'The Second EEC Directive on Company Law' (1978) 15 CML Rev 43, 43–6, and Schmitthoff, C M, 'New Concepts in Company Law' [1973] JBL 312, 313–16.

[19] See, for example, the House of Lords Select Committee (n 6 above): 'The inclusion in the Directive of private companies, would, in the view of the Committee, have consequences upon a very widely used method of conducting small businesses in the United Kingdom which are so serious as to be unacceptable. Every effort should be made to obtain their exclusion . . .' (5).

[20] (a) The company cannot issue bearer shares; (b) its shares cannot be quoted on a stock exchange; (c) the law restricts the right to transfer the shares; and (d) the name of the company must include the word 'private'. This proposed definition was uncontroversial, since the first three conditions were already requirements of UK law (Companies Act 1948, s 28(1) and Table A, Part II, reg 2) and the Government had indicated that it proposed to introduce the fourth (White Paper on Company Law Reform (Cmnd 5391) (HMSO, 1973)).

account;[21] subsequently however it relented, so that the final version of the Directive applies in the United Kingdom and Ireland only to public companies.

Article 1(2) permits Member States not to apply the Directive to 'investment companies with variable capital and to cooperatives incorporated as' a public company provided that such companies identify themselves as such in all letters and order forms. The latter exception was designed for France and Italy, where such a form of company exists. The former covers open-ended investment companies, for example unit trusts, which satisfy the conditions set out in Article 1(2), the rationale being that such companies are in fact regulated in the various Member States by separate legislation specifically designed for them, to be harmonized in due course by a further directive,[22] and that subjecting them to restrictions on the purchase of their shares would fundamentally interfere with their activities.

The Court of Justice has confirmed that the Second Directive remains applicable to companies in financial difficulties, even if subject to special collective liquidation or rejuvenation procedures, 'as long as the company's shareholders and normal bodies have not been divested of their powers'.[23] Even where the company's organs have been temporarily divested of their powers, the Directive will be applicable.[24]

Proposed extension of scope

In 1992, a report exploring the possibility of extending the Directive to private limited companies and limited partnerships with shares was published.[25] The report analyses the existing legislation of the Member States relating to such companies and partnerships and contains a series of recommendations on extending the Directive to them. Limited partnerships with shares exist—although they are little used in practice[26]—in all Member States[27] except the United Kingdom, Ireland and the Netherlands; they are subject to the same rules as those applicable to public companies and hence extension of the Directive to them would not cause prob-

---

[21] See n 52 below.

[22] Council Directive (EEC) 85/611 of 20 December 1985 on the coordination of laws, regulations and administrative provisions relating to undertakings for collective investment in transferable securities (UCITS) [1985] OJ L375/3.

[23] Joined Cases C 19–20/90 *Karella and Karellas* [1991] ECR I–2691, considered further below, pp 79–80. See Tridimas, T, 'The Case Law of the European Court of Justice on Corporate Entities' (1993) 13 Yearbook of European Law 335 for a discussion of the implication of this finding.

[24] Case C–441/93 *Pafitis and Others v TKE and Others* [1996] ECR I–1347. The Court also ruled, unsurprisingly since there is nothing in the Directive to suggest otherwise, that banks constituted in the form of public limited companies fall within the scope of the 2nd Directive.

[25] Boden de Bandt de Brauw Jeantet & Uria, *Report on Possible Extension of the Second Company Law Directive to Private Limited Companies and Limited Partnerships with Shares* (1992).

[26] The report notes the recent trend towards transforming a public company into such a partnership in order to use it as a defensive weapon against takeover bids, citing recent transformations of Yves Saint-Laurent, Hermès, Banque Worms, Eurodisneyland and Matra-Hachette.

[27] The names by which such partnerships are known in the various Member States are set out in ch II, at pp 17–18 above.

lems. The report concludes that if the Directive were so extended 'Member States in which this form of corporate organisation does not yet exist, would be required to introduce it in accordance with the rules laid down in the Second Directive'.[28] It is not clear why this should be so, however; the First Directive, after all, extends to such partnerships in those Member States where they exist but imposes no express or implied requirement that the other Member States introduce the form.

In relation to private limited companies, the report concludes that extending the Directive to them is in principle desirable, since the same considerations of creditor protection, and possibly also shareholder protection, enshrined in the Directive apply to private as to public companies. It points to the introduction of a minimum capital requirement[29]—described as 'the cornerstone of the capital protection rules of the Second Directive'[30]—as the major obstacle to such an extension, particularly in the United Kingdom and Ireland, where there is no minimum capital requirement,[31] and in Greece, Portugal and Spain, where it is very low. (It should be noted that the report does not advocate extending the same minimum capital requirement to private as to public companies, and suggests a minimum issued capital of ECU 10,000, possibly with a minimum paid-up capital of ECU 5,000.) Further difficulties in simply extending the Directive to private companies arise because of the very different nature of private and public companies: the former require greater financial and organizational flexibility and relief from administrative burdens where possible. A number of the provisions of the Directive are accordingly inappropriate for private companies. One solution proposed in the report is for any directive applying the principles of the Second Directive to private companies to provide that some of the stricter capital protection rules need not be applied on condition that the company's shareholders guarantee its commitments.

The Commission has not yet officially responded to the report, but a response is presumably being considered and change may be expected.

Nature of the Directive

In *Meilicke v ADV/ORGA*[32] Advocate General Tesauro considered the question whether the provisions of the Second Directive were minimum standard provisions or whether they constituted an exhaustive code of rules on the topics covered. He noted that the second recital in its preamble explicitly stated that its objective was

---

[28] At p 83.

[29] See also Lutter, M, 'A Mini-Directive on Capital', in De Kluiver and Van Gerven (eds), *The European Private Company* (1995), for a brief comparative review of minimum capital requirements for private companies in the EC. Lutter argues for requiring a minimum paid-up capital of 20,000 ECUs.

[30] *Report* (n 25 above) 84.

[31] For a discussion of some of the policy considerations involved in the decision to impose a minimum capital requirement on UK private companies, see Freedman, J, 'Small Businesses and the Corporate Form: Burden or Privilege?' (1994) 57 MLR 555.

[32] Case C–83/91 [1992] ECR I–4871, considered further below, at pp 63–6.

to ensure, inter alia, 'minimum equivalent protection for both shareholders and creditors' of public companies, which suggested prima facie that Member States could provide for more rigorous protective measures. Directives with the express objective of 'minimum equivalence' did not necessarily however give Member States unfettered discretion to impose stricter standards: that objective could equally be realized by setting limits in the directive within which Member States could lay down stricter provisions. Even a cursory examination of the Second Directive revealed that, while certain provisions (such as Articles 2, 3 and 26) left Member States free to adopt stricter measures, others (such as Articles 7, 8(1) and 11(2)) conferred no discretion on the national legislature. That fact suggested that Member States could supplement rules laid down in the Directive by stricter provisions only where there was express provision or authorization.[33] This view was implicitly affirmed by the Court of Justice in the series of rulings given in the Greek capital cases, considered further below.[34]

Structure of the Directive

There are unfortunately no headings or sections in the Second Directive. Underlying virtually all its provisions are the two principles that a company's capital must be initially adequate and subsequently maintained and that shareholders have certain rights in relation to the issue of new capital. Within that wider framework, the provisions fall with relative ease into a structure which reflects the original section headings in the first draft (formation of the company, maintenance of the company's capital, increase of capital, reduction of capital) and is, broadly, followed here. There are however apparent anomalies: in particular, Articles 7, 8 and 12, which contain general principles relating to capital, are in the section of the Directive otherwise devoted to the formation of companies[35] and Article 17, relating to serious loss of capital, is sandwiched uncomfortably between the provisions on distributions and those on acquisition of own shares. Those Articles are here dealt with together, after the section devoted to those Articles relevant to formation. Article 42, lingering at the end of the Directive between general procedural and derogating provisions[36] and the commencement provisions, enunciates an important general principle underlying the Directive which it seems appropriate to set out at the outset, before the remainder of the Directive.

---

[33] Para 12 of the Opinion.   [34] At pp 79–83.

[35] The dissonance was less apparent in the first draft, where there was no equivalent of Art 8 and the drafts of Arts 7 and 12 appeared together at the end of the section of formation on companies, immediately before the section on maintenance of capital generally.

[36] Arts 40 and 41, dealt with in this chapter together with the articles to which they relate.

Equal Treatment of Shareholders

Article 42 states that for the purposes of the implementation of the Directive, Member States' laws shall ensure equal treatment of all shareholders who are in the same position. This principle of non-discrimination is reflected in United Kingdom company law.[37]

Formation of Public Companies

Articles 2 to 5 of the Directive contain miscellaneous provisions relating to the disclosure of information, liabilities incurred before authorization to commence business, and the minimum number of members. Articles 6 and 9 to 11 concern a company's initial capital, requiring a minimum amount of capital on formation and laying down conditions for the amount and the type of consideration for a company's first issue of shares. Article 13 contemplates the formation of a public company by conversion from a private company, rather than by original registration as a public company, and is intended to prevent the provisions applicable on such registration from being avoided by conversion. It requires Member States to provide 'at least the same safeguards as are laid down in Articles 2 to 12 in the event of the conversion of another type of company into a public limited liability company'. Since those provisions include requirements as to the value of consideration for shares, this Article in effect requires a valuation of the assets and liabilities of companies so converting.[38]

Information to be disclosed

Articles 2 and 3 prescribe an irreducible minimum of information to be disclosed by a public company, complementing Section I of the First Directive which prescribes the method of disclosure. Article 2 provides that the statutes (in the United Kingdom, memorandum of association and articles of association) or instrument of incorporation (in the United Kingdom, memorandum of association) must indicate:

---

[37] See, e g, Davies, P L, *Gower's Principles of Modern Company Law* (6th edn, 1997) 303: 'the initial presumption of the law is that all shares confer the same rights and impose the same liabilities. As in partnership equality prevails in the absence of agreement to the contrary'. *The City Code on Take-overs and Mergers* (1996) makes this principle explicit in relation to takeovers by public (not just listed) companies, requiring that all shareholders of the same class of an offeree company should be treated similarly by an offeror (General Principle 1). There is a corresponding principle known as *Gleichsbehandlung* in Germany.

[38] Art 13 is implemented in the UK by the Companies Act 1985, ss 43–5. Section 43(3)(b) requires a statement by the company's auditors that according to the relevant balance sheet the amount of the company's net assets is not less than the aggregate of its called-up share capital and undistributable reserves.

(1) the company's type and name;[39]

(2) its objects;[40]

(3) the amount of its subscribed capital or, if it has an authorized capital, the amount thereof and of its subscribed capital, both initially and on any change in the authorized capital;[41]

(4) in so far as 'they are not legally determined, the rules governing the number of and the procedure for appointing members of the bodies responsible for representing the company with regard to third parties, administration, management, supervision or control of the company and the allocation of power among those bodies';

(5) the duration of the company, unless indefinite.

The Council issued a statement incorporated in the minutes of the relevant session seeking to clarify the meaning (in (4) above) of 'the bodies responsible for . . . supervision or control of the company': those terms are intended to refer to the relevant organ in a public company which has adopted a two-tier management structure, namely the French *conseil de surveillance*, the German *Aufsichtsrat* and the Dutch *raad van commissarissen*. It was expressly stated that auditors under any name[42] were not among the above-mentioned bodies.[43]

Most British public companies have both executive and non-executive directors, and although articles of association normally lay down the procedure for appointing directors neither they nor the Companies Act 1985 regulate the allocation of powers between the two types or the allocation of powers to any managing director. Some commentators consider that, since the issue has not been addressed by the implementing legislation, the United Kingdom must therefore be considered not to have adequately implemented Article 2(d), although it is perhaps more likely that 'the bodies' referred to in the provision means the two types of board discussed above rather than the members of the board.[44]

Article 3 requires further information to be given in either (a) the statutes or the instrument of incorporation or (b) a separate document published in accordance

---

[39] Implemented in the UK by the Companies Act 1985, ss 1 and 2.

[40] Implemented in the UK by the Companies Act 1985, s 2.

[41] The Companies Act 1985, s 2, requires a company's memorandum to state the amount of its authorized capital and the number of shares taken by the subscribers to the memorandum. Beyond this, Art 2(c) does not appear to have been implemented in the UK, which is ironic given that it was widely hailed by UK commentators as a welcome and overdue change to the law: see, for example, Morse, G, 'The Second Directive: Raising and Maintenance of Capital' [1977] ELR 126, 127, describing the existing capital clause in the UK (restricted to authorized capital) as 'at best irrelevant and at worst misleading'.

[42] *Abschlussprüfer, expert comptable, commissaire, commissaire-reviseur, commissaire aux comptes, auditor, revisor.*

[43] See Keutgen, G, 'La deuxième directive en matière de sociétés' (1977) 5925 Revue pratique des sociétés 1, 4, n 11.

[44] See Morse (n 41 above) 127–8, and Wooldridge, F, 'The Harmonization of Company Law' [1978] Acta Juridica 327, 335–6, who also argue that the same considerations apply to the division of powers between the board and individual directors and between the board and the general meeting, both of which are governed by uncodified—and sometimes obscure—principles of common law.

with Article 3 of the First Directive. The option of disclosure in a separate document is attributable to the German delegation, and is intended to avoid the requirement to include certain details which are of only ephemeral significance (for example the identity of the subscribers, the costs of incorporation and advantages granted to promoters) in the instrument which will govern the company throughout its existence and require republication every time it is amended. The requirements are straightforward: to disclose (a) the registered office,[45] (b) to (h) details of the issued share capital and classes thereof,[46] (i) the identity of the subscribers to the statutes or instrument of incorporation,[47] (j) the total amount or an estimate of the formation costs[48] and (k) any special advantage granted to promoters.[49] The *Exposé des motifs* in the first draft explains why Article 3(i) refers to subscribers rather than promoters: it was felt that no purpose would be served by the disclosure requirement if the persons targeted by it varied between the different Member States, and that a definition based on signature was the most objective and therefore the most certain for third parties. It was not thought that failing to require identification of promoters in the broader sense would erode the duties of promoters since that topic would be dealt with in the wider context of the duties of managers etc generally.

Liabilities incurred before authorization to commence business

Article 4 provides that, where the laws of a Member State require a company to have authorization before starting business, they shall also provide for responsibility for liabilities incurred by or on behalf of the company before the grant or refusal of such authorization other than liabilities under contracts which are conditional on the grant of authorization.[50]

Number of members

Article 5 provides that where the laws of a Member State require a company to be formed by more than one member, the company shall not be automatically dissolved if the number of members or shareholders falls below the legal minimum.[51]

---

[45] Implemented in the UK by the Companies Act 1985, s 10.
[46] Implemented in the UK by the Companies Act 1985, ss 88 and 128.
[47] Implemented in the UK by the Companies Act 1985, s 1(1).
[48] Implemented in the UK by the Companies Act 1985, s 117.
[49] Implemented in the UK by the Companies Act 1985, s 117.
[50] Implemented in the UK by the Companies Act 1985, s 117(8).
[51] Since there is no concept of automatic dissolution in UK company law, Art 5 did not require implementation.

Minimum capital

Article 6 requires Member States to prescribe a minimum capital of not less than 25,000 European units of account[52] to be subscribed before a company may be incorporated or obtain authorization to commence business.[53] The first draft specified 25,000 units of account as a mandatory amount rather than a minimum, subject to a 10 per cent margin of adjustment to accommodate national currencies which would not convert into round figures, and subject to specified exceptions where Member States could impose a higher amount (one of which—carrying on activities whose specific nature involves special requirements—was dangerously vague; the other exception was as a condition of listing). The approach of the final version is more flexible, giving Member States the option of setting a higher level.[54]

The original Member States had minimum capital requirements ranging from 20,000 to 160,000 units of account[55] (FFr100,000 in France, rising to FFr500,000 if the company sought to raise funds from the public; DM100,000 in Germany; BFr1,250,000 in Belgium; L100,000,000 proposed in Italy; fl25,000 in the Netherlands[56]); the United Kingdom and Ireland had no such requirement, except where there was a prospectus and even then at the directors' discretion. Clearly wide divergences in the requirement were capable of affecting freedom of establishment and distorting competition, for example by discouraging companies from setting up cross-border subsidiaries in Member States with higher limits. The final figure chosen was inevitably a compromise: France, for example, wanted less and Italy more. It is interesting to note that it was stated in the *Exposé des motifs* in the first draft that the purpose of the minimum capital was deterrent rather than protective: 'so that small undertakings will not use the public company'; the European Parliament however thought that the figure of 25,000 units of account was appropriate because small and medium-sized businesses would also be able to obtain that amount. The figure is unquestionably on the small side if the purpose is to ensure

[52] As defined by Decision (ECSC) 3289/75 of the Commission of 18 December 1975 on the definition and conversion of the unit of account to be used in decisions, recommendations, opinions and communications for the purposes of the Treaty establishing the European Coal and Steel Community [1975] OJ L327/4. At the time of adoption of the Directive, the amount was equivalent to US$25,000, or approximately £16,000. The unit of account was replaced by the 'European Currency Unit' or ECU by Council Regulation (EEC) 3180/78 changing the value of the unit of account used by the European Monetary Cooperation Fund [1978] OJ L379/1 and references in legislation changed accordingly by Council Regulation (EEC, EURATOM) 3308/80 on the replacement of the European unit of account by the ECU in Community legal instruments [1980] OJ L345/1. As from 1 January 1999 references in legal instruments to the ECU are to be replaced by references to the euro: Regulation (EC) 1103/97 on certain provisions relating to the introduction of the euro [1997] OJ L162/1.
[53] Implemented in the UK by the Companies Act 1985, ss 117–18.
[54] The UK, for example, set the figure at £50,000.
[55] Original Proposal, *Exposé des motifs*, 10.
[56] Keutgen, G, 'La deuxième directive en matière de sociétés' (1977) 5925 Revue pratique des sociétés 1, 8; Schmitthoff, C M, 'The Second EEC Directive on Company Law' (1978) 15 CML Rev 43, 47.

that the company's capital is a genuine guarantee for third parties and to reserve the public company for undertakings of a certain scale.

Payment for shares

Article 9(1) requires shares issued for cash to be paid up at the time the company is incorporated or authorized to commence business[57] as to at least 25 per cent of their nominal value or, if none, their accountable par.[58] The 25 per cent was an average of the prevailing national rates in the original Member States. Article 9(2) requires non-cash consideration for shares to be paid in full within five years of constitution.[59] The final version is more flexible than the initial draft, which reflected French law where the requirement is for payment of non-cash consideration in full on allotment, although cash consideration may be paid up within five years.[60] The rationale, as stated in the *Exposé des motifs*, is that the requirement to pay up in full was a form of protection against fictitious consideration and one of the simplest ways of ensuring that someone subscribing non-cash consideration actually delivers.

Member States may derogate from Article 9(1) to the extent necessary 'for the adoption or application of provisions designed to encourage the participation of employees, or other groups of persons defined by national law, in the capital of undertakings'.[61] The Court of Justice has held that in order to fall within this derogation the practical application of the provisions in question must help to achieve the objective set out. The mere fact that a national rule provides for the hypothetical and ancillary possibility of transferring shares to employees is not sufficient. The Court also confirmed the view of Advocate General Tesauro that the reference in the article to 'other groups of persons refers to shareholding by private individuals and is not concerned with the transfer of shares to credit institutions or to public-law bodies'.[62]

Valuation of non-cash consideration

The intention behind Article 9 would be futile if non-cash consideration were not subject to objective and hence independent monitoring carried out before the

[57] There is a parallel requirement in Art 26 for subsequent issues: see p 83 below.
[58] Implemented in the UK by the Companies Act 1985, s 101, which goes further than the Directive in that it also requires payment in full of any premium.
[59] There is a parallel requirement in Art 27 for subsequent issues: see pp 83–4 below. Art 9(2) is incompletely implemented in the UK by the Companies Act 1985, s 102, which is restricted to consideration which is or includes an undertaking which is or may be performed more than five years after the date of the allotment.
[60] See Keutgen (n 56 above), 10.   [61] Art 41(1).
[62] Joined Cases C–19–20/90 *Karella and Karellas* [1991] ECR I–2691, at paras 32–5 of the judgment. The judgment is considered further below, pp 79–80.

company was incorporated or authorized to commence business.[63] Article 10 accordingly requires a report on 'consideration other than in cash' to be drawn up by 'independent experts appointed or approved by an administrative or judicial authority', describing the assets and the methods of valuation used and stating whether the values so arrived at correspond[64] to the nominal or accountable par value of, and where appropriate the premium on, the shares to be issued.[65] Article 10(3) requires the report to be published in accordance with Article 3 of the First Directive.[66]

Continental systems[67] generally accepted the principle of valuation of non-cash consideration for shares, at least for large companies (although as the European Parliament pointed out, it is just as—or even more—necessary for smaller companies). There was no parallel, however, in United Kingdom and Irish law against the concealed issue of shares at a discount by the issue of shares for assets of inadequate value,[68] and Article 10 was welcomed by commentators as an important safeguard.[69]

An exception to the valuation requirement was added at the instigation of the Dutch delegation in the Council: Article 10(4) permits Member States to relax the requirement where 90 per cent of the nominal value or accountable par is issued to one or more companies for a non-cash consideration, provided that a number of specified conditions are satisfied. This exception is designed to cater for certain intra-group issues and corporate reorganizations involving the creation by one or more companies of a subsidiary. The prescribed conditions require the subscribers to the recipient company's memorandum to agree to dispense with the expert's report and the company furnishing the consideration to have certain undistributable reserves and to guarantee certain debts of the recipient company; both the

[63] There is a parallel requirement in Art 27 for subsequent issues: see pp 83–4 below.

[64] Denecker, J, points out that this is ambiguous: does the valuer have to assess the value of the shares issued for the non-cash consideration, or merely satisfy himself that there is some 'mathematical' equivalence between their nominal value and the non-cash consideration? He inclines to the latter view: see 'La deuxième directive du Conseil des Communautés Européennes relative à la constitution de la société anonyme, au maintien et aux modifications de son capital' (1977) 95 Revue des sociétés 661, 667.

[65] Implemented in the UK by the Companies Act 1985, ss 103 and 108.

[66] See pp 19–20 above.

[67] See Stein, E, *Harmonization of European Company Laws* (1971) 321, n 21 for a note of the pre-implementation requirements in the six original Member States. A more detailed outline of the French and German requirements may be found in Lutter, M, 'L'Apport en numéraire fictif: une théorie allemande et un problème de droit européen' (1991) 109 Revue des sociétés 331.

[68] In the UK, the parties' own valuation of consideration for shares was (and for private companies still is) in general accepted as conclusive: *Re Wragg* [1897] 1 Ch 796. Tunc, A, reported how it was 'a great surprise for a French lawyer before the Companies Act 1980 to find that you [the UK] had no procedure whatsoever for the control of the payments of shares in kind': 'A French lawyer looks at British company law' (1982) 45 MLR 1.

[69] See, for example, Temple Lang, J, 'Three EEC Draft Directives on Company Law—Capital, Mergers and Management' (1972) 7 Irish Jurist 306. Cf the view of the House of Lords Select Committee: 'The Committee doubt whether in the United Kingdom the trouble and expense of obtaining such a valuation would be justified by any additional safeguard that it might provide': 24th Report (n 6 above), 6.

agreement to dispense with the report and the guarantee must be published.[70] A further exception was added by the Third Directive:[71] where a new company is formed to acquire an existing company or companies by a merger within the meaning of that directive, Article 23(4) provides that Member States need not apply the valuation rules laid down in Article 10 of the Second Directive to the formation of that company.

The concept of 'consideration other than in cash' was considered by Advocate General Tesauro in *Meilicke v ADV/ORGA*.[72] German courts had developed a theory of 'disguised contributions in kind' in order to pre-empt transactions effected to avoid the German law requirements (reflecting Article 10) for the valuation of non-cash consideration subscribed for shares. German law classifies as a disguised contribution in kind—and hence as subject to the valuation requirements—any contribution in cash which, albeit in full formal compliance with company law, is linked in time and substance with a legally-binding transaction under which the funds received by the company by virtue of the cash subscription are returned to the subscriber, for example in repayment of a debt.[73] The *Landgericht* (Regional Court), Hanover, referred a number of questions to the Court of Justice for a preliminary ruling, essentially concerned with whether the German case-law treating contributions made in such circumstances as contributions in kind was compatible with the Second Directive. The Court of Justice did not rule on the questions referred, since it decided that the problem raised was a hypothetical one and that it had not been provided with the factual and legal information necessary to enable it to give a useful judgment.[74] Advocate General Tesauro, howver, having reformulated the extremely detailed and lengthy questions submitted by the *Landgericht*,[75] considered the issue whether repayment of a debt due by the

[70] Art 10(4)(a) to (f). The conditions are not reflected in the exception provided for in the UK legislation implementing Art 10: see the Companies Act 1985, s 103(3) and (5).

[71] 3rd Council Directive (EEC) 78/855 of 9 October 1978 based on Art 54(3)(g) of the Treaty concerning mergers of public limited liability companies [1978] OJ L295/36. See ch IV.

[72] Case C–83/91 [1992] ECR I–4871.

[73] For further discussion of the German theory, see Lutter (n 67 above) and Meilicke, W, and Recq, J-G, 'Plaidoyer pour un droit européen des sociétés: l'apport de créances détenues sur une société en difficulté financière' [1991] Revue trimestrielle de droit européen 587.

[74] See the judgment, in particular paras 27–33. See also Arnull, A's summary of and comment on the case in [1993] CMLR 613, Kennedy, T, 'First Steps towards a European Certiorari?' (1993) 18 ELR 121; Tridimas, T, 'The Case-Law of the European Court of Justice on Corporate Entities' (1993) 13 Yearbook of European Law 335 and Benoit-Moury, A, 'Droit européen des sociétés et interprétations des juridictions communautaires' [1993] Revue de droit international et de droit comparé 105. For a detailed analysis of the case, see Wooldridge, F, 'Disguised Contributions in Kind; the European Court Refuses a Preliminary Ruling on Hypothetical Questions' (1993) Legal Issues of European Integration, vol 2, 69.

[75] The questions had in fact been drafted by Dr Meilicke, who was a company lawyer and author of a number of books and articles on the compatibility of the theory of disguised contributions in kind with the Second Directive. He also held one share in ADV/ORGA, which had recently increased its capital. Dr Meilicke brought proceedings ostensibly seeking an order that the company disclose certain information to him to enable him to establish whether the increase in capital was a disguised contribution in kind and, if so, whether the requirements as to valuation imposed by German case-law in such circumstances had been satisfied. Dr Meilicke's written observations to the Court, to which a copy of one of

company to a shareholder using the proceeds of a fresh issue was consideration in cash or in kind.

The Advocate General noted that to permit Member States to formulate their own definition of contribution in kind would in effect enable them to decide the scope of the Directive, since the Directive prescribed two different sets of rules depending on the nature of the contribution. Although the Directive did not expressly define the two concepts, the reference in Article 9 to 'consideration other than in cash' was a residual definition and thus precluded any third category. Interpretation of the concepts must be formulated at a Community level and not left to the discretion of the Member States, since the variation inherent in the latter would not be conducive to ensuring even a minimal level of harmonization.[76] In the light of the objective of the rules on non-cash consideration—avoiding the danger of over-valuation to the detriment of the company—the critical factor in deciding whether contribution by waiver of a debt amounted to cash or non-cash consideration was whether there was a risk of overvaluing the debt. There was no such risk in the case of a debt which was liquid and due. Even where the company was in financial difficulties, the value for it of a liquid and due debt was necessarily its face value.[77] Where therefore the subscriber's claim against the company arose from a debt in money, liquid and due, there was no reason, in the light of the rationale of the provisions on consideration in kind, not to treat it as cash consideration: it was a method of fulfilling an obligation to furnish consideration in cash. Where, however, a debt had, for example, not fallen due, it could only be consideration in kind and it would be necessary to value it.[78]

Nachgründung

Although the provisions of Article 10 for the valuation of non-cash consideration for shares do much to prevent avoidance of the basic prohibition in Article 8 on the issue of shares at a discount,[79] those provisions themselves[80] could be avoided if promoters subscribed for shares for cash and the company subsequently used that cash to buy assets from them at an overvalue. Article 11,[81] which draws heavily on the German

---

his books was annexed, argued strenuously that the theory of disguised contributions in kind was incompatible with the Directive. As the Advocate General pointed out, Dr Meilicke was advocating a ruling by the Court which would deprive him of the remedy he was allegedly seeking (see para 4 of the Opinion).

[76] Para 13 of the Opinion.   [77] Para 15 of the Opinion.   [78] Para 16 of the Opinion.
[79] See below, p 67.

[80] And indeed others: the Jenkins Committee in the UK advised against a statutory minimum capital on the ground that it would be too easy to evade by concealed distribution of assets to the promoters after the initial subscription: *Report of the Company Law Committee* (Cmnd 1749 (1962), para 27).

[81] Implemented in the UK by the Companies Act 1985, s 104. The provision is unimportant in practice in the UK, since the subscribers are almost invariably employees of a firm of solicitors or of a company registration agent and have no further involvement with the company. Although s 104 also applies where a private company re-registers as public and agrees to acquire a non-cash asset from a member at the date of re-registration, such agreements are rare in practice.

Nachgründung (post-incorporation)' law,[82] seeks to prevent such abuse. It extends the valuation and disclosure provisions of Article 10 to acquisitions by a company from subscribers to its statutes or instruments of incorporation within a period laid down by national law of at least two years after incorporation or authorization to commence business for a consideration which is not less than 10 per cent of its subscribed capital, and imposes an additional requirement of approval by the general meeting.[83] Member States may extend the provisions to acquisitions from shareholders or others.[84] The provisions are expressed not to apply to acquisitions which are effected in the normal course of the company's business, at the instance or under the supervision of an administrative or judicial authority, or on a stock exchange.[85]

There has been some debate as to whether Article 11 constitutes an exhaustive provision to counter avoidance of Article 10 the Directive or whether it leaves Member States free to legislate against further avoidance.[86] It was accepted in the original Proposal that ways of circumventing Article 10 could doubtless be dreamt up, but stated that it was intended to leave national law to provide for anti-avoidance.[87] In the *Meilicke* case,[88] Advocate General Tesauro considered the scope of Articles 10 and 11. He concluded that Article 10 as a whole could not be considered to lay down minimum standards, since the limits within which Member States may adopt stricter or less strict regulations were spelt out explicitly (Article 10(2) specifies that the experts' report must contain 'at least' certain information, and Article 10(4) states that Member States may decide not to apply the Article in specified circumstances).[89] Article 11, on the contrary, raised greater problems, from the point of view of both literal and teleological interpretation, in particular as to its role as protection against avoidance of the rules on non-cash consideration. Article 11 specifically conferred on the national legislature the power to adopt stricter measures, in that it expressly provided for increasing the two-year period

---

[82] Art 52 *AktienGesetz* on post-incorporation acquisition of assets by a company.

[83] Cordoliani, A considers that requiring a simple majority whatever the conclusions of the report is an insufficient guarantee which may prejudice minority shareholders: 'Constitution de la société anonyme. Maintien et modifications de son capital dans les Etats Membres de la Communauté Économique Européenne' (1978) 12649 La semaine juridique 129, 132.

[84] It is interesting to note the contrasting attitudes of a Belgian commentator, who expresses the hope that the Belgian legislation will make use of this option to ensure that the requirement to control non-cash consideration is fully effective and to avoid possible abuse by the intervention of men of straw (Keutgen, G, 'La deuxième directive en matière de sociétés' (1977) 5925 Revue pratique des sociétés 1, 11–12, author's translation) and a Scottish commentator, who states: 'It is, one hopes, unlikely that the British government [sic] will accept that kind invitation until the principal provision of article 11 is expressed in terms more juristically precise than they at present appear to be' (Bennett Miller, J, in 'Harmonisation of Company Law: The Second EEC Directive' (1977) 22 Journal of the Law Society of Scotland 370, 372).

[85] The UK implementing legislation does not include the third exception.

[86] See Lutter, M, 'L'Apport en numéraire fictif: une théorie allemande et un problème de droit européen' (1991) 109 Revue des sociétés 331, and Meilicke and Recq, 'Plaidoyer pour un droit européen des sociétés' [1991] Revue trimestrielle de droit européen 587, both with particular reference to the theory of disguised contributions in kind developed by the German courts to counter schemes designed to avoid the German law requiring valuation of non-cash consideration.

[87] *Exposé des motifs*, 11.   [88] Cited in n 72.   [89] Para 17 of the Opinion.

and broadening the circle of persons subject to the provision. The fact that it expressly envisaged two circumstances in which national law may adopt stricter measures supported the view that Member States may implement the Second Directive by stricter measures only where and within the limits which the Directive itself provided. Similarly, the fact that Article 11(2) set out in unequivocal and mandatory terms circumstances where Article 11(1) was not to apply suggested that Article 11(1) was not to be applied to circumstances not expressly envisaged thereby which in substance avoided the provisions on contributions in kind.[90] Article 11 was an exceptional provision which could not be applied by analogy so as to cover general categories of transactions.[91] However, Member States may apply their own rules relating to the universal concept of anti-avoidance to penalize transactions in which intent to circumvent the law—in particular, that on contributions in kind—was specifically proved rather than presumed.[92]

General Provisions as to Capital

Consideration for shares

Article 12 sets out the general principle that, subject to the provisions relating to reduction of capital, 'the shareholders may not be released from the obligation to pay up their contributions'. This principle flows from the dual nature of capital, which itself is a leitmotiv running through the Directive: capital represents at once the total of contributions enabling the company to be established and the creditors' guarantee fund.[93]

General principles as to the nature and adequacy of consideration provided for shares subscribed are set out in Articles 7 and 8. Article 7 provides that the subscribed capital may be formed only of assets capable of economic assessment and may not include an undertaking to perform work or supply services.[94] Advocate General Tesauro expressed the view in his Opinion in the *Meilicke* case[95] that Article 7 must be interpreted as meaning that 'economic assessment' could only mean assessment from the point of view of the company, although his reasoning is somewhat circular.[96] The final version of Article 7 is wider than that in the origi-

---

[90] Para 18 of the Opinion.   [91] Para 19 of the Opinion.
[92] Para 21 of the Opinion.   [93] See original Proposal, *Exposé des motifs*, 11.
[94] Implemented in the UK by the Companies Act 1985, s 99.   [95] Cited in n 72.
[96] The Advocate General invokes Art 7 to confirm the view he has earlier expressed that the value of a debt must be its face value, which is its value for the company. Art 7 requires that consideration for shares be capable of objective assessment in monetary terms: 'a claim certainly can be valued in . . . cash terms. A contribution comprising the waiver of a claim against the company at its nominal value . . . must therefore be regarded as permitted by [Art 7]. Moreover, the letter and purpose of that provision . . . support . . . the view that the economic assessment of a claim made against the company must be made from the company's point of view . . . For the aforesaid reasons, Article 7 must therefore be interpreted as meaning that the claim may be valued only from the company's point of view: it is clear that, from that point of view, the valuation of a claim (or rather, from the company's point of view, a debt) may not be based on anything other than its nominal value' (paras 15 and 16 of the Opinion).

nal Proposal, which excluded items which could not be realized; this was itself wider than the alternative apparently considered of requiring asset values to be calculated by reference to their value on a forced sale. Consideration was also given to allowing capital to be constituted by intangible assets up to a threshold of 25 per cent provided that those assets were written off before any distribution of profit. This would however still have meant that the subscriber in question was providing an unrealizable asset in exchange for a realizable share.[97] The first draft expressly stated that it did not preclude knowhow and goodwill from being considered as assets capable of realization.

Article 8 provides that shares may not be issued at a price lower than their nominal value or, if none, their accountable par, subject to commission for those placing shares in the exercise of their profession.[98] The reference to shares with no nominal value catered for Luxembourg and Belgium: 'accountable par' was defined in the *Exposé des motifs* in the original Proposal (albeit in connection with the forerunner of Article 9, there being no express prohibition on the issue of shares at a discount in the original Proposal). Unsurprisingly, it is obtained by dividing the authorized capital by the number of shares representing it.

Serious loss of capital

Article 17 requires a general meeting in the event of a serious loss of capital, 'serious loss' to be defined by national law at a figure not higher than half the subscribed capital. The meeting must be called within a period to be specified by national law and 'consider whether the company should be wound up or any other measures taken'. There is thus a positive obligation to consider measures, including specifically whether the company should be wound up, and not just to provide information. The first draft went further, requiring the meeting to take the necessary measures or consider dissolution: both the Economic and Social Committee and the European Parliament considered that this was too draconian, since steps may already have been taken to deal with the situation. The Article was inspired by German law, although a number of Member States had analogous provisions in their legislation[99] and the figure of one half reflects the search for a reasonable compromise between the different levels. The Article does not prescribe the basis of valuation for determining the existence or extent of the loss.

Implementation in Great Britain

Article 17 is implemented in Great Britain by s 142 of the Companies Act 1985. The provision was opposed by the House of Lords Select Committee, which

---

[97] See original Proposal, *Exposé des motifs*, 11.

[98] Implemented in the UK by the Companies Act 1985, ss 97 and 100.

[99] The *Exposé des motifs* in the original Proposal notes that harmonization was particularly difficult because of the wide divergence between national laws in this area.

concluded that it 'might well precipitate the disaster it was intended to prevent',[100] but in general welcomed by commentators.[101] Section 142 applies only to public companies, unlike much of the British legislation implementing the Second Directive which extends to private companies; as Gower points out, since most private companies 'are mainly financed by bank overdrafts repayable on demand (and thus "liabilities") . . . they might have had to convene such a meeting almost immediately after they were launched'.[102] Section 142 has been criticized for not requiring the company to consider any specific measure when the meeting is called, simply providing that the meeting shall be 'for the purpose of considering whether any, and if so what, steps should be taken to deal with the situation.'[103]

More recently, the Company Law Committee of The Law Society has made representations to the European Commission seeking revision of Article 17: it considers that notification to members of a serious loss of capital would suffice. In its view, experience indicates that no benefit flows from the holding of a meeting under s 142 and that the holding of a meeting may even be detrimental, causing unnecessary expense and commercial damage to the company and the loss of management time. It also points to uncertainty as regards a company the value of whose assets is liable to fluctuate regularly: is there a continuing requirement to convene a further meeting if the value of the assets falls again after a subsequent rise?[104]

Maintenance of Capital

The provisions of the Second Directive so far considered mainly lay down requirements for a company's initial capital, intended to ensure that public companies start their existence with adequate funds. Articles 15 to 24a[105] seek to ensure that those funds are properly used, and in particular are not returned to shareholders. Articles 15 and 16 define the circumstances in which distributions to shareholders may be made and make provision for the recovery of unlawful distributions. Articles 18 to 24a define the circumstances in which a company may acquire its own shares

[100] 24th Report from the Select Committee of the House of Lords on the European Communities (Session 1974–75, HL Paper 239), 9.

[101] Schmitthoff, for example, hailed it as 'an important and sound innovation' ('The Second EEC Directive on Company Law' (1978) 15 CML Rev 43, 52) and Temple Lang, while pointing out some of the practical problems of valuation and timing, stated: 'Taken together with the articles of the directive on the issue of new shares, the overall effect will be to put the decision as to the company's future into the hands of the existing shareholders rather than the directors . . .' ('The Second EEC Company Law Directive' (1976) 9 Irish Jurist 37, 50).

[102] Davies, P L, *Gower's Principles of Modern Company Law* (6th edn, 1997) 248, n 95.

[103] Wooldridge, F, *Company Law in the United Kingdom and the European Community: Its Harmonization and Unification* (1991) 161, n 94. The absence of a requirement to take any steps led Gower to describe the legislation as 'somewhat fatuous': n 102 above, 248.

[104] *European Commission Consultation Paper on Company Law*, Memorandum No 346 of the Company Law Committee, June 1997, 6.

[105] With the exception of Art 17, considered above, which lays down a procedure to be followed where capital has been lost.

(whether directly or indirectly by subscription, purchase, financing or as security)[106] and lay down conditions applying where a company holds its own shares whether lawfully or in contravention of those provisions.

Distributions to shareholders

Article 15(1)[107] provides that, except on a reduction of capital, no distribution (including the payment of dividends or interest[108] on shares; excluding capitalization of reserves, or 'bonus issues') may be made when the company's last annual accounts show that its net assets are, or following such a distribution would become, less than its subscribed capital (excluding any uncalled capital) and undistributable reserves.[109] The amount of any distribution may not exceed the previous financial year's net profits plus any profits brought forward and distributable reserves, less any losses brought forward and sums placed to reserve in accordance with the law or the statutes. Until implementation of the Fourth Directive,[110] the method of determining net assets and profits and losses was that defined by national law. It was accepted in the original Proposal[111] for the Second Directive that this provision would not be wholly effective until the Fourth Directive was implemented, but it was considered that it was none the less apposite to state the principle in the context of guarantees relating to the maintenance of capital. The prohibition on paying dividends before making good past losses required a fundamental change to United Kingdom law, which previously permitted a company with net losses forward to distribute dividends out of any profit made.[112]

Article 15(2) imposes requirements where a Member State's law allows the payment of interim dividends.[113] The conditions, which provide for interim accounts and reflect, *mutatis mutandis*, the requirements laid down in Article 15(1) as to source and amount of distributions, are designed to ensure that the provisions of that article are not circumvented.

[106] But not by redemption of redeemable shares, which is dealt with in Art 39: see below.

[107] Implemented in the UK by the Companies Act 1985, ss 263–4 and 270–6.

[108] The first draft permitted, subject to specified conditions, companies not yet in full operation to pay shareholders fixed-rate, fixed-term interest in the absence of profit; that article was however dropped.

[109] In relation to investment companies with fixed capital, as defined, Member States may derogate from this requirement subject to certain disclosures being made; such a company may not however make a distribution when its total assets as shown in its last annual accounts are less than 150% of its total liabilities to creditors as there shown: Art 15(4), implemented in the UK by the Companies Act 1985, ss 265–6.

[110] See ch V.   [111] See *Exposé des motifs*, 11.

[112] So-called 'nimble dividends'. The House of Lords Select Committee (n 100 above, 6–7) considered that the proposed restriction was too strict and suggested as a compromise the recommendation of the Jenkins Committee on Company Law (Cmnd 1749 (1962), paras 340–1), 'that companies should not be required to make good losses of fixed capital before striking the profit available for dividend, but . . . that past trading losses should be made good . . .' For a discussion of the previous position in the UK, see Savage, N, 'Law and Accounting—the Impact of EEC Directives on Company Law (1)' (1979) 1 *The Company Lawyer* 24.

[113] Implemented in the UK by the Companies Act 1985, ss 263–4 and 272.

Article 16 requires any distribution made contrary to Article 15 to be returned by the recipient if the company proves that he knew of its irregularity or could not in view of the circumstances have been unaware of it.[114] The original Proposal referred to lack of good faith rather than to knowledge.

Acquisition by a company of its own shares

Article 18[115] prohibits a company from subscribing for its own shares, whether directly or through an intermediary or by means of a controlled company.[116] This basic prohibition was uncontroversial, since it already existed in all the Member States, although not all expressly prohibited indirect subscription. Where shares are subscribed in contravention of the prohibition, the subscribers to the statutes or instrument of incorporation (on an initial issue) or the 'members of the administrative or management body' (on an increase of capital) are to be liable to pay for them. The original Proposal imposed strict liability on such persons, but the Economic and Social Committee considered that only those responsible for the irregularity should be liable. The final version is a compromise: the Member States may provide for such a person to be released from the obligation to pay for the shares 'if he proves that no fault is attributable to him personally'. Note that Article 17 does not require such subscriptions to be void.[117]

Some Member States imposed an absolute prohibition on the acquisition (other than by subscription) by a company of its own shares, while others permitted it within certain (always narrow) parameters. For that reason, and also because such an acquisition may sometimes be useful and legitimate[118] provided that the interests of shareholders and creditors are not harmed, the Directive did not contain an absolute prohibition. The protection accorded by national laws permitting acquisitions in certain circumstances took very different forms: some prescribed the source of the funds to be used and required each transaction to be approved by the general meeting, others authorized acquisitions by the company's management in order to avoid serious harm to the company, with fewer restrictions but subject to a threshold for such acquisitions of 10 per cent of subscribed capital. Although the

---

[114] Implemented in the UK by the Companies Act 1985, s 277. In *Precision Dippings Ltd v Precision Dippings Marketing Ltd* [1986] Ch 447, the Court of Appeal sidestepped the problem of imputing knowledge to a company by holding that since an unlawful dividend paid by a subsidiary was unlawful the parent company had received it as a constructive trustee and as such was liable to repay it under general principles of English law.

[115] Implemented in the UK by the Companies Act 1985, ss 143–4.   [116] Art 24a: see below.

[117] Keutgen, G, 'La deuxième directive en matière de sociétés' (1977) 5925 Revue pratique des sociétés 1, 14, states that the Directive does not impose such a sanction in the interests of third parties, although it is not clear how such interests are thereby served. The UK legislation provides that any acquisition by a company of its own shares, whether by purchase, subscription or otherwise, in contravention of the statutory prohibition shall be void: Companies Act 1985, s 143(2).

[118] The *Exposé des motifs* for the original Proposal (12) gives as examples acquisitions in the interest of price stabilization (apparently permitted in France at least: see Denecker, J, 'La deuxième directive du Conseil des Communautés Européenes' (1977) 95 Revue des sociétés 661, 672) or with a view to using the shares to pay creditors or distribute to employees.

two approaches are conceptually different, neither constitutes an appreciable danger for third parties and shareholders and it was decided to provide for both in the Directive, subject to strict regulation. Article 19(1) thus lays down the following conditions to be observed by Member States permitting a company to acquire its own shares, whether itself or through a nominee or by means of a controlled company:[119]

(1)   the general meeting must authorize such acquisitions;[120]

(2)   the aggregate nominal value or, if none, the accountable par of shares acquired by or on behalf of the company may not exceed 10 per cent of the subscribed capital;

(3)   the acquisitions may not reduce the net assets below the total of the subscribed capital plus undistributable reserves;

(4)   only fully paid-up shares may be acquired;[121]

(5)   members of 'the administrative or management body' must satisfy themselves that for each transaction the conditions set out in (2) to (4) are respected.[122]

Member States may derogate from the requirement for authorization by the general meeting in two circumstances: where the acquisition 'is necessary to prevent serious and imminent harm to the company', provided that the next general meeting after the acquisition is fully informed of the 'reasons for and nature of' the acquisitions, the number and nominal value or accountable par of, the proportion of subscribed capital represented by, and the consideration for, the shares acquired,[123] and where shares are acquired for distribution to, and distributed within twelve months to, employees of the company or an associate company.[124]

The first of those two derogations reflects German law, which permitted a company to acquire its own shares in order to prevent serious harm (*schweren Schaden*) to it; acquisitions have been made pursuant to that law 'to prevent persistent depreciation of the price of shares on the Stock Exchange;[125] . . . to get rid of shares owned by troublesome minorities; and . . . to release the company from a creditor's claims'.[126] Presumably Article 19(2) would apply equally in those circumstances; it would probably also apply to certain takeover defences, for example to avert an imminent bid in favour of an alternative bid more beneficial to the

---

[119] Art 24a: see below.

[120] The authorization does not have to be for each specific transaction; it must however be limited to a specified period not exceeding 18 months. The terms and conditions of the acquisitions, the maximum number of shares to be acquired, and, in the case of an acquisition for value, the maximum and minimum consideration, must be determined.

[121] The *Exposé des motifs* for the original Proposal stated that restricting acquisitions to fully paid shares seemed an important guarantee, since otherwise payment of the balance would be impossible, the company becoming a creditor of itself.

[122] Art 19(1) is implemented in the UK by the Companies Act 1985, ss 162–70, with the surprising lacuna that the threshold for acquisitions of 10% of the subscribed capital is not provided for.

[123] Art 19(2), not implemented in the UK.   [124] Art 19(3), not implemented in the UK.

[125] Also permitted in France: see Denecker (n 118 above) 672.

[126] Wooldridge, F, 'The Harmonization of Company Law' [1978] Acta Juridica 327, 338.

majority of the shareholders.[127] The possible danger posed by the flexibility of the concept of 'serious and imminent harm' is tempered by the conditions imposed, particularly the 10 per cent ceiling, which will discourage abuse by directors.

The second permitted derogation reflects the German and French policies of encouraging employee participation in companies. It is echoed in more general terms by Article 41(1), which provides that Member States may derogate from the requirements for approval of the general meeting and for the 10 per cent aggregate ceiling for shares so acquired if necessary for the adoption or application of provisions 'designed to encourage the participation of employees, or other groups of persons defined by national law, in the capital of undertakings'.[128]

Article 20 provides for further derogations, permitting Member States to exempt the following from Article 19 (and hence from all the conditions for acquisitions set out in that article, rather than merely from the requirement for authorization of the general meeting):

(1) shares acquired on a reduction or redemption of capital; as part of a universal transfer of assets; pursuant to a court order to protect minority shareholders;[129] by way of forfeiture; and to indemnify minority shareholders in associated companies;

(2) fully paid-up shares acquired by way of underwriting commission; by way of execution of a debt; and by a fixed-capital investment company or an associate company at the investor's request, provided that the company's net assets are not reduced below the total of its subscribed capital and undistributable reserves.

Article 22 prescribes certain minimum[130] conditions which Member States permitting acquisitions must impose on the holding of shares so acquired. Voting rights in respect of such shares are to be suspended; if the shares are included among the assets shown in the balance sheet an equivalent undistributable reserve is to be included among the liabilities; and the company's annual report is to contain specified minimum information as to the acquisitions.[131]

Shares acquired in contravention of Article 19 or 20 must be disposed of within one year or cancelled.[132] Shares acquired pursuant to an exemption in Article 19,

---

[127] See Wooldridge, 'The Harmonization of Company Law' [1978] Acta Juridica 327, 338.

[128] See p 61 above for a note as to the scope of this provision. In addition, Art 41(2) empowers Member States to exempt from the requirement for authority of the general meeting acquisitions of own shares by companies incorporated under a special law which issue a separate class of workers' shares to their employees as a body, who are represented at general meetings of shareholders by delegates having the right to vote.

[129] Particularly on a merger, change in company object or form, transfer abroad of registered office, or introduction of restrictions on transfer of shares.

[130] German law, for example, goes further, and deprives shares so held of all rights attaching thereto: Art 71b of the AktienGesetz.   [131] Art 22.

[132] Art 21. Member States need not apply this article where the shares are acquired by a controlled company (see below) on condition that they provide for suspension of the voting rights attaching to the shares and for their repurchase at the purchase price by the members of the public company's administrative or management organ, unless those members prove that the public company played no part in the acquisition: Art 24a(6).

other than on a reduction or redemption of capital or by an investment company, must be disposed of within three years or cancelled unless their nominal value or, if none, accountable par does not exceed 10 per cent of the subscribed capital.[133] Such cancellation in either event may be made subject to a corresponding reduction of capital, and must be so subject where the net assets as a result fall below the total of subscribed capital and undistributable reserves.[134] Pending disposal or cancellation, the holding of the shares is of course subject to the restrictions imposed by Article 22 (see above).

Article 23 supplements the preceding articles by prohibiting, subject to specified exceptions, a company from advancing funds,[135] making loans or providing security with a view to the acquisition of its own shares by a third party. Such a provision is clearly necessary in order to prevent disguised acquisitions; the article was modelled on the pre-existing United Kingdom legislation. Transactions effected (a) by financial institutions in the normal course of business or (b) with a view to the acquisition of shares by or for employees of the company or an associated company or (c) with a view to the acquisition by a fixed-capital investment company or associated company of its shares at the investor's request are permitted, provided in all cases that they do not result in the company's net assets falling below the total of its subscribed capital and undistributable reserves.

As a further anti-avoidance measure, Article 24 assimilates to an acquisition for the purposes of the preceding provisions the acceptance by or on behalf of a company of its shares as security, although Member States may exclude from this treatment transactions concluded by financial institutions in the normal course of business. Both this rule and the exception are directly inspired by German law.

Implementation of Article 23 in the United Kingdom

It is interesting to focus briefly on the recent history of the legislative prohibition in the United Kingdom on financial assistance by a company for the acquisition of its own shares. Section 54 of the Companies Act 1948 prohibited a company from giving, 'whether directly or indirectly, and whether by means of a loan, guarantee, the provision of security or otherwise, any financial assistance for the purpose of or in connection with a purchase or subscription made or to be made by any person of or for any shares in the company, or . . . in its holding company', subject to exceptions for lending by financial institutions in the ordinary course of their business and for financing the acquisition of shares by employees. As indicated above, the inclusion of a similar prohibition in the final version of the Directive is

---

[133] Art 20(2)(3). Member States need not apply these paragraphs in the circumstances set out in n 132 above: Art 24a(6).

[134] Arts 20(3) and 21.

[135] Presumably intended to encompass a gift, notwithstanding the arguments that on a literal interpretation 'advance funds' 'might be taken to describe merely a kind of credit transaction consisting of a payment in advance of the normal date of payment': see *Company Law Reform: Proposals for Reform of Sections 151–158 of The Companies Act 1985*, Memorandum No 293 of the Company Law Committee of The Law Society (1994), para 14.

attributable to the influence of the United Kingdom and Ireland, and Schmitthoff describes Article 23 as 'evidently modelled on' s 54.[136] In 1980 two cases[137] suggested that s 54 was wider than previously thought and might catch transactions entered into with a genuine view to the commercial interests of the company if they involved putting a purchaser of shares in the company in funds to complete his purchase. In an attempt to redress the balance and ensure that unobjectionable transactions were not caught by the prohibition, s 54 was replaced by the much more elaborate provisions of ss 42 to 44 of the Companies Act 1981,[138] the major novelty being the introduction of new exemptions. Sections 42 to 44 were subsequently re-enacted as ss 151 to 158 of the consolidating Companies Act 1985.

Section 153(1) provides that financial assistance is not prohibited if (a) the company's principal purpose in giving it is not to give it for the purpose of acquisition of the shares or if the giving of the assistance for that purpose is but an incidental part of some larger purpose of the company and (b) the assistance is given in good faith in the interests of the company; s 153(2) makes analogous provision for assistance given after the acquisition. This exemption—which appears to go beyond the scope of Article 23—was considered by the House of Lords in *Brady v Brady* [1989] AC 755. Lord Oliver of Aylmerton, with whose speech the other Law Lords concurred, described the section as 'not altogether easy to construe' and the ambit of its operation as 'far from easy to discern'. He concluded, 'with a measure of regret', that a larger purpose was not the same as a more important reason, even where that reason was, as a matter of commercial sense, excellent:

the financial or commercial advantages flowing from the acquisition, whilst they may form the reason for forming the purpose of providing assistance, are a by-product of it rather than an independent purpose of which the assistance can properly be considered to be an incident . . . I do not think that a larger purpose can be found in the benefits considered to be likely to flow or the disadvantages considered to be likely to be avoided by the acquisition which it was the purpose of the assistance to facilitate.

Notwithstanding its rationale,[139] that interpretation severely restricted the scope of the exemption[140] and, like the two earlier decisions which prompted the

---

[136] 'The Second EEC Directive on Company Law' (1978) 15 CML Rev 43, 50.

[137] *Belmont Finance Corpn v Williams Furniture Ltd (No 2)* [1980] All ER 393 and *Armour Hick Northern Ltd v Whitehouse* [1980] 1 WLR 1520.

[138] *Gower's Principles of Modern Company Law* (6th edn, 1997) 264 states that 'probably more midnight-oil was burnt on this subject than on all the rest of that Act'.

[139] As Lord Oliver stated: 'If one postulates the case of a bidder for control of a public company financing his bid from the company's own funds—the obvious mischief at which the section is aimed—the immediate purpose which it is sought to achieve is that of completing the purchase and vesting control of the company in the bidder. The reasons why that course is considered desirable may be many and varied . . . [They] may be excellent reasons but they cannot, in my judgment, constitute a "larger purpose" of which the provision of assistance is merely an incident.'

[140] 'The logic is, of course, impeccable and the House of Lords is infallible. But the result seems to reduce s 153(1) and (2) to very narrow limits indeed and to make one wonder whether the midnight oil burnt on [their] drafting . . . has achieved anything worthwhile': Gower (n 138 above) 270.

introduction of s 153, caused great concern in legal circles.[141] As a result, the Department of Trade and Industry issued a consultative document in October 1993[142] seeking views on a possible reform of the legislation which would split the prohibition into two tiers, the first of which would 'simply implement Article 23 of the Second Directive. It would therefore apply only to public companies and would cover only those types of financial assistance prohibited by the Second Directive.'[143] The DTI advocated this approach on the ground that, by 'bringing UK legislation closer to that [sic] of the Second Directive, it should reduce the scope for uncertainty which may arise from having UK legislation which is different from the EC legislation it implements'.[144]

The DTI published a further consultation paper on financial assistance in November 1996 (*Company Law Reform: Financial Assistance by a Company for the Acquisition of its own Shares*, 21 November 1996). The paper proposed major changes to the private company regime, including a proposal to remove private companies from the scope of the prohibition subject to a requirement for shareholder approval in certain cases, together with certain changes to the public company regime, in particular the replacement of the principal and larger purpose tests in s 153 with a 'predominant reason' test, thus in effect reversing *Brady v Brady*. Subject to concerns that the latter proposal could if not carefully framed go beyond what was permitted by the Directive,[145] the paper received a positive reception from the legal profession. The DTI published its conclusions on the main elements of its proposals for reform in April 1997: broadly, it would seek to introduce a 'predominant reason' test, but private companies would remain subject to the prohibition albeit with a more flexible 'whitewash' procedure (*Company Law Reform: Financial Assistance by a Company for the Acquisition of its own Shares*, 21 April 1997). The DTI concluded that primary rather than, as had initially been hoped, secondary legislation[146] would be required to implement its proposed reforms, which will delay matters; the reforms are understood not to be a high legislative priority for the current Labour Government.

---

[141] In fact, the transaction in question in *Brady v Brady* was ultimately upheld, since as the company in question was a private company it could lawfully give financial assistance by following the 'whitewash' procedure laid down by ss 155–8 which relax the prohibition for private companies provided certain steps are followed. While this has nothing to do with the Second Directive, it is interesting—if disheartening—to note that this solution was not raised until the case was before the House of Lords, which gave leave for one of the parties to raise further points of law not argued before the trial judge or the Court of Appeal. As Gower points out, 'Having regard to the wealth of legal and accountancy talent available to the parties, it seems almost incredible that this course had not occurred to anyone earlier': ibid, 271.

[142] *Company Law Review: Proposals for Reform of the Companies Act 1985, ss 151–8.*

[143] The second tier would apply to other types of financial assistance by public companies (e g by a subsidiary for the purpose of an acquisition of shares in its parent) and financial assistance by private companies, which could be effected subject to a 'gateway' procedure.

[144] See n 142 above, 4.

[145] See Gower (n 138 above) and the response of the Company Law Committee of The Law Society, Memorandum No 344.

[146] Pursuant to the Deregulation and Contracting Out Act 1994.

The Company Law Committee of The Law Society, in its response to the *Commission Consultation Paper on Company Law*, has argued strongly for changes to Article 23, which would facilitate simplification of the British regime. In particular, it advocates, instead of the absolute prohibition currently contained in Article 23, that financial assistance should be prohibited unless the transaction concerned has been approved by a resolution of shareholders, and that the prohibition should in any event be subject to a *de minimis* exception defined by reference to reduction in net assets.[147]

Extension of Articles 18–24 to transactions by controlled companies

It was accepted in the *Exposé des motifs* in the original Proposal[148] that it was possible for a company to use an associated company to circumvent the provisions of the Directive relating to the subscription and acquisition by a company of its own shares by procuring such a company to effect the transaction without however doing so sufficiently openly or directly for it to be 'on behalf of' the company. It was therefore seen as essential to extend the rules to such companies, but that issue was postponed until it could be resolved in the context of the regulation of groups of companies generally, to be separately harmonized at a later date. This loophole[149] has now been stopped, although not as part of such an ambitious scheme. A new Article 24a has been inserted in the Second Directive by Council Directive (EEC) 92/101 of 23 November 1992 amending Directive (EEC) 77/91 on the formation of public limited-liability companies and the maintenance and alteration of their capital[150] ('the amending Directive').

The effect of the amendment is to extend Articles 18 to 24 of the Second Directive to the subscription, acquisition or holding of shares in a public company effected by another company under the public company's control. Where a public company 'directly or indirectly holds a majority of the voting rights' in or 'can directly or indirectly exercise a dominant influence on' a company within the meaning of the First Directive,[151] or with a comparable legal form but governed by the law of a third country, the subscription, acquisition or holding of shares in the public company by the controlled company is regarded as having been effected by the public company itself.[152] Pending coordination of national laws on groups of companies, Member States may define the circumstances in which a public company will be regarded as directly or indirectly (a) holding voting rights or (b) able to exercise a dominant influence, provided that the definition applies at least where a public company is a member of the putative controlled company and has either

---

[147] Memorandum No 346 (n 104 above) 7–8.　　　　　　　　　　　　[148] At p 13.

[149] Described variously as 'a necessary consequence of the "salami" tactics of harmonization [and] not an important' omission (Wooldridge, 'The Harmonization of Company Law' [1978] Acta Juridica 327, 339), and 'a serious omission' (Temple Lang, J, 'Three EEC Draft Directives on Company Law' (1972) 7 Irish Jurist 306, 310).

[150] [1992] OJ L347/64. Member States are required to enact before 1 January 1994 implementing provisions to come into effect not later than 1 January 1995.

[151] See above, pp 17–18, for a list of such companies.　　　　　　　　　　[152] Art 24a(1).

the right to appoint or dismiss a majority of the board of that company or sole control of a majority of the voting rights in that company under an agreement with other members.[153]

Member States need not apply Article 24a(1) where:

(1)   the companies are linked by indirect shareholding or indirect influence if they provide for the suspension of the voting rights attached to the shares in question;[154] or

(2)   the transaction is effected on behalf of a person other than the public company or another controlled company[155] or by the controlled company *qua* professional dealer in securities;[156] or

(3)   the shares were acquired before the relationship of control satisfied the criteria set out in the Article[157] or before the entry into force of its implementing legislation.[158]

If either derogation in (3) is invoked, the voting rights attached to those shares must be suspended.[159]

A much-needed effect of the amendment has been to preclude a tactic which had developed in the context of takeovers, whereby during the period for which a takeover bid remained open the target company in effect circumvented the 10 per cent limit on acquiring its own shares imposed by the Second Directive by having a subsidiary acquire its shares with no such limit.

Increase in Capital

Article 25 enshrines the basic principle that a decision to increase a company's capital must ultimately rest with the shareholders, and Article 29 takes this protection of the position of shareholders in the company further by providing that shares issued for cash must be offered on a pre-emptive basis to existing shareholders. Articles 26 and 27 reflect the provisions of Articles 9 and 10, applying to a company's initial capital, as to the amount and type of consideration for shares. Article 28 makes provision for issues which are not fully subscribed.

Article 25(1) provides that any increase in capital must be decided on by the general meeting.[160] The history of the provision reflects the dichotomy between those

---

[153] Art 24a(3). The terms in question follow closely those used in the 7th Directive on Consolidated Accounts to determine whether an undertaking is a 'subsidiary undertaking'. See ch VI, pp 163–70, and see in the UK the Companies Act 1985, s 258 and Sch 10A.

[154] Art 24a(2).   [155] Art 24a(4)(a).

[156] Provided that it is a member of a Stock Exchange or approved or supervised by an authority competent to supervise such dealers: Art 24a(4)(b).

[157] Art 24a(5).   [158] Art 2(1) of the amending Directive.

[159] Both Art 24a(5) and Art 2(1) provide that the shares must be taken into account in calculating the 10% threshold on permitted acquisitions of own shares for the purpose of Art 19(1)(b): see p 71 above. In the latter, there is a transitional provision in favour of Belgium: Art 2(2) of the amending Directive.

[160] Implemented in the UK by the Companies Act 1985, s 80. Temple Lang, J, 'Three EEC Draft Directives on Company Law' (1972) 7 Irish Jurist 306, 312, expresses the view that, in shifting the

Member States (all the original ones except the Netherlands) which did not distinguish between authorized and issued capital, and the Netherlands, joined by the United Kingdom and Ireland during the course of negotiation of the Directive, which did. If only one concept of capital is recognized and stated in the statutes, then inevitably fresh issues will require those statutes to be amended. The original Proposal had accordingly assimilated the requirements for quorum, majority etc on an increase in capital to those required on an alteration of the statutes; the provision was subsequently deleted to take account of the position in those Member States which recognized authorized capital as distinct from subscribed capital. The final version leaves it to national law to prescribe the procedural requirements for such a meeting.[161] The decision of the meeting and the capital increase itself are required to be published in accordance with Article 3 of the First Directive.[162]

Article 25(2) provides that an increase in subscribed capital up to a maximum amount may be authorized by the statutes or instrument of incorporation or by the duly published decision of the general meeting. Individual decisions to increase capital may then be taken by the body on whom the authority was conferred, normally of course the management organ. The authority may not be for more than five years, although it may be renewed by the general meeting. This provision has been described as 'the nearest the directive gets to the Irish and British concept of authorised but unissued capital',[163] although it is drawn from the French and German systems where the concept is not recognized as such. The practical inconvenience of not having authorized but unissued capital, so that every time the management wished to issue new shares they had to seek the approval of the general meeting, had led those legal systems to develop the principle of conferring limited authority on the management.[164]

Where there are several classes of shares, each class of shareholder 'whose rights are affected by the transaction' shall have the right to vote separately on decisions of the general meeting pursuant to either of the above provisions.[165] The Directive gives no guidance as to what is meant by 'rights . . . affected'.

authority to decide on fresh issues from the board to the general meeting, the Directive lessens minority shareholders' protection against share issues for improper purposes, since the principle that directors' decisions can be upset if not taken bona fide in the interests of the company does not apply to shareholders' decisions. It was presumably in part to guard against this, however, that the requirement that equity shares issued for cash be offered to existing shareholders on a pre-emptive basis was included in the Directive: Art 29, see pp 84–7 below.

[161] Compromises requiring the authorization to be by a two-thirds majority, or by a simple majority of votes at a meeting where at least half the subscribed capital is represented, were rejected. See the 24th Report of the House of Lords Select Committee on the European Communities (Session 1974–75, HL Paper 239), 10.

[162] See pp 19–20 above.

[163] Temple Lang (n 160 above) 311. Keutgen, G, 'La deuxième directive en matière de sociétés' (1977) 5925 Revue pratiques des sociétés 1, 19, gives the heading 'Legalization of authorized capital' (author's translation) to his discussion of Art 25(2).

[164] See Schmitthoff, C M 'The Second EEC Directive on Company Law' (1978) CML Rev 43, 48–9, and Keutgen, ibid, 19.

[165] Art 25(3).

The issue of securities convertible into shares is subject to the above requirements, but not the conversion itself, since it is regarded as the simple execution of the decision which has already been authorized in principle by the general meeting.[166] This provision reflects Belgian law. Note that the Directive gives holders of convertible securities no rights to be consulted on an increase of capital or to have new shares offered to them under the pre-emption rights considered below.

Member States may derogate from Article 25 if necessary for the adoption or application of provisions 'designed to encourage the participation of employees, or other groups of persons defined by national law, in the capital of undertakings'.[167]

Article 25 has been considered by the Court of Justice in a series of cases referred from Greece. The first three cases[168] all concerned a Greek law ('the Law') setting up the Organization for the Restructuring of Enterprises ('ORE'), a State-controlled public company whose object was to contribute to the economic and social development of the country through, inter alia, the financial rationalization of undertakings. In the *Karella* case,[169] the ORE took over the administration of a public limited company and decided to increase its capital pursuant to the Law, which empowered it to do so, by way of derogation from the general law, by decision subject to ministerial approval. The Karellas, shareholders in the company, sought judicial review of the ministerial decree approving the decision. The Council of State referred to the Court of Justice two questions on the direct effect and scope of Article 25(1).[170]

The Court stated that Article 25(1) was clearly and precisely worded and unconditionally laid down a rule enshrining the general principle that the general meeting has the power to decide upon increases in capital. The derogation in Article 25(2) was exhaustive. Article 25(1) could accordingly be relied upon by individuals against the public authorities before national courts.[171]

As to the scope of Article 25(1), the Greek Government had argued that the relevant provisions of the Law were outside the Article since they did not form part of the basic legal system governing capital increases generally but provided, by way of exception and in the public interest, for special measures in connection with the restructuring of undertakings which were in difficulty. The Court was not

---

[166] Art 25(4); original Proposal, *Exposé des motifs*, 14.

[167] Art 41(1), implemented in the UK by the Companies Act 1985, s 80(1)(a); see p 61 above for a note as to the scope of the derogation.

[168] See for a full analysis Tridimas, T, 'The Case-Law of the European Court of Justice on Corporate Entities' (1993) 13 Yearbook of European Law 335. See also Benoit-Moury, B, 'Droit européen des sociétés et interprétations des juridictions communautaires' [1993] Revue de droit international et de droit comparé 105.

[169] Joined Cases C–20/90 *Karella and Karellas* [1991] ECR I–2691. See Tridimas, T, 'Direct Effect and the Second Company Law Directive' (1992) 17 ELR 158. Identical issues were raised in Joined Cases C 134–135/91 *Kerafina v Greek State and Others* [1992] ECR I–5699 in which the Court reiterated the answers given in *Karella and Karellas*.

[170] A third question on the direct effect and scope of Art 42 (see p 57 above) was also referred, but the Court decided that in the light of its answers to the first two questions there was no need to reply to it.

[171] Paras 19–23 of the judgment.

persuaded. It stated that the objective of the Directive, to provide a minimum level of protection for shareholders in all the Member States, would be seriously frustrated if those States were entitled to derogate from its provisions by rules—even special or exceptional ones—depriving shareholders of involvement in increases in capital. While the Directive conferred express powers to derogate from certain provisions, there was no such power to derogate from Article 25(1) in crisis situations. On the contrary, Article 17(1) provided for a general meeting to be held in the event of a serious loss of capital, which confirmed that Article 25(1) applied even where the company was in serious financial difficulties. The relevant provisions of the Law were thus contrary to the Directive.[172]

In *Sindesmos Melon tis Eleftheras Evangelikis Ekklisias and Others v Greek State and Others*,[173] where the facts were similar, it had been argued on behalf of the ORE that the shareholders, by requesting that the company be made subject to the Law, had tacitly consented to the full application of the Law and thus to the increase in capital by administrative measure. Advocate General Tesauro rejected that argument, which was not dealt with by the Court, stating:

To accept that the general assembly may delegate to a body outside the company the power to increase the capital, without any limit having been fixed and without, moreover, any express deliberations having taken place, merely inferring such a desire from the request to be made subject to a procedure in which recourse to increases in capital is only a possibility, means not only reconstructing a desire which in fact probably never existed, but also accepting that the general assembly has the power to withdraw the company completely from the scope of the beneficial provision of the Directive.[174]

A further case, *Pafitis and Others v TKE and Others*,[175] concerned the compatibility with the Second Directive of national legislation under which, on appointment of a temporary administrator of a bank in financial difficulties, all the powers and competencies of the organs of the bank were to lapse automatically and be vested, together with the management of the bank, in the temporary administrator. Pursuant to that legislation and acting in the stead of the general meeting, the temporary administrator of the defendant bank, which was constituted as a public company, decided to increase the bank's capital and invited existing shareholders by notice published in the political and financial press to exercise their pre-emptive rights within thirty days. The plaintiff shareholders having failed to exercise their rights within that period, the temporary administrator allotted fresh shares to third parties. The plaintiffs challenged the increase in capital. The Athens Court of First Instance requested a preliminary ruling on certain issues from the Court of Justice.

---

[172] Paras 26–31 of the judgment.
[173] Case C–381/89 [1992] ECR I–2111; discussed further below in relation to Art 29(1): see p 86.
[174] Para 6 of the Opinion.
[175] C–441/93 [1996] ECR I–1347. In Case C–235/98 *Pafitis and Others v Trapeza Kentrikis Ellados and Others*, pending the Court has been asked to consider whether the relevant provisions of the Second Directive have direct effect as between, on the one hand, a company under ORE management and the new shareholders after an increase in capital and, on the other hand, certain of the old shareholders.

It was argued that the increase in capital was not subject to Article 25 because it was a measure for the reorganization of a credit institution. The Court of Justice, unimpressed, referred to its previous decisions in the *Karella*, *Sindesmos* and *Kerafina* cases, and stated that it was not open to Member States to adopt reorganization measures for banks or public companies generally which ran counter to the Directive.[176] The Court also dismissed an attempt to distinguish the previous cases on the basis that the national provisions there at issue merely brought to an end the powers of management of the undertaking, leaving the general meeting in existence, whereas the measure at issue in the *Pafitis* case caused all the powers of the company's organs, including the general meeting, to lapse and become vested in the temporary administrator. It ruled that the Directive continued to apply where ordinary reorganization measures were taken in order to ensure the company's survival, even if those measures meant that the shareholders and organs were temporarily divested of their powers.[177] The Court accordingly concluded that Article 25 precluded national legislation under which the capital of a bank constituted in the form of a public limited-liability company which, as a result of its debt burden, was in exceptional circumstances, could be increased by an administrative measure without a resolution of the general meeting.[178]

Finally the Court considered of its own motion the effect of a provision of Greek law (Article 281 of the Civil Code) which the defendants had sought to invoke before the national court, pursuant to which 'the exercise of a right is prohibited where it manifestly exceeds the bounds of good faith or morality of the economic or social purpose of that right'. The national court had stated in the order for reference, without raising the issue in a question referred, that that provision allowed objection to be made against the exercise of rights conferred by Community law if, in a particular case, those rights were exercised abusively. The Court affirmed that, in relation to rights relied on by an individual on the basis of Community provisions, it was for the Court to verify whether the judicial protection available under national law was appropriate. In this case, the uniform application and full effect of Community law would be undermined if a shareholder relying on Article 25(1) were deemed to be abusing his rights merely because he was a minority shareholder of a company subject to reorganization measures or had benefited from the reorganization of the company. Since Article 25(1) applied without distinction to all shareholders, regardless of the outcome of any reorganization procedure, to treat an action based on Article 25(1) as abusive for such reasons would be tantamount to altering the scope of that provision.[179]

---

[176] Paras 39–41.   [177] Paras 54–9.

[178] Para 60. Advocate General Tesauro had summarized the effect of the earlier rulings more colourfully: 'the Court made it clear that not even a special law designed to ensure the recovery of a company can deprive the shareholders of a most "intimate" and unrelinquishable right: that of making changes to the capital structure of the company' (para 13 of the Opinion).

[179] Paras 67–70.

The Court was expressly asked in *Kefalas and Others v Elleniko Dimosio and Others*[180] to consider the compatibility with Community law and the effect on Article 25 of the principle of abuse of rights discussed above. In that case, shareholders in a company, Khartopiia, subject to ORE administration, had unsuccessfully challenged an increase in capital effected by the ORE. The national court considered that the applicants' claim manifestly exceeded the bounds of good faith, morality and the economic or social purpose of the right since (a) when it was made subject to the Law, Khartopiia had been heavily indebted with an acute liquidity problem and insufficient assets to cover its liabilities; (b) the increase in capital had led to its financial recovery and resumption of trading and averted the risk of massive job losses, all with beneficial effects on the national economy, whereas, had the capital not been increased, it would have been declared insolvent to the detriment of the shareholders, the workers would have been laid off and the national economy would have been deprived of an important undertaking; and (c) when the capital was increased, the shareholders had been given a preferential right to acquire shares which they had not used.

The Court ruled that, although the application by national courts of domestic rules such as Article 281 for the purposes of assessing whether the exercise of a right arising from a provision of Community law was abusive could not be regarded as contrary to the Community legal order, the application of such a rule must not prejudice the full effect and uniform application of Community law in the Member States. In particular, it was not open to national courts, when assessing the exercise of a right arising from a provision of Community law, to alter the scope of that provision or to compromise its objectives.

Referring to its earlier rulings, discussed above, the Court stated that the decision-making power of the general meeting provided for in Article 25(1) applied even where the company in question was experiencing serious financial difficulties. Since an increase in capital was, by its very nature, designed to improve the company's economic situation, to characterise an action based on Article 25(1) as abusive on the ground that the contested increase in capital resolved the company's financial difficulties and enured to the shareholder's economic benefit would mean that a shareholder of a company in financial crisis could never rely on Article 25(1), thus altering the scope of that provision.

Similarly, the uniform application and full effect of Community law would be prejudiced if a shareholder's failure to exercise his preferential right to acquire new shares issued on the contested increase of capital were deemed to be an abuse of his right under Article 25(1). By exercising his preferential right, the shareholder would in effect have endorsed the very decision which he was contesting. However, Community law did not preclude a national court, on the basis of suffi-

---

[180] Case C–367/96, judgment of 12 May 1998. In Case C–373/97 *Diamantis v Greek State and Organismos Oikonomikis Anasygkrotis Epicheiriseon*, pending, the Court has been asked to consider further aspects of the principle of abuse of rights in connection with an increase of capital by a company under ORE management.

cient telling evidence, from examining whether, by bringing an action under Article 25(1) for a declaration that an increase in capital was invalid, a shareholder was seeking to derive, to the detriment of the company, an improper advantage, manifestly contrary to the objective of that provision, which was to ensure, for the benefit of shareholders, that an increase in capital affecting their share of equity was not taken without their participation.

Payment for shares

Article 26 provides that shares issued for a consideration must be paid up to at least 25 per cent of their nominal value or, if none, accountable par, plus the whole of any premium.[181] The first draft contained an additional rule that where an increase in capital was subscribed in cash, shares already issued should be paid up first, although Member States could derogate from this where the needs of the company could not be met by unpaid capital. That rule reflected French and Italian law, which took the view that it was logical to have recourse first to uncalled capital, and that maintaining the company's rights as a creditor of its shareholders was an illusory guarantee for third parties since the debt constituted by uncalled capital was often irrecoverable in fact. Other national laws took the more optimistic view that it could be advantageous if a company's capital included debts due by way of uncalled capital because that capital could be mobilized at any point, and that even paid-up capital could not be regarded as constituting a cast-iron guarantee of funds since it might have been dissipated by imprudent investment. The Commission in drafting the Directive espoused the first view,[182] the Economic and Social Committee promoted the second, which ultimately prevailed.

Member States may derogate from Article 26 if necessary for the adoption or application of provisions 'designed to encourage the participation of employees, or other groups of persons defined by national law, in the capital of undertakings'.[183]

Article 27 contains provisions relating to the issue of shares for non-cash consideration on an increase in capital which are parallel to those contained in Articles 9(2) and 19 in relation to the issue of shares at the time of formation. Thus Article 27(1) requires such consideration to be paid in full within five years of the decision to increase the capital.[184] Article 27(2) requires such consideration to be subject to a report prepared in accordance with Article 10(2) and (3) (minimum contents and publication requirement).[185] Article 27(3) empowers Member States to derogate from the requirement for a report in the case of a merger or public offer for the

[181] Implemented in the UK by the Companies Act 1985, s 101.

[182] See original Proposal, *Exposé des motifs*, 13–14.

[183] Art 41(1), implemented in the UK by the Companies Act 1985, s 101(2); see p 61 above for a note as to the scope of the derogation.

[184] Incompletely implemented in the UK by the Companies Act 1985, s 102, which is restricted to consideration which is or includes an undertaking which is or may be performed more than five years after the date of the allotment.

[185] See p 62 above. Implemented in the UK by the Companies Act 1985, s 103.

purchase or exchange of shares where the issued shares are used as payment for the shareholders in the target company: either such operation will give rise to valuations and reports which there is no need to duplicate.[186] The original Proposal contained no such exception; the Economic and Social Committee pointed out that in the context of an acquisition obtaining a valuation in advance was impracticable and could hinder acquisitions by Community companies, thus putting companies from third countries at a competitive advantage.[187] There is also a permitted derogation where all the shares issued on an increase in capital are issued to one or more companies, on condition that all the shareholders in the issuing company have agreed to dispense with the expert's report and the conditions set out in Article 10(4)(b) to (f) are satisfied.[188]

Partial subscription

Article 28 provides that an increase in capital which is not fully subscribed may proceed only if the conditions of the issue so provide.[189] The first draft suggested, less flexibly, that the general meeting could decide on the validity of such an increase and in default of a decision within three months the subscribers would be released from their commitment.

Pre-emption rights

The provisions of Article 29 giving existing shareholders pre-emption rights on an increase in capital have been described as 'an illustration of the skilful blending of comparative legal material, taken from the laws and practices of several Member States'.[190] Although welcomed by commentators as an important safeguard for shareholders against improper issues by directors of shares to themselves, the Directive has been criticized for failing to go further towards shareholder protec-

---

[186] Implemented in the UK by the Companies Act 1985, s 103(3) and (5).

[187] The House of Lords Select Committee also made the point that insisting on an expert valuation in the context of a share-for-share takeover would greatly complicate such transactions, and 'the process of valuation could be very difficult if the company for which the bid is made has a special value to the bidder or if the company for which the bid is made opposes the acquisition': 24th Report (n 161 above), 6.

[188] Art 27(4). The conditions require the company furnishing the consideration to have certain undistributable reserves and to guarantee certain debts of the recipient company; both the agreement to dispense with the report and the guarantee must be published.

[189] Implemented in the UK by the Companies Act 1985, s 84. Before the original implementing provision (Companies Act 1980, s 16) there was no statutory provision to this effect in the UK, although in practice the Stock Exchange required that all issues by listed companies were fully underwritten.

[190] Schmitthoff, C M, 'The Second EEC Directive on Company Law' (1978) CML Rev 43, 53. See Rodière, R, 'L'harmonisation des législations européennes dans le cadre de la C.E.E.' [1965] Revue trimestrielle de droit européen 336, 353 ff. for a summary of the provisions in the six original Member States for the protection of existing shareholders against dilution of their holdings on a new issue. Rodière argues that imposing one method with this aim to the exclusion of others goes beyond harmonization.

tion by requiring that on an increase in capital shares should be issued at the best price.[191]

Mandatory pre-emption rights were provided for in most but not all national laws, subject to variations of detail. Article 29 is principally derived from German law, although that law was wider than the Article in that it did not limit pre-emption rights to issues for cash. The inclusion of this provision in the Directive was resisted by the Netherlands, where pre-emption rights were common for close companies but not for listed companies.[192] There was no legal provision in the United Kingdom or Ireland for pre-emption rights on an increase in capital, although the Stock Exchange required offers by listed companies of equity issues for cash to be offered to existing shareholders pro rata unless the general meeting agreed otherwise.[193]

The basic, and mandatory, principle is that on an issue of shares[194] for cash[195] the shares must be offered on a pre-emptive basis to shareholders in proportion to the capital represented by their shares.[196] Member States may exempt shares which carry a limited right to participate in distributions or the company's assets on liquidation[197] and, where there are several classes of shares carrying different voting or participation rights, may provide that new shares of one class shall be offered to shareholders of that class before shareholders of the other classes.[198] Article 29(3) lays down publication and procedural requirements: where all a company's shares are registered, all the shareholders must be informed in writing; in other cases, publication in the national gazette designated for the purpose of the First Directive suffices. The Court ruled in the *Pafitis* case[199] that publication of an offer of subscription in daily newspapers does not constitute information given in writing to shareholders as required by Article 29(3).

Article 29(4) states that the statutes or instrument of incorporation may not restrict or withdraw the right of pre-emption but that the general meeting may do so,[200]

---

[191] See Temple Lang, J, 'Three EEC Draft Directives on Company Law' (1972) 7 Irish Jurist 306, 312 and Hurst, J E, 'Harmonization of Company Law in the EEC' (1974) 2 Legal Issues of European Integration 63, 71. Hurst suggests that it might 'be better to provide that should the shareholder participation be diluted by an unduly low issue price of new shares, the existing shareholders should have a claim for damages, and that this should be an occasion where the minority could sue'.

[192] See Stein, E, *Harmonization of European Company Laws* (1971) 326.

[193] See Tunc, A, 'Petrification' in Buxbaum, R M, Hertig, G, Hirsch, A and Hopt, K L (eds), *European Business Law* (1991) 200–2 for an interesting account of the English and French experience in implementing Art 29.

[194] Or securities convertible into shares or carrying the right to subscribe for shares, but not the conversion of or subscription for such shares: Art 29(6).

[195] There will thus be no need for pre-emption rights to be waived on a share-for-share takeover.

[196] Art 29(1); implemented in the UK by the Companies Act 1985, s 89.

[197] Art 29(2)(a). The UK has made use of this option, limiting s 89 to 'equity shares' as defined in the Companies Act 1985, s 94.

[198] Art 29(2)(b); implemented in the UK with considerable obscurity by the Companies Act 1985, s 89(2). [199] Case C–441/93 [1996] ECR I–1347.

[200] By a majority which Member States must provide is not less than two-thirds of the votes attaching to the capital represented or (at the Member State's option) a simple majority provided that at least half the subscribed capital is represented: Art 40.

provided that the administrative or management body justifies the proposed issue price to the meeting. This ensures that the shareholders will know the proposed price before issue, thus enabling them to block an under-priced issue which would dilute the value of their shares. The Economic and Social Committee criticized the requirement for justification of the proposed issue price; its gloomy forecast that Article 29(4) would in practice inhibit the system of authorized capital has fortunately not been realized, and appears to stem in part from a confusion between authorized and issued capital.[201] Member States may however provide that the statutes, the instrument of incorporation or the general meeting may for a renewable maximum period of five years give the power to restrict or withdraw the right to the body empowered to decide on an increase in subscribed capital.[202] Finally, Article 29(7) makes it clear that the right of pre-emption is not regarded as excluded where on an increase of capital shares are issued to financial institutions for placing among the company's shareholders on a pre-emptive basis.

Member States may derogate from Article 29 if necessary for the adoption or application of provisions 'designed to encourage the participation of employees, or other groups of persons defined by national law, in the capital of undertakings'.[203]

Article 29(1) was considered by the Court of Justice in the *Sindesmos* case.[204] Shareholders of a company whose administration had been taken over by the ORE contested the validity of an increase in capital made pursuant to another provision of the Law which provided for such increases to be made without regard to existing shareholders' pre-emption rights. The Court followed the same line of reasoning which it had applied in the *Karella* case and concluded that Article 29(1), as well as Article 25(1), was both applicable in the circumstances and of direct effect.[205]

In *Siemens*[206] the Court was asked whether it was compatible with Article 29 for a Member State to provide for shareholders to have a right of pre-emption on an issue of shares for non-cash consideration and to subject a decision withdrawing that right to judicial review. German law conferred on shareholders a right of pre-emption on an increase of capital both for cash and for non-cash consideration. The right of pre-emption may be withdrawn by the general meeting in certain strictly defined circumstances, reflecting those set out in Article 29; in addition, the case-law of the Bundesgerichtshof (Federal Court of Justice) had, by imposing supplementary conditions, subjected resolutions of the general meeting providing for the withdrawal of the right of pre-emption to substantive review, including that the

---

[201] The Committee's argument was that such justification would be 'wholly impossible in the case of capital authorized pursuant to Art 22(2) [Art 25(2) of the final version] since, at the time when that capital is authorized, the price has not been fixed' (author's translation).

[202] In accordance with Art 25(2): see p 78 above. Implemented in the UK by the Companies Act 1985, s 95.

[203] Art 41(1), implemented in the UK by the Companies Act 1985, s 89(5); see p 61 above for a note as to the scope of the derogation.

[204] Case C–381/89 *Sindesmos Melon tis Eleftheras Evangelikis Ekklisias and Others v Greek State and Others* [1992] ECR I–2111. The background facts are set out at pp 79–80 above.

[205] Paras 39–43.   [206] Case C–42/95 [1996] ECR I–6017.

measure be justified on objective grounds in the company's interests. Siemens AG proposed to increase its capital by an issue of shares for cash and non-cash consideration (holdings in other companies). The Bundesgerichtshof ruled that the resolution did not satisfy the conditions imposed by its case-law in so far as it withdrew the right of pre-emption on the proposed issue for non-cash consideration; it expressed doubts however as to the compatibility of its case-law with Article 29 of the Second Directive, and accordingly requested a preliminary ruling from the Court of Justice.

The Court noted that Article 29 in terms applied only to issues of shares for cash. Following the Opinion of Advocate General Tesauro, it ruled that that did not preclude Member States from extending its provisions to issues for non-cash consideration, or from subjecting a decision to withdraw the pre-emption right in those circumstances to a substantive review of the kind laid down by the Bundesgerichtshof.[207] The Court lent weight to the fact that a national rule extending the right of pre-emption was consistent with one of the aims of the Directive, namely ensuring more effective protection for shareholders.[208]

Reduction in Capital

Articles 30 to 39 contain provisions governing the circumstances in which a company may reduce its capital, including by the redemption of shares.

Article 30 provides that the general meeting[209] must approve any reduction in the subscribed capital, except under a court order.[210] The meeting shall act 'in accordance with the rules for a quorum . . . laid down in Article 40 without prejudice to Articles 36 and 37'. It is not clear what this means. Article 40 requires Member States to provide that such decisions 'must be taken at least by a majority of not less than two-thirds of the votes attaching to the securities or the subscribed capital represented' (Article 40(1)), and adds that Member States may 'lay down that a simple majority of the votes specified in paragraph 1 is sufficient when at least half the subscribed capital is represented' (Article 40(2)). Since the Article is itself expressed to apply to, inter alia, decisions referred to in Article 30, the reference in Article 30 presumably is not there simply to invoke Article 40 as such: it can only mean that the quorum requirement in Article 40(2), which on a reading of Article 40 as a whole is optional, applies in any event to decisions to reduce capital. Presumably however it is simply the quorum requirement which applies, and not—unless the Member State concerned has taken advantage of the option—the

---

[207] Para 22.   [208] Para 19. See also paras 15–19 of the Opinion.

[209] The notice convening the meeting must specify at least the purpose and proposed method of the reduction, and the decision must be published in accordance with Art 3 of the 1st Directive (see above ch II): Art 30.

[210] Companies Act 1985, s 135, requires both a special resolution of the general meeting and a court order to effect a reduction of capital.

sufficiency of a simple majority. This seems an unnecessarily complicated way to legislate. The reference to Articles 36 and 37 is also puzzling: those Articles, which concern a method of reducing capital specific to Germany, are themselves expressed not to be subject to Article 40.

Where there are several classes of shares, the decision of the general meeting must be subject to a separate vote, at least for each class of shareholders whose rights are affected by the transaction.[211] No guidance as to the circumstances in which rights will be regarded as 'affected' is given. This requirement was welcomed by commentators[212] in the United Kingdom and Ireland, where the existing law was widely perceived as giving inadequate protection to class rights on a reduction of capital: reducing capital by repaying preferential shareholders, for example, was a common practice and was not regarded as involving their class rights.[213] Although the Companies Act 1985 requires the approval of the class of shareholders whose rights are varied,[214] the narrow common law interpretation of 'variation' of rights has not been modified and it is thus arguable that Article 31 has not been fully implemented.

Article 32 lays down provisions for the protection of creditors on a reduction of capital. To accommodate the multiplicity of existing national laws, some of which provided for creditors to consent to or to have the right to contest the reduction of capital, while others guaranteed a right to security or payment or required authorization of the reduction, the Directive states the principle that on a reduction[215] in the subscribed capital[216] at least the creditors whose claims antedate publication of the decision to reduce capital shall be entitled at least to obtain security for claims which have not fallen due by the date of that publication, and leaves national law to prescribe the conditions for the exercise of that right and to grant further rights if required.[217] The final sentence of Article 32(1) states that Member States may not set aside the right to security unless the creditor has adequate safeguards or the latter are not necessary in view of the company's assets: this was inspired by French law. Until the creditors have obtained satisfaction or a court has decided that their application should not be granted, the reduction is to be ineffective.[218] The Economic and Social Committee proposed adding to Article 32 a requirement for Member States to ensure preferential status on a reduction of capital by an insolvent company for debts to employees by way of salary; this was not accepted.

---

[211] Art 31.

[212] See, e g, Morse, G, 'The Second Directive: Raising and Maintenance of Capital' [1977] ELR 126, 131, and Temple Lang, J, 'Three EEC Draft Directives on Company Law' (1972) 7 Irish Jurist 306, 312.

[213] See cases cited in Davies, P L, *Gower's Principles of Modern Company Law* (6th edn 1997) 724, n 10.

[214] Section 125.

[215] Not beyond the minimum capital prescribed pursuant to Art 6 (see pp 60–61 above) except where conditional on a subsequent increase in capital to at least that amount: Art 34.

[216] Including a reduction by waiver of the payment of the balance of the shareholders' contributions: Art 32(3), excluding a reduction to offset losses incurred or to set aside an undistributable reserve of up to 10% of the reduced capital to be used only to offset losses incurred or to increase subscribed capital (a German structure): Art 33(1).

[217] Art 32(1).   [218] Art 32(2).

Article 35 relates to French and Belgian law, which provide for procedures analogous to a reduction of capital by way of redemption without reduction. It lays down a series of minimum conditions concerning authorization, publication, the source of the funds to be used and the rights retained by redeemed shareholders. Article 36 concerns an analogous German procedure of reduction by compulsory withdrawal of shares, and similarly prescribes a series of minimum conditions concerning authorization, procedure, creditor protection and publication; Article 37 adds to these where the shares to be withdrawn were acquired by or on behalf of the company. Article 38 ensures that on any such redemption or compulsory withdrawal class rights are protected by a separate voting requirement. These two types of procedure are described in terms which are transposable into other laws and brought within the net of the Directive, in order to forestall other countries from trying to avoid the rules on reduction of capital by providing for variations on such processes.[219]

Finally, Article 39 applies where Member States permit companies to issue redeemable shares. It imposes a series of minimum conditions for redemption, closely modelled on the United Kingdom legislation on redeemable preference shares in force at the time the Directive was being negotiated.[220] The company's statutes or instrument of incorporation must authorize redemption[221] and lay down the terms and manner of redemption; the shares must be fully paid; only sums available for distribution in accordance with Article 15(1)[222] or the proceeds of a new issue made for the purpose may be used to fund the redemption, and in the former case a sum equal to the nominal value or, if none, accountable par of the redeemed shares must be included in an undistributable[223] reserve; any premium payable on redemption may be paid only from sums available for distribution or from another undistributable reserve; and notification of the redemption must be published in accordance with Article 3 of the First Directive.[224]

---

[219] See original Proposal, *Exposé des motifs*, 16.

[220] Companies Act 1948, s 58. This has now been replaced by the Companies Act 1985, ss 159–60, which reflect the broader scope of Art 39 in that they are not limited to preference shares but permit the issue of redeemable equity shares.

[221] And must have done so before the shares were subscribed for.

[222] See p 69 above.

[223] Except on a reduction of capital; otherwise it may be used only by way of capitalization for the purpose of increasing the subscribed capital.

[224] See pp 19–20 above.

IV

The Third and Sixth Directives

Introduction

The Third Directive on mergers of public companies[1] and the Sixth Directive on divisions of public companies[2] derive from a single Proposal, originally intended to regulate both types of operation. The Commission's Proposal[3] for a third Council directive to co-ordinate the safeguards which Member States require of companies as defined in Article 58, paragraph 2, of the Treaty in order to protect the interests of members and other parties in mergers of joint-stock companies[4] was submitted to the Council in June 1970. Despite its name, it was also expressed to extend to 'other transactions akin to a merger',[5] including divisions. However, shortly before the Third Directive was adopted the Council decided that further work on divi-

---

[1] 3rd Council Directive (EEC) 78/855 of 9 October 1978 based on Art 54(3)(g) of the Treaty concerning mergers of public limited liability companies [1978] OJ L295/36. The literature is not extensive: see Wooldridge, F, 'The Third Directive and the Meaning of Mergers' (1980) 1 The Company Lawyer 75; Shields, L K, 'The Third and Sixth Directives: Their Effects on Irish Law' (1984) 7 Journal of the Irish Society for European Law 47; Cordoliani, H F A, 'Le droit des fusions et la Communauté Européenne' [1979] La semaine juridique, édition commerce et industrie, nos 28–9, Etudes et commentaires, no 13078, 365; Heenen, J, 'La directive sur les fusions internes' [1981] Cahiers de droit européen 15, and Keutgen, G, 'La directive européenne sur les fusions nationales' (1979) 78 Revue pratique des sociétés 98.

[2] 6th Council Directive (EEC) 82/891 of 17 December 1982 based on Art 54(3)(g) of the Treaty, concerning the division of public limited liability companies [1982] OJ L378/47. The literature on the 6th Directive is even sparser: for a brief discussion of the background and a good summary of both Directives, see Barbaso, F, 'The Harmonisation of Company Law with regard to Mergers and Divisions' [1984] JBL 176.

[3] COM (70) 633 final, 12 June 1970; [1970] OJ C89/20: published in English with Explanatory Memorandum in EC Bull Supp 5/70. The draft is discussed in Stein, E, *Harmonization of European Company Laws* (1971) 378–83 and Temple Lang, J, 'Three EEC Draft Directives on Company Law—Capital, Mergers and Management' (1972) 7 Irish Jurist 306, 313–19. It is comprehensively analysed in Van Ommeslaghe, P, 'La proposition de troisième directive sur l'harmonisation des fusions de sociétés anonymes' in Zonderland, P (ed), *Quo Vadis Ius Societatum?* (1972) 123–50.

[4] A somewhat archaic term: joint-stock companies were a common form of business association in the UK in the 17th and 18th centuries; the common stock (in the sense of stock-in-trade) was contributed by a large group of persons. The name developed to distinguish such associations from groups of persons (principally merchant adventurers trading overseas) in which each member traded with his own stock and on his own account. After the crash of the biggest joint-stock company, the South Sea Company, in 1720, the so-called Bubble Act prohibited the formation of new joint-stock companies unless authorized by Crown charter or private Act. See generally Davies, P L, *Gower's Principles of Modern Company Law* (6th edn, 1997) 18–28. 'Public companies' might have been a preferable translation (in this context) of the French terms *sociétés anonymes* and *sociétés de capitaux* in the Proposal, the essence of which in either case is that the shares are freely transferable.

[5] Heading to Ch V of the original Proposal, comprising Art 21.

sions was needed in view of the extra risks involved in one company's assets being distributed among several others, and such transactions were made the subject of the separate and subsequent Sixth Directive.

The operations to which the Third and Sixth Directives apply are little used in the United Kingdom, and hence are relatively unfamiliar to lawyers from those jurisdictions. Corporate restructuring in the United Kingdom is more commonly effected by way of a takeover, whereby one company acquires another by purchasing shares in it from the latter's shareholders in return for either cash or shares in the former company; that type of transaction is not covered by the Third Directive. Divisions, although technically possible, are even less practised.[6] Before further considering the history and scope of the Third and Sixth Directive, therefore, it is helpful briefly to describe the types of operation to which they apply. The definitions are derived from French, German and Italian law, and will be considered in more detail below.

The Third Directive applies where:

(1)   one or more companies transfer all their assets and liabilities to another existing company, which issues shares[7] to the shareholders of the transferring company or companies which are then dissolved;[8]

(2)   several companies transfer all their assets and liability to a company they have formed, which issues shares[9] to the shareholders of the transferring companies which are then dissolved;[10] or

(3)   one or more wholly-owned subsidiaries transfer all their assets and liabilities to their parent and are then dissolved.[11]

The Directive will accordingly not apply to:

(1)   transfers of a company's assets and liabilities which do not involve the dissolution of the transferring company and the issue of shares by the acquiring company, such as the disposal of a branch or the sale of certain assets;

(2)   takeovers in the sense of acquisitions of shares in a company which involve neither the transfer of assets and liabilities nor the dissolution of the acquired company;

(3)   the reconstruction or reorganization of a single company, since only one company is involved; or

---

[6] The 6th Directive was known in the UK as the 'scissions' Directive. The Chairman of the HL Select Committee on the EC opened the oral proceedings on the draft 6th Directive by stating that he understood that the Department of Trade had introduced the word into the English language: the Department responded that they could not take credit for inventing the word, but had found it in the Shorter Oxford Dictionary: 43rd Report (Session 1979–80, HL Paper 206), 9.

[7] The company may also make a cash payment not exceeding 10% of the nominal value of the shares so issued.

[8] Art 3(1).

[9] The company may also make a cash payment not exceeding 10% of the nominal value of the shares so issued.

[10] Art 4(1).   [11] Art 24.

(4)   the transfer of one company's assets and liabilities to a newly formed company, since the definitions in the Directive require that there should be more than one existing company involved.

The Sixth Directive applies where a company transfers all its assets and liabilities to more than one other company (already existing or newly formed), which issue shares[12] to the shareholders of the transferring company which is then dissolved.[13]

Background and History

At the time of the Commission's initial Proposal, the First Directive had been adopted, and the Proposal for the Second Directive published. There were clearly many candidates for the next phase of the company law harmonization programme: one reason the relatively unexciting topic of domestic mergers and divisions was chosen was the draft Convention on international mergers of public companies then under discussion. Without harmonization of national laws in this area, it would be all the more difficult for the Member States to reach agreement on the draft Convention; work accordingly proceeded in parallel on both documents, preliminary drafts of which were started in 1967. Many of the detailed provisions of the Convention reflect those of the Proposal for the Third Directive, and there are numerous references to the internal law of the Member States as to mergers. (The Convention, based on Article 220(3) of the Treaty, was prepared in 1967, was eventually abandoned, amid disagreements over, in particular, employee protection, and resurrected as the draft Tenth Directive, which is still deadlocked for much the same reason.)[14]

In 1970, when the Proposal was submitted, five[15] of the six original Member States had provision for mergers, the exception being the Netherlands which was more familiar with takeovers by acquisition of shares.[16] France had detailed provision in its laws for divisions (and appears to have been the main driving force behind the adoption of the Sixth Directive,[17]) but they were also practised in other Member States, such as Italy, Belgium and Luxembourg, which had no formal code governing them.

---

[12] The company may also make a cash payment not exceeding 10% of the nominal value of the shares so issued.

[13] Arts 2 and 21.   [14] See further ch XIX.

[15] France, Germany and Italy had legislation specifically providing for mergers, while Belgium and Luxembourg, where in practice mergers occurred, had provision for their tax treatment: Van Ommeslaghe, P, 'La proposition de troisième directive' in Zonderland, P (ed), *Quo Vadis Ius Societatum?* (1972) 126.

[16] For a brief survey, see Stein, E, *Harmonization of European Company Laws* (1971) 374–8. For a discussion of the drafting process of the proposal, see Van Ommeslaghe, ibid, 124–5.

[17] See the Report of the HL Select Committee (n 6 above), 9–11. At one point in the discussion, Viscount Amory suggested rather testily 'How about re-naming it fission ['fusion' is the French term for merger in the 3rd Directive] instead of scission: the French might lose all interest.'

The Economic and Social Committee delivered its Opinion in May 1971[18] and the European Parliament in November 1972.[19] The Commission submitted an amended Proposal in January 1973[20] in order to take account of both those opinions, of the accession of the United Kingdom, Ireland and Denmark and of the current text of the draft Convention on international mergers.[21] The European Parliament approved the amended Proposal in April 1975[22] subject to its own amendments, which were substantially reflected in the second amended Proposal submitted by the Commission in December 1975.[23] The Third Directive was adopted on 9 October 1978[24] and the Sixth Directive on 17 December 1982. As a result of the curious feature that the two directives started life as one Proposal, the Sixth Directive received no scrutiny as such from the Economic and Social Committee or the Parliament,[25] an omission to which the Netherlands, United Kingdom and Irish delegations objected strongly, as did the Parliament.[26]

Legal Basis

Both directives are based on Article 54(3)(g) of the Treaty. Doubts have been expressed as to whether, in the case of the Third Directive, the compulsory introduction into the laws of certain Member States of a type of transaction not hitherto provided for strictly fell within the concept of coordination of safeguards.[27] There were also doubts at the time of the Proposal, which contained provisions for the protection of employees, as to whether employees could be regarded as 'others' within the meaning of Article 54(3)(g): those doubts however became otiose since, as indicated below, employees' interests were subsequently dealt with in a separate instrument, the Transfer of Undertakings Directive,[28] founded on Article 100.

Aims

As is apparent from the above, the principal aim of the Third Directive was to harmonize national laws relating to domestic mergers and in particular to require

[18] [1971] OJ C88/18.

[19] [1972] OJ C129/50.

[20] COM (72) 1668 final, 4 January 1973.

[21] See the *Exposé des Motifs*.

[22] [1975] OJ C95/8.

[23] COM (75) 671 final, 22 December 1975.

[24] Confusingly, some couple of months after adoption of the 4th Directive on 25 July 1978.

[25] The preamble to the 6th Directive refers to the fact that the Proposal for the 3rd Dir covered division operations, and states somewhat airily 'the opinions of the European Parliament and of the Economic and Social Committee were in favour of the regulation of such operation': 3rd recital.

[26] See the Report of the HL Select Committee: 43rd Report (Session 1979–80, HL Paper 206), paras 11–13, and the Minutes of Evidence, 9–13.

[27] See Van Ommeslaghe, 'La proposition de troisième directive' in Zonderland, P (ed), *Quo Vadis Ius Societatum?* (1972) 126; Heenen, J, 'La directive sur les fusions internes' [1981] Cahiers de droit européen 15.

[28] Council Directive (EEC) 77/187 of 14 February 1977 on the approximation of the laws of the Member States relating to the safeguarding of employees' rights in the event of transfers of undertakings, businesses or parts of businesses [1977] OJ L61/26.

Member States (for example, the Netherlands) which did not provide for mergers as defined to introduce the concept into their legislation. This is expressed in the preamble to the Directive as required for the protection of the interests of members and third parties.[29] Those third parties were originally intended to include employees;[30] by the time of adoption however employees' interests were already comprehensively regulated by the Transfer of Undertakings Directive,[31] and the preamble to the Third Directive merely refers to that instrument.[32] There is specific reference however to the need to keep shareholders informed,[33] to protect creditors' interests[34] and to keep third parties informed through appropriate disclosure.[35] Finally, the preamble refers to the need to extend the Directive to cover 'certain legal practices which in important respects are similar to merger, so that the obligation to provide such protection cannot be evaded'[36] and the desirability, in order 'to ensure certainty in the law as regards relations between the companies concerned', of limiting the cases in which nullity can arise.[37]

In contrast to the Third Directive, the Sixth Directive does not seek to impose on all Member States the concept of division as defined; instead it states that 'the protection of the interests of members and third parties requires that the laws of the Member States relating to divisions of public limited liability companies be coordinated where the Member States permit such operations'.[38] The objective is thus to ensure that the Directive's safeguards are observed where divisions are permitted. The remaining specific aims of the Third Directive are, however, all shared by the Sixth Directive.

Scope

The Third and Sixth Directives apply only to public limited companies as listed in Article 1 of the Third Directive.[39] As already noted, the Sixth Directive applies only where Member States permit such companies to carry out the division operations defined by the Directive.[40]

Member States need not apply the Directives to co-operatives incorporated as public companies[41] or to cases where the companies being acquired or divided are the subject of 'bankruptcy proceedings, proceedings relating to the winding-up of insolvent companies, judicial arrangements, compositions and analogous proceedings'.[42]

---

[29] 3rd recital.   [30] See the 5th recital in the preamble to the Proposal.
[31] Cited in n 28.
[32] 5th recital. Art 12 similarly refers to Directive (EEC) 77/187: see p 109 below.
[33] 4th recital.   [34] 6th recital.   [35] 7th recital.
[36] 8th recital.   [37] 9th recital.   [38] 5th recital.
[39] See 6th Directive, Art 1.   [40] Art 1(1)(2)(3).
[41] 3rd Directive, Art 1(2) and 6th Directive, Art 1(4); at the time of the Proposal, such companies were permitted in France and Italy.
[42] 3rd Directive, Art 1(3) and 6th Directive, Art 1(4).

The Directives cover domestic mergers and divisions only, namely those involving companies governed by each Member State's national laws.[43] The criteria for determining which companies are governed by a Member State's national laws vary according to whether the State subscribes to the incorporation theory (company governed by the laws of its State of incorporation) or the real seat theory (company governed by the laws of the State where it has its real seat).[44] Since the Directives are expressly restricted to mergers and divisions involving companies governed by a given Member State's national laws, there appears to be nothing—pending adoption and implementation of the proposed Tenth Directive—to prevent Member States from imposing different or additional rules on operations involving companies from other Member States.

Definition of Merger

The Third Directive requires Member States to make provision, as regards companies governed by their national laws, for rules governing 'merger by the acquisition of one or more companies by another and merger by the formation of a new company'[45] and for the acquisition of one company by another which holds all its shares.[46] The common feature of all these operations is that all the assets and liabilities of the acquired company are transferred to the acquiring company; the acquired company is then dissolved, without going into liquidation.

Mergers by acquisition

Article 3(1) defines 'merger by acquisition' as follows:

the operation whereby one or more companies are wound up without going into liquidation and transfer to another all their assets and liabilities in exchange for the issue to the shareholders of the company or companies being acquired of shares in the acquiring company and a cash payment, if any, not exceeding 10% of the nominal value of the shares so issued or, where they have no nominal value, of their accounting par value.

A merger by acquisition may be illustrated by the diagram on p. 96.

There is no acquisition of one company by another in the usual sense in which that concept is used by Anglo-American lawyers; the undertaking rather than the company as separate entity is the subject of the acquisition. Perhaps 'absorption' (the concept used in the French text) might have been a better choice of term.

---

[43] Art 2 of the 3rd Directive and Art 1 of the 6th Directive.
[44] See further chs XVI and XVIII.   [45] Art 2.   [46] Art 24.

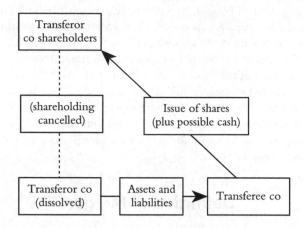

Mergers by the formation of a new company

This type of merger is defined by Article 4(1) as follows:

the operation whereby several companies are wound up without going into liquidation and transfer to a company that they set up all their assets and liabilities in exchange for the issue to their shareholders of shares in the new company and a cash payment, if any, not exceeding 10% of the nominal value of the shares so issued or, where they have no nominal value, of their accounting par value.

A merger by the formation of a new company may be illustrated by the following diagram:

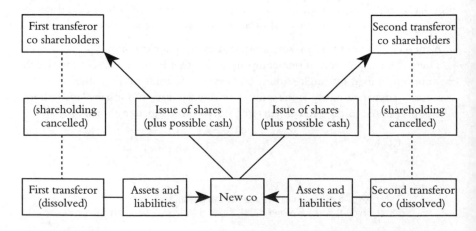

Features common to both types of merger

The concept of being wound up without going into liquidation would perhaps be better expressed in English as being dissolved without being wound up.[47] The essential element is that the company ceases existence without going through a separate winding-up process entailing the realization and distribution of assets to creditors and shareholders: since all assets and liabilities pass to the successor company, there would in any event be nothing to liquidate. As a matter of common sense, it would seem that the transfer of assets and liabilities would have to be effected before the dissolution; Article 19(1), however, provides that the transfer of assets, the change of shareholders and the ceasing to exist of the company being acquired are to happen simultaneously.

The possibility of a cash top-up is designed to facilitate calculating the amount of shares to be allotted in consideration of the transfer, enabling fractions of shares to be avoided. The 10 per cent threshold was borrowed from German law. Member States may permit a threshold higher than 10 per cent; the provisions of the Directive will still apply.[48] The reference to shares without nominal value was inserted to cater for Belgium and Luxembourg; the 'accounting par value' of such a share is obtained by dividing the company's capital by the number of shares issued.

Member States may provide[49] that merger by acquisition may also be effected where one or more of the companies being acquired is in liquidation,[50] or that merger by the formation of a new company may also be effected where one (or more) of the companies ceasing to exist is in liquidation,[51] provided that the company or companies in liquidation have not yet begun to distribute assets to the shareholders in the course of the liquidation.[52] That provision is borrowed from German law. Where a merger is effected by a company in liquidation which has paid off all its creditors, the transfer will be of net assets rather than of assets and liabilities.

Acquisition of wholly-owned subsidiary

Article 24 requires Member States to make provision, in respect of companies governed by their laws, for the operation whereby one or more companies are wound up without going into liquidation and transfer all their assets and liabilities to

---

[47] cf the terminology used in Council Directive (EEC) 90/434 of 23 July 1990 on the common system of taxation applicable to mergers, divisions, transfers of assets and exchanges of shares concerning companies of different Member States [1990] OJ L225/1, Art 2(a): the definition of merger is substantially the same, but the English reads 'one or more companies, on being dissolved without going into liquidation, transfer all their assets and liabilities . . .' The original Proposal used the terms 'dissolution without liquidation': Art 2(2) and (3).

[48] Art 30.   [49] This option derives from German law.   [50] Art 3(2).

[51] Art 4(2).   [52] If so, the rules of liquidation will have to be followed instead.

another company which is the holder of all their shares and other securities conferring the right to vote at general meetings. The operation is illustrated by the following diagram:

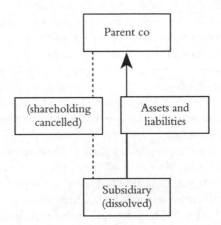

Member States may apply Article 24 to operations as described where all the shares and other securities referred to are held by and/or on behalf of the acquiring company.[53] Such operations will not fall within the definition of merger by acquisition of one company by another since there is no allotment of shares by the acquiring company in consideration of the transfer of assets. In contrast, where a subsidiary is held as to less than 100 per cent there will be an allotment; in such circumstances the protection afforded by the full procedure is deemed necessary in any event in the interests of the minority shareholders, although subject to certain exceptions.

Article 24 requires acquisitions of wholly-owned subsidiaries to be regulated by the Directive with the exception of certain provisions relating to the issue of shares which would in other circumstances be made,[54] the drawing up of draft terms of merger and reports thereon[55] and the civil liability of directors and experts.[56] Moreover Member States may dispense with the need for a general meeting of the parent and subsidiary to approve the merger, subject to certain provisos.[57]

Analogous operations

In order to avoid circumvention of its provisions by the use of operations analogous but not identical to those to which it explicitly applies, the Directive extends to 'Other operations treated as mergers'.[58] Article 30 has already been men-

---

[53] Art 26.   [54] Arts 5(2)(b) (c) (d) and 19(1)(b).   [55] Arts 9, 10 11(1)(d) (e).
[56] Arts 20 and 21.   [57] Art 25; see further below.
[58] Heading of Ch V, comprising Arts 30 and 31.

tioned:[59] it provides that where Member States permit a threshold for cash consideration higher than 10 per cent of the nominal (or accounting par) value of the shares issued, the Directive none the less applies. Article 31 provides that where the laws of a Member State permit mergers by acquisition or by the formation of a new company or by the acquisition of a wholly-owned subsidiary 'without all of the transferring companies thereby ceasing to exist'—in effect, the transfer of part of an undertaking—the Directive will apply to the operation.

As indicated above, the original Proposal had a significantly broader scope than the Directive as adopted: it extended to transactions 'through which a company transfers to one or more companies . . . all or part of its assets in return for the allotment to its shareholders of shares in the beneficiary company or companies as full or partial consideration for this transfer'.[60] That definition encompassed not only divisions, subsequently separately dealt with in the Sixth Directive, but also simple transfers of assets in return for shares. As the Economic and Social Committee pointed out, such transfers were already regulated in part by the Second Directive, since they are contributions in kind.

Definition of Divisions

As indicated, the Commission's Proposal included an article covering divisions of companies, namely the splitting-up of a company and the transfer of its assets to more than one acquiring companies, whether previously existing or newly formed, in consideration of the allotment of shares in the acquiring companies to the split company's shareholders. Such operations would not fall within the definitions of merger since there is more than one acquiring company. The Commission felt however that they were:

none the less akin to mergers in many legal and economic respects. In order to ensure that there is no evasion of the safeguards required for mergers, it would appear indispensable that the rules laid down for mergers should be applied to these transactions also, though in a slightly amended form.[61]

The similar features included the transfer of all assets and liabilities, the exchange of shares and the dissolution of the company being divided or acquired without the need to go through cumbersome liquidation procedures. During the negotiation of the Third Directive however there was much disagreement as to whether special rules on divisions were necessary, France being the only original Member State with detailed provision for divisions in its law. Eventually, in order to prevent further delay in the adoption of the Third Directive, the provision was dropped and the Council, which considered that further work was necessary given the extra risks involved in one company's assets being distributed among several others, indicated

---

[59] See pp 97.   [60] Art 21(1).   [61] Explanatory Memorandum, 5 (see n 3 above).

that the matter would continue to be examined. The definitions closely follow the definitions of the equivalent type of merger in the Third Directive, *mutatis mutandis*.

Member States are not required by the Sixth Directive to permit the types of divisions of companies discussed below, but where they do so permit, the operations must be subjected to the provisions of the Directive.

Division by acquisition

Article 2(1) defines 'division by acquisition' as follows:

the operation whereby, after being wound up without going into liquidation, a company transfers to more than one company all its assets and liabilities in exchange for the allocation to the shareholders of the company being divided of shares in the companies receiving contributions as a result of the division (hereinafter referred to as 'recipient companies') and possibly a cash payment not exceeding 10% of the nominal value of the shares allocated or, where they have no nominal value, of their accounting par value.

A division by acquisition may be illustrated by the following diagram:

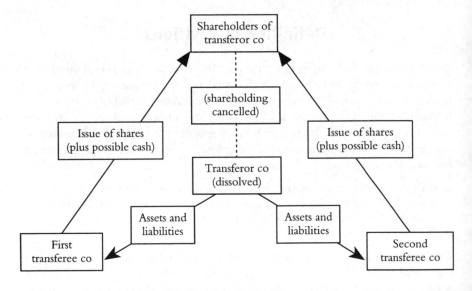

Division by the formation of new companies

This type of division is defined by Article 21(1) as follows:

the operation whereby, after being wound up without going into liquidation, a company transfers to more than one newly-formed company all its assets and liabilities in exchange for the allocation to the shareholders of the company being divided of shares in the recipient companies, and possibly a cash payment not exceeding 10% of the nominal value of the shares allocated or, where they have no nominal value, of their accounting par value.

A division by the formation of new companies thus has the same structure as a division by acquisition, the only difference being that the recipient companies are newly formed rather than existing companies.

Division by combined method

Member States may permit companies to carry out operations whereby a division by acquisition is combined with a division by the formation of one or more new companies: at least one recipient company is an existing company and at least one recipient company is newly formed. Such operations are to be subjected to both sets of requirements covering the two types of division.[62]

Division under the supervision of a judicial authority

The Sixth Directive provides for the relaxation of certain of its provisions concerning publication and inspection of documents (considered separately below) where division operations are subject to the supervision of a judicial authority with the power (a) to call a general meeting of the shareholders of the company being divided in order to decide upon the division; (b) to call any meeting of creditors of each of the companies involved in order to decide upon the division; (c) to ensure that the shareholders and creditors of the companies involved have received or can obtain at least certain specified documents[63] in time to examine them before the general meeting of their company and (d) to approve the draft terms of the division.

These provisions are reportedly the fruit of long and animated discussion, and reflect a compromise between two opposing views.[64] The United Kingdom sought a general system of derogations from the provisions of the Directive for divisions under the supervision of its national courts, on the basis that such supervision comported equivalent guarantees. That argument was rejected by the Commission and the other delegations, which did not consider that guarantees deriving from the discretionary authority of the national courts could compare with specific guarantees laid down in the Directive to apply in all cases.

Features common to all types of division

Notwithstanding the wording of Articles 2 and 21, which firmly (if incomprehensibly) place the transfer later in time than the dissolution of the company being divided, Article 17 states that the transfer, the change of shareholders and the ceasing to exist of the company being divided are simultaneous.

---

[62] Art 1(3).   [63] Referred to in Art 9: see below.
[64] See Barbaso, F, 'The Harmonisation of Company Law' [1984] JBL 176, 183, and Welch, J, 'The Harmonisation of Company Laws in the EEC' in Panebianco, M (ed), *Europa Comunitaria e America Latina* (1983).

Member States may provide that divisions[65] by acquisition or by the formation of new companies may also be effected where the company being divided is in liquidation, provided that it has not yet begun to distribute assets to the shareholders in the course of the liquidation.[66]

Analogous operations

The Sixth Directive contains anti-avoidance provisions analogous to those in the Third Directive. Article 24 provides that where Member States permit a threshold for cash consideration higher than 10 per cent of the nominal (or accounting par) value of the shares issued, the Directive none the less applies. Article 25 provides that where the laws of a Member State permit divisions by acquisition or by the formation of new companies 'without the company being divided ceasing to exist', the Directive will apply to the operation.

Procedure

The Third Directive lays down detailed rules to be followed on a merger. Chapter II, comprising Articles 5 to 22, contains the procedure on a merger by acquisition. Chapter III, consisting solely of Article 23, applies to mergers by the formation of a new company; since, however, with only one or two exceptions it simply applies Chapter II to such mergers, the procedure for both types will be considered together. For that purpose, Article 23(1) provides that 'merging companies' and 'company being acquired' means the companies which will cease to exist and 'acquiring company' means the new company.

The Sixth Directive follows a similar pattern: Chapter I, comprising Articles 2 to 20, lays down the procedure to be followed on a division by acquisition; Chapter II, consisting of Articles 21 and 22, applies to divisions by the formation of new companies and similarly incorporates by reference most of Chapter I. For that purpose, Article 22(1) provides that 'companies involved in a division' means the company being divided and 'recipient companies' means each of the new companies. The procedure in general follows closely that laid down for mergers; as will be seen, what differences there are tend to take the form of extra disclosure obligations on the companies involved with a view to increased protection for shareholders and creditors on a division.

---

[65] Art 2(3) of the 6th Directive provides generally that, in so far as the 6th Directive refers to the 3rd Directive, 'merging companies' means 'the companies involved in a division', 'company being acquired' means 'company being divided', 'acquiring company' means 'each of the recipient companies' and 'draft terms of merger' means 'draft terms of division'.

[66] Art 2(2) applying to divisions by acquisition Art 3(2) of the 3rd Directive and Art 21(2) applying to divisions by the formation of new companies Art 4(2) of the 3rd Directive.

Draft terms

Mergers

Article 5 of the Third Directive requires the boards[67] of the merging companies to draw up written draft terms of merger.[68] The neutral concept of 'draft terms', or *projet de fusion* in French, was chosen to accommodate the divergent practice in the five (of the original six) Member States where mergers occurred: some required the management to conclude a merger contract or draw up a draft contract before the general meetings of the companies concerned approved the merger, others prohibited the conclusion of a contract before the general meetings had approved the merger in principle.[69] All however had, as might be expected, a similar pattern of negotiation, agreement and approval by members of the conditions of merger. The Directive, rather than seeking to eliminate the differences, lays down the core requirements that the essential conditions of the merger are fixed before the general meetings and set out in a document accessible to shareholders and others.

The draft terms are to specify at least the following details:

(a)   the type, name and registered office of each of the merging companies [and, in the case of a merger by formation of a new company, the new company];[70]

(b)   the share exchange ratio and the amount of any cash payment;

(c)   the terms relating to the allotment of shares in the acquiring company;

(d)   the date from which the holding of such shares entitles the holders to participate in profits and any special conditions affecting that entitlement;

(e)   the date from which the transactions of the company being acquired shall be treated for accounting purposes as being those of the acquiring company;

(f)   the rights conferred by the acquiring company on the holders of shares to which special rights are attached and the holders of securities other than shares, or the measures proposed concerning them;

(g)   any special advantage granted to the experts referred to in Article 10(1) and members of the merging companies' administrative, management, supervisory or controlling bodies.[71]

However, where the merger involves the acquisition by one company of a wholly-owned subsidiary, (b) (c) and (d) do not apply since there is no allotment of shares in the acquiring company.[72]

---

[67] The Directives refer to 'the administrative or management bodies'. The Proposal specified that, in the case of a company with a two-tier management structure, this meant the executive rather than the supervisory board: Art 22(1).

[68] Art 5(1).

[69] Explanatory Memorandum, 6; see further Stein, E, *Harmonization of European Company Laws* (1971) 375; Van Ommeslaghe, P, 'La proposition de troisième directive' in Zonderland, P (ed), *Quo Vadis Ius Societatum?* (1972) 130–1, and Cordoliani, H F A, 'Le droit des fusions' [1979] La semaine juridique (see n 1 above) 268–9.

[70] Art 23(2); see also 6th Directive, Art 22(2).   [71] Art 5(2).   [72] Art 24.

Divisions

Article 3 of the Sixth Directive echoes Article 5 of the Third Directive, *mutatis mutandis*. In addition to the information listed above, Article 3(2) requires the draft terms of division to include:

(h)   the precise description and allocation of the assets and liabilities to be transferred to each of the recipient companies;

(i)   the allocation to the shareholders of the company being divided of shares in the recipient companies and the criterion upon which such allocation is based.

The Sixth Directive accordingly envisages divisions in which shares in the recipient companies are not allocated in proportion to the holdings of the shareholders of the company being divided. In such a case, the Directive permits Member States to provide that the minority shareholders of the company being divided may exercise the right to have their shares purchased. If so, the minority shareholders must be entitled to receive consideration corresponding to the value of their shares; in the event of a dispute concerning such consideration, it must be possible for the consideration to be determined by a court.[73]

The Sixth Directive moreover makes provision for the situation where an asset or liability is not allocated by the draft terms of division and where the interpretation of those terms does not make a decision on its allocation possible. In the case of an asset, the asset or the consideration therefor shall be allocated to all the recipient companies in proportion to the share of the net assets allocated to each of those companies under the draft terms.[74] In the case of a liability, each of the recipient companies shall be jointly and severally liable for it; Member States may provide for the limitation of such liability to the net assets allocated to each company.[75]

Publication

The draft terms must be published for each of the merging companies or the companies involved in the division in accordance with Article 3 of the First Directive[76] at least one month before the general meeting which is to decide on the operation.[77]

On a division under the supervision of a judicial authority, that authority may relieve the companies involved in the division from the obligation to publish the draft terms provided that (a) it establishes that the draft terms, accounts and reports[78] are available to the shareholders and creditors of all the companies involved in time to be examined before the general meeting called to decide upon the division; (b) it establishes that no prejudice would be caused to shareholders or creditors and (c) the national system of protection of creditors' interests covers all claims regardless of their date.[79]

---

[73] Art 5(2).   [74] Art 3(3)(a).   [75] Art 3(3)(b).
[76] See pp 19–20 above.   [77] 3rd Directive, Art 6; 6th Directive, Art 4.
[78] Referred to in Art 9: see below.   [79] Art 23(2)(a).

Reports on draft terms

Except in the case of the acquisition of a wholly-owned subsidiary,[80] two separate reports must be made on the draft terms.

First, the boards[81] of each merging company or each company involved in the division must draw up a detailed written report explaining the draft terms and setting out the legal and economic grounds for them, in particular the share exchange ratio and, in the case of a division, the criterion determining the allocation of shares.[82] The report must also describe any special valuation difficulties which have arisen and, in the case of a division, disclose the preparation of the report on non-cash consideration required by Article 27(2) of the Second Directive[83] for recipient companies and the register where that report must be lodged.[84] Moreover, in the case of a division the board of the company being divided must inform both that company's general meeting when it is deciding on the draft terms and the boards of the recipient companies so that they can inform their general meetings of any material change in the assets and liabilities since the draft terms were prepared.[85]

Second, one or more experts,[86] acting on behalf of each of the merging companies or the companies involved in the division[87] but independent of them, appointed or approved by a judicial or administrative authority, must examine the draft terms and draw up a written report to the shareholders.[88] The experts must state whether in their opinion the share exchange ratio is fair and reasonable and describe any special valuation difficulties which have arisen. The experts' statement must at least:

(a) indicate the method or methods used to arrive at the share exchange ration proposed;
(b) state whether such method or methods are adequate in the case in question, indicate the values arrived at using each such method and give an opinion on the relative importance attributed to such methods in arriving at the value decided on.[89]

The experts are to be entitled to obtain all relevant information and documents from the merging companies and to carry out all necessary investigations.[90]

---

[80] Art 24.   [81] See n 67.   [82] 3rd Directive, Art 9; 6th Directive, Art 7(1).
[83] See p 83 above.   [84] 3rd Directive, Art 9, second para; 6th Directive, Art 7(2).
[85] 6th Directive, Arts 7(3) and 20(d).
[86] Which may, depending on the laws of each Member State, be natural or legal persons or companies or firms: 3rd Directive, Art 10(1), 6th Directive, Art 9(1). The definition of 'expert' is substantially the same as that in the 2nd Directive, Art 10(1), in connection with the valuation of non-cash consideration for shares: see ch II above. Indeed the 6th Directive provides that the same expert may act in both capacities: Arts 8(3) and 22(4).
[87] Member States may provide for the appointment of one or more experts for all the companies if such appointment is made by a judicial or administrative authority at the joint request of those companies: 3rd Directive, Art 10(1), 6th Directive, Art 8(1).
[88] Art 10(1).   [89] 3rd Directive, Art 10(2), applied by 6th Directive, Art 8(2).
[90] 3rd Directive, Art 10(3), applied by 6th Directive, Art 8(2).

The Directives do not (as did the Proposal) expressly state that the company's auditors may act as experts for this purpose: nor however does there appear to be anything to prevent it.[91]

Member States need not apply the relevant Directive's requirements for management and experts' reports in the following circumstances. First, where 90 per cent or more (but not all) of the voting securities of the company being acquired are held by or, at Member States' further option,[92] on behalf of, the acquiring company, provided that the minority shareholders of the company being acquired are entitled to have their shares acquired by the acquiring company for a consideration corresponding to the value of the shares and that a court has jurisdiction to determine the value of the consideration in the event of disagreement.[93] Second, where all the shareholders and the holders of other voting securities of the companies involved in a division have so agreed.[94] Third, where on a division by the formation of new companies the shares in each new company are allocated to the shareholders of the company being divided in proportion to their rights in the capital of that company.[95]

General meeting

Agenda and procedure

The draft terms and any consequential alterations to the companies' statutes must be approved at the general meeting of each of the merging companies, by either[96] (a) at least two thirds of the votes attaching either to the shares or to the subscribed capital represented, or (b) a simple majority of such votes when at least half the subscribed capital is represented.[97] Where there is more than one class of share, there must be separate voting for each class of shareholder whose rights are affected by the proposed merger or division.[98] Moreover, if the company's statutes require alteration (for example, to authorize the requisite issue of shares), any procedure governing such alteration must also be followed.[99] (The original Proposal required that procedure to be followed in any event, even where no alteration to the statutes was involved; following a suggestion by the Economic and Social Committee, the provision was amended so as to apply only 'where appropriate' (*le cas échéant*).) The rules as to quorum and other procedural requirements are a matter for the relevant national law.

---

[91] The UK implementing legislation permits the company's auditors to act as experts: see the Companies Act 1985, para 5(3) of Sch 15B. See Cordoliani, H F A, 'Le droit des fusions' [1979] La semaine juridique (n 1 above) 370, for a discussion of this and other problems raised by the wording of Arts 10(1) and 8(1).

[92] 3rd Directive, Art 29.   [93] 3rd Directive, Art 28.   [94] 6th Directive, Art 10.

[95] 6th Directive, Art 22(5).   [96] At the Member States' option.

[97] 3rd Directive, Art 7(1)(3); 6th Directive, Art 5(1).

[98] 3rd Directive, Art 7(2); 6th Directive, Art 5(1).

[99] 3rd Directive, Art 7(1) and 6th Directive, Art 5(1).

In the case of a merger or division by formation of a new company, the company's statutes must in addition be approved at a general meeting of each of the companies that will cease to exist or of the company being divided; the requisite majority is not specified.[100] It may be noted that, on a merger by the formation of a new company (but not on a division), the Member States need not apply to the new company the rules governing the verification of any consideration other than cash for the issue of shares, laid down in Article 10 of the Second Directive.[101] Although those rules would in principle be applicable, it was considered acceptable to permit their exclusion since the shareholders should be sufficiently protected by the merger procedure, in particular the requirement for an experts' report.

Shareholders' rights of inspection

At least one month before the general meeting, all shareholders must be entitled to inspect at the registered office[102] (a) the draft terms of merger or division, (b) the annual accounts and reports of the merging companies or the companies involved in the division for the preceding three financial years, (c) if the last financial year ended more than six months before that date,[103] an accounting statement drawn up as at a date within the three months preceding the date of the draft terms, (d) the reports of the boards of the merging companies or the companies involved in the division and (e) the experts' reports.[104] Where an accounting statement is required to be drawn up, the same methods and layout as the last annual balance sheet must be used;[105] the Member States may however provide that it is not necessary to take a fresh physical inventory[106] and that the valuations shown in the last balance sheet are to be altered only to reflect entries in the books of account, provided that (a) interim depreciation and provisions and (b) material changes in actual value not shown in the books are taken into account.[107] Member States may moreover permit the requirement for an accounting statement to be dispensed with on a division if all the shareholders and the holders of other voting securities of the companies involved have agreed.[108]

The period and manner prescribed for the inspection of the documents specified above need not be applied on a division under the supervision of a judicial authority where that authority establishes that the documents are available to the shareholders and creditors of all the companies involved in time to be examined before the general meeting and that no prejudice would be caused to shareholders or creditors.[109]

---

[100] 3rd Directive, Art 23(3); 6th Directive, Art 22(3).
[101] Art 23(4). Such an exemption is in effect already provided for in the 2nd Directive, Art 27(3): see ch. III.
[102] And to obtain on request free copies of: 3rd Directive, Art 11(3) and 6th Directive, Art 9(3).
[103] i e one month before the general meeting.
[104] 3rd Directive, Art 11(1); 6th Directive, Art 9(1).
[105] Art 11(2) and Art 9(2).   [106] Art 11(2)(a) and Art 9(2)(a).
[107] Art 11(2)(b) and Art 9(2)(b).   [108] 3rd Directive, Art 10.
[109] 3rd Directive, Art 23(2)(c).

More generally, Member States need not apply Article 11 of the Third Directive (entitlement of shareholders to inspect documents) where 90 per cent or more (but not all) of the voting securities of the company being acquired are held by or, at Member States' further option,[110] on behalf of, the acquiring company, provided that the minority shareholders of the company being acquired are entitled to have their shares acquired by the acquiring company for a consideration corresponding to the value of the shares and that a national court has jurisdiction to determine the value of the consideration in the event of disagreement.[111]

Circumstances where no general meeting is necessary

First, Member States need not require a general meeting of the *acquiring company* in a merger[112] or any *recipient company* in a division[113] (which may, if the company is large, save it much expense) provided that at least one month before the general meeting of the company or companies being acquired or the company being divided (a) the draft terms are published as required by the relevant Directive and (b) all shareholders of the acquiring company or each recipient company are entitled to inspect the draft terms, the accounting documents[114] and the board and experts' reports. Where however the merger or division is by the formation of a new company, the general meeting of that company cannot be dispensed with.[115] On a division under the supervision of a judicial authority, that authority may dispense with the above-mentioned specific requirements of publication and shareholder inspection where there is no general meeting of a recipient company provided that the authority establishes that the documents are available to the shareholders and creditors of all the companies involved in time to be examined before the general meeting and that no prejudice would be caused to shareholders or creditors.[116]

Second, Member States need not require a general meeting of *either company* in the case of the acquisition of a wholly-owned subsidiary provided that, at least one month before the operation takes effect, the draft terms are published as regards each company and the shareholders of the acquiring company are entitled to inspect, and obtain free copies of, the draft terms and accounting documents.[117]

Third, Member States need not require a general meeting of the *company being divided* where the recipient companies together hold all its shares and all other voting securities provided that, at least one month before the operation takes effect, the draft terms are published as regards each company and the shareholders of all companies are entitled to inspect, and obtain free copies of, the draft terms, accounting documents and reports.[118]

---

[110] 3rd Directive, Art 29.
[112] 3rd Directive, Arts 8 and 27.
[114] Those specified in the 3rd Directive, Art 11(1) and in the 6th Directive, Art 9(1).
[115] 3rd Directive, Art 23(1) and the 6th Directive, Art 22(1).
[116] 3rd Directive, Art 23(2)(b).
[118] 6th Directive, Art 20.

[111] 3rd Directive, Art 28.
[113] 6th Directive, Art 6.
[117] 3rd Directive, Art 25.

In all the above cases, one or more shareholders of the acquiring company or the company being divided holding a minimum percentage to be fixed at not more than 5 per cent[119] of the subscribed capital must be entitled to require a general meeting to be called.[120]

In cases where the approval of the general meeting has been dispensed with in a merger, the draft terms of merger must be drawn up and certified in due legal form.[121]

Protection of employees' rights

Protection of the rights of the employees of each of the merging companies or each of the companies involved in a division is to be regulated in accordance with Directive (EEC) 77/187.[122]

Protection of creditors' interests

The rules for the protection of creditors' interests varied between the Member States which provided for mergers. Some gave creditors a right of objection blocking the merger as long as the objections had not been withdrawn or overruled by a court. Others provided for a right of objection but did not permit the objection to block the merger, which however could not be relied upon as against creditors who had not been paid off or given security for their claim. Others gave no right of objection, merely providing for creditors to be paid off or given security. Moreover, some national rules on the protection of creditors applied only to creditors of the company being acquired whereas others extended to creditors of all the merging companies.[123]

The Third Directive does not standardize these various rules in the case of mergers. Article 13 requires the Member States to provide for an adequate system of protection of the interests of creditors of the merging companies whose claims ante-date, but have not fallen due by, the publication of the draft terms.[124] The

---

[119] The Member States may provide for non-voting shares to be excluded from this calculation.

[120] 3rd Directive, Arts 8(c), 25(c) and 27(c); 6th Directive, Arts 6(c) and 20(c).

[121] 3rd Directive, Art 16(1); 6th Directive, Art 14.

[122] 3rd Directive, Art 12; 6th Directive, Art 11. Directive (EEC) 77/187 is cited in n 28. See further McMullen, J, *Business Transfers and Employee Rights* (1992); de Groot, C, 'The Council Directive on the Safeguarding of Employees' Rights in the Event of Transfers of Undertakings: an Overview of the Case Law' (1993) 30 CML Rev 331; de Groot, C, 'The Council Directive on the Safeguarding of Employees' Rights in the Event of Transfers of Undertakings: An Overview of Recent Case Law' (1998) 35 CML Rev 707; Davies, P L, 'Acquired Rights, Creditors' Rights, Freedom of Contract, and Industrial Democracy' (1990) 9 *Yearbook of European Law* 21; *Acquired Rights of Employees: the Transfer of Undertakings Directive (77/187/EEC) and Statutory Instrument No 306/80*; *Papers from the I.C.E.L. Conference November 1988* (1988).

[123] Explanatory Memorandum, 11–12; Stein, E, *Harmonization of European Company Laws* (1971) 377–8; Van Ommeslaghe, P, 'La proposition de troisième directive' in Zonderland, P (ed), *Quo Vadis Ius Societatum?* (1972) 136–9.

[124] Art 13(1).

protection may be different for the creditors of the acquiring company and for those of the company being acquired[125] (the acquiring company, after all, continues to exist; until adoption of the Directive, its creditors were protected in France and Italy alone[126]), but all creditors must at least be entitled to obtain adequate safeguards where the financial situation of the merging companies makes such protection necessary and where they do not already have such safeguards.[127] Those provisions reflect the compromise reached between the diverging views expressed during negotiation of the Directive[128] on the question whether the creditors of the acquiring company needed special protection in line with the law of France and Italy but not of Germany, Belgium or Luxembourg.

The Sixth Directive follows the same pattern with respect to divisions, but provides additional protection for creditors. Article 12 requires the Member States to provide for an adequate system of protection of the interests of creditors of the companies involved in a division whose claims ante-date, but have not fallen due by, the publication of the draft terms.[129] The protection may be different for the creditors of the recipient companies and for those of the company being divided[130] but all creditors must at least be entitled to obtain adequate safeguards where the financial situation of the company being divided and that of the company to which the obligation will be transferred in accordance with the draft terms makes such protection necessary and where they do not already have such safeguards.[131]

All the above provisions apply to debenture-holders of the merging companies or companies involved in the division, without prejudice to national rules permitting or requiring the collective exercise of debenture-holders' rights, except where they have approved the operation either individually or by a debenture-holders' meeting in accordance with national law.[132]

The Directives contain further protection for debenture-holders. They provide that holders of securities, other than shares, to which special rights are attached must be given rights in the acquiring company or the relevant recipient companies[133] at least equivalent to those they possessed in the company being acquired or divided, unless they have approved the alteration of those rights either individually or by a meeting of the holders of such securities in accordance with national law or unless the holders are entitled to have their securities repurchased (in the case of a merger, by the acquiring company). Article 15 would apply not only to certain debenture-holders (for example, 'debentures convertible into shares, debentures exchangeable against shares, debentures giving preferential rights to subscribe for

---

[125] Art 13(3).

[126] Barbaso, F, 'The Harmonisation of Company Law' [1984] JBL 176, 181.

[127] Art 13(2).

[128] Both by the governmental experts at an early stage and later in the Council. See generally Van Ommeslaghe (n 123 above) 136–7.

[129] Art 12(1).   [130] Art 12(4).   [131] Art 12(2).

[132] 3rd Directive, Art 14; 6th Directive, Art 12(5).

[133] 'the recipient companies against which such securities may be invoked in accordance with the draft terms of division': Art 13.

shares in the company or giving a right to a share in the profits'[134]) but also to 'holders of other subscription rights'[135] and holders of certain special types of security recognized in certain Member States, such as '*parts bénéficiaires* which represent no capital and . . . *jouissance* shares or dividend-right certificates (*Genusscheine*)'.[136]

Member States need not however apply Articles 13, 14 and 15 of the Third Directive or Articles 12 and 13 of the Sixth Directive as regards the holders of convertible debentures and other convertible securities if the rights attaching to such securities had already been determined by the conditions of issue by the time the implementing legislation of a Member State had come into force.[137]

In the cases of divisions, the Sixth Directive provides, as mentioned, certain additional protection for creditors.

First, Article 12(3) provides for the joint and several liability of the recipient companies in so far as a creditor of the company to which the obligation has been transferred in accordance with the draft terms has not obtained satisfaction, although Member States may limit such liability to the net assets allocated to each of those companies other than the one to which the obligation has been transferred. Moreover, Member States need not provide for such liability where the division is subject to the supervision of a judicial authority[138] and a majority in number representing three-fourths in value of the creditors or any class of creditors of the company being divided have agreed to forego such liability at a meeting called by the judicial authority.[139]

Second, and more generally, the Directive permits[140] Member States to provide that the recipient companies shall in any event be jointly and severally liable for the obligations of the company being divided, in which case they need apply none of the foregoing specific provisions for the protection of creditors.[141] Where however Member States combine those specific provisions with the general imposition of joint and several liability on the recipient companies, they may limit such liability to the net assets allocated to each of those companies.[142]

Formalities

The Directives require either the minutes of the general meetings which decide on the merger or division, together with any subsequent contract, or, where the operation need not be approved by general meetings, the draft terms, to be drawn up

---

[134] Art 13(1) of the original Proposal.   [135] ibid.
[136] Art 14 of the original Proposal.   [137] 3rd Directive, Art 32(3); 6th Directive, Art 26(4).
[138] Pursuant to Art 23: see below.   [139] In accordance with Art 23(1)(c): see below.
[140] The common law countries were reportedly opposed to the imposition of mandatory joint and several liability as a matter of course: Barbaso, F, 'The Harmonisation of Company Law' [1984] JBL 176, 182.
[141] Art 12(6). The provisions which Member States need not in such circumstances apply are paras (1)–(5) of Art 12.
[142] Art 12(7).

and certified in due legal form, unless the Member State provides for judicial or administrative preventive supervision[143] of the legality of mergers or divisions which extends to all the legal acts required for the operation.[144] The notary or the authority competent so to draw up and certify the document must check and certify the existence and validity of the legal acts[145] and formalities required of the company for which he is acting and of the draft terms.[146]

The merger or division must be publicized in accordance with Article 3 of the First Directive[147] in respect of each of the merging companies or companies involved in the division.[148] The acquiring company or any recipient company may however itself carry out the publication formalities relating to the company or companies being acquired or the company being divided.[149]

Timing and consequences

The date on which a merger or division takes effect is to be determined by national law.[150] That provision reflects the impossibility of arriving at a uniform solution given the diversity of practice in the five (of the original six) Member States which provided for mergers[151] (although an unsuccessful attempt was made, following reservations expressed by the Economic and Social Committee[152] and the European Parliament,[153] to specify three alternative possible dates[154]).

The Third Directive states, however, that a merger shall have the following consequences *ipso jure* and simultaneously:

(a)   the transfer, both as between the company being acquired and the acquiring company and as regards third parties, to the acquiring company of all the assets and liabilities of the company being acquired;

(b)   the shareholders of the company being acquired become shareholders of the acquiring company;

(c)   the company being acquired ceases to exist.[155]

The effect of Article 19(1)(a)[156] is that, as between the companies involved, the transfer of the assets and liabilities will be valid notwithstanding non-compliance

---

[143] *Contrôle préventif*: the essence appears to be that, without the judicial or administrative approval, the merger cannot go ahead.

[144] 3rd Directive, Art 16(1); 6th Dir, Art 14. See Cordoliani, H F A, 'Le droit des fusions' [1979] La semaine juridique (n 1 above) 372 for a discussion.

[145] Presumably in the sense of formal documents.

[146] 3rd Directive, Art 16(2); 6th Directive, Art 14.   [147] See pp 19–20 above.

[148] 3rd Directive, Art 18(1); 6th Directive, Art 16(1).

[149] 3rd Directive, Art 18(2); 6th Directive, Art 16(2).

[150] 3rd Directive, Art 17; 6th Directive, Art 15.

[151] Explanatory Memorandum, 10; see further Van Ommeslaghe, P, 'La proposition de troisième directive' in Zonderland, P (ed), *Quo Vadis Ius Societatum?* (1972) 141–2, and Cordoliani (n 144 above) 372.

[152] [1971] OJ C88/20.   [153] [1972] OJ C129/51.

[154] First amended Proposal, Art 9.   [155] Art 19(1).

[156] Described by Van Ommeslaghe (n 151 above) as one of the cornerstones of the directive (143).

with any formalities normally required for the transfer of property. Article 19(3) however provides that that shall not affect any national laws which require the completion of such formalities in order for the transfer of assets or liabilities to be effective against third parties. Thus where the law of a Member State provides that the transfer of certain property is effected only by inscription in a register (for example, real property in a land register) and protects third parties who relied in good faith on entries in such a register, those rules will continue to apply.[157] Any such formalities may be carried out by the acquiring company, although Member States may permit the company being acquired to continue to carry them out for a limited period which cannot, save in exceptional cases, be more than six months from the date on which the merger takes effect.[158] Without such a provision, the company would of course be unable to take any further action, since by virtue of Article 19(1)(c) it ceases to exist as a consequence of the merger.

The provisions of Article 19 of the Third Directive are broadly reflected in Article 17 the Sixth Directive, *mutatis mutandis*. Article 17(1) corresponds closely to Article 19(1) ('the company being divided' replacing 'the company being acquired' and 'the recipient companies' replacing 'the acquiring company'), although sub-paragraphs (a) and (b) specify that the transfer and the substitution of shareholders shall be 'in accordance with the allocation laid down in the draft terms'. Article 17(3) corresponds to Article 19(3).

The early draft of the proposed directive provided for an exception to the principle of universal transmission in the case of rights and obligations *intuitu personae*, namely those essentially linked to the identity of the company. That exception did not survive, on the ground that certain systems of law did not recognize that a legal person's rights and obligations could be dependent on its identity for such purposes.[159] The draft moreover provided for the possibility of renegotiating certain contracts which, as a result of the merger, would either be incompatible with contractual obligations of the acquiring company or lead to serious injustice (*graves iniquités*). It was considered however that renegotiation would be incompatible with the law of certain Member States.[160]

Article 19(1)(b) of the Third Directive, providing for the substitution of shareholders, does not apply to the acquisition by a company of a wholly-owned subsidiary.[161] It may be noted that Article 19(1)(b) was the subject of a declaration by the Italian delegation in the Council of Ministers to the effect that the provision was without prejudice to provisions of national law providing a 'right of withdrawal' for minority shareholders in the event of a merger.[162] Italy was the only original Member State whose law granted dissenting shareholders the right to require redemption of their shares.[163]

---

[157] Explanatory Memorandum to the Proposal, explanation of Art 15.   [158] Art 19(3).
[159] Van Ommeslaghe (n 151 above) 145.   [160] Ibid, 144.   [161] Art 24.
[162] Keutgen, G, 'La directive européenne sur les fusions nationales' (1979) 78 Revue pratique des sociétés, 114; Heenen, J, 'La directive sur les fusions internes' [1981] Cahiers de droit européen 15, 20.
[163] See Stein, E, *Harmonization of European Company Laws* (1971) 376.

Both Directives contain a provision[164] designed to prevent the absorbing company from acquiring its own shares as a consequence of the merger or division: it prohibits the exchange of shares in the acquiring or recipient company for shares in the company being acquired or divided held by or on behalf of either company. The original Proposal specified that shares in the company acquired held by the acquiring company should be cancelled.[165]

Civil Liability Arising Out of the Merger or Division

The Directives require the Member States to lay down rules governing the civil liability towards the shareholders of the company being acquired or divided of (a) the members of its administrative or management bodies in respect of misconduct on their part in preparing and implementing the merger or division[166] and (b) the experts responsible for drawing up on its behalf the experts' report in respect of misconduct on their part in the performance of their duties.[167]

Member States are free to regulate the details of such liability as they see fit. The original Proposal required that the liability should be towards the individual shareholders (subject to provision, if required, for class actions) and that the liability should be joint and several, although a board member or expert may be discharged from liability if he could prove that no blame attached to him.[168] Those provisions, in particular the reversal of the burden of proof, proved highly controversial and were ultimately dropped from the Third Directive (and accordingly did not appear in the Sixth Directive) on the basis that the matter would be dealt with in the more general context of the Fifth Directive.

Nullity of Mergers and Divisions

The Explanatory Memorandum to the original Proposal explains that annulment of a merger may result either from subsequent annulment of the general meeting of one of the merging companies or from the invalidity of one of the documents drawn up during the implementation of the merger. The rules on the grounds for annulment of general meetings and the invalidity of legal documents vary between Member States and it was accepted that it was not appropriate to seek to harmonize them by the proposed Third Directive, although at the time of the Proposal the intention was to harmonize the rules on the annulment of decisions of general meetings in a subsequent directive on the structure of joint-stock companies.[169] It

---

[164] 3rd Directive, Art 19(2); 6th Directive, Art 17(2).   [165] Art 9(3).

[166] 3rd Directive, Art 20; 6th Directive, Art 18.

[167] 3rd Directive, Art 21; 6th Directive, Art 18.   [168] Arts 16 and 17 of the Proposal.

[169] Subsequently proposed as the draft 5th Directive, which has not yet been adopted: see further ch XIX.

was however felt desirable to protect members and other parties by adopting uniform arrangements ruling out the annulment of mergers as far as possible. Article 22 of the Third Directive restricts the circumstances in which Member States may provide for the nullity of mergers,[170] laying down a series of conditions to be observed. Article 19 of the Sixth Directive is almost identical.[171]

Nullity must be ordered in a court judgment[172] or, at Member States' option, by an administrative authority subject to appeal to a court.[173] That provision reflects the requirement of the First Directive that the formation of a company may only be annulled by a court decision.[174] The judgment shall be published in accordance with Article 3 of the First Directive[175] and may be challenged by a third party, if such challenge is permitted by the laws of the Member State concerned, only within six months of such publication.[176]

A merger or division which has taken effect in accordance with the law of the Member States as provided by the Directives[177] may be declared void only in three circumstances: (a) if there has been no judicial or administrative preventive supervision of its legality; (b) if it has not been drawn up and certified in due legal form; and (c) if it is shown that the decision of the general meeting is void or voidable under national law.[178] Moreover nullification proceedings may not be initiated more than six months after the date on which the merger or division becomes effective as against the person alleging nullity (or, where nullity is sought from an administrative authority, not more than six months after the date on which the merger or division took effect in national law[179]), nor may they be initiated if the situation complained of has been rectified.[180] The Directives provide generally that where it is possible to remedy a defect liable to make a merger or division void, the competent court shall grant the companies involved a period of time within which to rectify the situation.[181] That approach is reminiscent of that of the Second Directive to the dissolution of companies with fewer than two members: if the laws of a Member State permit the company to be wound up in such circumstances by order of the court, the judge having jurisdiction 'must be able to give the company sufficient time to regularise its position'.[182]

---

[170] Except for the nullity of a merger pronounced following any supervision other than judicial or administrative preventive supervision of legality, in which case Art 22 is expressed not to apply: Art 22(3).

[171] With a proviso in Art 19(3) reflecting that in the 3rd Directive, Art 22(3).

[172] 3rd Directive, Art 22(1)(a); 6th Directive, Art 19(1)(a).

[173] Arts 22(2) and 19(2). All the provisions of Arts 22 and 19 concerning the judgment apply equally to a decision of an administrative authority.

[174] Art 11: see ch II above.

[175] 3rd Directive, Art 22(1)(e); 6th Directive, Art 19(1)(e). Art 3 of the 1st Directive requires publication in the Member State's designated national gazette either of the full or partial text concerned or of a reference to the document which has been deposited in the companies' files in the register kept for the purpose or entered in that register: see ch II above.

[176] Arts 22(1)(f) and 19(1)(f).   [177] 3rd Directive, Art 17; 6th Directive, Art 15.

[178] Arts 22(1)(b) and 19(1)(b).   [179] Arts 22(2) and 19(2).

[180] Arts 22(1)(c) and 19(1)(c).   [181] Arts 22(1)(d) and 19(1)(d).   [182] Art 5(2).

As for the consequences of nullity, it is provided that a judgment declaring a merger or division void shall not of itself affect the validity of obligations owed by or in relation to the acquiring company or the recipient companies which arose between the date when the merger or division became effective and the date of publication of the judgment annulling it.[183] Companies which have been parties to a merger shall be jointly and severally liable in respect of such obligations of the acquiring company.[184] In the case of a division, each of the recipient companies shall be liable for its obligations arising between those dates; the company being divided shall also be liable for such obligations, but Member States may limit the latter liability to the share of net assets transferred to the recipient company on whose account such obligations arose.[185]

In relation to mergers by the formation of a new company, the Third Directive provides[186] that the provisions on nullity of mergers are without prejudice to Articles 11 and 12 of the First Directive, which lay down rules on the nullity of companies.[187]

Implementation in the United Kingdom

Unlike the Third Directive, the Sixth Directive, as indicated above, does not require Member States to legislate for the operations which it covers, it merely provides that, where divisions as defined are permitted, the Directive must be implemented. Although historically neither divisions nor mergers as defined by the Third Directive were widely practised in the United Kingdom, ss 425 to 427 of the Companies Act 1985 (formerly ss 206 to 208 of the Companies Act 1948), which concern arrangements and reconstructions of companies made under the supervision of the court, were sufficiently broad to encompass mergers and divisions as defined in the Directives but conferred too much discretion on the court to comply with all the procedural requirements and safeguards of the Directives. It was accordingly necessary to tailor the legislation in order properly to implement the Directives. That was effected by the addition of s 427A of and Sch 15B to the Companies Act 1985, inserted by the Companies (Mergers and Divisions) Regulations 1987.[188] Those provisions in effect leave the original system intact for operations which fall outside the definitions in the Directives (including such operations involving private companies only) but impose the procedure required by the Directives on operations falling within those definitions.

---

[183] Art 22(1)(g) and 19(1)(g).   [184] Art 22(1)(h).   [185] Art 19(1)(h).
[186] Art 23(1).   [187] See ch II.   [188] SI 1987/1991.

V

The Fourth Directive

Background

The Fourth Directive on annual accounts, like the companion Seventh Directive on consolidated accounts, is an uneasy compromise between two fundamentally different traditions: the prescriptive continental[1] approach, with detailed legislation governing the format of accounts and the methods of valuation and rates of depreciation to be used, and the more pragmatic and flexible Anglo-Dutch practice based on accounting principles[2] subject to a general requirement of a true and fair view.[3] The concessions which were inevitably made in the course of negotiating such difficult middle ground manifest themselves in the numerous options available in the Directive: one commentator quotes 'no less than 41 options open to the Member States in addition to 35 options left to the business enterprises themselves'.[4] However, although full harmonization may have proved an elusive goal[5] the achievement of the Fourth Directive in imposing certain common minimum reporting and disclosure requirements should not be underestimated.[6] Even though the existence and number of options mean that accounts prepared in compliance with the Directive can appear very different, the minimum information required to be given should enable the system which has been applied to be ascertained and the

[1] The early versions of the 4th Directive, before the UK's influence was felt, were closely modelled on the relevant French and German legislation. The Netherlands' approach was closer to that of the UK.

[2] Set by the accountancy profession. The other significant non-statutory source of disclosure requirements in both the UK and the Netherlands has historically been the listing rules of each country's Stock Exchange.

[3] The UK terminology. See below, pp 128–30, for a discussion of the concept in the UK and in the Directive.

[4] Buxbaum, R M and Hopt, K J, *Legal Harmonization and the Business Enterprise* (1988) 235, quoting Niehus, 'Zur Transformation der 4. EG-(Bilanz-)Richtlinie in den Mitgliedstaaten der Europäischen Gemeinschaft' (1985) 14 Zeitschrift für Unternehmens- und Gesellschaftsrecht 536, 537. There is a useful list of the options for Member States in Whinney Murray Ernst & Ernst, *The Fourth Directive: Its Effect on Reporting and Accounting in the UK and Ireland* (1978) 98–100.

[5] One commentator states that even after the 4th Directive has been fully implemented 'the European world of harmonized corporate financial reporting will remain something of a scaled-down tower of Babel': McComb, D, 'Accounting', in Buxbaum, R M, Hertig, G, Hirsch, A and Hopt, K J (eds), *European Business Law* (1991) 280.

[6] The extent of the disparity between accounting practice in the Member States before implementation of the Directive should not be overlooked. For an interesting discussion of the position in the various States and the reasons for the variations, see Savage, N, 'Law and Accounting—the Impact of EEC Directives on Company Law' (1980) 1 The Company Lawyer 24 and 91.

accounts interpreted accordingly, so that the objective of comparability has been attained. The Directive is also important in that it is the first of the company law harmonization directives to have a major impact on the vast number[7] of limited companies operating throughout the Community, since the First Directive dealt with discrete topics of limited relevance in practice[8] and the Second and Third[9] Directives on capital and mergers respectively applied to public companies only.

The Fourth Directive has its roots in the discussions leading up to the First Directive, and in particular the proposal to require disclosure of companies' balance sheets and profit and loss accounts. The First Directive was to apply to both public and private limited-liability companies, and the prospect of requiring the latter to publish their accounts met with fierce resistance, in particular from Germany where no financial disclosure was required of such companies. One of the arguments raised by opponents of the extension of disclosure was that, in the absence of harmonized rules on the content and layout of accounts, little of practical value would be achieved. This led to the eventual compromise reached for the purposes of the First Directive, namely postponing application of the disclosure requirement to private limited-liability companies until 'implementation of a Directive concerning co-ordination of the contents of balance sheets and of profit and loss accounts and concerning exemption of such of those companies whose balance sheet total is less than that specified in the Directive from the obligation to make disclosure, in full or in part, of the said documents'.[10]

In the mean time and against the background of the Commission's apparent reluctance to tackle the complex and politically sensitive issue of harmonized accounting requirements, the German Institute of Public Accountants grasped the nettle. In 1966 it organized a study group under the chairmanship of the President of the German Institute of Auditors, Dr Elmendorff, consisting of accounting experts from the six original Member States excluding Luxembourg, and offered assistance to the Commission. The latter 'gratefully accepted' the assistance of the group and entrusted it with drawing up a preliminary draft of a directive on annual financial documents.[11] The group's preliminary proposal, in which the German influence was manifest, was submitted to the Commission in 1968;[12] it formed the basis for the first Commission Proposal for the Directive.

An awareness of the factors which influenced the Proposal is helpful to an understanding of the legislative history of the Directive.[13] In Germany in 1966, when the

---

[7] Estimated at the time of adoption of the Directive at 1.5m: Ernst & Whinney, *The Fourth Directive: Its Effect on the Annual Accounts of Companies in the European Economic Community* (1979) 8, where it is suggested that the Directive 'may cause businessmen to recognise, for the first time, what the vast company law harmonisation programme is going to mean to the business and commercial life of the Community as a whole'. By 1993, the figure was 3m.

[8] Disclosure, validity of company obligations and nullity.

[9] Which was in fact adopted after the 4th.   [10] Art 2(1)(f) of the First Directive.

[11] See Stein, E, *Harmonization of European Company Laws* (1971) 270–1 and 354.

[12] The text of this proposal is discussed in some detail in Stein, ibid, 355–64.

[13] The development of specific provisions in the Directive is discussed below, in the context of the relevant Article of the final version.

Elmerdorff group was constituted, there were fewer than 2,500 *Aktiengesellschaften*, broadly equivalent to the English concept of a public company, compared with over 58,000 *Gesellschaften mit beschränkter Haftung*, or private limited-liability companies.[14] German (and most other continental) capital markets were very different from those of the United Kingdom: the tendency was for major investors to have special links with the (relatively few) companies in which they invested, for ownership to be highly concentrated and for debt capital to be raised on a short-term basis from banks. In the United Kingdom, by contrast, markets were very much more open, with few special links between investors and companies and a long tradition of widespread share ownership;[15] companies preferred to raise capital by equity investment, necessitating developed and liquid capital markets which in turn depended on effective investor protection. Although German public companies were at the time required to disclose their accounts, the principal concern of that requirement was creditor protection rather than shareholder information. This manifested itself particularly in conservative rules on valuation. Like France (the other main influence on the Elmendorff proposal), Germany regarded accounting regulation as a matter for the statute book rather than for guidelines issued by the accountancy profession, as was the tradition in the United Kingdom.[16] In most continental countries other than the Netherlands, detailed legislation prescribed the format and content of accounts; moreover, the accounts which a company was required to disclose were also used by the Revenue: in general, accounting profit and tax profit had to be measured on the same basis.[17]

The Elmendorff proposal was prescriptive in tenor, laying down detailed rules for the layout of the balance sheet (based on the then French formula), the profit and loss account (based on the German and French practice of disclosure of gross income, with consolidation of revenue and expenses being prohibited), valuation

[14] See Stein (n 11 above) 244–5. The former figure includes *Kommanditgesellschaften mit Aktien*, or limited partnerships with shares, effectively a form of public company.

[15] By way of example, in 1972 it was estimated that the number of quoted companies, market capitalization and equity turnover in the UK were greater than the combined totals of the five main original Member States (Savage, N, 'Law and Accounting' (1980) 1 The Company Lawyer 24, 25).

[16] There is a useful comparison of the pre-implementation accounting systems of these three Member States in the Commission's document *The Fourth Company Accounts Directive of 1978 and the accounting systems of the Federal Republic of Germany, France, Italy, the United Kingdom, the United States and Japan* (1986). There is also an informative discussion of these and other issues by McKinnon, S M, in Newman, A D H (ed), *The Seventh Directive: Consolidated Accounts in the EEC* (1984) 19–24.

[17] This is still the case in, inter alia, France, Germany and Italy. As will be seen, this has consequences for valuation and depreciation rules: in times of inflation, a system of current cost accounting may be unacceptable to a tax-driven legislature since it will erode taxable profit. At an early stage in the legislative history of the 4th Directive, the Economic and Social Committee drew attention to what it termed the 'regrettable phenomenon' of the 'contamination of accounting by tax laws', and called for progress in the harmonization of company tax laws ([1973] OJ C39/33). The Ruding Committee recommended the Commission, as part of the general harmonization of the tax base which it advocated, to take appropriate measures to reduce the differences between financial reports and company accounts used for tax purposes (*Report of the Committee of Independent Experts on Company Taxation* (1992)). For a discussion of this specific recommendation, see van der Tas, L G, 'European Accounting Harmonization: Achievements, Prospects and Tax Implications' [1992] Intertax 178, 187.

and depreciation (designed to raise the rules to the level of France and Germany, where reforms in 1966 and 1965 respectively prohibited the creation of hidden reserves by deliberate undervaluation, common practice at the time elsewhere in the original Member States), and the compulsory audit of accounts by an independent auditor. The proposal was to apply to public companies only. There was no requirement as such that the accounts give a true and fair view or equivalent. Although there was no provision for consolidated accounts, the idea that accounts should to some extent reflect the economic reality of the corporate structure found expression in the requirement for disclosure of economic ties with other undertakings and the results of transactions with them and of information regarding holdings in related undertakings and participation in controlling and controlled companies.

History

The first formal Proposal for the Directive, drawn up by a working group constituted in 1969, was submitted by the Commission to the Council in November 1971.[18] In the same year the *Groupe d'Etudes* (EEC Accountants Study Group, an informal committee of accountants from each Member State formed at the request of the Commission to facilitate consultations) invited representatives from the United Kingdom, Ireland and Denmark, then potential new Member States, to discuss the proposals. The group was persuaded of the value of many Anglo-Dutch concepts,[19] and as a result of its influence and direct governmental pressure from the United Kingdom, Ireland and the Netherlands significant changes were made to the 1971 Proposal.[20] The European Parliament delivered its Opinion on the proposed directive in November 1972[21] and the Economic and Social Committee in February 1973.[22] An amended Proposal was issued in 1974,[23] incorporating further changes which took into account the accession in the interim of the United Kingdom,[24] Ireland and Denmark. Between 1974 and 1977 the Proposal underwent three readings[25] by Council of Ministers' *ad hoc* working parties and lengthy

[18] COM (71) 1232 final, 29 October 1971; [1972] OJ C7/11; English text with Statement of Grounds in EC Bull Supp 7/71.

[19] Such as the true and fair view: see below, pp 128–30.

[20] And later to the 1974 amended Proposal.   [21] [1972] OJ C129/38.

[22] [1973] OJ C39/31.   [23] COM (74) 191 final, 21 February 1974; EC Bull Supp 6/74.

[24] See Nobes, C W, 'The Harmonisation of Company Law Relating to the Published Accounts of Companies' (1980) 5 ELR 38, 41, and Savage, N, 'Law and Accounting' (1980) 1 The Company Lawyer 24. The latter states that 'the final version represents something of a success for the UK negotiators bearing in mind that the original framework was conceived at a time when the UK had no voice within the Community': 28.

[25] It was explained to the UK HL Select Committee on the EC that the first reading of the Council of Ministers' working party had 'taken about nine months, of sessions perhaps once every two months or thereabouts, varying in length from one day to three days'. Viscount Amory on the Committee responded with astonishment: 'That is a very different practice to that of the House of Lords where our first reading never takes more than 25 seconds!': 4th Report (Session 1975–76, HL Paper 24) Minutes of Evidence, 42.

examination by the Council of Permanent Representatives. The Fourth Council Directive based on Article 54(3)(g) of the Treaty on the annual accounts of certain types of companies (EEC) 78/660 was adopted on 25 July 1978.[26]

Legal Basis

The Fourth Directive is based on Article 54(3)(g) of the Treaty,[27] the rationale being expressed to be that 'the coordination of national provisions concerning the presentation and content of annual accounts and annual reports, the valuation methods used therein and their publication in respect of certain companies with limited liability is of special importance for the protection of members and third parties'.[28] The theme of protecting the investing public is taken further later in the preamble with the statement that 'it is necessary . . . to establish in the Community minimum equivalent legal requirements as regards the extent of the financial information that should be made available to the public by companies that are in competition with one another'.[29]

Structure

The Directive is divided into twelve sections comprising 62 Articles. Article 1 is an introductory provision which describes the scope of the Directive and lists the types of company to which it is to apply. Section 1 consists of Article 2, the core provision: it defines the accounts as the balance sheet, the profit and loss account and the notes on the accounts and lays down the basic requirement that they give a true and fair view and the parameters within which a company may depart from that requirement. Sections 2 to 6 (Articles 3 to 30) deal with presentation of accounts. Section 7 (Articles 31 to 42) prescribes valuation rules. Section 8 (Articles 43 to 45) deals with the disclosure of additional information in the notes to the accounts. Section 9 (Article 46) prescribes the contents of the annual report. Section 10 (Articles 47 to 50) comprises requirements for the publication of accounts and provides for certain smaller companies to publish abridged accounts. Section 11

---

[26] [1978] OJ L222/11. The best general commentary is by Cordoliani, H F A, 'La normalisation communautaire des comptes annuels des sociétés' La semaine juridique, édition commerce et industrie (1979) vol II, 297. There is also a useful by summary by Clayton, M R, and de Vallois, C, 'The Fourth Company Law Directive on the Annual Accounts of Limited Liability Companies' (1978) 4 Droit et pratique du commerce international 405. The impact of the Directive on the first nine Member States is discussed in Ernst & Whinney, *The Fourth Directive* (1979) and on the first twelve Member States in the Commission's publication *The Fourth Company Law Directive—Implementation by Member States* (1987).

[27] Which confers power on the Council to issue directives 'coordinating to the necessary extent the safeguards which, for the protection of members and others, are required by Member States of companies or firms . . . with a view to making such safeguards equivalent throughout the Community'.

[28] First recital in the preamble; see further pp 123–4 below.   [29] 3rd recital.

(Article 51) requires annual accounts to be audited subject to a permitted derogation in favour of smaller companies. Section 12 consists of miscellaneous final provisions: Article 52 provides for a Contact Committee to be set up; Article 53
defines the European Unit of Account, used to determine the thresholds for certain derogations; Article 54 has been superseded by the Eleventh Directive;[30]
Article 55 lays down time limits for implementation; Articles 56 to 61 originally
contained transitional provisions (pending the entry into force of the Seventh
Directive on Consolidated Accounts) concerning consolidated accounts and have
since been replaced by that Directive.[31]

Scope

Limited-liability companies

The original proposal of the Elmendorff group, reflecting the position in Germany,
applied only to companies of the *société anonyme* type,[32] broadly equivalent to public companies in the United Kingdom. The first Commission Proposal for the
Fourth Directive stated that the bulk of the Directive applied only to such public
companies,[33] but contained in Section 11 special provisions for private limited-
liability companies. Private companies were to draw up accounts in accordance
with the Directive, with the addition of balance sheet items showing claims on and
debts to members.[34] The accounts were to be audited and published unless
Member States took advantage of various options to exempt smaller companies as
defined[35] from these requirements. The amended Proposal retained the same pattern but included in the list of public companies all UK limited-liability companies
with the exception of Northern Ireland private companies.[36] This distinction was
resisted by the United Kingdom.[37] The final version applies to public and private
limited-liability companies of the same types as are covered by the First Directive,[38]
with the exception of banks and other financial institutions and insurance companies which were initially excluded pending subsequent coordination[39] and which

---

[30] See ch VIII.   [31] See pp 123, 133, 142–4 and 194–5 below.
[32] And entities equivalent to the *société en commandite par actions*: see the list on pp 17–18.
[33] With an option for Member States to permit smaller companies as defined to prepare slightly
abridged accounts: Art 24.
[34] Art 48.   [35] Arts 49 and 50.
[36] It is stated in the Explanatory Memorandum to the amended Proposal that this distinction followed Art 2(1)(f) of the First Directive as amended by the Act of Accession. See pp 23 (n 45) and 53–4
above for further discussion of this issue.
[37] More as a matter of principle, since the relaxation for audit was not thought to be necessary in the
UK and the publicity requirements were thought to be wholly unworkable in any event for UK companies: see below, pp 149–50. The firm stance taken was presumably influenced by the contemporaneous and analogous debate in connection with the 2nd Directive where much more than principle was
at stake: see above, p 53–4.
[38] See pp 17–18 above for the full list.   [39] Art 1(2).

are now covered by separate directives.[40] Limited liability was chosen as the criterion for application of the Directive both because 'such companies' activities frequently extend beyond the frontiers of their national territories and [because] they
offer no safeguards to third parties beyond the amounts of their net assets'.[41]

Where a limited-liability company to which the Fourth Directive applies has a
branch in another Member State, the company's audited accounts must be disclosed not only in the Member State where it is incorporated but also in any
Member State where it has a branch.[42]

Subsidiary undertakings

Subsidiary undertakings are prima facie subject to the requirements of the Fourth
Directive even where they are included in the consolidated accounts drawn up by
their parent undertaking in accordance with the Seventh Directive.[43] Article 57[44]
however provides that a Member State need not apply the provisions of the Fourth
Directive concerning the content, auditing and publication of annual accounts to
companies governed by their national laws which are subsidiary undertakings[45] of,
and included in the consolidated accounts of, an EC parent undertaking provided
that (a) all shareholders or members have declared their agreement to the exemption in respect of the financial year concerned; (b) the parent undertaking has
declared that it guarantees the subsidiary undertaking's commitments; (c) the
exemption is disclosed in the notes to the consolidated accounts; and (d) the subsidiary undertaking publishes[46] the declarations referred to in (a) and (b) above, the
consolidated accounts, consolidated annual report and auditors' report.

Certain unlimited-liabllity entities

The entities covered by the Fourth Directive were extended in 1990 to deal with
a practice which had developed in certain Member States, in particular Germany,
of avoiding application of the Directive. As indicated above, the Directive established a link between limited-liability and disclosure and on that basis listed the various types of limited-liability company in the different Member States in defining

---

[40] Council Directive (EEC) 86/635 of 8 December 1986 on the annual accounts and consolidated
accounts of banks and other financial institutions [1986] OJ L372/1 and Council Directive (EEC)
91/674 of 19 December 1991 on the annual accounts and consolidated accounts of insurance undertakings [1991] OJ L374/7.

[41] 2nd recital in the preamble. The latter rationale has a familiar ring for lawyers in the UK, where
it has long been the accepted view that extensive disclosure is the price of limited liability.

[42] This provision is considered in more detail in connection with publication of accounts: see below,
pp 150–52. There is an analogous requirement for non-EC limited-liability companies with branches
in the EC.

[43] See ch VI.   [44] As replaced by Art 43 of the 7th Directive.

[45] As defined in the 7th Directive: see pp 163–70 below.

[46] In accordance with Art 3 of the First Directive, namely by filing in the company's file in a central
register, commercial register or companies register.

the entities to which it applied. In addition, all Member States recognize certain types of partnerships, limited partnerships[47] and (in the United Kingdom and Ireland) unlimited companies (here together referred to as 'unlimited-liability entities') which, not being limited-liability companies, were not within the original scope of the Directive.[48] Where however all the partners with unlimited liability (or in the case of unlimited companies all the members) are limited-liability companies, for practical purposes such an entity is a limited-liability company 'at one remove'.[49] The practice was particularly prevalent in Germany, using the *GmbH & Co KG* (*Kommanditgesellschaft*), a limited partnership between a private company (the general partner) and its members (the limited partners).[50]

The Commission took the view that 'it would run counter to the spirit and aims of [the Fourth and Seventh] Directives to allow such partnerships and partnerships with limited liability not to be subject to Community rules'.[51] This loophole was stopped in 1990 by an amending Directive,[52] Article 1(1) of which adds to the list of entities covered by the Directive[53] partnerships, limited partnerships and unlimited companies under various national names if all members with unlimited liability are limited-liability companies or, where not governed by the law of a Member State, have a comparable legal form. As a further anti-avoidance measure, the list also includes unlimited-liability entities if all members with unlimited liability are themselves unlimited-liability entities.[54]

The amending Directive provides for the Fourth Directive not to apply directly to unlimited-liability entities in two circumstances.[55]

First,[56] Member States may require limited-liability companies governed by

---

[47] The term 'limited partnership' is liable to mislead: at least one partner must have unlimited liability.

[48] Although Member States had the option of applying the Directive to them, and this was done by Belgium and the Netherlands.

[49] Written Question No 2332/85 by Herman, F (PPE-B) to the Commission of 10 January 1986; [1986] OJ C182/24.

[50] Petite, M, 'The Conditions for Consolidation under the 7th Company Law Directive' (1984) 21 CML Rev 81, 101, n 42, gives a figure (in 1984) of 60,000 *GmbH & Co KG* in the Federal Republic, with an average size between the *AG* (of which there were then fewer than 2,000) and the *GmbH* (around 200,000).

[51] 5th recital in the preamble to the 1990 Directive.

[52] Council Directive (EEC) 90/605 of 8 November 1990 amending Directive (EEC) 78/660 on annual accounts and Directive (EEC) 83/349 on consolidated accounts as regards the scope of those Directives [1990] OJ L317/60; implemented in the UK by The Partnerships and Unlimited Companies (Accounts) Regulations 1993 (SI 1993/1820). Germany's resistance to the amendment was overcome by agreement on further extensions of the exemptions available to small companies (see below, n 242 and pp 147–8), although as at July 1997 it had still not implemented the amending Directive and the Commission brought an action under Art 169: Case C–272/97 *Commission* v *Germany*, still pending.

[53] Set out in Art 1(1) of the 4th Directive.

[54] The English text simply refers to 'companies', but all other language versions make it clear that, as might be expected given the aim, all types of entity added by the amendment are covered. The UK implementing legislation however follows the English version, presumably in order to avoid bringing within the scope of the Directive numerous professional partnerships with unlimited-liability service companies.

[55] There is a separate exemption from publication in certain circumstances: see p 153 below.

[56] Art 57a(1) of the 4th Directive, added by Art 1(4) of the amending Directive.

their law which are members with unlimited liability of an unlimited-liability entity to draw up, have audited and publish with their own accounts the accounts of the unlimited-liability entity concerned in conformity with the Fourth Directive, in which case that Directive does not apply to the unlimited-liability entity.

Second,[57] Member States need not apply the requirements of the Fourth Directive to an unlimited-liability entity where (a) its accounts are drawn up, audited and published in conformity with the Fourth Directive by a company which is a member with unlimited liability of the unlimited-liability entity and is governed by the law of another Member State, or (b) it is included in consolidated accounts drawn up, audited and published in accordance with the Seventh Directive by a member with unlimited liability or by a parent undertaking governed by the law of a Member State.[58]

In both these cases, the unlimited-liability entity concerned must reveal on request the name of the entity publishing the accounts.[59]

The apparent complexity of these provisions is an inevitable, if unfortunate, consequence of the cumbersome terminology necessitated by repeatedly referring to two separate categories of entity and the nexus between them. As in the case of most anti-avoidance legislation, however, its substance may more readily be grasped if its rationale is borne in mind. In this case, the aim is to ensure that a limited-liability company cannot trade through the medium of an unlimited-liability entity and thereby avoid disclosing in its accounts details of what are in effect its activities. The primary technique of attaining that objective is subjecting the unlimited-liability entity to the requirements of the Directive relating to the drawing up, publication and auditing of accounts. Where the accounts of the unlimited-liability entity are required to be published with the accounts of one of its members (first exemption and first limb of second exemption) or form part of the consolidated accounts of the group concerned (second limb of second exemption) this objective is in any event attained and therefore the primary requirement of separate disclosure is otiose.

Small and medium-sized companies

The early versions of the Fourth Directive distinguished between public and private companies and drew further distinctions between certain categories of private company, determined by reference to balance sheet total, turnover and average number of employees.[60] Although in the final version the emphasis shifted so that

---

[57] Art 57a(2) of the 4th Directive, added by Art 1(4) of the amending Directive.
[58] In the case of (b), the exemption must be disclosed in the notes on the consolidated accounts.
[59] Art 57a(3) of the 4th Directive.
[60] The Statement of Grounds in the first Proposal explains this tie between the extent of the disclosure and the size of the company by reference to the 1st Directive. The final version of that Directive however itself makes no provision for any such threshold (although it anticipates that a distinction will be drawn in the 4th Directive: see Art 2(1)(f)), and the reference in fact dates back to an earlier draft of

the Directive no longer drew any distinction between public and private companies, the concept of less rigorous requirements for smaller companies was retained. The Directive defines two categories of smaller company which may benefit from various exemptions and derogations.[61] The categories apply to both public and private companies.[62]

Small companies are those which on their balance sheet date[63] do not exceed the limits of two of the following three criteria:[64]

- Balance sheet total: ECU 2.5 million[65]
- Net turnover: ECU 5 million
- Average number of employees during the financial year: 50.[66]

Small companies may be permitted to draw up and publish abridged balance sheets and abridged notes to their accounts and may be exempted from all or any of the requirements to prepare annual reports, to publish their profit and loss accounts, annual reports and audit reports, and to have their accounts audited.

Medium-sized companies are those which on their balance sheet date[67] do not exceed the limits of two of the following three criteria:[68]

- Balance sheet total: ECU 10 million
- Net turnover: ECU 20 millon.
- Average number of employees during the financial year: 250.[69]

---

the Directive which imposed a threshold of a balance sheet total of 1m units of account (the same as the highest of the three different thresholds in the first Proposal for the 4th Directive: see Art 50) for the disclosure of accounts by private companies: see pp 22–3 above.

[61] Considerably extended by Council Directive (EEC) 90/604 of 8 November 1990 amending Directive (EEC) 78/660 on annual accounts and Directive (EEC) 83/349 on consolidated accounts as concerns the exemptions for small and medium-sized companies and the publication of accounts in ECUs [1990] OJ L317/57.

[62]Although it should be noted that the UK has not used the option to its full extent, denying the exemptions which would otherwise apply where the company is, or was at any time within the relevant financial year, a public company, a banking or insurance company or an authorized person under the Financial Services Act 1986 (broadly, dealing in or managing investments or giving investment advice) or a member of a group any one of whose members is such a company: Companies Act 1985, s 247A(1)(2).

[63] In two successive financial years. If after qualifying as a small company for two successive years the company fails to qualify for one year but requalifies the following year, it will not lose the privilege. This is the effect of the mysteriously worded Art 12(1).

[64] Art 11 as amended most recently by Council Directive (EC) 94/8 of 21 March 1994 amending Directive (EEC) 78/660 as regards the revision of amounts expressed in ECUs [1994] OJ L82/33.

[65] Art 12(2) provides that for the purposes of translating these thresholds into national currencies the amounts in ECUs may be increased by not more than 10%.

[66] The UK equivalents are £2.8m, £1.4m and 50: Companies Act 1985, s 247(3) as amended by the Companies Act 1985 (Accounts of Small and Medium-Sized Enterprises and Publication of Accounts in ECUs) Regulations 1992 (SI 1992/2452).

[67] See n 63 above.

[68] Art 27 as amended most recently by Directive (EC) 94/8, cited in n 64.

[69] The UK equivalents are £11.2m, £5.6m and 250: Companies Act 1985, s 247(3) as amended by SI 1992/2452, cited in n 66.

Medium-sized companies may be exempted from the requirements to disclose turnover and gross margins in their profit and loss accounts and to disclose turnover in the notes to the accounts.

In 1997 the Commission circulated a Questionnaire on Simplification of the Accounting Directives for Small and Medium-sized Enterprises.[70] The vast majority of responses were in favour of maintaining the existing thresholds and options for small and medium-sized companies.[71]

Implementation in the United Kingdom

The Fourth Directive was implemented in the United Kingdom by the Companies Act 1981, the relevant provisions of which are now consolidated in the Companies Act 1985.[72] The major changes made as a result of the Directive were the introduction of standard layouts for the balance sheet and profit and loss account and of statutory valuation rules, both required by the Directive, and the introduction of derogations for certain categories of smaller private companies, permitted by the Directive.

The Annual Accounts

Article 2 states that the annual accounts are to comprise the balance sheet, the profit and loss account and the notes to the accounts.[73] There is no mention in Article 2 or elsewhere in the Directive of the statement of source and application of funds, which is therefore not mandatory.[74] The annual report, in contrast, is mandatory by virtue of Article 46[75] of the Directive, although it is not among the documents which constitute 'annual accounts' as defined by Article 2.

The documents comprising the annual accounts are to constitute a composite whole[76] and be drawn up clearly and in accordance with the provisions of the Directive.[77] The former provision was apparently intended to underline the

---

[70] XV/7023/97–EN. See also Commission Recommendation (EC) 96/280 of 3 April 1996 concerning the definition of small and medium-sized enterprises [1996] OJ L107/4.

[71] See Summary of responses, XV/7040/98–EN.

[72] Part VII and Sch 4. The Companies Act 1989 replaced Part VII in its entirety and amended Sch 4. Issues relating to implementation were canvassed in the UK Government's Green Paper *Accounting and Disclosure—A Consultative Document* (Cmnd 7654; HMSO, 1979).

[73] Art 2(1).

[74] To that extent the 4th Directive does not go so far as International Accounting Standard No 7.

[75] See p 148 below.   [76] Art 2(1).

[77] Art 2(2). The original Proposal required the accounts to 'conform to the principles of regular and proper accounting', a provision presumably reflecting Netherlands influence: the 1970 Act on Annual Accounts of Enterprises had just introduced a requirement that accounts be drawn up using standards regarded as acceptable in economic and social life.

importance of the notes to the accounts 'as a necessary complement for a proper understanding of the balance sheet and the profit and loss account'.[78]

Article 2(6) makes it clear that the Fourth Directive is a minimum standards directive, stating that the Member States 'may authorize or require the disclosure in the annual accounts of other information as well as that which must be disclosed in accordance with' the Directive.

The True and Fair View

Article 2(3) requires the annual accounts to 'give a true and fair view of the company's assets, liabilities, financial position and profit or loss'. The evolution of this provision illustrates the shift in emphasis which the draft Directive underwent as a result of the influence of the United Kingdom and Ireland. The original Proposal required the annual accounts to 'conform to the principles of regular and proper accounting'[79] and, 'in the context of the provisions regarding the valuation of assets and liabilities and the lay-out of accounts, [to] reflect as accurately as possible the company's assets, liabilities, financial position and results'.[80] The intermediate amended Proposal included requirements that the accounts 'give a true and fair view of the company's assets, liabilities, financial position and results'[81] and be 'drawn up clearly and in conformity with' the Directive,[82] reflecting criticisms made by both the Economic and Social Committee[83] and the European Parliament,[84] representations from the *Groupe d'Etudes* and governmental pressure from the United Kingdom, Ireland and the Netherlands. This did not however go far enough to satisfy the United Kingdom and Ireland, primarily because the true and fair view was not expressly stated to be overriding.[85] As pointed out by the United Kingdom House of Lords Select Committee on the European Communities considering the amended Proposal:

It does not necessarily follow that to draw up accounts according to . . . the draft Directive would achieve the more desirable object of presenting a true and fair view. The two con-

---

[78] Statement of Grounds in the original Proposal.   [79] Art 2(2).   [80] Art 2(3).

[81] Art 2(2), replacing the reference to accounting principles on the questionable assumption that 'the requirement of a true and fair view necessarily implies that such principles must be observed': Explanatory Memorandum in amended Proposal.

[82] Art 2(3).

[83] Which took exception to the first provision in its original French version (*donner . . . une image aussi sûre que possible*), considering it 'too vague'. After suggesting the formula 'as true a view as possible', the Committee mysteriously omitted to use it in its proposed amended text: 'The annual accounts should [sic] give a true view of assets, of the financial situation and of the company's results' [1973] OJ C39/34–5.

[84] Which suggested replacing the original French text with '*donner . . . une image fidèle*': [1972] OJ C129/40.

[85] Although it was thought by the draftsman that the principle as restated 'implies that should the specific provisions of the Directive be of themselves insufficient to ensure that this objective is attained, the company will be legally obliged to provide further information': Explanatory Memorandum in amended Proposal.

cepts may well be incompatible, as exemplified by the rules provided in the draft Directive for the valuation of items in the balance sheet. In some instances the application of these rules will fail to capture the essence of the true and fair approach.[86]

This issue is dealt with in the final version by Article 2(4), which states: 'Where the application of the provisions of this Directive would not be sufficient to give a true and fair view . . . additional information must be given',[87] and Article 2(5), which reads as follows:

Where in exceptional cases the application of a provision of this Directive is incompatible with the obligation laid down in paragraph 3, that provision must be departed from in order to give a true and fair view . . . Any such departure must be disclosed in the notes on the accounts together with an explanation of the reasons for it and a statement of its effects on the assets, liabilities, financial position and profit or loss. The Member States may define the exceptional cases in question and lay down the relevant special rules.[88]

The Commission has emphasized that the final sentence of Article 2(5) is not intended to allow Member States to introduce an accounting rule of a general nature which is contrary to the Directive or to create additional options allowing for accounting treatments which are not in conformity with the Directive.[89]

The concept of a true and fair view continues both to fascinate and to mystify continental commentators, perhaps in part because the notion of a criterion so important as to override detailed prescriptions but itself undefined is alien to the continental legal tradition.[90] Even were it less elusive, however, the English concept[91] cannot be

---

[86] 4th Report (Session 1975–76, HL Paper 24) Minutes of Evidence, 5. The reference to the valuation rules was made in the context of the very limited provision in the early versions of the Directive for any form of inflation accounting, which was at the time being formalized in the UK in a draft accounting standard which was the subject of lively professional debate. See further nn 185–6 below.

[87] Implemented in the UK by the Companies Act 1985, s 226(4).

[88] Implemented in the UK by the Companies Act 1985, s 226(5). See also Abstract 7 issued by the UK Accounting Standards Board's Urgent Issues Task Force, *True and Fair View Override Disclosures*, in December 1992, setting out the profession's consensus as to how the statutory disclosure requirement implementing Art 2(5) is to be interpreted.

[89] In its 1997 *Interpretative Communication Concerning Certain Articles of the Fourth and Seventh Council Directives on Accounting* (XV/7009/97–EN), para 6. For a commentary on the Communication, see Van Hulle, K's article of the same title (1998) 9 European Business Law Review 114.

[90] See, e g, Vitrolles, H: '*Nos confrères britanniques revendiquent, à juste titre, la paternité du concept de l'image fidèle, sans toutefois pouvoir définir cette idée construite à partir de cinquante années d'expérience. Conception innée, diront les uns, bien subjective, affirmeront les autres: de toute façon diamétralement opposée à celle des pays imprégnés de droit romain depuis des siècles*' (Our British colleagues rightly claim that they created the concept of the true and fair view, without however being able to define the notion developed out of fifty years' experience. Some assert that the concept is innate, others that it is purely subjective: in any event it is diametrically opposed to that used in those countries imbued for centuries with Roman Law): 'Editorial', [1982] Revue française de comptabilité 433.

[91] Of which it has been said that, 'like all concepts of equity and fairness, it eludes definition; its interpretation is a matter of judgment in the circumstances of particular cases': HL Select Committee on the EC (n 86 above) 24. Gower, L C B, *Principles of Modern Company Law* (3rd edn, 1969) 524 cites a 1965 article in which it was 'estimated that, using various accepted methods, it is possible to arrive at over a million different "true and fair" views'. See further McComb, D, 'Accounting' in Buxbaum, Hertig, Hirsch and Hopt (eds), *European Business Law* (1991) 282–3; Bird, P, 'What is "A True and Fair View"?' [1984] JBL 480; Lasok, K P E, and Grace, E, 'Fair Accounting' [1988] JBL 235.

assumed to be identical in meaning and scope to the term as used in the Fourth Directive. Ultimately, the only body competent to interpret the term is the Court of Justice, which if called upon to rule on the matter is likely to adopt an autonomous Community meaning for the term.[92] Pending such interpretation, it must be doubted whether the incorporation of the concept in the implementing legislation of Member States previously unfamiliar with the concept has necessarily resulted in a significant change in practice.[93]

Although the issue was potentially relevant in *Tomberger v Gebrüder von der Wettern*,[94] the Court made no attempt to grapple with the notion beyond commenting that compliance with the principle was the primary objective of the Directive and that its application must, as far as possible, be guided by the general principles (concerning valuation rules) contained in Article 31 and, perhaps more questionably, stating that it was clear from various specific provisions in Article 31 that 'taking account of all elements—profits made, charges, income, liabilities and losses—which actually relate to the financial year in question ensures observance of the requirement of a true and fair view.'[95] Advocate General Tesauro, however, made the following brief observation:

That principle requires the balance sheet to be drawn up so as to give not only a true (even in the relative sense in which that adjective is traditionally and necessarily used as regards balance sheets) but also a fair (essentially with regard to the good faith of the person drawing up the balance sheet) representation of the company's assets and liabilities, its financial position and its profit or loss.[96]

The Advocate General's interpretation of 'fair' is, at least from a British perspective, somewhat surprising, and it is unfortunate that the Court did not deal further with the issue. Further guidance from the Court may be forthcoming in the pending case of *DE + ES Bauunternehmung GmbH v Finanzamt Bergheim*.[97]

---

[92] See by analogy the case-law of the Court of Justice on the meaning of 'consideration' in the 6th Directive, e g Case 154/80 *Staatssecretaris van Financiën v Coöperatieve Aardappelenbewaarplaats* [1981] ECR 445, where the Court stated that 'the expression in issue is part of a provision of Community law which does not refer to the law of the Member States for the determining of its meaning and its scope; it follows that the interpretation, in general terms, of the expression may not be left to the discretion of each Member State': para 9.

[93] See e g Hopt, K J,: 'I remember the bitter fights about this "foreign Anglo-Saxon concept" we had in Germany. Of course now it is beautifully incorporated into the German commercial law statute. But I tell you, not much has changed. Everything is more or less like before. This is true even in the book: the new statutory text is generally interpreted in the light of the old legal situation. Even less has changed in the actual accounting process' (*European Business Law* (1991) 299). See also Arden, M, 'A True and Fair View: Do the Member States of the EU Approach the Company Accounting Directives in Different Ways?' [1995] Butterworths Journal of International Banking and Financial Law 295.

[94] Case C–234/94 [1996] ECR I–3133; the case is considered in more detail below.

[95] Paras 18 and 22 of the judgment. Art 31 is considered further below, pp 134–57.

[96] Para 4 of the Opinion.   [97] Case C–275/97.

The Balance Sheet and Profit and Loss Account

Introduction

Sections 2 to 6 contain provisions concerning the balance sheet and the profit and loss account. The detailed requirements as to layout, nomenclature and terminology of items are not dealt with here;[98] the outline below merely indicates some of the more significant provisions. The following items are defined for accounting purposes in the Directive: fixed assets,[99] participating interests,[100] provisions,[101] net turnover[102] and extraordinary items.[103]

Layouts

Sections 3 and 5 prescribe[104] the permitted[105] formats for the balance sheet (two alternative layouts, horizontal and vertical, set out in Articles 9 and 10 respectively) and the profit and loss account (four alternative layouts, set out in Articles 23 to 26; two are in vertical form[106] and two in horizontal form[107]). The alternative vertical and horizontal layouts differ in the method of categorizing expenditure and income: Articles 23 and 24 classify expenses and revenue according to their nature (for example raw material costs, staff costs) and Articles 25 and 26 according to their function (for example production costs of sales, distribution expenses, administrative expenses). The layout may not be changed from one financial year to the next except in exceptional cases with disclosure in the notes to the accounts and an explanation of the reasons.[108] More detailed sub-divisions within the prescribed layouts are permitted and may be required by Member States.[109] There is a limited degree of flexibility within the prescribed formats where the special nature of an undertaking so requires[110] or in the interests of materiality[111] or clarity.[112] In

---

[98] Readers are referred to the sources cited in n 26 and to Whinney Murray Ernst & Ernst, *The Fourth Directive: Its Effect on Reporting and Accounting in the UK and Ireland* (1978) for further details of the requirements of the Directive and its implications in the UK, and to Pennington, R R *Company Law* (1995), ch 17, for an exposé of the requirements of the UK implementing legislation.

[99] Art 15(2).

[100] Art 17. The definition is considered in connection with the various definitions introduced by the 7th Directive: see below, pp 190–92.

[101] Art 20. See also Art 42. See p 140 below.

[102] Art 28. See also the Commission's Interpretative Communication (n 89 above), paras 22 and 23.

[103] Art 29. See also the Commission's Interpretative Communication (n 89 above), paras 24–6.

[104] Legislating for mandatory layout was one of the major changes brought about by the 4th Directive in the UK.

[105] Member States may prescribe one or more of the alternatives; if the latter, they may allow companies to choose between them: Arts 8 and 22. The UK permits all the formats, which are set out in the Companies Act 1985, s B of Pt I of Sch 4.

[106] Arts 23 and 25   [107] Arts 24 and 26.   [108] Art 3.   [109] Art 4(1).

[110] Art 4(2): such adaptations may be required by the Member States of undertakings forming part of a particular economic sector.

[111] Art 4(3)(a).   [112] Art 4(3)(b).

respect of each item in the balance sheet and the profit and loss account, the corresponding item for the previous financial year must be shown, adjusted (with disclosure in the notes to the accounts) if it is not comparable.[113] Adaptation of the layouts may be authorized or required in order to include the appropriation of profit or the treatment of loss.[114] Any set-off between asset and liability items or between income and expenditure items is prohibited.[115] Among the more significant items required to be disclosed in the accounts are contingent liabilities, value adjustments in respect of each fixed asset item,[116] and a detailed breakdown of expenses, including purchases.

Derogations and relaxations

Article 5(1) allows Member States to prescribe special layouts for the annual accounts of investment companies and financial holding companies,[117] provided that the layouts give a true and fair view of those companies' assets, liabilities, financial position and profit or loss. This concession reflects the fact that such companies tend to have little by way of stocks, machinery etc and tend to have a low turnover.

Articles 11 and 12 allow Member States to permit small companies[118] to draw up abridged balance sheets omitting a significant level of detail which would otherwise be required. This reflects a common practice in the original Member States (and indeed in the United Kingdom between 1908 and 1967). Article 27 allows Member States to permit medium-sized companies[119] to avoid disclosure in the profit and loss account of the items (turnover and gross margins) making up gross profit by grouping certain items under the operating result.[120]

Accounting for Holdings in Other Undertakings

The Directive requires disclosure in the balance sheet and profit and loss account of specified information[121] about affiliated undertakings and participating interests.[122]

---

[113] Art 4(4).

[114] Art 6. Art 50 requires this information to be published together with the accounts in any event: see p 149 below.

[115] Art 7. See further the Commission's Interpretative Communication (n 89 above), paras 7–9.

[116] See p 137 below.

[117] As defined in Art 5(2) and (3). The exemption for financial holding companies was included at the request of Luxembourg. See further pp 178–9 below.

[118] As defined: see p 126 above. Implemented in the UK by the Companies Act 1985, s 246, and paras 2–5 of Sch 8.

[119] As defined: see p 126 above. Implemented in the UK by the Companies Act 1985, s 246A.

[120] The UK has not implemented this provision, although it permits such disclosure to be omitted in the profit and loss account published by medium-sized companies: see n 286 below.

[121] Capital held, loans to and debts to and from, income from and interest and similar charges payable to.

[122] The rules on valuation of participating interests are summarized on pp142–3.

Affiliated undertakings

Affiliated undertakings were not defined in the Fourth Directive: the provisions governing their accounting treatment were originally suspended until a directive on consolidated accounts came into force. Article 41 of the Seventh Directive[123] defines them by reference to the group relationships set out in Articles 1 and 12 of the Seventh Directive for the purpose of the preparation of consolidated accounts, and hence in effect as any subsidiary, fellow subsidiary or parent undertaking as those terms are defined in the national law implementing the Seventh Directive. As a result of the optional nature of some of the group relationships in Article 1, the definition of 'affiliated undertaking' may vary slightly between Member States. Moreover, a Member State which has not used the optional definitions in Articles 1 and 12 in determining which entities must be included in consolidated accounts may none the less use them in defining 'affiliated undertaking' for the purpose of disclosing the specified information in a company's annual accounts, and hence the definitions of group relationships and 'affiliated undertaking' may not be identical even within the same Member State.

Participating interests

Participating interests are defined in Article 17 of the Fourth Directive as:

rights in the capital of other undertakings, whether or not represented by certificates, which, by creating a durable link with those undertakings, are intended to contribute to the company's activities. The holding of part of the capital of another company shall be presumed to constitute a participating interest where it exceeds a percentage fixed by the Member States which may not exceed 20%.[124]

The Commission has indicated its view that, where the company holding the participating interest and the company in which the interest is held are governed by different Member States and where the presumption of a participating interest is based on different percentages, the question whether a participating interest exists is decided by reference to the law of the Member State in which the reporting company is established.[125]

---

[123] Art 56 of the 4th Directive (as replaced by Art 42 of the 7th Directive) incorporates this definition into the 4th Directive. Art 41 itself cross-refers to Art 1(1) of the 7th Directive.

[124] Implemented in the UK by the Companies Act 1985, s 260, which sets the threshold at 20%.

[125] Interpretative Communication (n 89 above), para 14.

Valuation Rules

General principles

Article 31(1) requires the items shown in the annual accounts to be valued in accordance with the following general principles: (a) the company must be presumed to be carrying on its business as a going concern; (b) the methods of valuation must be applied consistently from one financial year to the next; (c) valuation must be made on a prudent basis; (d) account must be taken of income and charges relating to the financial year, irrespective of the date of receipt or payment thereof; (e) the components of asset and liability items must be valued separately;[126] and (f) the opening balance sheet for each financial year must correspond to the closing balance sheet for the preceding financial year. Departures from these principles is permitted in exceptional cases; they must be disclosed in the notes to the accounts and the reasons for them given together with an assessment of their effect on the assets, liabilities, financial position and profit or loss.[127] The effect of Article 32, which provides that the items shown in the annual accounts are to be valued in accordance with subsequent Articles[128] based on the principle of purchase price or production costs, is to add another general principle, that of historical-cost accounting; disclosed departures from this principle are also permitted, within certain defined limits.[129]

Prudence

Article 31(1)(c) adds to the general requirement of prudence the following specific requirements: (aa) only profits made at the balance sheet date may be included; (bb) account must be taken of all foreseeable liabilities and potential losses arising in the course of the financial year concerned or a previous one, even if such liabilities or losses become apparent only between the balance sheet date and the date on which the balance sheet is drawn up; and (cc) account must be taken of all depreciation, whether the result of the financial year is a loss or a profit.

The original Proposal for the Directive did not refer to any general principle under this head, but merely listed the above-mentioned three requirements as general principles themselves. The amended Proposal, purporting to 'take account of certain principles which are more particularly observed in professional practice in

---

[126] The interpretation and scope of this requirement are at issue in Case C–275/97 *DE + ES Bauunternehmung GmbH v Finanzamt Bergheim*, currently before the Court.

[127] Art 31(2). As pointed out by the Economic and Social Committee, the only practicable way of attaining some degree of harmonization of a practice varying widely between the Member States 'is to legislate for the majority and to made provision for derogations; since the latter are likely to run counter to the aim of the Directive, it must be insisted upon that they be explained and assessed' in the notes.

[128] Arts 34–42. See pp 137–40 below for a discussion of the general rules laid down by these provisions. Further guidance on some of the more technical valuation rules, not further discussed in this chapter, may be found in the Commission's Interpretative Communication (n 89 above), paras 29–45.

[129] See pp 140–42 below.

certain of the new Member States',[130] incorporated a reference to a general principle that valuation be made 'on a conservative basis',[131] and recast the three
requirements as specific examples of this principle. The United Kingdom objected
to the term 'conservative' on the ground that accounts prepared on a conservative
basis may understate the strength of a company's financial position, which misleads
users as much as overstatement. There was also concern that the requirement of
conservatism coupled with the provisions in the amended Proposal that depreciation be calculated 'according to a method that satisfies the requirements of good
management'[132] and that 'provisions for contingencies and charges shall not exceed
in amount the sums which a reasonable business man would consider necessary'[133]
might result in excessive amounts being written off for depreciation or excessive
reserves being made for contingencies, thus creating secret reserves not disclosed in
the accounts.[134] The United Kingdom suggested amending the English text in line
with both the existing United Kingdom terminology[135] and the French version of
the amended Proposal, which referred to *le principe de prudence*; this was done in the
final version.

It is noteworthy that there is no guidance in the Directive as to when a profit is
to be regarded as 'made'[136] for the purpose of Article 31(c)(aa). The question of
when a profit is regarded as realized itself varies among the Member States, depending on the extent to which the principle of prudence has historically dominated
national accounting practice: in Germany, for example, a profit is in general not
regarded as realized until received, whereas in the United Kingdom it is accepted
that there can be a realized profit in anticipation of cash receipts, provided that it is
reasonably certain that cash will be received at a date not too remote.[137] Again, the
Court of Justice has competence to interpret the term in the event of a dispute.

The question arose in *Tomberger v Gebrücker von der Wettern*, decided in 1996,[138]
although the Court failed to give any genuine guidance on the issue, instead couch-
ing its ruling in terms which were both highly specific and extremely cautious. The
parent company in that case had two wholly-owned subsidiaries. The subsidiaries'
annual accounts for the financial year ending 31 December 1989 were approved at
their general meetings on 29 June 1990. Those accounts showed the appropriation

---

[130] i e Denmark, the United Kingdom and Ireland. See Explanatory Memorandum. The going-
concern principle was also added at this stage.

[131] Art 28(1)(c).   [132] Art 33(1)(b).   [133] Art 39.

[134] This practice, formerly common in the UK, was effectively outlawed by the Companies Act
1948, paras 6 and 7 of Sch 8.

[135] Statement of Standard Accounting Practice 2.

[136] 'Realized' might have been a better term, being consistent with UK accounting terminology. The
French use *réalisé*. The UK implementing legislation also uses 'realized'.

[137] See Renshall, M, The Distribution of Profits and Assets (1980) 1 The Company Lawyer 194. The
UK Accounting Standards Board noted in its discussion paper on Derivatives and other Financial
Instruments issued in July 1996 that the Directive's prohibition of reporting unrealized gains prevented
implementation of its proposal that changes in the current value of financial instruments, whether realized or unrealized, should be recognized in the profit and loss account.

[138] Cited in n 94. For further background to the case and a helpful discussion of the Opinion and
the judgment see Schön, W,'s case-note in (1997) 34 CML Rev 681.

but not the payment of profits to the parent. The parent's accounts for the same period, which did not show the profits appropriated to it by its subsidiaries, were approved at its general meeting on 19 October 1990. Mrs Tomberger, a shareholder in the parent company, sought annulment of the resolution approving the parent company's accounts, arguing that they should have included the profits appropriated to it by the subsidiaries for that same year (which would presumably have led to a higher dividend). The Bundesgerichtshof (Federal Court of Justice) referred the question whether in those circumstances the parent's accounts infringed Article 31(1)(c)(aa).[139]

The Court noted that the Directive sought to coordinate national provisions concerning the presentation and content of annual accounts of certain types of companies. In order to coordinate the content of annual accounts, the Directive laid down the principle of the 'true and fair view', compliance with which was the primary objective of the Directive and which required the accounts to give a true and fair view of their assets and liabilities, financial position and profit or loss: see Article 2(3) and (5).

The Court stated that application of that principle must, as far as possible, be guided by the general principles contained in Article 31. It considered the following principles to be of particular importance: first, only profits made at the balance-sheet date may be included in the balance sheet;[140] second, account must be taken in the balance sheet for a financial year of all income and charges relating to that year, irrespective of the date of receipt or payment of such income or charges;[141] third, account must be taken of liabilities and losses arising in the course of a financial year even if they became apparent only between the end of the financial year and the date on which the balance sheet for that year was drawn up.[142] The Court stated that it was clear from those provisions that taking account of all elements— profits made, charges, income, liabilities and losses—which actually related to the financial year in question ensured observance of the requirement of a true and fair view.

The Court concluded that, if the national court was satisfied that the subsidiary's accounts themselves complied with the principle of the true and fair view, it was not contrary[143] to Article 31(1)(c)(aa) for that court to consider that, in the circumstances described (which were listed in detail by the Court, thus narrowing the ruling), the profits in question must be entered in the parent company's balance sheet for the financial year in respect of which the subsidiary appropriated them. This conclusion differed from that reached by Advocate General Tesauro, who was of the view that a parent company's accounts should not show its subsidiaries' profits for the same year even in the circumstances of this case. The Advocate General

---

[139] The Bundesgerichthof also asked whether the accounts infringed the principles laid down in Art 59 on the 'equity method' (see p 143 below). The Court stated that, since Germany had not made use of the option conferred by Art 59, it could have no bearing on the case, and considered it no further.

    [140] Art 31(1)(c)(aa).   [141] Art 31(1)(d).   [142] Art 31(1)(c)(bb).

    [143] The wording, of course, does not necessarily mean that other methods would be contrary.

argued that the subsidiaries' profits could not be regarded as 'made' for the purposes of the parent's accounts until the decision to distribute, which occurred after their balance sheet date and hence, in the circumstances of this case, after the parent's balance sheet date. That view—unlike the final judgment—would have entailed a significant change in practice in the United Kingdom. Although the judgment may be expected to have more effect in Germany, it is difficult to predict the likely extent of its impact in view of the extremely careful terms in which it is couched.

Historical-cost valuation

Fixed assets

Article 35(1) requires fixed assets to be valued at purchase price[144] or production cost,[145] to be reduced in the case of fixed assets with limited useful economic lives by value adjustments[146] calculated to write off the value of such assets systematically over their useful economic lives. Value adjustments may be made in respect of financial fixed assets to reflect fluctuations of value,[147] and must be made in respect of other fixed assets if it is expected that the reduction in their value will be permanent.[148] Such 'value adjustments', reflecting depreciation of the asset, must be charged to the profit and loss account and, if they are not shown separately there, be disclosed separately in the notes to the accounts.[149] In addition, cumulative value adjustments (movements between initial purchase price or production cost[150] and balance sheet date) must be disclosed either in the balance sheet or in the notes to the accounts.[151]

---

[144] The total of the price paid and incidental expenses: Art 35(2).

[145] The total of the purchase price of the raw materials and consumables and the costs directly attributable to the product (Art 35(3)(a)), together with, to the extent that they relate to the period of production, (i) a reasonable proportion of costs indirectly attributable to the product (Art 35(3)(b)) and (ii) interest on capital borrowed to finance production (Art 35(4)).

[146] 'Value adjustments' are defined in Art 19 as 'all adjustments intended to take account of reductions in the values of individual assets established at the balance sheet date whether that reduction is final or not'. A deliberate decision was taken by the draftsman to avoid terminology in contemporary use in the Member States (e g depreciation, *amortisation*) describing apparently similar but essentially different phenomena, and to create instead a neutral Community terminology so as to increase the likelihood of uniform application of the rules: see the Statement of Grounds in the first Proposal. The requirement to disclose value adjustments was welcomed in the UK, as it makes clear the conservative revaluations common on the continent (apart from the Netherlands).

[147] Art 35(1)(c)(aa).   [148] Art 35(1)(c)(bb).

[149] Art 35(1)(c)(cc). If fixed assets are depreciated solely for fiscal reasons, the amount of the adjustments and the reasons for making them must be disclosed in the notes to the accounts: Art 35(1)(d). Member States may derogate from Art 35(1)(c)(cc) in the case of investment companies (as defined in Art 5(2)), which may be allowed to set off value adjustments to investments directly against 'Capital and reserves', showing the amounts separately under 'Liabilities' in the balance sheet (Art 36). The UK has implemented this derogation in the Companies Act 1985, para 71(2) of Sch 4.

[150] Or, where inflation accounting is applied, the purchase price or production cost resulting from revaluation: Art 15(3)(c).

[151] Art 15(3)(a).

Formation expenses

National law may permit formation expenses[152] and research and development costs[153] to be shown on the balance sheet as an asset, in which case they must be explained in the notes to the accounts[154] and written off within a maximum period of five years.[155] There may be no distribution of profits until formation expenses have been completely written off unless total distributable reserves and profits brought forward at least equal the expenses not written off. In exceptional cases,[156] Member States may permit derogations from these provisions in the case of research and development costs, in which case the derogations and the reasons for them must be disclosed in the notes to the accounts.[157]

Goodwill

To the extent that it was acquired for valuable consideration, goodwill must be shown as an asset on the balance sheet, and written off within a maximum period of five years.[158] Member States may however permit companies to write goodwill off systematically over a longer period provided that that period does not exceed the useful economic life of the asset and is disclosed in the notes to the accounts together with supporting reasons.[159] There is no restriction on distributing profits before goodwill is fully written off. The Directive does not state how the goodwill is to be written off, but it is generally assumed that the write-off can be through the profit and loss account or directly against reserves.[160]

The first Proposal[161] made no provision for derogation from the five-year rule

[152] See item B in each of the permitted balance sheet formats set out in Arts 9 and 10.

[153] See item C.I.1 in each of the permitted balance sheet formats set out in Arts 9 and 10.

[154] Art 34(2).   [155] Art 34(1)(a).

[156] To cater in particular for industries with development over a long timescale, e g the aerospace industry.

[157] Art 37(1). The UK does not permit preliminary expenses or research costs to be treated as an asset: Companies Act 1985, para 3(2) of Sch 4. In exceptional cases however development costs may be so treated in the balance sheet, subject to the disclosures required by the Directive: para 20 of Sch 4.

[158] Art 37(2).   [159] Art 37(2); para 21 of Sch 4 to the Companies Act 1985.

[160] See e g in the UK SSAP 22, Accounting for Goodwill, which permits both of these treatments, preferring the latter. Accounting for goodwill has been the subject of continual debate in the UK since this standard was adopted in 1984, and it will be replaced for accounting periods ending on or after 23 December 1999 by FRS 10 on goodwill and intangible assets, which provides inter alia that (a) goodwill should be rebuttably presumed to have a finite life not exceeding 20 years and be amortized to profit and loss account over its expected useful economic life and (b) significant goodwill which is expected to be maintained indefinitely and readily measurable is not to be written down but is to be subject to an annual impairment review; a true and fair override is required. FRS 10 is supplemented by FRS 11, issued in 1998, setting out the principles and methodology for accounting for impairments of fixed assets and goodwill.

[161] Art 34(2), which simply stated 'Article 32(1)(a) [writing off of formation expenses within five years] shall apply to item C.I.3 under Articles 8 and 9 [the balance-sheet entry for goodwill]', the terse drafting causing the UK HL Select Committee on the EC to comment that the paragraph 'at any rate shows that the device of legislation by reference is not confined to English draftsmen': 4th Report (Session 1975–76, HL Paper 24) Minutes of Evidence, 30. The Committee concluded with the robust recommendation that 'the writing-off of goodwill should be left to the good sense of the company's directors' (31).

for writing off goodwill. This provoked extreme resistance from the United Kingdom, in particular because, pending the Seventh Directive on consolidated accounts,[162] there was concern about the effect of the provision's applying not only to purchased goodwill by a single company—on the acquisition of an unincorporated business for example—but also to the goodwill arising on consolidation in the case of a takeover of another company. Takeovers by acquisition of shares were at the time (and still are) very much more common in the United Kingdom than elsewhere in the Community, and there was concern that requiring the substantial figures for goodwill which arise in such takeovers to be amortized over five years would be financially crippling to the acquiring company, seriously reducing its ability to pay dividends and hence making its shares unattractive to investors and making it difficult for it to raise capital. As a result of representations made by the United Kingdom, the option of writing off over a longer period not exceeding the useful economic life[163] of the asset was included.

Ancillary assets

By way of exception to the general rule requiring separate valuation,[164] tangible fixed assets, raw materials and consumables which are constantly being replaced and the overall value of which is of secondary importance to the undertaking may be shown at a fixed quantity and value if their quantity, value and composition do not vary materially.[165] This simplified method of valuation, intended for such ancillary items as repair equipment, tools etc., reflects a practice recognized in the majority of the Member States before implementation of the Directive.[166]

Current assets

Current assets must be valued at purchase price or production cost,[167] subject to value adjustments with a view to showing them at market value if lower or in particular circumstances another lower value.[168] Member States may permit exceptional value adjustments, subject to disclosure of the amount in the profit and loss account or the notes to the accounts,[169] which on the basis of a reasonable

---

[162] Which makes provision for alternative accounting treatment for goodwill arising on a takeover by the acquisition of at least 90% of the equity of the target company: see below, pp 189–90.

[163] Described by Grenside, J P, Deputy President of the Institute of Chartered Accountants and Vice President of the EEC Accountants Study Group, in giving evidence to the HL Select Committee as 'about as long as a piece of string': (n 161 above) 43.

[164] In Art 31(1)(e).   [165] Art 38.   [166] See the Statement of Grounds in the first Proposal.

[167] Art 39(1)(a). The terms are defined in Art 35(2), (3) and, at the Member States' option, (4): see nn 144–5 above. In addition, Member States may permit the purchase price or production cost of stocks of goods of the same category and all fungible items including investments to be calculated whether on the basis of weighted average prices or by the 'first in, first out' or 'last in, first out' or other similar method: Art 40(1). Where the balance sheet value so calculated differs materially from the last known market value, the difference must be disclosed in total by category in the notes to the accounts: Art 40(2).

[168] Art 39(1)(b). Where the adjustments are made solely for tax purposes, the reasons for making them must be disclosed in the notes to the accounts (Art 39(1)(e)).

[169] Art 39(1)(c).

commercial assessment are necessary if the valuation of the items is not to be modified in the near future because of fluctuations in value. This derogation is intended to apply to particular goods such as non-ferrous metals, the value of which is subject to sizeable fluctuations: since their value on the balance sheet date may be arbitrary, the principle of prudence requires that account be taken of later falls in value.[170] There is provision for the specific case of debts where the amount repayable is greater than the amount received, in which case, provided it is shown separately in the balance sheet or the notes to the accounts, the difference may be shown as an asset[171] and must be written off by a reasonable amount each year so as to be completely written off by the time of repayment of the debt.[172] This situation will principally arise on the issue of bonds below par.

Provisions[173]

The general principle of prudence requires account to be taken of all foreseeable liabilities and potential losses arising in the course of the financial year concerned or a previous one.[174] Article 42 states that provisions for liabilities and charges may not exceed in amount the sums which are necessary;[175] Article 20 defines the concept in some detail and makes it clear that provisions may not be used to adjust the values of assets.[176] The draftsman's intention was that, by defining provisions 'strictly and precisely, the unwarranted inflation of these items that could result from it should be avoided'.[177]

Both the Commission and the Accounting Advisory Forum[178] have recently stated that the Directive requires provisions for environmental risks and liabilities.[179]

Inflation accounting

The extent to which departures from the general principle of historical-cost accounting[180] may be authorized was a thorny problem during negotiation of the

[170] See the Statement of Grounds in the first Proposal.   [171] Art 41(1).   [172] Art 41(2).

[173] The interpretation and scope of Arts 20 and 42 are at issue in Case C–275/97 *DE + ES Bauunternehmung GmbH v Finanzamt Bergheim*, currently before the Court.

[174] Art 31(1)(c)(bb); see pp 134–5 above.

[175] A questionable improvement on the original version (Art 39 in the first Proposal), which required provisions not to exceed 'the sums which a reasonable businessman would consider necessary'.

[176] Art 20(3). In Case 161/78 *Conradsen v Ministeriet for Skatter og Afgifter* [1979] ECR 2221 the Court briefly considered Art 20 in the context of a case concerning assessment to capital duty, and stated that Art 20(3) made it clear that entering provisions in the accounts related to the requirements for the presentation of balance sheets but could not alter the basis for the assessment of a tax such as capital duty which in substance is based on the actual value of the assets (para 17 of the judgment).

[177] Statement of Grounds in the first Proposal. See further as to provisions the Commission's Interpretative Communication (n 89 above), paras 17–19.

[178] See below, pp 155–61.

[179] Commission's Interpretative Communication (n 89 above), paras 20 and 21, and *Environmental Issues in Financial Reporting*, published by the Accounting Advisory Forum in 1996.

[180] In the combined provisions of Arts 32 and 35, requiring valuation at the original cost price less any depreciation written off since acquisition.

Directive. Germany in particular was strongly opposed to permitting any form of inflation accounting,[181] presumably because of the fiscal implications in a system in which tax is assessed on the basis of a company's annual accounts.[182] The Netherlands, on the other hand, had made significant progress in the 1970s in developing standards of replacement-cost accounting, avoiding tax repercussions by requiring fiscal accounts to be drawn up on the historical-cost basis.[183] The compromise in the original Proposal was to permit methods of valuation which departed from the classic historical-cost method within narrowly defined limits.[184] These limits were broadened in the amended Proposal,[185] but were still not sufficiently flexible to accommodate the method of inflation accounting that was at the time gaining credence in the United Kingdom.[186] The final version authorizes Member States[187] to 'permit or require'[188] not only valuation by the replacement value method for tangible fixed assets with limited useful economic lives and for stocks (Article 33(1)(a)) and revaluation of tangible fixed assets and financial fixed assets (Article 33(1)(c)), but also 'valuation by methods other than that provided for in (a) which are designed to take account of inflation for the items shown in annual accounts, including capital and reserves' (Article 33(1)(b)). The objective of

---

[181] Account may be taken of the effect of inflation in arriving at the balance sheet value of an asset in a number of ways, of which the most important in practice are valuation at the current cost of a replacement (replacement cost, calculated at the end of each financial year) or at the sum which it would realize if sold (periodic revaluation).

[182] There was also concern that permitting inflation accounting might 'institutionalize' inflation, a view which seems somewhat ingenuous 20 years later.

[183] See generally Ernst & Whinney, *The Fourth Directive: Its Effect on the Annual Accounts of Companies in the European Economic Community* (1979).

[184] See Arts 30 and 31 of the original Proposal, and the discussion in the Statement of Grounds, 51–54. Art 30 permitted replacement-cost valuation of tangible fixed assets with a limited useful life and of stocks, reflecting the Netherlands influence; Art 31 authorized revaluation of certain fixed assets. In either case the difference was to be shown as a revaluation reserve.

[185] Arts 30 and 31, mainly by allowing for current-cost valuation, presumably reflecting the UK influence exerted through the *Groupe d'Etudes* (see p 120 above). Current-cost accounting was a highly topical issue in the 1970s in the UK, where it was estimated that in 1974 stock appreciation amounted to nearly 50% of the gross trading profit of companies (*Report of the Inflation Accounting Committee*, Cmnd 6225, para 290, 80).

[186] Current-cost accounting, as recommended by the Sandilands Inflation Accounting Committee, reporting in 1975. Using this method, a balance sheet shows not the historical cost of assets but their 'value to the business' at the balance sheet date, generally at the amount it would cost the company to replace the asset in its existing condition. The depreciation figure shown in the profit and loss account is a proportion of the 'value to the business' of the asset shown in the balance sheet, rather than a proportion of its cost; stock appreciation is removed from the profit and loss account by making a 'cost of sales adjustment' so that the profit and loss account is debited with the 'value to the business' of stock as it is consumed, rather than with its historical cost. Current-cost accounting was eventually enshrined as SSAP 16 in 1979.

[187] The Commission must be notified if a Member State wishes to make use of this derogation, which is expressed to be available 'pending subsequent coordination': Art 33(1).

[188] In respect of all companies or any classes of companies: Art 33(1). In the UK, current-cost accounting is permitted for fixed assets excluding goodwill in accordance with the rules laid down in paras 29–33 of Sch 4 to the Companies Act 1985.

coordinating valuation methods,[189] increasingly remote with each stage of the Directive, seems to have reached vanishing point.

The aim of comparability by full disclosure[190] however is firmly upheld: the final subparagraph of Article 33(1) provides: 'The application of any such method, the balance sheet and profit and loss account items concerned and the method by which the values shown are calculated shall be disclosed in the notes to the accounts.' In addition the historical–cost valuation or the difference between it and inflation–accounting valuation of each balance sheet item except for stocks must be disclosed in the balance sheet or the notes to the accounts.[191] Moreover, the amount of the difference between valuation by the inflation-accounting method used and valuation in accordance with historical–cost accounting must be entered in a revaluation reserve in the balance sheet; whenever the amount of this reserve has been changed in the course of the financial year, the notes to the accounts must include a table showing movements to and from the reserve.[192] The reserve may be capitalized in whole or in part at any time[193] and must be reduced to the extent that the amounts transferred thereto are no longer necessary for implementation of the valuation method used and the achievement of its purpose;[194] otherwise, the reserve may not be reduced[195] and in particular no part of the reserve may be distributed unless it represents gains actually realized.[196]

A final point to be made about inflation accounting in accordance with the Directive is that Member States may permit or require companies otherwise using inflation accounting to draw up their profit and loss accounts on the basis of historical cost, provided that value adjustments reflecting the difference arising are shown separately in the layouts.[197]

Certain participating interests

Article 59[198] lays down rules for the valuation of participating interests[199] in the capital of undertakings over the operating and financial policies of which signifi-

---

[189] See the 1st and 5th recitals in the preamble.

[190] Underlying the 3rd and 5th recitals in the preamble.   [191] Art 33(4).

[192] Art 33(2)(a). The treatment of the reserve for tax purposes must also be explained in the balance sheet or the notes to the accounts, which in Member States where accounting treatment is directly affected by fiscal legislation will help show the impact of the latter.

[193] Art 33(2)(b).

[194] Art 33(2)(c). Transfers to the profit and loss account may be made only to the extent that the amounts transferred have been entered as charges or reflect increases in value which have been actually realized; the amounts must be disclosed separately in the profit and loss account.

[195] Art 33(2)(d). This and the previous two provisions are implemented by para 34(3)(3A)(3B), added by the Companies Act 1989. Before the amendment, para 34 did not reflect the prohibition in Art 33(2)(d), and the amendment sought to put an end to the practice which had arisen of writing goodwill off the revaluation reserve.

[196] Art 33(2)(c). This reflects the provisions of the 2nd Directive on distributable profits: see p 69 above.

[197] Art 33(3).   [198] As replaced by Art 45 of the 7th Directive.

[199] As defined by Art 17: see p 133 above. The Article need not be applied where a participating interest is not material for the purposes of Art 2(3) (the true and fair view requirement): Art 59(9).

cant influence is exercised. An undertaking shall be presumed to exercise a significant influence over another undertaking where it has 20 per cent or more of the shareholders' or members' voting rights[200] in that undertaking. The Article provides that Member States may require or permit such an interest to be shown in the balance sheet either[201] (a) at book value calculated in accordance with Articles 31 to 42[202] or (b) at the amount corresponding to the proportion of the capital and reserves represented by it.[203] In either case, (i) the difference between these two values, calculated[204] as at the date as at which the method is applied for the first time,[205] is to be disclosed separately in the balance sheet or in the notes to the accounts; (ii) the value or amount used is to be adjusted to reflect variations over the financial year in the proportion of capital and reserves represented and reduced by the amount of the dividends relating to the interest;[206] and (iii) a positive difference, in so far as it cannot be related to any category of asset or liability, is to be dealt with in accordance with the rules applicable to goodwill,[207] namely written off within five years or over a longer period not exceeding its useful economic life.

The Directive requires the proportion of the profit or loss attributable to participating interests to be shown separately in the profit and loss account;[208] where it exceeds the amount of dividends paid or payable, the amount of the difference must be placed in an undistributable reserve.[209] Member States may require or permit that the attributable proportion be shown in the profit and loss account only to the extent of the amount of dividends paid or payable.[210] The adjustments made for consolidation purposes to eliminate profits and losses resulting from intra-group transactions and included in the book value of assets[211] must also be made when calculating the figures to be used in single company accounts in so far as the facts are known or can be ascertained.[212]

---

[200] Art 59(1) incorporates certain rules laid down by Art 2 of the 7th Directive for the calculation of the percentage, so as to exclude certain voting rights and include others. These are discussed in connection with the 7th Directive: see pp 164–5 below.

[201] A Member State may prescribe the application of one or other of these methods; the balance sheet or the notes to the accounts must indicate which has been used: Art 59(2)(c).

[202] Art 59(2)(a).   [203] Art 59(2)(c). This is known as the equity method of valuation.

[204] Where the assets or liabilities of the undertaking in which the interest is held have been valued by methods other than those used by the company drawing up the annual accounts, they may (or at Member States' option must) for the purpose of this calculation be revalued by the latter company's methods (Art 59(3)). If not so revalued, this must be disclosed in the notes to the accounts.

[205] Member States may require or permit calculation of the difference as at the date of acquisition of the interest or, where the acquisition took place in several stages, as at the date at which the holding became a participating interest (Art 59(2)(d)).

[206] Art 59(4).   [207] Art 59(5).   [208] Art 59(6)(a).

[209] Art 59(6)(b).   [210] Art 59(6)(c).

[211] Pursuant to Art 26(1)(c) of the 7th Directive. The derogations permitted by Art 26(2)(3) apply. See p 185 below.

[212] Art 59(7).

Investment companies

Member States may prescribe that investments in which investment companies (as defined) have invested their funds shall, pending subsequent coordination, be valued on the basis of their market value, in which case the Member States may waive the obligation on investment companies with variable capital to show separately the value adjustments referred to in Article 36.[213]

The Notes to the Accounts

Contents

Article 43(1) lists certain minimum information which must be disclosed in the notes to the accounts,[214] without specifying any format or order. The Article makes no reference to the overall objective of the notes to the accounts, unlike the original version[215] which stated that they 'shall contain commentary on the balance sheet and profit and loss account in such manner as to give as true and fair a view as possible of the company's assets, liabilities, financial position and results'.[216] The information listed is expressed to be over and above the extensive information required under other provisions of the Directive, principally disclosure of departure from prescribed practice and use of concessions, most of which have been referred to above and are summarized below:[217]

- any departure from the Directive in order to give a true and fair view (Article 2(5));
- any departure from the prescribed layout of the accounts (Articles 3, 4(3)(b) and 4(4));
- the relationship to other items of assets or liabilities relating to more than one balance-sheet item★ (Article 13(1));
- contingent liabilities★ (Article 14);
- movements in fixed assets★ (Article 15(3)(a));
- material accrued income (Article 18);
- material accrued charges (Article 21);
- extraordinary income and extraordinary charges (Article 29);
- taxes on profit or loss on ordinary activities and taxes on extraordinary profit or loss shown as total (Article 30);

---

[213] Art 60; for Art 36, see above, n 149.

[214] In the UK, much of this information was previously required to be disclosed in the directors' report, thus the effect of Art 43 on the extent of disclosure was limited. Its significance lies in the fact that the information, once shifted to the notes to the accounts, became subject to audit. The current UK requirements are set out in Pt III of Sch 4 to the Companies Act 1985.

[215] And amended Proposal.   [216] Art 40.

[217] The items marked with an asterisk may be disclosed either in the notes to the accounts or in the balance sheet or profit and loss account as appropriate.

- any departures from general accounting principles (Article 31(2));
- the use of inflation accounting (Article 33(1));
- tax treatment* and movements of the revaluation reserve (Article 33(2)(a));
- comparable historical-cost figures* (Article 33(4));
- depreciation of fixed assets* (Article 35(c)(cc));
- depreciation of fixed assets solely for tax purposes (Article 35(d));
- interest on capital included in production costs (Article 35(4));
- research and development costs and goodwill written off over more than five years (Article 37(1) and (2));
- depreciation of current assets* (Article 39(1)(c));
- depreciation of current assets solely for tax purposes (Article 39(1)(e));
- any difference between the balance sheet value and market value of stock (Article 40(2));
- the difference where the amount repayable on account of a debt is greater than the amount received* (Article 41(1));
- material provisions other than for pensions and taxation (Article 42);
- where small companies are exempt from the obligation to prepare annual reports,[218] specified information concerning the acquisition by the company of its own shares (Article 46(3));[219]
- specified items where medium-sized companies publish abridged balance sheets* (Article 47(3)(a));
- where the accounts are published in ECUs, the exchange rate prevailing at the balance sheet date (Article 50a);[220]
- details of any parent undertaking which draws up consolidated accounts for the group[221] and of the place where copies of such consolidated accounts may be obtained provided that they are available (Article 56(2));[222]
- use of the exemption for parent undertakings from auditing and publishing the profit and loss account (Article 58);
- the method of valuing certain participating interests* (Article 59).

The additional matters required to be disclosed by Article 43(1) comprise information relating to the following:

- the methods used for valuation and for calculating value adjustments (Article 43(1)(1));

---

[218] See p 148 below.
[219] Added by Art 6 of Directive 90/604. The information, set out in Art 22(2) of the 2nd Directive, is set out on p 148 below.
[220] Added by Directive 90/604.
[221] i e, in the case of a group consisting of more than one tier, both the ultimate parent preparing consolidated accounts for the group as a whole and the parent closest to the subsidiary preparing consolidated accounts for a sub-group. See further pp 173–6 below.
[222] As replaced by Art 42 of the 7th Directive.

- undertakings in which the company directly or indirectly holds at least a percentage of the capital which the Member States cannot fix at more than 20 per cent (Article 43(1)(2));[223]
- undertakings of which the company is a member with unlimited liability (Article 43(1)(2));[224]
- share capital (Article 43(1)(3), (4) and (5));
- long-term or secured debts (Article 43(1)(6));
- off balance sheet financial commitments, with separate disclosure of commitments relating to pensions and affiliated undertakings (Article 43(1)(7));
- net turnover broken down by categories of activity and into geographical markets in so far as the categories and markets differ substantially from one another (Article 43(1)(8));
- employees (Article 43(1)(9));
- the effect of valuations made with a view to obtaining tax relief (Article 43(1)(10));[225]
- taxation (Article 43(1)(11));
- directors' and former directors' emoluments and pensions (Article 43(1)(12) and loans etc to directors (Article 43(1)(13)).

In addition, the Seventh Directive requires the following disclosures:

(1)   where a parent undertaking has been exempted from the requirement to consolidate pursuant to Article 7 of the Seventh Directive,[226] the name and registered office of the parent undertaking drawing up the consolidated accounts and the exemption from the obligation to draw up consolidated accounts and a consolidated annual report;[227] and

(2)   where consolidated accounts omit a parent undertaking pursuant to Article 15 of the Seventh Directive,[228] the annual accounts of the parent[229] must either

---

[223] Implemented in the UK by the Companies Act 1985, s 231 and Sch 5. The percentage is fixed at 10% (para 7(2) of Sch 5). Pending subsequent coordination, Member States need not apply Art 43(1)(2) to financial holding companies as defined in Art 5(3) (see p 178 below) (Art 43(2)). This relaxation has now been modified where the financial holding company has been exempted from the requirement to prepare consolidated accounts (Art 5(2) of the 7th Directive; see p 179 below).

[224] As amended by Directive (EEC) 90/605, Art 1(2).

[225] This is designed to limit the impairment of the true and fair view in cases where, in certain Member States in which tax laws require that items be presented in the accounts in accordance with their treatment for tax purposes, fixed assets are depreciated at accelerated rates over less than their estimated useful lives, leading to a misstatement of profitability and assets.

[226] Where the parent is also a subsidiary undertaking and its own parent undertaking is governed by the law of a Member State and either (a) that parent holds all its shares or (b) that parent holds 90% or more of its shares and the remaining shareholders have approved the exemption, provided in either case that the exempted undertaking and all its subsidiary undertakings are included in audited consolidated accounts for a larger group drawn up in accordance with the Directive by an EC parent.

[227] Art 7(2)(c) of the 7th Directive.

[228] Under which Member States may, for the purposes of giving a true and fair view, permit the omission from consolidation of any parent undertaking not carrying on any industrial or commercial activity which holds shares in a subsidiary undertaking on the basis of a joint arrangement with one or more undertakings not included in the consolidated accounts: see ch p 182 below.

[229] Which must be attached to consolidated accounts: Art 15(2).

account for its investment in subsidiaries by the equity method or disclose equivalent information in the notes.[230]

Exceptions and exemptions

Member States may allow the prescribed disclosures relating to undertakings in which the company holds a fixed percentage of the capital or of which it is a member with unlimited liability to take the form of a statement deposited in the company's file set up in a central register, commercial register or companies register;[231] they may also allow omission of such disclosures,[232] or the prescribed disclosures as to turnover,[233] where their nature is such as to be seriously prejudicial to any of the undertakings concerned. Member States may exempt companies which are parent undertakings[234] from disclosing the amount of capital and reserves and profits and losses of undertakings in which the company holds a fixed percentage or of which it is a member with unlimited liability provided that the undertakings concerned are included in consolidated accounts drawn up by an EC parent undertaking or the holdings have been dealt with by the parent undertaking in its annual accounts in accordance with Article 59[235] or in its consolidated accounts.[236]

Member States may permit small companies to draw up abridged notes to their accounts,[237] complying with Article 32 only to the extent of information on valuation, minority holdings, undertakings of which they are unlimited-liability members, simple share capital,[238] total long-term and secured debt, and loans to directors,[239] and may exempt medium-sized companies from the requirement to disclose details of turnover.[240] Finally, a 1990 amendment permits Member States to waive the requirement to provide information as to directors' emoluments where such information makes it possible to identify the position of a specific member of such a body[241] and to exempt small companies from the obligation to

---

[230] Art 15(3).

[231] In accordance with Art 3 of the First Directive: see pp 19–20 above. Use by the company of this option must itself be disclosed in the notes to the accounts: Art 45(1)(a).

[232] Art 45(1)(b), implemented in part in the UK by the Companies Act 1985, s 231(3). Art 45(1)(b) states that the Member States may make such omissions subject to prior administrative or judicial authorization (improving on the version in the first Proposal which used the criterion of 'a reasonable business man' (Art 42(b)); in the UK, the Secretary of State's consent is required. Art 45(1)(b) requires that the fact of omission must itself by disclosed in the notes to the accounts.

[233] Art 45(2), implemented in the UK by the Companies Act 1985, para 55(5) of Sch 4. The requirement to disclose turnover was added on the suggestion of the Economic and Social Committee, which stressed that derogations must be provided: 'Disclosure finds its proper limits when it respects professional secrets, if the latter do not hide a deliberate wish to conceal what should not be concealed'.

[234] As defined in the 7th Directive: see pp 163–70 below.

[235] See pp 142–3 above.   [236] Art 61 as replaced by Art 46 of the 7th Directive.

[237] Art 44, implemented in the UK by the Companies Act 1985, s 246 and Part III of Sch 8.

[238] i e excluding information otherwise required under Art 43(1)(5) on participation or conversion rights.

[239] Art 44.   [240] Art 45(2).

[241] Art 43(3), added by Art 4 of Directive (EEC) 90/604.

disclose in the notes to their accounts certain information prescribed elsewhere in the Directive.[242]

The Annual Report

Article 46 requires the annual report[243] to include 'at least a fair review of the development of the company's business and of its position'[244] and to give an indication of (a) any important events that have occurred since the end of the financial year; (b) the company's likely future development; (c) activities in the field of research and development; (d) the information concerning acquisitions of own shares prescribed by Article 22(2) of the Second Directive; and (e) the existence of branches of the company.[245] The underlying principle is that the annual report 'must set out all the facts that do not directly relate to the various items in the annual accounts but do affect the overall appreciation of the economic position of the company. In this report the organs of the company express their personal opinions on the development and future prospects of the company.'[246] Unlike the notes to the accounts, the annual report does not form part of the annual accounts as defined in Article 2(1); it thus does not require auditing and as will be seen it is subject to less stringent publication requirements.[247]

The information required by Article 22(2) of the Second Directive comprises the reasons for acquisitions made during the financial year, the number and nominal value or accountable par of the shares acquired or disposed of both during the financial year and cumulatively and the proportion of the subscribed capital which they represent, and the consideration if any.

The Commission and the Accounting Advisory Forum[248] have recently given guidelines as to the type of information regarding environmental matters which could usefully be included in the annual report.[249]

Member States may exempt small companies from the obligation to prepare annual reports, provided that the notes to the accounts give the above information concerning the acquisition by a company of its own shares.[250]

---

[242] Art 44(2), added by Art 5 of Directive (EEC) 90/604. The relevant provisions of the Directive are Arts 15(3)(a) and (4), 18, 21, 29(2), 30 (part), 34(2), 40(2), and 42 (part), most of which are mentioned above.

[243] Corresponding to the pre-implementation directors' report and chairman's statement in the UK.

[244] Art 46(1). The basic requirement is implemented in the UK by the Companies Act 1985, s 234 and the contents prescribed by Sch 7.

[245] Art 46(2) as amended by Art 11 of the 11th Directive.

[246] Statement of Grounds in the original Proposal.

[247] Unless of course the company chooses to publish the notes to its accounts and the annual report as a single document, in which case the stricter requirements will apply.

[248] See pp 155–6 below.

[249] See the Commission's Interpretative Communication (n 89 above), para 49, and the Accounting Advisory Forum's *Environmental Issues in Financial Reporting* (1996).

[250] Art 46(3), added by Art 6 of Directive (EEC) 90/604. The 1990 amendment resolves the previous legislative conflict: Art 22(2) of the 2nd Directive required public companies to include the

Publication of Accounts

Section 10 of the Directive provides for publication of accounts. The primary requirement is that the 'annual accounts, duly approved,[251] and the annual report, together with the opinion submitted by the person responsible for auditing the accounts' be published in accordance with the First Directive.[252] It must also be possible to obtain a copy of all or part of the accounts and report upon request, at a price not exceeding its administrative cost.[253]

Whenever the annual accounts and annual report are published in full, the form and text published must be those which were audited and be accompanied by the full text of the audit report and include disclosure and reasons for any qualification or refusal to report on the accounts made by the auditor.[254] If the annual accounts are not published in full—for example if extracts are published for publicity purposes—their incomplete character must be disclosed, together with (a) the register in which the accounts have been filed in accordance with Article 47 or, if relevant, the fact that such filing has not yet been effected and (b) whether the auditors' report was issued with or without qualification or was refused; the auditors' report itself may not be published with incomplete accounts.[255]

Where the annual accounts do not include the proposed and actual appropriation of the profit or treatment of the loss, those items must be published together with the accounts and in like manner.[256]

The original Proposal required the annual accounts to be published in full in a designated national gazette in addition to being filed in the company's file.[257] This was intended to make the accounts more readily available to third parties, including future shareholders.[258] The requirement was subsequently dropped, presumably in part at least as a result of protests by the United Kingdom where it would

---

above-mentioned information in their annual report while Art 47(2) of the 4th Directive permitted Member States to relieve small companies (which for the purposes of the Directive may be public companies) from the obligation to publish the annual report.

[251] By the competent organs of the company. The Directive does not legislate for approval, the procedure for which will therefore be a matter for each Member State's domestic law. In the UK, a company's annual accounts are required to be approved by the board of directors, signed on behalf of the board by a director and laid before the company in general meeting: Companies Act 1985, ss 233(1) and 241(1).

[252] Art 47(1). The relevant provision of the First Directive (Art 3) requires filing in the company's file in a central register, commercial register or companies register. Art 6 of the First Directive requires Member States to provide for appropriate penalties for failure to disclose accounts; in 1997 the Court ruled in Case C–97/96 *Verbund deutscher Daihatsu Händler eV v Daihatsu Deutschland GmbH* [1997] ECR I–6843 that German penalties for failure to disclose accounts were inadequate. That ruling was confirmed in proceedings brought under Art 169 of the Treaty in Case C–191/95 *Commission v Germany*, judgment of 29 September 1998. See for a full discussion pp 26–8 above.

[253] Art 3(3) of the 1st Directive and second subpara of Art 47(1) of the 4th Directive as substituted by Art 38(3) of the 7th Directive.

[254] Art 48.   [255] Art 49.   [256] Art 50.   [257] Art 44(2).

[258] See the Statement of Grounds.

have called for a 'publishing feat of startling magnitude'[259] given that in 1975 there were some 16,000 public companies and 585,000 private companies.

The accounts may be published in the currency in which they were drawn up and in ECUs,[260] translated at the exchange rate prevailing on the balance sheet date and disclosed in the notes to the accounts.[261] It is anticipated that companies may publish their accounts using the Euro unit instead of the ECU in addition to their national currency unit as from 1 January 1999.[262]

Branches

Subsidiary companies clearly fall within the scope of the Fourth Directive;[263] branches of a company do not. If a subsidiary is required to disclose its accounts whereas the branch is subject to no financial reporting requirement in the Member State where it is established in respect of its activities or those of its 'parent', there is an obvious disparity in third party protection. In 1989, this anomaly was removed by the Eleventh Directive[264] concerning disclosure requirements in respect of branches opened in a Member State by certain types of company[265] governed by the law of another State.

The effect of the Eleventh Directive in the area of company accounts is tantamount to extending the disclosure requirements of the Fourth Directive[266] by

[259] HL Select Committee on the EC, 4th Report (Session 1975–76, HL Paper 24) Minutes of Evidence, 31.

[260] As defined in Reg (EEC) 3180/78 ([1978] OJ L379/1) as amended by Reg (EEC) 2626/84 ([1984] OJ L247/1) and Reg (EEC) 1971/89 ([1989] OJ L189/1): Art 53(1) as amended by Art 3 of Directive 90/604. Implemented in the UK by the Companies Act 1985, s 242B, added by the Companies Act 1985 (Accounts of Small and Medium-Sized Enterprises and Publication of Accounts in ECUs) Regulations 1992 (SI 1992/2452) reg 3. In September 1997, Avis cars was reported as being the first company on the London Stock Market to report its results in ECUs.

[261] Art 50a, inserted by Art 8 of Directive (EEC) 90/604.

[262] See *Accounting for the Introduction of the Euro*, guidelines issued by the Commission (1997). The guidelines, which are not legally binding, consider that there is no need to amend Art 50a.

[263] Although there is a possible exemption for certain subsidiaries: see p 123 above.

[264] Council Directive (EEC) 89/666 of 21 December 1989 [1989] OJ L395/36; implemented in the UK by the Oversea Companies and Credit and Financial Institutions (Branch Disclosure) Regulations 1992 (SI 1992/3179), inserting inter alia ss 690A and 699A and Schs 21A and 21D into the Companies Act 1985, and the Companies Act 1985 (Disclosure of Branches and Bank Accounts) Regulations 1992 (SI 1992/3178). The original Proposal for the 11th Directive was submitted in July 1986 (COM (86) 397 final, 23 July 1986: [1986] OJ C203/12); the Economic and Social Committee delivered its Opinion in September 1987 ([1987] OJ C319/61) and the European Parliament in November 1987 ([1987] OJ C345/74). An amended Proposal was submitted in July 1988 COM (88) 153 final, 28 March 1988; [1988] OJ C105/6 and the Parliament adopted its decision in September 1989: [1989] OJ C256/72.

[265] Credit and other financial institutions and insurance companies are excluded from the provisions of the 11th Directive concerning disclosure of accounts. The former are covered by Council Directive (EEC) 89/117 of 13 February 1989 on the obligations of branches established in a Member State of credit institutions and financial institutions having their head offices outside that Member State regarding the publication of annual accounting documents [1989] OJ L44/40, implemented in the UK by the regulations cited in n 264 above.

[266] The remainder of the 11th Directive is discussed in ch IX.

making the existence of a foreign branch an additional trigger for disclosure of the parent's accounts: there is no requirement for disclosure of branch accounts. Unfortunately there is no definition of 'branch' in the Eleventh Directive.[267] The Economic and Social Committee suggested a definition in line with that used in Directive (EEC) 77/780 on credit institutions,[268] namely 'a place of business which forms a legally dependent part of a credit institution and which conducts directly all or some of the operations inherent in the business of credit institutions'.[269] That definition is incorporated *mutatis mutandis* in Directive (EEC) 89/117 on branches of credit institutions,[270] which has obvious analogies with the Eleventh Directive. It is echoed in part by the definition of 'branch, agency or other establishment' framed by the Court of Justice for the purposes of the Brussels Convention,[271] which although given in a different context reflected a similar need to develop a definition independent of the domestic law of a particular Member State and common to all Member States. The Court ruled:

the concept of branch, agency or other establishment implies a place of business which has the appearance of permanency, such as the extension of a public body, has a management and is materially equipped to negotiate business with third parties so that the latter, although knowing that there will if necessary be a legal link with the parent body, the head office of which is abroad, do not have to deal directly with such parent body but may transact business at the place of business constituting the extension.[272]

In the case of branches of companies from other Member States, the Eleventh Directive[273] requires the accounting documents of the company as drawn up, audited and disclosed pursuant to the law of the Member State by which the company is governed in accordance with the Fourth, Seventh and Eighth Directives to be disclosed pursuant to the law of the Member State of the branch[274] in accordance with Article 3 of the First Directive.[275] The Member State of the branch may stipulate that the accounting documents must be published in another official language of the Community and that the translation of such documents

---

[267] Notwithstanding the purported definition of the term in the UK implementing legislation by reference to its meaning in the 11th Directive: see the Companies Act 1985, s 698(2)(b).

[268] Council Directive (EEC) 77/780 of 12 December 1977 on the coordination of laws, regulations and administrative provisions relating to the taking up and pursuit of the business of credit institutions [1977] OJ L322/30.

[269] Art 1.   [270] Cited in n 265 above.

[271] Convention of 27 September 1968 on Jurisdiction and Enforcement of Judgments in Civil and Commercial Matters [1978] OJ L304/77.

[272] Case 33/78 *Somafer v Saar-Ferngas* [1978] ECR 2183, para 12. See also n 6, p 343 below.

[273] Arts 1(1), 2(1)(g) and 3. In contrast with the provisions relating to branches of companies from non-Member States, these provisions are maximum provisions: Art 3, for example, states that the 'compulsory disclosure provided for . . . shall be limited to the accounting documents [as defined]'.

[274] In the UK, by filing with the Registrar of Companies: the Companies Act 1985, s 699AA and Sch 21D.

[275] Namely, filing in the company's file in a central register, commercial register or companies register. Art 1(2) of the 11th Directive provides that where there is a conflict between the disclosure requirements in respect of the branch and those in respect of the company, the former shall take precedence.

must be certified.[276] Where the company has opened more than one branch in a Member State, the disclosure may be made in the register of the branch of the company's choice, in which case the other branches must disclose the particulars of the branch register where disclosure was made.[277] In the case of branches of companies from third countries which are of a legal form comparable to the types of company to which the First Directive applies, the accounting documents of the company as drawn up, audited and disclosed pursuant to the law of the State which governs the company are to be disclosed in accordance with the law of the Member State of the branch as laid down in Article 3 of the First Directive.[278] Where those documents are not drawn up in accordance with or in a manner equivalent to the Fourth and Seventh Directives, Member States may require that accounting documents relating to the activities of the branch be drawn up and disclosed.[279]

Derogations and exemptions

Small and medium-sized companies[280]

As stated above,[281] Member States may permit small companies to draw up abridged balance sheets and abridged notes to the accounts.[282] Article 47(2) extends the scope of that exemption so that Member States may also permit such companies to publish such abridged accounts instead of full accounts; in addition, Member States may relieve small companies from the obligation to publish their profit and loss accounts and annual reports and the auditors' report.[283]

Medium-sized companies may publish the slightly less detailed profit and loss accounts which they may be permitted to draw up under Article 27;[284] they may in addition publish slightly abridged balance sheets[285] and notes to the

---

[276] Art 4.

[277] Art 5. The drafting of this article is somewhat inept, appearing to cater for only one of the three possible methods of disclosure permitted by the First Directive. The objective of course is to exempt multiple branches of the same company from making identical full disclosure, provided that it is clear from the permitted limited disclosure made by any branch where full disclosure may be found.

[278] Arts 7(1), 8(j) and 9(1). The combined effect of these provisions is that in relation to branches of companies from third countries the disclosure requirement is a minimum provision.

[279] Art 9(1). The same provisions apply in the case of conflicting disclosure requirements, language and translation and companies with more than one branch as for branches of companies from another Member State: Arts 7(2) and 9(2).

[280] For definitions, see p 126 above.   [281] Pp 132 and 147–8.   [282] Arts 11 and 44.

[283] The UK has taken advantage of this option, exempting small companies from the need to deliver to Companies House their profit and loss accounts and annual reports and permitting disclosure of abbreviated balance sheets and notes to the accounts and an abbreviated auditors' report: ss 246 and 247B of and Sch 8A to the Companies Act 1985 (inserted by the Companies Act 1985 (Accounts of Small and Medium-sized Companies and Minor Accounting Amendments) Regulations 1997 (SI 1997/220)).

[284] The UK permits medium-sized companies to disclose such accounts rather than the full profit and loss account (s 246A of the Companies Act 1985, inserted by SI 1997/220), although the latter must still be prepared.

[285] Art 47(3)(a).

accounts.[286] Medium-sized companies may not however be exempted from the requirements to publish their profit and loss accounts and annual report and the auditors' report.

Parent undertakings

Article 58[287] provides that Member States need not apply the provisions of the Directive concerning inter alia publication of the profit and loss account to companies which are parent undertakings as defined in the Seventh Directive[288] provided that (a) the parent undertaking draws up consolidated accounts in accordance with the Seventh Directive; (b) the exemption is disclosed in the notes to the parent undertaking's annual and consolidated accounts; and (c) the profit or loss of the parent company is shown in its balance sheet.

Subsidiary undertakings

The possible exemption for subsidiary undertakings in certain circumstances is discussed above.[289]

Unlimited-liability entities[290]

The Member State of an unlimited-liability entity may exempt it from publishing its accounts provided that (a) those accounts are available to the public at its head office with copies obtainable on request at a price not exceeding their administrative cost[291] and (b) all its members with unlimited liability are either (i) limited-liability companies governed by the laws of another Member State none of which publishes the accounts of the unlimited-liability entity concerned with its own accounts[292] or (ii) not governed by the laws of a Member State but with a comparable legal form to limited-liability companies.[293] This exemption is designed to cater for unlimited-liability entities established in a Member State where there is no central register for such entities.[294]

---

[286] Art 45(2) already permits Member States to exempt medium-sized companies from disclosing the breakdown of turnover by category otherwise required by Art 43(8). Art 47(3)(b) extends the possible abridgements which such companies may make to the published notes to their accounts. The UK permits medium-sized companies to omit breakdown of turnover by category from the notes to the accounts delivered to the Registrar of Companies: the Companies Act 1985, s 246A(3)(b), inserted by SI 1997/220.

[287] As inserted by Art 44 of the 7th Directive; implemented in the UK by the Companies Act 1985, s 230.

[288] See pp 163–70 below.   [289] See p 123 above.   [290] See pp 123–5 above.

[291] Appropriate sanctions must be provided for failure to comply with this publication obligation.

[292] In which case the second exemption considered below would apply.

[293] Art 47(1a) of the 4th Directive, inserted by Art 1(3) of Directive (EEC) 90/605.

[294] See 9th recital in the preamble to Directive 90/605. Since such entities are not subject to the First Directive, Member States are not under any obligation to ensure that a register is opened for them. The exemption is implemented in the UK by reg 6 of the Partnerships and Unlimited Companies (Accounts) Regulations 1993 (SI 1993/1820).

Auditing

Article 51 requires companies to have their annual accounts audited by one or more persons authorized by national law to audit accounts.[295] The auditors must also verify that the annual report is consistent with the annual accounts.[296]

Member States may exempt small companies from the audit requirement,[297] in which case they must introduce appropriate sanctions for cases in which the annual accounts or annual reports of such companies are not drawn up in accordance with the Directive.[298] Moreover, Article 58[299] provides that Member States need not apply the provisions of the Directive concerning inter alia auditing of the profit and loss account to companies which are parent undertakings as defined in the Seventh Directive[300] provided that (a) the parent undertaking draws up consolidated accounts in accordance with the Seventh Directive; (b) the exemption is disclosed in the notes to the parent undertaking's annual and consolidated accounts; and (c) the profit or loss of the parent company is shown in its balance sheet. The possible exemption for subsidiary undertakings in certain circumstances is discussed above.[301]

There is an obvious lacuna in that the provisions relating to auditing contain no rules on the scope of the audit or, indeed, the duties and responsibilities of auditors. At the time the Fourth Directive was being negotiated, the draft Fifth Directive was being discussed: the latter instrument included provision for the duties of auditors of public companies. That was considered to be an adequate complement to the relevant provisions of the Fourth Directive, given the option for Member States to exempt private companies from the audit requirement. Unfortunately progress on the Fifth Directive subsequently stalled and hence there is no provision at Community level governing the scope of the audit report or the duties of the auditor.[302]

---

[295] Art 51(1)(a). The 8th Directive seeks to harmonize the qualifications required of auditors: see ch VII.

[296] Art 51(1)(b). The annual report will necessarily contain statements of opinion by the managers of the company on present and future developments, and the auditor obviously cannot in his certificate give any guarantee as to the outcome of such forecasts; hence the more limited duty as regards this document: see the Explanatory Memorandum in the amended Proposal.

[297] Art 51(2). The exemption was included to assist Member States such as Germany which had too few qualified accountants to undertake the audit of all small companies. The UK took advantage of this option with the Companies Act 1985 (Audit Exemption) Regulations 1994 (SI 1994/1935), inserting ss 249A to 249E in the Companies Act 1985. These provisions, as amended by the Companies Act 1985 (Order Exemption) (Amendment) Regulations 1997 (SI 1997/936), abolish the statutory audit requirement for small companies whose turnover is not more than £350,000 for the year in question.

[298] Art 51(3).

[299] As inserted by Art 44 of the 7th Directive; implemented in the UK by the Companies Act 1985, s 230.

[300] See pp 163–70 below.   [301] See p 123 above.

[302] See also ch VII on the 8th Directive, on auditors and pp 409–10 below.

Contact Committee

Article 52 seeks to assuage the fears of Anglo-Dutch accountants that legislating in detail on the form and content of company accounts will be insufficiently flexible to accommodate commercial developments. It provides for the setting up[303] of a Contact Committee composed of representatives of the Member States and of the Commission[304] to facilitate harmonized application of the Directive 'through regular meetings dealing in particular with practical problems arising in connection with its application'[305] and to advise the Commission if necessary on additions or amendments to the Directive.[306] The Committee, which is convened by the chairman (a Commission representative[307]) either on his own initiative or at the request of one of its members,[308] meets twice yearly; some of the results of its discussions have been published.[309]

Discussions in the Contact Committee prompted the Commission to issue in 1997 an Interpretative Communication on the Fourth and Seventh Directives[310] commenting on topics where authoritative[311] clarification appeared to be required.

Developments since the Fourth Directive[312]

Accounting Advisory Forum[313]

In 1990, the Commission decided that it was time to review the accounting harmonization process and organized a conference on future harmonization.[314] As a consequence of the conference, the Commission decided to set up the Accounting Advisory Forum[315] to provide a platform for discussion and exchange of views on developments in the accounting field; to offer views and advice, particularly in areas not covered by the directives; to resolve accounting issues which impede the comparability of accounts; and to advise on the position which the Commission should take in bodies such as the International Accounting Standards Committee.[316]

---

[303] Under the auspices of the Commission.   [304] Art 52(2).   [305] Art 52(1)(a).
[306] Art 52(1)(b).   [307] Art 52(2).   [308] Art 52(3).
[309] e g Commission of the EC, *Accounting Harmonization in the European Communities: Problems of Applying the Fourth Directive on the Annual Accounts of Limited Companies* (1990).
[310] *Interpretative Communication Concerning Certain Articles of the Fourth and Seventh Council Directives on Accounting* (XV/7009/97–EN).
[311] The Commission's terminology. The interpretation suggested in the Communication will not, of course, prejudge the interpretation which the Court of Justice may be called upon to give.
[312] See also pp 197–8 below.
[313] See van der Tas, L G, 'European Accounting Harmonization: Achievements, Prospects and Tax Implications' [1992] Intertax 178.
[314] The report was published by the Commission: *The Future of Accounting Standards Harmonization* (1990).
[315] Consisting of representatives of European organizations of preparers and users of accounts and auditors, of the national accounting standards setting bodies in the EC and of accounting academics.
[316] On which it has observer status.

In 1996, the Commission issued a paper drawn up by the Accounting Advisory Forum, *Environmental Issues in Financial Reporting*.

Possible amendment of Fourth Directive

In April 1997, the Commissioner for the Internal Market, Mario Monti, indicated[317] that he was examining the possibility of amending the Fourth Directive in order to make various technical changes to reflect International Accounting Standards[318] in certain areas, particularly to deal with accounting for derivatives and other financial instruments and to make adaptations to the thresholds for small and medium-sized companies as a result of the introduction of the Euro.

[317] In a speech at the annual dinner of the UK Institute of Chartered Accountants.

[318] The moves to coordinate international and Community accounting requirements are discussed further in ch VI, pp 197–8.

VI

The Seventh Directive

Background

The Fourth Directive on annual accounts and the Seventh Directive on consolidated accounts have much more in common than their subject-matter. In both cases, the original Proposal, drawing heavily on German concepts, proved unacceptable in a number of essential areas to representatives of the United Kingdom and the Republic of Ireland and, to a lesser extent, the Netherlands; the protracted negotiations necessary to resolve the seemingly irreconcilable positions adopted by on the one hand representatives of the continental Member States, in particular Germany, and on the other hand the Anglo-Dutch countries resulted in strikingly long legislative gestation periods (from first formal Proposal to final adoption, seven years in both cases: however, the real period is somewhat longer, since both Proposals had been preceded[1] by informal drafts); and the final version differed significantly from the earliest Proposal, the differences representing to a substantial extent either acceptance and incorporation of the Anglo-Dutch arguments (for example, in relation to the true and fair view) or an unwieldy compromise between the two positions (for example, in relation to the definition of the relations between undertakings which will trigger the requirement to prepare consolidated accounts).

The Directives taken together form a whole: the Seventh Directive complements the Fourth, extending the latter's requirements as to format and content of accounts, valuation rules, publication and audit to the consolidated accounts which it requires to be prepared in certain defined circumstances. In the same way as the need for the Fourth Directive was foreseen in the First Directive,[2] the Fourth Directive itself called for harmonization of legislation on consolidated accounts, stating in its preamble that 'when a company belongs to a group, it is desirable that group accounts giving a true and fair view of the activities of the group as a whole be published'.[3]

The points made in chapter V on the Fourth Directive[4] about the contrasting attitudes of the German–French and the Anglo–Dutch accounting traditions apply

[1] By three years in the case of the 4th Directive and two years in the case of the 7th Directive.

[2] See above, pp 22–3.

[3] 12th recital. Although the original Proposal for the 4th Directive, issued in 1971, did not contain this recital, it provided in Art 51(2) for the deferral of certain provisions concerned with accounting for holdings in associated undertakings until the entry into force of a Council Directive relating to consolidated accounts.

[4] See pp 118–9 above.

equally to the background to the Seventh Directive. Consolidation practice[5] in the ten Member States at the time of adoption of the Seventh Directive diverged widely, with at one extreme the Netherlands, Denmark, the United Kingdom and Ireland, where companies were required to draw up group accounts, and at the other Luxembourg and Greece, where there was no such obligation or convention.[6] Within those Member States where consolidated accounts were prepared, there were significant differences in the relationship which triggered consolidation and the consolidation techniques used. Harmonization was thus considered desirable both to iron out the differences which put parent companies in some Member States at an advantage over those in others and to extend the information available to members and others.

History

As indicated above, the need for a directive on consolidated accounts was envisaged at an early stage, and the Commission's first Proposal for a Seventh Directive pursuant to Article 54(3)(g) of the Treaty concerning group accounts[7] was submitted to the Council in May 1976, two years before adoption of the Fourth Directive. The European Parliament delivered its Opinion in June 1978[8] and the Economic and Social Committee in February 1977.[9] The Commission issued an amended Proposal in December 1978,[10] taking into account those opinions and the adoption[11] of the Fourth Directive, and the Seventh Council Directive (EEC) 83/349 based on Article 54(3)(g) of the Treaty on consolidated accounts[12] was

---

[5] There is an interesting historical account of the development of the practice of consolidation in Barker, B, 'The Seventh and Eighth Directives on Company Law' (1984) 7 Journal of the Irish Society for European Law, 65.

[6] German public companies and parents of large groups had to consolidate domestic subsidiaries. In France and Italy, listed parents prepared consolidated accounts (in France on a voluntary basis) and in Belgium listed parents of large groups did so. See McKinnon, S M, in Newman, A D H (ed), *The Seventh Directive: Consolidated Accounts in the EEC* (1984) for further details.

[7] [1976] OJ C121/2; COM (76) 170 final; EC Bull Supp 9/76. This Proposal is the subject of a number of useful if summary articles: Savage, N, 'Law and Accounting—the Impact of EEC Directives on Company Law (2)' (1980) 1 The Company Lawyer 91; van Hulle, K, 'The EEC Accounting Directives in Perspective: Problems of Harmonization' (1981) 18 CML Rev 121; Nobes, C W, 'The Harmonisation of Company Law Relating to the Published Accounts of Companies' (1980) 5 ELR 38; Niessen, H, 'La proposition de septième directive concernant les comptes du groupe' (1981) 17 Cahiers de droit européen 26; Timmermans, C W A, 'Les comptes consolidés dans la CEE' (1977) 55 Revue de droit international et de droit comparé 341; Pevtchin, G J, 'La proposition de septième directive sur les comptes du groupe' (1981) 17 Cahiers de droit européen 38 and Gelders, G, 'La proposition de septième directive de la C.E.E. relative aux comptes consolidés' in Juridische aspecten van de geconsolideerde jaarrekening/Aspects juridiques des comptes consolidés (1980). There is a very detailed analysis from the UK's point of view in the Report of the HL Select Committee on the EC, 25th Report (Session 1976–77, HL Paper 118).

[8] [1978] OJ C163/60.   [9] [1977] OJ C75/5.
[10] [1979] OJ C14/2; COM (78) 703 final.   [11] On 25 July 1978.
[12] [1983] OJ L193/1. There is an excellent study of the Directive (including an analysis of its effects on all the present Member States except Finland) by McKinnon, S M, in Newman, A D H (ed), *The*

adopted on 13 June 1983. The final version differed substantially from the original Proposal.[13] The major changes were made during the negotiations in the Council of Ministers working party, which involved four readings rather than the usual three and took over four years.[14]

Legal Basis and Aims

The Seventh Directive is based on Article 54(3)(g) of the Treaty. The requirement of that Article that coordination of safeguards[15] be for the protection of the interests of members and others is echoed in the first and third recitals, which state that 'consolidated accounts must be drawn up so that financial information concerning . . . bodies of undertakings may be conveyed to members and third parties' and that 'the aim of coordinating the legislation governing consolidated accounts is to protect the interests subsisting in companies with share capital'.[16] Generally, the preamble refers to the 'objectives of comparability and equivalence in the information which companies must publish within the Community',[17] the agreed conditions of consolidation and the permitted and mandatory exemptions,[18] the effect on consolidated accounts of the true and fair view requirement[19] and the need for consistency and comparability.[20] The final recitals make specific reference to accounting for certain participating interests, the notes to the consolidated accounts and the maintenance of certain originally transitional derogations in the Fourth Directive.

Structure

Section 1 of the Directive, comprising Articles 1 to 15, sets out the conditions for the preparation of consolidated accounts, namely the inter-undertaking relationships necessary or sufficient to trigger the requirement and the permitted or required exemptions. As indicated, this section of the Directive proved the most

Seventh Directive: Consolidated Accounts in the EEC (1984). There are useful summaries by Cooke, T E, 'The Seventh Directive—An Accountant's Perspective' (1984) 9 ELR 143, including an overview of pre-implementation practice and major changes required in the first ten Member States, by Wooldridge, F, 'The EEC Council Seventh Directive on Consolidated Accounts' (1988) 37 ICLQ 714, and by Pennington, R, 'Consolidated Accounts: the Seventh Directive' (1984) 5 The Company Lawyer 63.

[13] It was also nearly double the length: 51 Articles rather than the original 27.

[14] See for further discussion Schneebaum, S, 'The Company Law Harmonization Program of the European Community' (1982) 14 Law & Policy in International Business 293, 315.

[15] The Economic and Social Committee questioned the soundness of Art 54(3)(g) as the legal basis of the Directive, given that a number of Member States had no such safeguards to coordinate. Taken to its logical conclusion, this argument would make most of the company law harmonization programme unlawful.

[16] The Proposal referred to protecting the interests of members, employees and third parties (1st recital); this survived the amended Proposal but was changed before adoption.

[17] 2nd recital.   [18] 2nd, 3rd and 4th recitals.   [19] 5th recital.
[20] 6th recital.

difficult to negotiate: as will be seen, a major shift of emphasis took place between the first Proposal and the final version. Section 2, comprising Articles 16 to 35, concerns the preparation of consolidated accounts, laying down accounting principles, requirements as to format and content, rules for valuing interests in undertakings, and information to be included in the notes to the accounts. Sections 3, 4 and 5, comprising Articles 36, 37, and 38 to 38a respectively, cover the consolidated annual report, the auditing of consolidated accounts, and the publication of consolidated accounts. Section 6 comprises Articles 39 to 51, transitional and final provisions including replacements of Articles 56 to 59 and 61 of the Fourth Directive.[21]

Implementation in the United Kingdom

Member States were required to bring into force legislation implementing the Seventh Directive by 1 January 1988,[22] although the implementing legislation could first apply to consolidated accounts for financial years beginning during 1990.[23] The Directive was implemented in the United Kingdom by the Companies Act 1989, which inter alia replaced Pt VII of the Companies Act 1985 (accounts and audit) and the related schedules so as to bring the Act into line with the Directive.

The most fundamental change resulting from implementation was the new definition of parent and subsidiary undertakings in the new s 258 and Sch 10A. The definition of 'subsidiary undertaking' is much wider than that of the previous term 'subsidiary', a mechanistic definition which had presented many opportunities to devise corporate structures which, notwithstanding de facto group control, remained off the controlling company's balance sheet. Implementation also required new exemptions from the requirement to consolidate, so as to exempt inter alia subsidiary undertakings with a parent established in another Member State and small and medium-sized groups.

Implementation of the requirements as to the preparation of consolidated accounts involved legislating for many matters which had been previously dealt with by Accounting Standards. Although this required new provisions in the Companies Act, it obviously had little effect in practice. There was however substantive change to the permitted practice relating to merger and acquisition accounting. The conditions for using merger accounting[24] became much stricter, so that many more acquisitions would have to be accounted for under the acquisition method. Previously, the requirement[25] to amortize goodwill in a company's accounts over a period not exceeding its 'useful economic life' did not apply to

---

[21] See ch V above. The transitional provisions, now otiose, are mentioned below briefly or not at all.
[22] Art 49(1).   [23] Art 49(2).   [24] Formerly dealt with in SSAP 23.
[25] Derived from the 4th Directive: see pp 138–9 above.

goodwill arising on consolidation. That relaxation[26] was repealed in the context of implementing the Seventh Directive, so that goodwill arising on consolidation would have to be amortised through the profit and loss account. The opportunity was also taken to make it clear in the legislation that the questionable practice of eliminating goodwill by writing it off against the revaluation reserve was not permissible.[27]

Conditions for Consolidation[28]

The major issue dividing the Member States during discussions of the Seventh Directive was whether the criterion for consolidation should be the existence of an economic unit or the existence of a legal power to control. France and Germany led the other continental Member States in favouring an economic definition of the group, depending on the unity of decision making: if different entities are in fact managed as a single economic unit, they should be regarded as constituting a group. The United Kingdom and Ireland, on the other hand, preferred a definition which depended on whether there was a legal power to control. These contrasting concepts can best be illustrated by tracing the development of the relevant provisions in the Directive, from the 'economic' approach of the original Proposal to the 'legal' approach which underlies the central provisions in the final version.[29]

The original Proposal

The original Proposal drew heavily on the German legislation on group accounts.[30] Article 3(1) defined a group[31] as consisting of 'a dominant undertaking and one or more undertakings dependent[32] on it . . . if the dominant undertaking exercises, in practice, its dominant influence to the effect that all such undertakings are managed on a central and unified basis[33] by the dominant undertaking'. A 'dependent

---

[26] Companies Act 1985, para 66 of Sch 4.

[27] Companies Act 1985, para 34(3) of Sch 4, inserted by the Companies Act 1989.

[28] This aspect of the Directive is the subject of a thorough and lucid analysis by Petite, M, 'The Conditions for Consolidation under the 7th Company Law Directive' (1984) 21 CML Rev 81.

[29] See further for an interesting discussion of the 'contrasting philosophies' the Memorandum submitted by the UK accountancy bodies to the HL Select Committee on the EC, published with the Committee's 25th Report (Session 1976–77, HL Paper 118), 18–20.

[30] See further Wooldridge, F, 'The Definition of a Group of Companies in European Law' [1982] JBL 272.

[31] There was also a separate definition of a 'horizontal group', which is considered below, p 170.

[32] The concepts of 'dominant undertaking' and 'dependent undertaking' were imported from German law.

[33] A representative of the UK Department of Trade, asked before the HL Select Committee on the EC whether he could give any indication as to how this concept worked in Germany, replied: 'We have been making considerable efforts, including sending some of our colleagues to Germany, to discuss with British firms of accountants who operate there and with the German Institute of Auditors how the system works but I cannot say that we have gained a satisfactory grasp of the situation or one that would

undertaking' was defined as 'an undertaking over which another undertaking, referred to as the dominant undertaking, is able, directly or indirectly, to exercise a dominant influence'.[34] Article 2(2) listed three circumstances where one undertaking was presumed to be dependent on another: majority shareholding, majority voting control, and power to appoint a majority of the board. Article 3(3) adds a further presumption: where an undertaking is dependent on another undertaking, the two undertakings are presumed to constitute a group. This means that, for example, where an undertaking is dominant by virtue of *being able* to exercise a dominant influence, it will be presumed to exercise that influence *in practice*. The inherent weakness of the economic approach is already apparent: *de facto* influence is a subtle and elusive concept which too easily slips away from a formal definition, and any attempt to reduce the reliance on detailed verification on a case-by-case basis by the enactment of presumptions instantly complicates the definition.

The Economic and Social Committee endorsed the use of the economic unit and unified management as the basis for consolidation, albeit subject to doubts about the vagueness of terms such as 'dominant influence' which reflect the unsatisfactory nature of the approach. The European Parliament on the other hand gave unqualified approval to the definition. The accountants' study group, the *Groupe d'Etudes*, presented a detailed submission to the Commission in 1977, criticizing the economic definition. No change however was made to the definition in the amended Proposal, except that in the English text the term 'managed on a central and unified basis' was replaced by 'managed on a unified basis'. The major changes were agreed during the difficult negotiations in the Council of Minister working parties between 1979 and 1983.

The final version

The concept of 'group' was dropped in the course of negotiations, primarily so as not to prejudice the work that was then in progress on what is still an embryonic Proposal for a draft directive on groups.[35] The Seventh Directive as adopted instead lists a series of relationships between undertakings which will give rise to the obligation to consolidate. The cluster of undertakings so linked are referred in the Directive to as 'the undertakings to be consolidated taken as a whole', although the more accessible term 'group' is used throughout this chapter. The presumptions have gone and a number of objective legal links have been incorporated in place of the 'economic unit' concept.[36]

be helpful to the Committee. It has been put to us that central and unified management is like an elephant in the sense that one recognises it when one sees it but you cannot describe it. I do not find this terribly helpful either.' (n 29 above, 11–12).

[34] Art 2(1).

[35] An amended Proposal for a draft 9th Company Law Directive on groups was prepared by the Commission in 1983 but has not progressed beyond an unpublished draft: see ch XIX.

[36] Luxembourg was the only Member State which remained unconvinced at the end of the negotiating period of the benefits of a definition based on the existence of an objectively verifiable legal

The parent–subsidiary relationships

Article 1(1) provides that a Member State must require an undertaking[37] governed by its national law to draw up consolidated accounts and a consolidated annual report if that undertaking (a parent undertaking) either has a majority of the shareholders' or members' voting rights in another undertaking[38] or is a shareholder or member of another undertaking and either (a) it controls a majority of that undertaking's board;[39] (b) it has the right to exercise a dominant influence over that undertaking pursuant to a contract with it or a provision in its memorandum or articles;[40] (c) a majority of that undertaking's board who have held office from the beginning of the preceding financial year until the time when the consolidated accounts are drawn up have been appointed solely as a result of the exercise of its voting rights;[41] or (d) it controls alone or pursuant to an agreement with other shareholders or members a majority of voting rights in that undertaking.[42]

In addition, Article 1(2)[43] provides that pending subsequent coordination Member States may require an undertaking (a parent undertaking) governed by their national law to draw up consolidated accounts and a consolidated annual report if it holds a participating interest[44] in another undertaking and either (a) it actually exercises a dominant influence over the other undertaking or (b) it and the other undertaking are managed on a unified basis by the parent undertaking.

In all the above cases, the other undertaking concerned is referred to as a 'subsidiary undertaking'. The various definitions are considered in more detail immediately below.

Mandatory link: majority voting rights

Article 1(1)(a)[45] requires a parent undertaking to draw up consolidated accounts if it has a majority of the shareholders' or member' voting rights in another undertaking. A definition based on holding a majority of the capital was rejected because the existence of non-voting shares and weighted voting rights might mean that a majority shareholder did not in fact have the degree of effective control which was still regarded as necessary.

---

relationship. It 'remained fully committed to a purely economic viewpoint, by consistently maintaining that a legal power of control, which was not accompanied by the effective exercise of the control, should not lead to a consolidation, even where it was based on a holding of the majority of the voting rights': Petite, M, 'The Conditions for Consolidation under the 7th Company Law Directive' (1984) 21 CML Rev 81, 89, n 19. The reason was presumably the large number and economic importance of financial holding companies in Luxembourg; this problem was subsequently resolved by the introduction of an exemption from consolidation for such companies in certain circumstances: see below, pp 178–9.

[37] Not necessarily a limited-liability company: see pp 172–3 below.   [38] Art 1(1)(a).
[39] Art 1(1)(b).   [40] Art 1(1)(c). This provision is an option: see pp 166–7 below.
[41] Art 1(1)(d)(aa). This provision is an option: see pp 167–9 below.   [42] Art 1(1)(d)(bb).
[43] Implemented in the UK by the Companies Act 1985, ss 258(4) and 260.
[44] As defined in Art 17 of the 4th Directive: see p 133 above.
[45] Implemented in the UK by the Companies Act 1985, s 258(2)(a).

The Commission has expressed the view[46] that, for the purposes of Article 1(1)(a), the majority of voting rights should always be taken to mean a simple majority of all voting rights in a company, even where the law or the company's constitution requires that all or certain decisions can be taken only on the basis of a qualified majority or limits the voting power of a shareholder or member to a given percentage of the total voting rights which is less than a majority of all the voting rights, irrespective of the size of his shareholding and the associated voting rights. It notes, however, that such restrictions must be seen in the light of Article 13(3)(a)(aa)[47] which allows an undertaking not to be included in consolidated accounts where severe long-term restrictions substantially hinder the parent undertaking in the exercise of its rights over the assets or management of that undertaking.

Article 2[48] lays down various rules for determining the percentage of voting rights held by the putative parent undertaking:

(1)   The rights of any other subsidiary undertaking[49] and those held on behalf of the parent undertaking or of another subsidiary undertaking by any person acting in his own name must be added to those of the parent undertaking.[50] This provision ensures that the basic definition is not avoided by the use of nominee holdings.

(2)   Rights attaching to shares held by the parent or a subsidiary undertaking on behalf of any person who is neither the parent nor a subsidiary undertaking must be ignored in calculating the parent undertaking's voting rights.[51]

(3)   Rights attaching to shares held by the parent of a subsidiary undertaking by way of security must be ignored provided that 'the rights in question are exercised in accordance with the instructions received, or held in connection with the granting of loans as part of normal business activities, provided that the voting rights are exercised in the interests of the person providing the security'.[52] It is not clear from the wording whether, in the event of shares held both by way of security and in connection with the granting of loans, the secured creditor must comply with both conditions in order for the shares not to be included in the calculation.[53] A comparison of the French, German, Dutch, Italian and Spanish versions, which are drafted differently, suggests that the English text of the proviso would more accurately read: 'either the rights are exercised in accordance with the instructions

---

[46] In its 1997 *Interpretative Communication Concerning Certain Articles of the Fourth and Seventh Council Directives on Accounting* (XV/7009/97–EN), paras 52 and 53.

[47] See p 180 below.

[48] Implemented in the UK by the Companies Act 1985, paras 7, 8 and 9 of Sch 10A.

[49] The Directive does not provide that a subsidiary undertaking of a subsidiary undertaking is to be regarded as a direct subsidiary of the ultimate parent. Thus voting rights of a sub-subsidiary are not automatically aggregated with those of the ultimate parent, although they may be so aggregated if the sub-subsidiary is acting on behalf of its or the ultimate parent.

[50] Art 2(1).　　　　　　　　　[51] Art 2(2)(a).　　　　　　　　　[52] Art 2(2)(b).

[53] See further Wooldridge, F, 'The EEC Council Seventh Directive on Consolidated Accounts' (1988) 37 IQLQ 714, 719.

received, or the shares are held in connection with the granting of loans as part of normal business activities and the voting rights are exercised in the interests of the person providing the security.'[54]

(4)   The total voting rights in the subsidiary undertaking must be reduced by rights attaching to any shares held by or on behalf of that undertaking or a subsidiary undertaking thereof:[55] thus only those rights capable of being exercised by outside interests are relevant for the purposes of calculating a majority.

Mandatory link: power of control of board

Article 1(1)(b)[56] refers to the right to appoint or remove a majority of the members of the administrative, management or supervisory board of the putative subsidiary undertaking. In determining whether an undertaking has such a right, the first three rules set out above for the calculation of a majority of voting rights apply.[57]

The right to appoint or remove directors may arise in a number of ways: for example, pursuant to an agreement between two 50 per cent shareholders (neither of whom of course will be a parent under the first definition) that one of them can appoint the chairman of the board of directors, or under a provision in a company's articles of association that the appointment of a person as director of its parent company automatically entails his appointment as director of that company. In the Netherlands in particular it may arise as a result of priority shares (*prioriteitsaandelen*) which entitle their holders to retain control over a company by making binding proposals for the nomination, suspension and dismissal of the members of its management and supervisory boards.

In countries such as Germany and the Netherlands where the two-tier board system operates, it is control over the composition of the supervisory board which will be critical since the management or administrative board is appointed by the supervisory board. The provision is however more relevant to countries with unitary board structures, since the presence on the supervisory board of a mandatory proportion of employee representatives in most two-tier systems is liable to complicate attempts to give a minority shareholder control of the overall composition of the board.

The Commission has expressed the view[58] that Article 1(1)(b) does not apply where a company is entitled to appoint a minority of the board of the putative subsidiary and that minority holds a majority of the voting rights.[59] In such circumstances however the former company will, assuming that it holds shares in the latter

---

[54]   That is the sense in which Art 2(2)(b) has been implemented in the UK (by the Companies Act 1985, para 8 of Sch 10A).

[55]   Art 2(3).   [56]   Implemented in the UK by the Companies Act 1985, s 258(2)(b).

[57]   Art 2(1).   [58]   In its 1997 *Interpretative Communication* (n 46 above), para 56.

[59]   The UK has taken the contrary view in its implementation of Art 1(1)(b), providing in the Companies Act 1985, para 3(1) of Sch 10A, that the reference in s 258(2)(b) to the right to appoint or remove a majority of the board of directors is to the right to appoint or remove directors holding a majority of the voting rights at meetings of the board on all, or substantially all, matters.

company, be required to account for it in its own and (if it is a member of a group) consolidated accounts by the equity method of accounting, since it will fall within the definition of an affiliated or associated company.[60]

Optional link: control by agreement

Article 1(1)(c)[61] covers the situation where an undertaking 'has the right to exercise a dominant influence over an undertaking (a subsidiary undertaking) of which it is a shareholder or member, pursuant to a contract entered into with that undertaking or to a provision in its memorandum or articles of association'.

Germany is the only Member State where this type of 'control contract' (*Beherrschungsvertrag*[62]) exists, under which one undertaking gives all responsibility for management to another undertaking which may direct the former's affairs in its own interests. Although there can be no dispute that an undertaking so controlled should be consolidated, the issue created difficulties during negotiations. Member States where such contracts were unlawful were reluctant to endorse a requirement that their national implementing legislation provide for them. Attempts in the Council of Ministers' negotiations to draw up a sufficiently wide definition to be acceptable to all Member States were abandoned, as any general definition would have caught arrangements where consolidation would be inappropriate, for example arrangements between investment management firms and the unit trusts they manage.[63] By way of compromise, Article 1(1)(c) defines control contracts narrowly and requires mandatory consolidation in the event of a control contract, but then states: 'Those Member States the laws of which do not provide for such contracts or clauses shall not be required to apply this provision'.[64] This solution[65] leaves a lacuna in the mandatory consolidation sought in such circumstances: if a parent undertaking established in a Member State whose law does not provide for control contracts and which has taken advantage of the option not to apply Article 1(1)(c) enters into a control contract with, say, a German company, it will not be required to consolidate.[66]

---

[60] Art 59 of the 4th Directive (pp 142–3 above) and Art 33 of the 7th Directive (see pp 190–2 below).

[61] Implemented in the UK by the Companies Act 1985, s 258(2)(c).

[62] *Aktiengesetz*, Arts 291 *et seq*.

[63] See McKinnon, S M, in Newman, A D H (ed), *The Seventh Directive: Consolidated Accounts in the EEC* (1984), 35.

[64] Academic debate as to whether UK law 'provided for' such contracts and hence as to the correctness of the UK's expected approach of not enacting this provision was rendered irrelevant by its decision to implement Art 258(2)(c) after all: see the Companies Act 1985, s 258(2)(c)(ii). 'Control contract' is further defined by para 4(2) of Sch 10A as a contract in writing conferring a right to exercise dominant influence which (a) is of a kind authorized by the memorandum or articles of the undertaking in relation to which the right is exercisable and (b) is permitted by the law under which that undertaking is established.

[65] As well as resulting in the grammatical infelicity of including what amounts to an option in a list of provisions prefaced with the words: 'A Member State shall require . . .'

[66] See further Petite, M, 'The Conditions for Consolidation under the 7th Company Law Directive' (1984) 21 CML Rev 81, 90–1.

It should be noted that there is no definition of 'dominant influence', nor has the approach of German law and the original Proposal, of raising a presumption of dominant influence in certain circumstances, been followed. The definition is accordingly left to the Member States. The United Kingdom's implementing legislation provides that for the purpose of this provision:[67]

an undertaking shall not be regarded as having the right to exercise a dominant influence over another undertaking unless it has a right to give directions with respect to the operating and financial policies of that other undertaking which its directors are obliged to comply with whether or not they are for the benefit of that other undertaking.[68]

The apparent requirement in the introductory words of Article 1(1)(c) that the parent undertaking be a shareholder or member of the subsidiary undertaking is contradicted in the following sentence, which provides that a Member State 'need not prescribe that a parent undertaking must be a shareholder in or member of its subsidiary undertaking'.

Optional link: actual appointment of a majority of the board

Article 1(1)(d)(aa)[69] permits[70] Member States to require consolidation where an undertaking is a shareholder or member of another undertaking the majority of the members of whose administrative, management or supervisory bodies who have held office during the financial year, the preceding financial year and up to the time when the consolidated accounts are drawn up, have been appointed solely as a result of the exercise of its voting rights. Member States may specify that in order for this definition to apply the parent undertaking's holding represents 20 per cent or more of the shareholders' or members' voting rights.

This and the following two provisions represent the culmination of attempts to legislate for circumstances in which the *actual exercise of control* based on a minority shareholding should give rise to the requirement to consolidate: they are the surviving remnants of the economic approach.[71] Italy and France in particular wanted consolidation to be compulsory when an undertaking actually exercises control even if none of the legal nexuses agreed applies. This could arise, for example, where the holder of a significant minority of voting rights is able to use his stake to appoint a majority of the board as a result of the inertia of other shareholders. This is particularly relevant in the continental Member States where in general, and in contrast to the United Kingdom and Ireland, bearer shares are both common and

---

[67] But not for that of s 258(4)(a) which implements Art 1(2) and hence uses the term 'actually exercises a dominant influence': the Companies Act 1985, para 4(3) of Sch 10A.

[68] The Companies Act 1985, para 4(1) of Sch 10A.   [69] Not implemented by the UK.

[70] Again by means of the cumbersome route of first stating that a Member State 'shall require' consolidation in the specified circumstances and subsequently providing (obliquely in this case, by a provision towards the end of Art 1(1)(d)) that the Member States 'shall prescribe at least the arrangements referred to in (bb) above'.

[71] This and the following provision differ from the 'unified management' criterion in the original Proposal (which has survived in somewhat emasculated form in the optional Art 1(2), discussed below) because France wanted objective criteria against which the actual exercise of control could be measured.

popular.[72] Article 1(1)(d)(aa) is designed to cater for such a situation: for that reason, the final sentence of Article 1(1)(d) states that subparagraph (aa) is not to apply where another undertaking has the rights referred to in subparagraphs (a), (b) or (c) with regard to that subsidiary undertaking, thereby ensuring that it will not apply where the right to exercise control is in fact concentrated in other hands. An alternative proposal, which would have had the same effect, was based on majority voting power at general meetings called to appoint board members.

A number of Member States, including the United Kingdom, objected that the principle of relying on absenteeism of shareholders as a basis for the parent–subsidiary relationship was unsound: shareholders who are content to be passive during good years, when the company is prospering and they have a good return on their holdings, may start taking more interest in the company's affairs when profits dwindle; the question whether the company should be consolidated by a more evenly active minority shareholder would therefore vary from year to year and the group picture would fluctuate with the economic wind. Against that view it can be argued that since consolidation is intended to procure a true and fair view of the position at the end of a financial year, it is the actual situation in that year rather than possible changes in the future which is critical; in any event, the requirement of continuity ultimately incorporated in Article 1(1)(d)(aa), albeit limited, will ensure a degree of consistency.[73]

It was finally agreed that, on the basis that the criterion for factual control spelt out in Article 1(1)(d)(bb)[74] would be mandatory, that in Article 1(1)(d)(aa) would be optional, notwithstanding its position in the list in Article 1(1) of circumstances in which consolidation is apparently compulsory.[75]

For the purposes of determining whether the requisite appointments were made solely as a result of the putative parent's voting rights, the provisions of Article 2[76] apply. It is unclear however at what point the aggregation of the voting rights of the putative parent and those of any other subsidiary undertaking and nominees of either required by Article 2(1) takes place. By definition there will be a time span of over two years[77] between the appointment at issue and the date of determining whether the parent–subsidiary relationship exists, namely the date when the consolidated

---

[72] Notice of meetings must be given to holders of bearer shares by newspaper announcements: inevitably their attendance is very irregular.

[73] A more pragmatic counter-argument is that there is little practical difference whether or not the putative subsidiary is consolidated in these circumstances, since if it is not it will in any event normally have to be accounted for on an equity basis by the putative parent as a participating interest (Art 59 of the 4th Directive; see pp 142–3 above), which will give the same group profit as consolidation (although other profit and loss account and balance sheet figures would differ).

[74] See below.

[75] Petite suggests that one reason for this 'legal curiosity' may be to pave the way for the provision to become compulsory as a result of the review of the Directive originally proposed for 1995: (n 66 above) 94.

[76] See pp 164–5 above.

[77] Because the office must have been held for the financial year in question, the preceding financial year and up to the time of drawing up the accounts: see above.

accounts are drawn up. If the calculation is carried out at the latter date by reference to the combined votes cast on the appointment by the putative parent and those undertakings which at the latter date are its other subsidiaries and nominees, the requirement to consolidate may bite even though the appointment was in fact made as a result of the voting rights exercised by, inter alia, companies which were not at that time subsidiaries of the putative parent: this would be the case if the group structure had changed between appointment and drawing up the accounts.[78]

It is also unclear precisely what is meant by 'appointed solely as the result of . . .'. It obviously covers resolutions on which the only votes in favour were cast by the putative parent and any other subsidiaries or nominees. It is not however obvious that it would cover the situation where those undertakings cast only a majority of the votes cast in favour of the resolution to appoint, or *a fortiori* where their combined vote, albeit a minority of the total cast in favour, was critical in that without it the resolution would not have been carried.

Mandatory link: actual control of majority voting rights

Article 1(1)(d)(bb)[79] describes an alternative circumstance in which a minority shareholder could have actual control: where it 'controls alone, pursuant to an agreement with other shareholders in or members of [an undertaking of which it is shareholder or member] a majority of shareholders' or members' voting rights in that undertaking'.

This provision may cover, for example, shareholders' agreements. Its precise scope will vary between the Member States however since the second sentence permits Member States to 'introduce more detailed provisions concerning the form and contents of such agreements'. Thus a Member State reluctant to endorse the concept of factual control alone as a criterion for consolidation may require that in order to fall within this definition an agreement be, for example, legally binding, of a given duration and unconditional in the assignment of the voting rights;[80] another State with more enthusiasm for the actual control approach could so define the relevant agreements as to embrace a wide array of informal arrangements. In the final analysis, however, the term 'agreement' may fall to be interpreted by the Court of Justice.

Optional links: participating interest and either (a) actual exercise of dominant influence or (b) management on a unified basis

Article 1(2)[81] permits Member States, 'pending subsequent coordination', to require any undertaking governed by its national law to draw up consolidated

---

[78] See further Pennington, R, 'Consolidated Accounts: the Seventh Directive' (1984) 5 The Company Lawyer 63, 65.

[79] Implemented in the UK by the Companies Act 1985, s 258(2)(d).

[80] In which case, the putative subsidiary would probably already be subject to the requirement to consolidate by virtue of the combined effect of Arts 1(1)(a) and 2(1).

[81] Implemented in the UK by the Companies Act 1985, s 258(4). 'Participating interest' is defined in s 260.

accounts and a consolidated annual report if that undertaking (a parent undertaking) holds a participating interest[82] in another undertaking (a subsidiary undertaking) and either '(a) it actually exercises a dominant influence over it; or (b) it and the subsidiary undertaking are managed on a unified basis by the parent undertaking'.[83] The purpose of this provision was to accommodate German law, but since the definitions proved unpalatable to a number of Member States they were made optional. The concepts of 'dominant influence' and 'managed on a unified basis' are not defined.

Horizontal groups

All the definitions considered above are concerned with the existence of a parent–subsidiary relationship between undertakings, giving rise to the conventional 'vertical' group. As indicated above, the original Proposal also provided for compulsory consolidation of groups of undertakings 'between which no relationship of dependency . . . exists . . . managed on a [central and] unified basis',[84] embodying the statement in the preamble that 'a group sometimes consists of undertakings which exist on an equal footing with one another'.[85] This provision was designed to require consolidation of all EC subsidiaries of a non-EC parent; it would also have caught some joint ventures.

That proposal encountered considerable resistance, in particular from the United Kingdom. Moreover, once it had been agreed that the concept of unified management should not be included in the criteria for mandatory consolidation of vertical groups it was difficult to justify retaining it as the linchpin of the definition of horizontal groups. For those reasons, the Directive as adopted tempered the original requirement by (a) incorporating objectively verifiable criteria as evidence of management on a unified basis and (b) making consolidation for such horizontal groups as fell within the revised definition optional.

Article 12(1)[86] accordingly permits Member States to require any undertaking governed by its national law to draw up consolidated accounts and a consolidated annual report incorporating the results of any undertaking with which it has no parent–subsidiary relationship[87] if (a) the undertakings are managed on a unified basis pursuant to a contract concluded between them or provisions in their memorandum or articles of association or (b) their administrative, management or supervisory bodies consist for the major part of the same persons in office during the financial year and until the consolidated accounts are drawn up.

---

[82] As defined in Art 17 of the 4th Directive: see p 133 above.

[83] Where the interest is 'significant' rather than 'dominant', it will normally have to be accounted for using the equity method: see pp 142–3 above, and pp 190–2 below.

[84] Art 4(1). The words in square brackets seem to have been included in the original Proposal as a result of a translation error and were deleted from the amended Proposal.

[85] 2nd recital.   [86] Not implemented by the UK.

[87] And of all subsidiary undertakings of the undertakings: Art 12(2).

The definition, if implemented, will catch so-called 'horizontal groups' of which
the classic example is the Anglo-Dutch group Unilever, which essentially consists
of two independent companies managed by identical boards.[88] It will not however,
unlike the controversial predecessor of Article 12 in the original Proposal, catch so-
called 'fictitious horizontal groups'. These are vertical groups of which the parent
is not caught as a parent undertaking within the meaning of the Directive, either
because it is established outside the Community or because it is not one of the legal
entities covered by the Directive.[89] The original Proposal[90] treated the subsidiaries
of such a parent as a horizontal group provided that at least one subsidiary had its
registered office in the Community, and required each such subsidiary 'at the same
level within the group and nearest to the dominant group undertaking' to draw up
consolidated accounts of all such subsidiaries together with all their subsidiaries,
regardless of where their registered offices were situated. The concept however
encountered stiff resistance.[91] First, it was questionable whether consolidated
accounts which did not include the results of the parent and hence could not give
a view of the group as a whole were in any event useful. Second, it made little sense
to require a number of subsidiaries each to prepare consolidated accounts. Third,
there was an obvious risk that the undertaking drawing up such accounts would
encounter difficulties in obtaining the necessary financial information from the
other undertakings to be consolidated, particular where they were situated outside
the Community; it may indeed not even be aware of the existence of all such
undertakings. The requirement for consolidation in the case of fictitious horizontal groups was accordingly abandoned.

The Undertakings to be Consolidated

The Fourth Directive, which the Seventh Directive is intended to complement,
applies to a variety of types of limited-liability company and, by virtue of a recent
anti-avoidance amendment, to certain types of partnership and unlimited company
constituted in a particular way. Because consolidated accounts by definition
embrace a number of undertakings in a prescribed relationship, there are obviously
a number of possible ways in which the legal form of the undertakings in question
may be relevant. The original Proposal[92] required every parent undertaking,

---

[88] For an interesting analysis of a recent merger of UK and Australian companies which adopted a
similar structure, see King, P, Radford, N, and Read, S, 'RTZ/CRA: The Mining Merger' in [1996] 1
Practical Law for Companies 27–34.

[89] See below. The original Proposal would in fact have required any parent undertaking in the EC,
regardless of legal form, to prepare consolidated accounts; however it became apparent during negotiations that that requirement would have to be watered down.

[90] Arts 6(1)(a) and 6(2)(b).

[91] It was in fact only the Commission which had any real enthusiasm for the consolidation of subsidiaries of a non-EC parent. Its aim to require disclosure of the scale of operations of multinational
groups in the EC was made explicit in the Explanatory Memorandum of the original Proposal: see 19.

[92] Graphically described in this context as 'coherent but radical': Petite, M, 'The Conditions for
Consolidation under the 7th Company Law Directive' (1984) 21 CML Rev 81, 99.

regardless of its legal form, to draw up consolidated accounts, provided that one of the undertakings within the group was established in one of the limited-liability corporate forms prescribed.[93] This requirement was not acceptable to a majority of delegations,[94] which during negotiations in Council expressed a number of criticisms. First and foremost, it would mean that a requirement to draw up consolidated accounts would be imposed on undertakings which were not required by the Fourth Directive[95] to draw up individual company accounts. Second, among those undertakings would be natural persons: requiring natural persons to draw up consolidated accounts raises both problems of principle and practical difficulties in distinguishing between commercial assets and private wealth. Third, there was concern that extending the reach of the Directive beyond limited-liability companies in any way would be the thin end of the wedge, and that it would end up applying to entities such as non-profit-making associations. Finally, the practical difficulties of monitoring compliance in the case of Member States with no pre-existing system of registration of non-corporate entities were raised.

The final result, after a number of possible compromises had been discussed and rejected,[96] was embodied in Article 4 of the Directive as adopted. Article 4(1) reflects the original provision, stating that a parent undertaking and all of its subsidiary undertakings are to be undertakings to be consolidated where either the parent or one of more subsidiaries is established as one of the listed types of company.[97] Article 4(2) however permits Member States to exempt a parent undertaking from the requirement[98] to draw up consolidated accounts where it is not established as one of the listed types of company.[99] By virtue of a 1990 amending directive,[100]

[93] Art 6(1)(a), which listed various forms of public and private limited-liability company in the then Member States.

[94] It was supported by, inter alia, Denmark and the Netherlands, which argued that information should be disclosed about all groups of significant size, and Italy, which wished to ensure that its numerous State holding companies were treated on an equal footing with the private sector. The Commission regarded it as an important anti-avoidance measure given the existence in Germany of the *GmbH & Co KG*, an entity which makes it possible to clothe the limited liability of its members with the appearance of unlimited liability (see above, pp 123–5). See further McKinnon, S M, in Newman, A D H (ed), *The Seventh Directive: Consolidated Accounts in the EEC* (1984) 45–6 and 318–19, and Petite (n 92 above) 101, n 42.

[95] It must be remembered that at the time the 7th Directive was being negotiated, the scope of the 4th Directive had not been extended so that the only undertakings to which it applied were limited-liability companies. Some of the criticisms of the wide scope of the original Proposal of the 7th Directive—expressed to be motivated in part by anti-avoidance factors (see the Explanatory Memorandum, 23)—have in fact now been met by the extension of scope of the 4th and 7th Directives: see below.

[96] See Petite (n 92 above) 101.

[97] Broadly, public or private limited-liability companies. The list is the same as that set out in Art 1 of the 4th Directive, which itself covers the same companies as Art 1 of the First Directive as amended: see pp 17–18 above.

[98] In Art 1(1).

[99] The UK has taken advantage of this option. Thus the Companies Act 1985, s 227(1), states: 'If at the end of a financial year a company is a parent company the directors shall . . . prepare group accounts.' 'Parent company' is defined in s 258(1) as a parent undertaking which is a company.

[100] Council Directive (EEC) 90/605 of 8 November 1990 amending Directive (EEC) 78/660 on annual accounts and Directive (EEC) 83/349 on consolidated accounts as regards the scope of those Directives [1990] OJ L317/60. See pp 123–5 above for a full discussion of this Directive.

Article 4(1) is extended so as also to apply where either the parent undertaking or one or more subsidiary undertakings is constituted as one of the types of entity mentioned in the second or third sub-paragraphs of Article 1(1) of the Fourth Directive.[101] The permitted exemption in Article 4(2) is extended in parallel, so that Member States may exempt from the requirement to draw up consolidated accounts a parent undertaking not within the amended list of entities.

Article 3(1) states that a parent undertaking and all of its subsidiary undertakings are undertakings to be consolidated regardless of where the registered offices of such subsidiary undertakings are situated. Thus the requirement to consolidate is triggered by the presence in a Member State of a parent undertaking; once so triggered, it will extend to all subsidiary undertakings, wherever established, within or without the Community.

Exemptions

There are numerous further exemptions from the requirement to draw up consolidated accounts, some mandatory and some optional.

Sub-consolidation

It will be apparent that under Article 1(1), referred to above,[102] consolidation is prima facie required at every level of a vertical group with multiple tiers (see diagram overleaf).

The original Proposal[103] required sub-consolidation at every level in such a group. In the diagram below undertakings A, B and C, being parent undertakings, would each have had to draw up consolidated accounts for themselves and all their subsidiary undertakings. This requirement met with fierce criticism from a number of delegations, echoing the view of the European Parliament that it was 'unduly onerous and of limited value'.[104] The requirement remains in the final version but is heavily tempered by a number of exemptions, all subject to conditions designed to ensure that the parent's 'members and third parties are sufficiently protected'.[105] It was on the basis that the level of protection agreed in the course of negotiating the exemptions was sufficiently high that it was decided appropriate to make certain exemptions mandatory, so that undertakings could benefit from them as of right rather than being dependent on the Member State's discretion in implementing an optional exemption.

---

[101] See p 124 above.   [102] See pp 163–9 above   [103] Art 6(2)(a).

[104] Unilever in giving evidence to the UK HL Select Committee for the EC stated that it would as a result have to produce over 200 additional sets of consolidated accounts: 25th Report (Session 1976–77, HL Paper 118) Minutes of Evidence, 56.

[105] 3rd recital in the preamble.

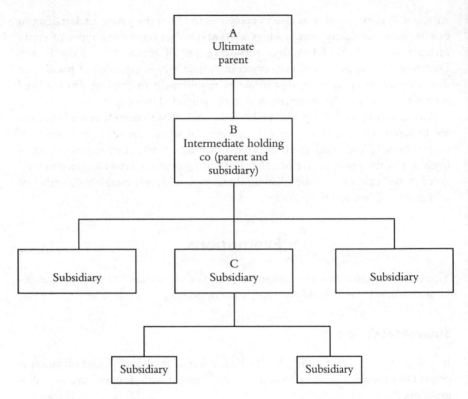

As will be seen, the mechanics of the exemption in effect achieve a degree of mutual recognition of accounts: very broadly, a parent undertaking in one Member State which is itself a subsidiary of a parent in another Member State may or in some cases must be exempted from the requirement to draw up consolidated accounts on the basis that its parent draws up consolidated accounts under the law of that other Member State.

Mandatory exemption: 90 per cent plus subsidiary of EC parent

Article 7 requires Member States to exempt from the requirement to consolidate any parent undertaking governed by its national law which is also a subsidiary undertaking if its own parent undertaking is governed by the law of a Member State and either (a) that parent holds all[106] its shares[107] or (b) that parent holds 90 per cent or more of its shares and the remaining shareholders have approved the exemption,[108] provided in either case that the exempted undertaking and all its

---

[106] Ignoring shares held by members of its administrative, management or supervisory bodies pursuant to an obligation in law or in the memorandum or articles of association.

[107] Implemented in the UK by the Companies Act 1985, s 228.

[108] Art 7(1). Member States which at the time of adoption of the Directive required sub-consolidation in the second case (90%) have an additional ten years for implementation, i e until 2000. This concession was primarily for the benefit of the UK, which has not yet implemented it.

subsidiary undertakings are included in audited consolidated accounts for a larger group drawn up in accordance with the Directive by an EC parent.[109] Those consolidated accounts, including any additional information required under Article 9,[110] the accompanying consolidated annual report and the auditors' report, must be published[111] for the exempted undertaking, and the notes to the annual accounts of the exempted undertaking must disclose the name and registered office of the parent undertaking drawing up the consolidated accounts and the exemption from the obligation to draw up consolidated accounts and a consolidated annual report.[112]

This exemption, although expressed to be mandatory, is not absolute: Member States need not extend it to companies whose securities are listed on an EC Stock Exchange,[113] nor will it override any legislation on the drawing up of consolidated accounts or consolidated annual reports in so far as they are required for the information of employees or their representatives or by an administrative or judicial authority for its own purposes.[114] Moreover, a Member State may make the exemption dependent upon (a) the disclosure in the consolidated accounts[115] of any additional information required to be included in consolidated accounts drawn up by undertakings governed by its national law[116] and/or (b) the disclosure in the notes to the consolidated accounts or in the annual accounts of the exempted undertaking of any of the following information regarding the exempted undertaking and its subsidiary undertakings: the amount of fixed assets, net turnover, the result for the financial year, the amount of capital and reserves, and the average number of employees during the financial year.[117]

Optional exemption: other subsidiaries of an EC parent

Article 8(1)[118] permits Member States to extend the Article 7 exemption to cases where the shareholders in or members of the exempted undertaking who own a minimum proportion of its subscribed capital have not requested the preparation of consolidated accounts at least six months before the end of the financial year. The Member States may fix the proportion at not more than 10 per cent for public companies[119] and not more than 20 per cent for undertakings of other types. The conditions set out in Article 7(2) and the conditions permitted by Article 9 apply.

The Directive spells out that this exemption must not be implemented in a discriminatory manner: a Member State may not make it a condition of the

---

[109] Art 7(2)(a) and 7(2)(b)(aa).   [110] See below.

[111] In the manner prescribed by the law of the Member State governing that undertaking in accordance with Art 38 (see p 196 below); that Member State may require the documents to be published in its official language and the translation to be certified (Art 7(2)(b)(bb)).

[112] Art 7(2)(c).

[113] Art 7(3); the UK Companies Act 1985, s 228(3), reflects this qualification.   [114] Art 10.

[115] Or in an appendix.   [116] Art 9(1).   [117] Art 9(2).

[118] Implemented in the UK by the Companies Act 1985, s 228. The proportion of capital is fixed at 5%.

[119] And limited partnerships with share capital.

exemption that the parent undertaking preparing the consolidated accounts be also governed by its national law,[120] nor impose conditions concerning the preparation and auditing of the consolidated accounts.[121]

Optional exemptions: subsidiary of a non-EC parent

Article 11(1)[122] permits Member States to exempt intermediate parents which themselves have a non-EC parent provided that the exempted undertaking and all its subsidiary undertakings are included in audited consolidated accounts for a larger group drawn up in accordance with the Directive or in an equivalent manner.[123] There is no holding threshold as in the case of EC groups; the provisions as to publication and disclosure in the notes to the accounts however apply.[124]

Member States may also extend the optional exemption provided for in Article 8[125] to intermediate parents with non-EC parents.[126]

In all the above cases, Articles 9 and 10 apply.[127] The exemptions cannot be extended under Article 11 unless their equivalents under Articles 7 to 9 apply to EC groups.[128]

Small groups

The original Proposal permitted Member States to exempt small and medium-sized groups from including certain details in their consolidated accounts.[129] This approach closely shadowed that of the Fourth Directive in relation to small and medium-sized companies, even to the extent of adopting identical criteria. It was not however acceptable to a number of Member States, which felt strongly that it should be possible wholly to exempt smaller groups from any obligation to prepare consolidated accounts.[130] Once that principle had been accepted, it became apparent that there was a wide divergence of views as to the appropriate group limits: some delegations urged that the small-company criteria in the Fourth Directive be extended to groups in order to provide the strongest possible disincentive against fragmenting an existing company in order to avoid consolidation, while others advocated limits of up to 25 times those thresholds. The ultimate compromise involved two stages: for a transitional period of ten years[131] the figures are ten times

---

[120] Art 8(2).   [121] Art 8(3).   [122] Not implemented by the UK.
[123] The Directive leaves it to the Member States to decide how to determine equivalence. Proposals during negotiations that equivalence would have to be verified by an EC auditor or defined in conventions between the EC and other countries were rejected as unworkable. See for further discussion Schneebaum, S, 'The Company Law Harmonization Program of the European Community' (1982) 14 Law and Policy in International Business 293, 310–15.
[124] By virtue of Art 11(2). The provisions are Art 7(2)(b)(bb) (see n 111 above) and Art 7(2)(c) (see p 175 above).
[125] See above.   [126] Art 11(2).   [127] See p 175 above.
[128] Art 11(3).   [129] See Arts 21(2), 23(2) and 24(2).
[130] In general, either for the pragmatic reason that exempting smaller groups would reduce the scale of the task of legislating for consolidated accounts for the first time or as a result of believing as a matter of economic principle that there is little public interest in small groups.   [131] Until 2000.

the small company criteria in the Fourth Directive; thereafter the figures are the same as the medium–sized company criteria.[132] The figures are as follows:[133]

	Transitional Limits (Available until the year 2000)	*Permanent Limits* (medium–sized company under Fourth Directive)	*Small-company limits under Fourth Directive*
Balance sheet total	ECU 25 million	ECU 10 million	ECU 2.5 million
Net turnover	ECU 50 million	ECU 20 million	ECU 5 million
Average number of employees	500	250	50

To qualify for the exemption from the requirement to consolidate, the group must satisfy two of the three criteria on a parent undertaking's balance sheet date in two successive financial years[134] and must not include a company whose securities are listed on an EC Stock Exchange.[135]

It is relatively simple for an individual company to determine whether it falls within the Fourth Directive thresholds. Whether or not a group comes within the balance sheet total and net turnover limits however may vary significantly depending on whether the figures are calculated before or after elimination of intra–group transactions. The Directive allows for this difference by permitting Member States to require or permit that qualification for the exemption be determined before elimination of intra–group transactions, thus avoiding the conceptually unsatisfactory position of requiring that accounts be consolidated in order to establish entitlement to exemption from consolidation. In that case, however, the Directive provides for the limits for the balance sheet total and net turnover criteria to be increased by 20 per cent.[136]

It is interesting to note that the overwhelming majority of replies to a Questionnaire issued by the Commission in 1997 on Simplification of the Accounting Directives for Small and Medium-Sized Enterprises[137] were in favour of maintaining the possibility of exempting small and medium-sized groups from

---

[132] Art 6(1) and 6(5).

[133] After the most recent quinquennial amendment by Council Directive (EC) 94/8 of 21 March 1994 amending Directive (EEC) 78/660 as regards the revision of amounts expressed in ECUs [1994] OJ L82/33. The UK has implemented this option; the current figures are £5.6 million, £11.2 million and 250: the Companies Act 1985, s 249, as amended by the Companies Act 1985 (Accounts of Small and Medium-Sized Enterprises and Publication of Accounts in ECUs) Regulations 1992 (SI 1992/2452).

[134] Art 6(3), applying Art 12 of the 4th Directive: see above, p 126, n 63.

[135] Art 6(4).   [136] Art 6(2).

[137] XV/7023/97–EN. A Summary of the responses was published in January 1998 (XV/7040/98–EN).

the consolidation requirement. Where however Member States had not made use of the option to exempt such groups, there was a similar majority against making further dispensations (including an exemption from the audit requirement) available.

Financial holding companies

The question of whether, and if so to what extent, financial holding companies should be relieved of accounting requirements applicable to other parent companies had already been canvassed in negotiating the Fourth Directive. The outcome of those discussions were two relatively minor concessions for financial holding companies. First,[138] Member States were permitted to enact special formats for their annual accounts to reflect the fact that they have little by way of stock, machinery etc., and tend to have a low turnover; the accounts must none the less give a true and fair view of the company's assets, liabilities, financial position and profit or loss equivalent to that required of other companies. Second,[139] Member States were permitted, 'pending subsequent coordination', to exempt financial holding companies from the requirement[140] to disclose detailed information in the notes to the accounts concerning undertakings in which they had participating interests. For the purposes of those exemptions, the Fourth Directive defined financial holding companies as

companies the sole object of which is to acquire holdings in other undertakings, and to manage such holdings and turn them to profit, without involving themselves directly or indirectly in the management of those undertakings, the aforegoing without prejudice to their rights as shareholders. The limitations imposed on the activities of these companies must be such that compliance with them can be supervised by an administrative or judicial authority.[141]

The limited exemptions in the Fourth Directive had been agreed largely to appease Luxembourg, which was concerned that imposing extensive disclosure requirements on such companies would seriously impair its attractiveness as a financial centre.[142] When it came to negotiating the Seventh Directive, the issue was reopened. It was argued by Luxembourg that financial holding companies, although technically parents by virtue of their portfolios, did not in practice involve themselves in the operation or management of their subsidiaries and hence should not be assimilated to 'genuine' parents for accounting purposes. After protracted discussion, the possibility of exempting financial holding companies from consolidation was included in the Seventh Directive; the circumstances in which the

---

[138] Art 5(1) of the 4th Directive.   [139] Art 43(2) of the 4th Directive.
[140] In Art 43(1)(2).   [141] Art 5(3) of the 4th Directive.
[142] Petite cites the following figures as at the end of 1981 to illustrate the importance of financial holding companies in Luxembourg: of the 9,619 limited companies then registered there, 5,350 were financial holding companies: 'The Conditions for Consolidation under the 7th Company Law Directive' (1984) 21 CML Rev 81, 102, n 43.

exemption could be available were defined with much greater rigour however than in the Fourth Directive and companies taking advantage of the exemption lose the benefit of some of the exemptions from disclosing information as to their holdings in their annual accounts.

Article 5(1)[143] of the Seventh Directive permits Member States to exempt financial holding companies from the requirement to prepared consolidated accounts provided that the following conditions are satisfied. The exemption must be granted by an administrative authority after it has checked that the second, third and fourth conditions have been fulfilled.[144]

First, the company must fall within the definition of 'financial holding company' in the Fourth Directive, set out above.

Second, it must not have intervened directly or indirectly in the management of any subsidiary undertaking during the financial year in question.[145]

Third, it must not have exercised any voting rights attaching to its shares to appoint any director[146] during that or the five preceding financial years; the six-year period reflects the maximum term of office for directors in most Member States. Where a financial holding company has had to use its voting rights for the operation of the board (for example, to ensure a quorum or where that company has all the voting rights), it may still fall within the exemption provided that neither its majority shareholder nor any of the directors of it or its majority shareholder is a director of the subsidiary undertaking concerned and that the directors so appointed have fulfilled their functions without any interference or influence on the part of the holding company or any of its subsidiary undertakings.

Fourth, the company must have made loans only to undertakings in which it holds participating interests; any loans to other parties must have been repaid by the end of the previous financial year.[147]

Article 5(2) disapplies the relaxation in Article 43(2) of the Fourth Directive, entitling financial holding companies to reduced disclosure concerning undertakings in which they have participating interests, in the case of exempted financial holding companies. However, such disclosures may be omitted when their nature is such that they would be seriously prejudicial to the company, its shareholders or any subsidiary, provided that the omission is disclosed in the notes to the accounts.[148] A Member State may make such omissions subject to prior authorization.

Miscellaneous exemptions

Articles 13 to 15 describe a number of further circumstances in which a subsidiary undertaking may, or sometimes must, be omitted from the consolidation. Where a

[143] Not implemented by the UK.
[144] Art 5(1)(d). This requirement was included largely in response to the collapse in 1982 of Banco Ambrosiano.
[145] Art 5(1)(a) of the 7th Directive.
[146] 'member of [the] administrative, management or supervisory bodies'.   [147] Art 5(1)(c).
[148] Art 5(2)(b).

subsidiary undertaking is exempted pursuant to Article 13 or 14, details of it must none the less be disclosed in the notes to the consolidated accounts, together with, in the case of Article 13 exemptions, an explanation for the exclusion.[149]

Undertaking not material—optional exemption[150]

An undertaking need not be included in consolidated accounts where it is not material for the purpose of the true and fair view of the group's assets, liabilities, financial position and profit or loss to be given by the consolidated accounts.[151] If two or more subsidiary undertakings are individually immaterial but taken together are material for that purpose, they must none the less be included in the consolidation.[152]

Severe long-term restrictions—optional exemption[153]

An undertaking need not be included in consolidated accounts where severe long-term restrictions substantially hinder either its parent from exercising its rights over the assets or management of the subsidiary or, in the case of a horizontal group, the exercise of unified management of the undertaking.[154] This may occur, for example, because the subsidiary is located in a country which restricts the remittance abroad of its profits or otherwise controls its activities.[155]

The Commission has expressed the view[156] that this exemption may be applicable to permit exclusion from consolidation where the subsidiary would otherwise require consolidation in accordance with Article 1(1)(a) because the parent holds a simple majority of all voting rights in a company but where the law or the company's constitution requires all or certain decisions to be taken only on the basis of a qualified majority or limits a shareholder's voting power to a given percentage of the total voting rights which is less than a simple majority. Whether the exemption will apply in such circumstances, however, will often be questionable: if, for example, a shareholder holds two-thirds of the voting rights and the constition requires a three-quarters majority for certain decisions but a two-thirds majority for altering that provision of the constitution, it is clear that there are no 'severe long-term restrictions'.

Necessary information unobtainable—optional exemption

An undertaking need not be included in consolidated accounts where the information necessary for the preparation of consolidated accounts cannot be obtained without disproportionate expense or undue delay.[157]

---

[149] Art 34(2)(b).   [150] Implemented in the UK by the Companies Act 1985, s 229(2).
[151] Arts 13(1) and 16(3).   [152] Art 13(2).
[153] Implemented in the UK by the Companies Act 1985, s 229(3)(a).   [154] Art 13(3)(a).
[155] See McKinnon, S M, in Newman, A D H (ed), *The Seventh Directive: Consolidated Accounts in the EEC* (1984), 52, for further examples.
[156] In its 1997 *Interpretative Communication Concerning Certain Articles of the Fourth and Seventh Council Directives on Accounting* (XV/7009/97–EN), paras 52 and 53.
[157] Art 13(3)(b); implemented in the UK by the Companies Act 1985, s 229(3)(b).

Shares held for resale—optional exemption

An undertaking need not be included in consolidated accounts where its shares are held exclusively with a view to their subsequent resale,[158] for example where a merchant bank acquires shares in a company in the course of arranging an offer of its shares to the public.

Subsidiaries with different activities—mandatory exemption

Where the activities of one or more subsidiary undertakings are so different that their inclusion in the consolidated accounts would be incompatible with the requirement[159] that those accounts give a true and fair view of the assets, liabilities, financial position and profit or loss of the group, they must be excluded from the consolidation.[160] This exemption is expressed not to be applicable merely because the undertakings concerned are partly industrial, partly commercial and partly provide services, or carry on industrial or commercial activities involving different products or provide different services.[161] The exemption would apply, for example, to a group which encompassed both industrial or commercial and banking or insurance activities or which included separate entities funding employee pensions or providing employee accommodation.

The Commission notes[162] that accounting practice in this context has developed since the Directive was adopted, so that subsidiaries tend to be included in the consolidated accounts regardless of the nature of their business compared with the parent's. It accordingly considers that Article 14 should be read in the light of this development, and that a subsidiary should be excluded from consolidation pursuant to that provision only in very rare circumstances where the application of the true and fair view principle so requires.

Where the Article 14 exemption is invoked, the accounts of the excluded undertaking must, if they are not published in the same Member State, be either attached to the consolidated accounts or made available to the public. Application of the exemption and the reasons therefor must be disclosed in the notes to the accounts.[163]

Non-trading parent—optional exemption

A further optional exemption is provided by Article 15.[164] This provision was included in order to cater specifically for the Royal Dutch–Shell group structure,

---

[158] Art 13(3)(c). The Companies Act 1985, s 229(3), implements this exemption, adding a requirement that the undertaking has not previously been included in consolidated group accounts prepared by the parent company.

[159] In Art 16(3).

[160] Art 14(1); implemented in the UK by s 229(4) of the Companies Act 1985. The provision is expressed to be without prejudice to Art 33, which requires certain associated undertakings to be accounted for on an equity basis: see pp 190–2 below.

[161] Art 14(2).   [162] In its *Interpretative Communication* (n 156 above) para 58.

[163] Art 14(3).   [164] Not implemented in the UK.

which involved two parallel companies together holding a number of operating subsidiaries in the ratio 60:40 per cent. Neither parent traded. Consolidated accounts were produced in respect of all the operating companies; without this exemption, the Dutch parent would have been included in the consolidation with the UK parent shown as an outside interest. This was felt to be unsatisfactory, since both parents acted in unison. Article 15(1) accordingly provides that Member States may, for the purposes of giving a true and fair view, permit the omission from consolidation of 'any parent undertaking not carrying on any industrial or commercial activity which holds shares in a subsidiary undertaking on the basis of a joint arrangement with one or more undertakings not included in the consolidated accounts'. The annual accounts of the parent must be attached to the consolidated accounts,[165] and must either account for its investment in subsidiaries by the equity method or disclose equivalent information in the notes.[166]

The Preparation of Consolidated Accounts

In contrast to the provisions concerning the scope of the requirement to consolidate, the more technical provisions of the Directive concerning the preparation of consolidation accounts were relatively uncontroversial, at least from the standpoint of the United Kingdom.[167] The only major problem was the treatment of goodwill arising on consolidation; the United Kingdom's difficulty with the initial proposal[168] that goodwill should be written off over a maximum period of five years was however resolved in the course of negotiating the Fourth Directive.[169]

Consolidated accounts, defined as comprising the consolidated balance sheet, the consolidated profit and loss account and the notes to the accounts,[170] are required to be drawn up clearly and in accordance with the Seventh Directive[171] and, more specifically, with the principles set out in Articles 25 to 28.[172] The Commission stated in the Explanatory Memorandum to the Proposal that the use of the adjective 'consolidated' made it clear that group accounts were required to incorporate in consolidated form the annual accounts of the undertakings belonging to the group: the Directive did not allow group accounts to be submitted in the form of a collection of the annual accounts of the undertakings concerned.[173] It may be noted that the Seventh Directive, like most of the company law and securities directives, lays down minimum standards: a Member State may require or permit the disclosure in consolidated accounts of information additional to that required to be disclosed by the Directive.[174]

---

[165] Art 15(2).   [166] Art 15(3).
[167] Those provisions are implemented in the UK by the Companies Act 1985, Schs 4 and 4A. UK implementation is considered further below only to the extent that it illustrates a point of interest.
[168] Art 16 of the original Proposal (1976).   [169] Adopted in 1978. See pp138–9 above.
[170] Art 16(1).   [171] Art 16(2).   [172] Art 24. The principles are considered below.
[173] Commentary on Art 9.   [174] Art 16(6).

General principles

True and fair view

Consolidated accounts must give a true and fair view of the assets, liabilities, financial position and profit or loss of the group.[175] As in the case of individual company accounts, where the application of the Directive would not be sufficient to give a true and fair view additional information must be given[176] and where, in exceptional cases which may be defined and provided for by special rules by the Member States, the application of one of its provisions is incompatible with the obligation to give a true and fair view that provision must be departed from and the departure disclosed in the notes to the accounts, together with an explanation of the reasons for it and a statement of its effect on the assets, liabilities, financial position and profit or loss.[177]

Consistency

The methods of consolidation must be applied consistently from one financial year to the next;[178] derogations are permitted only in exceptional cases and must be disclosed in the notes to the accounts with reasons and an assessment[179] of their effect on the assets, liabilities, financial position and profit or loss of the group.[180]

Layout

The provisions of the Fourth Directive on the layout of the balance sheet and profit and loss account[181] apply to consolidated accounts without prejudice to the provisions of the Seventh Directive and taking account of 'the essential adjustments resulting from the particular characteristics of consolidated accounts as compared with annual accounts.'[182] Those adjustments involve those items for which the Seventh Directive specifically provides to supplement those of the Fourth Directive and which follow naturally from the consolidation process.[183] They comprise (a) the positive or negative consolidation difference (namely goodwill arising on the acquisition of a subsidiary);[184] (b) the amount of capital and profit or loss attributable to minority shareholders;[185] and (c) where a participating interest[186] is accounted for using the equity method (i) the difference between its book value and the proportion of capital and reserves it represents[187] and (ii) the proportion or the profit or loss of the associated undertaking concerned.[188]

---

[175] Art 16(3). On the true and fair view, see further the discussion in ch V, pp 128–30.
[176] Art 16(4).   [177] Art 16(5).   [178] Art 25(1).
[179] The Commission stated in the Explanatory Memorandum to the Proposal: 'Precise figures are not required under this provision, for to do so would rob the exception of much of its sense. It is sufficient to give an indication of its overall effects.' (commentary on Art 14(2)(a)).
[180] Art 25(2).   [181] Arts 3–10, 13–26 and 28–30: see pp 131–2 above.   [182] Art 17(1).
[183] Commission's *Interpretative Communication* (n 156 above), para 59.
[184] Art 19(1)(c); see further pp 186–7 below.   [185] Arts 21 and 23; see p 183 below.
[186] See p 190 below.   [187] Art 33(2)(a)(b); see p 191 below.
[188] Art 33(6); see p 191 below.

Where however there are specific circumstances[189] which would entail undue expense, a Member State may permit stocks to be combined in the consolidated accounts[190] rather than, as would otherwise be required,[191] breaking stock down into raw materials and consumables, work in progress, finished goods and goods for resale and payments on account. Stocks may therefore be classified in accordance with the purpose most frequently used during the financial year.[192]

Financial year

Consolidated accounts must be drawn up as at the same date as the parent undertaking's annual accounts.[193] Subsidiary undertakings' accounts may however be drawn up on the basis of a different financial year: it may be group policy for subsidiaries, particularly those based abroad, to complete their own accounts in advance of the preparation of consolidated accounts. Where an undertaking's balance sheet date precedes the consolidated balance sheet date by more than three months, that undertaking must draw up interim accounts for the purpose of consolidation as at the consolidated balance sheet date.[194] The original Proposal required that such interim accounts be audited,[195] but that requirement was dropped on the basis that it would be unduly burdensome; the interim accounts would in any event have to be considered by the auditors of the consolidated accounts in forming their view on the consolidated accounts.

Member States may require or permit consolidated accounts to be drawn up as at a date different from that of the parent's annual accounts in order to take account of the balance sheet dates of the largest number or the most important of the consolidated undertakings, with disclosure of the derogation and the reasons therefor in the notes to the consolidated accounts. The consolidated accounts must also take account of or disclose important events which have occurred between the consolidated balance sheet date and that of a consolidated undertaking which concern the latter's assets and liabilities, financial position or results.[196]

Valuation

The Seventh Directive refers[197] to the relevant provisions of the Fourth Directive[198] for the principles and rules to be applied in the valuation of items shown in the consolidated accounts. It requires a parent drawing up consolidated accounts to apply the same methods of valuation as it applies in its annual accounts, unless Member States require or permit the use in consolidated accounts of other methods complying with the Fourth Directive.[199] In that case, the use of other methods and the reasons therefor must be given in the notes to the consolidated accounts.[200]

---

[189] For example, substantial intra-group trading.   [190] Art 17(2).
[191] By the sub-headings prescribed by the alternative balance sheet formats set out in Arts 9 and 10 of the 4th Directive.
[192] Commission's *Interpretative Communication* (see n 156 above), para 60.   [193] Art 27(1).
[194] Art 27(3).   [195] Art 14(1)(e).   [196] Art 27(2).   [197] Art 29(1).
[198] Arts 31–42 and 60: see pp 134–44 above.   [199] Art 29(2)(a).   [200] Art 29(2)(b).

Subsidiary undertakings are not required to use the same methods of valuation as those used by the parent in drawing up the consolidated accounts, but where the methods differ the assets and liabilities concerned must be revalued in accordance with the methods used for the consolidation unless the results of such revaluation are not material for the purposes of giving a true and fair view. Departures from this principle are permitted in exceptional cases, subject to disclosure of the departure and the reasons therefor in the notes to the accounts.[201]

Tax

The Directive requires the consolidated accounts to take account of any difference arising on consolidation between the tax chargeable for the current and preceding financial years and the amount of tax paid or payable in respect of those years where it is probable that an actual charge to tax will arise within the foreseeable future for a consolidated undertaking.[202] Exceptional value adjustments (for example write-downs and revaluations) made solely for tax purposes must also be eliminated from the consolidated balance sheet except where Member States require or permit no elimination in such circumstances, in which case the amounts of the adjustments and the reasons for them must be disclosed in the notes to the accounts.[203]

Consolidation techniques

Elimination of intra-group transactions

Consolidated accounts are required to show the assets, liabilities, financial positions and profits or losses of the group as if the consolidated undertakings were a single undertaking.[204] Thus the assets and liabilities of those undertakings are required to be incorporated in full in the consolidated balance sheet[205] and their income and expenditure incorporated in full in the consolidated profit and loss account.[206] That principle however is subject to the elimination of intra–group transactions, namely debts and claims between the consolidated undertakings,[207] income and expenditure relating to transactions between the consolidated undertakings,[208] and profits and losses resulting from transactions between the consolidated undertakings where they are included in the book values of assets.[209]

Derogations from any of the above three requirements are required to be permitted where the amounts concerned are not material for the purpose of the true and fair view.[210] In addition, there are two further possible derogations in the case

---

[201] Art 29(3).
[202] Art 29(4). The Explanatory Memorandum on the Proposal gives as an example of deferred tax the case 'in which the undistributed profits of a [subsidiary] undertaking established outside the Community have been taxed on a scale much lower than that applicable to the [parent] undertaking . . . Insofar as these profits will be distributed to the latter undertaking, account should be taken in advance in the group accounts of the effects of the distribution on the amount of tax to be paid.' (commentary on Art 15(d)).
[203] Art 29(5).   [204] Art 26(1).   [205] Art 18.   [206] Art 22.   [207] Art 26(1)(a).
[208] Art 26(1)(b).   [209] Art 26(1)(c).   [210] Art 26(3).

of intra-group profits and losses. First, Member States may, pending subsequent coordination, allow elimination in proportion to the parent undertaking's interest in each of the subsidiary undertakings included in the consolidation.[211] Thus intra-group profits and losses attributable to minority shareholders need not be eliminated. Second, a Member State may permit derogations for transactions concluded according to normal market conditions where the elimination would entail undue expense; the derogation must be disclosed and, where the effect on the assets, liabilities, financial position and profit or loss of the group is material, that fact must be disclosed in the notes to the accounts.[212]

Minority interests

In the case of wholly-owned subsidiary undertakings, the requirement[213] to incorporate in full their assets, liabilities, income and expenditure clearly makes economic sense. In the case of subsidiary undertakings owned as to less than 100 per cent, that requirement still applies: proportional consolidation is not permitted by the Directive. The economic picture is instead adjusted by the minority interests being shown separately in the accounts. The Directive requires the amount attributable to shares in consolidated subsidiary undertakings held by persons other than the consolidated undertakings to be shown in the consolidated balance sheet as a separate item with an appropriate heading[214] and the amount of any profit or loss attributable to such shares to be similarly shown in the consolidated profit and loss account.[215]

Changes in composition of group

Before implementation of the Directive, acquisitions and disposals in the course of a financial year were dealt with in two different ways by Member States. Some States, including the United Kingdom, included a subsidiary's results only since acquisition or up to disposal; others, including Germany, restated comparative figures. The Directive provides in effect for both methods. Where the composition of the group has changed significantly in the course of a financial year, the consolidated accounts must contain information making the comparison between successive sets of consolidated accounts meaningful. Where however the change is major, Member States may require or permit that obligation to be fulfilled by the preparation of an adjusted opening balance sheet and an adjusted profit and loss account.[216]

Goodwill arising on consolidation

When one undertaking acquires another, the price paid may, if the acquired undertaking is thriving, exceed the value of its net assets at the time of the acquisition. The difference is generally known as goodwill. If the acquired undertaking is not thriving and the purchase price is less than the value of its net assets, the difference

---

[211] Art 26(1)(c); implemented in the UK by the Companies Act 1985, para 6(3) of Sch 4A.
[212] Art 26(2).   [213] In Arts 18 and 22.   [214] Art 21.   [215] Art 23.   [216] Art 28.

is generally known as negative goodwill.[217] The Directive refers to these amounts as positive or negative consolidation differences. The accounting treatment of goodwill arising on acquisitions has been the subject of much debate.

Goodwill in the more general sense is required by the Fourth Directive to be shown as an asset on the balance sheet and written off within a maximum period of five years, although Member States may permit a longer period not exceeding its useful economic life.[218] Goodwill arising on consolidation is similarly required to be shown as an asset on the consolidated balance sheet[219] and, in general, dealt with in accordance with the Fourth Directive.[220] Member States may however permit goodwill arising on consolidation to be deducted 'immediately and clearly' from reserves.[221]

A negative consolidation difference may be transferred to the consolidated profit and loss account only in two circumstances, which reflect the underlying assumption that negative goodwill on consolidation will arise either because unfavourable results or costs are anticipated or from a bargain purchase. The circumstances are (a) where the difference corresponds to the expectation at the date of acquisition of unfavourable future results in the undertaking acquired, or to the expectation of costs which the undertaking acquired would incur, in so far as such an expectation materializes, and (b) in so far as the difference corresponds to a realized gain[222] (namely when, a subsidiary having been acquired for less than its fair value, the subsidiary or the related fixed assets are sold or depreciated).

Acquisition accounting

The acquisition method of accounting is the principal method prescribed by the Directive for calculating the amount to be shown in the accounts as goodwill arising on consolidation (positive or negative consolidation differences). In essence, goodwill is the difference between the fair value of the purchase consideration and the fair value of all the subsidiary's identifiable net assets (tangible and intangible). The Directive reaches the same result via a different route, in effect using the book value of the subsidiary's net assets as a starting point. In practice, the amount by which the purchase price for a company exceeds the book value of its net assets may in part reflect the fact that those assets have not been recently revalued, so that the book values are less than the current market value used to negotiate the purchase price. Thus not all of that excess will correspond to goodwill. In order to identify the amount of the excess which may properly be regarded as the excess of the purchase price over the fair value of the net assets, those parts of the excess

---

[217] For a discussion of the concept of negative goodwill and related issues, see McKinnon, S M, in Newman, A D H (ed), *The Seventh Directive: Consolidated Accounts in the EEC* (1984) 72.

[218] Art 37(2) of the 4th Directive; see pp 138–9 above.   [219] Art 19(1)(c).

[220] Art 30(1) of the 7th Directive. Art 39(3) gives Member States the option of slightly more favourable accounting treatment of goodwill on consolidation which arose before the date of the first consolidated accounts drawn up in accordance with the Directive. For the treatment of goodwill in accordance with the 4th Directive and in the UK, see ch V, pp 138–9.

[221] Art 30(2).   [222] Art 31.

which are due merely to overdue revaluation must be subtracted.[223] This is what the Directive requires, with the further difference that the Directive expresses the preliminary equation not in terms of the purchase consideration and the net assets but in terms of the book value of the shares in the subsidiary acquired by the parent and the book value of its capital and reserves. Since however the book value of the shares in the subsidiary will be the same as the purchase consideration and the total of a company's capital and reserves will be the same as the total of its net assets, this comes to the same thing.

Article 19 thus requires the book values of shares in the capital of consolidated undertakings to be set off against the proportion which they represent of the capital and reserves of those undertakings. The primary rule is that the set-off is to be effected on the basis of book values as at the date at which the undertakings are included in the consolidation for the first time.[224] As indicated, since book values are used in this calculation the resulting differences are not automatically regarded as goodwill on consolidation since they are, so far as possible, to be entered directly against those items in the consolidated balance sheet with values above or below their values.[225] The remaining difference is regarded as goodwill arising on consolidation.

The reference to the date at which the undertakings are included in the consolidation for the first time suggests the first balance sheet date at which the newly acquired subsidiary is consolidated. That seems contrary to the underlying rationale of acquisition accounting, which seeks to show the cost to the group of the net assets acquired and any premium or discount, which will not necessarily be reflected in their book value as at the first balance sheet date after acquisition. Article 19(1)(b) however authorizes Member States to require or permit a slightly different method of calculating the goodwill arising on consolidation, namely on the basis of the values of identifiable assets and liabilities as at the date of acquisition of the shares or, in the event of acquisition in two or more stages (a situation apparently not envisaged in Article 19(1)(a)), as at the date on which the undertaking became a subsidiary. It will be observed that Article 19(1)(b) refers to values, rather than book values. The option in Article 19(1)(b) was included for the benefit of the United Kingdom, so as to permit the continuation of existing accountancy practice.

Whichever method of calculating the difference is used, the Directive requires the resultant difference to be shown as a separate item in the consolidated balance sheet with an appropriate heading and an explanation in the notes to the accounts of the difference, the methods used and any significant changes in relation to the preceding financial year.[226] Member States may permit positive and negative

---

[223] This very simplistic discussion is based on the assumption that (a) the purchase price exceeds the fair value of the assets and (b) the fair value of the assets exceeds the book value of the assets. In the rather less likely event of the fair value of the assets being either more than the purchase price or less than the book value of the assets, there will be negative rather than positive goodwill, discussed further below.

[224] Art 19(1)(a).   [225] Art 19(1)(a).   [226] Art 19(1)(c).

goodwill arising on the consolidation of different subsidiaries to be offset, provided that a breakdown of the differences is given in the notes to the accounts.[227]

The requirements of acquisition accounting do not apply to shares in the parent which are held either by the parent itself or by another consolidated undertaking: such shares are to be treated in the consolidated accounts as own shares in accordance with the Fourth Directive.[228]

There is a specific transitional provision for acquisition accounting when a group first prepares consolidated accounts in accordance with the Directive: Member States may permit or require the use, for the purposes of determining the book value of a holding and the proportion of capital and reserves which it represents, of a date preceding or coinciding with that first consolidation.[229]

Merger accounting

Merger accounting[230] is an alternative method of accounting for acquisitions which avoids accounting both for any premium[231] on shares issued by the parent and for goodwill on consolidation. Merger accounting, little known on the continent before its introduction as an option in the Seventh Directive, was popular in the United Kingdom (although not always regarded as lawful[232]) for both those reasons: the pre-acquisition profits of the subsidiary remained distributable and there was no goodwill requiring amortization and consequent reduction of profits. Where an acquisition is accounted for in accordance with merger accounting, the book value of the parent's investment in the subsidiary (namely, the nominal value of the shares issued in consideration of the shares acquired) is set off against the nominal value of the shares acquired, and any difference is added to or deducted from the consolidated reserves.

At the request of the United Kingdom, this method was at a relatively late stage included in the Directive as an option.[233] Member States may require or permit the book value of shares in a subsidiary undertaking to be set off in the consolidated accounts against the corresponding percentage of capital only (as opposed to capital and reserves) in the following strictly defined circumstances:[234]

(1)   The parent must hold at least 90 per cent of the nominal value (or, if they have no nominal value, the accounting par value) of the shares, other than shares which carry a limited right to participate in distributions and/or in the subsidiary's assets on liquidation.[235]

---

[227] Art 19(1)(c).
[228] Art 19(2).
[229] Art 39(1).
[230] In the US, pooling of interests. For a full discussion of merger accounting, see McKinnon, S M, in Newman, A D H (ed), *The Seventh Directive: Consolidated Accounts in the EEC* (1984) 78–82.
[231] By way of the (undistributable) share premium account.
[232] Although ruled in effect unlawful in 1952, it continued to be practised until a more explicit ruling in 1980. It was then legalized, subject to certain conditions, in the 1981 Companies Act (the relevant provision is now the Companies Act 1985, s 131).
[233] Implemented in the UK by the Companies Act 1985, paras 10 and 11 of Sch 4A.
[234] Art 20(1).   [235] Art 20(1)(a).

(2)   That shareholding must have been obtained pursuant to an arrangement providing for the issue of shares by the parent.[236]

(3)   Any cash payment involved must not have exceeded 10 per cent of the nominal value (or accounting par value) of the shares issued.[237]

Any difference resulting must be added to or deducted from the consolidated reserves.[238] The application of merger accounting must be disclosed in the notes to the accounts together with the resulting movement in reserves and the names and registered offices of the undertakings concerned.[239]

Equity accounting

The Directive lays down rules for the accounting treatment in consolidated accounts of certain holdings in associated undertakings. An associated undertaking is an undertaking which is not itself consolidated but over whose operating and financial policy a consolidated undertaking exercises a significant influence. Where a consolidated undertaking holds a 'participating interest' in an associated undertaking, that interest must in general be accounted for using what is known as the equity method,[240] under which the investing company's balance sheet shows its investments in such interests at cost plus a share of undistributed profits (or less a share of losses) and the profit and loss account shows a share of the associated undertaking's earnings.

'Participating interest' is defined as:

rights in the capital of other undertakings, whether or not represented by certificates, which, by creating a durable link with those undertakings, are intended to contribute to the company's activities. The holding of part of the capital of another company shall be presumed to constitute a participating interest where it exceeds a percentage fixed by the Member States which may not exceed 20%.[241]

An undertaking shall be presumed to exercise a significant influence over another undertaking where it has 20 per cent or more of the shareholders' or members' voting rights[242] in that undertaking. 'Significant interest' is not otherwise defined: it was stated in the Explanatory Memorandum to the Proposal that the 'criterion used to define an associated undertaking is of necessity somewhat vague. The introduction of strict and precise criteria would make it impossible to cover the many forms and means existing in economic practice for exercising a significant influence on the running of an undertaking.'

---

[236] Art 20(1)(b).   [237] Art 20(1)(c).   [238] Art 20(2).   [239] Art 20(3).

[240] Unless the participating interest is not material for the purposes of a true and fair view (Art 33(9)) or is accounted for as a joint venture pursuant to Art 32 (Art 32(3)).

[241] Art 17 of the 4th Directive, incorporated by reference by Art 33(1) of the 7th Directive; implemented in the UK by the Companies Act 1985, s 260.

[242] Art 33(1) applies Art 2 which lays down rules for the calculation of the percentage, so as to exclude certain voting rights and include others. These are discussed above, pp 164–5.

The Directive requires participating interests to be shown in the consolidated balance sheet as a separate item with an appropriate heading.[243] There are detailed rules for establishing the initial valuation of the associated undertaking. When such an investment is first accounted for in the consolidated accounts, it must be included in the consolidated balance sheet either[244] at book value calculated in accordance with the Fourth Directive[245] (namely at cost or valuation) or at the amount corresponding to the proportion of the capital and reserves represented by it (the equity method).[246] In either case, the difference between these two values, calculated as at the date as at which the method is applied for the first time, is to be disclosed separately in the consolidated balance sheet or in the notes to the accounts. It will be apparent that, whichever method of initial accounting is used, the difference will be attributable to the fact that the book value of the associated undertaking's assets is less than their fair value and/or to goodwill. Unsurprisingly therefore a positive difference, in so far as it cannot be related to any category of asset or liability, is to be dealt with in accordance with the rules applicable to goodwill.[247]

Further provisions govern the process of calculation summarized above. Where the assets or liabilities of the associated undertaking have been valued by methods other than those used for consolidation, they may (or at Member States' option must) for the purpose of this calculation be revalued by the latter methods; if not so revalued, this must be disclosed in the notes to the accounts.[248] Member States may require or permit calculation of the difference as at the date of acquisition of the shares or, where the acquisition took place in several stages, as at the date at which the undertaking became an associated undertaking.[249] Where the associated undertaking itself draws up consolidated accounts, the calculation must be based on the capital and reserves shown in such accounts.[250]

In subsequent years, the value or amount stated as above must be adjusted to reflect variations over the financial year in the proportion of capital and reserves represented by the interest and reduced by the amount of the dividends relating to the interest.[251] The equity method must therefore be used to account for a participating interest in associated undertakings after its first inclusion in the consolidated accounts.

The Directive requires the proportion of the profit or loss attributable to participating interests to be shown separately in the consolidated profit and loss account.[252] The adjustments made for consolidation purposes to eliminate profits and losses resulting from intra-group transactions and included in the book value of assets[253] must also be made in so far as the facts are known or can be ascertained.[254]

[243] Art 33(1).

[244] A Member State may prescribe the application of one or other of these methods; the balance sheet or the notes to the accounts must indicate which has been used: Art 33(2)(c).

[245] Art 33(2)(a).   [246] Art 33(2)(c).   [247] Art 33(5).   [248] Art 33(3).

[249] Art 33(2)(d).   [250] Art 33(8).   [251] Art 33(4).   [252] Art 33(6).

[253] Pursuant to Art 26(1)(c). The derogations permitted by Art 26(2)(3) apply. See pp 185–6 above.

[254] Art 33(7).

There is a specific transitional provision for equity accounting when a group first prepares consolidated accounts in accordance with the Directive: Member States may permit or require the use, for the purposes of determining the book value of a holding and the proportion of capital and reserves which it represents, of a date preceding or coinciding with that first consolidation.[255]

Joint ventures

Member States may permit or require proportional consolidation of joint ventures, namely undertakings managed jointly by a consolidated undertaking and one or more other undertakings not included in the consolidation.[256] The jointly managed undertaking would thus be included in the consolidated accounts in proportion to the rights in its capital held by the consolidated undertaking subject to the exemptions in Articles 13 to 15.[257] The provisions of the Directive as to the preparation of consolidated accounts will apply *mutatis mutandis*,[258] as does the specific transitional provision available for acquisition and equity accounting.[259] Where an associated undertaking in which a consolidated undertaking has a participating interest is also a joint venture and is accounted for by proportional consolidation, the requirement in Article 33 to account for by the equity method does not apply.[260]

The Notes to the Accounts

Contents

Article 34(1) lists certain minimum information which must be disclosed in the notes to the consolidated accounts in addition to the extensive information required under other provisions of the Directive,[261] principally disclosure of departure from prescribed practice and use of concessions, most of which has been referred to above and is summarized below:[262]

(1)   any exclusion of an undertaking from the consolidated accounts pursuant to Article 14 (different activities making inclusion incompatible with true and fair view), with reasons (Article 14(3));

---

[255] Art 39(2).
[256] Art 32(1). The UK permits proportional consolidation of joint ventures: the Companies Act 1985, para 19 of Sch 4A.
[257] Applied by Art 32(2). See pp 179–82 above for those exemptions.
[258] Arts 16–32, discussed above; applied by Art 32(2).   [259] Art 39(1)(2): see above.
[260] Art 32(3).
[261] And by the 4th Directive, where provisions of the 4th Directive are applied to consolidated accounts, namely Arts 3–10, 13–26, 28–42 and 60. See ch V, pp 144–6, for a list of disclosures required by the 4th Directive.
[262] See also Art 9(2), p 175 above.

(2) any departure from the Directive in order to give a true and fair view (Article 16(5));

(3) goodwill arising on consolidation, the method of calculating it and significant changes in relation to the preceding financial year together with a breakdown of any positive or negative goodwill offset (Article 19(1)(c));

(4) the use of merger accounting, the resulting movement in reserves and details of the undertakings concerned (Article 20(3));

(5) any departure from the principle of consistency with the reasons and an assessment of the effect (Article 25(2));

(6) any departure from the requirement to eliminate intra-group profits and losses and, if material, its effect on the consolidated accounts (Article 26(2));

(7) the use of different dates for the consolidated accounts and the parent's accounts with the reasons (Article 27(2));

(8) the use of different valuation methods for the consolidated accounts and the parent's accounts with the reasons (Article 29(2)(b)) and any departure from the requirement to revalue where different valuation methods have been used by consolidated undertakings, with the reasons (Article 29(3));

(9) the amount of exceptional value adjustments which have not been eliminated, with the reasons (Article 29(5));

(10) the method used for valuing participating interests in associated undertakings and the amount of goodwill arising, if not disclosed in the consolidated balance sheet (Article 33(2)(a)(b)(c));

(11) any decision not to revalue an associated undertaking's assets and liabilities which have been valued by methods other than those used in the consolidated accounts (Article 33(3));

(12) where the consolidated accounts are published in ECUs, the exchange rate prevailing at the balance sheet date (Article 38a).

The additional matters required to be disclosed by Article 34 comprise specified information relating to the following:

(1) the methods used for valuation and for calculating value adjustments (Article 34(1));

(2) undertakings included in the consolidation, the structure of group holdings and the basis on which the undertakings are consolidated[263] (Article 34(2)(a));

(3) undertakings excluded from the consolidation pursuant to Articles 13 and 14[264] (Article 34(2)(b));

(4) associated undertakings (Article 34(3)(a)), including those not accounted for on the equity basis pursuant to Article 33(9)[265] with reasons (Article 34(3)(b));

(5) undertakings proportionately consolidated pursuant to Article 32[266] (Article 34(4));

---

[263] Unless that is Art 1(1)(a) (see pp 163–5 above) and the proportion of capital and voting rights held are the same.
[264] See pp 180–1 above.   [265] See pp 190–2. above.   [266] See p192.

(6)   other undertakings in which undertakings included in the consolidation or excluded pursuant to Article 14 directly or indirectly hold at least a percentage of the capital which the Member States cannot fix at more than 20 per cent (Article 34(5));

(7)   long-term (due and payable after more than five years) or secured debts (Article 34(6));

(8)   off balance sheet financial commitments, with separate disclosure of commitments relating to pensions and affiliated undertakings not included in the consolidation (Article 34(7));

(9)   consolidated net turnover broken down by categories of activity and into geographical markets in so far as the categories and markets differ substantially from one another (Article 34(8));

(10)   employees, with staff costs if these are not disclosed in the profit and loss account (Article 34(9)(a)), including details of employees of proportionally consolidated joint ventures (Article 34(9)(b));

(11)   effect of valuations made with a view to obtaining tax relief[267] (Article 34(10));

(12)   taxation (Article 34(11));

(13)   emoluments and pensions of the parent undertaking's directors and former directors and, at Member States' option, emoluments of directors of joint ventures or associated undertakings in which a consolidated undertaking has a participating interest (Article 34(12));

(14)   loans etc to the parent undertaking's directors and, at Member States' option, to directors of joint ventures or associated undertakings in which a consolidated undertaking has a participating interest (Article 34(13)).

Member States may allow the disclosures required by Article 34(2)(3)(4)(5) to take the form of a statement deposited in the company's file set up in a central register, commercial register or companies register;[268] they may also allow omission of such disclosures,[269] or the prescribed disclosures as to turnover,[270] where their nature is such as to be seriously prejudicial to any of the undertakings concerned.

In addition, the Fourth Directive requires disclosure in the notes to the consolidated accounts where a Member State has opted to exempt (a) subsidiary undertakings included in the consolidated accounts of an EC parent undertaking from the requirements of the Fourth Directive concerning the content, auditing and

---

[267] This is designed to limit the impairment of the true and fair view in cases where, in certain Member States in which tax laws require that items be presented in the accounts in accordance with their treatment for tax purposes, fixed assets are depreciated at accelerated rates over less than their estimated useful lives, leading to a misstatement of profitability and assets.

[268] In accordance with Art 3 of the First Directive: see pp 19–20 above. Use by the company of this option must itself be disclosed in the notes to the accounts: Art 35(1)(a).

[269] Art 45(1)(b). The Member States may make such omissions subject to prior administrative or judicial authorization; the fact of omission must itself by disclosed in the notes to the accounts.

[270] Art 45(2).

publication of annual accounts under Article 57 of the Fourth Directive[271] and (b) parent undertakings from auditing and publishing the profit and loss account under Article 58 of the Fourth Directive.[272]

The Consolidated Annual Report

Article 36 requires the consolidated annual report to include 'at least a fair review of the development of business and the position' of the group[273] and to give an indication of (a) any important events that have occurred since the end of the financial year; (b) the likely future development of the group; (c) the activities of the group in the field of research and development; and (d) the number and nominal value[274] of shares in the parent undertaking held by or on behalf of itself or its subsidiary undertakings.[275] Unlike the notes to the accounts, the annual report does not form part of the consolidated accounts as defined in Article 16(1); it thus does not require auditing and as will be seen it is subject to less stringent publication requirements.

Auditing

Article 37 requires an undertaking which draws up consolidated accounts to have the accounts audited by one or more persons authorized by national law to audit accounts.[276] The auditors must also verify that the consolidated annual report is consistent with the consolidated accounts.[277]

---

[271] As substituted by Art 43 of the 7th Directive. Art 57 requires in addition that (a) all shareholders or members have declared their agreement to the exemption in respect of the financial year concerned; (b) the parent undertaking has declared that it guarantees the subsidiary undertaking's commitments; and (c) the subsidiary undertaking publishes the declarations referred to in (a) and (b) above, the consolidated accounts, consolidated annual report and auditors' report.

[272] As substituted by Art 44 of the 7th Directive. The other requirements are that (a) the parent undertaking draws up consolidated accounts in accordance with the 7th Directive; (b) the exemption is disclosed in the notes to the parent undertaking's annual accounts and (c) the profit or loss of the parent company is shown in its balance sheet.

[273] Art 36(1).   [274] Or, if none, accounting par value.

[275] Art 36(2)(d). A Member State may require or permit the disclosure of these particulars in the notes to the accounts.

[276] Art 37(1). The 8th Directive seeks to harmonize the qualifications required of auditors: see below, ch X.

[277] Art 37(2). The annual report will necessarily contain statements of opinion by the managers of the parent undertaking on present and future developments, and the auditor obviously cannot in his certificate give any guarantee as to the outcome of such forecasts; hence the more limited duty as regards this document: see the Explanatory Memorandum in the amended Proposal for the 4th Directive.

Publication of Consolidated Accounts

Section 5 of the Directive provides for publication of consolidated accounts. The primary requirement is that the 'consolidated accounts, duly approved,[278] and the consolidated annual report, together with the opinion submitted by the person responsible for auditing the accounts' be published in accordance with the First Directive.[279] It must also be possible to obtain a copy of all or part of the accounts and report upon request, at a price not exceeding its administrative cost.[280]

Where the undertaking which drew up the consolidated accounts is not a limited company and is not required by national law to publish consolidated accounts as required by the First Directive, it must at least make them available to the public at its head office and provide copies on request at a charge not exceeding the administrative cost of the copy.[281]

Whenever the accounts and annual report are published in full, the form and text published must be those which were audited and be accompanied by the full text of the audit report and include disclosure and reasons for any qualification or refusal to report on the accounts made by the auditor.[282] If the accounts are not published in full—for example if extracts are published for publicity purposes—their incomplete character must be disclosed, together with (a) the register in which the accounts have been filed or, if relevant, the fact that such filing has not yet been effected and (b) whether the auditors' report was issued with or without qualification or was refused; the auditors' report itself may not be published with incomplete accounts.[283]

Member States must provide for appropriate sanctions for failure to comply with the above publication requirements.[284]

The consolidated accounts may be published in the currency in which they were drawn up and in ECUs, translated at the exchange rate prevailing on the consolidated balance sheet date and disclosed in the notes to the accounts.[285] It is anticipated that consolidated accounts may be published using the Euro unit instead of the ECU in addition to their national currency unit as from 1 January 1999.[286]

---

[278] By the competent organs of the company. The Directive does not legislate for approval, the procedure for which will therefore be a matter for each Member State's domestic law.

[279] Art 38(1). The relevant provision of the First Directive (Art 3) requires filing in the company's file in a central register, commercial register or companies register: see above, pp 19–20.

[280] Art 3(3) of the First Directive and Art 38(2) of the 7th Directive.   [281] Art 38(4).

[282] Art 48 of the 4th Directive, applied by Art 38(5) of the 7th Directive.

[283] Art 49 of the 4th Directive, applied by Art 38(5) of the 7th Directive.

[284] Art 38(6). See the discussion on pp 26–8 above on the question of appropriate sanctions.

[285] Art 38a, inserted by Art 9 of Council Directive (EEC) 90/604 of 8 November 1990 amending Directive (EEC) 78/660 on annual accounts and Directive (EEC) 83/349 on consolidated accounts as concerns the exemptions for small and medium-sized companies and the publication of accounts in ECUs [1990] OJ L317/57. Member States may provide that this provision shall first apply to the consolidated accounts for financial years beginning on 1 January 1995 or during the 1995 calendar year (Art 3(2) of Directive (EEC) 90/604).

[286] See *Accounting for the Introduction of the Euro*, guidelines published by the Commission (1997). The guidelines, which are not legally binding, consider that there is no need to amend Art 38a.

Contact Committee

Article 47 provides that the Contact Committee set up under the Fourth Directive[287] shall also facilitate harmonized application of the Seventh Directive 'through regular meetings dealing, in particular, with practical problems arising in connection with its application'[288] and to advise the Commission if necessary on additions or amendments to the Directive.[289]

In 1995, the Commission finally resolved a long-standing area of speculation by publicly disowning any intentions of setting up its own accounting standards board: instead, the Commission announced plans[290] to examine the possibility for EC companies with an international vocation to prepare their consolidated accounts on the basis of international accounting standards set by the International Accounting Standards Committee.[291] The new approach was prompted by the perceived need to help major EC companies gain access to capital on world markets; the principal objective was to ensure that accounts prepared in accordance with the Community requirements also satisfied international requirements, so that companies operating internationally could rely on one set of accounts for their listings worldwide. Since the International Accounting Standards Committee was seeking jointly with the International Organisation of Securities Commissions to agree a core set of international standards which would be accepted by Stock Exchanges across the world,[292] it was an ideal opportunity for the Community legislation to be scrutinized for the same purpose.

In December 1996, the Commission published the results of an analysis by the Contact Committee of the compatibility between the international standards issued up to the end of 1995 and the requirements of, inter alia, the Fourth and Seventh Directives.[293] The work focused on consolidated accounts because they are the accounts requested by capital markets worldwide. The Contact Committee concluded that, with minor exceptions, the international and Community requirements did not conflict. The document, although important in the context of the new approach, is only a first step: as the Contact Committee points out, EC companies are not in fact subject directly to the Fourth and Seventh Directives but to the national implementing legislation and national accounting standards. National authorities were accordingly invited to reflect on the contents of the document and possibly carry out a similar exercise relating to the national rules.

---

[287] See p 155 above.   [288] Art 47(a).   [289] Art 47(b).

[290] *Accounting Harmonisation: A New Strategy* vis-à-vis *International Harmonisation* COM (95) 508 final, 14 November 1995.

[291] A private organization representing the accounting profession. The IASC has developed a number of international standards; although not mandatory, some countries have adopted as national standards all the international standards issued, and some multinational companies prepare their accounts in accordance with international standards.

[292] Scheduled to be presented to IOSCO for endorsement in the course of 1998.

[293] *An Examination of the Conformity between the International Accounting Standards and the European Accounting Directives* (European Commission).

More recently still, discussions in the Contact Committee prompted the Commission to issue in 1997 an Interpretative Communication on the Fourth and Seventh Directives[294] commenting on topics where authoritative[295] clarification appeared to be required. It may be noted that in this document[296] the Commission confirmed that an undertaking required to prepare its consolidated accounts in conformity with the Seventh Directive which wishes simultaneously to satisfy international or United States requirements may do so only to the extent that the consolidated accounts remain in conformity with the Seventh Directive. In particular, no adjustments to the layouts of the accounts prescribed in the Fourth Directive may be made other than those allowed by Article 4 of the Fourth Directive[297] and no valuation methods may be used which are in conflict with the Fourth Directive.

---

[294] *Interpretative Communication Concerning Certain Articles of the Fourth and Seventh Council Directives on Accounting* (XV/7009/97–EN). For a commentary see Van Hulle, K's article of the same title (1998), 9 European Business Law Review 114.

[295] The Commission's terminology. The interpretation suggested in the Communication will not, of course, prejudge the interpretation which the Court of Justice may be called upon to give.

[296] Para 61.   [297] See pp131–2 above.

VII

The Eighth Directive

Introduction and Aims

The Eighth Directive on the approval of auditors[1] is an essential complement to the Fourth and Seventh Directives on company accounts,[2] which impose an audit requirement for both annual and consolidated accounts:[3] the imposition of a Community-wide standard for the preparation and certification of company accounts would in practice have limited effect if those required to audit the accounts themselves had divergent qualifications and were not subject to equivalent requirements of independence and integrity. The Eighth Directive seeks to ensure that auditors in all Member States have equivalent minimum qualifications. It does not seek to go beyond the harmonization of minimum qualifications: in particular, it does not aim to realize the mutual recognition of degrees or other qualifications,[4] to achieve freedom of establishment or freedom to provide services in favour of persons qualified as auditors[5] or to deal with the issue of auditors' liability.[6] Instead, it establishes a requirement of approval by national authorities, to be granted only subject to the fulfilment of specified conditions relating to legal status and structure, reputation, qualifications, professional integrity and

---

[1] 8th Council Directive (EEC) 84/253 of 10 April 1984 based on Art 54(3)(g) of the Treaty on the approval of persons responsible for carrying out the statutory audits of accounting documents [1984] OJ L126/20. There is little literature: see however Wooldridge, F, *Company Law in the United Kingdom and European Community* (1991); Barker, P, 'The Seventh and Eighth Directives on Company Law' (1984) 7 Journal of the Irish Society for European Law, 65 and Feuillet, P, 'La huitième directive du Conseil des Communautés européennes et le commissariat aux comptes' (1984) 102 Revue des sociétés 26.

[2] And was also intended to complement the draft 5th Directive and the European Company Statute, which both provided for the audit of accounts.

[3] Art 51 of the 4th Directive and Art 37 of the 7th Directive.

[4] See now however Council Directive (EEC) 89/48 of 21 December 1988 on a general system for the recognition of higher degrees and diplomas [1989] OJ L19/6. The Commission has recently flagged the possibility of a sectoral directive in the field of professional qualifications with a view to helping to overcome some of the current obstacles to the freedom of establishment for accountants and auditors: *Communication from the Commission on the Statutory Audit in the European Union: The Way Forward* [1998] OJ C143/12.

[5] See for a discussion of this more general context Olivier, H, 'Perspectives du contrôle légal des comptes dans la Communauté Européenne' (1989) 66 Revue de droit international et de droit comparé 209 and Case C–106/91 *Ramrath v Ministre de la Justice* [1992] ECR I–3351.

[6] See however the Commission's Green Paper *The Role, the Position and the Liability of the Statutory Auditor within the European Union* [1996] OJ C321/1, and its *Communication on the Statutory Audit* (n 4 above) discussed further in ch XX. See also Andenas, M, 'Disciplining Auditors—Problems of Parallel Disciplinary and Civil Proceedings' (1998) 9 European Business Law Review 12.

independence, coupled with a requirement that basic information about those so approved be available to the public.

As the Commission pointed out in the Explanatory Memorandum on its Proposal,[7] the approval required by the Directive is limited to those responsible for carrying out a specific task, namely the statutory audit of accounts, rather than those exercising a specific profession: in certain Member States, more than one profession is authorized to carry out the statutory audit, and the Commission saw no need to change that state of affairs.

The Eighth Directive dates back to a Commission working paper prepared in 1972. The original Proposal was submitted by the Commission to the Council in April 1978. The Economic and Social Committee delivered its Opinion in April 1979[8] and the European Parliament in May 1979.[9] In December 1979 the Commission submitted an amended Proposal[10] but the Directive was not finally adopted until April 1984, the delay being attributable to strong differences of views between the various delegations as to, in particular, the independence of auditors.

Scope

Article 1 provides that the measures prescribed in the Directive shall apply to the laws, regulations and administrative provisions of the Member States concerning persons responsible for carrying out the statutory audits of the annual accounts of companies and firms or the consolidated accounts of bodies of undertakings[11] and verifying that the annual reports are consistent with those accounts in so far as such audits and such verification are required by Community law.[12]

The original Proposal had, rather than describing the type of undertaking, listed the types of company specified in the Fourth Directive. As pointed out by the Economic and Social Committee however that approach had the disadvantage that, if the Community adopted further directives prescribing audits for the accounts of other types of company, it would be necessary to make special arrangements for the authorization of persons to carry out such audits. The United Kingdom professional bodies had originally been of the view that that provision should be extended so as to refer to the companies and firms which are the subject of Article 58 of the Treaty, but decided not to press for such an amendment on the pragmatic grounds

---

[7] Proposal for an 8th Directive pursuant to Art 54(3)(g) of the EEC Treaty concerning the approval of persons responsible for carrying out statutory audits of the annual accounts of limited liability companies COM (78) 168 final, 24 April 1978; [1978] OJ C112/6; for the Explanatory Memorandum, see EC Bull Supp 4/78. See generally van Hulle, K, 'The EEC Accounting Directives in Perspective: Problems of Harmonization' (1981) 18 CML Rev 121, 135–40 and Feuillet, P, 'Le projet de huitième directive de la Commission des Communautés Européennes et le commissariat aux comptes' [1979] Revue des sociétés 47. The Report on the proposal of the UK HL Select Committee on the EC is also very informative: 12th Report (Session 1979–80, HL Paper 60).

[8] [1979] OJ C171/30.   [9] [1979] OJ C140/154.
[10] COM (79) 679 final, 30 November 1979; [1979] OJ C317/6.
[11] Throughout the rest of this chapter called 'auditors' for simplicity.   [12] Art 1(1).

that, first, it was unlikely to be accepted and, second, if it were it would entail significant work at national level determining precisely which bodies were so subject.[13]

Approval of Auditors

The cornerstone of the Directive, the rule that statutory audits of the accounts as defined in Article 1(1) shall be carried out only by approved persons, is set out in Article 2(1). The remainder of Section II of the Directive, 'Rules on approval' (comprising Articles 2 to 22), lays down numerous conditions for the granting of such approval.

Legal status and structure

Article 1(2) provides that the persons responsible for the statutory audit may, depending on the legislation of each Member State,[14] be natural or legal persons or other types of company, firm or partnership, together defined as 'firms of auditors'.

Article 2(1) provides that the authorities[15] of the Member States may approve only (a) natural persons who satisfy at least the conditions laid down in Article 3 to 19 or (b) firms of auditors satisfying at least the following conditions. First, the natural persons who actually carry out the audits on behalf of the firms must satisfy at least the conditions imposed in Articles 3 to 19; moreover, the Member States may provide that such natural persons must also be approved.[16] Second, a majority of the voting rights in the firm must be held by, *and* a majority of the members[17] of the administrative or management board must be, natural persons or firms of auditors who themselves satisfy at least the conditions imposed in Articles 3 to 19;[18] the Member States may provide that such natural persons or firms of auditors must themselves be approved.[19]

Member States which did not impose an equivalent condition as to majority of voting rights at the time of adoption of the Directive need not impose it provided that all the shares in a firm of auditors are registered and can be transferred only with the agreement of the firm and/or, where the Member State so provides, with the approval of the competent authority.[20] The original Proposal provided that the requirement as to majority holding (originally expressed as holding of capital, which as the Economic and Social Committee pointed out was insufficient to

---

[13] See the Report of the HL Select Committee (n 7 above) Minutes of Evidence, 21–2.

[14] Which varied greatly: see Olivier, H, 'Perspectives du contrôle légal' (1989) 66 Revue du droit international et de droit comparé 209, 214.

[15] Which may be professional associations provided that they are authorized by national law to grant approval: Art 2(2).

[16] Art 2(1)(b)(i).   [17] Or, where the body has only two members, at least one member.

[18] With the exception in the case of holders of voting rights of Art 11(1)(b), as to which see below.

[19] Art 2(1)(b)(ii) and (iii).   [20] Art 2(1)(b)(ii).

express effective control) was to apply only to firms constituted after the entry into force of measures implementing the Directive.[21] That provision was strongly criticized, both by the European Parliament and the Economic and Social Committee and by commentators from Member States which imposed a similar requirement,[22] with the result that it was replaced by the current exemption which, though more general, is coupled with a specific safeguard designed to ensure that the control exercised by approved persons cannot be further watered down. Moreover, the Member States may fix a period of not more than five years from 1 January 1990 (the date by which implementing measures must apply) for compliance with Article 2(1)(b)(i) and (ii).[23]

Article 2(1) continues by providing that the approval of a firm of auditors must be withdrawn when any of the conditions it imposes on firms are no longer fulfilled. Member States may however provide that in such circumstances firms have a period of two years to regularize the situation.

The original Proposal also provided that, in the case of a firm of auditors, partners, members or managers who did not personally fulfil the conditions for approval should exercise no influence over the audit and the audit reports and related documents should be withheld from the knowledge of such persons.[24] The Economic and Social Committee sensibly pointed out that auditing would be 'seriously impeded' by the latter provision, 'since it precludes the use of such specialists as data-processing experts and statisticians'. The Committee accordingly proposed deleting the withholding requirement; the European Parliament proposed the same amendment. The United Kingdom House of Lords Select Committee on the European Communities pointed out[25] a similar problem which would arise from the original wording for the many continental firms which include both locally qualified and United Kingdom qualified partners: those partners who are not locally qualified, but who may be senior partners and, in the case of a local subsidiary, may even be the auditors of the holding company, and who would in any event be jointly liable as partners for any negligence on the part of the locally qualified partner in connection with the audit, would not only be prohibited from taking part in, or even using influence over, audits, but would even be prohibited from seeing any of the documents concerned with the audits. The withholding provision was subsequently deleted; the prohibition on exercising influence was also dropped by the Commission, to be reintroduced in a less stringent format by way of Article 27, which requires such persons not to 'intervene in the execution of audits in any way which jeopardizes the independence of the natural persons' actually carrying out the audit on behalf of the firm.

---

[21] Art 2(2)(a).
[22] Feuillet, P, 'Le projet de huitième directive' (1979) 97 Revue des sociétés 47, 62.
[23] Arts 14(2) and 30(2).   [24] Art 2(2)(a).
[25] Report of the HL Select Committee (n 7 above), para 10.

Reputation

Member States' authorities may grant approval only to persons of good repute (*personnes honorables*) who are not carrying on any activity which is incompatible, under the law of that State, with the statutory auditing of annual accounts.[26] This provision too was watered down from its equivalent in the Proposal, Article 3 of which referred to 'persons who are of good repute and independent'. There was concern that the concept of independence, being difficult to define, should not be included in such bald terms.[27] The Commission had sought to justify the requirement in the Explanatory Memorandum by stating that 'the role of an auditor can be said to be incompatible with any activity which is of a kind that may limit his independence'; in the final version, the condition is spelt out in substantially the same terms, preserving the situation in certain Member States where auditors were prohibited from carrying on certain specified activities regarded as incompatible.

It may be noted that the requirement of good repute is expressed to apply at the time of approval of an auditor by the authorities. In contrast, the provisions of Section III of the Directive concerning professional integrity and independence[28] impose a continuing requirement, since they are couched by reference to the situation at the time of each audit carried out. These two aspects of integrity reflect the different approaches within the Community. In some continental countries, the concept of good repute is regarded as an objectively verifiable state which may be evidenced at any given time by an extract from the Ministry of Justice or the police. The approach of the professional bodies in the United Kingdom, by contrast, has tended to focus rather on the independence of auditors from the client company in the context of specific audit assignments. The combined effect of Article 3 and Section III was briefly considered by the Court of Justice in *Ramrath v Ministre de la Justice*,[29] discussed below.[30]

Qualifications

Natural persons may be approved only after having (a) attained university entrance level; (b) completed a court of theoretical instruction; (c) undergone practical training; and (d) passed an examination of professional competence of university final examination level organized or recognized by the Member State.[31]

The criterion of attainment of university entrance level was chosen because that concept was understood and recognized in all the Member States, notwithstanding

---

[26] Art 3.

[27] See the Opinion of the Economic and Social Committee [1979] OJ C171/30 and the UK HL Select Committee Report: 12th Report (Session 1979–80, HL Paper 60).

[28] Arts 23 to 27: see pp .207–10 below.   [29] Cited in n 5.   [30] See pp 208–10.

[31] Art 4. The Commission indicated in 1998 that it proposed to organize a closer coordination of the curricula for the training of auditors with a view to ensuring higher and more closely equivalent professional standards: see the *Communication from the Commission on the statutory audit in the European Union: the way forward* [1998] OJ C143/12, para 3.16.

their widely divergent teaching techniques and notwithstanding that in some but not all States an auditing qualification could be conferred by a university.[32]

Member States may approve auditors even if they do not fulfil the above conditions if they can show that they have engaged in professional activities which have enabled them to acquire sufficient experience in the fields of finance, law and accountancy (a) for fifteen years and have passed the examination of professional competence or (b) for seven years and have in addition undergone the practical training.[33] Member States may deduct periods of theoretical instruction in the above-mentioned fields lasting not less than one year, totalling not more than four years and attested by an examination recognized by the State, from the fifteen or seven year periods,[34] provided that the period of professional activity as well as the practical training is not shorter than the programme of theoretical instruction and practical training otherwise required.[35] The periods of professional activity necessary to benefit from this exemption were deliberately pitched on the long side, with a view to discouraging too many putative auditors from choosing this route rather than the intended generally applicable standard.[36]

The examination of professional competence must be at least partly written and must guarantee the necessary level of theoretical knowledge, and the ability to apply such knowledge in practice, of subjects relevant to the statutory auditing of annual accounts.[37]

The test of theoretical knowledge must include (a) auditing, analysis and critical assessment of annual accounts, general accounting, consolidated accounts, cost and management accounting, internal audit, standards relating to the preparation of annual and consolidated accounts and to methods of valuing balance sheet items and of computing profits and losses, legal and professional standards relating to the statutory auditing of accounting documents and to those carrying out such audits; and (b) in so far as they are relevant to auditing, company law, the law of insolvency and similar procedures, tax law, civil and commercial law, social security law and law of employment, information and computer systems, business, general and financial economics, mathematics and statistics, basic principles of the financial management of undertakings.[38] It must be borne in mind that, although the Directive lists subject headings for the test of theoretical knowledge, it prescribes no standards as to the contents of the different courses; there appears moreover to be no common understanding as to this.[39]

A Member State may however provide that a person with university or equivalent qualification in any of the above subjects is exempt from the relevant part of the test of theoretical knowledge;[40] such persons who have in addition received practical training in such subjects attested by an examination or diploma recognized

---

[32] Explanatory Memorandum (n 7 above).   [33] Art 9.   [34] Art 10(1).
[35] Art 10(2).   [36] Explanatory Memorandum (n 7 above).   [37] Art 5.
[38] Art 6.
[39] See the Commission's Green Paper *The Role, the Position and the Liability of the Statutory Auditor within the European Union* [1996] OJ C321/1, paras 4.3 and 4.5.
[40] Art 7(1).

by the State may also be exempted from the test of the ability to apply in practice his theoretical knowledge.[41]

Trainees must also complete at least three years' practical training in inter alia the auditing of annual and consolidated accounts or similar financial statements. At least two-thirds of that training must be completed under a person approved in accordance with the Directive under the law of the Member State or, at that State's option, under the law of another Member State.[42] Member States are moreover required to ensure that all training is carried out under persons providing adequate guarantees regarding training.[43]

Member States may approve persons who have obtained all or part of their qualifications in another State[44] provided (a) the authorities consider the qualifications equivalent to the local qualifications required in accordance with the Directive and (b) either the authorities consider legal knowledge obtained in the other State to be sufficient or the persons concerned furnish proof of the legal knowledge required locally for statutory auditing of accounts.[45]

A Member State may consider to be approved in accordance with the Directive professional persons and firms of auditors who had been approved by that State's competent authorities before its legislation implementing the Directive becomes applicable.[46] In the case of natural persons, such approval may be either specific to the person or flow from admission to a recognized professional association where under the law of the State concerned such admission confers the right to carry out statutory audits of annual and consolidated accounts.[47] In the case of firms, the conditions as to voting control and management imposed in Article 2(1)(b)(ii)[48] must however be complied with within a period of no more than five years from when the State's implementing legislation becomes applicable.[49] Natural persons who, before a State's implementing legislation became applicable, carried out statutory audits in the name of a firm of auditors may subsequently be authorized to continue so to do even if they do not fulfil all the conditions imposed by the Directive.[50]

Audits of small and medium-sized companies and groups

A major cause of the delay in adopting the Eighth Directive was the interaction between the system of approval of auditors and the exemptions from the audit requirement permitted by the Fourth and Seventh Directives on small companies and groups.[51] Denmark has not made use of that exemption, so that under Danish law the accounts of such companies and groups still require audit. Denmark has two categories of auditors, for one of which no university degree is necessary so

---

[41] Art 7(2).   [42] Art 8(1).   [43] Art 8(2).
[44] Whether a Member State or a third country.   [45] Art 11(1).
[46] Arts 12(1) and 14(1).   [47] Art 12(1)(2).   [48] See above.   [49] Art 14(2).
[50] Art 14(3).
[51] Arts 11, 27 and 51(2) of the 4th Directive and Art 6 of the 7th Directive. See further chs V and VI..

that they cannot be approved in accordance with the Directive. The latter category audit the accounts of small companies: that in itself poses no problem because, since statutory audit of such accounts is not required by Community law, auditors of such accounts are not within the scope of the Directive.[52] However, Denmark also permitted the less qualified auditors to audit the accounts of medium-sized companies; since statutory audit of such accounts is required by Community law, the continuance of this practice would have infringed the Eighth Directive as originally envisaged. Denmark was unwilling to restrict the permitted activities of its less qualified auditors to small companies, of which at the time there were only some 5,000, which would not provide a sufficient work load for the less qualified auditors.[53] The Commission proposed a compromise which was finally included as Articles 20 and 21.

Article 20 permits a Member State which does not make use of the exemption from audit for small companies and in which, at the time of adoption of the Directive, there were several categories of auditors, to approve as auditors of medium-sized companies natural persons acting in their own names who (a) fulfil all the conditions of the Directive (save that the level of the examination of professional competence may be lower than that otherwise required[54]) and (b) had audited the accounts of the company in question when it was still a small company. Such persons may not however audit the company's accounts if it is part of a group requiring consolidation exceeding the thresholds laid down by the Fourth and Seventh Directives for small groups. Member States may permit the practical training of such persons to be completed under a person who is himself approved pursuant to Article 20.[55]

Article 21 permits a Member State which does not make use of the exemption from consolidation (and hence of audit of consolidated accounts) for small groups and in which, at the time of adoption of the Directive, there were several categories of auditors, to approve as auditors of consolidated accounts a person approved pursuant to Article 20 if on the parent undertaking's balance sheet date the body of undertakings to be consolidated does not, on the basis of those undertakings' latest annual accounts, exceed the thresholds for small groups, provided that he is empowered to audit the accounts of all the undertakings included in the consolidation.

Both exemptions are expressed to be available only until subsequent coordination of the statutory auditing of accounting documents.

---

[52] See Art 1(1), discussed above, p 200.
[53] This account drawn from Todd, J, 'La directive sur les qualifications aux portes d'adoption' (1984) La vie judiciaire, no 1980, 7.
[54] By Art 4: see pp 203–5 above.   [55] Art 22.

Professional Integrity and Independence

The Directive requires Member States to prescribe that persons approved as auditors, and natural persons who carry out audits on behalf of a firm of auditors,[56] shall carry out audits with professional integrity[57] and shall not carry out audits required by law if they are not independent in accordance with the law of the Member State requiring the audit.[58] Approved persons must be liable to appropriate sanctions for infringement of those provisions.[59] Finally, Member States must ensure that the members and shareholders of approved firms of auditors and the members of their management[60] who do not personally fulfil the conditions for approval in a particular Member State do not intervene in the execution of audits in any way which jeopardizes the independence of the natural persons carrying out the audits on behalf of such firms.[61]

Those provisions are the much-changed successor of Article 11 of the original Proposal, which proved a major sticking point in the negotiations. Article 11 provided as follows:

1. An approved person whose independence does not appear to be sufficiently guaranteed in relation to the persons who are members of the body which represents, administers, directs or supervises a company, or its majority shareholders or members, shall not audit the accounts of that company.

2. An auditor of a company's accounts may, neither directly nor through another person, receive benefits from that company or from the persons specified in paragraph 1 and may not have an interest in the capital of that company.

3. A person may only audit the annual accounts of a company or group of companies where more than 10% of his turnover is derived from that client if the disciplinary authorities consider that, in view of the circumstances, this situation is not such as to limit his independence.

4. Member States shall ensure that approved persons fulfil their obligations either through appropriate administrative measures or by making such persons subject to professional discipline. In particular, approved persons shall, as a minimum, be liable to disciplinary sanctions if they fail to carry out their duties as auditors with all due professional care and complete moral and financial independence.

The United Kingdom found unacceptable the prohibition on auditors' holding shares in the companies whose accounts they audit. First, where the audit firm was a large partnership the prohibition would, since all the partners have an interest in all the work done by the firm, have extended to any partner, or even any partner's spouse. Second, the big firms, or some of the partners in those firms, frequently have partnership arrangements with many smaller local firms: it would be burdensome and impractical to exchange and constantly update lists of companies in which no partner in these often wide and informally linked arrangements may not

---

[56] Art 25.   [57] Art 23.   [58] Art 24.   [59] Art 26.
[60] 'the administrative, management and supervisory bodies'.   [61] Art 27.

hold shares. Third, the restriction meant that no auditor nor any of his partners could be a trustee of a trust fund including in its portfolio shares in the company. Fourth, it would apply to holdings via a unit trust or similar fund, even though the unit-holder could not generally be expected to know from day to day the identity of the underlying shares. Finally, the prohibition would as drafted instantly disqualify a person who had inherited shares in a company from auditing the accounts of that company; it was felt that it would be more appropriate to allow a reasonable period for divestment of the holding in such circumstances.

The United Kingdom had further problems with the restriction on an auditor's obtaining more than 10 per cent of his turnover from a single client. That limit would present problems for an auditor with fewer than ten clients; even with ten clients, it would prevent any client being charged more than 10 per cent of turnover, and with more than ten clients, the loss of one or two in a given year might result in the contribution of a remaining client in that year exceeding 10 per cent. Finally, the prohibition appeared to be capable of evasion and almost impossible to supervise.[62] The solution ultimately adopted was increased renvoi to national law.

The requirements of professional integrity and independence were considered briefly by the Court of Justice in *Ramrath v Ministre de la Justice*,[63] which concerned the validity of the decision of the Luxembourg Minister of Justice to withdraw Mr Ramrath's authorization to practise as an auditor in Luxembourg when he became employed by a firm of auditors established in Germany. Although an associated firm of auditors established and approved in Luxembourg employed Mr Ramrath as regards his duties in Luxembourg, the Minister gave as reasons for withdrawing the authorization that Mr Ramrath (a) had no professional establishment in Luxembourg contrary to Article 3 of the Law of 28 June 1984 and (b) was not authorized as an auditor under Luxembourg law contrary to Article 6 of that Law. It was argued that the requirements laid down by the Law were necessary in order to ensure the professional independence of auditors in Luxembourg. In particular, the Minister submitted that it followed from the recitals in the preamble to the Eighth Directive and from Articles 3, 23, 24, 25 and 26 thereof that it was for each Member State to determine the criteria of independence and integrity for auditors. Supervision of compliance with the rules of professional practice by an auditor within a Member State's territory presupposed that the auditor was under an obligation to have a permanent infrastructure and minimum presence within that State. Compliance with those rules by an employed auditor could be guaranteed only through his employer, and supervision by the authorities of compliance with such rules would be possible only at the level of the employer, who would therefore have to be approved by those authorities.

---

[62] See generally the Report of the HL Select Committee (n 27 above) on the EC and Todd, J, 'Projet de directive communautaire sur les qualifications des auditeurs' (1984) La vie judiciaire, no 1979, 4.

[63] Cited in n 5.

The Court's ruling was based solely on the Treaty provisions on the freedom of establishment and the freedom to provide services. In brief, it held that those provisions precluded a Member State from prohibiting a person from becoming established on its territory and practising as an auditor there on the grounds that that person was established and authorized to practise in another Member State. They did not however preclude a Member State from imposing conditions on practice as an auditor by a person already authorized to practise in another Member State, provided that the conditions were objectively necessary for ensuring compliance with professional practice rules and related to a permanent infrastructure for carrying out the work, actual presence in that Member State and supervision of compliance with professional conduct rules, unless compliance with such rules and conditions was already ensured through an auditor established and authorized in that State and in whose service the intended auditor was employed for the duration of the work.[64] Although the Directive was not referred to in the ruling, both the Court and Advocate General Jacobs commented on it.

The Court noted that the Eighth Directive left to Member States inter alia the task of assessing in accordance with national law the independence and integrity of auditors practising within their territory. A Member State could carry out that task by requiring compliance with rules of professional practice, justified by the public interest, relating to the integrity and independence of auditors and applying to all persons practising as auditors within the territory of that State. In that respect, requirements relating to the existence of infrastructure within the national territory and the auditor's actual presence appeared to be justified in order to safeguard that interest. Such requirements were no longer objectively necessary however where the audit was carried out by an auditor who, while established and authorized to practise in another Member State, was temporarily in the service of a person authorized to practise as an auditor by the authorities of the Member State in which that audit was carried out, since the Member State could ensure through that person that an auditor who from time to time carried out audits in its territory complied with its rules.[65]

Advocate General Jacobs was of the view that Article 24 could clearly be implemented by forbidding an auditor to be employed by any person or firm which was not itself an auditor, but that it was less clear that it was permissible to exclude employment with a person or firm authorized as an auditor under the law of another Member State. Such a Member State must be presumed to have implemented the Eighth Directive, including the obligations laid down by Articles 23 and 24.

The Advocate General referred also to Article 3, which requires Member States to grant approval only to persons of good repute who are not carrying on any activity which is incompatible under national law with statutory auditing. He noted that definitions of what activities were incompatible with statutory auditing, and of

---

[64] Operative part of the judgment.   [65] Paras 34–36 of the judgment.

what constituted professional independence (although not perhaps professional integrity), could vary as between Member States. If therefore it were shown that the particular circumstances of an auditor's employment with a person or firm authorized in another Member State were such as to offend against national requirements of professional independence, or against other legitimate requirements, that might be a reason for requiring such employment to cease. Similarly, such an employment might preclude the auditor in question from carrying out particular audits, by virtue of a connection between the audited company and his employer. It would be for the national court to decide whether such an infringement of standards had occurred in any individual case. On the other hand, he did not consider that a Member State was permitted to assume, without proof, that its standards had been infringed by the mere fact of employment by an auditor authorized in another Member State. However, in order to ensure compliance with the relevant rules of professional conduct and independence, it might not always be sufficient simply to compare the regulations governing the matter in the two Member States concerned. Thus, even if German rules governing professional independence of auditors contained requirements identical to those laid down in Luxembourg, it might still be necessary for the Luxembourg authorities to examine whether the condition of professional independence was satisfied in any particular case. In the case of an audit performed by Mr Ramrath, the Luxembourg authorities were, in particular, entitled to require that there be no connection between the audited company and the German firm such as to impair his independence, and if such requirements were to be enforced it might be necessary for the regulatory authorities in the two countries to cooperate and to exchange information. Such cooperation did not however seem excessively onerous. In any event, the mere possibility of a conflict of interest resulting from employment in another Member State was clearly not sufficient to justify a prohibition on practice in Luxembourg. The Advocate General accordingly concluded that it was manifestly disproportionate for Luxembourg to lay down an absolute and *a priori* prohibition against employment with a firm of auditors established in another Member State.[66]

Publicity

Article 28 requires Member States to ensure that the following information is made available to the public: (a) the names and addresses of all approved natural persons and firms of auditors;[67] (b) in respect of each approved firm, the names and addresses of (i) the natural persons who carry out audits on behalf of the firm; (ii) the firm's members or shareholders; and (iii) the members of the firm's administrative or management body.[68] Finally, where a natural person is permitted to audit

---

[66] Paras 17–19 of the Opinion. [67] Art 28(2). [68] Art 28(2).

the accounts of medium-sized companies or small groups, the category of company or firm or the bodies of undertakings in respect of which such an audit is permitted must also be indicated.[69]

Contact Committee

Article 29 provides that the Contact Committee set up by the Fourth Directive[70] shall also facilitate harmonized application of the Eighth Directive through regular meetings dealing in particular with practical problems arising in connection with its application and advise the Commission if necessary on additions or amendments to the Directive. Such a committee will be of particular relevance in the context of an instrument such as the Eighth Directive which prescribes details such as educational course content, which may need to develop with the passage of time.

Implementation

Member States are required to bring into force the implementing laws, regulations and administrative provisions before 1 January 1988.[71] They may however provide that the implementing legislation does not become applicable for a further two years.[72] There are in addition numerous transitional provisions designed to ease the effect of the introduction of new requirements for approval of auditors.[73] Since however the latest of the various transitional periods[74] has now expired, it is unnecessary to consider those provisions.

The Eighth Directive was implemented in the United Kingdom by Pt II of the Companies Act 1989, most of which was brought into force on 1 March 1990.[75]

---

[69] Art 28(3).   [70] See p 155 above.   [71] Art 30(1).   [72] Art 30(2).

[73] Arts 13 and 15–19. For a brief discussion of the interaction between Arts 18 and 30, see Case C–157/91 *Commission v Netherlands* [1992] ECR I–5899.

[74] Six years after 1 January 1990: Art 18, relating to persons training at that time.

[75] Companies Act 1989 (Commencement No 2) Order 1990 (SI 1990/142).

VIII

The Eleventh Directive

The Eleventh Directive on disclosure by branches[1] seeks to stop a lacuna in the system of protection of third parties by the mandatory disclosure of certain information relating to companies. As has been seen, the First, Fourth, Seventh and Eighth Directives impose a series of disclosure requirements on companies. Where a company incorporated in one Member State seeks to exercise its right of establishment by setting up a subsidiary in another Member State, that subsidiary, being a company, will be subject to those requirements in the Member State where it is incorporated. Where however a company establishes a branch rather than a subsidiary in another Member State, that branch, not being a corporate entity, will not be so subject. Although information about the company will be available in its State of incorporation, it may not be readily accessible to third parties dealing with it through the medium of the branch. That difference in treatment may be seen as both affecting the exercise of companies' rights of establishment and prejudicing the protection of third parties in certain circumstances. Moverover, certain Member States had imposed their own disclosure requirements on branches, which differed between Member States, leading to further discrepancies within the Community.[2] The Eleventh Directive aims to redress the balance[3] by subjecting branches to certain of the disclosure requirements.

Disclosure is in general limited to information relating to the branch with a reference to the register of the company of which the branch is part, since the company is already required to make its own disclosure in that register; certain items relating to the company which are of particular interest to third parties, namely 'the powers of representation, the name and legal form and the winding-up of the company and the insolvency proceedings to which it is subject', are however required to be disclosed in the State of the branch.[4] The Directive extends to branches of companies governed by the law of countries outside the Community, 'to ensure

---

[1] 11th Council Directive (EEC) 89/666 of 21 December 1989 concerning disclosure requirements in respect of branches opened in a Member State by certain types of company governed by the law of another State [1989] OJ L395/36. See for a brief discussion Dine, J and Hughes, P, *EC Company Law* (1991) and Wooldridge, F, *Company Law in the United Kingdom and the European Community* (1991) 95–8.

[2] See the Explanatory Memorandum on the Commission's Proposal for an 11th Council Directive based on Art 54(3)(g) of the Treaty concerning disclosure requirements in respect of branches opened in a Member State by certain types of companies governed by the law of another State, COM (86) 397 final, 23 July 1986.

[3] See the 1st–6th recitals in the preamble.

[4] See the 8th recital in the preamble and the Explanatory Memorandum to the Proposal, para 10.

that [its] purposes . . . are fully realized and to avoid any discrimination on the basis of a company's country of origin'.[5]

The original Proposal for the Eleventh Directive was submitted in July 1986;[6] the Economic and Social Committee delivered its Opinion in September 1987[7] and the European Parliament in November 1987.[8] An amended Proposal was submitted in July 1988[9] and the Parliament adopted its decision in September 1989.[10] The Directive was adopted in December 1989.

Scope

The Directive concerns (a) branches opened in a Member State by a company which is governed by the law of another Member State and to which the First Directive applies[11] and (b) branches opened in a Member State by a company which is not governed by the law of another Member State but which is of a legal form comparable with the types of company to which the First Directive applies.[12]

Unfortunately there is no definition of 'branch' in the Directive.[13] The Economic and Social Committee suggested a definition in line with that used in Directive (EEC) 77/780 on credit institutions,[14] namely 'a place of business which forms a legally dependent part of a credit institution and which conducts directly all or some of the operations inherent in the business of credit institutions'.[15] That definition is incorporated *mutatis mutandis* in Directive (EEC) 89/117 on branches of credit institutions,[16] which has obvious analogies with the Eleventh Directive. It is echoed in part by the definition of 'branch, agency or other establishment' framed by the Court of Justice for the purposes of the Brussels Convention,[17] which although given in a different context reflected a similar need to develop a definition independent of the domestic law of a particular Member State and common to all Member States. The Court ruled:

---

[5] 11th recital in the preamble.

[6] COM (86) 397 final, 23 July 1986; [1986] OJ C203/12. For a brief commentary see Dine, J, 'Company Law Directives: A Protective Proposal' (1989) 33 SJ 30.

[7] [1987] OJ C319/61.   [8] [1987] OJ C345/74.

[9] COM (88) 153 final, 28 March 1988; [1988] OJ C105/6; EC Bull, Supp 5/88.

[10] [1989] OJ C256/72.

[11] Art 1(1); for such companies, see the list on pp 17–18 above.   [12] Art 7(1).

[13] Notwithstanding the purported definition of the term in the UK implementing legislation by reference to its meaning in the 11th Directive: see the Companies Act 1985, s 698(2)(b).

[14] Council Directive (EEC) 77/780 of 12 December 1977 on the coordination of laws, regulations and administrative provisions relating to the taking up and pursuit of the business of credit institutions [1977 OJ L322/30.

[15] Art 1.

[16] Council Directive (EEC) 89/117 of 13 February 1989 on the obligations of branches established in a Member State of credit institutions and financial institutions having their head offices outside that Member State regarding the publication of annual accounting documents [1989] OJ L44/40.

[17] Convention of 27 September 1968 on Jurisdiction and Enforcement of Judgments in Civil and Commercial Matters [1978] OJ L304/77. See however n 6, p 343 below.

the concept of branch, agency or other establishment implies a place of business which has the appearance of permanency, such as the extension of a public body, has a management and is materially equipped to negotiate business with third parties so that the latter, although knowing that there will if necessary be a legal link with the parent body, the head office of which is abroad, do not have to deal directly with such parent body but may transact business at the place of business constituting the extension.[18]

The Commission appears to assume in its Explanatory Memorandum to the Proposal that the Court's above definition is generally applicable.[19]

Branches opened by credit and other financial institutions are excluded from the provisions of the Directive concerning disclosure of accounts (Articles 3 and 9).[20] They are instead covered by Directive (EEC) 89/117 on branches of credit institutions.[21] Branches opened by insurance companies are similarly excluded from those provisions pending subsequent coordination.[22]

The Directive does not affect disclosure requirements for branches imposed by other provisions, for example in the field of employees' rights to information or tax law, or for statistical purposes.[23] Such requirements will however not necessarily be valid, since they will be subject to scrutiny in accordance with general provisions of Community law: for an example of a fiscal disclosure requirement relating to branches which the Court held to be excessive and hence invalid in part, see *Futura Participations and Singer v Administration des Contributions*.[24]

Branches of Companies from other Member States

Article 1(1) requires documents and particulars relating to such a branch to be disclosed pursuant to the law of the Member State of the branch in accordance with Article 3 of the First Directive, namely in a public register maintained for the purpose.[25] Where there are conflicting disclosure requirements in respect of branch and company, those applying to the branch take precedence with regard to transactions carried out with the branch.[26]

Article 2(1) exhaustively lists the documents and particulars which must be disclosed pursuant to Article 1; Article 2(2) adds further items which the Member State of the branch may require to be disclosed. The wording of Article 2 suggests that no additional disclosure requirements may be imposed on branches of companies from other Member States; this may be contrasted with Article 8, discussed below, which imposes minimum rather than maximum requirements on branches

---

[18] Case 33/78 *Somafer v Saar-Ferngas* [1978] ECR 2183, 2192.   [19] Note 3 to para 3.
[20] Art 14(1).   [21] See n 16 above.
[22] Art 14(2). Council Directive (EEC) 91/647 of 19 December 1991 on the annual accounts and consolidated accounts of insurance undertakings [1991] OJ L374/7 now coordinates accounting requirements for insurance companies; presumably a Directive will follow in due course coordinating the obligations of cross-border branches of such companies regarding the publication of accounts.
[23] 12th recital in the preamble.   [24] Case C–250/95 [1997] ECR I–2471.
[25] See pp 19–20 above.   [26] Art 1(2).

of companies from third countries. In relation to accounting documents, the pre-amble to the Directive specifically underlines this policy, stating:

. . . national provisions in respect of the disclosure of accounting documents relating to a branch can no longer be justified following the coordination of national law in respect of the drawing up, audit and disclosure of companies' accounting documents; . . . it is accord-ingly sufficient to disclose, in the register of the branch, the accounting documents as audited and disclosed by the company.[27]

The following must be disclosed pursuant to Article 2(1):

(1)   the address and activities of the branch;[28]

(2)   the register in which the company file mentioned in Article 3 of the First Directive is kept, and the registration number in that register;[29]

(3)   the name and legal form of the company and the name of the branch if dif-ferent;[30]

(4)   the appointment, termination of office and particulars of the persons autho-rized to represent the company as a lawful company organ or member thereof as disclosed in accordance with the First Directive[31] and[32] as permanent representa-tives of the company for the activities of the branch, with in the latter case an indication of the extent of their powers;[33]

(5)   details of any liquidators (including their appointment and powers), liqui-dation, winding up, striking off, insolvency proceedings, arrangements, composi-tions etc;[34]

(6)   the company's accounts as drawn up, audited and disclosed pursuant to the law of its Member State in accordance with the Fourth, Seventh and Eighth Directives;[35]

(7)   the closure of the branch.[36]

The Member State of the branch may additionally require disclosure of:

(1)   the signature of those authorised to represent the company;[37]

---

[27] 9th recital.   [28] Art 2(1)(a)(b).   [29] Art 2(1)(c).   [30] Art 2(1)(d).

[31] See pp 21–2 above. Note that it must appear from such disclosure whether the persons so autho-rized may act alone or must act jointly: see Art 2(1)(d) of the First Directive.

[32] The Directive uses neither 'and' nor 'or', merely setting out the two provisions consecutively. It is clear from the Proposal however that they were intended to be cumulative.

[33] Art 2(1)(e).   [34] Art 2(2)(f).

[35] Arts 2(1)(g) and 3. If the company is a subsidiary, it may in certain circumstances not be required to draw up its own accounts in accordance with the 4th Directive: see Art 57 of the 4th Directive as amended, discussed in ch V above, p 123. In that case, disclosure pursuant to the 11th Directive will presumably be of the relevant consolidated accounts, required by Art 57 to be published for the sub-sidiary in accordance with the laws of the Member State in which it is established. The Proposal included a specific provision to that effect (Art 3(2)). An attempt by the Economic and Social Committee to require the parent to guarantee the commitments of its subsidiary in those circumstances was unsuccessful.

[36] Art 2(1)(h).   [37] Art 2(2)(a).

(2)   the company's instruments of constitution[38] and statutes (if contained in a separate instrument) and any amendments thereto;[39]

(3)   an attestation from the register in which the company file is kept attesting to the company's existence;[40]

(4)   charges on the company's property situated in that Member State, provided that the disclosure relates to the validity of those charges.[41]

Additional rules apply to disclosure of the company's accounts and, if required to be disclosed, its statutes. First, the Member State of the branch may require that those documents be published in another official language of the Community and that such translation be certified.[42] Second, a company with more than one branch in a Member State which does not have a single, central register for disclosure may decide in which register those documents may be disclosed; the other branch or branches must then simply disclose the particulars of that register and the number of the branch in that register.[43]

The Directive also requires Member States to prescribe that letters and order forms used by a branch state, in addition to the information required by the First Directive,[44] the register in which its file is kept together with its number in that register.[45]

Finally, Article 11 of the Directive amends the Fourth Directive so as to require companies incorporated in a Member State to indicate in their annual report the existence of branches.[46]

Branches of Companies from Third Countries

The provisions discussed above (Articles 1 to 6) constitute Section I of the Directive. Section II in effect applies Articles 1 to 6, with certain amendments, to branches of companies from third countries.

As indicated above, the list[47] of particulars which require disclosure is, in the case of branches of companies from third countries, expressed as a minimum requirement. The list includes all the items required by Article 2(1) to be disclosed in the case of a branch of a company from another Member State, together with the company's instruments of constitution and statutes (if contained in a separate instrument) and any amendments thereto. In addition, disclosure is required of three items which, in the case of companies incorporated in another Member State, are required to be disclosed by the First Directive, namely (a) the company's principal place of business;[48] (b) the amount of subscribed capital if that is not apparent from

---

[38] *Acte constitutif:* in the case of a United Kingdom company, the memorandum of association.
[39] Art 2(2)(b).   [40] Art 2(2)(c).   [41] Art 2(2)(d).   [42] Art 4.   [43] Art 5.
[44] Namely the register in which the company's file is kept, its number in that register, its legal form, the location of its seat and, where appropriate, the fact that it is being wound up.
[45] Art 6.   [46] Art 46(2)(e) of the 4th Directive.   [47] In Art 8.
[48] *Siège* in French, translated as 'seat' in the First Directive.

the company's constitution, with annual updates; and (c) whether those authorized to represent the company may do so alone or must act jointly. Finally, disclosure is required of the law of the State by which the company is governed and its object.

The disclosure requirement is expressed[49] to apply to the accounting documents of the company as drawn up, audited and disclosed pursuant to the law of the State which governs the company. Where they are not drawn up in accordance with, or in a manner equivalent to, the Fourth and Seventh Directives, Member States may require that accounting documents relating to the activities of the branch be drawn up and disclosed.

Articles 4 (translation) and 5 (disclosure of accounts and constitution where there is more than one branch) apply.[50] Finally, Member States must prescribe that letters and order forms used by a branch state the register in which its file is kept together with its number in that register and, where the law of the State by which the company is governed requires entry in a register, the register in which the company's file is kept and its number in that register.[51]

Miscellaneous General Provisions

Each Member State is to determine who is to carry out the disclosure formalities required by the Directive.[52] Member States are required to provide for appropriate penalties in the event of failure to comply with the requirements of the Directive.[53] This provision is analogous with Article 6 of the First Directive, discussed in chapter II above.[54]

Finally, the Directive is brought within the remit of the Contact Committee set up pursuant to the Fourth Directive.[55]

Implementation in the United Kingdom

The Directive required implementing provisions to be adopted by 1 January 1992 and to apply (a) to annual accounts for the financial year beginning on 1 January 1993 or during 1993 and (b) for other purposes, from 1 January 1993.[56]

The bulk of the Directive was implemented in the United Kingdom by the Oversea Companies and Credit and Financial Institutions (Branch Disclosure) Regulations 1992,[57] inserting inter alia ss 690A and 699A and Schs 21A and 21D into the Companies Act 1985 (disclosure regime for branches); in addition, the Companies Act 1985 (Disclosure of Branches and Bank Accounts) Regulations 1992,[58] adding para 6(d) to Sch 7 Companies Act 1985, implements Article 11 (disclosure of the existence of branches in a company's annual report). Although

---

[49] By Art 9(1).   [50] Art 9(2).   [51] Art 10.   [52] Art 13.
[53] Art 12.   [54] See pp 26–8.   [55] See p 155 above.   [56] Art 16(1)(2).
[57] SI 1992/3179.   [58] SI 1992/3178.

relatively painless in terms of legislation, implementation has been effected in such a way as to result in two separate regimes applying to two slightly different categories of foreign companies which have established themselves in Great Britain. Before implementation of the Eleventh Directive, the Companies Act 1985 required the disclosure of certain information by companies incorporated outside Great Britain which established a place of business in Great Britain.[59] Rather than replace that regime with the requirements of the Eleventh Directive, the United Kingdom when implementing the Directive provided for a parallel system of disclosure by companies incorporated outside the United Kingdom and Gibraltar which have a branch in Great Britain.[60] Although the regimes are similar, the disclosure requirements are not identical. The critical factor determining which regime applies is whether the company has established a place of business within the meaning of national law[61] or a branch, defined as 'a branch within the meaning of the . . . Eleventh Directive'.[62] Since, as discussed, there is no definition of 'branch' in the Directive, this situation must be regarded as unclear and confusing.[63]

---

[59] Section 691.   [60] Section 690A and Sch 21A.

[61] See for a brief discussion of this concept Davies, P L, *Gower's Principles of Modern Company Law* (6th edn, 1997), 130, and Dine, J and Hughes, P, *EC Company Law* (1991).

[62] Section 698(2).

[63] The confusion is even worse than the above brief summary indicates, since there is a third regime for companies incorporated in the Channel Islands and the Isle of Man (s 699), which for most but not all purposes are assimilated to companies incorporated within Great Britain, as well as (in accordance with the Bank Branches Directive) additional disclosure requirements on branches of credit and financial institutions (s 699A).

IX

The Twelfth Directive

Background and History

In 1988, when the Commission submitted its Proposal for a Twelfth Council Directive on company law concerning single-member private limited companies,[1] Belgium, Denmark, France, Germany and the Netherlands all permitted the formation of single-member companies, Luxembourg had introduced draft legislation to that end and Portugal permitted single-person businesses to have limited liability. Denmark, Germany and the Netherlands permitted single-member companies to be formed by artificial as well as by natural persons, while Belgium required the member of such a company to be a natural person; France, and the proposed legislation in Luxembourg, permitted single-member companies to be formed by artificial persons but prohibited the creation of one single-member company by another. The other Member States made no provision for single-member companies, and either imposed personal liability on a sole shareholder[2] or required a company with a sole shareholder to be wound up.[3] The Proposal sought to overcome the divergences between the laws of the Member States in this area by providing a legal instrument allowing the limitation of liability of the individual entrepreneur throughout the Community.[4]

It was only relatively recently that national laws had become so accommodating to the notion of a single-member company.[5] The legal systems in the Latin countries had historically regarded the company as essentially a contract. The French civil code, for example, provided until 1985: '*La société est un contrat par*

---

[1] [1988] OJ C173/10: COM (88) 101 final, 18 May 1988; Bull EC, Supp 5/88. For a commentary on the Proposal see Wooldridge, F, 'The Draft Twelfth Directive on Single-Member Companies' [1989] European Business Law 86.

[2] See, for example, UK Companies Act 1985, s 24.

[3] Explanatory Memorandum, 3–4; Wooldridge, F, 'The Draft Twelfth Directive' and Wooldridge, F, *Company Law in the United Kingdom and the European Community* (1991) 98–101. For a survey of the historical approaches taken by France, Germany and Italy, see Ducouloux-Favard, C, 'Société d'un Seul, Entreprise Unipersonelle' [1990] La Gazette du Palais (Doctrine) 577; for more detail of the systems of those States and of Belgium and Greece, see Karayanni, F A, *Les sociétés d'une seule personne dans le droit des états membres de la Communauté Européenne* (1992). For a more detailed discussion of the French law, see Daigre, J-J, 'La société unipersonelle en droit français' [1990] Revue internationale de droit comparé 665.

[4] 4th and 5th recitals in the preamble.

[5] Denmark 1973, Germany 1980, France 1985, the Netherlands 1986 and Belgium 1987. The Portuguese law dates from 1986 and the Luxembourg draft law had been proposed in 1985 (Explanatory Memorandum, 3).

lequel deux ou plusieurs personnes conviennent de mettre quelque chose en commun . . .'[6]
Stein[7] recounts that, in the discussions surrounding the finalization of the grounds
of permitted nullity of a company set out in Article 11 of the First Directive,[8] 'since
the laws of the Six, with a single *prospective* exception of the Belgian reform, precluded incorporation by a single founder, a new ground was added . . . allowing
invalidity where the number of *founder*-shareholders was less than two.' (The
Belgian legislative proposal referred to, which appears not to have reached the
statute book, permitted a company to act as a single incorporator of its own subsidiary; its existence explains the final wording of Article 11(2)(f): 'Nullity may be
ordered [on the ground] that, *contrary to the national law governing the company*
[emphasis added], the number of founder members is less than two.')

Although Article 11(2)(f) was prompted by the general intolerance in the then
Community of the concept of a company with fewer than two founder members,
the Member States adopted different approaches to an existing company the shares
in which were acquired by one person.[9] Those differences led to the inclusion of
a specific provision to deal with single-member companies in the 1968 Convention
on the Mutual Recognition of Companies and Bodies Corporate.[10] Article 9 of that
Convention permits a Member State to refuse to recognize a foreign company on
the ground that its objects or activities are contrary to public policy. The second
paragraph of that Article provides however that, if the law of the State of incorporation permits companies lawfully to exist with a single shareholder, a company
may not for that reason alone be considered by a Contracting State to be contrary
to its public policy within the meaning of private international law.[11]

By the time the proposed Second Directive was being discussed[12] however a
shift of emphasis by the Community legislature was apparent. Stein recounts:

The doctrinal concept of the company as a contract which used to dominate the 'Latin' legal
systems could not tolerate a 'one-man' company in any form whatsoever. The proposed
directive, however, recognizes the 'one-man' company in a limited sense, only if all the

    [6] Art 1832 (A company is a contract whereby two or more persons agree to do something jointly
(author's translation)).
    [7] Stein, E, *Harmonization of European Company Laws* (1971), 308.
    [8] Adopted in 1968. See pp 45–7 above.
    [9] Germany, Italy and the Netherlands acknowledged the continuing existence of the company in
such circumstances (although in Italy the sole member lost the benefit of limited liability), and France
followed that view as regards foreign companies when the law governing those companies did so;
Belgium however refused to recognize single-member companies on grounds of public policy: Stein (n
7 above) 419; Ducouloux-Favard (n 3 above).
    [10] 29 February 1968. The text may be found in [1968] Revue trimestrielle de droit européen 400;
an English text is in [1969] EC Bull Supp 2 and an unofficial translation by Stein in Stein, E,
Harmonization of European Company Laws (1971), 525. See further ch XVIII below.
    [11] Although the 1968 Convention is unlikely ever to come into effect as such, the Belgian Cour de
Cassation used Belgium's approval of it as the basis for departing from its earlier case-law and holding
in 1978 in *Anstalt Del Sol v Space Age Plastics Cy Inc* that the requirement for two persons to constitute
a company was no longer an essential principle of public policy for the purposes of private international
law (judgment of 13 January 1978, [1979] Revue critique de jurisprudence belge, 40; see Karayanni, F
A, *Les sociétés d'une seule personne* (1992) 53–4 and 78).
    [12] The Proposal was submitted in 1970.

shares are acquired by a single person *after* the company's formation by more than a single founder. In that event, the company may no longer be held automatically dissolved . . . however, the Member States would remain free to require the liquidation of such a company. If a judicial proceeding for dissolution is instituted, the court must allow the company a period of not less than six months 'to regularize its situation.' This proposed text appeared acceptable to both the industry and the bankers. However, a more 'radical' Belgian proposal to allow a single person to organize a 'one-man company' was not accepted in the working group, reportedly because it had 'nothing to do with the protection of creditors or shareholders.' The true reason may have been the lingering attachment to the doctrine of the company as a contract . . . It would be in the interest of creditors, at least, to coordinate national rules regarding the liability of the single shareholder.[13]

The less radical provision survived as Article 5 of the Second Directive, although, like the remainder of that Directive, it applies only to public companies.[14]

The legislative progress of the Commission's Proposal for a directive on single-member companies was rapid, the process from first draft to adopted text being completed in little more than eighteen months despite the submission of two amended texts. The Economic and Social Committee delivered its Opinion on the first Proposal in September 1988[15] and the European Parliament approved the Proposal with suggested amendments in March 1989.[16] The Commission presented an amended Proposal in May 1989[17] on which the Council adopted a common position in June 1989. The Parliament gave it a second reading under the cooperation procedure in October 1989 and voted in favour of three amendments,[18] one of which was accepted by the Commission which submitted a re-examined Proposal in November 1989.[19] The Twelfth Council Company Law Directive on single-member private limited-liability companies was adopted on 21 December 1989.[20] It was required to be implemented by 1 January 1992, although Member States were permitted to provide that, in the case of companies already in existence on that date, the Directive would not apply until 1 January 1993.[21]

Legal Basis and Aims

The doubts referred to by Stein as to whether provision at the Community level for single-member companies involved 'coordinating to the necessary extent the

---

[13] *Harmonization of European Company Laws* (1971) 327–8.   [14] See p 59 above.

[15] [1988] OJ C318/9.   [16] [1989] OJ C96/90.

[17] COM (89) 193 final, 24 May 1989; [1989] OJ C152/10.   [18] [1989] OJ C291/53.

[19] COM (89) 591 final, 29 November 1989.

[20] Directive (EEC) 89/667; [1989] OJ L395/40. There is a summary by Murray, J, in his chapter in *Corporate Law: the European Dimension* (1991), 17–21, and good commentaries by Karayanni, F A, in *Les sociétés d'une seule personne* (1992) and by Mousoulas, S, 'La société unipersonelle à responsabilité limitée communautaire—Appréciation de la XIIe directive du Conseil en matière de sociétés' [1990] Revue des sociétés 395.

[21] Art 8.

safeguards which, for the protection of the interests of members and others, are required by Member States of companies or firms' within the meaning of Article 54(3)(g) of the Treaty, the legal basis of the Directive, remain: Wooldridge, for example, describes the draft directive as 'based upon a somewhat bold interpretation' of the Article.[22] It is arguable however that legislation on single-member companies safeguards creditors' interests: it will presumably encourage sole traders to assume a corporate form pursuant to 'a legal framework which under existing Community measures and the present directive provides a series of equivalent safeguards, particularly regarding disclosure and the drawing up and auditing of accounts, which allows the company's funds to be kept separate from the sole member's private assets and liabilities'.[23] In any event, the legal basis is doubtful only in so far as it *requires* provision for single-member companies: in so far as it harmonizes safeguards for creditors or extends to single-member companies the rules (for example on disclosure) applicable to other types of company, the Directive clearly falls within Article 54(3)(g). Moreover, it is sensible to interpret Article 54(3)(g) broadly in the light of the aims of that section of the Treaty, namely to eliminate obstacles to free movement.

Besides the above-mentioned aims of third-party protection, the Proposal was clearly intended to complement Community initiatives to encourage the creation and development of small and medium-sized enterprises.[24] Partly[25] for that reason, private companies were considered to be the most appropriate vehicle for single-member companies, although as will be seen there is provision for Member States to extend the option to public companies.

Whether the overriding aim of harmonization can be said to have been achieved in any real sense by the Directive is also doubtful: since the Directive permits private or public single-member companies or sole traders with limited liability, and permits Member States to restrict the number of single-member companies which an individual may form and to prohibit a company from forming a single-member company, the divergences between the laws of the Member States are unlikely to be much eroded by the Directive. However, it will at least ensure that all Member States provide for some form of limited-liability trading for an individual.

Form of Single-member Company

Article 1 of the Directive provides that it is to apply to the laws, regulations and administrative provisions of the Member States relating to listed types of company:

[22] 'The Draft Twelfth Directive on Single-Member Companies' [1989] European Business Law 86.
[23] Explanatory Memorandum, 4.
[24] See the Explanatory Memorandum, 3, and the 3rd recital in the preamble.
[25] See further below.

the list which follows comprises those companies equivalent in each Member State to a private company.[26]

As indicated above, one reason for making private companies the principal vehicle for single-member companies was the desire to encourage small and medium-sized enterprises. Other factors were that some Member States required public companies to have more than two members, so that reducing minimum membership to one would have been more controversial, or more than one director, which would run counter to the concept of a one-man company, and that, as required by the Second Directive, public companies must have a minimum capital, thus making them a less attractive option (although some Member States also require a minimum capital of private companies).

Article 6 however permits Member States to allow single-member companies in the case of public limited companies,[27] in which case the 'Directive shall apply'. That presumably means that the requirements of the Directive concerning publicity, general meetings and contracts between the sole member and his company[28] are to apply.

Article 7 provides as follows:

A Member State need not allow the formation of single-member companies where its legislation provides that an individual entrepreneur may set up an undertaking the liability of which is limited to a sum devoted to a stated activity, on condition that safeguards are laid down for such undertakings which are equivalent to those imposed by this Directive or by any other Community provisions applicable to the companies referred to in Article 1.

This provision was designed to accommodate the fact that 'for theoretical reasons certain Member States are reluctant to accept the idea of a one member company'.[29] Since such Member States may nevertheless provide for limited liability for sole traders, as Portugal had already chosen to do, that option was included in the Directive. The Portuguese legislation[30] provides that an individual trader may constitute an 'individual limited-liability business' (*estabelecimento individual de responsabilidade limitada*; 'EIRL') by allocating to it a proportion of his assets, to represent the EIRL's initial capital. That capital must be put into a separate bank account in the name of the owner of the EIRL. The EIRL must be constituted by a notarized document and the notary must confirm that the provisions as to capital have been complied with. There are various requirements as to formation, publicity, accounts, maintenance of capital, separation of assets and liquidation. In particular, the EIRL's assets are to be used solely for obligations arising from the business activity[31] and those assets are the only assets to be used for such obligations.

---

[26] For the full list, see those types of company listed in the First Directive as amended and described as such, set out on pp 17–18 above.

[27] The Netherlands permits this.   [28] Arts 3–5; see below.

[29] Explanatory Memorandum, 9.

[30] Decreto-lei no 248/86 of 25 August 1986. See Karayanni, F A, *Les sociétés d'une seule personne* (1992) 59–67.

[31] Subject to exceptions concerning obligations of the owner which arose before publication of the document setting up the EIRL and the case of forced execution against the EIRL's owner if his own

It is clear from Article 7 that, where a Member State takes advantage of the option, it must impose safeguards equivalent to those which would apply to a single-member company. Those safeguards will of course include the specific requirements of the Twelfth Directive as to publicity, administration and contracts; they will also extend to safeguards imposed by the other company law directives, concerning, for example, disclosure of information, audit and accounts.[32]

Creation and Membership

Article 2(1) provides that a company 'may have a sole member when it is formed and also when all its shares come to be held by a single person'. Thus a single-member company may either be created as such *ab initio* or arise as a result of the concentration of all the shares in an existing company in the hands of a single share-holder. Article 11(2)(f) of the First Directive, which provides that the latter circumstance is a permitted ground of nullity of companies, is accordingly now redundant in so far as concerns private companies.

In the original Proposal, Article 2(1) included a requirement that 'Shares in such a company shall be nominative'.[33] That requirement was subsequently dropped. As the Commission explained:

the only purpose of such a requirement is to indicate the identity of the shareholder. Since this identity is already shown in the company's statutes—which must be made public by virtue of the First Directive when the company is originally formed as a single-member company and by virtue of Article 3 of the [Twelfth Directive] in all other cases—this requirement is superfluous.[34]

Article 2(2) of the original Proposal prohibited a single-member company whose sole member was a legal person from being the sole member of another company. The aim of that prohibition was to avoid the creation of chains of companies.[35] Article 2(3) of the Proposal provided further that, where the sole member was a legal person, Member States were to impose one of two conditions. First, Member States could provide for unlimited liability of the sole member during the period of sole membership, subject to a possible exception where the sole membership arose after the company's formation, in which case Member States could provide that unlim-ited liability would not be incurred unless another member was not found within one year.[36] Alternatively, Member States could both fix a minimum capital (of an

goods are insufficient. In the case of bankruptcy of the owner however the rights of the EIRL's credi-tors against its assets are protected.

[32] 1st, 4th and 8th Directives. They will not however include the requirements as to capital con-tained in the 2nd Directive, which is not applicable to private companies.

[33] i e, bearing the name of a person. The term is not generally used of shares in English, 'registered shares' being the more general contrast to bearer shares. In French, however, the term *titre nominatif* is accepted as a contrast to bearer shares.

[34] COM (89) 591 final, 29 November 1989, 3.   [35] Explanatory Memorandum, 5.

[36] Art 2(3)(a).

unspecified amount) for single-member companies and require both the company and its sole member to be companies which at their balance sheet dates did not exceed the limits of two of the three criteria for medium-sized companies within the meaning of Article 27 of the Fourth Directive on Annual Accounts.[37] If one of the companies exceeded the limits and the situation was not regularized in the year following the balance sheet date, the sole member would have unlimited liability for obligations of the company arising after the balance sheet date.[38]

The proposed restrictions on the freedom of a company to be the sole shareholder of another company met with resistance, particularly on the part of Germany. It was argued that they were too restrictive for groups, and in any event unlikely to be effective, since in practice ways would be found around them. Moreover, it was considered inappropriate to include in a directive of limited scope provisions which would directly affect other areas, in particular the law of groups.[39] It appears to have been the final point which persuaded the Commission to amend its Proposal so as to replace the prohibition in Article 2(2) and the conditions in Article 2(3) with a new provision which survived as Article 2(2) of the adopted Directive.[40] Article 2(2) provides:

Member States may, pending coordination of national laws relating to groups, lay down special provisions or sanctions for cases where:
(a)   a natural person is the sole member of several companies;
(b)   a single-member company or any other legal person is the sole member of a company.

Article 2(2) is further explained in the preamble to the Directive:

the sole aim of this provision is to take account of the differences which currently exist in certain national laws; . . . for that purpose, Member States may in specific cases lay down restrictions on the use of single-member companies or remove the limits on the liabilities of sole members; . . . Member States are free to lay down rules to cover the risks that single-member companies may present as a consequence of having single members, particularly to ensure that subscribed capital is paid.[41]

Publicity Requirements

Where a company is incorporated as a single-member company, that fact will be apparent from the disclosure made in accordance with Article 3 of the First Directive, which requires the company's instrument of constitution to be lodged in the companies register or equivalent in the Member State of incorporation.[42] Article 3 of the Twelfth Directive complements that provision with a requirement for disclosure where a company becomes a single-member company because all its

---

[37] See p 126 above.   [38] Art 2(3)(b).
[39] Karayanni, F A, *Les sociétés d'une seule personne* (1992) 87.
[40] Explanatory Memorandum relating to the 1st amended Proposal, 2–3.   [41] 6th recital.
[42] Arts 2(1)(a) and 3(1)(2). See pp 19–21 above.

shares come to be held by a single person. It requires that fact, together with the identity of the sole member, to be either disclosed in the companies register or equivalent or 'entered in a register kept by the company and accessible to the public'. It is surely unfortunate that the Directive permits the latter option: not only do the alternative permitted methods of publicity undermine the coordination achieved, but also the option of disclosure in the company's own register means that the central register may not contain information which is clearly of relevance for third parties.

The Commission's amended Proposal included an Article 2a reflecting a proposal by the European Parliament that a company must state on its letters and order forms[43] that it is a single-member company. However, the Council objected that 'this extremely bureaucratic and expensive requirement would be contrary to the directive's objective of creating conditions more favourable to small businesses'.[44] The Commission also made the sensible point that 'to show this information on the company's stationery does not provide any safeguard for creditors. Since liability is limited to the company's assets, the essential point for creditors is that the accounting directives are fully applied, and provision is made for this irrespective of the number of shareholders.'[45]

Administration

Article 4 provides that the sole member shall exercise the powers of the general meeting of the company[46] and that decisions taken by him in that capacity shall be recorded in minutes or drawn up in writing.[47] It is for the individual Member States to make provision for appropriate penalties for failure to comply with that rule.[48] A prohibition in the original Proposal against delegation by the sole member of the powers of the general meeting was dropped in accordance with a suggestion by the Parliament, with a view to simplifying the functioning of the single-member company.[49] A suggestion by the Economic and Social Committee that, with a view to greater transparency and as an aid to enforcement, the right of interested parties to have access to minutes and other documentation should be specifically stated[50] was in contrast not taken up.

Transactions between Member and Company

Article 5 provides that contracts between the sole member and his company as represented by him shall be recorded in minutes or drawn up in writing,[51] although

---

[43] Referred to in Art 4 of the First Directive; see p 24 above.
[44] Explanatory notes to the re-examined Proposal, 3.   [45] Ibid.   [46] Art 4(1).
[47] Art 4(2).   [48] Explanatory Memorandum, 8.
[49] Explanatory Memorandum with regard to the amended Proposal, 4.
[50] [1988] OJ C318/10, para 2.4.1.   [51] Art 5(1).

Member States need not apply that provision to 'current operations concluded under normal conditions'.[52] As the Commission explained, any agreement between any company and one of its members carries the risk of a conflict of interest; legislation has been enacted on the subject in all Member States. The danger however is clearly much greater in the case of the single-member company.[53] The original Proposal required the possibility of any agreement between the sole member and the company represented by him to be provided for in the company's statutes or instrument of incorporation, on the basis that such documents were accessible to any interested party at the companies register in accordance with the First Directive.[54] That additional restriction did not survive.

As with Article 4, the Directive leaves it to the individual Member States to legislate on the effects of non-compliance with the requirement imposed by Article 5(1).

Implementation in the United Kingdom

The Directive has been implemented in the United Kingdom by the Companies (Single Member Private Limited Companies) Regulations 1992.[55] In so far as it has attracted comment, the Directive has received a cautious welcome.[56] The need for a single-member company has perhaps not been felt so keenly in the United Kingdom, where the concept of nominee shareholders is firmly entrenched, as in civil law jurisdictions which are not so familiar with that device. Conversely, the United Kingdom experiences no conceptual difficulties with the principle of a single-member company: contract is not the essence of incorporation, and the concept of a corporation sole, a corporate entity with a single member,[57] has been recognized in England and Wales[58] since medieval times.

---

[52] Art 5(2).   [53] Explanatory Memorandum, 8.
[54] Art 5(2); Explanatory Memorandum, 8. For the background to this provision, much influenced by German law, see Karayanni, F A, *Les sociétés d'une seule personne* (1992) 90–2.
[55] SI 1992/1699.
[56] See, for example, Wooldridge, F, 'the principle . . . would seem to be generally worthy of support', *Company Law in the United Kingdom and the European Community* (1991), 100.
[57] Historically, corporations sole have been mainly ecclesiastical offices, from archbishop down to vicar; the sovereign is also a corporation sole at common law.
[58] But not in Scotland, except where created by statute applicable also to Scotland.

X

Background to the Securities Directives

Conspectus

The Treaty contains no reference to securities markets: none the less the European Community has been described as 'the most active and influential organization in the nascent field of international securities regulation'.[1] That recent assessment reflects the fruits of the Commission's progress in a number of directions spanning three decades.

At an early stage, between 1960 and 1965, Community action focused on liberalizing capital movements in general and exploring the possibilities of liberalizing capital markets in particular. The 1970s saw the parallel approaches of a non-binding code of conduct and the launching of a major harmonization programme, which culminated in a raft of directives adopted at the turn of the decade concerned with the admission of securities to official listing. In 1985 the Commission's White Paper *Completing the Internal Market*[2] made liberalization of capital markets, including those relating to securities transactions, a high priority, and the end of the decade saw the adoption of a further parcel of directives concerned with mutual recognition of listing particulars, public offer prospectuses, disclosure of major shareholdings and insider dealing. The original goal of the 1980s, the creation of a single pan-European market, has largely been recognized as over-ambitious; the current goal is rather to give investors within the Community direct access to securities quoted Europe-wide by linking existing markets into an information network.[3]

Paving the Way

Progress in the liberalization of capital movements was made at an early stage, with directives of 1960[4] and 1962[5] concentrating on facilitating capital movements in

---

[1] Wolff, S, 'Securities Regulation' in Folsom, R H, Lake, R B and Nanda, V P (eds), *European Community Law after 1992* (1993) 501.

[2] COM (85) 310 final, 14 June 1985. The White Paper identified the three leading principles of an integrated European capital market: total freedom of the movement of capital, freedom of financial services and cooperation of the public authorities with reference to operations on the financial markets.

[3] The Eurolist project: see further pp 234–5 below.

[4] 1st Directive of 11 May 1960 for the implementation of Art 67 of the Treaty [1960] JO L43/921; [1959–62] OJ Spec Ed, 49.

[5] 2nd Council Directive (EEC) 63/21 of 18 December 1962 adding to and amending the First Directive for the implementation of Art 67 of the Treaty [1963] JO L9/62; [1963–4] OJ Spec Ed, 5.

certain fields and, inter alia, liberalizing capital transactions in unlisted securities. In 1964 the Commission appointed a committee of experts, under the chairmanship of Professor Segré, 'to examine and make recommendations on the factors conducive to the creation of a viable European capital market'.[6] In its report, *Development of a European Capital Market* (1966), the Committee stressed the importance of investors having 'at their disposal sufficient and reasonably homogeneous information on securities dealt in other markets'. This led to the Committee's recommendation of a greatly improved scheme of mandatory disclosure on issue, followed by various continuing disclosure obligations, and of a harmonized prospectus on public offers. A draft sample prospectus for both public offers and admission to listing was annexed to the Segré report, which largely formed the basis for what ultimately became the Listing Particulars Directive (see chapter XI). A further working group was set up by the Commission in 1969 under the chairmanship of de Barsy, E G, then president of the Belgian Banking Commission, which recommended a number of measures to liberalize securities markets. The recommendations of both these bodies are largely reflected in the Listing Particulars[7], Interim Reports[8] and Public Offer Prospectus[9] Directives.

The Segré report also recommended the elimination of legal, regulatory and administrative barriers which put issuers from other Member States at a disadvantage compared with national issuers. Increased integration of the various markets, by way of multiple quotation to be obtained by the admission of the same shares to listing on the Stock Exchanges of several Member States, was recommended, on the basis that introducing foreign shares on various exchanges would facilitate dealing and reduce its cost. Various suggestions in the report were ultimately reflected in some of the major reorganizations of EC Stock Exchanges, for example the 'Big Bang' in London and the reforms elsewhere in Europe.[10]

The central theme of disclosure was the dominant principle in the subsequent developments. The goal was ultimately market integration, with as a first step interpenetration of the markets in which transactions in the same securities take place in a number of different markets subject to the same requirements of disclosure and comparable supervision at the national level. Drafts of what were to become the Listing Particulars and the Admissions Directives were published in 1972 and 1976 respectively, but progress towards adoption was slow.[11] The Commission decided

---

[6] See Rider, B, and Ffrench, H L, *The Regulation of Insider Trading* (1979) 263.

[7] Council Directive (EEC) 80/390 of 17 March 1980 coordinating the requirements for the drawing up, scrutiny and distribution of the listing particulars to be published for the admission of securities to official stock exchange listing [1980] OJ L100/1.

[8] Council Directive (EEC) 82/121 of 15 February 1982 on information to be published on a regular basis by companies the shares of which have been admitted to official stock exchange listing [1982] OJ L48/26.

[9] Council Directive (EEC) 89/298 of 17 April 1989 coordinating the requirements for the drawing-up, scrutiny and distribution of the prospectus to be published when transferable securities are offered to the public [1989] OJ L124/8.

[10] e g Amsterdam, Copenhagen, Paris, Madrid and Lisbon.

[11] See further ch XI below.

that it would approach the matter from another angle in the mean time, and issued a recommendation concerning a European code of conduct relating to transactions in transferable securities.[12] The document referred to investors' 'lack of full information on the securities . . . and ignorance or misunderstanding of the rules governing the various markets' as obstacles to interpenetration. The code, annexed to the recommendation, set out a fundamental objective, certain general overriding principles and a number of supplementary principles. The fundamental objective was to 'establish standards of ethical behaviour on a Community-wide basis, so as to promote the effective functioning of securities markets . . . and to safeguard the public interest'. The general principles focused on timely disclosure of 'fair, accurate, clear, adequate' information; fair and equal treatment of shareholders; and equitable dealings by directors and financial intermediaries. The supplementary principles included the following, which have since been elaborated and formalized by the Interim Reports and Public Offer Prospectus Directives respectively:

12.   Every company whose securities are dealt in on the market should publish periodically, and at least every six months, information which is clear, precise, complete and up-to-date concerning its business operations, results and financial position. Any fact or important decision capable of having an appreciable effect on the price of securities should also be made public without delay.

. . .

14.   It is desirable that a public issue of securities should be preceded by the publication of a prospectus . . .

The recommendation had little effect in practice. Although certain national regulatory bodies issued statements requiring operators within their jurisdiction to respect the code,[13] the recommendation had no binding force.[14] Its significance lies more in its status as the first articulation by the Commission of its general approach to promoting 'the proper working and the interpenetration of [the securities] markets'.[15] It firmly established the principle of disclosure, the bedrock of the subsequent legislation. It also crystallized the Commission's approach to insider dealing,[16] which is noteworthy given that at the time only one Member State (France) had even attempted to grapple with the problem by legislation,[17] and

---

[12] Commission Recommendation (EEC) 77/534 of 25 July 1977 [1977] OJ L212/37. For a full commentary see Lempereur, C, 'Le code de conduite européen concernant les transactions relatives aux valeurs mobilières' (1978) 55 Revue de droit international et de droit comparé 249.

[13] Belgium, France and Luxembourg: see Wymeersch, E, 'L'action de la Communauté Européenne dans le domaine des valeurs mobilières' (1988) 3 Revue de droit des affaires internationales 365, 373.

[14] Buxbaum, R M, and Hopt, K, recount that, since the recommendation emanated from the then British-led DG XV (Financial Institutions and Taxation) rather than DG III (Internal Market and Industrial Affairs), which included the predominantly German-staffed Directorate usually responsible for harmonization, its structure reflected the British tradition of self-regulation rather than the more legalistic German preference: Legal Harmonization and the Business Enterprise (1988) 231.

[15] Explanatory Memorandum, para 1.

[16] Supplementary principle 9 enjoined insiders in possession of price-sensitive information to refrain from dealing or disclosing.

[17] See ch XV below.

included a reference (in supplementary principle 17) to the rights of minority share-holders on changes of controlling interests,[18] which again were in general not pro-tected by national law at the time.[19] Moreover, the fact that the code has been overtaken by directives covering much of the same ground does not necessarily mean that it has become obsolete, since the Court of Justice has held that national courts are bound to take recommendations into consideration in order to decide disputes, in particular where they cast light on the interpretation of national imple-menting measures or where they are designed to supplement binding Community provisions.[20]

Harmonizing the Regulatory Framework

These various strands were woven together and ultimately reissued as the directives adopted at the turn of the 1970s relating to conditions for the admission of securi-ties to listing, the listing particulars and interim information to be published on and after admission to listing and, a decade later, the disclosure of major shareholdings, the prospectus to be published on the public offer of securities and insider dealing.

The securities directives[21] comprise the Admissions Directive,[22] the Listing Particulars Directive, the Interim Reports Directive, and the Public Offers Prospectus Directive (the last three directives cited at notes 7–9). The first three of these directives were originally intended to standardize listing requirements throughout the Community, so that admission to listing in any Member State would have entailed the right to admission to listing in any other Member State. This proved over-ambitious, and the directives settled instead for the more limited aim of harmonizing minimum requirements. They impose obligations on a com-pany on and after an application for the listing of its securities on a Stock Exchange in a Member State: the Admissions Directive lays down the conditions to be satis-fied and the Listing Particulars Directive defines the information to be published by a company seeking such listing, and the Interim Reports Directive harmonizes the information to be published on a continuing basis by companies whose shares are listed. The three directives are considered together in the next chapter. The

[18] That principle and the following one condemning undisclosed acquisitions of controlling hold-ings were apparently omitted from the text published in Germany since they were difficult to reconcile with German law and practice: Buxbaum and Hopt (n 11 above).

[19] See 'Remarks by R. J. Goebel' in the *Proceedings of the 82nd Annual Meeting of the American Society of International Law* (1988) 299.

[20] Case C–322/88 *Grimaldi v Fonds des Maladies Professionnelles* [1989] ECR 4407. See Wouters, J, 'EC Harmonisation of National Rules Concerning Securities Offerings, Stock Exchange Listing and Investment Services: An Overview' (1993) 4 European Business Law Review 199, 200.

[21] A good succinct summary of the salient provisions of all four directives may be found in Warren, M G, 'Global Harmonization of Securities Laws: the Achievement of the European Communities' (1990) 31 Harvard Law Review 209–18, and Wolff, S, 'Securities Regulation' (see n 1 above).

[22] Council Directive (EEC) 79/279 of 5 March 1979 coordinating the conditions for the admission of securities to official stock exchange listing [1979] OJ L66/21.

Public Offers Prospectus Directive prescribes the information to be published when previously unlisted securities, whether or not they are subsequently to be listed, are offered to the public for the first time; it is considered in chapter XII. The Listing Particulars and Public Offers Prospectus Directives also include provisions for mutual recognition of the documents with which they are concerned; this aspect is considered in chapter XIII.

The interaction of the Admissions and Listing Particulars Directives and the Public Offers Prospectus Directive[23] will be more readily understood if it is borne in mind that in most continental countries the admission of securities to listing is regarded as a separate operation from the offer of securities to the public, even if the two operations occur simultaneously or nearly so. The issue and public placing of the shares normally precedes their admission to listing by several weeks,[24] whereas in the United Kingdom the two operations are normally simultaneous. In the early 1970s, when the various possibilities for harmonization were being discussed, a prospectus on the admission of securities to listing was compulsory in five of the original six Member States, which also had existing supervisory authorities, whereas a prospectus on public offers was compulsory in only three.[25] Offers of securities directly to the public were moreover relatively rare on the continent.[26] The Commission accordingly decided to work initially towards harmonizing requirements for the prospectus on admission, or listing particulars:[27] a directive harmonizing conditions for admission to listing was the logical complement to the proposed Listing Particulars Directive, and the Interim Reports Directive completed the first tier of the legislative structure regulating the securities market at Community level.

The Commission's energy in this field was then directed to harmonizing the content of public offer prospectuses. The proposed directive proved controversial

[23] Described by a head of the DTI's Financial Services Division as 'a rather complex tangle of directives': Willott, B, 'EC Capital Markets', *Corporate Law—The European Dimension* (1991) 69.

[24] This pattern also explains the one-way recognition of prospectuses as listing particulars: the absence of a requirement for recognition in the opposite direction, which appears prima facie to be anomalous in an otherwise coherent and seamless structure, is presumably designed to slot in with continental practice.

[25] The five excluded Italy; the three comprised France, Belgium and Luxembourg. See Suckow, S, 'The European Prospectus' (1975) AJCL 50, 52–3 and Lempereur, C, 'La proposition de directive sur le prospectus à publier en cas d'offre publique de souscription ou de vente de valeurs mobilières' (1981) 58 Revue de droit international et de droit comparé 223, 224–5. See also the latter half of the 4th recital in the preamble to the Listing Particulars Directive.

[26] See Warren, M G, 'The Common Market Prospectus' (1989) 26 CML Rev 687, 707 at n 86 for a description of the pattern of major issues.

[27] The distinction between the prospectus on issue and listing particulars is elegantly reflected in the French terms *prospectus d'émission* and *prospectus d'admission*. The confusion between the two documents was for a while intensified by the English practice before and around adoption of referring to the Listing Particulars Directive as the 6th Directive on Prospectuses: see, e g, the title of Morse, G's article 'Sixth Directive on Prospectuses Adopted' (1980) 5 ELR 316. The term 'listing prospectus' has recently been coined in the UK in the wake of the implementation of the Public Offer Prospectus Directive to describe the document to be published on a first public offer of securities for which a listing is being sought.

in a number of respects, and its passage through the legislative process culminating in adoption in 1989 took the better part of a decade.[28]

A logical progression from having similar requirements governing information to be disclosed at various stages is for Member States to recognize disclosure documents issued in another State, and this was addressed in further directives concerned with the mutual recognition of listing particulars and prospectuses.[29]

Like any securities market, the Community-wide market being sculpted by this legislation will need to ensure a solid base of investor confidence in order to flourish. A coherent framework for the prohibition and detection of insider dealing is an essential element in inspiring such confidence, and the Insider Dealing Directive[30] seeks to impose this, requiring insider dealing to be prohibited within harmonized parameters. Mandatory disclosure of significant shareholdings contributes further to the transparency of the market, ensuring that both investors and issuers themselves have the means of knowing the pattern of control; this has been achieved by the Major Shareholdings Directive,[31] which provides for disclosure of major holdings and changes to holdings in listed companies.

Harmonization may from today's standpoint seem an ambitious and elusive target. As will be seen, the securities directives are honeycombed with numerous exceptions and derogations,[32] so that it is tempting to conclude that the sought-after harmonization remains an illusion. It must however be borne in mind that the Directives were conceived and developed against a background of widely divergent securities regulation, the spectrum in the original Member States ranging from regulatory anarchy in Italy to a sophisticated system of control in France.[33] A latticework of minima governing the conditions for admission to listing, disclosure on and after listing, public offers, mutual recognition and market transparency has been constructed: while this remains remote from the concept of a uniform and all-encompassing regulatory framework, it is none the less a laudable achievement.[34]

[28] See ch XII below for further discussion.

[29] Council Directive (EEC) 87/345 amending Directive (EEC) 80/390 coordinating the requirements for the drawing-up, scrutiny and distribution of the listing particulars to be published for the admission of securities to official stock exchange listing [1987] OJ L185/81; and Council Directive (EEC) 90/211 of 23 April 1990 amending Directive (EEC) 80/390 in respect of the mutual recognition of public offer prospectuses as stock exchange listing particulars [1990] OJ L112/24; see ch XIII below.

[30] Council Directive (EEC) 89/592 of 13 November 1989 coordinating regulations on insider dealing [1989] OJ L334/30. See ch XV.

[31] Council Directive (EEC) 88/627 of 12 December 1988 on the information to be published when a major holding in a listed company is acquired or disposed of [1988] OJ L348/62; see ch XIV.

[32] So much so that one commentator has described the Public Offers Prospectus as appearing 'to constitute a mandatory disclosure scheme in search of an issuer': Warren (n 26 above) 702.

[33] See for an outline of the positions in the original Member States Buxbaum, R M, and Hopt, K, *Legal Harmonization and the Business Enterprise* (1988), 189–92.

[34] Although it is perhaps not perceived as particularly significant in the UK, where companies have tended to view multiple European listings as unnecessary given the traditional pre-eminence of the London markets. In 1996, only eleven UK companies were (in addition to their London listings) listed on more than two European Stock Exchanges, and only five on more than three: Kehoe, J, and Bannister, J A, 'International Listings: Access to New Markets' (May 1996) Practical Law for Companies 23, 27.

For companies seeking listings throughout Europe however even this degree of harmonization has been eroded by the practice of competent authorities in certain Member States of supplementing the minimum requirements laid down by the Directives with additional obligations, in particular requiring the translation of documents and the inclusion of local tax and other information. That problem is being tackled by other initiatives, in particular Eurolist.[35]

Eurolist and Beyond

As mentioned above, the current goal at a European level for the further integration of securities markets is the linking of markets into an information network. 'Euroquote', the early private initiative of the Federation of European Stock Exchanges, 'collapsed under the weight of the divergent interests of its members'.[36] The Eurolist project, developed by the Federation of European Stock Exchanges in agreement with the Stock Exchange authorities in the fifteen Member States, Switzerland and Norway, is designed to provide for the simultaneous listing and trading of major European shares on several European exchanges. The system aims to provide cross-exchange information services to facilitate trading in shares in up to 250 European companies on a number of different member Stock Exchanges of the Federation. The authorities agree to grant listings on the basis of a certificate of good conduct from the issuer's home State authorities, which are responsible for monitoring the company on behalf of all member exchanges. Listing requirements and continuing obligations are standardized rather than imposed as minimum requirements. To use Eurolist, companies need to be listed on at least one participating Stock Exchange and seeking secondary listing on at least a further two, and have a market capitalization of at least ECU 1 billion together with annual share turnover of at least ECU 250 million.

There are also now two rival Europe-wide markets for growth companies wanting to raise capital. EASDAQ (European Association of Securities Dealers Automated Quotation) is based on the United States' NASDAQ (National Association of Securities Dealers Automated Quotation), the world's first electronic Stock Market, and will operate as a screen-based pan-European Stock Market focusing on high growth companies.[37] Its launch in September 1996 coincided with or preceded the creation of junior markets in several Member States:

---

[35] At a wider international level, the International Organisation of Securities Commissions issued a consultative document in 1997 proposing international disclosure standards for cross-border equity offerings and initial listings by foreign issuers. The intention is to develop internationally agreed standards so that a company could issue a single disclosure document when seeking a listing on any of the world's major Stock Markets.

[36] Steil, B, *Illusions of Liberalization: Securities Regulation in Japan and the EC* (1995) 28.

[37] See Vanassche, C, 'EASDAQ—the new Pan-European Stock Market for High Growth Companies' [1996] European Financial Services Law 258 and Stoakes, C, 'EASDAQ: A Truly European Exchange?' (1996) European Counsel, I(2), 22.

the Alternative Investment Market in London, Le Nouveau Marché in Paris, Deutsche Börse's Neuer Markt in Frankfurt, Italy's Mercado Telematico Delle Impresse and Amsterdam's NMAX (Nieuwe Markt Amsterdam). EURO.NM (official name 'Nouveau Marché'/'Nieuwe Markt') is a European Economic Interest Grouping formed between the Paris, Frankfurt, Amsterdam and Brussels new markets. It aims to create a Europe-wide trading network based on the existing markets, linking trading systems so as to increase the pool of available investors.[38]

Now that Eurolist, EASDAQ and EURO.NM are established, the question arises whether further steps should be taken in pursuit of market integration.[39] Several commentators have advocated the creation of a European securities commission.[40] While it may be thought unlikely that such a proposal would survive the combined resistance of jealously guarded national sovereignty and the move towards subsidiarity, it is noteworthy that in 1993 the Council published a draft common position with a view to adopting a directive setting up a securities committee. The purpose of the committee would be to consider measures for adapting acts adopted by the Council in the field of securities, securities markets and securities intermediaries to technical progress, examine any question relating to the application of Community provisions in those fields and be consulted by the Commission on new proposals as regards further coordination in those fields.

The Contact Committee—Watching the Directives

It is convenient to conclude this introductory chapter with a brief reference to the Contact Committee, common to all the directives in this area. Article 20 of the Admissions Directive provides that a Contact Committee is to be set up alongside the Commission, to be composed of persons appointed by the Member States and representatives of the Commission, to facilitate (a) the harmonized implementation of the Directive through regular consultations on any practical problems arising from its application and on which exchanges of views are deemed useful and (b) the establishment of a concerted attitude between Member States on the more stringent and additional conditions and obligations which they may require

---

[38] See 'New Markets Compete' in European Counsel (May 1997) II, 11. For further discussion of both markets, see Blumberg, J-P, De Bauw, F, Sunt, C, Van Hulle, H, Macq, V, Van Lancker, J, Lohest, T and Ponnet, E, *EASDAQ and EURO.NM BELGIUM* (1997).

[39] See Garzaniti, L, 'Single Market-Making: EC Regulation of Securities Markets' (1993) 14 The Company Lawyer 43 for a useful summary of various options for a future European securities market. Wymeersch, E, sets out a detailed proposal for an integrated European securities market in 'From Harmonization to Integration in the European Securities Markets' (1981) 3 Journal of Comparative Corporate Law and Securities Regulation 1, 10–25.

[40] See e g Warren, M G, 'Global Harmonization of Securities Laws' (1990) Harvard Law Review 231, and Leleux, P, 'Corporation Law in the United States and in the EEC' (1967–68) 5 CML Rev 133. There is a useful overview of the issues by Lee, R, in 'Should There Be a European Securities Commission? A Framework for Analysis' (1992) 3 European Business Law Review 102.

pursuant to Article 5 and to advise the Commission if necessary on any supplements or amendments to be made to the Directive, including in particular adjustments pursuant to Article 21 (see below). The Committee's functions were extended to encompass analogous tasks in relation to the Listing Particulars Directive,[41] the Interim Reports Directive[42] and the Public Offers Prospectus Directive,[43] as well as the Major Shareholdings Directive[44] and the Insider Dealing Directive.[45]

The Impact of the Euro

In July 1997 the Commission issued a Communication *The Impact of the Introduction of the Euro on Capital Markets*.[46] The report was prepared by a group of market participants, chaired by A Giovannini. It focuses on technical and other issues that will have a direct impact on the functioning of the capital markets after the introduction of the euro and sets out recommendations on redenomination of the bond and equity markets and on the market conventions to be applied to the new euro market.

With regard to the bond market, the report recommends that non-government bonds follow the practice for government bonds, namely, as decided at the Madrid European Council in December 1995, all new issues should be denominated in euro from 1 January 1999. Since the Madrid Council, some Member States have announced that they will convert a substantial part of their outstanding debt into euro after that date. The report considers various models for redenomination and makes recommendations on market rules and conventions, price sources, issuing procedures, benchmarks, ratings, and the repo market.

With regard to the equity market, the report recommends that trading and quoting in euro should also start on 1 January 1999, although intermediaries will have to make conversions when necessary in order to settle their clients' accounts in the currency denomination of the clients' choice. The European Stock Exchanges have since endorsed this recommendation, announcing that they intend to switch all trading and quotation to the euro in a 'big bang' from 1 January 1999. It suggests that it would be sensible for redenomination of shares to take place at the same time as the change in the accounting unit, although synchronization is not essential since the denomination of share capital should affect neither its economic value nor investors' ability to trade in shares. The report further recommends, as a way of avoiding redenomination, that companies should move to non par value shares, namely shares expressed simply as a fraction of the company's total capital. The report notes that non par value shares are permitted by the Second Company Law Directive, although implementation of this solution would require national legislation to be adopted in most of the Member States.

---

[41] Art 26.   [42] Art 11.   [43] Art 25.   [44] Art 16.   [45] Art 12.

[46] COM (97) 337 final, 2 July 1997. See also the Opinion of the Economic and Social Committee on the Communication [1998] OJ C73/141.

In the United Kingdom, where the companies legislation contains no procedure whereby a company can redenominate its share capital into another currency, the Department of Trade and Industry issued a consultative document[47] regarding possible legislative changes to assist the redenomination of share capital into euros. Legislation is likely in the near future.[48]

[47] *The Euro: Redenomination of Share Capital*, January 1998.
[48] For further discussion see Proctor, C, 'Share Capital and the Euro—Redenominating shares' (April 1998) Practical Law for Companies, vol IX, 17.

XI

The First Stage—Harmonizing the Conditions of Listing

It is convenient to consider the Admissions, Listing Particulars and Interim Reports Directives together (collectively referred to in this chapter as 'the Listing Directives'), since, as stated in the preamble to a directive amending the Admissions and Listing Particulars Directives:[1]

there is a close link between these three Directives, not only because the purpose of all three is to coordinate a number of rules relating to securities which have been admitted to official stock exchange listing or whose admission to such official listing is requested, but above all because the three Directives aim to establish at Community level a coordinated information policy on the securities in question.[2]

Legal Basis of the Listing Directives

All three Listing Directives are based on Articles 54(3)(g)[3] and 100[4] of the Treaty. The rationale for reliance on Article 54(3)(g) is clear:[5] investor protection is promoted by mandatory disclosure of information and the imposition of minimum requirements with which companies seeking admission of their securities to listing must comply. The preamble to the Admissions Directive states that recourse to Article 100 was required because, since the Directive applies to 'securities issued by non-member States or their regional or local authorities or international public bodies', it extends to entities not within the second paragraph of Article 58[6] of the

---

[1] Council Directive (EEC) 82/148 of 3 March 1982 amending Directive (EEC) 79/279 coordinating the conditions for the admission of securities to official stock exchange listing and Directive (EEC) 80/390 coordinating the requirements for the drawing up, scrutiny and distribution of the listing particulars to be published for the admission of securities to official stock exchange listing [1982] OJ L62/22.

[2] 4th recital in the preamble.

[3] Which at the time of adoption of the Directives referred to 'coordinating to the necessary extent the safeguards which, for the protection of the interests of members and others, are required by Member States of companies or firms within the meaning of . . . Article 58 with a view to making such safeguards equivalent throughout the Community'.

[4] 'The Council shall, acting unanimously on a proposal from the Commission, issue directives for the approximation of such provisions . . . as directly affect the establishment or functioning of the common market.'

[5] And was the sole legal basis recited in the Proposals for the three directives.

[6] 'companies or firms constituted under civil or commercial law, including cooperative societies, and other legal persons governed by public or private law, save for those which are non-profit-making'.

Treaty, thus going 'beyond the scope of Article 54(3)(g) while directly affecting the establishment and functioning of the common market within the meaning of Article 100'.[7] The preamble to the Listing Particulars Directive states that the coordination which it seeks to impose 'must apply to securities independently of the legal status of the issuing undertaking', so that the Directive similarly applies to entities not within the second paragraph of Article 58 and thus goes beyond the scope of Article 54(3)(g).[8] The Interim Reports Directive does not explicitly address the issue of legal basis, but since it applies to all companies with shares listed on a Stock Exchange of a Member State,[9] it extends to companies incorporated outside the Community and hence also goes beyond Article 54(3)(g).

Some commentators[10] have expressed surprise that the Admissions Directive at least did not also cite Article 67 *et seq* (progressive abolition of restrictions on the movement of capital) of the Treaty as a legal basis. Those Treaty provisions however confer only a limited power on the Commission to initiate harmonizing legislation, confined to the coordination of exchange policies,[11] so that the omission appears justified.[12]

Scope of the Listing Directives

The Admissions, Listing Particulars and Interim Reports Directives apply respectively to 'securities which are admitted to official listing or are the subject of an application to official listing on a stock exchange situated or operating within a Member State', 'securities which are the subject of an application for admission to official listing on a stock exchange situated or operating within a Member State' and 'companies the shares of which are admitted to official listing on a stock exchange situated or operating in a Member State'.[13] There is no definition in any

---

[7] 2nd recital in the preamble to the Admissions Directive.

[8] 5th recital in the preamble.   [9] See in particular the 8th recital in the preamble.

[10] e g Wymeersch, E, 'La directive sur les conditions d'admission en bourse' (1980) 6 Revue de la banque 7, paras 3 and 22–5, and Izquierdo, M, *Los Mercados de Valores en la CEE* (1992) 61.

[11] Art 70(1). Schmitthoff, C M, makes the wider point that the Treaty basis for company law harmonization in general might be expected 'to be contained in the chapter on the Free Movement of Capital because that is the true reason why it is necessary to have at least some degree of conformity in the national company laws. But when dealing with the free movement of capital, the draftsmen of the Treaty were only thinking of the abolition of exchange control restrictions and neglected everything else over that preoccupation': 'The European Prospectus' in Recht und Wirtschaft in Geschichte und Gegenwart: Festschrift für Johannes Bärmann zum 70. Geburtstag (1975) 859.

[12] See further Seidel, M, 'Escape Clauses in European Community Law' [1978] CML Rev 283–308, 293.

[13] Art 1(1) in each case. The Interim Reports Directive recites that the protection of debenture-holders by the publication of a half-yearly report is not essential because of the rights conferred on them by the debentures. The Proposal had envisaged including convertible, exchangeable or warrant-backed debentures in the scope of the Directive, but between Proposal and adoption the Admissions Directive was adopted under which such debentures may be admitted to listing only if the related shares are also listed; hence regular information needs to be coordinated only for companies whose shares are admitted: see the 5th recital in the preamble.

of the directives of 'securities',[14] 'official listing' or 'stock exchange',[15] although the schedules to both the Admissions and the Listing Particulars Directives setting out respectively the conditions with which shares must comply and the layout of listing particulars[16] seem to envisage straightforward shares to the exclusion of even the most straightforward derivative instruments.[17] Since all the Listing Directives[18] require Member States to designate competent authorities to oversee their execution, it seems both reasonable and consistent with the scheme of the legislation that those authorities should be able to determine the scope of those terms, provided that the definition accords with the aim of the Directives. The United Kingdom Listing Rules define 'securities' as shares, debt securities, units in a collective investment scheme, miscellaneous warrants, certificates representing debt securities, warrants or options to subscribe or purchase securities and other securities of any description.[19] The implementing legislation also defines 'the Official List' as the Official List maintained by the competent authority, which is the London Stock Exchange.[20]

All three Listing Directives provide for the exclusion from their scope of open-ended investment companies (unit trusts) and the units they issue.[21] Member States may decide not to apply the Admissions Directive to securities issued by a Member State or its regional or local authorities; the Listing Particulars Directive shall in any event not apply to securities issued by a State or its regional or local authorities.[22] Member States may exclude central banks from the Interim Reports Directive.[23]

---

[14] cf the Commission Recommendation concerning a European code of conduct (EEC) 77/534 of 25 July 1977 [1977] OJ L212/37 (pp 230–1 above), which included the not particularly illuminating definition of 'transferable securities' as 'all securities which are or may be the subject of dealings on an organized market'. Cf also the definition in the Public Offer Prospectus Directive: see pp 271–3 below.

[15] Wymeersch (n 10 above) considers all three undefined concepts at length: 11–18.

[16] Sch A in each case.

[17] Although the Admissions and Listing Particulars Directives make express provision for certificates representing shares (Arts 4(3) and 16 of the former and Sch C to the latter), this concept is intended to cater for a particular Dutch practice of holding shares: see n 72 below.

[18] Art 9 of the Admissions and the Interim Reports Directives and Art 18 of the Listing Particulars Directive.

[19] There is a wider and less fluent definition in the Financial Services Act 1986, including shares and stock in the share capital of a company; debentures, including debenture stock, loan stock, bonds, certificates of deposit and other instruments creating or acknowledging indebtedness (other than under a contract for the supply of goods or services or a cheque or other bill of exchange, banker's draft or letter of credit); warrants or other instruments entitling the holder to subscribe for shares or stock, whether or not the shares or stock are for the time being in existence or identifiable; and certificates or other instruments conferring property rights in respect of shares or stock, any right to acquire, dispose of, underwrite or convert shares or stock, or a contractual right (other than an option) to acquire such shares or stock otherwise than by subscription: s 142 and Sch 1, paras 1, 2, 4 and 5.

[20] Financial Services Act 1986, s 142(7), as amended by the Official Listing of Securities (Change of Competent Authority) Regulations 1991 (SI 1991/2000).

[21] Art 1(2) in all cases. Member States may decide not to apply the Admissions Directive to such units; the Listing Particulars and Interim Reports Directives are expressed not to apply to such units or companies respectively. The relevant terms are defined in Art 2(a) and (b) of the Admissions and Listing Particulars Directives and Art 1(2) of the Interim Reports Directive. Unit trusts are governed by their own EC legislation, in particular Council Directive (EEC) 85/611 of 20 December 1985 on the coordination of laws, regulations and administrative provisions relating to undertakings for collective investment in transferable securities (UCITS) [1985] OJ L375/3.

[22] Art 1(2) in each case.   [23] Art 1(3).

Both the Admissions and the Listing Particulars Directives use the term 'issuer', although the schedules to the Admissions Directive setting out the conditions of listing and the continuing obligations thereafter refer to 'company' (in relation to the admission of shares) and 'undertaking' (in relation to the admission of debt securities). The Listing Particulars Directive defines 'issuer' as 'companies and other legal persons and any undertaking whose securities are the subject of an application for admission to official listing on a stock exchange'.[24] The Interim Reports Directive applies to companies.[25]

Implementation in the United Kingdom

The United Kingdom was one of the first Member States to implement the Admissions, Listing Particulars and Interim Reports Directives, originally by statutory instrument made under powers conferred by the European Communities Act 1972.[26] That legislation might be described as tertiary rather than secondary, since it legislated by the simple expedient of annexing the Directives to the Regulations, reg 3(1) provided simply 'the requirements of the directives . . . shall have effect and be applied . . .'. It might also, less charitably, be described as ineffective, since the relevant provisions of the European Communities Act[27] do not permit conferment by secondary legislation of the 'power to legislate by orders, rules, regulations or other subordinate instrument',[28] and the Council of The Stock Exchange as competent authority for the purposes of the Directives[29] needed such power. The Regulations were subsequently repealed as part of the implementation of the Financial Services Act 1986;[30] its provisions are now in the main reflected in the Listing Rules[31] issued by the London Stock Exchange (which became the 'competent authority' in 1991), acting pursuant to powers conferred on it by Pt IV of the Financial Services Act.[32] Although there is no express statutory requirement on the Stock Exchange to comply with the Directives in framing and administering its rules, the Secretary of State is empowered[33] to direct the Stock Exchange to take or not to take specific action if it appears to be contravening Community obligations.

---

[24] Art 2(c).
[25] Art 1(1).
[26] The Stock Exchange (Listing) Regulations 1984 (SI 1984/716).
[27] Section 2(2) and Sch 2.
[28] Para 1(1)(c) of Sch 2.
[29] See pp 246–8 below.
[30] By the Financial Services Act (Commencement No 3) Order 1986 (SI 1986/2246).
[31] Formerly entitled 'The Admission of Securities to Listing', the Listing Rules, currently in a 1993 edition updated by regular supplements, are also known as 'the Yellow Book'. Certain provisions of the Directives are implemented by provisions of the Financial Services Act rather than by the Listing Rules: these are indicated in footnotes.
[32] See, e g, s 143(1): 'An application for listing shall be made to the competent authority in such manner as the listing rules may require' and s 144(1): 'The competent authority shall not admit any securities to the Official List . . . unless satisfied that—(a) the requirements of the listing rules . . . are complied with'.
[33] By the Financial Services Act 1986, s 192.

The United Kingdom influenced the scope and drafting of both the Admissions[34] and the Interim Reports Directives and had little difficulty in accepting the final versions; the Listing Particulars Directive however had started its passage through the legislative process before the accession to the European Communities of the United Kingdom, whose influence was proportionately less as a result.[35]

Prior to implementation of the Listing Directives, there were no legislative requirements as to the content of prospectuses to be published on the admission of securities to official Stock Exchange listing[36] although in practice the Stock Exchange invariably required a company seeking an official listing to comply with its stringent disclosure provisions as a condition of admission to listing and subsequently to comply with continuing obligations imposed on it by way of a listing agreement. In many respects implementation of the Listing Directives merely gave legal status to existing practice. The distinction is however more than academic: before implementation, the Stock Exchange's application and interpretation of its rules were not subject to review by the courts; after implementation, they were required to be so subject.[37] Furthermore the distinction between those of the Stock Exchange's listing rules which implement a requirement of the Listing Directives and those which are additional requirements[38] imposed by the Stock Exchange of its own initiative remains relevant since the Exchange has power to waive compliance with the latter but not with the former.[39]

Admission to Listing

History and aims of the Admissions Directive

Although the Proposal for the Listing Particulars Directive pre-dated that for the Admissions Directive,[40] the latter was adopted first and logically merits consideration before the former. The Commission's Proposal for a Directive coordinating the

[34] Which was based on a report prepared by a Commission Working Party on which the UK was represented and in which a representative of the Stock Exchange was involved.

[35] It is interesting to speculate on whether the requirement for the designation of competent authorities, enunciated for the first time in the Listing Particulars Directive and leading ultimately to the reconstitution of the UK Stock Exchange, would have been incorporated in the Directives in the same form had the UK been more involved in the drafting of the Listing Particulars Directive. The concept of a statutory body regulating the financial markets, commonplace in the founding Member States, was for historical reasons alien to the UK, which might have fought to change the emphasis. See for an interesting discussion Schmitthoff, C M, 'The European Prospectus' cited in n 11 above, 859–64.

[36] The content of prospectuses published when securities were offered to the public was in contrast prescribed by statute (Companies Act 1948, ss 37–55 and 417–23 and Schs 3, 4 and 5).

[37] See further below, pp 247–51.

[38] All three Listing Directives impose minimum requirements which may be added to by the competent authorities: see Arts 5(1) of the Admissions and Listing Particulars Directives and Art 3 of the Interim Reports Directive.

[39] The helpful annotations to the Listing Rules, indicating where relevant which provision of which directive is being implemented, greatly facilitate drawing this distinction.

[40] By far the most comprehensive analysis of the Admissions Directive is Wymeersch, E, 'La

conditions for the admission of securities to official stock exchange quotation[41] was submitted to the Council in January 1976. The Economic and Social Committee delivered its Opinion in July 1976[42] and the Parliament in September 1976.[43] Council Directive (EEC) 79/279 coordinating the conditions for the admission of securities to official stock exchange listing was adopted on 5 March 1979.[44]

The first recital in the preamble to the Admissions Directive sets out the three intertwined aims of coordinating the conditions for the admission of securities to official listing, stating that it will

provide equivalent protection for investors at Community level, because of the more uniform guarantees offered to investors in the various Member States . . . facilitate both the admission to official stock exchange listing, in each such State, of securities from other Member States and the listing of any given security on a number of stock exchanges in the Community [and] accordingly make for greater interpenetration of national securities markets and therefore contribute to the prospect of establishing a European capital market . . .

Subsequently it is expressly recited that, because of the different structures of the securities markets in the different Member States, coordination should be limited to the establishment of minimum conditions for admission to listing, without giving issuers any right to such listing,[45] such partial coordination to be seen as 'a first step towards subsequent closer alignment of the rules of Member States'.[46]

The requirements for admission

Article 3[47] requires Member States to ensure that securities may not be admitted to official listing on any Stock Exchange situated or operating within their territory unless the conditions laid down in the Directive are satisfied, and that issuers of securities admitted to such official listing[48] are subject to the obligations provided for in the Directive. The conditions are set out in Schs A (for shares) and B (for

directive sur les conditions d'admission en bourse' (1980) 6 Revue de la banque 7. There is reasonably detailed coverage by Wooldridge, F, in 'Some Recent Community Legislation in the Field of Securities Law' (1985) 10 ELR 3 and a summary by Morse, G, 'Directive on the Admission of Securities to Official Stock Exchange Listing' (1979) 4 ELR 201.

[41] [1976] OJ C56/2.   [42] [1976] OJ C204/5.   [43] [1976] OJ C238/38.

[44] [1979] OJ L66/21. The Directive was amended by Directive (EEC) 82/148 (see n 1 above), but solely in relation to time for implementation.

[45] See, however, Wymeersch (n 40 above) 26–9, and 'From Harmonization to Integration in the European Securities Markets' (1981) 3 Journal of Comparative Corporate Law and Securities Regulation 1, 6–7. Wymeersch argues that the effect of the Directive is to abolish discretion in admitting securities to listing. The argument, however, is not persuasive: in the final analysis it reduces to deducing from the proposition in Art 3 that 'securities may not be admitted . . . unless the conditions laid down by this Directive are satisfied' the proposition that they must be admitted if the conditions are satisfied, which at least as a matter of formal deductive logic is an example of a standard textbook fallacy.

[46] 5th and 6th recitals in the preamble.

[47] Implemented in the UK by the Financial Services Act 1986, ss 142(1) and 144(1).

[48] Including securities already so admitted before implementation of the Directive, which thus had some retroactive effect.

debt securities) and the obligations in Schs C (for shares) and D (for debt securities).[49] Member States may impose 'more stringent' or additional conditions and obligations, excluding in the case of EC companies a requirement that the securities have already been admitted to official listing in a Member State,[50] provided that they apply generally for all issuers or individual classes of issuer and, in the case of conditions, have been published before application for admission is made.[51] By way of derogation however Member States may, solely in the interests of investor protection, give the competent authorities[52] power to impose any special condition on the admission of a security to listing which they consider appropriate and of which they have explicitly informed the applicant.[53] Certain derogations from the prescribed conditions are authorized, provided that both those derogations and any derogations permitted from more stringent or additional conditions imposed 'apply generally for all issuers where the circumstances justifying them are similar'.[54] In accordance with the philosophy of disclosure underlying the securities directives, Member States may require issuers of securities admitted to official listing to inform the public on a regular basis of their financial position and the general course of their business.[55] Furthermore such issuers are required to provide the competent authorities with 'all the information which the latter consider appropriate in order to protect investors or ensure the smooth operation of the market',[56] published in such a form and within such time limits as the authorities consider appropriate. Should the issuer fail to comply with such a requirement, the competent authorities may themselves publish such information after hearing the issuer.[57] An application for admission of certificates representing shares shall be considered only if the competent authorities consider that the issuer of the certificates is offering adequate safeguards for the protection of investors.[58]

The Proposal included a provision for official quotation without application in exceptional cases where there was in fact a market in the security and it was in the interests of the investor to make the relevant dealings subject to the disciplines and controls of official quotation.[59] This was dropped, presumably because of foreseeable practical difficulties with the imposition and monitoring of conditions and obligations.

The conditions for admission to listing set out in Schs A and B[60] are detailed and numerous; only the most noteworthy are mentioned here. The obligations set out in Schs C and D[61] are considered in the section 'Continuing Obligations under the Admissions Directive' below.[62]

---

[49] Art 4(1) and (2).   [50] Art 6.   [51] Art 5(1).
[52] See below, pp 246–8.   [53] Art 10.   [54] Arts 5(3) and 7.
[55] Art 5(4).   [56] Art 13(1).   [57] Art 13(2).   [58] Art 16.   [59] Art 16.
[60] Member States may decided not to apply Sch B and the requirements in Sch D to inform the public of major new developments and new loan issues in the case of debt securities issued by certain public sector EC companies where capital and interest repayments are guaranteed by the State: Art 8.
[61] In fact, only Schs B(A) and D(A) are relevant to companies, since B(B) and D(B) concern debt securities issued by a State or its regional or local authorities or by a public international body.
[62] See pp 259–61.

Information about the issuer

The issuer of shares to be listed must have published or filed annual accounts in accordance with national law for the three financial years preceding the application for listing, subject to derogation by the competent authorities where this is desirable in the interests of the company or investors and the latter have the necessary information available to arrive at an informed judgment concerning the company and the shares.[63] Except where the shares for which admission is sought are of the same class as those already listed, their foreseeable market capitalization (or if this cannot be assessed the company's capital and reserves, including profit or loss, from the last financial year) must be at least one million European units of account;[64] Member States may provide for admission without this condition being satisfied if the competent authorities are satisfied that there will be an adequate market for the shares.[65]

The original Proposal required a company seeking first time admission of a class of shares to give proof of its profit-making capacity for the previous two financial years and provide satisfactory evidence that it would maintain a profit-making capacity for the current and following financial years.[66] This was deleted on the suggestion of the Economic and Social Committee, who considered that an automatic substantive examination of the issuer's financial status was not the job of the competent authorities, and that in any event it was impossible to give any reliable indications as to forthcoming profitability.

Information about the shares

The shares to be listed must be freely negotiable[67] and by the time of admission[68] at least 25 per cent of the class of shares concerned must be in public hands in one

---

[63] Sch A, para I(3). The requirement for conformity with national law means that consolidated accounts will normally be required for the applicant company and its subsidiary undertakings, in accordance with the 7th Directive.

[64] Sch A, para I(2). The unit of account is defined in Council Reg (EC) 3320/94 of 22 December 1994 on the consolidation of the existing Community legislation on the definition of the ECU following the entry into force of the Treaty on European Union [1994] OJ L350/27; provision is made in Sch A for adjustment of the threshold to reflect fluctuations in national currencies. A higher threshold may be prescribed only if there is another regulated exchange operating in the State with an equivalent threshold of ECU 1m or less. See further n 52, p 60 above

[65] Sch A, para I(2).

[66] Proposal, Sch A, para 1(3).

[67] Sch A, para II(2), which further states that partly paid shares may be treated as freely negotiable if their negotiability is not restricted and the public has appropriate information to enable open and proper dealing. Although the word 'negotiable' is used in the Directive, it does not carry its normal meaning in UK law, entailing in particular transfer simply by delivery or by endorsement and delivery and the right of a bona fide transferee for value to obtain a better title than the transferor. Share certificates are not negotiable in this sense under UK law (although share warrants in respect of bearer shares are), and it would have been preferable for the draftsman to use the term 'transferable' instead.

[68] Or, where shares are to be distributed to the public through the stock exchange after admission, within a short period. This reflects the continental practice of a public offer of shares followed by an application for listing. In such a case, the first listing may be made only after the end of the period during which subscription applications may be submitted: Sch A, para II(3).

or more Member States (although a lower percentage may be acceptable if, in view of the large number of shares of the same class and the extent of their distribution to the public, the market will operate properly with a lower percentage). The application for listing must cover all shares of the same class already issued;[69] moreover, where shares have been admitted to official listing and the company makes further issues of shares of the same class it must, unless the new shares are automatically admitted, apply for their admission to listing either within a year of issue or when they become freely negotiable.[70] Shares issued by a non–EC company not listed in the country of origin or the country where most of the shares are held may not be admitted unless the competent authorities are satisfied that the lack of a listing is not due to the need to protect investors.[71]

Certificates representing shares

Certificates representing shares may be admitted only if the issuer of the underlying shares and the certificates fulfil the conditions set out above.[72]

Information as to debt securities

Debt securities to be listed must be freely negotiable[73] and the amount of the loan may not be less than ECU 200,000.[74] Convertible debentures may be admitted only if the related shares are already or simultaneously listed on the same exchange or another regulated, regularly operating, recognized open market.[75] There are special provisions in Pt B of Sch B for the admission of public-sector debt securities.

Powers and duties of the competent authorities

Member States are required to designate the national authority or authorities competent to decide on admissions covered by the Directive, and to ensure that such authorities have such powers as may be necessary for the exercise of their duties.[76]

---

[69] Sch A, para II(5). Member States may derogate from this requirement for controlling blocks of shares or shares not freely transferable pursuant to agreements, provided that the public is informed and there is no danger of prejudice to the interests of the holders of the shares for which admission is sought.
[70] Sch C, para 1.   [71] Sch A, para II(7).
[72] Art 4(3). The provision is intended primarily to cater for the Dutch practice of representing shares by bearer certificates issued by an *administratiekantoor*, usually a subsidiary of a bank or a related company of the issuer.
[73] Sch B(A), para II(1); see notes at n 67 above.
[74] Sch B(A), para III(1). Member States may provide for admission to listing when this condition is not fulfilled where the competent authorities are satisfied that there will be a sufficient market for the debt securities concerned; the threshold does not in any event apply to 'tap issues', i e issues of the same type of debt securities issued on an occasional basis.
[75] Sch B(A), para III(2). Member States may by way of derogation provide for admission if the competent authorities are satisfied that holders have available all the information necessary to form an opinion concerning the value of the underlying shares.
[76] Art 9(1)(2). In the UK, the Council of The Stock Exchange was designated as competent authority in the original implementing legislation, The Stock Exchange (Listing) Regulations 1984 (SI

The competent authorities may reject an application for admission if they consider that the issuer's situation is such that admission would be detrimental to investors' interests.[77] Moreover, those authorities may refuse to admit a security already listed in another Member State where the issuer fails to comply with the obligations resulting from admission in that State,[78] in which case, without prejudice to any other sanction contemplated for failure to comply with those obligations, the competent authorities may make public the fact that an issuer is failing to comply.[79] The Directive does not prescribe other sanctions, leaving them to the discretion of Member States, although it provides that the competent authorities may decide on the obvious response of suspension or discontinuance of listing.[80]

The combined wording of Articles 4(1) and 9(1) means that Member States are not required to make the competent authorities responsible for monitoring compliance with the continuing obligations laid down in Schs C and D, although the Member States are specifically required to ensure that the Directive applies.[81] In practice it will inevitably be the competent authorities designated under Article 9(1) which will be entrusted with this task, and certain provisions of the applicable schedules assume this.[82]

Article 14 empowers the competent authorities to suspend the listing of a security 'where the smooth operation of the market is, or may be, temporarily jeopardized or where protection of investors so requires', or to discontinue listing where they are satisfied that, owing to special circumstances,[83] 'normal regular dealings in a security are no longer possible'. Article 15 requires decisions refusing admission or discontinuing a listing to be 'subject to the right to apply to the courts'; failure to give a decision within six months of receipt of the application or of the applicant's supplying any further information requested within the initial period shall be deemed a rejection of the application and likewise be subject to review by a

---

1984/716). Under the Financial Services Act 1986, s 142(6), as amended by the Official Listing of Securities (Change of Competent Authority) Regulations 1991 (SI 1991/2000), the UK's competent authority is now the London Stock Exchange Limited ('the Stock Exchange').

[77] Art 9(3). The forerunner of Art 9(3) in the original Proposal required 'explicit reasons' for the decision to be given to the applicant (Art 10(1)), although Member States were authorized to empower the competent authorities, 'for the purpose of protecting the investor', to withhold the reasons for rejection (Art 11(b)). Both the Economic and Social Committee and the European Parliament objected to the latter derogation. The final version reflects the search for a compromise.

[78] Art 11.   [79] Art 12.

[80] See Art 14, discussed further below. A further possible sanction might be a refusal to admit securities issued in the future by the offending company. The Stock Exchange was asked during the hearings on the Interim Reports Directive before the HL Select Committee on the EC whether it considered that an application to the courts for an injunction or an order might additionally be available; the Exchange stated that it was not convinced that the listing agreement, the private-law agreement between Exchange and issuer which before implementation of the Listing Directives laid down the terms of listing, would be held by the courts to be specifically enforceable: see 69th Report (Session 1979–80, HL Paper 360), 18. This seems likely to remain the case with regard to the Listing Rules.

[81] Art 9(1).   [82] See, e g, paras 3(a) and 5(a) of Sch C.

[83] Expressed in the UK implementing regulations as normally including a suspension lasting longer than six months without the issuer taking adequate action to obtain restoration of listing.

court.[84] It is further stated in the preamble to the Directive that 'such right to apply must not be allowed to restrict the discretion' of the competent authorities.[85]

The competent authorities are required by Article 18 to cooperate wherever necessary, in particular by the exchange of any requisite information, for the purpose of carrying out their duties. In the case of applications for multiple listing of securities, the competent authorities are to communicate with each other and make the necessary arrangements to expedite the procedure and simplify as far as possible the relevant formalities and any additional conditions. To this end, applications for admission to listing must state whether a similar application has been, is or will shortly be made.[86]

Article 19 requires Member States to provide that present and former employees of competent authorities shall be bound by professional secrecy, so that they may not divulge any confidential information received in the course of their duties except as required by the law or, in the case of confidential information exchanged pursuant to requirements of the Directive, to the competent authorities of other Member States, in which latter case the information will remain subject to the obligation of professional secrecy.

Article 15 in the United Kingdom

The seemingly innocuous requirement that decisions refusing or suspending a listing be subject to review by the courts necessitated a radical innovation, not only in the law but also in the legal structure of the financial services sector, in the United Kingdom, where it must be remembered there was already in place a sophisticated framework for the admission of securities to listing and the subsequent monitoring of companies so listed. Before implementation of the Listing Directives, the Stock Exchange was an unincorporated and unregistered company formed under a Deed of Settlement and operating with no statutory or regulatory authority; in order for the remedy of judicial review[87] to lie against it as competent authority a change in its status was necessary, since there can be no judicial review in the United Kingdom of purely private law measures. This was one of the factors contributing

---

[84] In the UK, this will be by way of judicial review of the decision of the Quotations Committee, to which an appeal lies from a decision of the Executive (composed of senior staff of the Listing Department), to which an appeal lies from the original decision of the Listing Department. The six-month time limit is implemented in the UK by the Financial Services Act 1986, s 144(4).

[85] 3rd recital.

[86] The requirement for cooperation between competent authorities, which surfaces at various points of the Listing Directives, is a precursor to the more recent device of mutual recognition. See for a list of the circumstances in which the obligation to cooperate is imposed, and further discussion, Lambrecht, P, 'Mutual Recognition of Listing Particulars and Prospectuses and the New Possible Exemptions' [1994] Revue de droit d'affaires international / International Business Law Journal 721, 723–4.

[87] Accepted as the appropriate method of 'appeal' in the context of the British judicial system, which in contrast to continental systems has no separate system of administrative courts.

to the Stock Exchange's 'transformation from a club to a statutorily-recognised regulatory body'[88] as part of the City of London's 'Big Bang'.[89]

The scope of the right to apply to the courts in respect of decisions refusing admission or discontinuing a listing was considered by the Court of Appeal of England and Wales in *R v International Stock Exchange of the United Kingdom and the Republic of Ireland Ltd, ex p Else (1982) Ltd*.[90] The issue was whether the right extended to shareholders in the issuer. Listing of the issuer's shares was first suspended and then cancelled, inter alia because the chairman was arrested on suspicion of insider dealing offences[91] and the Exchange was concerned about the adequacy of the financial information provided by the issuer and about its accounts. After an unsuccessful appeal to the Quotations Committee, the issuer took the matter no further. Three shareholders however sought judicial review of the decision to cancel the issuer's listing, arguing that it was irrational, disproportionate and tainted by bias or the appearance of bias. The judge hearing the application at first instance decided to seek a preliminary ruling from the European Court of Justice on the questions whether Article 15 gave a shareholder the right (a) to apply to the relevant national court and (b) to be heard by the competent authorities in relation to a decision to discontinue the listing of the company in which he held shares. The Stock Exchange appealed to the Court of Appeal against the decision to make a reference, arguing inter alia that it was *acte clair* that Article 15 gave no such rights.

The Court of Appeal closely scrutinized the relevant provisions of the Directive, including the third[92] recital in the preamble which reads as follows:

Whereas there should be the possibility of a right to apply to the courts against decisions by the competent national authorities in respect of the application of this Directive, although such right to apply must not be allowed to restrict the discretion of these authorities . . .

It noted that the original Proposal for the Directive contained no precursor of this recital, although its Article 10(2) required Member States to provide for a right of appeal to the courts against a decision to refuse an application for listing. The Economic and Social Committee had suggested that provision should be made for a right of appeal against any decision of the competent authorities, and not just against a decision to refuse an application.[93] The European Parliament also considered that there should be greater rights of appeal against the decisions of the competent authorities, and proposed an amended Article 10(2) requiring Member States to provide for a right of administrative appeal or appeal to the courts against a decision to refuse an application and against decisions taken pursuant to Articles

---

[88] Davies, P L, *Gower's Principles of Modern Company Law* (6th edn, 1997) 395. The London Stock Exchange is now a registered limited company operating within a statutory framework.

[89] For a fascinating account of the background to 'Big Bang', see Gower, L C B, '"Big Bang" and City Regulation' (1988) 51 MLR 1.

[90] [1993] QB 534.   [91] And subsequently acquitted.

[92] Referred to throughout the judgment of the CA as the 7th recital.

[93] Mystifyingly, the Committee's proposed amendment does not appear to take the matter further, since it requires Member States to 'provide for an appeal procedure against the rejection of an application'.

14(2),[94] 15(2)[95] and 16.[96] As the Court of Appeal pointed out however there was no suggestion that the right of appeal should be conferred on additional parties.

The applicants had argued that the third recital and Article 15 imposed no restriction on the parties granted a right to apply to the courts. Given that (a) the Directive is a measure intended to protect investors, including shareholders, and (b) shareholders are (i) likely to suffer loss or prejudice if the listing of their company is cancelled and (ii) cannot resist such cancellation unless they are notified of an impending decision and its potential grounds and have the opportunity to make representations which the competent authority is bound to consider before making the decision, the intention of Article 15 is or may be[97] to confer rights on shareholders to be notified of an impending decision whether a listing should be cancelled, to be informed of the grounds relied on and to be given an opportunity to make representations and to challenge the decision once made.

The judgments given by two of the members of the Court of Appeal[98] make a number of points of general interest relating to the intention, construction and effect of the Directive. Sir Thomas Bingham MR stated that he was compelled to what he regarded as 'an inevitable conclusion that the right is conferred on a company or an issuer alone' by a number of considerations. These included the grave restrictions on the competent authorities' discretion—explicitly safeguarded by the third recital—which would follow recognition of the rights for which the applicants contended. The procedure which would be triggered by a proposal to cancel a listing would involve substantial delays in effecting the cancellation; this, however, would subvert the intention ascribed to the Directive reflecting 'the need for regulatory authorities to take quick and decisive action where the situation requires it'. The procedure, which would involve circularizing all shareholders and giving them the information they need to make a decision, would moreover be 'a substantial and expensive task. If the Directive envisaged such a procedure it could scarcely avoid all reference to the questions: who is to carry out this task? And who is to pay? Spare though the style of Community draftsmanship may be, it would be surprising to find a lacuna as gross as this.' Similar considerations arise from the Directive's failure to address obvious problems which would arise on the applicants' construction if a majority of shareholders accepted the proposal. Finally, the lack of definition in the Directive of 'investors' means that it is 'an instrument of such uncertain scope [that it] cannot properly be given direct effect'.

---

[94] Broadly equivalent to Art 13(2) of the final version.   [95] Art 14(2).

[96] Art 16, which was not reflected in final version, empowered the competent authorities in exceptional cases to list a security without application where there was in fact a market in the security.

[97] The submission is couched in these somewhat startling terms because the issue before the CA was whether the judge at first instance was right to decide to make a reference: for that purpose, ambiguity would suffice.

[98] McCowan LJ agreed with the judgment of Sir Thomas Bingham MR, adding only the beguilingly ingenuous observation that 'it would be very odd if Art 15 contemplated that a wider class of persons than the company should have the right to apply to the courts in respect of discontinuance of listing than in respect of admission to listing but neglected to say so'.

Leggatt LJ also concluded that 'the correct application of Community law in this case is so obvious as to leave no scope for any reasonable doubt'. He regarded the applicants' argument that because the Directive is for the protection of investors it is they who must have a right to apply to the court as a *non sequitur*, being fortified in that conclusion by the 'commercially intolerable' consequences of extending the right to persons other than the company, which 'might even allow the will of a majority to be thwarted, if not overborne, by the protestation of an individual shareholder'.

Listing Particulars

History and aims of the Listing Particulars Directive[99]

Concrete proposals for a directive harmonizing the content and layout of the document to be published on the admission of securities to listing date back to 1972, when the Commission submitted a Proposal for a directive concerning the content, supervision and distribution of the prospectus to be published when securities issued by companies or firms within the meaning of the second paragraph of Article 58 of the Treaty are admitted to official stock exchange listing.[100] The Parliament delivered its Opinion in January 1974[101] and the Economic and Social Committee in July 1974.[102] Council Directive (EEC) 80/390 coordinating the requirements for the drawing up, scrutiny and distribution of the listing particulars to be published for the admission of securities to official Stock Exchange listing was adopted on 17 March 1980.[103]

The Directive has been amended four times. The first amendment in 1982 merely extended the period for implementation.[104] The second and third amendments were made in 1987 and 1990 and concern mutual recognition.[105] The fourth amendment in 1994 sought to facilitate the transition from second-tier to offical markets and provided for simplified listing particulars for cross-border listing of major companies.[106]

---

[99] The Listing Particulars Directive is given good coverage in Wooldridge, F, 'Some Recent Community Legislation in the Field of Securities Law' (1985) 10 ELR 3, and summarized by Morse, G, in 'Sixth Directive on prospectuses adopted' (1980) 5 ELR 316. The 1972 Proposal is dealt with in detail by Suckow, S, 'The European Prospectus' (1975) 23 AJCL 50 and in summary by Schmitthoff, C M, 'The European Prospectus' in Recht und Wirtschaft in Geschichte und Gegenwart: Festschrift für Johannes Bärmann zum 70. Geburtstag (1975) 859, 857–72.

[100] [1972] OJ C131/61.   [101] [1974] OJ C11/24.

[102] [1974] OJ C125/1.   [103] [1980] OJ L100/1.

[104] Directive (EEC) 82/148, cited in n 1 above.

[105] Council Directive (EEC) 87/345 of 22 June 1987 amending Directive (EEC) 80/390 coordinating the requirements for the drawing-up, scrutiny and distribution of the listing particulars to be published for the admission of securities to official stock exchange listing [1987] OJ L185/81 and Council Directive (EEC) 90/211 of 23 April 1990 amending Directive (EEC) 80/390 in respect of the mutual recognition of public offer prospectuses as stock exchange listing particulars [1990] OJ L112/24. Both are considered in ch XIII.

[106] Directive (EC) 94/18, cited in n 141 below; the amendment is considered in the accompanying text.

The evolving philosophy of disclosure as the bedrock for harmonization of securities regulation is crystallized for the first time in the Directive, the preamble to which invokes investor protection in widening markets as the *raison d'être* for requiring sufficient and objective information concerning the financial circumstances of the issuer and particulars of the securities to be admitted.[107] It notes however that such information, although required in most Member States, differs between Member States 'both as regards the contents and the layout of the listing particulars and the efficacy, methods and timing of the check on the information given therein',[108] and that the effect of such differences is to hinder multiple listing and cross-border investment and thus the capital structure of the Community. The Directive accordingly proposes to eliminate such divergence by co-ordination of national disclosure regulations on admission to listing.

The objectives of the Listing Particulars Directive can no longer be considered in isolation: since the adoption of the Public Offer Prospectus Directive, the standards and procedure prescribed for listing particulars by the former directive apply equally, *mutatis mutandis*, to a prospectus in relation to a public offer of transferable securities where an application to list those securities is to be made or where recognition of the prospectus as listing particulars or as a prospectus elsewhere in the Community is sought.[109] Moreover, since the two amending Directives were adopted the aims of the Listing Particulars Directive must be taken to encompass the achievement of the full mutual recognition of listing particulars, 'an important step forward in the creation of the Community's internal market',[110] and the recognition of a public offer prospectus as listing particulars where admission to official listing is requested shortly after a public offer.[111]

Information to be disclosed

The Directive requires Member States to ensure that the admission[112] of securities to official listing on a Stock Exchange situated or operating in their territories is conditional upon the publication of an information sheet, or listing particulars,[113]

---

[107] The Directive strongly influenced the US Securities and Exchange Commission in its development of US disclosure forms for foreign issuers: see Warren, M G, 'Global Harmonization of Securities Laws: the Achievement of the European Communities' (1990) 31 Harvard International Law Journal 185, 211, n 159.

[108] 3rd recital in the preamble.

[109] See chs XII and XIII. Warren, M G, states that in its new role the Listing Particulars Directive 'will serve as the core of a supranational disclosure system applicable to multi-jurisdictional offerings within the common market': 'The Common Market Prospectus' (1989) 26 CML Rev 687, 689.

[110] 3rd and 4th recitals in the preamble to Directive (EEC) 87/345.

[111] Directive (EEC) 90/211. The mutual recognition provisions of the Listing Particulars Directive as amended are considered in ch XIII.

[112] The Economic and Social Committee's adventurous suggestion that the requirement of issuing a prospectus should apply also on a reduction of capital was unsurprisingly stillborn.

[113] Art 3, implemented in the UK by the Financial Services Act 1986, ss 144(1), (2) and (2A) and the Listing Rules. Section 144(2A) is permissive rather than mandatory to enable the Stock Exchange to take advantage of certain of the exemptions from publishing listing particulars. As a result of the

and to appoint a competent authority[114] to monitor and approve the drawing up and publication of those listing particulars. The Directive does not require or impose any sanction for non-compliance, which is left to the discretion of the Member States.

Article 4(1) imposes a general requirement for listing particulars to:

contain the information which, according to the particular nature of the issuer and of the securities for the admission of which application is being made, is necessary to enable investors and their investment advisers to make an informed assessment of the assets and liabilities, financial position, profits and losses, and prospects of the issuer and of the rights attaching to such securities.[115]

Member States are to ensure that the general requirement 'is incumbent upon the persons responsible for the listing particulars' or part thereof (for example auditors' reports).[116]

Article 5 requires Member States to ensure that, subject to the permitted exemptions, listing particulars contain 'at least' the items of information prescribed in the Schedules[117] 'in as easily analysable and comprehensible form as possible'. Schedule A prescribes the layout and minimum contents of listing particulars for the admission of shares to official Stock Exchange listing and Sch B those for the admission of debt securities. The separation reflects the fact that in some Member States, for example France, the requirements for listing of debt securities were less onerous than those for listing shares.[118] In addition, Sch C contains requirements for listing particulars for the admission of certificates representing shares.[119] The schedules cover sixteen pages; Articles 8 to 17, which lay down rules for tailoring the requirements of the schedules to specific cases warranting exemptions from or

Public Offer Prospectus Directive, a prospectus rather than listing particulars is required where the securities in question are being offered to the public for the first time, but the Listing Particulars Directive still governs the content, approval and publication of the prospectus. See further ch XII below.

[114] Art 18. In the UK the competent authority is the London Stock Exchange: see n 76 above.

[115] Implemented in the UK by the Financial Services Act 1986, s 146. This general disclosure obligation prompted an increase in the level of disclosure required in the UK: see Reid, D and Ballheimer, A, 'The Legal Framework of the Securities Industry in the European Community under the 1992 Programme' (1991) 29 Columbia Journal of Transnational Law 103, 126. Gower, *Principles of Modern Company Law* (5th edn, 1992) 325, describes how 'the prospect of finding such an open-ended obligation laid down by statute caused shivers to run down the spine of the City Establishment'.

[116] Art 4(2) read with para 1.1 of Schs A and B. This is implemented in the UK by the Financial Services Act 1986, ss 146 and 152 and the Listing Rules—in practice the responsibility statement attributes responsibility solely to directors which prima facie does not fully comply: see Gower (ibid), 348.

[117] Gower (n 115 above, 321, n 56) argues that it is 'distinctly dubious' whether the Listing Particulars Directive is a minimum standards directive. The words 'at least', however, suggest that the Directive imposes minimum standards for the detailed requirements.

[118] Wooldridge, F, 'Some Recent Community Legislation in the Field of Securities Law' (1985) 10 ELR 3, 12. Wooldridge gives a detailed account of how the requirements of Schs A and B differ from the pre-implementation listing rules of the London Stock Exchange (then entitled *The Admission of Securities to Listing*).

[119] All three schedules are implemented in the UK by Chapter 6 of the Listing Rules.

modifications to the prescribed information,[120] cover a further three pages. The following outline reflects only a few of the more noteworthy points applicable to the admission of shares, under the headings used in Sch A. To the extent that the information required under Sch A is given in the company's annual accounts, which must themselves be included by virtue of chapter 5 of Sch A, it does not need to be duplicated under other chapter headings.[121] Where headings prescribed by the Schedules 'appear inappropriate to the issuer's sphere of activity or legal form', the headings may be adapted to give equivalent information.[122]

Information concerning those responsible for listing particulars and the auditing of accounts[123]

This includes a requirement for a declaration by those responsible 'that, to the best of their knowledge, the information given in that part of the listing particulars for which they are responsible is in accordance with the facts and contains no omissions likely to affect the import of the listing particulars' and a requirement for details of the company's auditors and disclosure of any qualification of the audit report on the annual accounts. The competent authorities may refuse to accept the audit report or require an additional audit report.[124]

Information concerning admission to official listing and the shares for the admission of which application is being made[125]

This includes details of the issue and justification of the issue price, the rights attaching to the shares, any restriction or withdrawal of shareholders' pre-emption rights with reasons therefor, the procedure for exercising or negotiating any pre-emption rights, the receiving agents and underwriters and their remuneration or commission, any Stock Exchange on which shares of the same class are already listed and any takeover bids received or made by the issuing company in the last and current financial years.

General information about the issuer and its capital[126]

This includes details of issued and authorized but unissued capital including changes to the issued capital in the preceding three years, an indication of persons who to the issuer's knowledge (a) 'directly or indirectly, severally or jointly, exercise or could exercise control over the issuer' with particulars of the proportion of the voting capital which they hold and (b) directly or indirectly hold a proportion of the issuer's capital which the Member States may not fix at more than 20 per cent and a brief description of the group the company belongs to, if any.

---

[120] Namely rights issues (Art 8), securities issued by financial institutions (Art 11) or in connection with a takeover (Art 15), certificates representing shares (Art 16) and debt securities with (Art 14) and without (Art 9) associated rights in shares, normally bought and traded by professional investors (e g Euro-bonds) (Art 10), issued in a continuous or repeated manner by credit institutions (Art 12) or guaranteed by a legal person (Art 13) or a State (Art 17).

[121] Sch A, para 5.6.   [122] Art 5(3).   [123] Sch A, ch 1.   [124] Art 19.
[125] Sch A, ch 2.   [126] Sch A, ch 3.

Information concerning the issuer's activities[127]

This includes a breakdown of net turnover[128] during the preceding three financial years by categories of activity and into geographical markets where such categories and markets differ substantially from each other and information about material contracts, patents and licences, average numbers employed and the company's investment policy. Where the issuer is a 'dominant undertaking forming a group with one or more dependent undertakings', the information required under this heading must be given for both the issuer and the group.[129]

Information concerning the issuer's assets and liabilities, financial position and profits and losses[130]

This includes the company's last three balance sheets and profit and loss accounts together with the notes on the accounts for the last financial year, which must not have ended more than eighteen months before the draft listing particulars are filed with the competent authorities, the profit or loss and the dividend per share for the last three financial years and specified information relating to undertakings in which the issuer holds a proportion of the capital 'likely to have a significant effect on the assessment of its own assets and liabilities, financial position or profits and losses'.

Information concerning administration, management and supervision[131]

This includes remuneration paid and benefits in kind granted during the last completed financial year 'under any heading whatsoever' to each of the administrative, management and supervisory boards, shown as total amounts for each category of body, and also total remuneration paid and benefits in kind granted by any dependent undertakings with which the issuer forms a group; the number of shares in the issuer and options over such shares held by and total outstanding loans and guarantees granted by the issuer to members of those bodies; details of interests of such members in any unusual transactions effected by the issuer in the preceding and current financial years; and employee share schemes.

Information concerning the recent development and prospects of the issuer[132]

Subject to derogation by the competent authorities, this comprises information on the trend of the issuer's business since the end of the financial year to which the last published annual accounts relate and on the issuer's prospects for at least the current financial year. Where the issuer is a 'dominant undertaking forming a group

---

[127] Sch A, ch 4.

[128] The seemingly unexceptionable requirement to disclose turnover was in fact a radical innovation for half the original Member States. When the Proposal for the Directive was published in 1972, only France, Luxembourg and Germany had such a requirement: see Suckow, S, 'The European Prospectus' (1975) 23 AJCL 50, 61.

[129] Sch A, para 5.5.   [130] Sch A, ch 5.   [131] Sch A, ch 6.   [132] Sch A, ch 7.

with one or more dependent undertakings', the information required under this heading must be given for both the issuer and the group.[133]

Permitted omissions and exemptions[134]

Member States may allow the competent authorities responsible for checking the listing particulars to provide for partial or complete exemption from the obligation to publish listing particulars in a number of cases, including where the securities (a) have been issued to the public or in connection with a takeover or merger and within the previous twelve months a document containing equivalent information has been published in the same Member State;[135] (b) are to be allotted pursuant to a bonus issue or conversion rights;[136] (c) are of the same class as those already listed and increase them by less than 10 per cent;[137] or (d) are to be allotted to employees if shares of the same class are already listed.[138]

The competent authorities may authorize omission of information (a) which it considers insignificant or (b) disclosure of which would be contrary to the public interest or seriously detrimental to the company, provided that the omission is immaterial to a potential purchaser's informed assessment of the securities.[139] There is a further provision concerning debt securities whose admission coincides with their public issue: if some of the terms of the issue are not finalized until the last moment, information as to those may be omitted from the listing particulars provided that they indicate how it will be given; it must be published before the start of the listing.[140]

An important amendment was made to the Listing Particulars Directive in 1994 with the objective of facilitating the transition from second-tier to official markets in Member States having parallel exchanges by extending the circumstances in which Member States may provide for partial or complete exemption from the obligation to publish listing particulars. Article 6(5) was added,[141] permitting Member States to allow the competent authorities to provide for partial or complete exemption from the requirement to publish listing particulars where an application is made for the admission of securities to official listing in a Member State and for at least the preceding two years the issuer's shares have been dealt with on

---

[133] Sch A, para 5.5.
[134] As well as the general provisions discussed here, there are also a number of specific exemptions and omissions applicable in specific cases: see summary in n 120 above.
[135] Art 6(1).   [136] Art 2.   [137] Art 6(3)(a).   [138] Art 6(3)(d).
[139] Art 7, implemented in the UK by the Financial Services Act 1986, s 148, and the Listing Rules. The Economic and Social Committee criticized the string of 'imprecise legal expressions' in this provision, considering that 'the accumulation of such expressions here conflicts with the need for legal certainty'.
[140] Art 21(3).
[141] By Art 1(2) of Directive (EC) 94/18 of the European Parliament and of the Council of 31 May 1994 amending Directive (EEC) 80/390 coordinating the requirements for the drawing up, scrutiny and distribution of the listing particulars to be published for the admission of securities to official stock exchange listing, with regard to the obligation to publish listing particulars [1994] OJ L135/1.

an official second-tier market in the same Member State whose competent authorities consider that information equivalent in substance to that required by the Directive is already available to investors.[142]

Simplified listing particulars for cross-border listing

A further significant amendment was made by Directive (EC) 94/18, aiming to simplify cross-border listing of blue-chip companies. Article 6(4)[143] provides that, where application is made for the admission of securities to official listing in a Member State and for at least the preceding three years the securities have been officially listed in another Member State whose competent authorities confirm that during that period[144] the issuer has complied with 'the requirements concerning information and admission to listing imposed by Community Directives',[145] Member States may allow the competent authorities to provide for publication of the following simplified set of documents instead of fresh listing particulars: (a) the issuer's latest annual report, audited annual accounts and, if already published, half-yearly statement for the year in question; (b) any listing particulars, prospectus or equivalent published by it in the preceding twelve months; (c) a document containing a brief description of the securities, details of any significant change or development since (a) and (b), information specific to the market of the country of admission concerning in particular income tax, the issuer's paying agents and publication of notices to investors, and a responsibility statement; (d) specified information about the company, its capital, major shareholders and reports concerning accounts.[146] Member States may 'establish non-discriminatory minimum quantitative criteria', such as current market capitalization, for entitlement to this exemption; alternatively, competent authorities may extend the option to smaller companies.[147]

Approval and publication

Article 18 provides that no listing particulars may be published until they have been approved by the competent authorities[148] who may approve publication only if

---

[142] Art 6(5).   [143] Added by Art1(1) of Directive (EC) 94/18.

[144] The Directive as amended appears contradictory: Art 6(4)(a) requires the securities to have been officially listed 'in another Member State for not less than three years' before the application, while Art 6(4)(b) requires compliance 'during the preceding three years or during the entire time the issuer's securities have been listed, if that is less than three years'. A possible explanation is that, notwithstanding the reference in (a) to 'another Member State', (b) refers to the case where the securities have been admitted to official listing in more than one Member State, in at least one of which they have been admitted for less than three years.

[145] Art 6(4)(b). Presumably these comprise the Admissions, Listing Particulars, Interim Reports and Major Shareholdings Directives.

[146] Art 6(4)(c). The documents do not have to be published in the or an official language of the Member State concerned, provided that the language used is customary in the sphere of finance and accepted by the competent authorities: Art 6a.

[147] 12th recital in the preamble to Directive (EC) 94/18.   [148] Art 18(2).

they consider that the listing particulars satisfy all the requirements of the Directive.[149] Publication must be either by setting out the listing particulars in a newspaper circulated throughout, or at least widely circulated in, the Member State concerned or by including them in a brochure available to the public free of charge at the Stock Exchange concerned, the registered office of the issuer and the registered offices of the issuer's paying agents.[150] In addition, either the listing particulars or a notice stating where they have been published and where they may be obtained must appear in a publication designated by the Member State where admission is sought.[151] Publication must be within a reasonable period, to be prescribed by national legislation or the competent authorities, before the date on which official listing becomes effective or, on a rights issue, before the earlier start of trading in the pre-emptive subscription rights.[152]

Preliminary and supplementary listing particulars

Article 22 requires that all 'notices, bill, posters and documents announcing [the forthcoming publication of listing particulars] and indicating the essential characteristics of [the] securities, and all other documents relating to their admission and intended for publication' by or on behalf of the issuer be first communicated to the competent authorities, who are to decide whether they should be submitted to scrutiny before publication. Such preliminary announcements must state that listing particulars exist and indicate where they are being or will be published. In practice there are many preliminary advertisements and announcements of a forthcoming major public issue, including, in the United Kingdom at least, 'pathfinder' prospectuses intended to gauge and arouse interest in the offer and 'mini-prospectuses' summarizing the full listing particulars.[153]

Article 23[154] requires a supplement to the listing particulars to be prepared, scrutinized and published in the same way as full particulars to cover every 'significant new factor capable of affecting assessment of the securities' which arises after adoption of the listing particulars and before Stock Exchange dealings begin.

---

[149] Art 18(3). Art 18(4) states that the competent authorities' liability continues to be governed by national law and is not affected by the Directive: this provision was inserted to allay national Stock Exchanges' fears that designation as competent authorities might involve them in increased liabilities (Wooldridge, 'Some Recent Community Legislation in the Field of Securities Law' (1985) 10 ELR 3, 11).

[150] Art 18(1). In the UK, the Financial Services Act 1986, s 149, requires in addition that the listing particulars be filed at the Companies Registry.

[151] Art 20(2). In the UK the Listing Rules require publication of a notice of availability, the Exchange's *Weekly Official Intelligence* being the designated publication, and publication of the full particulars, a mini-prospectus, a formal notice or an offer notice in at least one national newspaper.

[152] Art 21(1). In the UK the Listing Rules require publication at least two business days prior to the expected date of the consideration of the application for admission to listing. Art 21(2) provides for postponement of publication in 'exceptional, properly justified cases' in the case of securities of a class already listed on the same exchange and issued for non-cash consideration and of rights issues.

[153] Art 22 is implemented in the UK by the Financial Services Act 1986, s 154.

[154] Implemented in the UK by the Financial Services Act 1986, s 147, and the Listing Rules.

Cooperation between Member States

Article 24c(1)[155] requires the competent authorities to cooperate wherever necessary for the purpose of carrying out their duties and to exchange any information required for that purpose. A specific obligation to cooperate is imposed in two cases.

(1) Where (a) an application for admission to listing concerns securities giving a right to participate in company capital, either immediately or at the end of a maturity period; and (b) the application is made in a Member State or States other than that in which the issuer of the underlying shares has its registered office; and (c) the issuer's shares have already been admitted to official listing in that State. In those circumstances, the competent authorities of the Member State where admission is sought may act only after consulting their counterparts in the Member State in which that registered office is situated.[156]

(2) Where an application for admission to listing is made for securities which have been listed in another Member State less than six months previously, the second competent authorities concerned are to contact the first and so far as possible exempt the issuer from preparing new listing particulars, subject to any national requirement for updating, translating or issuing supplements.[157] In practice in such circumstances the listing particulars used for the first application should attract recognition.[158]

Present and former employees of the competent authorities are to be bound by professional secrecy and thus may not divulge any confidential information received in the course of their duties except as required by law,[159] other than information exchanged pursuant to the Directive which is to be covered by the obligation of professional secrecy in the hands of the recipient authority.[160]

Continuing Obligations under the Admissions Directive

The Admissions Directive imposes a number of continuing obligations on companies whose securities[161] are admitted to official listing on a Stock Exchange.

---

[155] Added by Directive (EEC) 87/345.   [156] Art 24c(2) added by Directive (EEC) 87/345.
[157] Art 24c(3) added by Directive (EEC) 87/345.   [158] See further ch XIII below.
[159] Art 25(1).   [160] Art 25(2).
[161] The obligations also apply to issuers of shares represented by certificates admitted to official listing: see Art 4(3).

Treatment of shareholders

The Admissions Directive, echoing the Code of Conduct,[162] requires the company to ensure equal treatment for all shareholders in the same position. All the necessary facilities and information must be available, at least in each Member State in which its shares are listed, to enable shareholders to exercise their rights. In particular the company must notify shareholders of meetings, enable them to exercise their voting rights, publicize the allocation and payment of dividends and the issue of new shares including allotment, renunciation and conversion arrangements and, unless the company itself provides financial services, designate a financial institution through which shareholders may exercise their financial rights.[163]

Equivalence of information

A company with shares listed on Stock Exchanges in different Member States must ensure that equivalent information is made available to each market in question, and a company with shares listed on Stock Exchanges both in and outside the Community must make available to the EC markets where its shares are listed information which is at least equivalent to that which it makes available to the non-EC markets, if such information may be important for the evaluation of the shares.[164] The proviso is intended to avoid duplication of all the very comprehensive disclosure requirements imposed by the US Securities and Exchange Commission.[165]

Accounts and reports

The company must make its most recent annual accounts and its last annual report available to the public as soon as possible; where the company prepares both consolidated and own accounts both must be so made available unless the competent authorities exempt one set from the requirement, which they may do if that set contains no significant additional information as against the other. If the accounts do not comply with the Fourth and Seventh Directives, more detailed or additional information must be provided.[166]

---

[162] See pp 230–31 above.

[163] Admissions Directive, Sch C, para 2. Sch D, para A(1) contains an analogous requirement for issuers of debt securities.

[164] Admissions Directive, Sch C, para 6; para 9.9 of the Listing Rules.

[165] Wymeersch, E, 'La directive sur les conditions d'admission en bourse' (1980) 6 Revue de la banque 7, para 75.

[166] Admissions Directive, Schs C and D, para 4.

Additional information

Draft amendments to the instrument of incorporation or statutes of a company with listed shares or debt securities must be communicated to the competent authorities by the date of the relevant general meeting.[167]

The company must inform the public:

(1) as soon as possible of any major new developments in its sphere of activity which are not public knowledge and which may, in the case of a company with listed shares, lead to substantial movements in the prices of its shares by virtue of their effect on its assets and liabilities or financial position or on the general course of its business or, in the case of a company with listed debt securities, significantly affect its ability to meet its commitments;[168]

(2) without delay of any changes in the rights attaching to the various classes of shares[169] or the rights of holders of debt securities;[170]

(3) in the case of a company with listed shares, of any changes in its capital structure as compared with previously published information as soon as such changes come to its notice;[171] and

(4) in the case of a company with listed debt securities, without delay of any new loan issues and in particular any underlying guarantee or security.[172]

Article 17 requires the information to be made available to the public by publication in at least one widely distributed newspaper or in writing in places indicated by announcements in such a newspaper or 'by other equivalent means approved by the competent authorities'. In the United Kingdom, the London Stock Exchange requires such information to be channelled through its Company Announcements Office, which then disseminates it electronically through its Regulatory News Service. The information is to be published in a language customary in the sphere of finance and accepted by the competent authorities.[173]

The Interim Reports Directive[174]

History and aims

The Interim Reports Directive started life sandwiched among the continuing obligations imposed on companies with listed shares by Sch C to the Admissions

---

[167] Sch C, para 3; Sch D(A), para 2.

[168] Sch C, para 5(a) and Sch D(A), para 4(a). In both cases there is provision for exemption by the competent authorities if the disclosure of particular information is such as to prejudice the company's legitimate interests.

[169] Including, in the case of listed debt securities which are convertible or exchangeable or warrant-backed, shares to which those debt securities relate: Sch D(A), para 4(d).

[170] Sch C, para 5(b) and Sch D(A), para 4(b).   [171] Sch C, para 5(c).

[172] Sch D(A), para 4(c).   [173] Art 17(2).

[174] There is a summary analysis of the Directive from the UK angle in Wooldridge, F, 'Some Recent Community Legislation in the Field of Securities Law' (1985) 10 ELR 3, 15–17.

Directive.[175] As a result of early difficulties encountered in reaching agreement between the Member States as to the detailed scope of the provision, it was decided to deal with the matter by a discrete directive which could be negotiated separately without hindering adoption of the Admissions Directive. A Proposal for a Council Directive on information to be published on a regular basis by companies whose transferable securities are admitted to official stock exchange listing was submitted by the Commission in January 1979.[176] The Economic and Social Committee delivered its Opinion in October 1979[177] and the European Parliament in March 1980.[178] The Commission submitted an amended Proposal to the Council in June 1980[179] and Council Directive (EEC) 82/121 on information to be published on a regular basis by companies the shares of which have been admitted to official Stock Exchange listing was adopted on 15 February 1982.[180]

The Interim Reports Directive, although ultimately a slender[181] and unassuming instrument, is interesting in that it changed comprehensively between first Proposal and adoption, largely as a result of strongly felt reservations by the United Kingdom Stock Exchange, Department of Trade and various bodies representative of commercial interests. These reservations focused on two major issues. First, it was felt that as originally framed the Directive would require disclosure of irrelevant, unhelpful and inappropriate information rather than the most obviously apposite interim information, namely financial results. Second, the Stock Exchange made it clear that it would have grave difficulty in accepting appointment as the competent authority unless it was made clear that it would not thereby assume potentially unlimited and unquantifiable liability towards investors for any damage flowing from failure by companies to comply.

The original Proposal required half-yearly disclosure of net turnover, other operating income, operating charges, gross operating result and any interim dividends paid or proposed, together with an explanatory statement including at least the number of persons employed, investment carried out and decisions taken as to future investment, state of the order book, the general situation regarding stocks of finished products, the degree of capacity utilization, and any new products or activities which had had a significant effect on turnover.[182] Many of these requirements are appropriate only for companies operating in the manufacturing sector and cannot easily be extrapolated to other sectors, for example insurance, banking and, travel. Some would be disproportionately burdensome to marshall in a suitable

---

[175] See para 4 of Sch C to the Proposal for the Admissions Directive ([1976] OJ C56/14) requiring companies to make available to the public, at least half-yearly, ' sufficient information to enable the public to evaluate the assets and financial position of the company and the general progress of its business . . .'. The Economic and Social Committee felt that this went ' far beyond what is required as regards an interim report', referring to what subsequently proved a major sticking point for the UK, namely that the provision is mandatory and it is not stated what is to be regarded as ' sufficient' information: [1976] OJ C204/9.

[176] COM (78) 759 final, 15 January 1979; [1979] OJ C29/5.   [177] [1980] OJ C53/54.
[178] [1980] OJ C85/69.   [179] COM (80) 332 final, 18 June 1980; [1980] OJ C210/5.
[180] [1982] OJ L66/21.   [181] Eleven substantive articles take up less than three pages.
[182] Art 5(2) and (4) of the original Proposal.

form;[183] moreover, some are not reflected in the requirements of the Fourth Directive on annual accounts, so that the interim financial disclosure requirement would have been more rigorous than the annual one. Perhaps most striking to a commentator from the United Kingdom, where the Stock Exchange had for many years required listed companies to publish their unaudited half-yearly results, is the omission of the most useful figures, the profit or loss after tax: this was because in certain Member States, for example Luxembourg and Italy, there was legislation prohibiting the publication of unaudited profit figures.

The second perceived problem with the original Proposal was the strict liability which it imposed on the competent authorities. Member States were required to designate the competent authorities 'responsible for ensuring that the rules laid down in this Directive applied'.[184] Since those rules were expressed in absolute and inflexible terms—'companies . . . shall publish';[185] the report 'shall be published within three months . . .'[186] and 'shall consist of . . .'[187]—it was feared, at least in the United Kingdom, that the competent authorities would be assuming strict liability on a continuing basis for companies' failure to report promptly or fully. The approach in the Proposal contrasted with that of the Admissions and the (then proposed) Listing Particulars Directive, which merely obliged the competent authorities not to do certain things—namely admit the securities to listing—unless certain prescribed conditions were satisfied. The wording was changed to cater for these concerns, so that the Directive as adopted puts the primary responsibility for ensuring compliance on the Member States.

The preamble to the Directive as adopted states that the Listing Particulars Directive's aim of ensuring improved and more equivalent protection of investors,[188] facilitating multiple listings and thereby contributing to the establishment of a genuine Community capital market is also served by coordinating the requirements for supplying investors in listed securities with appropriate regular information.[189] It adds that the half-yearly report 'must enable investors to make an informed appraisal of the general developments of the company's activities during the period covered . . . [but] need contain only the essential details of the

---

[183] The Law Society made the innovative suggestion that both these problems could be resolved by the simple expedient of disapplying most of the proposed Directive most of the time: noting that ' full compliance with the directive might be undesirable . . . on the grounds that the information is of little relevance to the recipients and the preparation of it could be unduly burdensome', it proposed giving the competent authorities power to exempt companies from publishing information required by the Directive which 'would be of no material relevance or [if] compliance would be unduly burdensome': Written Submission to the HL Select Committee on the EC, 69th Report (Session 1979–80, HL Paper 360), 31. Perhaps fortunately, the more conventional approach of amending the undesirable provisions prevailed.

[184] Art 11(1).   [185] Art 2.   [186] Art 4.   [187] Art 5(1).

[188] The original Proposal for the Interim Reports Directive included in this list of objectives 'to make securities more attractive to investors' (2nd recital). As the CBI drily pointed out in its submission to the HL Select Committee, 'If the main purpose of information is to protect the investor by enabling him to judge whether or not a company is a good investment the information provided should not always make securities more attractive' (n 183 above, 22).

[189] 1st and 2nd recitals in the preamble.

financial position and general progress of the business of the company in question',[190] and that to ensure effective investor protection and the proper operation of Stock Exchanges it should apply not only to companies from Member States but also to companies from non-member countries.[191]

The interim report

Article 2 requires the Member States to ensure that companies whose shares are admitted to official listing in their territory publish half-yearly reports on their activities and losses during the first six months of each financial year;[192] more stringent or additional obligations may be imposed provided that they apply generally to all companies or to all companies of a given class.[193] The half-yearly report is to be published within four months[194] of the end of the relevant six-month period, subject to extension by the competent authorities in 'exceptional, duly substantiated cases'.[195] The report is intended to 'enable investors to make an informed appraisal of the general development of the company's activities during the period covered [but] need contain only the essential details on the financial position and general progress of the business of the company . . .'.[196] It must include tables showing net turnover, profit or loss before or after deduction of tax[197] and any interim dividend paid or proposed,[198] in each case with figures for the corresponding period in the previous financial year.[199] If the accounting information has been audited, the auditor's report and any qualification must be reproduced in full.[200]

The report must also contain an explanatory statement relating to the company's activities and profits and losses during the period covered,[201] including any significant information enabling investors to make an informed assessment of the trend of the company's activities and profits or losses and an indication of any special factor which has influenced those activities and profits or losses during the period in question; the statement must enable a comparison to be made with the corresponding period of the preceding financial year and so far as possible refer to the company's likely future development in the current financial year.[202]

---

[190] 6th recital in the preamble.   [191] 8th recital in the preamble.   [192] Art 2.
[193] Art 3.
[194] Originally three months; the Economic and Social Committee suggested extending the period since three months 'could cause the interim figures to follow too soon after the final results for the previous year, leaving a long interval of up to nine months before any further results are forthcoming'.
[195] Art 4. Examples might be where there has been difficulty obtaining information from abroad or where the company has changed its financial year end.
[196] 6th recital in the preamble.
[197] The terms have the same meaning as in the 4th and 7th Directives on accounts: Art 5(2).
[198] Art 5(4).   [199] Art 5(5).   [200] Art 8.
[201] Art 5. Art 5(3) provides that Member States may allow the competent authorities, exceptionally and on a case-by-case basis, to authorize companies whose shares are listed in only one Member State to supply estimated profits and losses; this must be indicated in the report and must not mislead investors.
[202] Art 5(6).

Article 9 provides for the appointment of competent authorities,[203] who may, inter alia, adapt particular requirements of the Directive which are unsuited to a company's activities or circumstances,[204] authorize the omission of certain prescribed information[205] if they consider that disclosure would be 'contrary to the public interest or seriously detrimental to the company'[206] and authorize publication of a half-yearly report published in a non-member country containing equivalent information.[207] The competent authorities are not however required to approve interim reports in advance.

The report is to be published in at least one newspaper widely distributed in the State or in the national gazette or made available to the public in places indicated by announcement in such a newspaper or by other means approved by the competent authorities[208] and not later than the time of first publication the company is to send a copy to the competent authorities of each Member States in which its shares are admitted to official listing.[209] It must be drawn up in a language 'customary in the sphere of finance and . . . accepted by the competent authorities'.[210]

---

[203] In the UK, the London Stock Exchange: see n 76 above.

[204] Art 9(3). This provision was of more relevance to the earlier versions of the Directive, which as indicated above was originally framed in terms singularly inappropriate for companies outside the manufacturing sector. The final version, although much improved in this respect, may none the less require adaptation for, e g, companies whose business is very seasonal and companies in the assurance and reinsurance sectors, where results cannot be assessed until, respectively, full actuarial valuation has taken place and estimates from reinsured companies have been received, both of which normally occur on an annual basis.

[205] The Article provides that the company or its representatives are to be responsible for the correctness and relevance of the facts on which any application for such exemption is made. This is a further attempt to make it clear that the competent authorities are not intended to assume potential liability; see the comments of the Economic and Social Committee expressing the concerns which led to its inclusion.

[206] The second ground is subject to the proviso that the omission 'would not be likely to mislead the public with regard to facts and circumstances knowledge of which is essential' for assessing the shares concerned: Art 9(4). The UK Listing Rules purport to give the Stock Exchange an unfettered power to authorize the omission of any information if it considers such omission otherwise necessary or appropriate, which appears to go well beyond the Directive. The power to exempt in the Proposal for the Directive originally extended to information 'of minor importance only'; this was dropped following the European Parliament's description of it as 'contrary to the objective of the proposed Directive'.

[207] Art 9(6).   [208] Art 7(1).

[209] Art 7(3). The amended Proposal for the Directive had added a requirement that the interim report be published according to the requirements of the 1st Directive (see ch II above); this was subsequently dropped, no doubt to the relief of the HL Select Committee on the EC who had somewhat opaquely commented that in the UK it would merely add to statutory filing requirements which were already 'more than sufficiently difficult to police': (n 183 above) para 12(2).

[210] Art 7(2).

XII

The Second Stage—Harmonizing Public Offer Prospectuses

History, Aims and Legal Basis

When the first Proposal for a directive coordinating the information to be disclosed when unlisted securities are offered to the public for the first time (whether or not they are subsequently listed)[1] was submitted by the Council to the Commission in January 1981, the Admissions and Listing Particulars Directives had already been adopted and the amended Proposal for the Interim Reports Directive was pending before the Council. The Commission saw the Public Offers Prospectus Directive as 'the final link in a natural chain',[2] complementing the disclosure requirements imposed by the other three Directives on and after admission of securities to listing. At that time, Germany, the Netherlands, Italy, Denmark and Greece had no legislation on prospectuses, and there would have been a fundamental flaw in the developing edifice of investor protection if disclosure on offers to the public had continued to be unregulated. Moreover, the contribution made to investor protection by the introduction of harmonized information requirements on admission to listing through implementation of the Listing Particulars Directive would have been seriously undermined if, on offers to the public of shares for which a listing was subsequently[3] sought, inadequate disclosure was required on the initial offer. Unlisted shares offered to the public on the continent were furthermore much more likely to remain unlisted than in the United Kingdom, where public offers uncoupled with a contemporaneous application for listing were relatively rare (although they had been regulated by statute since the turn of the century[4]): a

---

[1] Proposal for a Council Directive coordinating the requirements for the drawing up, scrutiny and distribution of the prospectus to be published when securities are offered for subscription or sale to the public COM (80) 893 final, 31 December 1980; [1980] OJ C355/39. That draft is analysed in detail by Lempereur, C, 'La proposition de directive sur le prospectus à publier en cas d'offre publique de souscription ou de vente de valeurs mobilières' (1981) 58 Revue de droit international et de droit comparé 223.

[2] Henriksen, O B, then Director-General of DG XV (Financial Institutions and Taxation) of the Commission, giving evidence to the HL Select Committee on the EC, 30 June 1981; 43rd Report (Session 1980–81, HL Paper 271), Minutes of Evidence, 10. The Commission also described it as 'a logical follow-up' to the Listing Particulars Directive in the Explanatory Memorandum to the Proposal for what became Directive (EEC) 87/345 COM (87) 129 final, 24 March 1987.

[3] In the original six Member States, public offers normally preceded admission to listing.

[4] Companies Act 1900. The relevant provisions were subsequently consolidated in the Companies Act 1948, ss 37–55 and Sch 4, and re-enacted in the Companies Act 1985, Pt III. After Pt IV of the

failure to impose information requirements on such issues would accordingly have left a significant sector of the investing public unprotected.

The Economic and Social Committee delivered its Opinion on the first Proposal in September 1981[5] and the European Parliament in April 1982.[6] The Commission submitted an amended Proposal in July 1982,[7] which sought to accommodate some of the perceived lacunae in the first draft: for example, it included an exemption for Euro-bonds and incorporated a provision for mutual recognition. Many further problems remained however, and negotiations ground to a halt for several years while issues such as the exclusion of Euro-equities, the need for pre-vetting of prospectuses, the question whether there should be uniform disclosure for listed and unlisted securities and the scope of various key terms and exemptions were debated. Eventually Council Directive (EEC) 89/298 coordinating the requirements for the drawing-up, scrutiny and distribution of the prospectus to be published when transferable securities are offered to the public[8] was adopted on 17 April 1989.

The preamble to the Directive recites the familiar litany of investor protection through disclosure, contributing to the proper functioning of securities markets and thereby promoting the interpenetration of national markets and encouraging the creation of a pan-European capital market.[9] The preamble then refers to the framework for disclosure on listing set up by the Listing Particulars Directive as an important step in the implementation of a genuine Community information policy and recites that such an information policy also requires that a prospectus containing analogous information should be made available to investors and that the contents should be harmonized in order to achieve equivalence of minimum safeguards.[10]

The seventh recital is remarkable, admitting the impossibility of defining what is in effect the name of the Directive. It reads: 'Whereas, so far, it has proved impossible to furnish a common definition of the term "public offer" and all its constituent parts'. This question is considered further below.

Finally, the preamble expresses the policy adopted in the final version of distinguishing between two levels of disclosure depending on whether a listing is sought

Financial Services Act 1986 was brought into force, Pt III of the Companies Act 1985 applied only to offers of unlisted securities, now governed by the Public Offer of Securities Regulations 1995 (SI 1995/1537). See further n 14 below.

[5] [1981] OJ C310/50. The weight to be given to the Committee's Opinion is somewhat undermined by its misunderstanding of the nature of the Directive, which it explained 'lays down what information is to be published in the form of a prospectus when securities which are not to be given a stock market quotation are issued or offered to the public' (para 1).

[6] [1982] OJ C125/176.

[7] COM (82) 441 final, 27 July 1982; [1982] OJ C226/4. This version is analysed in detail by Pennington, R, 'Prospectuses for Securities Offered to the Public' (1983) 4 The Company Lawyer 151.

[8] [1989] OJ L124/8. The best review of the final text is by Warren, M G, 'The Common Market Prospectus' (1989) 26 CML Rev 687.

[9] 2nd, 3rd and 4th recitals in the preamble.   [10] 4th, 5th and 6th recitals.

for the securities being offered and the desire for mutual recognition of certain prospectuses and listing particulars.[11]

The original and amended Proposals for the Directive, in keeping with the Admissions, Listing Particulars and Interim Reports Directives, were based on Articles 54(3)(g) and 100 of the Treaty, on the basis that the coordination it sought to attain must apply to securities independently of the legal status of the issuing undertaking, thus going beyond the scope of Article 54 and requiring recourse to Article 100.[12] For no obvious reason the final version simply refers to Article 54, although 'issuers' are defined as including 'companies and other legal persons and any undertakings'[13] so that the rationale for Article 100 recited in the early versions would seem to be equally applicable.

Implementation in the United Kingdom

The United Kingdom's implementation of the Public Offers Prospectus Directive has been almost as bedeviled by delay and dissent as adoption of the Directive itself.[14] Ironically, given that the United Kingdom was one of the few Member States which historically had regulated prospectuses on public offers, from the earliest stages the proposed Directive met with intense and thinly veiled resistance on the part of, for example, the Department of Trade, The Stock Exchange, and The Law Society: it was felt that since the matter was efficiently and effectively regulated at national level, harmonization by the European Community was an unnecessary interference.[15] This hostility was to some extent defused by the changes which the original Proposal underwent before adoption nearly a decade later; in the mean time, the Financial Services Act 1986 had been adopted as part of the overhaul of the financial services industry in the City and in implementation of the first batch of securities directives. The Public Offers Prospectus Directive was originally intended to be implemented by Pts IV and V of the Financial Services Act governing listed and unlisted securities respectively. Part IV, substantially fleshed out by the London Stock Exchange's Listing Rules made pursuant to powers contained in it, was brought into force in February 1987: its effect was to require

---

[11] 8th recital. Neither the original nor the amended Proposal distinguished between listed and unlisted securities, requiring the same (highly detailed) level of information in respect of both. This had been one of the most controversial issues in the negotiations, as it was felt that small and medium-sized issuers of unlisted securities would be unduly burdened. The mutual recognition aspects of the Directive are dealt with in ch XIII below.

[12] 7th recital in the preamble.   [13] Art 3(c).

[14] The background to the statutory framework in the UK to 1985 is summarized in n 4 above. The interregnum between 1985 and implementation of the Directive in 1995 is described with commendable clarity, given the complex web of legislation, by Brazier, G, 'The Problem with Securities Law' [1994] NLJ 469.

[15] The HL Select Committee, however, saw the Proposal in the broader context and concluded that although there was no 'great practical need for the draft Directive' in the UK and the alterations required to UK law and practice would be small, there might be a gain in other Member States; on balance, the Proposal was therefore advantageous.

listing particulars to be published on a public offer of securities the subject of an application for listing. Part V was originally intended to replace Pt III of the Companies Act 1985, requiring a prospectus to be published on a public offer of securities for which no listing was sought. By the time the Public Offers Prospectus Directive was adopted, Pt V had still not been brought into force and it had become clear that, in part because of the changes which the Directive had undergone between the Commission's amended Proposal and the final version adopted, the Directive could no longer simply be implemented by Pt V as it then stood.[16] In July 1990 the Department of Trade and Industry issued a consultative document[17] on implementation. In the light of responses received during the consultation process, the Treasury (which in the mean time had taken over responsibility for this area from the Department of Trade and Industry) decided on a new approach and issued a further consultation document and draft regulations in July 1994.[18] The Public Offers of Securities Regulations 1995[19] came into force on 19 June 1995, repealing Pt V,[20] requiring a person offering transferable securities to the public in certain circumstances to prepare and publish a prospectus according to requirements set out in the Regulations, and amending Pt IV of the Financial Services Act 1986 so that a prospectus may in certain circumstances be prepared, scrutinized and approved in accordance with the Listing Rules.[21]

A further complication arises from the fact that before implementation of the Directive there was in the United Kingdom a third, residual class of public offers not covered by either of the regimes outlined above (that is, public offers of securities for which no listing was sought, governed by Pt III of the Companies Act 1985, and public offers of securities for which a listing was sought, governed by Pt IV of the Financial Services Act 1986 and the Listing Rules). This third category

[16] For a detailed discussion of Pt V, see Ferran, E, 'The Public Offers Directive and Problems of Implementation' in Andenas, M, and Kenyon-Slade, S, *EC Financial Market Regulation and Company Law* (1993) 103–9.

[17] *Listing Particulars and Public Offer Prospectuses: Implementation of Part V of the Financial Services Act 1986 and Related EC Directives.*

[18] *Revised implementation of the EC Prospectus Directive.* HM Treasury stated: 'The previous discussions revealed a number of serious difficulties with the approach based on Pt V of the FSA. Although most of these could have been overcome the result would have been an extremely complex set of regulations, leading to additional costs for issuers for professional advice, but failing to produce a body of law which was clear and readily enforceable': 6.

[19] SI 1995/1537. There are useful summaries of the Regulations and the changes to UK law and practice which they introduce by Creamer, H, in 'The Prospectus Directive: A New Regime for Public Offers' (which despite its title is about the Regulations and not the Directive as such) (May 1995) Practical Law for Companies 25, and by Bates, C, in 'The New UK Prospectus Rules' [1995] Butterworths Journal of International Banking and Financial Law 296. In addition, the UK Treasury issued a guidance note, *Public Offers of Securities Regulations 1995* in March 1996 to assist issuers of securities, investors and their professional advisers in understanding the main features of the regime introduced by the Regulations.

[20] On the same date The Financial Services Act 1986 (Commencement) (No 13) Order 1995 (SI 1995/1538) brought into force the Financial Services Act 1986, s 212(3) and Sch 17, which repealed the Companies Act 1985, Pt III and Sch 3, which pending the entry into force of Pt V of the Financial Services Act 1986 (FSA 1986) had been governing prospectuses on public offers of unlisted securities.

[21] The Listing Rules were also amended on 16 June 1995 to reflect the changes to Pt IV.

included non-public offers of unlisted and listed securities and public offers of securities already listed. Documents making such offers were regulated as investment advertisements under s 57 of the Financial Services Act. In the absence of a specific derogation, the Directive would have required a prospectus in the case of this third category of offers. Article 13(3)[22] of the Directive accordingly permits Member States or the competent authorities to provide for partial or complete exemption from the obligation to publish a prospectus where by the time the offer is made investors have available information at least equivalent to that required by Section III by virtue of 'law, regulation or rules made by bodies enabled to do so by national laws'. This enables the United Kingdom to designate the Financial Services Authority[23] and the self-regulatory organizations and to exempt secondary offers covered by the FSA advertising rules under s 57 of the Financial Services Act provided that the offeror issues an advertising document containing information equivalent to a Section III prospectus.[24]

The final position in the United Kingdom is therefore that the Directive is implemented by two parallel sets of provisions with certain offers which would otherwise fall under the Directive being separately regulated by virtue of a specific derogation. Subject to that derogation, in so far as the Directive concerns public offers of securities the subject of an application for listing it is implemented by Pt IV of the Financial Services Act[25] and the Listing Rules,[26] and in so far as it relates to public offers of securities for which no listing is sought it is implemented by the Public Offers of Securities Regulations 1995.[27]

Scope

Article 1(1) of the Directive provides that it is to apply to 'transferable securities which are offered to the public for the first time in a Member State provided that these securities are not already listed on a stock exchange situated or operating in that Member State'.

---

[22] Secured by the UK, to whom alone it was relevant, in negotiations on the Directive: see Willott, B, 'EC Capital Markets', in *Corporate Law: The European Dimension* (1991) 72–3.

[23] Formerly the Securities and Investments Board.

[24] Art 13(3) has been implemented in this way by The Financial Services Act 1986 (Investment Advertisements) (Exemptions) Order 1995 (SI 1995/1266) and The Financial Services Act 1986 (Investment Advertisements) (Exemptions) (No 2) Order 1995 (SI 1995/1536), both of which came into force on 19 June 1995.

[25] In particular s 142(7A) and Sch 11A, both inserted by the Public Offers of Securities Regulations 1995 (POS Regulations).

[26] In both cases, as amended on 16 June 1995 in the light of the POS Regulations.

[27] In July 1998 the UK Treasury published the long-awaited draft Financial Services and Markets Bill, which will inter alia repeal the FSA 1986. UK financial services legislation will thereafter consist of the Financial Services and Markets Act and secondary legislation. The Treasury also issued a consultation document *Public Offers of Securities* proposing amendments to the Regulations and seeking views on reforming public offers of securities within the European Union.

Transferable securities

In contrast to the Admission, Listing Particulars and Interim Reports Directives, the Public Offers Prospectus Directive defines 'transferable securities'. The definition is as follows:

shares in companies and other transferable securities equivalent to shares in companies, debt securities having a maturity of at least one year and other transferable securities equivalent to debt securities, and any other transferable security giving the right to acquire any such transferable securities by subscription or exchange.[28]

The original Proposal applied to 'securities', which was not defined. A simple definition of 'securities' as meaning 'shares, debt securities or certificates representing shares' was added in the amended Proposal;[29] the concept of 'transferable securities' and its definition was added at a final stage. This has resulted in some untidiness: despite the definition in the final version, which includes 'other transferable securities equivalent to shares', Article 2 twice refers to 'transferable securities [which are] shares or transferable securities equivalent to shares'.[30]

In addition to debt securities having a maturity of less than one year, excluded as a consequence of the definition of 'transferable securities', the following transferable securities are expressly excluded from the ambit of the Directive:

- transferable securities offered in individual denominations of at least ECU 40,000[31] or in connection with a takeover bid or merger[32] or in exchange for shares in the same company resulting in no overall increase in issued capital[33] or by the employer or an affiliated undertaking to or for the benefit of past or present employees;[34]
- transferable securities issued by the public sector[35] or by non-profit-making bodies[36] or on the exercise of conversion or exchange rights provided that a public offer prospectus or listing particulars were published in the same Member States on the offer of the underlying securities;[37]
- bonus issues;[38]

---

[28] Art 3(e). [29] Art 3(h).

[30] e g the exclusions in Art 2(2)(g) and (k). The same untidiness applies to 'transferable debt securities', in respect of which Art 5 is similarly loosely worded.

[31] Art 2(2)(a).

[32] Art 2(2)(d)(e). The Directive defines neither 'take-over bid' nor 'merger'. The UK legislation defines 'takeover offer' as a takeover offer within the meaning of Pt XIIIA of the Companies Act 1985 (the definition is in s 428) or an offer made to all the holders of shares, or of shares of a particular class, in a body corporate to acquire a specified proportion of those shares (FSA 1986, Sch 11A, para 3(6); POS Regulations, reg 7(10)), and 'merger' by reference to the 3rd Directive ((EEC) 78/855; see ch IV).

[33] Art 2(2)(g). An example of such an exchange would be an exchange of part of holdings of ordinary shares for new preference shares under a scheme of arrangement: Pennington, R, 'Prospectuses for Securities Offered to the Public' (1983) 4 The Company Lawyer 151, 152.

[34] Art 2(2)(h). [35] Art 2(2)(c).

[36] Art 2(2)(j). The proceeds of the issue must be intended to be applied to the issuer's objects.

[37] Art 2(2)(i). [38] Art 2(2)(f).

- shares conferring rights to use the services provided by building societies and similar bodies;[39]
- unit trusts;[40] and
- Euro-securities[41] 'which are not the subject of a generalized campaign of advertising or canvassing'.[42]

The exemption for Euro-securities[43] was particularly hard fought[44] and one of the principal reasons for the delay in adopting the Directive. The original Proposal contained no exemption for either Euro-bonds or Euro-equities. Intensive lobbying from the International Primary Market Association[45] led to the inclusion of an exemption for the former in the amended Proposal.[46] Once this was achieved, the IPMA and other lobbyists on behalf of the Euro-markets concentrated on extending the exemption to Euro-equities, and this was attained[47] in the final version. The precise scope of the exemption is unclear: the terms 'generalized campaign', 'advertising' and 'canvassing' are undefined. In particular, it is not clear whether 'canvassing' includes unsolicited approaches to existing customers, or is restricted to cold calling in the narrow sense, that is, unsolicited approaches to clients with whom there is no existing business nexus.[48] The relevant wording of Article 2(2)(l) in the other language versions of the Directive seems to cover the entire spectrum from cold calling in the narrow sense to any publicity at all.[49]

Moreover, Euro-securities offers not subject to a generalized campaign were presumably considered by the drafters of the Directive to be prima facie offers to

---

[39] Art 2(2)(k).

[40] Arts 2(2)(b) and 3(a)(b). Unit trusts are not within the UK regimes: see FSA 1986 s 142(2) and POS Regulations, reg 3(1)(b), both read in conjunction with the FSA 1986, Sch 1.

[41] Defined in Art 3(f) as transferable securities which '—are to be underwritten and distributed by a syndicate at least two of the members of which have their registered offices in different States, and—are offered on a significant scale in one or more States other than that of the issuer's registered office, and—may be subscribed for or initially acquired only through a credit institution [defined in Art 3(d)] or other financial institution'.

[42] Art 2(2)(l).

[43] Gower, L C B, states that the definition in Art 3(f) is 'the best attempt so far to distinguish them from other international issues': Davies, P L, *Gower's Principles of Modern Company Law* (6th edn, 1997) 403.

[44] Willott, B, reports how 'there was an understandable difference of view between the UK, supported by the Commission, which saw Eurosecurities as principally a wholesale professional market, appropriate for exclusion; and countries like Belgium with the proverbial 'Belgian dentist' for whom bearer Eurosecurities were essentially a retail product': *Corporate Law: the European Dimension* (1991), 72.

[45] A trade association including the major investment firms syndicating euro-securities. The main tenets of the IPMA's attack are clearly summarized and discussed by Warren, M G, 'The Common Market Prospectus' (1989) CML Rev 687, 702–10. Luxembourg's concerns that the Euro-market would be 'driven off-shore to Zurich' suggests a somewhat hazy grasp of the course of the European coastline.

[46] Art 2(h); 'Eurobonds' were not defined.

[47] Apparently to the surprise of those pressing for it: see Warren (n 45 above) 705.

[48] The wording of the UK implementing legislation is different, if clearer: 'Euro-securities . . . not the subject of advertising likely to come to the attention of persons who are not professionally experienced in matters relating to investment': FSA 1986, para 2(r) of Sch 11A.

[49] For example, *Haustürgeschäften, colportagecampagne, offerte a domicilio, captación de clientes a domicilio, publicidade directa, personlig henvendelse*.

the public, since their exclusion would otherwise be unnecessary: this adds to the confusion as to the meaning of 'offered to the public' and implies that Euro-securities offers as defined are offers to the public whether or not they are the subject of a generalized campaign.[50]

There are in addition further optional exemptions under Article 5, which authorizes Member States to provide for partial or complete exemption from the obligation to publish a prospectus where the transferable securities being offered to the public are specified types of debt securities, including those issued on a continuous basis by credit or equivalent institutions and those issued by certain para-statal undertakings.

Offered to the public for the first time

As mentioned above, the drafters of the Directive abandoned their early attempts to give some definition to the central concept of a public offer, stating rather lamely that it 'proved impossible to furnish a common definition'.[51] This lacuna, hardly surprisingly, has been widely perceived as a major counterweight to any harmonizing effect which the Directive may otherwise have.[52]

The first Proposal stated that the Directive was to apply to securities which were 'offered for subscription or sale to the public within a Member State',[53] and provided that they would 'be considered to be offered for subscription or sale to the public where the offer is not addressed exclusively to a restricted circle of persons', the Member States to determine what is meant by 'restricted circle of persons' 'having regard to the number of persons to whom the offer is addressed and, if appropriate, having regard also to their nature, to the amount of the offer, and to the means of publicity used for making the offer'.[54] The Economic and Social Committee considered this definition insufficiently clear and felt that leaving the definition of the core element to be determined by the Member States 'runs counter to the proposed Directive's avowed aim of standardization.' It accordingly proposed the following definition, based on studies conducted by the Banking Federation:

Public offer means an offer of securities made directly or indirectly by the issuer . . . according to conditions established in advance through a public statement. An offer is not a public offer if it is addressed to a limited number of persons or bodies known to the offeror and falling within a certain category, who are personally informed by the issuer or his appointed agent. . . . An offer made indirectly by the issuer shall mean an issue originally subscribed by a bank or banking syndicate on condition that the securities so acquired are offered for sale

---

[50] See Warren (n 45 above), 707–8.   [51] 6th recital in the preamble.
[52] Although the DTI conceded that 'there are genuine arguments for the view that different definitions of offer to the public may be justified in view of the different social, commercial and market circumstances of the Member States': Further Memorandum to the HL Select Committee on the EC 43rd Report (Session 1980–81, HL Paper 271) Minutes of Evidence 30, para 8.
[53] Art 1(1).   [54] Art 1(2).

to the public, so that the bank or the syndicate concerned can be considered to be an agent of the issuer.

The Committee added a definition of 'by public statement' and stated strongly that the Directive should contain a definition of 'restricted circle of persons', to include 'investors, even where there are a great many of them, who have personal connections with the financial institution and are approached individually by it'.

The European Parliament suggested defining 'restricted circle of persons' as comprising:

an identifiable category of persons or bodies known to the offeror, to whom the offer is directly communicated by the offeror or his appointed agent so that only members of that category may accept the offer, and that such members undertake not to resell the securities offered within a specified period of time.

The first part of this suggestion was adopted by the Commission in its amended Proposal, in which the second paragraph of Article 1(2) (which had left it to the Member States to determine the definition) was replaced by the following:

An offer shall be considered to be made to a restricted circle of persons where it is addressed to an identifiable category of persons or bodies known to the offeror, to whom the offer is directly communicated by the offeror or his appointed agent so that only members of that category may accept the offer and such members are in possession of sufficient information to be able to make a reasonable evaluation of the offer.

Notwithstanding the foregoing, a Member State may consider that an offer is addressed to a restricted circle of persons where it is addressed to not more than a given number of persons to be specified by that Member State, which number shall not exceed 250.[55]

Agreement on this amendment proved impossible to secure however and it was dropped from the final version.

Difficulties with defining 'offer to the public' are hardly new, at least in the United Kingdom where there is a history of problems with the definition of 'public' in the context of the former legislation prohibiting private companies from offering securities to the public.[56] The United Kingdom's implementing legislation provides that 'A person offers securities to the public in the United Kingdom if, to the extent that the offer is made to persons in the United Kingdom, it is made to the public', which is unhelpful (if incontrovertible); the provision continues with the qualification that an offer made to any section of the public, 'whether selected as members or debenture holders of a body corporate, or as clients of the person

---

[55] This latter provision is similar to the one applied by the US SEC to determine whether a public offering is made for the purpose of registration under the US Securities Act 1933: Pennington, R, 'Prospectuses for Securities Offered to the Public' (1983) 4 The Company Lawyer 151, 153.

[56] Companies Act 1948, s 55. See Gower, L C B, *Principles of Modern Company Law* (4th edn, 1979) 350–3 for an overview of judicial interpretation of this provision. There is also a useful outline in the memorandum on the topic submitted by the DTI to the HL Select Committee on the EC on the Directive (n 52 above), 28–30.

making the offer, or in any other manner', is deemed to be made to the public.[57] Thus a vendor placing[58] may be regarded as an offer to the public, depending on how widely placed the shares are.

Some negative guidance is provided in the Directive by Article 2(1), which provides that it does not apply to certain types of offer,[59] including an exclusion for offers to a restricted circle of persons.[60] The other exclusions are offers to persons in the context of their trades, professions or occupations;[61] where the total selling price does not exceed ECU 40,000;[62] and where the minimum consideration per investor is ECU 40,000.[63]

The Directive will apply only where the securities are offered to the public 'for the first time'; it will thus not apply where securities already distributed in the course of a previous public offer are re-sold under a further public offer.

Provided that these securities are not already listed

Much of the literature on the Directive is dogged by persistent confusion as to the distinction it draws between listed and unlisted securities. The position is simple and unambiguous: the Directive has always applied to a public offer of securities (a) not listed at the time of the offer and (b) whether or not they are subsequently listed. The confusion results from a failure to distinguish between these two aspects. The restriction of the Directive to securities not listed at the time of the offer has

---

[57] FSA 1986, Sch 11A, para 1; POS Regulations, reg 6. There is an interesting discussion of the various options for defining 'offer to the public' in ch 7 of the DTI's 1990 consultative document, cited in n 17 above. The draft POS Regs provided that a person was to be 'regarded as offering securities to the public if he offers them to any section of the public, whether selected as members or debenture holders of a body corporate, or as clients of the person issuing the prospectus, or in any other manner.' It is tempting to speculate that the definition was broadened by the addition of the illuminating statement that a person offers securities to the public if the offer is made to the public to avoid the risk that an English court might refuse to interpret 'any section of the public' as including the public at large, by analogy with *Re a Company (No 00370 of 1983)*, *ex p Glossop* [1988] 1 WLR 1068 in which it was held that the Companies Act 1948, s 210, which sought to protect members against conduct which was oppressive to 'some part of the company's members', did not give a remedy where the conduct in question was oppressive to all the members.

[58] An arrangement whereby the vendor of property to a company is paid by an allotment of shares which are then 'placed' with investors by a merchant bank on the vendor's behalf so that the vendor ends up with cash.

[59] The numerous exceptions both for certain offers and for certain transferable securities led one commentator to describe the Directive as appearing 'to constitute a mandatory disclosure scheme in search of an issuer': Warren, M G, 'The Common Market Prospectus' (1989) CML Rev 687, 702.

[60] Art 2(1)(b); FSA 1986 Sch 11A, para 3(1)(d); POS Regs, reg 7(2)(d). Both the UK provisions are expressed in terms of offers to a restricted circle of persons 'whom the offeror reasonably believes to be sufficiently knowledgeable to understand the risks involved in accepting the offer'.

[61] Art 2(1)(a); FSA 1986 Sch 11A, para 3(1)(a); POS Regs, reg 7(2)(a). Both the UK provisions are defined in more detail than the source provision, making it clear that the primary thrust of the exclusion is offers to persons '(i) whose ordinary activities involve them in acquiring, holding, managing or disposing of investments (as principal or agent) for the purposes of their businesses; or (ii) who it is reasonable to expect will acquire, hold, manage or dispose of investments (as principal or agent) for the purposes of their businesses'.

[62] Art 2(1)(c). [63] Art 2(1)(d).

always been spelt out: the first Proposal contained an equivalent proviso to Article 1(1).[64] The amended Proposal dropped the proviso but this was purely cosmetic: it reappeared in a different guise but to the same effect under the list of securities to which the Directive was not to apply, which was extended to 'securities which are admitted to official listing on a stock exchange situated or operating in the Member State where the public offer is made'.[65] That the Directive applies whether or not the securities are to be subsequently listed has been made clear in the preamble to all versions.[66]

This confusion was exacerbated by the fact that the draft Directive was frequently referred to as 'the draft Directive on unlisted securities', which appears to have led many commentators to assume that it was only relevant to unlisted securities.[67] It was also no doubt aggravated by the fact that the original Proposal did not make any explicit distinction between listed and unlisted securities, leading the cursory reader to assume that it applied only to securities which were unlisted at the time of the offer and which remained unlisted. In fact, it applied to securities unlisted at the time of the offer whether or not they were subsequently listed, imposing identical disclosure requirements in each case. This itself was perceived as a major problem since it was felt that it was unduly burdensome to require the same level of information of smaller companies offering shares for which it was not intended to seek a listing. After four years of deadlock on the amended Proposal, the Commission decided to bisect the proposed regime and create two separate and different regimes for listed and unlisted securities.[68] The Directive would prescribe modified information to be published on a public offer of securities for which no listing was sought, while the prospectus to be published on a public offer of securities for which a listing was sought would be governed by the Listing Particulars

---

[64] Art 1(1).

[65] Art 2(j). Wooldridge, F, 'Some Recent Community Legislation in the Field of Securities Law' (1985) 10 ELR 3, unaccountably seems to have overlooked this, stating that the 'original proposal was applicable to unlisted securities, but the amended proposal no longer contains this limitation, being applicable to securities which are offered directly or indirectly by the issuer for subscription or sale in a Member State' (the amended version of Art 1(1), which he cites in support of the proposition without referring to Art 2(j) as amended).

[66] 6th recital in the preamble to all versions.

[67] Pennington makes this point, noting that the reasons for the delay between amended Proposal and adoption included 'reservations of a largely irrelevant nature . . . in respect of the effect of the proposals on the UK and French unlisted securities markets. [The Directive] will in no way affect the admission of securities to listing or to dealings on a regulated market without being listed, nor will it affect dealings in listed or unlisted securities which have already been issued': 'Prospectuses for Securities Offered to the Public' (1983) 4 The Company Lawyer 151, 151. The misapprehension as to the way in which the Directive applies to listed and unlisted securities perhaps explains some of the antipathy discernible in, for example, the evidence submitted to the HL Select Committee: The Stock Exchange, for example, questioned the need for the Directive inter alia because 'there appear to be very few cross-frontier issues of unlisted securities' so that the aim of 'interpenetration of national securities markets' was inapposite and because there were not enough domestic issues of unlisted securities to justify 'the heavy administrative expense' of setting up and operating the competent authority: 43rd Report (Session 1980–81, HL Paper 271) Minutes of Evidence, 16.

[68] See Warren (n 59 above), 698–9, n 45, citing EC Commission Staff Paper, SEC (86) 250 (12 February 1986).

Directive. In the final version, Section II deals with the contents and arrangements for the scrutiny and distribution of the prospectus for transferable securities for which admission to official Stock Exchange listing is sought and Section III with the contents and arrangements for the distribution of the prospectus for transferable securities for which admission to official Stock Exchange listing is not sought.

Prior Scrutiny of Prospectuses

The provisions for the prior scrutiny, or vetting, of prospectuses form part of the framework for mutual recognition, considered in the next chapter. However, it is appropriate to consider the basic issue of prior scrutiny at this point since it underlies certain Articles in the Directive relating to the publication of prospectuses, which cannot fully be understood without an awareness of the mechanism.

The original Proposal included a requirement that all prospectuses be approved by the competent authorities appointed by each Member State. Those authorities were to approve publication of the prospectus only if they considered that it satisfied all the requirements of the Directive.[69] That provision caused consternation in the United Kingdom in particular, where prospectuses in relation to securities for which no listing was sought had historically not been vetted (although a copy was required to be lodged with the Registrar of Companies). The proposed requirement, although limited to checking whether the information given corresponded to that required by the Directive[70] which was already undertaken by the Stock Exchange in respect of admissions to listing, was regarded as exceedingly onerous.[71] Furthermore, the Stock Exchange, reluctantly conceding that it was the most likely candidate for appointment as the competent authority, echoed the concerns which it had expressed in connection with the original Proposal for the Listing Particulars Directive[72] about incurring liability to investors who had suffered loss as a result of relying on an approved prospectus which did not strictly comply with the Directive. There was in addition concern that pre-vetting Euro-bond prospectuses (Euro-bonds at that stage were still covered by the Directive) would be impossible to reconcile with the need for speed in Euro-bond offers.[73]

---

[69] Art 17.

[70] As Lord Roberthall pointed out in evidence to the HL Select Committee on the EC, 'they could not very well consider whether the company was likely to be successful or not as that is the great problem of all investments. If they could do that, they would not be registering companies': 43rd Report (Session 1980–81, HL Paper 271) Minutes of Evidence, 4.

[71] The arguments adduced against this provision comprised two apparently contradictory strands advanced with equal heat, namely (a) pre-vetting would be onerous and involve heavy administrative expense and (b) there were not enough domestic issues of unlisted securities to justify such expense. See the Minutes of Evidence to the HL Select Committee (n 70 above) passim.

[72] See ch XI above.

[73] And the fact that their international character raises questions as to which would be the appropriate vetting authority. The Economic and Social Committee suggested an amendment dealing with both these issues. The European Parliament also made a somewhat ungrammatical attempt to deal with the international element.

Eventually the deadlock was resolved by limiting the requirement for pre-vetting to prospectuses issued in connection with a public offer of securities to be listed. Since in the final scheme of the Directive such prospectuses were regulated in accordance with the Listing Particulars Directive, in which the problems relating to potential liability to investors had ultimately been resolved to the satisfaction of the United Kingdom,[74] this dealt with the first problem; the second became irrelevant once Euro-securities had been lifted out of the Directive. Prospectuses relating to a public offer of securities for which no listing was to be sought did not have to be pre-vetted, although they had to be communicated to the bodies designated for that purpose.[75]

This apparent solution however gave rise to a further problem for the United Kingdom. As will be seen in the next chapter, public offer prospectuses meeting the listing particulars requirements and vetted in one Member State must be recognized as both listing particulars and public offer prospectuses in other Member States. As part of the framework for this, Article 12 permits Member States to provide that the person making the offer is to have the possibility of drawing up a prospectus the contents of which, subject to adaptations appropriate to the circumstances of a public offer, are to be determined in accordance with the Listing Particulars Directive; the prior scrutiny of such prospectuses is to be carried out by the bodies designated by the Member States even in the absence of an application for listing. Since the United Kingdom had no provision for vetting prospectuses where no listing was sought, it was potentially at a disadvantage from the point of view of mutual recognition. This has been resolved at national level by a legislative amendment establishing a procedure for the London Stock Exchange to approve prospectuses drawn up in accordance with listing particulars requirements even where no London listing is sought.[76]

The Obligation to Publish a Prospectus

The basic obligation to publish a public offer prospectus, unlike the requirements for content and scrutiny of the prospectus, applies whether or not the securities are to be listed. Member States are required by Article 4 to ensure that any offer of transferable securities to the public within their territories is subject to the publication of a prospectus by the person making the offer. If the offer is being made within twelve months of publication of a full prospectus in relation to an offer of different transferable securities by the same offeror in the same State, an abbreviated prospectus may be published on the second issue indicating only those changes 'likely to influence the value of the securities which have occurred' in the mean time, provided that that prospectus is made available only accompanied by the full prospectus or a reference thereto.[77] The prospectus must be published or made

---

[74] See ch XI above.   [75] Art 14.
[76] FSA 1986, s 156A, introduced by the POS Regs.   [77] Art 6.

available to the public not later than the time when the offer is made to the public.[78]

Prospectus where a Listing is Sought

Contents of the prospectus

Articles 7 to 10 deal with the contents and arrangements for the scrutiny and distribution of the prospectus for securities to be listed. Where a public offer relates to transferable securities which at the time of the offer are the subject of an application for official listing on a Stock Exchange situated or operating within the same Member State, the contents of the prospectus and the procedures for scrutinizing and distributing it are to be determined in accordance with the Listing Particulars Directive,[79] 'subject to adaptations appropriate to the circumstances of a public offer'.[80]

Although individual derogations and exemptions in accordance with the Listing Particulars Directive will be available in the circumstances there set out, there may be occasions where that Directive exempts the issuer completely from producing listing particulars, but where a prospectus may none the less be required because none of the exemptions under the Public Offers Prospectus Directive applies. For example, there is provision in the Listing Particulars Directive for exemption from the obligation to prepare listing particulars where the securities are of the same class as those already listed and increase them by less than 10 per cent;[81] there is however no corresponding exemption from the obligation to produce a prospectus if the securities are sufficiently widely distributed to amount to an offer to the public.[82]

Article 8 applies where a public offer is made in one Member State and admission to listing is sought in another. Provided that the Member State where the offer is made provides for the prior scrutiny of public offer prospectuses, the offeror must be able to draw up a prospectus in that State which complies with the Listing Particulars Directive.[83]

Publicity and publication

Announcements of a public offer of securities for which a listing is sought must be communicated in advance to the competent authorities and must mention that there is or (if the Member State authorizes the distribution of such announcements

---

[78] Arts 9 and 16; although this provision is duplicated in the sections dealing separately with securities to be listed and those not to be listed, it is identical for each regime.

[79] See ch XI above.   [80] Art 7.   [81] Art 6(3)(a).

[82] An example of this combination of circumstances might be a 1-for-12 rights issue.

[83] This will enable him to obtain mutual recognition of that prospectus as listing particulars on admission of the securities in the other Member State. See ch XIII below.

before the prospectus is available) will be a prospectus and state where it is published or where members of the public will be able to obtain it.[84]

Publication of the prospectus must be by insertion in a newspaper circulated throughout the Member State in which the offer is made or in the form of a brochure to be made available without charge to the public in that State and at the registered office of the offeror and the offices of its paying agents in that State.[85] In addition, either the prospectus or a notice stating where it has been published and where it may be obtained must be inserted in a publication designated by the Member State in which the offer is made.[86]

Prospectus where no Listing is Sought

Contents of the prospectus

The primary requirement where a public offer relates to transferable securities for which admission to listing is not sought is that the prospectus 'contain the information which, according to the particular nature of the issuer and of the transferable securities offered to the public, is necessary to enable investors to make an informed assessment of the assets and liabilities, financial position, profits and losses and prospects of the issuer and of the rights attaching to the transferable securities.'[87] Article 11(2) specifies certain minimum information which must be included in the prospectus 'in as easily analysable and comprehensible a form as possible' in order to fulfil the general obligation; where such information is inappropriate to the issuer's sphere of activity or its legal form or the securities being offered, equivalent information must be given.[88] The information is listed under the following headings: (a) those responsible for the prospectus; (b) the offer to the public and the transferable securities being offered; (c) the issuer and its capital; (d) the issuer's principal activities; (e) the issuer's assets and liabilities, financial position and profits and losses, interim accounts if any, the name of the auditor and details of any qualifications to audit reports; (f) the issuer's administration, management and supervision; and (g) to the extent that such information would have a significant impact on any assessment that might be made of the issuer, recent developments in its business and prospects. In the case of a public offer of debt securities, analogous information under most headings must be given about the guarantor,[89] and where such securities are convertible, exchangeable or warrant-backed, information must be given about the underlying securities, their issuer if different and the conditions of and procedures for conversion, exchange or subscription.[90]

---

[84] Art 10(1)(2); implemented in the UK by the FSA 1986, ss 154 and 154A and the Listing Rules.
[85] Art 10(3). In the UK, the FSA 1986, ss 149 and 154A, require in addition that the prospectus be filed at the Companies Registry.
[86] Art 10(4).   [87] Art 11(1).   [88] Art 11(6).   [89] Art 11(3).   [90] Art 11(4).

Omissions and exemptions

General derogations

Article 13[91] permits the Member States or the bodies designated by them to authorize omission from the prospectus of information (a) of minor importance only which is not likely to influence assessment of the issuer's assets and liabilities, financial position, profits and losses and prospects;[92] (b) the disclosure of which would be contrary to the public interest[93] or seriously detrimental to the issuer, provided in the latter case that omission would not be likely to mislead the public with regard to facts and circumstances essential for assessment of the securities;[94] and (c) which would not normally be in the possession of the initiator of the offer where that initiator is neither the issuer nor acting on the issuer's behalf.[95]

Derogations for shares admitted to unlisted markets

In the case of shares offered to existing shareholders on a pre-emptive basis on their admission to dealing on a Stock Exchange market,[96] the Member States may permit some of the specified information concerning the issuer's principal activities, assets and liabilities, financial position and profits and losses, and administration, management and supervision to be omitted provided that investors already possess equivalent up-to-date information as a result of the disclosure requirements of that exchange,[97] and where a class of shares has been admitted to dealing on such a market, the Member States may permit partial or complete exemption from the obligation to publish a prospectus if the number or value[98] of the shares offered is less than 10 per cent of the number or corresponding value of shares of the same class already admitted to dealing, provided that investors already possess up-to-date information about the issuer equivalent to that required by the Directive as a result of the disclosure requirements of that exchange.[99]

---

[91] The exemption provided for in Art 13(3) is considered above, at p 270. The three exemptions in Art 13(1) considered below all have parallels in the Listing Particulars Directive: see Art 7 and p 256 above. The exemption in Art 3(2) considered below has no parallel in the Listing Particulars Directive, presumably on the basis that a separate offeror will not act independently of the issuer where there is an application for listing.

[92] Art 13(1)(a). In the UK, the London Stock Exchange is authorized to administer this exemption, even though there is no application for listing.

[93] Art 13(1)(b); POS Regs, reg 11(1), which designates the Treasury of the Secretary of State as the body with power to authorize omission in this case.

[94] Art 13(1)(b). In the UK, the Stock Exchange is the designated body.

[95] Art 13(2); the UK implementation (POS Regs, reg 11(2)) does not require authorization to be obtained for omission in such circumstances.

[96] Not of course the official list, but an unlisted market such as, in the UK, the Alternative Investment Market.

[97] Art 11(7). In the UK, the Stock Exchange has been designated as the body competent to administer these derogations.

[98] Estimated market value or nominal value or, if there is no nominal value, accounting par value.

[99] Art 11(8).

Supplementary prospectus

Article 18 requires a supplementary prospectus to be published or made available to the public in the same way as the original prospectus or in accordance with procedures laid down by the Member States or the competent authorities, mentioning any significant new factor or correcting any significant inaccuracy in the original prospectus which is capable of affecting assessment of the securities and which arises or is noted between publication of the original prospectus and the definitive closure of the offer.[100]

Communication and publication of prospectus

A prospectus prepared under Section III must be communicated before publication to the bodies designated for that purpose in each Member State in which the securities are offered to the public for the first time[101] and published or made available to the public in that State in accordance with procedures to be laid down at national level.[102] Any announcements of the offer distributed or made available by the offeror to the public must state that a prospectus exists or (if the Member State authorizes the distribution of such announcements before the prospectus is available) will be published and indicate where it is published or will be available.[103] In addition, such announcements must be communicated in advance to the same bodies to whom the prospectus must be communicated if those bodies carry out prior scrutiny of public offer prospectuses, in which case those bodies must determine whether the documents should be checked before publication.[104]

Prospectuses drawn up as listing particulars

Article 12 permits Member States to provide for a person making a public offer to have the option of drawing up a prospectus the contents of which, subject to adaptations appropriate to the circumstances of a public offer, are to be determined in accordance with the Listing Particulars, to be vetted in advance by the competent authorities even where no application for listing is being made. This provision is designed to facilitate mutual recognition of prospectuses, and is accordingly dealt with in the next chapter.

---

[100] Not defined, although the word 'definitive' was added in response to the Economic and Social Committee's point that it is not clear when a public offer is closed. The Committee suggested specifying the end of the subscription or selling period.

[101] Art 14. The UK implementation (POS Regs, reg 4(2)) designates the Registrar of Companies for this purpose.

[102] Art 15.   [103] Art 17(1), final sentence, and (2).

[104] Art 17. In the UK, the Registrar of Companies, the body designated for the purposes of Art 14, does not carry out prior scrutiny.

Multi-national Offers

Article 20 tackles the question of whose competent authority is to regulate international issues. This problem was surprisingly not dealt with until the amended Proposal, which incorporated a provision[105] based on a suggestion by the Economic and Social Committee. The Article applies where there are public offers of the same transferable securities simultaneously or within a short interval in two or more Member States and where a prospectus is drawn up in accordance with the Listing Particulars Directive.[106] In that case, the authority competent for the approval of the prospectus is that of the Member State in which the issuer has its registered office provided that the public offer or any application for listing is made in that State,[107] unless that Member State makes no provision for the scrutiny of public offer prospectuses in which case the person making the public offer must choose an authority from another Member State in which the offer is made which provides for such scrutiny.[108] Since all Member States must, by virtue of the combined provisions of the Listing Particulars Directive and the Public Offer Prospectus Directive, provide for the scrutiny of public offer prospectuses in respect of securities for which admission to listing is to be sought, this provision will apply only where the securities are not to be listed in the same State in which the offer is made.

Failure to Comply with the Directive

The Directive makes no provision for sanctions for failure to comply with its requirements as to content and publication of prospectuses. The consequences of failing to meet the requirements of a Member State's implementing legislation will accordingly be governed by that Member State's national law.[109]

Cooperation between Member States and between Authorities

Article 19 requires the Member States to designate[110] bodies which are to cooperate with each other for the purposes of the proper implementation of the Directive and exchange all the information necessary to that end, and to ensure that they have

---

[105] Art 23(1). [106] i e, under Art 7, 8 or 12 of the Public Offer Prospectus Directive.
[107] Art 20(1). [108] Art 20(2).
[109] See Creamer, H, 'The Prospectus Directive: A New Regime for Public Offers' Practical Law for Companies (May 1995) 25, and Bates, C,'The New UK Prospectus Rules' [1995] Butterworths Journal of International Banking and Financial Law 296, for a brief summary of the current position in the UK.
[110] And inform the Commission, which must communicate the information to the other Member States.

the powers required therefor. Those bodies may be the same as those designated for the purposes of Article 14, which requires a prospectus to be communicated before publication to designated bodies in the Member State where the securities are first offered to the public.

Article 22(1) appears to echo Article 19, requiring the competent authorities to cooperate wherever necessary for the purpose of carrying out their duties and to exchange any information required for that purpose. The separate provisions reflect the drafting history of the Directive: the original Proposal contained a simple requirement that the Member States appoint competent authorities and notify the Commission thereof[111] followed by a separate requirement that, where relevant,[112] those authorities exchange information and cooperate. As indicated above,[113] that initial structure involving one set of authorities to monitor prospectuses on both type of offer—namely whether or not coupled with an application to list—was abandoned in the face of protests, mainly from the United Kingdom, as to the unacceptable liability such bodies may incur. Article 19 seeks to make it clear that the authorities responsible for prior scrutiny of a prospectus relating to a public offer of securities to be listed may be different[114] from the authorities to whom a prospectus relating to a public offer of securities for which no listing is sought is to be communicated pursuant to Article 14. Articles 19 and 22(1) also differ in scope, in that the former essentially sets out the requirement incumbent on Member States to designate the competent authorities while the latter describes the requirements of cooperation and exchange of information to be imposed on those authorities.[115] The same obligations of professional secrecy apply to employees of the competent authorities and information in their hands as in the case of the Admissions and Listing Particulars Directives.[116]

A specific obligation to cooperate is imposed where (a) a public offer concerns transferable securities giving a right to participate in company capital, either immediately or at the end of a maturity period and (b) the offer is made in a Member State or States other than that in which the issuer of the underlying shares has its registered office and (c) the issuer's shares have already been admitted to official listing in that State and (d) the prospectus is to be scrutinized. In those circumstances, the competent authorities of the Member State where the offer is made may act only after consulting their counterparts in the Member State in which that registered office is situated.[117]

---

[111] Art 17.   [112] i e in multi-national offers.   [113] See pp 277–8.

[114] And in the UK are different, the London Stock Exchange fulfilling the former role and the Company Registrar the latter.

[115] This difference is somewhat clouded by the wording of the English version of Art 19, which appears to do both. It is brought out more clearly in the other language versions.

[116] See pp 248 and 259 above.   [117] Art 22(2).

XIII

The Third Stage—Introducing Mutual Recognition

Background

Both applications for the listing of securities on an official Stock Exchange and public offers of securities may straddle national borders. The burden of complying with more than one regulatory system can be eased by harmonization of disclosure requirements; the residual duplication of effort can be eradicated by providing for mutual recognition throughout the Member States of the relevant disclosure documents. That state of affairs has now largely been accomplished: there is a framework for the mutual recognition of listing particulars as listing particulars (the 1987 amendment to the Listing Particulars Directive, or the First Mutual Recognition Directive), of public offer prospectuses as listing particulars (the 1990 amendment to the Listing Particulars Directive, or the Second Mutual Recognition Directive) and of public offer prospectuses as public offer prospectuses (the Public Offers Prospectus Directive).

The basic scheme and the legislative evolution of the relevant provisions are broadly similar in all cases. Both the Listing Particulars Directive[1] and the original Proposal for the Public Offers Prospectus Directive[2] provided for cooperation between the Member States concerned in the event of, respectively, simultaneous or near-simultaneous applications for admission of securities on exchanges situated or operating within several Member States and simultaneous or near-simultaneous public offers of the same securities within several Member States. The competent authorities were to exchange information and use their best endeavours to achieve maximum coordination of their relevant requirements, avoid a multiplicity of formalities and agree to a single text (subject to translation where appropriate and the issue of supplements where necessary) to meet each Member State's requirements. Where the applications or offers were made within six months of each other, the competent authorities of the State of the second transaction were to contact the competent authorities of the State of the first transaction and, so far as possible, exempt the issuer from the preparation of new listing particulars or a new prospectus subject to any requirements in that State for updating, translating or supplementing the document concerned.

---

[1] Art 24.   [2] Art 23.

The obligation to cooperate did not however go very far towards true mutual recognition. The first step towards that goal was taken in the context of the Proposal for the Public Offers Prospectus Directive, and was prompted by the European Parliament. The Parliament requested that in the case of multi-national public offers, a single public offer prospectus approved in only one Member State should suffice for the purposes of the offer in all the States, and in view of this the Commission provided for the principle of mutual recognition in Article 23 of its amended Proposal.[3] The provision evolved further in the course of the negotiations of the Public Offers Prospectus Directive, and finally became Article 21 of the Directive when, after much delay,[4] it was adopted in 1989. In the mean time however the Commission, inspired by the steps being taken with regard to the mutual recognition of public offer prospectuses and by the adoption in 1986 of a directive[5] abolishing exchange control restrictions on, inter alia, the admission of securities to official Stock Exchange listing (making it even more important to reduce to the minimum other types of obstacle to multi-national listings) presented a Proposal[6] on 24 March 1987 for a Council Directive amending the Listing Particulars Directive so as to apply the principle of mutual recognition to listing particulars in the same way as was being developed for public offer prospectuses. The Directive progressed with astonishing speed: the European Parliament approved the Proposal subject to one minor amendment on 10 April 1987[7] and the Economic and Social Committee on 14 April 1987,[8] and it was adopted on 22 June 1987.[9] Although an amending directive, inserting new Articles 24, 24a, 24b, 24c, 25 and 25a in the Listing Particulars Directive, the 1987 Directive is frequently and usefully referred to as the First Mutual Recognition Directive.

The next chronological step in the developing edifice of mutual recognition was the adoption of the Public Offers Prospectus Directive in April 1989, Article 21 of which established a scheme for the mutual recognition of public offer prospectuses which, as indicated above, closely paralleled that already adopted for listing particulars. The final brick was laid with the adoption in April 1990 of a further directive amending the Listing Particulars Directive, known as the Second Mutual Recognition Directive.[10] That Directive replaces Article 24b(1) of the Listing

---

[3] See the Explanatory Memorandum to the Proposal for the First Mutual Recognition Directive COM (87) 129 final, 24 March 1987.

[4] See ch XII above.

[5] Council Directive (EEC) 86/566 amending the First Directive of 11 May 1960 for the implementation of Art 67 of the Treaty [1986] OJ L332/22.

[6] COM (87) 129 final, 24 March 1987.   [7] [1987] OJ C125/172.

[8] [1987] OJ C150/18.

[9] Council Directive (EEC) 87/345 amending Directive (EEC) 80/390 coordinating the requirements for the drawing-up, scrutiny and distribution of the listing particulars to be published for the admission of securities to official Stock Exchange listing [1987] OJ L185/81.

[10] Council Directive (ECC) 90/211 of 23 April 1990 amending Directive (ECC) 80/390 in respect of the mutual recognition of public offer prospectuses as Stock Exchange listing particulars [1990] OJ L112/24. The Proposal was submitted on 22 March 1989 (COM (89) 133 final, [1989] OJ C101/13); the Opinion of the Economic and Social Committee was delivered on 21 June 1989 [1989] OJ C201/5; the European Parliament's Opinion on the Proposal (first reading under the cooperation

Particulars Directive, added by the First Mutual Recognition Directive, so as to provide for the mutual recognition of public offer prospectuses as listing particulars where admission to official Stock Exchange listing is requested within a short period of the public offer.

The Community Framework

The provisions for mutual recognition in all three cases covered by the scheme are very similar, and will be considered together.[11]

The two transactions (whether they are both public offers, both applications for listing, or a public offer followed by an application for listing[12]) must occur 'simultaneously or within a short interval' in the first two cases[13] and within three months[14] in the third case.

To attract recognition, listing particulars must be drawn up in accordance with the Listing Particulars Directive in the Member State in which the issuer has its registered office[15] and be approved by the competent authority of that State. If the issuer's registered office is not in one of the Member States where the applications are made, the listing particulars must be drawn up and approved under the legislation of one of those States, at the issuer's option.[16] Public offer prospectuses seeking recognition as such must be drawn up to listing particulars standard and approved by the competent authorities of the State in which the issuer has its registered office if the offer or any application for listing is made in that State, unless that State makes no provision in general for the prior scrutiny of public offer prospectuses in which case the prospectus must be approved by the authorities of one of the States in which the offer is made and which provides for prior scrutiny.[17] Public offer prospectuses seeking recognition as listing particulars must be drawn up to listing particulars standard and approved in any Member State.[18]

procedure) on 25 October 1989 [1989] OJ C304/34; and the Parliament's decision on the Council's common position (second reading under the cooperation procedure) on 17 January 1990 [1990] OJ C38/40. No substantive amendments were proposed by either body.

[11] See for an overview Lambrecht, P, 'Mutual Recognition of Listing Particulars and Prospectuses and the New Possible Exemptions' (1994) 6 Revue de droit d'affaires international 721.

[12] The fourth possibility is not catered for, presumably because of the pattern of practice in most Member States, where public offers and associated applications for listing are either contemporaneous or occur in that order.

[13] Arts 20(1) Public Offers Prospectus Directive (POPD) and 24 Listing Particulars Directive (LPD).

[14] Art 24b(1) LPD.

[15] This should discourage any 'forum shopping', ensuring that permitted variations in disclosure standards between Member States are not exploited by issuers seeking approval of listing particulars in the State with the least onerous requirements and securing recognition of those particulars elsewhere on the basis of the mutual recognition provisions.

[16] Art 24 LPD. This provision appears to dilute the anti-forum-shopping effect of the previous provision. Any temptation to restrict listings to foreign markets will however be counterbalanced by the tendency for securities to be more readily marketable and more liquid on domestic markets: see Warren, M G, 'Global Harmonization of Securities Laws: the Achievement of the European Communities' (1990) 31 Harvard International Law Journal 185, 213.

[17] Art 20 POPD.   [18] Art 24b(1) LPD.

Once so approved, subject to translation if required, the listing particulars or prospectus in question must be recognized by the other Member State(s) in which the second transaction is to occur; in particular those States cannot require the document to be approved by their competent authorities or to include additional information except that specific to the market of the country of admission concerning in particular income tax, the issuer's paying agents and publication of notices to investors.[19] There is however a specific obligation on the competent authorities of the State where recognition is sought to contact the competent authorities of the Member State in which shares are already listed where (a) an application for admission to listing or a public offer involving a prospectus to be scrutinized concerns securities giving a right to participate in company capital, either immediately or at the end of a maturity period and (b) the application or offer is made in a Member State or States other than that in which the issuer of the underlying shares has its registered office and (c) the issuer's shares have already been admitted to official listing in that State. In those circumstances, the competent authorities of the Member State where admission is sought or the offer is made may act only after consulting their counterparts in the Member State in which that registered office is situated.[20]

Where recognition of a public offer prospectus as listing particulars is sought, a supplement must be drawn up, scrutinized and published in accordance with the Listing Particulars Directive if any significant new factor capable of affecting assessment of the securities arises between the time when the content of the prospectus is adopted and the time when Stock Exchange dealings begin.[21]

Mutual recognition is not required (although it may be conferred by the Member State concerned) where the document in question benefits from partial exemption or partial derogation under the directive pursuant to which it was drawn up and approved and such exemption or derogation is not recognized in the rules of the other Member State concerned or the circumstances or conditions justifying the exemption or derogation also exist in the other Member State concerned, provided in the case of listing particulars that there are no other conditions concerning such exemption or derogation which might lead the competent authority in that Member State to refuse them.[22]

Mutual recognition is optional in the case of issuers whose registered office is outside the European Union.[23] The Community may enter into agreements with non-member countries for the mutual recognition of listing particulars and public offer prospectuses drawn up and scrutinized in accordance with their rules provided that those rules, even if different from those of the Listing Particulars and Public Offer Prospectus Directives, give investors equivalent protection to that afforded

---

[19] Art 24a(1) LPD, Art 21(1) POPD and Art 24b(1) LPD.   [20] Art 24c.
[21] Art 24b(3) LPD.   [22] Art 24a(2) LPD; Art 21(2) POPD and Art 24b(2) LPD.
[23] Art 24a(5) LPD; Art 21(4) POPD and Art 24b(2) LPD.

by those Directives.[24] This provision may ultimately be the basis for a multi-jurisdictional disclosure scheme between the United States and the Community.[25]

In the case of a request for recognition as listing particulars, the issuer of the shares for which admission is sought is to communicate to the competent authorities of the other Member States in which application is made the draft listing particulars[26] which it intends to use in that State.[27] When approving the listing particulars,[28] the primary competent authorities[29] are to provide their counterparts in the other Member States in which recognition is sought with a certificate of approval; if they have granted partial exemption or partial derogation the certificate is to state that fact and the reasons therefor.[30] In the case of a request for recognition as a prospectus, the person making the public offer is to communicate to the bodies designated by the Member States in which the offer is to be made the scrutinized and approved prospectus which it intends to use in that State.[31]

Information received by competent authorities in the course of a request for mutual recognition may be used only for the pursuit of those authorities' functions or in the context of administrative or judicial proceedings relating thereto.[32]

Implementation in the United Kingdom

Implementation in the United Kingdom of the mutual recognition provisions of the securities directives has, like the development of the provisions themselves, been piecemeal. The First and Second Mutual Recognition Directives were implemented by Stock Exchange Rules made pursuant to powers contained in the Financial Services Act 1986.[33] The mutual recognition provisions of the Public Offers Prospectus Directive were originally implemented in part, so as to provide for recognition in the United Kingdom of prospectuses approved by the competent authority of another Member State, by The Companies Act 1985 (Mutual Recognition of Prospectuses) Regulations 1991.[34] At that point recognition could not be mutual since there was no competent authority in the United Kingdom for the scrutiny of public offer prospectuses of securities for which no listing was sought. In 1995 that asymmetry was rectified as part of the revised framework for

---

[24] Art 25a LPD and Art 24 POPD. For a brief discussion of the external competence of the Community in a harmonized area, see p 330 below.

[25] See Wolff, S, 'Securities Regulation' in Folsom, R H, Lake, R B and Nanda, V P, *European Community Law after 1992* (1993) 510, n 73.

[26] And by implication, since Art 24a(4) is made applicable to the recognition of prospectuses as listing particulars by Art 24b(2), a prospectus sought to be so recognized.

[27] Arts 24a(4) and 24a(2) LPD.

[28] See comments in n 26.

[29] Normally those of the Member State in which the issuer has its registered office: see p 287 above.

[30] Arts 24a(3) and 24b(2) LPD.		[31] Art 21(3) POPD.

[32] Art 25 LPD and Art 23(3) POPD.

[33] Now replaced by the London Stock Exchange's Listing Rules: see p 241 above.

[34] SI 1991/823.

the implementation of the Prospectus Directive generally.[35] The mutual recognition provisions both of the Listing Particulars Directive and of the Prospectus Directive are now governed by the Public Offers of Securities Regulations 1995[36] and the Listing Rules.

[35] See pp 277–8 above.
[36] Reg 20 and Pt II of Sch 4, introducing a new s 156A into the Financial Services Act 1986.

XIV

The Major Shareholdings Directive

Background and History

In 1985, the Commission submitted its Proposal for a Council Directive on information to be published when major shareholdings in the capital of a listed company are acquired or disposed of.[1] At that time, only three Member States had a statutory regime for the disclosure of major shareholdings. Of those three, both France and Italy required disclosure of 10 per cent holdings in listed companies; only the United Kingdom had a more rigorous scheme, requiring disclosure when holdings in public companies, whether or not listed, reach 5 per cent and at each 1 per cent thereafter.[2] There were thus significant differences in the information made available to investors in the various Member States. The Council had already adopted the first three securities Directives (the Admissions Directive, the Listing Particulars Directive and the Interim Reports Directive), the cornerstone of each being the requirement to inform. The Commission's Proposal, providing for the disclosure of acquisitions or disposals of major shareholdings in the capital of listed companies, was 'aimed at reinforcing at Community level the information policy already adopted by the Council'.[3]

The Commission's rationale for proposing a framework for the compulsory disclosure of significant shareholdings was that investors would thereby be provided with information on persons liable to influence a company's management and so be able to follow developments in its ownership and gain a clearer idea of what was happening internally. That information might affect investors' assessment of the company's securities and hence be relevant to their investment or disinvestment decisions. Making such information available to the public moreover prevents uncontrollable rumours and stops misuse of price-sensitive information.[4]

To any Anglo-American commentator, for whom the concept of statutory disclosure is familiar as an aspect of takeover regulation, there is a striking omission from those reasons. In the United Kingdom, for example, where there has been mandatory disclosure of substantial shareholdings since 1967,[5] the principal aim of the legislation has always been seen as precluding a takeover bidder from secretly

---

[1] COM (85) 791 final, 23 December 1985; [1985] OJ C351/8.

[2] Section 199(2) Companies Act 1985; subsequently reduced to 3% by the Companies Act 1989, s 134(2).

[3] Explanatory Memorandum, 1–2.

[4] Explanatory Memorandum, 2.

[5] Companies Act 1967, s 33.

building up a sufficiently substantial stake to launch a bid which will take the company and the market by surprise.[6]

The Proposal was submitted to the Council on 23 December 1985. The Economic and Social Committee delivered its Opinion on 2 July 1986[7] and the European Parliament proposed its amendments on 9 April 1987.[8] The Commission submitted an amended Proposal on 4 September 1987[9] and the Parliament approved the common position on 26 October 1988.[10] Council Directive (EEC) 88/627 on the information to be published when a major shareholding in a listed company is acquired or disposed of was adopted on 12 December 1988.[11] Implementation was required by 1 January 1991.

Aims and Structure

The recitals in the preamble to the Directive dovetail neatly, as might be expected, with those in the previous securities directives. The preamble refers to the likelihood that a policy of adequate information will improve investor protection, increase confidence in securities markets and thus ensure that securities markets function correctly[12] and that coordination of that policy at Community level will, by making such protection more equivalent, make for greater interpenetration of Member States' transferable securities markets and therefore help to establish a true European capital market.[13]

The substantive provisions of the Directive are neither drafted nor structured as lucidly as they might be. In order better to understand the detail which follows, it is helpful to bear in mind the specific aims of the Directive. The principal aim is that 'investors should be informed of major holdings and of changes in those holdings'.[14] That aim is to be attained in two separate but complementary steps: first, a person acquiring or disposing of a major holding is to notify the issuing company and the competent authorities;[15] second, the company is to disclose that information to the public.[16] Definition of the type of transaction which gives rise to the obligation to notify and disclose is somewhat fragmentary, with different aspects to be found in various Articles.[17] Exemptions are similarly scattered.[18] The description which follows of the framework put in place by the Directive seeks to draw together the various threads.

It may be noted that the Directive is expressed to impose minimum standards: Article 3 provides that Member States may impose stricter or additional requirements, provided that such requirements apply generally to all those acquiring or disposing of holdings and all companies or to all those falling within a particular

---

[6] See, for example, Davies, P L, *Gower's Principles of Modern Company Law* (6th edn, 1997), 485.
[7] [1986] OJ C263/1. [8] [1987] OJ C125/141.
[9] COM (87) 422 final, 4 September 1987; [1987] OJ C255/6. [10] [1988] OJ C309/44.
[11] [1988] OJ L348/62. [12] 1st recital. [13] 2nd recital.
[14] 3rd recital. [15] Art 4(1). [16] Art 10(1).
[17] Arts 1, 2, 4, 7 and 8. [18] Arts 1(3), 6, 9 and 11.

category acquiring or disposing of holdings or of companies. The proviso appears to have been prompted by an amendment suggested by the Parliament. At the time the amendment was proposed, the Directive was still framed in terms of the proportion of subscribed capital, rather than voting rights, held; the amendment was presumably intended to permit Member States to require separate disclosure relating to voting shares. The provision would also give Member States the flexibility to apply stricter or additional requirements to, for example, acquisitions or disposals of holdings of certain classes of share, or holdings in the shares of public as opposed to listed companies (the approach taken by the United Kingdom since 1981).

The Competent Authorities

Member States are required to designate the competent authority or authorities for the purposes of the Directive, and to inform the Commission accordingly, specifying, where appropriate, any[19] division of duties between the authorities.[20] Member States are also required to ensure that the authorities have the necessary powers for the performance of their duties.[21] For the purposes of the Directive, the competent authorities are those of the Member State the law of which governs the company issuing the shares in question.[22]

The Directive additionally requires competent authorities in different Member States to cooperate with each other and exchange information[23] and imposes restrictions on the use to which such information may be put.[24] Those provisions are closely modelled on the equivalent provisions in the Admissions, Listing Particulars and Interim Reports Directives.[25]

Transactions Covered by the Directive

Article 1(1) of the Directive requires Member States to make certain acquisitions or disposals of shares subject to mandatory notification and disclosure. Those transactions are defined, either in Article 1(1) or elsewhere in the Directive, by reference to three elements: the nature of the acquirer or disposer (referred to hereafter as simply 'the acquirer'), the nature of the company which issued the shares and the effect of the transaction on the acquirer's holding.

---

[19] The published Directive has 'and'. It is clear from the Proposal and from other language versions that 'any' is meant.
[20] Art 12(1).   [21] Art 12(2).   [22] Art 13.   [23] Art 12(3).   [24] Art 14.
[25] See pp 248 and 259 above.

Persons required to disclose

The persons subject to the Directive are 'natural persons and legal entities in public or private law' who acquire or dispose of, 'directly or through intermediaries', certain holdings in such companies.[26] The definition is intended to encompass 'States or their regional or local authorities'.[27] The definition is moreover not restricted to nationals of or residents in the Community, although the practical effect of the broader definition may be doubted: the United Kingdom Stock Exchange noted in evidence to the House of Lords Select Committee on the European Communities that 'it is largely impossible to deal with overseas investors who are clearly determined not to disclose their indentities and who are able to hide behind and deal through foreign banks'.[28]

The nature of the issuer

Article 1(1) refers to companies incorporated under the law of a Member State whose shares are officially listed on a Stock Exchange or exchanges situated or operating within one or more Member States.

The Commission explained in its Proposal[29] that it was decided for practical reasons not to extend the Directive to holdings in companies incorporated outside the Community but listed on a Stock Exchange within a Member State. Where comparable provisions exist in such a company's country of origin, it will in any event have to declare major holdings in its capital in the Member State in which it is listed by virtue of the provisions on equivalence of information contained in the Admissions Directive.[30] Moreover, the final version of the Major Shareholdings Directive, reflecting a suggestion by the European Parliament, amends the Admissions Directive so that companies incorporated outside the Community but admitted to listing on a Stock Exchange in a Member State are subject to a specific requirement to inform the public within nine days of notice of the acquisition or disposal of a holding which would trigger the notification and disclosure requirement imposed by the Major Shareholdings Directive.[31]

The restriction of the requirement to holdings in *listed* companies is rather lamely justified on the ground that 'it is shares in listed companies which are dealt in regularly and the general public tends to invest primarily in those shares'.[32] At least in relation to the United Kingdom, that proposition is doubtful: many shares change hands on the unlisted market (formerly the Unlisted Securities Market, since 1995 the Alternative Investment Market) which historically has tended to run in parallel

---

[26] Art 1(1).　　　　　　　　　　　　　　　　　[27] See Explanatory Memorandum, 3.
[28] 16th Report (Session 1985–86, HL Paper 218), 9, para 28.
[29] Explanatory Memorandum, 4.　　　　　　　[30] See pp xx above.
[31] Annex to the Admissions Directive, para 5(c) of Sch C, as replaced by the Major Shareholdings Directive, Art 1(4).
[32] Explanatory Memorandum, 4.

with the Official List of the Stock Exchange.[33] Restricting the Directive to listed companies is however consistent with the three securities directives previously adopted, and that was no doubt a factor in the Commission's decision. In particular, those directives already required certain disclosures of changes in holdings of listed securities, but only in so far as they are known to the companies concerned.[34]

Although the Directive is restricted to holdings in companies with an official listing, it applies to acquisitions or disposals of any shares issued by such companies, whether or not the shares in question are themselves listed.

The Directive does not apply to the acquisition or disposal of major holdings in collective investment schemes.[35]

Types of transaction

Article 1(1) brings within the scope of the Directive acquisitions or disposals, made either directly or through intermediaries, of holdings 'meeting the criteria laid down in Article 4(1)'. Acquisition means not only purchase, but also 'acquisition by any other means whatsoever'.[36] The criteria laid down in Article 4(1) are expressed in terms of proportions of voting rights held which will trigger the disclosure requirement; Article 7 provides that in certain circumstances voting rights held by one person are to be attributed to another person for the purpose of calculating the voting rights held.

The Directive does not however extend to fluctuations in a person's holding of voting rights caused otherwise than by an acquisition or disposal by him. It does not therefore apply to a concentration of voting rights resulting from a company's purchasing or redeeming its own shares, or to voting rights in normally non-voting preference shares which have become exercisable because dividend payments are in arrears.[37]

Article 1(2) provides:

Where the acquisition or disposal of a major holding such as referred to in paragraph 1 is effected by means of certificates representing shares, this Directive shall apply to the bearers of those certificates, and not to the issuer.

---

[33] Although the disclosure requirement was restricted to shares in listed companies when it was first introduced in the UK (1967), it was extended to shares in any public company, whether or not listed, in 1981 (Companies Act 1981, s 63). Certain interests however are notifiable only in respect of listed companies (see p 305 below), and the requirement to disclose to the public, imposed by the Stock Exchange's Listing Rules, applies only to companies with a Stock Exchange listing. In its Consultative Document on Proposals for Reform of Part VI of the Companies Act 1985, issued in April 1995,the UK DTI proposed restricting the notification requirement to listed companies and those unlisted companies whose shares are 'publicly traded'.

[34] Listing Particulars Directive, Sch A, point 3.2.7; Admissions Directive, Sch C, point 5(c): see above, pp 254 and 261.

[35] Art 1(3).   [36] Art 2.

[37] By contrast, an obligation to notify does arise in such circumstances under the UK legislation: Companies Act 1985, s 199.

This provision is somewhat obscure. It is clear[38] that 'the issuer' refers to the issuer of the certificates rather than the issuer of the shares. Presumably, Article 1(2) concerns certificates issued to the beneficial owners of shares held by the issuer of the certificates.

The thresholds

Article 4 operates by laying down a series of thresholds. Where, following an acquisition or disposal, the proportion of voting rights held by the acquirer reaches, exceeds or falls below 10 per cent, 20 per cent, one-third, 50 per cent or two-thirds, the acquirer is within seven calendar days to disclose to the company and the competent authorities the proportion of voting rights he holds following the transaction.

The thresholds were chosen to correspond to percentages already laid down in earlier company law directives as criteria for various purposes.[39] Thus 10 per cent is used in the Seventh Directive for the purpose of exemption from consolidation;[40] 20 per cent is used in the Fourth Directive in the definition of a participating interest[41] and in the Seventh Directive for the purpose of determining when one undertaking is presumed to exercise a significant influence over another;[42] two-thirds is the majority required by the Second Directive for several important decisions concerning reduction, and redemption of capital,[43] by the Third Directive for a merger decision[44] and by the Sixth Directive for a decision on a division;[45] and 90 per cent is used in the Third Directive for the purpose of certain derogations from the rules on mergers or acquisitions.[46] The Commission explained the inclusion of one-third and 50 per cent as thresholds on the basis that a holding of one-third would make it possible for decisions requiring a majority of at least two-thirds to be blocked,[47] while 50 per cent signifies absolute control and hence it is essential that the public should be informed whenever that threshold was exceeded.

Article 4(1) further provides that Member States need not apply (a) the thresholds of 20 per cent and one-third where they apply a single threshold of 25 per cent or (b) the threshold of two-thirds where they apply the threshold of 75 per cent. It is likely that that qualification, which was not present in the Proposal, was introduced to take account of objections on behalf of the United Kingdom that, although its own disclosure system was in general much stricter than that proposed by the Commission, the Proposal would have required legislation for specific dis-

---

[38] See e g the French text: 'la présente directive s'applique aux porteurs de ces certificats et non à leur émetteur'.

[39] Explanatory Memorandum, 6–7.

[40] See p 175 above. [41] See p 133 above. [42] See p 190 above.

[43] See pp 87–9 above. [44] See p 106 above. [45] See p 106 above.

[46] See pp 106 and 108 above.

[47] Strictly speaking, it would require more than one third to block such decisions; however, since disclosure is required when the threshold is exceeded as well as when it is reached, the justification holds.

closure at 33.33 per cent and 66.66 per cent because those proportions are not whole percentage points and hence would not have caught by the existing legislation requiring disclosure of changes of each percentage point after 5 per cent.

The thresholds have been the subject of some criticism in the United Kingdom, where since 1989 there has been the much more rigorous system of disclosure at 3 per cent and every percentage point thereafter.[48] Giving evidence to the House of Lords Select Committee on the European Communities,[49] the Department of Trade and Industry questioned the value of disclosure where the points triggering the disclosure requirement were so widely spaced: much may happen to share prices between the first two thresholds of 10 and 20 per cent, and even before a holding reaches 10 per cent.[50] The Takeover Panel was similarly concerned about the large gap between the thresholds of one-third and 50 per cent, finding it 'strange' that someone could buy between 34 per cent and 49 per cent of a company without any disclosure obligation. That view may however reflect the slightly different rationale for disclosure in the United Kingdom, where the aim has traditionally been to prevent the market from being taken by surprise. Where the focus is rather on providing retrospective information about critical investments, a gradual increase is holdings between thresholds which are inherently significant is perhaps less important.

In the original Proposal, the thresholds (numerically the same as those in the Directive as adopted) were expressed as proportions of subscribed capital rather than of voting rights.[51] The Commission recognized that that approach was not the best way of ensuring that investors knew who was in a position to influence a company's management, since for that purpose it is clearly the proportion of voting shares held which is determinative. It considered however that it might be very difficult in certain cases for persons acquiring or disposing of holdings to know what percentage of the voting rights they held, since in certain countries shares may carry dual voting rights or voting rights held by any one shareholder may be subject to a ceiling; moreover in the case of convertible bonds it may be difficult to establish the total voting rights as that total depends on the number of bonds converted into shares. The original Proposal sought to ensure that investors were none the less informed of the proportion of voting rights held by any one shareholder by requiring the company to notify the public not only of the percentage of subscribed capital held by major shareholders but also of the percentage of voting rights held by such persons where those two percentages differed.[52] The final version of the Directive seeks to avoid the problems identified by the Commission in a different way: it uses voting rights as the yardstick for notification and disclosure, but provides in Article 4(2) that Member States shall, if necessary, establish in their national

---

[48] The original threshold, introduced in 1967, was 10%; any change to a notifiable holding was also to be notified. The threshold was reduced to 5% in 1976 (Companies Act 1976, s 26) and to 3% in 1989.
[49] Cited in n 28, at 11, paras 43 and 44.
[50] Although it may be noted that the UK threshold was 10% until 1976.   [51] Art 3.
[52] Explanatory Memorandum, 5–6.

law, and determine in accordance with it, the manner in which voting rights are to be brought to the notice of shareholders. In addition, the final paragraph of Article 4(1) of the Directive permits Member States to provide that a company must also be informed in respect of the proportion of capital held following an acquisition or disposal.

Attribution of voting rights

Article 4 applies where persons hold voting rights in their own name. There are however a number of ways in which a person may control voting rights attached to shares nominally held by someone else. Article 7 provides that, for the purposes of determining 'whether a natural person or legal entity as referred to in Article 1(1)' is required to notify under Article 4(1), 'the following shall be regarded as voting rights held by that person or entity:'. The various voting rights to which the provision applies are set out as a series of indents.

Article 2 provides that, for the purposes of the Directive, 'acquiring a holding' shall include 'acquisition in one of the situations referred to in Article 7'. There is no express corresponding provision that a disposal shall be regarded as having occurred when a situation described in Article 7 ceases to obtain. It might appear that Article 7 is framed in sufficiently broad terms that, where a divestment of voting rights covered by the article results in the total voting rights held by a person falling below one of the thresholds, there will be a requirement to notify. That is not however the case: although Article 7 appears to provide in general terms for the aggregation or attribution of interests, it cannot be considered in isolation, since it is expressed to apply for the purposes of determining whether there is an obligation 'to make a declaration as provided for in Article 4(1)'. Article 4(1) applies where, following an acquisition or disposal, a threshold is reached or crossed. An acquisition or disposal is accordingly necessary to trigger the obligation to notify in the first place.

Nominees and trustees

The first indent of Article 7 catches 'voting rights held by other persons or entities in their own names but on behalf of that person or entity'. Thus voting rights held by nominees or trustees will be attributed to those on whose behalf they are held. There appears however to be no exemption from the requirement on the nominal holders to notify, so that nominees and trustees will also be required to notify such rights in their own name.

It may be noted that there is no automatic attribution, as there is in the United Kingdom, of voting rights held by spouses and minor children.[53]

---

[53] Companies Act 1985, s 203(1).

Companies including subsidiaries

The second indent catches 'voting rights held by an undertaking controlled by that person or entity'. The forerunner of this provision in the original Proposal applied only where the shareholder was an undertaking, in which case it caught 'shares held by a subsidiary or shares held by other persons in their own name but on behalf of a subsidiary'.[54] The final version is considerably wider.

Article 8 defines 'controlled undertaking' in terms which overlap with the definition of 'subsidiary undertaking' used in the Seventh Directive.[55] For the purposes of Article 8, three of the five definitions in the Seventh Directive are used: namely an undertaking in which a person has a majority of voting rights, or in which a shareholder has the right to appoint or remove a majority of the members of the board, or in which a shareholder alone controls a majority of the voting rights pursuant to a shareholders' agreement.[56] Again echoing the Seventh Directive, Article 8(2) further provides that, for the purpose of calculating the proportion of the rights as regards voting, appointment or removal held by a putative parent undertaking, rights of any other controlled undertaking and of any person acting in his own name but on behalf of the parent undertaking or any other controlled undertaking are to be aggregated.

Concert parties

The third indent catches 'voting rights held by a third party with whom that person or entity has concluded a written agreement which obliges them to adopt, by concerted exercise of the voting rights they hold, a lasting common policy towards the management of the company in question'. This provision seeks to encapsulate what is commonly referred to as a 'concert party'. It will be seen from the wording that each party to whom the provision applies will be separately liable to disclose if the aggregate voting rights covered by the agreement reach, exceed or fall below one of the thresholds.

The precursor of this provision in the original Proposal adopted a different approach: it referred to 'persons acting in concert'[57] which it then defined as 'persons who have concluded an agreement which may lead to their adopting a common policy in respect of a company'.[58] That definition was based on a definition used in the Listing Particulars Directive for the purposes of requiring disclosure in listing particulars of persons who exercise or could exercise joint control over the issuer. 'Joint control' is there defined as 'control exercised by more than one company or by more than one person having concluded an agreement which may lead to their adopting a common policy in respect of the issuer'.[59] However, the excision of only half of that definition for the purposes of the proposed major shareholdings directive divorced the definition used from any notion of control. The effect was that, as the Law Society of Scotland pointed out in its evidence to the

---

[54] Art 4(2).   [55] See pp 163–70 above.   [56] Art 8(1).   [57] Art 6(1).
[58] Art 6(2).   [59] Annex, Para 3.2.6 of Sch A.

House of Lords Select Committee,[60] 'the definition of concert parties in the [proposed] Directive could cover environmental pressure groups'.

The final version of the attempted definition is far from perfect, although admittedly concert parties are notoriously difficult to define. The equivalent definition in the United Kingdom legislation spans three sections[61] comprising 21 subsections. The analogous provision in the *City Code on Take-overs and Mergers*, the extra-statutory code regulating the conduct of bids, reads more sympathetically, providing: 'Persons acting in concert comprise persons who, pursuant to agreement or understanding (whether formal or informal) actively co-operate, through the acquisition by any of them of shares in a company, to obtain or consolidate control . . . of that company.'[62]

It will be seen that the definition in Article 7 is narrower than the above definition in that a written agreement is necessary, although the Directive does not specify whether such an agreement must be legally binding (and given the difficulties of proving an unwritten agreement, the difference may for practical purposes be negligible). Nor would it cover an agreement as to specific voting tactics relating to one issue: the voting rights must be used in furtherance of 'a lasting common policy towards the management'. It is not clear whether 'the management' includes the composition of the board or merely means management strategy. If the former, it is not obvious whether a policy seeking to achieve a change in the composition of the board would be a 'lasting' policy, since it would in any event have a short-term objective. It may be noted however that the other language versions tend to the latter construction.[63]

The definition in the Directive is however in one sense broader, in that it does not require the parties to acquire shares:[64] it could extend to agreements between existing shareholders (although an acquisition or disposal remains necessary to trigger an obligation to notify). The United Kingdom's Department of Trade and Industry is currently considering changing the statutory definition, at least in relation to listed companies, in order properly to implement the Directive.

Transferred voting rights

The fourth indent catches 'voting rights held by a third party under a written agreement concluded with that person or entity or with an undertaking controlled by that person or entity providing for the temporary transfer for consideration of the voting rights in question'.

---

[60] Cited in n 28, at 10, para 32.   [61] Sections 204–6.

[62] Section C.1., defining 'acting in concert'.

[63] The Company Law Committee of the Law Society, in its response to the Commission's 1997 Consultation Paper on Company law, notes that 'considerable difficulties in interpreting the meaning of the expression' exist, and urges early revision of the Directive in order to deal with the matter: see Memorandum 346, *European Commission Consultation Paper on Company law* (June 1997), para 4.3.

[64] The Companies Act 1985 also requires the agreement to include provision for the acquisition of interests in shares (s 204(1)).

Shares held as security

The fifth indent catches 'voting rights attaching to shares owned by that person or entity which are lodged as security, except where the person or entity holding the security controls the voting rights and declares his intention of exercising them, in which case they shall be regarded as the latter's voting rights' (and presumably not the former's).[65]

Life interests

The sixth indent catches 'voting rights attaching to shares of which that person or entity has the life interest'.

Agreement to acquire

The seventh indent catches 'voting rights which that person or entity or one of the other persons or entities mentioned in the above indents is entitled to acquire, on his own initiative alone, under a formal agreement'. It is further provided that, in such a case, notification to the company in accordance with Article 4(1) is to be made on the date of the agreement.

Deposited shares

Finally, the eighth indent catches 'voting rights attaching to shares deposited with that person or entity which that person or entity can exercise at its discretion in the absence of specific instructions from the holders'. The second paragraph of Article 7 further provides that, by way of derogation from Article 4(1), where a threshold is reached or exceeded in such a case, Member States may relax the usual notification requirement so that the obligation to notify the company arises only twenty-one calendar days before its general meeting. The company is presumbly not relieved by this provision of its obligation to disclose to the public and, if relevant, to the competent authorities, since that obligation flows from Article 10(1) while the relaxation in Article 7 is expressed to be by way of derogation from Article 4(1).

Notification and Disclosure

As indicated, two separate obligations arise when a threshold is reached or crossed.

---

[65] The Law Society, considering that the precise meaning of the concepts in the 5th indent are unclear, has called for early revision of the Directive to deal with the matter: see Memorandum 346 (n 63 above) para 4.3.

The acquirer's obligation to notify the company and the competent authorities

Article 4(1) provides that the person or entity whose acquisition or disposal results in the proportion of voting rights held by him reaching, exceeding or falling below a threshold shall, within seven calendar days, notify the company and the competent authority or authorities of the proportion of voting rights held by him. There is no requirement as to form, or even that the notification be in writing; nor does there appear to be any obligation to identify the actual holder of the voting rights if the notification relates to a holding which consists of or includes rights attributed to the notifier under Article 7.[66] Although in most such cases the actual holder will be under a separate obligation to notify, the Directive does not require that it be possible to identify from the register the specific holding in respect of which two notifications have been made.[67]

The period of seven calendar days starts from the time when he learns of the acquisition or disposal or from the time when, in view of the circumstances, he should have learnt of it. The reference to his actual knowledge is presumably intended to cater for involuntary acquisitions, for example through gift or succession, or for situations where a transaction is effected on the acquirer's behalf by, for example, his investment manager. The reference to constructive knowledge is presumably intended to ensure that the notification period cannot be indefinitely prolonged by the acquirer's arranging not to be informed of transactions by his investment manager, or in other circumstances of deliberate lack of awareness. The relevance of constructive knowledge may pose problems for groups of companies, which will need to put in place systems to ensure prompt notification within the group of acquisitions and disposals.

Calendar days rather than the more usual concept of business or working days were presumably used because of the difficulties of prescribing a time limit based on business days to apply throughout the Community, given the different patterns of public holidays in the different Member States.

Exemptions from the obligation to notify

Where the acquirer is a member of a group of undertakings required under the Seventh Directive to draw up consolidated accounts,[68] it is exempt from the obligation to notify if its immediate or ultimate parent undertaking makes the notification required under Article 4(1).[69]

There is an additional optional exemption in Article 9(1): the competent authorities may exempt a professional dealer in securities who is either a member of a

---

[66] cf the position in the UK, where the notification must include, so far as known to the person making the notification, 'the identity of each registered holder of shares to which the notification relates and the number of such shares held by each of them': Companies Act 1985, s 202(3), substituted by Companies Act 1989, s 134(1)(4).

[67] Again, cf the position in the UK: (n 66 above).   [68] See ch VI above.   [69] Art 6.

Community Stock Exchange or approved or supervised by a competent authority from notifying an acquisition or disposal which is effected in his capacity as a professional dealer in securities provided that the acquisition is not used by the dealer to intervene in the management of the company concerned. This exemption replaces a much broader provision in the original Proposal, under which Member States were permitted to exempt transactions 'made by a market maker[70] in the pursuit of his activity'. The United Kingdom Department of Trade and Industry reportedly considered that exemption 'so wide that it could significantly reduce the effect of the Directive, particularly in Germany where the major banks are the predominant holders and traders of equity and the only people admissible to stock exchange membership'; the United Kingdom Takeover Panel had similar reservations, commenting that 'it would be possible to take significant stakes in companies in effect by working through a market maker'.[71] The Takeover Panel also made the point, equally applicable to the final version of the exemption, that for a market maker to hold 10 per cent of a listed company would in any event be unusual and should perhaps be disclosed.[72]

The type of conduct which will constitute intervention in the management of a company remains however unclear, although it is generally thought to involve something more than merely exercising the voting rights attaching to the shares.[73]

Transitional provision

Article 5 requires Member States to provide that, at a listed company's first annual general meeting more than three months after the Directive has been transposed into national law, any person holding 10 per cent or more of the company's voting rights must notify the company and the competent authority unless that person has already notified under Article 4.

The company's obligation to disclose to the public

Article 10(1) requires a company which has received a notification under Article 4(1) to disclose it to the public in each Member State where its shares are officially listed on a Stock Exchange. The disclosure must be made as soon as possible, but in any event not more than nine calendar days after receipt of the notification.

The time limit was seven calendar days in the Proposal, reflecting that for notification to the company under Article 4(1). The Commission commented that those 'relatively brief periods should make it possible to prevent, or at least restrict, misuse of such information, particularly through insider dealing.'[74] The Economic

---

[70] Broadly, persons who hold themselves out as buyers and sellers of particular securities.
[71] HL Select Committee (n 28 above) at 13, paras 55–6.
[72] Evidence to the Committee, 52, question 285.
[73] The Law Society has called for early revision of the Directive to deal with the matter: see Memorandum 346 (n 63 above) para 4.2.
[74] Explanatory Memorandum, 9.

and Social Committee, although it agreed that the information should be circulated very quickly, felt that a period of seven days could prove too short in some Member States.[75] The United Kingdom Stock Exchange, on the other hand, considered that seven days was too long a period;[76] in the United Kingdom, companies which have received notifications of major shareholdings are required to notify the Stock Exchange's Company Announcements Office 'without delay'. That provision reflects the obligation imposed on companies by the Admissions Directive to 'inform the public of any changes in the structure . . . of the major holdings in its capital . . . as soon as such changes come to its notice'.[77]

The second paragraph of Article 10(1) permits Member States to provide for the disclosure to the public under that provision to be made not by the company but by the competent authority, 'possibly in cooperation with the company'.[78]

Article 10(2) requires disclosure to be made by publication in newspapers or in writing at places indicated by announcements in newspapers or by other equivalent means approved by the competent authorities.[79] The details are identical to those laid down by Article 17 of the Admissions Directive for the provision of information to the public.[80]

Exemption from the obligation to disclose

Article 11 permits the competent authorities *exceptionally* to exempt companies from Article 10(1) where the authorities consider that the disclosure would be contrary to the public interest or seriously detrimental to the companies concerned, provided that, in the latter case, the omission 'would not be likely to mislead the public with regard to the facts and circumstances knowledge of which is essential for the assessment of the transferable securities in question.'[81] It is hard to see how an omission to disclose the fact that a shareholder's holding of voting shares had crossed one of the thresholds specified in the Directive could satisfy the proviso.

Transitional provision

Where notification to the company has been effected at its first annual general meeting more than three months after transposition of the Directive,[82] the public must be informed within one month of that meeting.[83]

---

[75] [1986] OJ C263/2, para 2.6.   [76] HL Select Committee (n 28 above) 12, para 52.
[77] Sch C, para 5(c); see p 261 above.
[78] In the United Kingdom, the Stock Exchange fulfils this function with respect to companies whose shares are listed there; where companies have shares listed in another Member State however it is for the shareholder to ensure that disclosure to the public is made in that State.
[79] In the UK, the company makes an entry in a register kept for the purpose and open for inspection by the public; listed companies in addition must inform the Stock Exchange as one of the continuing obligations of listing; the information will then appear on the Stock Exchange's announcements board and in its weekly Official Intelligence.
[80] See p 261 above.
[81] cf the parallel exemption from omission of information from listing particulars: Listing Particulars Directive, Art 7(b); see p 256 above.
[82] In accordance with Art 5: see p 303 above.   [83] Art 5.

Sanctions

Article 15 requires Member States to provide for appropriate sanctions for non-compliance with the Directive. The original Proposal made no provision for sanctions; that may have been because of concerns that they would be difficult, if not impossible, to enforce in the case of holdings of bearer shares and shareholders based outside the Community.[84]

Implementation in the United Kingdom

As indicated, at the time of the Proposal the United Kingdom had the most rigorous statutory system of disclosure of interests in shares in the Community. That system was moreover in many respects stricter[85] than that required by the Directive; since the Directive imposes minimum standards only, to a large extent the United Kingdom system could be left intact without compromising implementation. There were however a number of relatively minor changes required to be made.

The majority of the necessary changes were effected by the Disclosure of Interest in Shares (Amendment) Regulations 1993,[86] which came into force on 18 September 1993 and amended Pt VI of the Companies Act 1985.

First, certain categories of holdings, previously exempt from the Companies Act requirements, were brought within the notification and disclosure regime so as to comply with the Directive, but with a threshold of 10 per cent (either alone or aggregated with material interests) rather than 3 per cent. The Companies Act is expressed to operate by reference to interests in shares rather than holdings; such interests may be termed 'non-material interests' in order to distinguish them from the 'material interests' subject to the more stringent requirement. Non-material interests include (a) interests in public companies held by certain investment managers and operators of recognized collective investment schemes; (b) interests in listed (but not other public) companies under various charitable schemes and trusts; and (c) interests which exist because of the attribution of non-material interests of another person (for example, the interest otherwise attributable to a parent company of a fund manager).[87]

Second, the previous exemption for a market-maker carrying on business in the United Kingdom has been broadened to reflect more closely the exemption in Article 9; it now includes interests of dealers in securities and derivatives who carry

---

[84] In the UK, breach of the provisions of the Companies Act 1985 is a criminal offence punishable by imprisonment or a fine or both (s 210(4)). Moreover on conviction the Secretary of State may order restrictions on the transfer of the shares concerned, the exercise of voting rights in respect of the shares, the issue of further shares to the holder or the payment of dividends (ss 210(5) and 454).

[85] And more complex: the legislation is described by Gower as 'probably the most impenetrable [provisions] of any in the [Companies] Act' (*Principles of Modern Company Law* (5th edn, 1992) 613).

[86] SI 1993/1819.   [87] Companies Act 1985, s 199(2A).

on market–making activities and are authorized in any Member State, provided that the interests are 'not used by him for the purpose of intervening in the management of the company.'[88] The main effect of the amendment was to include market–makers elsewhere in the Community.

Third, the provision dealing with interests in shares exempt from the obligation to notify has been amended so as to make it clear that the exemptions are available only if the holder of the interest is not entitled to exercise or control the exercise of the voting rights in respect of the shares concerned.[89] That amendment was necessary to reconcile the United Kingdom system of disclosure, based on interests in voting shares, with the system required by the Directive, framed in terms of holdings of voting rights.

As mentioned above,[90] the definition of concert parties in the United Kingdom legislation is not coterminous with the definition in the Directive. Moreover, the time limit for disclosure in the United Kingdom runs from actual knowledge (of the existence of a notifiable interest) only, whereas the Directive requires that it run from actual or constructive knowledge (of the acquisition or disposal). In these two respects, the United Kingdom has not yet fully implemented the Directive. It was proposed to deal with both these issues in an overhaul of Pt VI of the Companies Act 1985.[91] It is now understood however that reform of Pt VI is not a high legislative priority of the Labour Government.

---

[88] Companies Act 1985, s 209(8)(9).   [89] Companies Act 1985, s 209(5)(6)(7).

[90] See p 300 above.

[91] See the Consultative Document on Proposals for Reform of Part VI of the Companies Act 1985 issued by the DTI in April 1995, and Memorandum No 320, 'Proposals for Reform of Part VI of the Companies Act 1985', issued in July 1995 by the Company Law Committee of The Law Society.

XV

The Insider Dealing Directive

Background

Much has been written about the theory of insider dealing and the need—or lack of need—for regulation.[1] The traditional view is that it is undesirable for securities to be bought or sold by someone in possession of confidential information which is not generally known and which, if it were known, would affect the price;[2] the traditional rationale is that investor confidence as a whole is undermined if potential investors fear that they will not be able to deal on an equal footing with others, and that this may 'prejudice the smooth operation of the market'.[3] The heterodox view, promoted in particular by Manne,[4] embraces a number of elements: insider dealing is a victimless crime; by increasing the volume of sales it increases market efficiency; it is justifiable remuneration for executives. Among advocates of the traditional view there is further scope for debate as to the best means of dealing with the problem: are criminal penalties either appropriate or effective and, if not, what sort of sanction would work?

Whatever the merits of the contrasting theories, regulation of insider dealing in one way or another is in fact fast becoming the norm. Within the European Community, France was the first to legislate in 1970;[5] in the same year, Germany introduced a voluntary code of conduct. In the United Kingdom, insider dealing in connection with takeovers was prohibited by the Takeover Panel's non-statutory code[6] in 1976; a

---

[1] See Hannigan, B, *Insider Dealing* (2nd edn, 1994) 5–13, for a lucid overview of the arguments, and Suter, J, *The Regulation of Insider Dealing in Britain* (1989) 14–49, for a thorough theoretical analysis. Both are comprehensively annotated. For a much more concise summary of the different theories, see Dine, J and Hughes, P, *EC Company Law* (1997) paras 13–2–13–9, and for an excellent distillation of the rationale for regulation see the introduction to Rider, B, *Insider Trading* (1983).

[2] For example, knowledge of an unannounced pending takeover bid likely to enhance the price of shares in the target company, or knowledge before the figures have been made public of a significant rise or fall in a company's profits.

[3] 6th recital in the preamble to the Directive.

[4] Manne, H G, *Insider Trading and the Stock Market* (1966).

[5] For subsequent developments see Dahan, F, 'The Impact of the 1989 EU Directive on Insider Dealing in France: Latest Developments' [1997] European Financial Services Law 194.

[6] *City Code on Take-overs and Mergers*, 1976 edn. See Suter (n 1 above) 264–80 for a discussion of the Code's rules on insider dealing. Note also that in the UK The Stock Exchange promulgated in 1977 a 'model code' for directors' share dealings which contained provisions relating to insider dealing: see Suter, ibid, 255–64. Notwithstanding France's lead in legislating against insider dealing, Tunc, A, describes the requirements of the Model Code as 'striking' in comparison with the French law, and states: 'It is a lesson to see how severely [the former Council for the Securities Industry, the pre-Big

general prohibition was enacted in 1980.[7] Sweden[8] passed insider dealing legislation in 1985, Denmark in 1987, Greece[9] and Finland in 1988, Belgium, the Netherlands and Austria in 1989, Ireland[10] in 1990, Spain,[11] Portugal,[12] Luxembourg and Italy[13] in 1991[14] and Germany in 1994.[15] Meanwhile in 1989, after more than twenty years' discussion within the Community of the regulation of insider dealing, the Council adopted the Insider Dealing Directive,[16] described variously as 'the most advanced cooperative effort among national securities regulators to date',[17] 'the first explicit step taken towards regulating the single financial market of the Community'[18] and 'a stellar model of international cooperation on securities regulation'.[19]

Bang City watchdog] considers unfair insider dealings': 'A French Lawyer Looks at British Company Law' (1982) 45 MLR 1, 3.

[7] Companies Act 1980, Pt V, subsequently re-enacted in the Company Securities (Insider Dealing) Act 1985. That legislation has now been repealed and replaced by the Criminal Justice Act 1993, Pt V, implementing the Directive. The Companies Bill 1973 prohibited insider dealing and included civil and criminal sanctions, but was never enacted.

[8] See Samuelsson, P, 'The Swedish Prohibition on Insider Trading' [1997] European Financial Services Law 89.

[9] See Avgouleas, E, 'The implementation of the Insider Dealing Directive in Greece' [1997] European Financial Services Law 131. Greece has recognized the problem for a long time: Hopt, K J, starts his article 'Insider Regulation and Timely Disclosure' (1996) 21 FORUM Internationale with a quotation from Aristotle's *The State of the Athenians*, written in the fourth century BC, attributing the wealth of certain Athenian families to the exploitation of inside information about a forthcoming law leaked by Solon, the 6th century legislator.

[10] See Linnane, H, 'Insider Dealing in Ireland and the Pressure for Changes to the Law' [1997] European Financial Services Law 101 and Linnane, H, 'The Insider Dealing Legislation' (1993) 3 European Business Law Review No 3, 55 and Ashe, M, and Murphy, Y, *Insider Dealing* (1992).

[11] See Bieger, P and Rojas, P, 'The Spanish Implementation of the Insider Dealing Directive' [1997] European Financial Services Law 204.

[12] See Castro, P O and Pritchard, P F, 'Reform of the Portuguese Securities Markets Legislation; the Financial Market Regulatory Structure and Insider Trading Legislation' (1991) 19 International Business Lawyer 501.

[13] See Serio, M, 'Insider Dealing in Italy' [1997] European Financial Services Law 201.

[14] See generally Gaillard, E, *Insider Trading: The Laws of Europe, the United States and Japan* (1992).

[15] See Standen, D J, 'Insider Trading Reforms Sweep Across Germany: Bracing for the Cold Winds of Change' (1995) 36 Harvard International Law Journal 177; Mennicke, P, 'Insider Regulation in Germany: Inside Information, Insider Status and Enforcement' [1997] European Financial Services Law 81, and Hopt, K J, 'Insider Regulation and Timely Disclosure' (n 9 above).

[16] Council Directive (EEC) 89/592 of 13 November 1989 coordinating regulations on insider dealing [1989] OJ L334/30.

[17] Written in 1991–92: Baltic, C V, 'The Next Step in Insider Trading Regulation: International Cooperative Efforts in the Global Securities Market' 23 Law & Policy in International Business 167.

[18] Fornasier, R, 'The Directive on Insider Dealing' (1989–90) 13 Fordham International Law Journal 149, 162.

[19] Ruiz, L, 'European Community Directive on Insider Dealing: A Model for Effective Enforcement of Prohibitions on Insider Trading in International Securities Markets' (1995) 33 Columbia Journal of Transnational Law, 217, 240.

History

Commentators on the Directive frequently refer to the 'speed with which it was adopted'.[20] While it is true that only twenty-nine months separated the Commission's first Proposal and its adoption,[21] the Directive should be seen in the wider historical context of moves by the Commission to address the perceived problem of insider dealing.[22] The first step was taken in 1966 with the publication of a report by the Committee of Experts appointed by the Commission to examine and make recommendations on the factors conducive to the creation of a viable European capital market. The report was entitled *The Development of a European Capital Market* (the 'Segré Report', after the chairman of the Committee, Professor Segré). The Committee recommended rules governing dealing by executives in securities of their companies, stating that the objective was, inter alia, 'to prevent those who, by virtue of their office in a company, have access to information which might influence the market from using their knowledge to secure a personal advantage denied to other investors'.

In 1970, the Commission put forward its initial Proposal for a European Company Statute,[23] largely based on a draft prepared in 1967 by Professor Sanders of the University of Rotterdam. The Proposal was amended by the Commission in 1975.[24] The draft statute imposed a duty of discretion on members of the boards 'in respect of information of a confidential nature concerning the company or its dependent undertakings'; that duty continued after members ceased to hold office (Articles 70 and 80). Where the shares of the European Company were quoted, Article 82 applied to board members and auditors who held shares and to 10 per cent shareholders, in all cases whether the shares were held directly or indirectly through an intermediary or constructively through a spouse or infant child. After providing for a system of registration of interests, that Article stipulated that any profit made by such a person on a sale and repurchase—or purchase and resale—within six months should automatically be the property of the company and was to be paid to it within eight days of completion of the transaction giving rise to the profit. Teeth were given to this provision by Article 72, which provided that holders of 5 per cent of the company's shares (or shares with a nominal value of 100,000 units of account)[25] could

---

[20] Pingel, I, 'The EC Directive of 1989' in Gaillard (n 14 above).

[21] 'a particularly short period by any standard of Community law-making records': Fornasier (n 18 above) 152.

[22] A detailed history of the developments, of which only a brief summary is given here, can be found in Rider, B, and Ashe, M, 'The Insider Dealing Directive', in Andenas, M, and Kenyon-Slade, S (eds), *EC Financial Market Regulation and Company Law* (1993), 211–22, and Rider, B and Ffrench, H L, *The Regulation of Insider Trading* (1979) 263–71.

[23] COM (70) 600 final, 24 June 1970; [1970] JO C124. The original concept was a uniform type of limited company which could be used throughout the Community without reliance on any system of domestic law for its validity. The current proposals are somewhat watered down, and have been politically stalled for some time, although a breakthrough now seems likey: see further ch XIX.

[24] COM (75) 150 final, 19 March 1975; EC Bull Supp 4/75.

bring an action on behalf of the company against members of the board for breach of duty, which would include a breach of Article 82. Moreover, Member States would have been required to introduce criminal penalties for breach, inter alia, of Article 82. Although the provision was dropped from the subsequent (1989) version of the draft Statute, its inclusion in the early drafts indicates that even at that time insider dealing was considered a problem to be addressed.[26]

The next step towards legislating at Community level against insider dealing was the setting up by the Directorate General for Financial Institutions and Taxation in 1976 of a working party on the coordination of the rules and regulations governing insider trading, following a survey of insider dealing regulation in the Member States carried out by that Directorate General. The report considered a number of issues relating to insider dealing; some of its recommendations are reflected in the Directive, notably the three prohibitions on insiders with inside information (from dealing, disclosing information or encouraging dealing), the nature of inside information, the timely disclosure obligation and the approach to enforcement.[27]

In 1977 the Commission issued a Recommendation concerning a European code of conduct relating to transactions in transferable securities.[28] The Code comprises a statement of its fundamental objective, namely 'to establish standards of ethical behaviour on a Community-wide basis, so as to promote the effective functioning of securities markets . . . and to safeguard the public interest', and a number of general and supplementary principles. These include the disclosure of information to the public and the improper use of confidential information. However, the provisions of the Code remained even further from legislative daylight than those of the draft European Company Statute: the Recommendation, not in any event binding, languished unknown and uninvoked, even though the years following its issue saw some of its principles reflected in regulatory initiatives at the national level. It is noteworthy that the Economic and Social Committee, in its Opinion on the proposed Insider Dealing Directive, cited the failure of the Code of Conduct as one of the factors leading to its 'conviction that binding regulations at EEC level are more desirable than a voluntary code', the other being the fact that the London Stock Exchange had pushed for legally binding regulations to replace the insider dealing provisions of the voluntary *City Code*.[29] The Code has however

---

[25] The substantial amount (a unit of account approximating to one US dollar at the time) is a reminder that the European Company was intended as a major commercial vehicle, to be set up by existing companies.

[26] Art 82 clearly drew on the US Securities Exchange Act 1934, s 16(b), which is framed in almost identical terms, and on the 1967/68 version of the French insider dealing law. The disclosure provision in the French legislation was amended in 1970 because the *Commission des Opérations de Bourse* 'could not keep pace with the large number of filings [more than 40,000 each year] required of insiders': Stutz, A E, 'A New Look at the European Economic Community Directive on Insider Trading' (1990) 23 Vanderbilt Journal of Transnational Law 135.

[27] See Cruickshank, C, 'Insider Trading in the EEC' (1982) 10 International Business Lawyer 345.

[28] Commission Recommendation (EEC) 77/534 of 25 July 1977: [1977] OJ L212/37; corrigendum at [1977] OJ L294/28. See above, pp 230–1, for further discussion of the Code.

[29] [1988] OJ C35/22, para 1.2.

not been entirely sterile: it provided a basis for cooperation within the Community, through meetings of the representatives of the regulatory authorities and between those authorities in the conduct of investigations.[30]

Finally, in May 1987, the Commission published the draft Directive,[31] submitting it to the Council in the same month. The Economic and Social Committee gave its Opinion in December 1987[32] and the European Parliament in June 1988.[33] The Commission then issued an amended Proposal in October 1988,[34] adopted by the Council in July 1989. The Directive was finally adopted on 13 November 1989.[35] It requires implementation by 1 June 1992. The United Kingdom implemented the substantive provisions in Pt V of the Criminal Justice Act 1993;[36] the provisions for enforcement and cooperation were in general already reflected in Pt III of the Companies Act 1989.[37]

Legal Basis[38]

The Directive was adopted on the basis of Article 100a of the Treaty, which (in the version applicable when the Directive was adopted) provides:

(1)   The Council shall, acting by a qualified majority on a proposal from the Commission in cooperation with the European Parliament and after consulting the Economic and Social Committee, adopt the measures for the approximation of the provisions laid down by law, regulation or administrative action in Member States which have as their object the establishment and functioning of the internal market.

The initial Proposal was based on Article 54(3)(g), which provides that, as part of the programme for abolishing restrictions on freedom of establishment, the Council shall coordinate 'to the necessary extent the safeguards which, for the

---

[30] See Suter, J, *The Regulation of Insider Dealing in Britain* (1989) 287.

[31] COM (87) 111 final, 21 May 1987; [1987] OJ C153/8.   [32] [1988] OJ C35/22.

[33] [1988] OJ C187/93.   [34] COM (88) 549 final, 4 October 1988; [1988] OJ C277/13.

[35] There is a detailed history of the drafting progress of the main provisions through the various legislative stages in Pingel, I, 'The EC Directive of 1989' in Gaillard, E, *Insider Trading: The Laws of Europe, the United States and Japan* (1992).

[36] These are very comprehensively discussed by Wotherspoon, K, 'Insider Dealing—The New Law: Part V of the Criminal Justice Act 1993' (1994) 57 MLR 419 and by Rider, B, and Ashe, T M, in *Insider Crime* (1993). There are good summaries by Finney, R, 'The New Insider Dealing Regime' [1993] Butterworths Journal of International Banking and Financial Law 525 and King, P, 'New Regime for Insider Dealing' (1993) 137 SJ 1242. For a practical analysis, see also White, M, 'The Implications for Securities Regulation of New Insider Dealing Provisions in the Criminal Justice Act 1993' (1995) 16 The Company Lawyer 163.

[37] For details of actual and proposed implementation as at 1992 in other Member States (including Austria, Finland and Sweden), see Gaillard (n 35 above) and the sources cited in nn 8–15 above. For a comparative study (with a practical angle) of the legislation in France, Germany, Italy, Switzerland and the UK, see Bombrun, N, Kersting, M O, Bauer, M, Salera, P, Grenbaum, J P, Daeniker, D, and Fergusson, L, 'Keeping it Secret' (May 1997) European Counsel 17.

[38] For a more detailed analysis of the legal basis of the Insider Dealing Directive, see Fornasier, R, 'The Directive on Insider Dealing' (1989–90) 13 Fordham International Law Journal 149, 154–62.

protection of the interests of members and others, are required by Member States of companies . . . with a view to making such safeguards equivalent throughout the Community'. The Proposal was seen to constitute 'an essential supplement' to the Admissions Directive, the Listing Particulars Directive and the Regular Information Directive, already adopted on the basis of both Article 54 and Article 100[39] of the Treaty, and the Major Shareholdings Directive, then a Proposal, based on Article 54 alone. The preamble to the Proposal referred to the need to combat insider trading by coordinated Community rules because such trading, 'by benefiting certain investors at the expense of others, is likely to undermine [investor] confidence and may therefore prejudice the smooth operation of the secondary market in transferable securities'. Although the aim of investor protection is clearly within the ambit of Article 54(3)(g), the wider goal of 'the smooth operation of the . . . market' is not; moreover, the 'safeguards' against insider dealing are not 'required . . . of companies', but rather form part of a wider framework regulating transactions in securities. Article 100a is accordingly a more appropriate basis, and the European Parliament's proposal that it be substituted for Article 54(3)(g) as the legal basis of the Directive was taken up.

Aims and Structure

The preamble to the Directive recites the importance of the secondary market in transferable securities in the raising of corporate finance and the associated need for its smooth operation. This in turn 'depends to a large extent on the confidence it inspires in investors', which depends inter alia on 'the assurance afforded to investors that they are placed on an equal footing and that they will be protected against the improper use of insider information . . . by benefiting certain investors as compared with others, insider dealing is likely to undermine that confidence'. Thus the main thrust of the Directive must be seen as the desire to place investors on an equal footing. As will be seen, some apparent difficulties with certain of its provisions resolve themselves when seen in the light of that overall aim.

The Directive is refreshingly concise: there are only fifteen Articles. Article 1 defines 'inside information'. Article 2 in effect defines primary insiders and imposes the primary prohibition on dealing; Article 3 adds prohibitions on disclosing information and recommending dealing; Article 4 extends the primary prohibition to secondary insiders, or 'tippees'. Article 5 defines the territorial scope of the prohibitions. Article 6 provides that Member States may adopt more stringent provisions

---

[39] 'The Council shall, acting unanimously on a proposal from the Commission, issue directives for the approximation of such provisions laid down by law, regulation or administrative action in Member States as directly affect the establishment or functioning of the common market.' Art 100a, expressed to be 'by way of derogation from Article 100', was inserted by the Single European Act as from 1 July 1987 and subsequently amended by the Treaty of Maastricht to reflect the greater powers conferred on the European Parliament.

than those laid down in the Directive. Article 7 extends an existing requirement on certain companies to disclose information. Articles 8 to 10 concern the designation and function of competent authorities to be set up by Member States. Article 11 concerns the competence of the Community to conclude agreements relating to insider dealing with non-member countries. Article 12 extends the powers of the Contact Committee, set up under the Admissions Directive. Article 13 concerns penalties. Article 14 sets the time scale for implementation and Article 15 states that the Directive is addressed to the Member States.

Articles 1 to 7, dealing with substantive law, will be dealt with first, followed by Articles 8 to 13 dealing with various aspects of enforcement.

Implementation in the United Kingdom

As noted above,[40] the Directive is implemented in the United Kingdom by Pt V of the Criminal Justice Act 1993. The provisions of that Act are annotated and discussed below only where a particular point of interest arises from the terms of implementation.[41]

Substantive Provisions

Inside information

Article 1(1) defines 'inside information' as:

information which has not been made public of a precise nature relating to one or several issuers of transferable securities or to one or several transferable securities, which, if it were made public, would be likely to have a significant effect on the price of the transferable security or securities in question . . .

Made public

No guidance is given as to when information is to be regarded as having been 'made public'. The original Proposal referred to 'information unknown to the public',[42] and the Explanatory Memorandum stated that this meant 'not yet published'; the European Parliament suggested amending this to 'information inaccessible or not available to the public', with the rider that publication 'involves the effective disclosure of inside information in such a manner sufficiently to ensure its availability to the investing public.' This amendment was intended to enable financial

---

[40] See n 7.
[41] They are more comprehensively footnoted in an earlier version of this chapter published as 'The Insider Dealing Directive and its Implementation in the United Kingdom' (1996) 3 Maastricht Journal of European and Comparative Law 287.
[42] Art 6.

analysts to work unimpeded, on the basis that 'though investment analysts' reports are unknown to the public, the information on which the analyst works is accessible'.[43] Although the Commission adopted the Parliament's suggestion, the Council preferred 'has not been made public'. It is arguable that a more appropriate criterion would be whether the information is accessible or available to the market, that is, to persons likely to deal in the relevant securities, rather than to the public at large.[44]

The Parliament's amendment would have resolved the ambiguity inherent in the final version as to whether the criterion is that information has been published or that it has become generally available to investors. The former interpretation could mean that insiders could be 'waiting at the starting gate', ready to act as soon as the inside information was released and before the public has had a chance to assimilate it. In the United States, where the concept of inside information has been developed incrementally by the courts in the absence of any legislative definition, it has been held that the information must not have 'been disseminated in a manner making it available to investors generally'.[45] Given the reference among the objectives of the Directive to placing investors on an equal footing,[46] this seems sensible,[47] notwithstanding the resulting need for a finding of fact in each case of the moment when the inside information can be regarded as having been so disseminated.[48] It is also consistent with the use of the term 'publicly available' in the 'analysts' exemption' in the preamble to the Directive.[49] It is interesting to note however that proposals in the United Kingdom to leave the term 'made public', reproduced in the implementing legislation,[50] unqualified, so that it would be for

---

[43] Opinion of the Committee on Economic and Monetary Affairs and Industrial Policy drawn up on behalf of the Committee on Legal Affairs and Citizens' Rights on the Proposal from the Commission for a Directive coordinating regulations on insider trading, Doc A2–0055/88, Series A, 5 May 1988, at 22, cited in Pingel (n 35 above) 7. The 'analysts' exemption' was eventually given lip service in the 13th recital in the preamble.

[44] See the Memorandum by the Company Law Committee of The Law Society, *Proposal for — Directive Co-ordinating Regulations on Insider Dealing*, January 1989, 7.

[45] See the chapter by McLaughlin, J T, and Macfarlane, M A H, in Gaillard, E, *Insider Trading: The Laws of Europe, the United States and Japan*, 285, 287 and n 5. For a note of French decisions to similar effect, see Gaillard, E, and Pingel, I, 'Les opérations d'initiés dans la Communauté Economique Européenne' (1990) 26 Revue trimestrielle de droit européen 329, 333.

[46] 5th recital in the preamble.

[47] It is borne out by the German version, which refers to information *nicht öffentlich bekannt* or not publicly known, and the Greek version, which refers to information *i opoia den ehei ginei gnosti sto koino*, or which has not become known to the public; all the other versions however follow the same pattern as the English.

[48] The US and French courts have developed guidelines as to when information will be regarded as having been 'made public': see Gaillard (n 45 above) 60 (France) and 287 (US). The American Stock Exchange Company Guide provides: 'Following dissemination of the information, insiders should refrain from trading until the public has had an opportunity to evaluate it thoroughly': s 401; see Schödermeier, M, and Wallach, E, 'The EEC Insider Directive Approaching Final Adoption' (1989) 5 Journal of International Business Law 234.

[49] 'Whereas estimates developed from publicly available data cannot be regarded as inside information . . .': 13th recital.

[50] Criminal Justice Act 1993, s 56(1)(c).

the courts to interpret it, 'met with vigorous opposition from several peers who felt that the absence of a definition left an unwelcome degree of uncertainty surrounding the content of offences carrying up to seven years' imprisonment'.[51] The Act now contains detailed guidelines (expressed to be non-exhaustive) according to which information is 'made public' if it is published in accordance with Stock Exchange rules, is contained in records which the public has a statutory right to inspect, can be 'readily acquired' by those likely to deal in the relevant securities, or is derived from information which has been made public.[52] A further provision lists circumstances in which information not falling within the preceding definition may nonetheless be treated as made public, mainly designed to offer some comfort to analysts and fund managers as to the sources of their information.[53]

Of a precise nature

This requirement is clearly intended to exclude rumours and speculation from the definition.[54] There has been some academic debate as to whether information that a bid is forthcoming would be 'precise';[55] the answer must depend on where, in the circumstances, the information came in the penumbra between hard fact and rumour, and is a question of fact not linguistics. It is interesting to note however that in drafting the implementing legislation the United Kingdom took the view that 'precise' alone was too narrow, meaning 'narrow, exact and definitive',[56] and settled instead on the term 'specific or precise information'. It was stated during the passage of the draft legislation that the word 'precise' alone 'might well have had the effect that, for example, information that there was to be a huge dividend increase would not be capable of being inside information. It would have been necessary to know also the quantum of the increase',[57] and that if, for example, the chairman of a company said to an analyst over lunch ' "Our results will be much

---

[51] Wotherspoon, K, 'Insider Dealing—The New Law: Part V of the Criminal Justice Act 1993' (1994) 57 MLR 419, 422.

[52] Section 58(2). See Parliamentary Debates, House of Commons Official Report, 10 June 1993, cols 180–8, for an interesting discussion of the ambit of the term in the UK implementing legislation.

[53] Section 58(3). See Skoyles, K J, 'Insider Dealing: When is Information "Made Public"?' (1993) 1 Journal of Asset Protection and Financial Crime. For a helpful discussion of the analysts' concerns, see Finney, R, 'The New Insider Dealing Regime' [1993] Butterworths Journal of International Banking and Financial law 525, 527.

[54] See para 2 of the Explanatory Memorandum (where the requirement was that the information be of 'a specific nature'): 'A simple rumour cannot therefore be regarded as inside information'.

[55] See, e g, Ashe, M, 'The Directive on Insider Dealing' (1992) 13 The Company Lawyer 15, citing Australian and Canadian cases. It was held in the former that a director who had been present at negotiations with an interested purchaser did not have specific information that a bid was in the offing, since the director 'was only deducing that [the other party] would buy the shares from the interest which they expressed during negotiations'. This is clearly wrong; it is also difficult to see why the Court of Justice would have regard to a decision of a New South Wales court of first instance on Australian legislation, since repealed, in construing a relatively unchallenging word.

[56] Said by Anthony Nelson, Economic Secretary to the Treasury; Parliamentary Debates, House of Commons Official Report, 10 June 1993, col 174.

[57] The Earl of Caithness in the House of Lords at the Report stage of the passage of the Criminal Justice Bill 1992: *Hansard*, HL 3 December 1992, col 1501.

better than the market expects or knows," that would not be precise. The person would not have disclosed what the results of the company were to be. However, it would certainly be specific . . .'.[58]

Relating to . . . issuers . . . or to transferable securities

Thus inside information can comprise information coming from within (for example, an increase in profits) or outside (for example, a takeover bid[59]) the issuer in question, 'information on the situation or prospects of one or more securities and information which is likely to influence the market as such (for example, the decision of a central bank to alter the discount rate)'.[60] By analogy, changes in exchange rates or new fiscal legislation could also come within the definition,[61] as could 'government decisions on passing a law which will bar exports to South Africa or will make investment in a certain branch more costly or news about the pending outcome of a major case for example at the Supreme Court'.[62] This is possibly stretching the concept of 'relating to' ('affecting' might have been a helpful alternative), but it is submitted that including advance information on such topics in the definition of inside information is in line with the objectives of the Directive. Concerns that the net is cast too wide[63] are misconceived given that this is only one aspect of a multi-faceted offence in which a number of different elements must coincide: the necessary limits to what can constitute inside information 'must be looked for elsewhere, namely in the concept of insider and the professional prohibitions and duties imposed on them by the directive'.[64] To this might be added the other elements of the definition of inside information itself, such as the likely effect on price, considered below. It may be noted however that the United Kingdom implementing legislation appears to exclude such wider information from its definition of inside information and to that extent must be regarded as defective. The Criminal Justice Act 1993 refers to information which 'relates to particular securities or to a particular issuer of securities or to particular issuers of securities and not to securities generally or to issuers of securities generally'.[65]

---

[58] *Hansard*, HL 3 December 1992, col 175.

[59] Knowledge of his own intentions will not prevent a bidder from completing his proposed bid (provided his purchases are made in his capacity as bidder): see the 11th recital in the preamble, and Gaillard, E, and Pingel, I, 'Les opérations d'initiés dans la Communauté Economique Européenne' (1990) 26 Revue trimestrielle de droit européen 329, 335.

[60] See para II.2 of the Explanatory Memorandum in the first draft.

[61] Bergmans, B, *Inside Information and Securities Trading* (1991).

[62] Hopt, K J, 'The European Insider Dealing Directive' in Hopt, K J and Wymeersch, E (eds), *European Insider Dealing* (1991) 132, at 134; the chapter is also published in (1990) 27 CML Rev 51.

[63] See, for example, Wymeersch, E, 'The Regulation of Insider Dealing within the European Community' in *Insider Dealing: Papers from the I.C.E.L. Conference October 1990* (1990) 3, 15.

[64] Hopt (n 62 above) 134.

[65] Criminal Justice Act 1993, s 56(1)(a).

Would be likely to have a significant effect on the price

This criterion or an analogous test couched in terms of materiality[66] is common to most national insider dealing legislation. As stated by the Commission in the Explanatory Memorandum, without such a restriction as to what constitutes inside information for regulatory purposes 'the managers or directors or even most of the employees of a company would never be able to carry out transactions in the securities of their companies, since they always have information which has not been published'.

Transferable securities

Article 1(2) defines 'transferable securities' as shares and debt securities and securities equivalent thereto; contracts or rights to subscribe for, acquire or dispose of such securities; and futures and index contracts, options and financial futures in respect of such securities,[67] when admitted to trading on a market which is regulated and supervised by authorities recognized by public bodies, operates regularly and is accessible directly or indirectly to the public. The definition, despite its width, includes neither unit trusts nor foreign exchange and commodities contracts and derivatives,[68] possibly in the case of the items other than unit trusts because they are regarded as, in practice, traded on professional markets.[69] The definition of 'market' for the purposes of Article 1(2) encompasses secondary markets, for example the various unlisted securities markets in the Community,[70] and trading on the 'off the floor' systems such as NASDAQ (National Association of Securities Dealers Automated Quotation), SEAQ (Stock Exchange Automated Quotations) etc. It would exclude privately run securities exchanges.

---

[66] The original Proposal referred to 'material effect'; the term was changed by the Council at the final stage. The Council also reinstated the words 'be likely to', which had been deleted at the Parliament's suggestion.

[67] This wide definition entailed one of the substantive changes to the UK insider dealing legislation. The securities, listed in the Criminal Justice Act 1993, Sch 2, now include (as well as shares, debentures, options and contracts for differences) futures, depositary receipts and loan stock or gilts issued by central government, local authorities and the Bank of England. The extension of the range of securities caught has brought within the UK legislation many 'Euro-securities', or derivatives dealt with on the Euromarkets, not previously covered: see Orosz, N, 'Insider dealing and the Euromarkets' [1994] International Financial Law Review 28.

[68] Nor, as Wymeersch points out, are transactions on the gold bullion and real estate markets caught: n 63 above, 14.

[69] Davies, P L, 'The European Community's Directive on Insider Dealing: From Company Law to Securities Markets Regulation?' (1991) 11 OJLS 92, n 2 on 93.

[70] It is not clear however whether it would extend to the *Hors cote* (over the counter) market in France, although French academics take the view that it does: Wymeersch (n 63 above) 11, n 22.

Primary insiders

Definition

The first part of Article 2(1) defines three categories of person whom Member States must prohibit from engaging in subsequently defined conduct. The prohibition is to apply to any person who possesses inside information:

—by virtue of his membership of the administrative, management or supervisory bodies of the issuer,

—by virtue of his holding in the capital of the issuer, or

—because he has access to such information by virtue of the exercise of his employment, profession or duties.

It is interesting to note that the first draft simply referred to 'any person who, in the exercise of his profession or duties, acquires inside information';[71] the first two categories were added at the instigation of Germany[72] and reflect the issuer-related definition in the German guidelines.[73]

The wording of the first category is wide enough to encompass not only members of the supervisory board in Member States which have the two-tier system but also the management of companies or forms of business enterprise other than public companies if those undertakings issue 'transferable securities'.[74]

Although there is no minimum holding required for a shareholder to fall within the second limb of the definition, the requirement that possession of the inside information be 'by virtue of his holding' will in practice have the effect of restricting the definition to substantial shareholders, in particular institutional shareholders, who are often regarded as being in a privileged position vis-à-vis corporate information because of their financial standing, their board nominees and their informal contacts with the company.[75] The provision will also cover cases where a substantial shareholder declines a secret offer from a potential bidder and subsequently deals in the expectation that a bid is forthcoming.[76] Within a group of companies, only an immediate parent will be caught by this provision: a horizontal or remoter vertical connection will not fall within the primary insider definition.

The third category is clearly the widest, liable to encompass not only employees but also lawyers, auditors, bankers, advisers, clients etc,[77] provided that they satisfy

---

[71] Art 1. See below for further discussion of the evolution and scope of this limb of the definition.

[72] Although the combination of a list of the principal insiders supplemented by a more general definition was already being favourably considered at a much earlier stage: see Cruickshank, C, 'Insider Trading in the EEC' (1982) 10 International Business Lawyer 345, 347.

[73] Bergmans, B, Inside Information and Securities Trading (1991) 70.

[74] Hopt, K J, 'The European Insider Dealing Directive' in Hopt, K J and Wymeersch, E (eds), European Insider Dealing (1991) 136.

[75] See Hannigan, B, Insider Dealing (2nd edn, 1994), 63.

[76] Wotherspoon, K, 'Insider Dealing—The New Law: Part V of the Criminal Justice Act 1993' (1994) 57 MLR 419, 425.

[77] Gaillard and Pingel note that French courts have found an architect and a head-hunter to be

the functional criterion that they have access to inside information 'by virtue of the exercise of' their employment, profession or duties. There is a division of academic opinion[78] as to whether there must be 'some kind of substantive connection between the profession or employment of the insider and the issuer',[79] or whether a total outsider, for example a taxi driver or waiter who overhears inside information in the course of his job, falls within the definition.[80] A study of the wording of the provision in the light of its legislative history supports the former view.

The first draft of this provision ('any person who, in the exercise of his profession or duties, acquires inside information'), reflecting the French approach, was explained by the Commission as intended to encompass 'those who by their profession or occupation are in a fiduciary relationship with or have a duty of confidentiality towards the company whose shares are in question'.[81] The Economic and Social Committee considered that that definition went 'further than the most usual concepts in business', by which apparently was meant the issuer-related criterion used in the German guidelines, and suggested a cumbersome alternative: 'any person who, in the occasional or regular performance of services in or for a company, acquires unpublished inside information about this company or another'. Although the Committee's amendment was not taken up, the wording of the provision underwent significant change before the final version.

The first change, prompted by the European Parliament, was the insertion of the word 'employment' before 'profession'. This was presumably intended to broaden the category by including those whose position *vis-à-vis* the company does not necessarily involve a fiduciary or confidential element. The resulting formula—'any person who, in the exercise of his employment, profession or duties, acquires inside information'—risked catching total outsiders who stumbled by chance on inside

within the analogous French provision: Gaillard, E, and Pingel, I, 'Les opérations d'initiés dans la Communauté Economique Européenne' (1990) 26 Revue trimestrielle de droit européen 329, 340.

[78] It is interesting that on the whole US commentators are not party to this debate, but on the contrary tend to welcome the definition of 'insider' as 'A major strength of the Directive . . . an excellent base' (Stutz, A E, 'A New Look at the European Economic Community Directive on Insider Trading' (1990) 23 Vanderbilt Journal of Transnational Law 135, 168); 'Perhaps the strongest point in the . . . directive', McGuinness, C A, 'Towards the Unification of European Capital Markets: The EEC's Proposed Directive on Insider Trading' (1988) 11 Fordham International Law Journal 432, 449. This presumably reflects the US experience of no statutory definition of insider dealing as such, with the courts accordingly playing a very active role in developing definitions. Stutz, 168, says that the EEC can learn from the US experience that 'clear definition of terms is necessary to prevent judicial abuse.'

[79] Tridimas, T, 'Insider Trading: European Harmonisation and National Law Reform' (1991) 40 ICLQ 919, 926–7.

[80] See Davies, P L, 'The European Community's Directive on Insider Dealing: From Company Law to Securities Markets Regulation?' (1991) 11 OJLS 92, 102, for a forceful statement of this view. It also seems to be endorsed by the UK government in debating the implementing legislation (Criminal Justice Act 1993, s 57(2)(a)(ii)): the Economic Secretary to the Treasury stated that the legislation 'therefore does not carry forward the connection text [in the previous legislation] . . . That is an important and desirable change which reflects the . . . directive, because it is quite possible for someone to have direct access to price-sensitive information without being connected to a company' (Parliamentary Debates, House of Commons Official Report, 10 June 1993, cols 189–90). The 'connection test' in the Company Securities (Insider Dealing) Act 1985, s 9, is summarized in n 83 below.

[81] Explanatory Memorandum, para II.1.

information while working in a capacity only incidentally overlapping with the company. It seems reasonable to assume that this lay behind the further major change in the final wording adopted by the Council: 'any person who [possesses inside information] *because he has access to such information by virtue of* the exercise of his employment, profession or duties'.[82] The relatively neutral criterion that the inside information be acquired in the exercise of the employment etc has been replaced by the much more specific requirement that the insider's employment etc involve his having access to inside information.[83]

In some respects the scope of the final version is wider than the Commission's initial intention, in that it is clear that the insider need no longer be 'in a fiduciary relationship with or have a duty of confidentiality towards' the issuer: it suffices that he possesses inside information because he has access to it by virtue of his position. An employee of a central bank with advance knowledge of, for example, a proposed change of interest rate could thus be an insider.[84] The requirement of access by virtue of status should however exclude the taxi driver who overhears inside information exchanged between customers, although the answer is not beyond doubt.[85]

Excluding the outsider with sharp ears from the definition of primary insider does not exonerate him from liability altogether: if he knowingly possesses inside information which must have come, directly or indirectly, from a primary insider, then he unequivocally comes within the definition of secondary insider[86] and must be prohibited at least from 'taking advantage of that information' by dealing. It may be thought that treating such persons as secondary insiders accords with the policy considerations which presumably underlay the creation of two classes of insider, primary and secondary, defined and treated differently.[87]

[82] Emphasis added. The suggested difference in meaning between the two versions is also borne out by a comparison of the wording of the French insider dealing legislation: '[les] personnes disposant à l'occasion de l'exercice de leur profession ou de leurs fonctions d'informations privilégiées' (persons with inside information available by virtue of the exercise of their occupation or their duties) (Ord 67–833, Art 10.1, para 1), accepted by French commentators as covering the apocryphal taxi driver (see Tridimas (n 79 above) 926), and the French wording of Art 2(1) of the Directive: '[les] personnes qui [disposent d'une information priviligiée] parce qu'elles ont accès à cette information en raison de l'exercise de leur travail, de leur profession ou de leurs fonctions'.

[83] This echoes elements of the UK's pre-implementation legislation, which included as primary insiders persons occupying a position as an employee (albeit expressed to be of the company or a related company) and persons in a position involving a professional or business relationship with the company or a related company 'which in either case may reasonably be expected to give him access to' inside information: Company Securities (Insider Dealing) Act 1985, s 9.

[84] See Hopt, K J, 'The European Insider Dealing Directive' in Hopt, K J and Wymeersch, E (eds), *European Insider Dealing* (1991) 138, for further examples.

[85] The issue is one on which a reference to the European Court of Justice on the construction of implementing legislation is expected in due course: see e g Dine, J, and Hughes, P, *EC Company Law* (1997) para 13.74, Wotherspoon, K, 'Insider Dealing—The New Law: Part V of the Criminal Justice Act 1993' (1994) 57 MLR 419, 426, Nystrom, D A, 'Securities—Insider Trading—The Effects of the New EEC Draft Insider Trading Directive' (1988) 18 Georgia Journal of International and Comparative Law 119, 133–4, n 110 (although Nystrom's argument that attempts to define, by using more words, merely create more problems has its limitations).

[86] Art 4: see below.

[87] In that secondary insiders need not—though may—be subject to the prohibition on disclosing and recommending. See pp 326–7 below.

Legal personality

Article 2(2) provides that where the insider as defined is a company or other type of legal person, the prohibition on dealing 'shall apply to the natural persons who take part in the decision to carry out the transaction for [its] account'. Most language versions of the Directive are ambiguous as to whether the prohibition substitutes or supplements, that is, whether the company or other legal person none the less remains itself subject to the prohibition.[88] For many continental legal systems this is academic, since the concept of criminal liability of corporations is not recognized, and it is against that background that the provision was included.[89]

Secondary insiders

Article 4 requires Member States to extend the basic prohibition on dealing to any person who 'with full knowledge of the facts possesses inside information, the direct or indirect source of which could not be other than a person referred to in Article 2'.[90] Although the Directive uses neither term,[91] it is convenient (and commonplace) to refer to such persons as 'secondary insiders' or 'tippees'[92] (although the latter term is not strictly correct since a deliberate tip is not necessary; see below).

[88] The Dutch is the only version which is unambiguous, stating that the prohibition is also (*eveneens*) applicable to the natural persons participating in the decision. The UK implementing legislation uses the word 'individual' in the definition of the offence (in s 52 of the Criminal Justice Act 1993), thus excluding legal persons from liability. Fornasier, R, 'The Directive on Insider Dealing' (1989–90) 13 Fordham International Law Journal 149, 164, takes the view that the prohibition in Art 2(2) substitutes, but that Member States may use Art 6 (see below, pp 327–8) to extend liability to legal persons.

[89] Hopt (n 84 above) 140. Reid, D and Ballheimer, A, suggest that the provision may also have been intended to endorse the practice of Chinese walls by permitting other persons in the company who do not have inside information to deal in the securities concerned, but it is hard to see how it could have this effect: if those other persons do not have inside information they are not in any event subject to the prohibition. See 'The Legal Framework of the Securities Industry in the European Community's 1992 Programme' (1991) 29 Columbia Journal of Transnational Law 103, 138.

[90] Included in the UK definition of 'insider' by the Criminal Justice Act 1993, s 57(2)(b).

[91] They both however appear in the Explanatory Memorandum in the first draft.

[92] Apparently coined by the 'guru of securities regulation', Professor Louis Loss of Harvard Law School who 'is rightly proud that the Oxford English Dictionary has credited him' with first use of the expression: Davies, P L, *Gower's Principles of Modern Company Law* (6th edn, 1997) 466, n 20. Members of the UK House of Lords were less enthusiastic about the term when debating the draft implementing legislation, which originally included it: 'any Act which as part of its new wording includes the creation of the word "tippee" is one which leaves me a total "flabbergastee". I am full of gloom at the thought that in cases in which the issue is the status of the recipient of the confidential information, judges for generations to come will begin their summings up by being unable to resist the temptation to say "Members of the jury, tippee or not tippee, that is the question"': Lord Wigoder, Second Reading, 3 November 1992. The term did not survive, although the rationale for its deletion given by Lord Renton, that it was ambiguous because 'tip' also means 'the projecting end of a pointed object; for example on a pencil . . . a gratuity—a tip to a taxi-driver . . . advice or suggestion; for example, a tip as regards a bet on a horse race' (Parliamentary Debates, House of Lords 3 December 1992, cols 1496–7), is hardly persuasive.

The first draft of Article 4 required the primary prohibition to be extended to 'any person who has knowingly obtained' the information from a primary insider.[93] It is clear that the main target was intended to be individuals who 'make a practice of procuring privileged information from "primary insiders" . . . and use it to their own advantage'.[94] The Economic and Social Committee suggested changing 'has knowingly' to 'is aware of the fact that he has obtained'. The final version goes further by dropping entirely the requirement to show that the secondary insider 'obtained', presumably in part at least in order to ensure that a person given unsolicited inside information cannot avoid liability, as occurred in the United Kingdom in 1988,[95] on the specious semantic ground that the dictionary meaning of 'obtain' is to 'procure or gain as the result of purpose and effort'.[96]

The Committee also suggested that further amendments could be made to the provision 'in such a way that the chain of persons who can be punished for passing on inside information does not end with the so-called "secondary insiders" but is continued further'. The latter proposal was translated into the final version of the provision by introducing the concept of 'direct or indirect source'. Although this may be thought to make the scope of the offence too wide by creating a potentially very long chain, the fact that the information must still retain all the defined characteristics of inside information, including precision, will inevitably restrict the number of links. The definition does however draw into the circle of potential insiders the apocryphal taxi driver and waiter overhearing a conversation: they may well not have 'obtained' the information, and may not even be what is commonly understood by 'tippees', but provided that they know that the information must have originally come from a primary insider they will be secondary insiders.

It has been argued[97] that the definition of secondary insider does not cover a person who obtains inside information directly from company documents rather than from another person. However, company documents of necessity originate with some person, almost certainly—in the case of documents containing inside infor-

---

[93] It is interesting to note that in the early 1980s 'the majority of national experts' consulted by the Commission considered 'that to include "tippees" in the text would be to go too far': Cruickshank, C, 'Insider Trading in the EEC' (1982) 10 International Business Lawyer 345, 346. The Proposal was drafted however in the wake of a number of well-publicized insider dealing scandals, in particular the Boesky affair, which doubtless shaped the view that secondary insiders should not be allowed to slip through the net.

[94] Explanatory Memorandum, para II.1.

[95] In *R v Fisher* (1988) 4 BCC 360, a recipient of unsolicited inside information who immediately bought and subsequently resold at a profit the shares in question was acquitted on that ground. The law was later brought back into line with common sense and the evident intention of Parliament by the House of Lords in *Attorney-General's Reference (No 1 of 1988)* [1989] AC 971 (pursuant to a procedure for review which does not affect the original outcome of the case).

[96] The first definition given in *The Shorter Oxford English Dictionary* (1973). The example given by the dictionary of such usage does not appear to support the construction: 'Blessed are the mercifull: for they shall obteyne mercy TINDALE *Matt.* 5:7'.

[97] See e g Standen, D J, 'Insider Trading Reforms Sweep Across Germany: Bracing for the Cold Winds of Change' (1995) 36 Harvard International Law Journal 177, 189, and Hopt, K J, 'The European Insider Dealing Directive' in Hopt, K J and Wymeersch, E (eds) *European Insider Dealing* (1991) 142.

mation—the board of directors or the company's advisers or auditors. The 'source' of the information for the purposes of Article 4 would therefore be a primary insider and the recipient in question a secondary insider.

Wotherspoon[98] expresses some disquiet that the Directive is ambiguous on the precise knowledge which the tippee must possess. This stems from concern that a United Kingdom court construing the implementing legislation, which refers to the tippee's knowledge that his direct or indirect source is a primary insider,[99] may be tempted by Lord Lowry's statement in *Attorney-General's Reference (No 1 of 1988)* that a tippee could not be liable under the original legislation[100] unless he knew the identity of the informant. Given that the statement was in any event made obiter, and referred to legislation drafted in a fundamentally different way (Lord Lowry was considering the meaning of 'knowingly' in 'knowingly obtained'), it is to be hoped that it will not be so extrapolated.

It is clear that Article 4 does not require that the information be originally disclosed unlawfully or in breach of confidence.[101]

Prohibited conduct

There are three categories of prohibited conduct. Member States must prohibit primary insiders from dealing, disclosing and recommending (all discussed further below) and secondary insiders from dealing. In addition, Member States may extend to secondary insiders the prohibition on disclosing and recommending. Article 5[102] lays down minimum rules of private international law to determine Member States' jurisdiction over transactions which frequently straddle frontiers.[103] It requires each Member State to apply all three prohibitions 'at least to actions undertaken within its territory to the extent that the transferable securities concerned are admitted to trading on a market of a Member State': thus provided the securities in question are admitted to trading on the market of one Member State, insider dealing in relation to such securities which occurs in another Member

---

[98] Wotherspoon, K, 'Insider Dealing—The New Law: Part V of the Criminal Justice Act 1993' (1994) 57 MLR 419, 426–7.

[99] Criminal Justice Act 1993, s 57.

[100] Company Securities (Insider Dealing) Act 1985, s 1(3), which extends the prohibition on dealing where (a) an individual 'has information which he knowingly obtained (directly or indirectly) from another individual who—(i) is connected with a particular company, or was at any time in the six months preceding the obtaining of the information so connected, and (ii) the former individual knows or has reasonable cause to believe held the information by virtue of being so connected, and (b) the former individual knows or has reasonable cause to believe that, because of the latter's connection and position, it would be reasonable to expect him not to disclose the information except for the proper performance of the functions attaching to that position.'

[101] Although disclosure by a primary insider will amount to a separate offence: see Art 3(1), discussed below.

[102] Imperfectly implemented in the UK by the Criminal Justice Act 1993, s 62.

[103] In this connection it should be noted that, by virtue of the Agreement on the European Economic Area [1994] OJ L1/3, Art 36(2) and Annex IX, the Directive applies to Switzerland and Liechtenstein (and Iceland).

State, for example making a disclosure or recommendation, or placing an order for purchase or sale, must be prohibited by that Member State. Furthermore, each Member State must in any event 'regard a transaction as carried out within its territory if it is carried out on a market [as defined] situated or operating within that territory',[104] regardless of the place where the order for purchase or sale originates. The territorial scope of the prohibitions is thus extremely wide, in accordance with the spirit of combating insider dealing at an international level.[105]

Dealing

Article 2(1), it will be recalled, applies to any person who possesses inside information by virtue of his membership of the issuer's administrative, management or supervisory bodies or his holding in the issuer's capital or 'because he has access to such information by virtue of the exercise of his employment, profession or duties'. It requires each Member State to prohibit any such person from 'taking advantage of that information with full knowledge of the facts by acquiring or disposing of for his own account or for the account of a third party, either directly or indirectly, transferable securities of the issuer or issuers to which that information relates'. Article 2(3) makes it clear that the prohibition applies to any acquisition or disposal of transferable securities 'effected through a professional intermediary', for example a stockbroker or a bank,[106] whether on or off a market. Member States may however exempt from the prohibition acquisitions or disposals of transferable securities effected 'without the involvement of a professional intermediary outside a market' as defined in Article 1(2),[107] such as privately arranged transactions effected off-market.[108]

The prohibition on dealing must be seen in the light of the eleventh recital in the preamble to the Directive, which states that:

since the acquisition or disposal of transferable securities necessarily involves a prior decision to acquire or to dispose taken by the person who undertakes one or other of these operations, the carrying-out of this acquisition or disposal does not constitute in itself the use of inside information . . .

This somewhat opaque provision is presumably designed to permit a potential bidder for a company to increase its stake in the target up to the threshold where a mandatory bid is required before making an announcement of the takeover. In

---

[104] Art 5, 2nd sentence.

[105] Contrast the manifestly inadequate criterion in the first draft of residence of the insider.

[106] 'Professional intermediary' is defined in the UK implementing legislation as a person 'who carries on a business consisting of [acquiring or disposing of securities (whether as principal or agent) or acting as an intermediary between persons taking part in any dealing in securities] and who holds himself out to the public or any section of the public . . . as willing to engage in any such business; or . . . is employed by [such] a person . . . to carry out any such activity': Criminal Justice Act 1993, s 59.

[107] See above, p 317.

[108] The UK's purported implementation of Art 2(3), in the Criminal Justice Act 1993, s 52(3), is flawed in that its effect is to exempt dealing which is either off-market or effected without a professional intermediary, whereas it is clear from the Article that the requirements are cumulative.

those circumstances, the putative bidder's intention to make a bid is of course itself inside information, and most countries where takeover activity is sufficiently developed to be subject to sophisticated regulation permit pre-announcement dealing.[109] The recital would also cover, for example, purchases by a fund manager which has decided to build up a stake in a company.

Note that although the prohibition extends to stockbrokers, portfolio managers, trustees etc, since it prohibits dealing 'for the account of a third party', it will not interfere with the simple execution of orders. This follows from the fact that, like so many of the core concepts in the Directive, the prohibited conduct has a composite definition: the insider must not only possess, he must also take advantage of the information by dealing. It is also spelt out in the twelfth recital in the preamble, which states:

the mere fact that market-makers, bodies authorized to act as *contrepartie*, or stockbrokers with inside information confine themselves, in the first two cases, to pursuing their normal business of buying or selling securities or, in the last, to carrying out an order should not in itself be deemed to constitute use of such inside information; . . . likewise the fact of carrying out transactions with the aim of stabilizing the price of new issues or secondary offers of transferable securities should not in itself be deemed to constitute use of inside information . . .[110]

This is a point of some importance, since it focuses on the intention required to commit the offence. Although the Directive does not refer in terms to intent, the dual requirement of 'full knowledge of the facts' and 'taking advantage'[111] of the information means that intention is clearly an element of the offence. Common sense suggests that the use of inside information on the stock market is unlikely to be the result of carelessness,[112] and it should normally be possible to infer the requisite intent from the circumstances. The concept of 'taking advantage' of the information should not be taken to imply that a profit must be made (or loss

---

[109] For a discussion of the rationale of this practice, see Davies, P L, 'The Take-over Bidder Exemption and the Policy of Disclosure' in Hopt, K J and Wymeersch, E (eds), *European Insider Dealing* (1991), 243–62. In the UK, the exemption is reflected in the Criminal Justice Act 1993, para 3 of Sch 1.

[110] These circumstances are excluded from the prohibition in the UK legislation by the Criminal Justice Act 1993, Sch 1.

[111] The UK implementing legislation, instead of incorporating the concept of 'taking advantage' in the offence of dealing, in effect builds it into the various defences in ss 52 and 53 of the Criminal Justice Act 1993. The Company Law Committee of The Law Society had expressed concern that the words 'taking advantage' 'may be construed as 'obtaining advantage'. It is, of course, possible to obtain an advantage without intent 'of any kind' (*Proposal for Directive—Co-ordinating Regulations on Insider Dealing*, January 1989, 3). The argument is unconvincing: 'taking advantage' has clear connotations of intent to turn to one's own benefit, and this interpretation is borne out by the other language versions, all of which use terms meaning at the least deliberate use and at the most exploitation of the information.

[112] Gaillard E, and Pingel, I, 'Les opérations d'initiés dans la Communauté Economique Européenne' (1990) 26 Revue trimestrielle de droit européen 329, 342. Ashe, M and Murphy, Y, *Insider Dealing* (1992) 50, note that Member States wishing to penalize insider dealing by negligence may do so, since the Directive is expressed to impose minimum standards: see Art 6. The notion of negligent insider dealing is somewhat elusive.

avoided):[113] there is nothing in the Directive to support the view that the insider who takes advantage of inside information for himself can avoid any penalty solely because the transaction was objectively not likely to make him any profit—incompetence cannot be an excuse for dishonesty.[114] The Explanatory Memorandum explained the criterion of taking advantage by reference to whether the insider's 'decision to buy or sell . . . has been taken in the light of [the inside] information. If a transaction is not triggered by inside information, therefore, it is not covered by the prohibition'.

Note finally that Article 2(4) excludes from the ambit of the Directive 'transactions carried out in pursuit of monetary, exchange-rate or public debt-management policies' by or on behalf of a State or its central bank or equivalent. This is the only exception provided for as such in the Directive.[115] It clearly covers Government activities in managing the economy, but would not extend to, for example, a sale of shares by a Government on a privatization.[116]

Disclosing

Article 3(a) requires Member States to prohibit primary insiders[117] who possess inside information from disclosing that information to any third party 'unless such disclosure is made in the normal course of the exercise of his employment, profession or duties'. No guidance is given as to when disclosure of inside information will be regarded as made 'in the normal course . . .', although the preamble makes the somewhat sweeping statement: 'communication of inside information to an authority, in order to enable it to ensure that the provisions of this Directive or other provisions in force are respected, obviously cannot be covered by the prohibitions laid down by this Directive'.[118]

The prohibition is—subject to the explicit qualification—an absolute one against disclosure, so that it will catch an insider even if he is not aware that the informa-

---

[113] The French insider dealing legislation originally included the same concept (*exploitation*); academic opinion was divided on the question whether a separate intention to profit was required, and the courts answered it in the negative. See Gaillard and Pingel (n 112 above) 343, and Pingel, I, 'The EC Directive of 1989' in Gaillard, E, *Insider Trading: The Laws of Europe, the United States and Japan* (1992) 14–15.

[114] Gaillard and Pingel (n 112 above) 343–4.

[115] This does not mean that defences provided for by national laws are necessarily contrary to the Directive: to the extent that such defences exempt conduct in which all the numerous essential elements of the offence are not present, they reflect the Directive. See Tridimas, T, 'Insider Trading: European Harmonisation and National Law Reform' (1991) 40 ICLQ 919, 923. The provisions in the preamble relating to market-makers, stockbrokers and stabilization are sometimes described as exemptions, but as explained above they rather illustrate situations where there is no improper use of inside information, and hence the offence is not complete.

[116] This may not be wholly academic: in 1995 the London Stock Exchange, after criticizing the UK Treasury's decision to float the Government's stake in the electricity generating companies without disclosing that the industry's regulator was considering a review of the electricity pricing formula, was reported to have passed its file on the matter to the DTI for consideration of breaches of insider dealing legislation ('Stock Exchange Criticises Treasury' (1995) Practical Law for Companies, Vol VI, 9).

[117] Art 6 makes it clear that Member States may extend the prohibition to secondary insiders.

[118] 14th recital.

tion disclosed is inside information[119] and even if he has no cause to believe that it will be used.

Recommending or procuring

Primary insiders are in addition—and secondary insiders may be[120]—prohibited from 'recommending or procuring a third party, on the basis of . . . inside information, to acquire or dispose of' securities as defined.[121] This provision is clearly designed to root out 'tipping' at the source, as a corollary to the prohibition on dealing applying to the tippee. It goes further than the previous restriction on disclosing in that it does not require that the information itself be imparted, merely that a recommendation to deal be made. Like the restriction on disclosing, it is not necessary that the 'tipper' be aware that the information on the basis of which he makes his recommendation is inside information.[122]

The provision as drafted could circumscribe directors of both the offeror and the target company in a takeover bid since, unlike the prohibition against disclosing, this prohibition is not relaxed where the recommending or procuring is done 'in the normal course of the exercise of [the person's] employment, profession or duties'. Directors of the offeror could be prevented from recommending their company to bid, and directors of the target from recommending their company's shareholders to accept the offer, but not, apparently, from recommending their shareholders not to accept an offer for their shares in the context of a hostile bid. That the prohibition appears to extend to the first two situations is unfortunate: that it falls short of the third is anomalous and supports the view that this consequence of Article 3(b) was unintended.

Extending the provisions

Article 6 makes it clear that the Directive seeks to impose minimum standards, and that Member States may go further.[123] It states that they may adopt 'more stringent' or additional provisions than those laid down in the Directive, provided that such provisions are applied generally.[124] The Article specifies that in particular

---

[119] Contrast the UK legislation which, by virtue of s 57(1)(a) of the Criminal Justice Act 1993 which provides that a person has information as an insider if and only if 'it is, and he knows that it is, inside information', does not make disclosing an offence in the absence of such knowledge.

[120] Art 6.

[121] Art 3(b), implemented in the UK by the Criminal Justice Act 1993, s 52(2)(a), with the additional gloss, going beyond Art 3(b), that for the offence to be committed the insider must know or have reasonable cause to believe that the dealing would take place.

[122] See n 121 above, which applies equally to the UK implementation of this provision.

[123] Fornasier argues convincingly that Art 6 'refers to the scope of the prohibition of insider trading and to the penalties attached to the violation of such prohibitions' rather than the definition of 'insider' and 'inside information', which he considers 'precise enough to warrant uniform implementation in all Members States [and] so comprehensive that it is difficult to imagine what could be left, as far as the definition of insider trading is concerned, to Member States' discretion': Fornasier, R, 'The Directive on Insider Dealing' (1989–90) 13 Fordham International Law Journal 49, 163–4.

[124] i e in a non-discriminatory manner.

Member States may extend the scope of the prohibition on dealing, and extend to secondary insiders the prohibitions on disclosing and recommending.

Disclosure

If insider dealing involves the abuse of unpublished information, it is obvious that it can be tackled not only be prohibiting such abuse but also—and indeed more effectively—by restricting to the minimum the period during which any given information is unpublished. Article 7 seeks to complement the preceding Articles by extending to companies and undertakings whose transferable securities are admitted to trading on a market as defined in Article 1[125] a disclosure provision applying pursuant to an existing directive to companies whose shares are admitted to official listing on a stock exchange.[126] That provision, in Sch C to the Admissions Directive,[127] requires as follows:

The company must inform the public as soon as possible of any major new developments in its sphere of activity which are not public knowledge and which may, by virtue of their effect on its assets and liabilities or financial position or on the general course of its business, lead to substantial movements in the prices of its shares.[128]

There is provision for exemption by the competent authorities 'if the disclosure of particular information is such as to prejudice the legitimate interests of the company'.

The original Proposal was stricter, requiring issuers 'immediately [to] inform the public . . . of any circumstance or decision which would be likely to have a material effect on the price' of the securities.[129] The Economic and Social Committee considered that the requirement to inform the public 'immediately' was too onerous and that 'any circumstance or decision . . .' was too wide, and should be restricted to facts or decisions which 'concern the company'. The Council accepted the Committee's suggestion that the equivalent requirement in Sch C to the Admissions Directive should in preference be incorporated by reference.

---

[125] See p 317 above.

[126] The extension therefore is to companies and non-corporate issuers whose securities are admitted to trading on a secondary market.

[127] Council Directive (EEC) 79/279 of 5 March 1979 coordinating the conditions for the admission of securities to official stock exchange listing [1979] OJ L66/21, discussed at p 261 above.

[128] Para 5(a), implemented in the UK by the Traded Securities (Disclosure) Regulations 1994 (SI 1994/188) which extend to all companies and undertakings with securities traded on a 'regulated market' the disclosure obligation on listed companies set out in the London Stock Exchange's Listing Rules. For a discussion of problems of interpretation of the former version of the relevant rule (para 9.1), see King, P, 'Insider Dealer v CJA' [1994] Compliance Monitor 54. The rule has now been amended to reflect much more closely the wording of para 5(a) (Amendment No 4 to The London Stock Exchange's Listing Rules, 9 January 1995).

[129] Art 7(1). Art 7(2) contained an analogous relaxation to that in Para 5(a).

Enforcement[130]

Articles 8 to 10[131] establish a comprehensive framework for the enforcement of the insider dealing laws derived from the Directive. Each Member State is to designate one or more competent authorities to ensure[132] application of their implementing legislation and to give such authorities 'all supervisory and investigatory powers that are necessary for the exercise of their functions'.[133] The Explanatory Memorandum in the first draft stated that the authorities 'should have sufficiently wide investigative powers to be able to ascertain from financial intermediaries their clients' true identities' (para 6). Strangely, however, the first draft itself merely required the authorities to be given 'all such supervisory powers as may be necessary for the exercise of their duties', and it was for the Parliament to suggest adding the words 'and investigatory'. Member States are to inform the Commission of the authority designated, and the Commission is to notify the other Member States.[134] Member States must provide for past and present employees of the competent authorities to be bound by professional secrecy; information covered by professional secrecy may not be divulged to any person or authority unless the law so provides.[135]

Article 10(1) requires the competent authorities throughout the Community to cooperate with each other 'whenever necessary for the purpose of carrying out their duties'. To this end they are to exchange any information required for that purpose:[136] this duty takes precedence over the professional secrecy obligation imposed by Article 9, but information so exchanged is to be subject to that obligation in the hands of the recipient authority. Except with the consent of the authority communicating information and subject to the recipient authority's obligations in criminal proceedings, that authority may use information received pursuant to this provision only for the exercise of its functions

---

[130] Note that the Council of Europe Convention on Insider Trading, opened for signature on 20 April 1989, also provides for mutual assistance and the exchange of information among the signatories. The broader range of potential signatories (which may include non-European countries on the invitation of the Council: see Art 15(1)) means that the Convention (which is reflected in the UK by the Companies Act 1989, Pt III), may prove a useful complement to the enforcement powers provided by the Directive.

[131] Implemented in the UK by the Companies Act 1989, Pt III. For an interesting and positive critique of the enforcement provisions of the Directive, see Ruiz, L, 'European Community Directive on Insider Dealing: A Model for Effective Enforcement of Prohibitions on Insider Trading in International Securities Markets' (1995) 33 Columbia Journal of Transnational Law 217, 240–2.

[132] If necessary in collaboration with other authorities.   [133] Art 8.   [134] Art 8(1).

[135] Art 9.

[136] Hopt asserts that it is clear from the German text (*erforderlichen*) that 'required' is to be understood as 'necessary': Hopt, K J, 'The European Insider Dealing Directive' in Hopt, K J and Wymeersch, E (eds), European Insider Dealing (1991) 146, n 53. Unfortunately there is no consistency in the various language versions. The Dutch (*vereiste*), Italian (*richieste*) and Portuguese (*requeridas*) terms suggest 'required' in the sense of 'requested, asked for'; the Spanish (*necesarias*), Danish (*nødvendige*) and French (*requis*) suggest 'necessary'; the Greek (*apaitoumenes*), like the English, is ambiguous and can mean either.

under Article 8(1) and in the context of proceedings relating to the exercise of those functions.[137]

The duty to exchange information required applies even where the request concerns actions which are not prohibited by the laws of the State receiving the request because it has not, although the State making the request has, made use of the options in Article 5 (territorial jurisdiction) or the second sentence of Article 6 (power to extend scope of primary prohibition and prohibit secondary insiders from disclosing or recommending).[138] The authorities may however refuse to act on a request for information where communication may adversely affect the 'sovereignty, security or public policy of the State addressed' or where legal proceedings are in process or final judgment has been given in respect of the same actions and against the same persons in the State addressed.[139]

Provisions for Further Development

There are two Articles which pave the way for extending or modifying the effect of the Directive. Article 11 provides that the Community may, in conformity with the Treaty, conclude agreements with non-member countries on the matters governed by the Directive. This provision appears simple and straightforward and indeed most commentators pass over it without comment. The use of the word 'may', however, implies that it purports to confer competence on the Community. If so, it is otiose, since the Court of Justice has made it clear that the Community in any event has such competence: '[W]henever Community law has created for the institutions of the Community powers within its internal system for the purpose of attaining a specific objective, the Community has authority to enter into the international commitments necessary for the attainment of that objective even in the absence of an express provision in that connexion'.[140] Until it has done so, the Member States are competent to do so, provided that there are no common rules likely to be affected and that they do not in so doing interfere with future developments of Community law.[141] Since it adds nothing of substance, the Article is therefore presumably intended merely as a statement of policy, meaning that 'the Community is prepared to conclude appropriate agreements on insider dealing with willing third countries'.[142]

---

[137] Hopt states that this is 'an important attempt to isolate the information given from tax authorities': ibid, 146.

[138] Art 10(1). Oddly, the option in the 1st sentence of Art 6, which provides that Member States may adopt more stringent provisions in general, is not mentioned in this context.

[139] Art 10(2).

[140] Opinion 1/76 *Opinion Given Pursuant to Article 228(1) of the EEC Treaty ('Laying-up Fund Opinion')* [1977] ECR 741, 755.

[141] This interpretation appears to be corroborated by the Declaration of the Commission for the Council Protocol No 9 concerning Art 11, according to Hopt (n 136 above), 147, and Bergmans, B, *Inside Information and Securities Trading* (1991) 77.

[142] Fornasier, R, 'The Directive on Insider Dealing' (1989–90) 13 Fordham International Law Journal 49, 174; Fornasier discusses the issue in depth at 170–6.

Article 12 adds to the powers of the Contact Committee set up by the Admissions Directive,[143] providing that it shall also have as its function: '(a) to permit regular consultation on any practical problems which arise from the application of this Directive and on which exchanges of view are deemed useful; (b) to advise the Commission, if necessary, on any additions or amendments to be made to this Directive'.

The Commission expressed its hope in the Explanatory Memorandum of the first draft that 'by providing a forum for regular contacts between the authorities in the different Member States this Committee should . . . promote effective cooperation between those authorities, which should help in combating insider trading'.

Sanctions

Article 13 provides: 'Each Member State shall determine the penalties to be applied for infringement of the measures taken pursuant to this Directive. The penalties shall be sufficient to promote compliance with those measures.'

The first draft of Article 13 consisted merely in the first sentence of the final version set out above. Both the Economic and Social Committee and the European Parliament stressed the desirability of harmonized penalties: the Committee suggested that the Commission 'should explore every possibility offered by the Contact Committee . . . to ensure that violations are penalised in a comparable manner from country to country', and the Parliament proposed adding to the Article a requirement that the Commission put forward proposals for harmonizing the penalties imposed in each Member State and a provision stating: 'Appropriate civil remedies for the purpose of this article shall involve the payment of an indemnity by those profiting by the use of inside information to those who can show that they have thereby suffered a loss.' The Commission's amended Proposal, although it did not incorporate the Parliament's suggested amendment, included a requirement that the penalties be 'sufficiently dissuasive to ensure respect for those measures'. Perhaps unsurprisingly, the Council rejected that amendment, stating that 'no matter how heavy penalties were, they could never ensure absolute compliance with the measures taken under the Directive'.[144]

Although there is a satisfying conceptual symmetry in the idea of harmonized penalties, the drafters of the Directive were fettered by the reluctance of the Community to prescribe criminal penalties, regarded by Member States as encroachments on their sovereignty. Article 13 therefore leaves Member States

---

[143] Cited in n 127 above. Art 20 sets up a Contact Committee 'to facilitate the harmonized implementation of this Directive through regular consultation on any practical problems arising from its application and on which exchanges of view are deemed useful . . . to advise the Commission, if necessary, on any supplements or adjustments to be made to this Directive'.

[144] SEC (89) 1207 final, SYN 85, 20 July 1986, at 6, cited by Pingel, I, in Gaillard, E, *Insider Trading: The Laws of Europe, the United States and Japan* (1992), 19, n 111. It is questionable whether the final criterion of sufficiency to promote compliance is much easier to apply.

complete discretion to determine sufficient penalties.[145] These clearly include criminal penalties, and *a fortiori* civil sanctions supplementing criminal penalties, provided in either case that the remedies can be shown to be 'sufficient' to promote compliance.[146] Whether the provision of private remedies—for example a right to compensation—alone would properly implement Article 13 is unclear. Although it is arguable that compensation is not a 'penalty',[147] the word 'penalty' in the English version of the Article is misleading:[148] almost all the other language versions use the wider term 'sanction',[149] which clearly covers private remedies provided, as always, that they are sufficient to promote compliance. It is interesting to note that the Irish implementing legislation imposes (in addition to criminal penalties) civil liability on primary and secondary insiders, providing for compensation of a party to a transaction who has lost and for an account at the instance of the issuer of the securities.[150] Portugal also provides for the insider to indemnify the injured parties.[151] The yardstick of sufficiency to promote compliance is, like any other requirement of the Directive, ultimately susceptible to review by the European Court of Justice; apart from extreme cases of manifestly lax sanctions, however, it is difficult to see on what basis the Court could assess the sufficiency of a particular measure.

[145] See Tridimas, T, 'Insider Trading: European Harmonisation and National Law Reform' (1991) 40 ICLQ 919, 932–7 for a full and interesting discussion of the issue of remedies.

[146] It is interesting to note that in 1996 both the London Stock Exchange and the former Securities and Investments Board (now the Financial Services Authority) called for changes so that there were civil law remedies against insider dealing, in view of the difficulties of bringing successful prosecutions under the criminal law. The Labour Government elected in the UK in 1997 is thought to be receptive to the idea, and the UK Treasury is reportedly looking at civil penalties.

[147] See e g Fornasier (n 142 above) 166.

[148] Wymeersch, E, 'The Regulation of Insider Dealing within the European Community' in *Insider Dealing: Papers from the I.C.E.L. Conference October 1990* (1990) 17; Bergmans (n 141 above) 76.

[149] The German, which uses a slightly different grammatical structure, uses the verb *ahnden*, to punish, in the first sentence and the word *Sanktionen* in the second.

[150] Companies Act 1990, s 109(1). See further Rider, B and Ashe, M, 'The Insider Dealing Directive' in Andenas, M and Kenyon-Slade, S (eds), *EC Financial Market Regulation and Company Law* (1993) 235–7. For a discussion of possible civil remedies in the UK under provisions other than the insider dealing legislation, see Tridimas (n 145 above) 934–5; Rider, B and Ashe, T M, *Insider Crime* (1993) 61–91 and Hannigan, B, *Insider Dealing* (2nd edn, 1994) 128–53.

[151] Commercial Companies' Code 1986, Art 449. See Gaillard (n 144 above) 154.

XVI

Freedom of Establishment of Companies— Introduction[1]

Article 52 of the Treaty requires Member States to abolish restrictions on the freedom of establishment of nationals of a Member State in the territory of another Member State. Freedom of establishment is expressed to include the right to take up and pursue activities as self-employed persons and to set up and manage companies or firms as defined by Article 58[2] under the conditions laid down for its own nationals by the law of the country where such establishment is effected. Restrictions on the setting up of agencies, branches or subsidiaries by nationals of any Member State established in the territory of any Member State are specifically required to be abolished. In considering the concept of freedom of establishment of companies, Article 52 must be read in conjunction with Article 58, which, in addition to defining 'companies or firms',[3] provides that companies or firms formed in accordance with the law of a Member State and having their registered office, central administration or principal place of business within the Community are, for the purposes of, inter alia, Article 52, to be treated in the same way as natural persons who are nationals of Member States.[4]

As will be seen however this attempted assimilation of companies to natural persons in the context of freedom of establishment has its limits. As a result of the artificial nature of the corporate entity, it is difficult simply to extrapolate to companies principles which, at the conceptual level, are easy to apply to individuals who generally have an unequivocal nationality, who may physically move across borders and who are unlikely, having done so, to be met by a refusal to recognize

---

[1] See generally Wouters, J and Schneider, H (eds), *Current Issues of Cross-Border Establishment of Companies in the European Union* (1995); Tridimas, T, 'The Case-Law of the European Court of Justice on Corporate Entities' (1993) 13 Yearbook of European Law 335; Cath, I G F, 'Freedom of Establishment of Companies: a New Step towards Completion of the Internal Market' (1986) 6 Yearbook of European Law 247; Cath, I G F, 'Free Movement of Legal Persons' in *Free Movement of Persons in Europe: Legal Problems and Experiences* (1993), 450; and Loussouarn, Y, 'Le droit d'établissement des sociétés' [1990] Revue trimestrielle de droit européen 229.

[2] As defined by Art 58: see further below. [3] See further below.

[4] The Court confirmed in Case 182/83 *Fearon v Irish Land Commission* [1984] ECR 3677, para 8, and C–70/95 *Sodemare v Regione Lombardia* [1997] ECR I–3395 para 25, that Art 58, by assimilating, for the purpose of giving effect to the chapter relating to the right of establishment, companies or firms as defined to natural persons who are nationals of one of the Member States, simply defines the class of persons to whom the right of establishment applies: it does not give rise to substantive rights different from those secured by the other provisions of Chapter 2, and in particular by Art 52. See also the Opinion of Fennelly AG in *Sodemare*, para 21.

their lawful existence. That has two consequences for an analysis of the scope of the freedom of establishment for companies.

First, the extensive case-law of the Court of Justice on individuals' freedom of establishment, although relevant in so far as it may involve restrictions on business activity, is not specifically related to companies, and is accordingly not considered except where it is of direct significance to companies' freedom of establishment. In contrast, the relatively few cases directly concerning companies are considered in some detail.[5]

Second, the most cursory discussion of companies' freedom of establishment will at an early stage run up against the related issue of recognition of foreign companies, in the broad sense of how Member States' laws deal with foreign companies seeking to relocate into their territory. Unlike natural persons, companies are creatures of the law and, in the present state of Community law, creatures of national law: they exist only by virtue of the varying national legislation which determines their incorporation and functioning.[6] Beyond the national confines of a company's State of incorporation, its existence depends on whether the other State is prepared to recognize it as a corporate entity. Although recognition is perhaps strictly speaking more a question of conflict of laws than of establishment, and although for a number of sound pragmatic reasons the issue arises rarely in practice, an awareness of at least the major contours of the field is essential for an understanding of some of the difficulties which arise in connection with the freedom of establishment of companies. The two conflicting approaches to the recognition of foreign companies which prevail in the Community are summarily sketched below;[7] the two Community initiatives to date seeking to grapple with the problems arising from the conflict are briefly discussed in chapter XVIII.

Corporate Nationality and Residence

A company will normally have some form of official address in the State in which it was incorporated, which will be registered in an official registry and may also be

---

[5] For a list of the extensive early literature on the freedom of establishment of companies, see Smit, H and Herzog, P E (eds), *The Law of the European Economic Community—A Commentary on the EEC Treaty* (1979), vol 2, 637–9. I G F Cath maps this shift of emphasis from companies to individuals, describing how, subsequent to the early cases giving Art 52 direct effect *vis-à-vis* private individuals, they have become 'the pioneers of cross-border establishment and, as a consequence, Article 58 of the Treaty dealing with the right of establishment of companies has taken a role secondary to that of Article 52': 'Freedom of Establishment of Companies: a New Step Towards Completion of the Internal Market' (1986) 6 Yearbook of European Law 247.

[6] Case 81/87 *The Queen v HM Treasury and Commissioners of Inland Revenue, ex p Daily Mail and General Trust PLC* [1988] ECR 5483, para 19.

[7] See further Stein, E, *Harmonization of European Company Laws* (1971) ch 2 and 396–402; Boyle, A J, 'The Recognition of Companies in the EEC' in Goode, R M and Simmonds, K R (eds), *Commercial Operations in Europe* (1978); Cath (n 5 above); Reindl, A, 'Companies in the European Community: Are the Conflict-of-Law Rules Ready for 1992?' (1990) 11 Michigan Journal of International Law 1270; Commission of the European Communities: *Study on Transfer of the Head Office of a Company from one Member State to another* (1993).

specified in its statutes. In the United Kingdom and Ireland this will be its registered office; in those States, the registered office need have no connection with the place where the company conducts its business or is managed (indeed the registered office is frequently no more than a brass plate in a solicitors' or accountants' premises, merely serving to identify an address where formal documents may be validly served on the company and where it keeps certain documents and registers required by the law to be available for inspection by the public). The incorporation theory, applied by the United Kingdom, Ireland, the Netherlands and Denmark,[8] regards a company as always subject to the law of the State where it is incorporated and where its registered office is situated, wherever the company's affairs are conducted or managed. It is not possible to change the law governing the company (although it may of course be dissolved and a new company incorporated in another State). If a company incorporated in one State moves its centre of operations to another, this gives rise to no conceptual problems, although it may have practical consequences.[9] Thus the incorporation theory accepts that a company's nationality and residence, like those of a natural person, may be severed.

Most continental Member States[10] however regard the locus of the company's central management and control, or 'real seat' (*siège réel*), as the factor which determines the law to which a company is subject. There is no apposite company law term for this concept in English since, as a result of the United Kingdom's application of the incorporation theory, the concept has no particular relevance in company law. The term 'central management and control' is drawn from tax terminology, where historically it was used as the test of a company's fiscal residence.[11] It is also the term used in the United Kingdom legislation enacting the Brussels Convention,[12] which uses a similar concept.[13] Other terms used by

[8] Cath, I G F, makes the interesting point that the theory of incorporation is especially popular in countries with a long-standing commercial maritime tradition where an open attitude to trade is expected to be met with reciprocity, as opposed to the more mercantilist attitude adopted in other countries: see 'Freedom of Establishment of Companies' (n 5 above) at 251. Latty, E R, reports that 'England apparently was the Delaware of the second half of the nineteenth century for French enterprises seeking to incorporate but to avoid the rigorous French law. In one litigated case, it appears that an attempt was even made to anglicize the Moulin Rouge': 'Pseudo-Foreign Corporations' (1955) 65 Yale Law Journal 137, n 130.

[9] e g, it may trigger tax liabilities or subject the company to disclosure requirements in the host State.

[10] Elegantly described as 'the juristic descendants of the Roman empire' by Conard, A F, 'Company Laws of the European Communities from an American Viewpoint' in Schmitthoff, C M (ed), *The Harmonisation of European Company Law* (1973). For further details of the variations on the real-seat theme applied by the different States, see the Commission's *Study on Transfer of the Head Office of a Company* (n 7 above) 5–13 and Frommel, S N, 'The Real Seat Doctrine and Dual-Resident Companies under German Law: Another View' [1990] European Taxation 267. For a clear analysis of the concept of real seat see Latty (n 8 above) 166–72.

[11] Companies incorporated in the UK are now resident for tax purposes in the UK: Finance Act 1988, s 66(1).

[12] Convention of 27 September 1968 on Jurisdiction and the Enforcement of Judgments in Civil and Commercial Matters [1978] OJ L 304/77.

[13] See Art 53 of the Convention and the Schlosser report para 75, and Civil Judgments and Jurisdiction Act 1982, s 42.

commentators include central administration, headquarters and head office[14] (although these terms risk underplaying the importance in civil law countries of the locus of shareholders' general meetings for determining a company's real seat).

The *siège réel* is distinguished from the *siège statutaire*. 'Registered office' is frequently given as the English translation of *siège statutaire*; the terms are not however precisely synonymous. The *siège statutaire* is simply the place where the company's statutes establish its seat and where the seat is accordingly presumed to be located. If the company's real seat appears to be located elsewhere, it is the location of the real seat which is significant and the *siège statutaire* is regarded as *fictif*. The law governing the company may be changed only by moving the company's real seat, which may not be permitted by the laws of the Member State concerned. In contrast to the incorporation theory, therefore, the real seat theory inextricably entwines a company's nationality and residence.

Under the 'real seat' theory, a company must in general comply with the full requirements of company law applicable in the State where it has its real seat. Since those laws include legislation governing incorporation and the location of the company's registered office or equivalent, the logical extension of this theory—applied in some States—requires that a company's real seat be located in the State in accordance with whose laws it has been validly formed. If a company incorporated in one Member State seeks to move its real seat to another State which applies the real seat theory, the latter State may[15] not recognize the company as validly constituted and lawfully operating unless it is reconstituted as a company incorporated in and with its registered office in that State, which may have, as mildly described by one commentator, '*des conséquences fiscales décourageantes*',[16] in addition to commercial implications such as the imposition of personal liability on directors and shareholders. Moreover, even where a real seat State is prepared to recognize foreign companies it will normally require them to be subject to certain provisions of its national company law.

There is an obvious conflict not only between the incorporation theory and the real seat theory but also between the real seat theory and the principle of unfettered freedom of establishment of companies. These issues are explored further in chapter XVIII.

The Treaty Provisions

Article 52 reads as follows:

Within the framework of the provisions set out below, restrictions on the freedom of establishment of nationals of a Member State in the territory of another Member State shall be

---

[14] See also Latty, 'Pseudo-Foreign Corporations' (1955) 65 Yale Law Journal 137 where he suggests the term 'brain or nerve-centre' (417).

[15] Some States may recognize the incoming company, either pursuant to a bilateral recognition convention or provided that the transfer has been approved by a specified majority (sometimes 100%) of the shareholders.

[16] Boutard-Labarde, M–C, case-note on Case 81/87 *The Queen v HM Treasury and Commissioners of Inland Revenue, ex p Daily Mail and General Trust PLC* [1989] Journal de droit international 428, 430.

abolished by progressive stages in the course of the transitional period. Such progressive abolition shall also apply to restrictions on the setting-up of agencies, branches or subsidiaries by nationals of any Member State established in the territory of any Member State.

Freedom of establishment shall include the right to take up and pursue activities as self-employed persons and to set up and manage undertakings, in particular companies or firms within the meaning of the second paragraph of Article 58, under the conditions laid down for its own nationals by the law of the country where such establishment is effected, subject to the provisions of the Chapter relating to capital.

Article 58 provides:

Companies or firms formed in accordance with the law of a Member State and having their registered office, central administration or principal place of business within the Community shall, for the purposes of this Chapter, be treated in the same way as natural persons who are nationals of Member States.

'Companies or firms' means companies or firms constituted under civil or commercial law, including cooperative societies, and other legal persons governed by public or private law, save for those which are non-profit-making.

It is helpful to reformulate Article 52 as it applies, by virtue of Article 58, to companies. For ease of reference, the definition of companies imported by Article 58 has been set out in italics. The Articles read together provide essentially that:

(1)   restrictions on the freedom of establishment of *companies formed in accordance with the law of a Member State and having their registered office, central administration or principal place of business within the Community* in the territory of another Member State shall be abolished;

(2)   as shall restrictions on the setting-up of agencies, branches or subsidiaries by *companies formed in accordance with the law of a Member State and having their registered office, central administration or principal place of business within the Community* established in the territory of any Member State;

(3)   freedom of establishment shall include the right to take up and pursue activities as self-employed persons and to set up and manage undertakings, in particular companies,[17] under the conditions laid down for its own nationals by the law of the country where such establishment is effected.

The third limb is complemented by Article 221, which requires Member States to accord nationals of other Member States the same treatment as their own nationals as regards participation in the capital of companies or firms within the meaning of Article 58.

It should be noted that it was held at an early stage—and has recently been reaffirmed in a case relating to the application of the Articles to companies—that Article 52 has direct effect.[18]

[17]   As defined in the second para of Art 58.
[18]   Case 2/74 *Reyners v Belgium* [1974] ECR 631; Case 71/76 *Thieffry v Conseil de l'Ordre des Avocats à la Cour de Paris* [1977] ECR 765, cited in Case C–1/93 *Halliburton Services v Staatssecretaris van Financiën* [1994] ECR I–1137.

Companies within the Scope of the Provisions

Article 58 refers to companies or firms (a) constituted under civil or commercial law, including co-operative societies, and other legal persons governed by public or private law, save for those which are non-profit-making (b) set up under the law of a Member State and (c) having their registered office, central administration or principal place of business within the Community. These three elements will be considered in turn.

Types of company covered

It was necessary to include a detailed definition in Article 58 because the term 'company' and its various linguistic equivalents do not have a uniform meaning throughout the Community: in some Member States, the concept embraces certain forms of partnership, whereas in others it is limited to entities with a genuine corporate persona.

The reference to civil and commercial law reflects the traditional continental view of these two areas as separate branches of the law. The reference to legal persons governed by public law extends the rights conferred by the article to State-controlled industries, economically important in many Member States.

The reference to firms is misleading to common law lawyers, suggesting as it does non-corporate entities: the terms of the Article suggest that only entities with a legal personality are covered, and thus that, for example, English law partnerships are not within the scope of the provisions (although of course the partners, *qua* natural persons, will be able to invoke freedom of establishment in their own right). The position is not however entirely clear, since there are many partnership-like forms of association in other Member States which, although they may not have legal personality *stricto sensu*, have capacity to hold assets and have rights and obligations in their own right.[19] It is interesting to note that the Convention on the Mutual Recognition of Companies and Legal Persons[20] uses the criterion of capacity to have rights and obligations to define the companies to which it applies.[21]

The terms of the Article would appear to exclude associations and organizations operating other than for profit, consistently with the exclusion from Article 48 of workers who are not remunerated and the exclusion from Article 59 of services not provided for remuneration. The Commission is currently seeking to regulate that

---

[19] For further discussion of the scope of the definition, see Smit, H, and Herzog, P (eds), *The Law of the European Economic Community—A Commentary on the EEC Treaty* (1979), vol 2, 641–2, and the articles cited; Cerexhe, E, *Le droit européen—La libre circulation des personnes et des entreprises* (1982) 40–1; and Burrows, F, *Free Movement in European Community Law* (1987); Wouters, J, 'The European Court of Justice and Fiscal Barriers to Companies' Cross-Border Establishment' in Wouters, J and Schneider, H (eds), *Current Issues of Cross-Border Establishment of Companies in the European Union* (1995).

[20] See ch XVIII.   [21] Art 1.

sector by way of a separate regulation on European associations, cooperatives and mutual companies.[22]

Formed in accordance with the law of a Member State

This requirement has been described by one commentator[23] as a significant concession to the incorporation theory. It is more likely that the requirement was merely intended to ensure that only companies incorporated within the Community could benefit from freedom of establishment within the Community, an understandable aim with no obvious conflict of laws angle.

Registered office, central administration or principal place of business within the Community

The beneficiaries of the freedom of establishment enshrined in the Treaty are, in the case of natural persons, defined as 'nationals of a Member State'.[24] As explained above, Member States subscribe to two irreconcilable theories determining the nationality of companies by reference in effect to the location of the registered office or the central administration (or principal place of business),[25] and there are genuine difficulties in evolving a Community theory of corporate nationality which bridges the gap between these two approaches. The Treaty could not therefore simply refer to corporate nationals of a Member State: instead, it seeks to lay down criteria for determining corporate nationality which are acceptable to holders of both theories. The Court of Justice has stated that it is the company's seat in the sense of these three factors which is the connecting factor determining a company's nationality[26] and that the Treaty places the three factors on an equal footing.[27]

These three alternative requirements have been interpreted by some commentators as abandoning the real seat theory in favour of the incorporation theory on the basis that, since the three requirements are alternatives and have equal weight, a company with its registered office but not its real seat in the Community would

[22] Amended Proposal for a Council Reg (EEC) on the statute for a European association [1993] OJ C236/1, amended Proposal for a Council Reg (EEC) on the statute for a European cooperative society [1993] OJ C236/17 and amended Proposal for a Council Reg (EEC) on the statute for a European mutual society [1993] OJ C236/40: all three proposals in COM (93) 252 final, 6 July 1993. See also Richards, H, 'What is EC Corporate Law?' in *Corporate Law—The European Dimension* (1991), 3.

[23] Benoit-Moury, A, in 'Droit européen des sociétés et interprétations des juridictions communautaires' [1993] Revue de droit international et de droit comparé 106, 111.

[24] Art 52.

[25] 'Principal établissement', of which 'principal place of business' is the translation, is used in Belgian law to mean a company's real seat. See further Stein, E, *Harmonization of European Company Laws* (1971), 28, n 17.

[26] Case 270/83 *Commission v France* [1986] ECR 273, para 18.

[27] Case 81/87 *The Queen v HM Treasury and Commissioners of Inland Revenue, ex p Daily Mail and General Trust PLC* [1988] ECR 5483, para 21.

fall within the definition.[28] The opposite argument would of course equally hold, although the scenario is perhaps less likely: a company with its registered office outside the Community and its real seat within it would also be covered. It seems likely that the alternatives were included to satisfy all Member States, whichever theory they applied, rather than with a view to endorsing one of the prevailing theories at the expense of the other (it may be thought particularly unlikely that it was intended to abandon the theory applied by five of the six original Member States). This appears to be the view taken by the Court of Justice, which stated in *The Queen v HM Treasury and Commissioners of Inland Revenue, ex p Daily Mail and General Trust PLC*:

. . . the legislation of the Member States varies widely in regard both to the factor providing a connection to the national territory required for the incorporation of a company and the question whether a company incorporated under the legislation of a Member State may subsequently modify that connecting factor. Certain States require that not merely the registered office but also the real head office,[29] that is to say the central administration of the company, should be situated on their territory, and the removal of the central administration from that territory thus presupposes the winding-up of the company with all the consequences that winding-up entails in company law and tax law. The legislation of other States permits companies to transfer their central administration to a foreign country but certain of them, such as the United Kingdom, make that right subject to certain restrictions, and the legal consequences of a transfer, particularly in regard to taxation, vary from one Member State to another. The Treaty has taken account of that variety in national legislation. In defining, in Article 58, the companies which enjoy the right of establishment, the Treaty places on the same footing, as connecting factors, the registered office, central administration and principal place of business of a company.[30]

Concern has been voiced[31] that the inclusion of the registered office alone as a sufficient link with the Community to confer on a company the right of establishment in other Member States would lead to an invasion of American and Japanese companies forming a subsidiary, managed from the parent's home country, in one Member State and using it as a springboard for Community-wide establishment notwithstanding the absence of any genuine economic link between the original subsidiary and any Member State. Despite the dramatic pictures painted of such developments,[32] there appears to be no evidence, after forty years of Article 58, that this has occurred. The Council's General Programme for the Abolition of

---

[28] Cerexhe, E, *Le droit européen—La libre circulation des personnes et des enterprises* (1982) 42; Loussouarn, Y, 'Le droit d'établissement des sociétés' (1990) 26 Revue trimestrielle de droit européen 229, 236.

[29] The French text reads *siège réel*; 'real seat' would perhaps have been a preferable rendering.

[30] Case 81/87 [1988] ECR 5483, paras 20 and 21.

[31] Particularly by the French. See eg Loussouarn, Y (n 28 above) and Scholten, Y, 'Company Law in Europe' (1967) 4 CMLR 377, 386, describing an unsuccessful attempt by the French delegation during the Treaty negotiations to write a caveat into Art 58 excluding foreign-controlled companies from the establishment chapter.

[32] See e g the desperate language of Loussouarn, '*Comment pallier les conséquences néfastes d'un tel laxisme?*': ibid, 236.

Restrictions on the Freedom of Establishment[33] however took this perceived threat sufficiently seriously to build into the Programme a requirement for an economic link with the Community before a company could avail itself of its right to create secondary establishments. It did this in its definition of beneficiaries of the Programme, conferring the right of establishment on companies within the meaning of the first paragraph of Article 58 but with the proviso, in the case of companies wishing to exercise their right of secondary establishment by setting up agencies, branches or subsidiaries in a Member State, that 'where only the seat prescribed by their statutes[34] is situated within the Community or in an overseas country or territory, their activity shows a real and continuous link with the economy of a Member State or of an overseas country or territory'.[35]

It is doubtful however whether this provision adds anything to the wording of the Treaty provisions: Article 58 does not stand alone, but has to be read in conjunction with Article 52, and the latter Article already restricts the right to set up secondary establishments to 'nationals of any Member State established in the territory of any Member State'. Extrapolating that statement to the corporate context means that the Treaty already requires that a company be established in one Member State before it can assert its right to create secondary establishments.[36] The Court of Justice has ruled that 'the concept of establishment within the meaning of Article 52 et seq. of the Treaty involves the actual pursuit of an economic activity through a fixed establishment in another Member State for an indefinite period';[37] although that ruling was not addressed to the situation in the State of origin, there is no reason to suppose that less would be required in that context.[38]

---

[33] 18 December 1961, OJ Spec Ed IX, Resolutions of the Council and of the Representatives of the Member States, 7. The Court of Justice has stated that the General Programme 'provides useful guidance for the implementation of the relevant provisions of the Treaty' (Case 71/76 *Thieffry v Conseil de l'Ordre des Avocats à la Cour de Paris* [1977] ECR 765, para 14 of the judgment and Case 79/85 *Segers v Bedrijfsvereniging voor Bank- en Verzekeringswezen, Groothandel en Vrije Beroepen* [1986] ECR 2375, para 15).

[34] *siège statutaire* in the French.

[35] There is a similar provision in the (unratified) 1968 Convention on the Mutual Recognition of Companies and Bodies Corporate, Art 3 of which permits Contracting States not to recognize a company whose real seat is outside the territories covered by the Convention if it has 'no genuine link with the economy of one of the said territories'. See further ch XVIII.

[36] This interpretation is borne out by the *travaux préparatoires* for Art 52, the text of which is accompanied by the comment: '*Cette disposition est rédigée de façon à exclure du bénéfice de la liberté d'établissement les ressortissants des Etats tiers, et, en ce qui concerne la seule liberté de créer des agences, des succursales et des filiales des ressortissants des Etats Membres qui ne sont pas établis à l'intérieur du marché commun.*' (This provision is drafted so as to exclude from the benefit of the freedom of establishment nationals of third countries and, solely in so far as concerns the freedom to create agencies, branches and subsidiaries, nationals of Member States who are not established within the common market.) See Scholten (n 31 above) 385.

[37] Case C–221/89, *The Queen v Secretary of State for Transport, ex p Factortame* [1991] ECR I–3905, para 20. See also Case C–55/94 *Gebhard v Consiglio dell'Ordine degli Avvocati e Procuratori di Milano* [1995] ECR I–4165, para 25 of the judgment.

[38] Suggestions to the contrary in Case 79/85 *Segers v Bedrijfsvereniging voor Bank- en Verzekeringswezen, Groothandel en Vrije Beroepen* [1986] ECR 2375 are in this author's view attributable to the Court's flawed analysis of the true circumstances of that case: see further the discussion in ch XVII. It may be noted however that La Pergola AG took the contrary view in his Opinion of 16 July 1998 in Case C–212/97 *Centros Ltd v Erhvervs- og Selskabsstyrelsen*: see para 18.

XVII

Secondary Establishment—the Case-Law

A company may seek to establish itself in a Member State other than that where it is incorporated either by transferring its real seat (primary establishment) or by setting up agencies, branches or subsidiaries[1] (secondary establishment). It may be thought that the first limb of Article 52, which requires the abolition of restrictions on the freedom of establishment of nationals of a Member State in the territory of another Member State, would encompass restrictions on the primary establishment of companies. The Court ruled however in *The Queen v HM Treasury and Commissioners of Inland Revenue, ex p Daily Mail and General Trust PLC*[2] that Article 52 confers no such right on a company. There are in any event sound practical reasons why companies rarely seek to transfer their real seat. Far more common is the creation by a company of a secondary establishment in another Member State, and it is that aspect of corporate freedom of establishment which will be considered first.

Forms of Secondary Establishment

Article 52 lists agencies, branches or subsidiaries as the secondary establishments which companies established in one Member State are entitled by the Treaty to set up in another Member State. It appears however that that list is not exhaustive of the forms of secondary establishment covered by the provision: the Court of Justice in *Commission v Germany*[3] stated that it was sufficient to come within the scope of the provisions of the Treaty on the right of establishment that an undertaking of one Member State maintained a permanent presence in another, even if that pres-

---

[1] Taking a lesser stake in the capital of a company established in another Member State is not expressly protected by the freedom of establishment provisions of the Treaty, but Art 221 requires Member States to accord nationals of the other Member States the same treatment as their own nationals as regards participation in the capital of companies or firms within the meaning of Art 58. Although Art 58 does not apply to Art 221 (being expressed to apply for the purposes of Ch 3 of Title III of the Treaty), so that there is no formal requirement to treat companies as natural persons, the Court in Case 81/87 *The Queen v HM Treasury and Commissioners of Inland Revenue, ex p Daily Mail and General Trust PLC* [1988] ECR 5483 assumed that Art 221 would guarantee equal treatment of foreign corporate investors as well as natural persons: para 17.

[2] Cited in n 1 above; discussed in ch XVIII.

[3] Case 205/84 [1986] ECR 3755. See Edward, D, 'Establishment and Services: An Analysis of the Insurance Cases' (1987) 12 ELR 231 for detailed analysis of this and connected cases concerning regulation of the insurance sector.

ence did not take the form of a branch or agency, but was exercised through the medium (a) of a mere office managed by the undertaking's own staff or (b) of a person who was independent but authorized to act on a permanent basis for the undertaking as an agency would do.[4]

None of the terms 'agency', 'branch' or 'subsidiary' is defined. Some guidance may however be found in decisions of the Court of Justice on the terms 'branch, agency or other establishment' used in Article 5(5) of the Brussels Convention.[5] In *Somafer v Saar-Ferngas*[6] the Court ruled:

the concept of branch, agency or other establishment implies a place of business which has the appearance of permanency, such as the extension of a parent body, has a management and is materially equipped to negotiate business with third parties so that the latter, although knowing that there will if necessary be a legal link with the parent body, the head office of which is abroad, do not have to deal directly with such parent body but may transact business at the place of business constituting the extension.

Similarly in *SAR Schotte v Parfums Rothschild*[7] Advocate General Slynn made the following observations:

A branch . . . is as I see it an outpost of the main business for the latter's benefit on a continuing basis and subject to the control of the main business. 'Agency' and 'establishment' I read in very much the same sense as indicating a place of business subsidiary to the business of the main business, though 'establishment' may be somewhat wider than 'branch'. I do not read 'agency' as covering simply the place where an agent acts for a principal.[8]

There is no guidance as to the meaning of the term 'subsidiary'. The criterion of effective control may be thought to be a sensible yardstick.

The Case-law of the Court of Justice

In contrast to the limited and unsatisfactory case-law on companies' rights of primary establishment,[9] the Court of Justice has had occasion in a series of cases to rule on what constitutes unlawful restrictions on the setting-up of agencies, branches or subsidiaries. *Commission v France*[10] (the avoir fiscal case), *Segers v Bedrijfsvereniging voor Bank- en Verzekeringswezen, Groothandel en Vrije Beroepen*,[11] *The Queen v The*

---

[4] Para 21 of the judgment. The text set out above is not taken from the ECR, which contains an error of translation; it is the version suggested by Judge Edward in 'Establishment and Services' (n 3 above) 244.

[5] Convention of 27 September 1968 on Jurisdiction and the Enforcement of Judgments in Civil and Commercial Matters [1978] OJ L304/77.

[6] Case 33/78 [1978] ECR 2183. La Pergola AG strongly disputed the relevance of this decision to the interpretation of Art 58 in his Opinion in Case C–212/97 *Centros Ltd v Erhvervs- og Selskabsstyrelsen*, delivered on 16 July 1998, para 19. In the absence however of more direct guidance by the Court, it seems reasonable to take account of the Court's approach to interpreting the same concept albeit in a different context.

[7] Case 218/86 [1987] ECR 4905.   [8] At 4912.   [9] Considered in ch XVIII.
[10] Case 270/83 [1986] ECR 273.   [11] Case 79/85 [1986] ECR 2375.

Secretary of State for Transport, ex p Factortame[12] and *Commission v United Kingdom*,[13] *The Queen v Inland Revenue Commissioners, ex p Commerzbank AG*,[14] *Halliburton Services v Staatssecretaris van Financiën*,[15] *Commission v Italy*,[16] *Futura Participations SA and Singer v Administration des Contributions*[17] and *ICI v Colmer*[18] are considered below[19] (although as will become apparent, the *Segers* case on a correct analysis concerned primary rather than secondary establishment). Each case is analysed in some depth; there is then some discussion of the principles to be drawn from the case-law and of possible justifications for prima facie unlawful restrictions on secondary establishment.

Case 270/83 *Commission v France*[20]

This was the first case directly concerning the Treaty provisions on the freedom of establishment of companies. The Commission brought Article 169 proceedings against France, arguing that French legislation which (subject to any applicable double-taxation convention) restricted shareholders' tax credits in respect of dividends[21] received from French companies to persons having their habitual residence or seat[22] in France infringed Article 52, in that the credit was not available to French branches or agencies of insurance companies[23] established in other Member States on the same terms as applied to French companies.

---

[12] Case C–221/89 [1991] ECR I–3905.   [13] Case C–146/89 [1991] ECR I–3533.
[14] Case C–330/91 [1993] ECR I–4017.   [15] Case C–1/93 [1994] ECR I–1137.
[16] Case C–101/94 [1996] ECR I–2691.   [17] Case C–250/95 [1997] ECR I–2471.
[18] Case C–264/96; judgment of 16 July 1998.

[19] A majority of these cases, together with the *Daily Mail* case, considered below in the context of primary establishment, are tax cases. Further analysis of the case-law from a fiscal angle may be found in Farmer, P and Lyal, R, *EC Tax Law* (1994), 311–22; Keeling, E and Shipwright, A, 'Some Taxing Problems Concerning Non-Discrimination and the EC Treaty' (1995) 20 ELR 580; Lyons, T, 'Discrimination Against Individuals and Enterprises on Grounds of Nationality: Direct Taxation and the Court of Justice' (1995–96) 1 EC Tax Journal 27; Knobbe-Keuk, B, 'Restrictions on the Fundamental Freedoms Enshrined in the EC Treaty by Discriminatory Tax Provisions—Ban and Justification [1994] EC Tax Review 74; Terra, B and Wattel, P, *European Tax Law* (2nd edn, 1997) 31–55; Wouters, J, 'The Case-Law of the European Court of Justice on Direct Taxes: Variations upon a Theme' (1994) 1 Maastricht Journal of European and Comparative Law 179 and van Raad, K, 'The Impact of the EC Treaty's Fundamental Freedoms Provisions on EU Member States' Taxation in Border-crossing Situations—Current State of Affairs' [1995] EC Tax Review 190, as well as in the specific articles cited in connection with individual cases.

[20] For a vigorous criticism, see Berlin, D, 'Jurisprudence fiscale européenne' (1987) 23 Revue trimestrielle de droit européen 105, 114–23.

[21] Since dividends are paid out of profits which have already been subject to corporation tax, the tax credit seeks to avoid double taxation as income in the hands of the recipients. See Glineur, P, 'Les revenus des participations: la compatablité des régimes différentiels d'imposition des établissements stables et des filiales avec le Traité de Rome' [1987] Journal de droit fiscal 65, for a clear explanation of the fiscal background to this case.

[22] '*domicile réel ou siège social*'. The latter is wrongly translated throughout the Opinion and judgment as 'registered office'. See further n 29 below.

[23] The case was brought in relation to the insurance sector alone, in part because the Commission had received complaints only in respect of that sector: see para 7 of the judgment and para 4 of the Opinion of Mancini AG. The Court expressed concern at the narrowness of the action: see para 9 of

The Commission advanced two principal submissions. First, it claimed that the French rules were contrary to the second paragraph of Article 52 inasmuch as they discriminated against companies incorporated under the law of another Member State, since (a) they treated French insurance companies (including French subsidiaries of foreign companies) differently from French agencies and branches of foreign insurance companies (b) the criterion for the different treatment was the location of the company's seat; since a company's seat served in the same way as nationality to connect it to a given system, using it as a criterion amounted to distinguishing on the basis of nationality; moreover, taking account of residence[24] constituted disguised discrimination and (c) foreign companies were disadvantaged by the different treatment. Second, it contended that the rules constituted an indirect restriction on the freedom to set up secondary establishments contrary to the first paragraph of Article 52 in that the different tax treatment discouraged secondary establishment by means of agencies or branches rather than subsidiaries.

The Court dealt with the two arguments together, considering them to be closely linked.[25] It stressed that Article 52 was intended to ensure that all nationals of Member States who established themselves in another Member State, even by secondary establishment, received the same treatment as nationals of that State and it prohibited as a restriction on freedom of establishment any discrimination on grounds of nationality resulting from the legislation of the Member State.[26] It was common ground that the effect of the French rules was that insurance companies whose seat was in another Member State and who pursued their activities in France through branches or agencies were treated differently from those whose seat was in France.[27]

The French Government had argued that that difference was justified by objective differences between the positions of such companies, based on the internationally accepted essential distinction in tax law between residents and non-residents, which is to be found in all legal systems.[28] The Court rejected that argument, stating that the freedom of establishment granted by Article 52 to nationals of another Member State included, by virtue of Article 58, the right of companies or firms formed in accordance with the law of a Member State and having their registered office, central administration or principal place of business within the Community to pursue their activities in the Member State concerned through a branch or agency. In the case of companies, it was their seat[29] in the above-mentioned sense (of the three alternative links) that served as the connecting factor

the judgment. The rule in fact posed a particular problem for the insurance sector because of the strict requirements of insurance regulation relating to assets and reserves. See further the judgment, 289–90, para 4 of the Opinion and Edward, D, 'Establishment and Services: An Analysis of the Insurance Cases' (1987) 12 ELR 231.

[24] Since as a matter of French law the company's *siège social* determines its *domicile*.
[25] Para 15 of the judgment.   [26] Para 14.   [27] Para 16.   [28] Para 17.
[29] *Siège*, wrongly translated in the English version of the judgment as 'registered office' (*siège statutaire*). Unfortunately the translation error has cast a long shadow, reaching several subsequent judgments and numerous commentaries on the case-law on Arts 52 and 58.

with the legal system of a particular State, like nationality in the case of natural persons. Article 58 would accordingly be deprived of all meaning were the Member State in which a company sought to establish itself able to treat it differently solely because its seat was situated in another Member State.[30]

The Court left open the possibility that a distinction based on the location of a company's seat (or the place of residence of a natural person) may under certain conditions be justified in an area such as tax law, but ruled it out in this case. The French law did not distinguish between companies with their seat in France and branches and agencies of companies with their seat abroad for the purpose of assessing their liability to corporation tax,[31] thus in effect admitting that there was no objective difference between their positions for fiscal purposes which could justify different treatment; accordingly, differential treatment concerning the grant of an advantage related to taxation, such as the tax credit in issue, was discriminatory.[32]

The Court thus appears to equate corporate seat with both nationality and residence, reflecting the difficulty of applying to companies a distinction which is conceptually unproblematic in relation to individuals. The French legislation, as might be expected, focused more on residence than on nationality: Article 158b of the French tax code restricted the tax credit to *'personnes qui ont leur domicile réel ou leur siège social en France'*.[33]

The French Government had sought to argue that the difference in treatment was compensated by advantages (such as not being subject to capital duty) which branches and agencies may enjoy as compared with companies, and hence justified. The Court rejected that argument, ruling that even if such advantages did exist, they could not justify a breach of the obligation laid down in Article 52 to accord foreign companies the same treatment in regard to the tax credit as was accorded to French companies. In that context, the Court stated that even discrimination of a limited nature would be contrary to Article 52.[34] It similarly rejected an argument that foreign insurance companies wishing to obtain the benefit of the tax credit for their secondary establishments in France were free to set up a subsidiary rather than

[30] Para 18. It is interesting to note that the French Conseil d'Etat had taken a step in the same direction ten years before the judgment of the Court of Justice, ruling that dividends paid by a French company to a Swiss company with an establishment in France should not be subject to tax deducted at source, as required by the legislation where the recipients had their real domicile or their seat outside France; the Conseil d'Etat stated that such an establishment should be assimilated to a seat in France. In 1985 the Conseil d'Etat reportedly reached the same result in relation to a French establishment of an Italian company, on the basis of the non-discrimination clause in the relevant double-taxation convention. See the case-note by de Moffarts d'Houchenée, S [1986] Annales de droit de Liège 429, 436–7, and 'Affiliation Privilege for Branch of Italian Company' (1986) 26 European Taxation 157.

[31] Both the method of determining taxable income and the rate of tax were the same.

[32] Paras 19–20. Berlin, D describes the Court as catching France *'en flagrant délit d'estoppel'* on this point: 'Jurisprudence fiscale européenne' (1987) 23 Revue trimestrielle de droit européen 105, 121. This is perhaps particularly so in the context of a tax credit, which is designed to relieve double taxation; denial of the credit to non-resident shareholders would therefore seem reasonable only if they were not paying the relevant tax in the first place.

[33] Para 4 of the judgment ('persons having their habitual residence or seat in France'—author's translation). See n 22.

[34] Para 21.

a branch or agency, ruling that the second sentence of Article 52 expressly left traders free to choose the appropriate legal form in which to pursue their activities in another Member State, and that freedom of choice must not be limited by discriminatory tax provisions.[35]

The French Government had put forward three further connected arguments. It contended first that, in the absence of fiscal harmonization, different measures were necessary in the two types of case to take account of the differences between the taxation systems. The Court summarily disposed of that argument, ruling:

the fact that the laws of the Member States on corporation tax have not been harmonized cannot justify the difference of treatment in this case. Although it is true that in the absence of such harmonization, a company's tax position depends on the national law applied to it, Article 52 of the EEC Treaty prohibits the Member States from laying down in their laws conditions for the pursuit of activities by persons exercising their right of establishment which differ from those laid down for its own nationals.[36]

France had also pleaded the danger of tax avoidance,[37] arguing that if the legislation were abolished, foreign companies owning shares in French companies might allocate those shares to a branch or agency operating in France solely in order to benefit from the tax credit. The Court ruled that 'risk of tax avoidance cannot be relied upon in this context. Article 52 of the EEC Treaty does not permit any derogation from the fundamental principle of freedom of establishment on such a ground.'[38] More pragmatically, the Court stated that the French Government had not in any event demonstrated that the perceived risk would materialize.

Finally, France had contended that it could not unilaterally extend the benefit of the tax credit, as proposed by the Commission, without disturbing the balance of the various double-taxation agreements already in existence between it and other Member States. Pending fiscal harmonization, the differential treatment could be resolved only in the context of those agreements, namely by adding reciprocal provisions. The Court dismissed that argument, stating that the rights conferred by Article 52 of the Treaty were unconditional and a Member State could not make respect for them subject to the contents of an agreement concluded with another Member State. In particular, that Article did not permit those rights to be made subject to a condition of reciprocity imposed for the purpose of obtaining corresponding advantages in other Member States.[39]

Case 79/85 *Segers v Bedrijfsvereniging voor Bank- en Verzekeringswezen, Groothandel en Vrije Beroepen*[40]

Academic analysis of this case is clouded by considerable confusion about the facts, which itself is partly attributable to errors in the English translation of the Opinion

[35] Para 22.   [36] Para 24.   [37] Wrongly translated as tax evasion; see n 144 below.
[38] Para 25.   [39] Para 26. See also para 7 of the Opinion of Mancini AG.
[40] See for an interesting discussion of certain aspects of this case Buxbaum, R M, Hertig, G, Hirsch, A and Hopt, K J (eds), *European Business Law* (1991) 153–8. The case was recently considered by La

of Darmon A G and the judgment. The facts are as follows.[41] Mr S, a Netherlands national, carried on a business as a sole trader in the Netherlands. He decided to incorporate his business, but, apparently because setting up a Netherlands company took considerably longer, he did so by acquiring a private limited company formed in accordance with English law and with a registered office in London. He and his wife became sole shareholders of the company and he became sole director. The company acquired the existing business established in the Netherlands, and that business, which continued to operate wholly in the Netherlands, comprised the entire activity of the company and was subject to Netherlands tax and social security. Mr S subsequently sought sickness insurance cover from the Netherlands organization which provided mandatory cover for employees. His claim was based on the then Netherlands law that a managing director who held 50 per cent or more of his company's shares was regarded as an employee of that company and as such covered. The organization refused cover, arguing that that rule applied only in the case of directors of companies incorporated and with a registered office in the Netherlands. Mr S appealed, and the Netherlands court referred to the Court of Justice the question whether, inter alia, Articles 52 and 58 of the Treaty precluded it from drawing a distinction for the purposes of social security cover between the director/major shareholder of a limited company incorporated under Netherlands law and a director/major shareholder of a limited company incorporated under the laws of another Member State, even if the foreign company clearly did not carry on any business in that other Member State but only in the Netherlands.

In order to understand the judgment it is helpful first to point to some linguistic confusion which unfortunately permeates the English (and to a lesser extent the French) versions of the judgment and of the Opinion of Darmon AG and second to mention a peculiarity of Netherlands commercial practice.

The critical linguistic error concerns the translation of the description in Dutch, presumably drawn from the order for reference and the written observations, of the English company's taking over the business as a *filiaal*, meaning branch or establishment (in this case, the latter). The French text of the judgment unfortunately uses the word *filiale*, meaning subsidiary, in the part of the judgment in which the facts are set out.[42] The English text uses 'subsidiary' at both relevant points of that

Pergola AG in his Opinion in Case C–212/97 *Centros Ltd v Erhvervs- og Selskabsstyrelsen*, delivered on 16 July 1998. Unfortunately the analysis in the Opinion is also based on a misunderstanding of the facts, discussed further below. It is to be hoped that the Court will take the opportunity in the forthcoming judgment to put the record straight.

[41] A more detailed exposition of the facts may be found in the summary of the case appearing in the article by Cath, I G F, Mr Segers' advocate in the proceedings before the Court, in 'Free Movement of Legal Persons' in *Free movement of persons in Europe: Legal Problems and Experiences* (1993), 450, 456–7. Mr Cath's comment in his other article cited, 'Freedom of Establishment of Companies: a New Step towards Completion of the Internal Market' (1993) 13 Yearbook of European Law 335, that upon analysis of the judgment 'the impression is obtained that the Court only discloses implicitly its reasoning in relation to certain legal issues involved' (248), is in the circumstances remarkably restrained.

[42] The final sentence of para 3; the second sentence refers to the company's acquiring the business as *succursale*, or branch.

paragraph, and perpetuates the error by stating that the registered office of the business acquired was in the Netherlands: the Dutch refers to that business as established in the Netherlands and the French to the business having its seat in the Netherlands, both of which are, unlike the English, correct.[43]

Common law lawyers are unaccustomed to drawing such a sharp distinction between the business operated by a company, in the sense of its commercial activities, and the legal entity which operates the business. It is however wholly natural in at least the Netherlands, whose law draws a distinction, even in respect of wholly domestic concerns, between a company as legal entity and the business which it runs;[44] the latter however is not normally regarded as a secondary establishment of the former.

Against the background of the correct terminology and the Netherlands practice of conceptually severing the owner-operator (the company) and the undertaking owned and operated (the business), it is clear that at issue was an empty 'shell' company bought (no doubt off the shelf) in England operating solely in the Netherlands, and thus in so far as the company was concerned it was exercising its right of primary establishment.[45] Unfortunately[46] neither the Court nor the Advocate General saw it that way.[47]

The Court referred to the judgment in *Commission v France*, reiterating its ruling in that case that the right of establishment includes the right of companies or firms formed in accordance with the law of a Member State and with their registered office, central administration or principal place of business within the Community to pursue their activities in another Member State through an agency, branch or

[43] It is unlikely that the problem which prompted the request for a preliminary ruling would have arisen had the facts been as the Court understood them: if the Netherlands business had been incorporated as a Netherlands subsidiary of the English company, there would have been no advantage in forming an English company and it may be supposed that Mr Segers would have been director of the subsidiary, and hence entitled to sickness cover under Netherlands law, in any event.

[44] See the explanation of the system in the Opinion of Jacobs AG in Case C–2/94 *Denkavit International v Kamer van Koophandel en Fabrieken voor Midden-Gelderland* [1996] ECR I–2827, paras 2–14. A further example may be found in the *Halliburton Services* case: in that case a Germany subsidiary in the US-owned group is described as having 'transferred its undertaking' (1139) and 'sold . . . its permanent establishment' (1153) to a Netherlands group subsidiary.

[45] A parallel may be discerned with the *Daily Mail* case, which concerned a company registered and incorporated in the UK seeking to move its economic centre of gravity to the Netherlands and which is unequivocally regarded as concerning primary establishment.

[46] This perhaps illustrates the weakness of the language system in the Court. The judges involved were German, Danish and Irish, and would almost certainly have been working from the French translations of the original Dutch documents, as would the French Advocate General. As indicated above, the Dutch *filiaal* and the French *filiale* are *faux amis*, and it may well have been through that route that the error was both introduced and perpetuated.

[47] C W A Timmermans makes the point forcefully, perhaps assisted by his nationality in understanding the structure: see Buxbaum, R M, Hertig, G, Hirsch, A and Hopt, K J (eds), *European Business Law* (1991) 137–8; it is also noted by Cath, I G F, Mr Segers' lawyer, who makes the pragmatic point that it mattered little to Mr Segers whether the case was decided on the basis of primary or secondary establishment since he was in any event granted his sickness cover as a result of the decision: 'Free Movement of Legal Persons' (n 41 above) 458.

subsidiary.[48] If the latter Member State were permitted to accord different treatment to a company seeking to establish itself there solely because its seat[49] was situated in another Member State, that would deprive Article 58 of all meaning.[50]

The Court then stated that, although entitlement to sickness cover pertained to a person and not a company, the requirement that a company formed in accordance with the law of another Member State must be accorded the same treatment as national companies meant that the employees of that company must have the right to be affiliated to a specific social security scheme since discrimination against employees in connection with social security protection indirectly restricted the freedom of companies in another Member State to establish themselves through an agency, branch or subsidiary in the Member State concerned.[51]

The national court's doubts as to the significance of the fact that the English company conducted no business in the United Kingdom, which should perhaps have provided a focus for correctly analysing the issue, were roundly dispelled by the Court, which stated that Article 58 required only that the company seeking to assert its right of establishment be formed in accordance with the law of a Member State and have its registered office, central administration or principal place of business within the Community. Provided those conditions are satisfied, the fact that the company conducts its business solely in another Member State is immaterial.[52] It must be doubted whether that is correct in relation to secondary establishment, the ostensible—if misconceived—basis of the decision: it appears to ignore the wording of the Treaty, which requires establishment in one Member State before a national, and by extension a company, can benefit from the right of secondary establishment in another Member State.[53]

The Court also dismissed an argument that the refusal to grant sickness cover was justified by the need to combat possible abuse and ensure the proper implementation of the national social security legislation, although it conceded that the need to combat fraud might justify a difference of treatment in certain (unspecified) circumstances.[54]

Fortunately the Court's conclusion was framed in terms which both transcend its misapprehension of the facts and apply comfortably to a company which has exercised its right of primary establishment. The Court ruled:

---

[48] Para 13 of the judgment.
[49] Wrongly translated as 'registered office' in the English text of the judgment.
[50] Para 14 of the judgment.   [51] Para 15 of the judgment.   [52] Para 16 of the judgment.
[53] See the 2nd sentence of the 1st para of Art 52, discussed in ch XVI above. See also Tridimas, T, 'The Case-Law of the European Court of Justice on Corporate Entities' (1993) 13 Yearbook of European Law 335, 339–40, and Timmermans, C W A, in Buxbaum, Hertig, Hirsch and Hopt (eds), *European Business Law* (1991) 134. It may be noted that in Case C–212/97 *Centros Ltd v Erhvervs- og Selskabsstyrelsen*, which concerned the refusal by one Member State to register the branch of a company validly formed in another Member State where it carried on no business on the ground that the business structure was designed to avoid compliance with the minimum capital requirements applicable to companies formed in the first State, La Pergola AG appears to follow the Court's approach in the *Segers* case since he concludes that Art 52 is infringed.
[54] Para 17.

The provisions of Articles 52 and 58 of the EEC Treaty must be interpreted as prohibiting the competent authorities of a Member State from excluding a director of a company from a national sickness insurance benefit scheme solely on the ground that the company in question was formed in accordance with the law of another Member State, where it also has its registered office, even though it does not conduct any business there.[55]

Advocate General Darmon, after dealing with the case on the basis of secondary establishment along similar lines to those followed by the Court,[56] had touched on the issue of primary establishment. He drew attention to the risk[57] that different treatment in the application of the Netherlands social security provisions may dissuade a Community national already established in the Netherlands from setting up a company abroad or from becoming a majority shareholder in such a company, curtailing the right of natural persons guaranteed by the second paragraph of Article 52 to set up and manage companies in another Member State. It is unfortunate that this line of reasoning was not pursued since it might, if better articulated, have paved the way for a clearer analysis in the *Daily Mail* case. It is difficult to resist the conclusion that the Court dealt with the *Segers* case in an excessively summary fashion: it is noteworthy that the case was allocated to a chamber of three judges, normally reserved for the least important cases, that the Advocate General delivered his Opinion at the hearing and that the judgment was delivered exactly one month later.[58]

Case C–221/89 *Factortame*[59] and Case C–146/89 *Commission v United Kingdom*[60]

The two cases of *Factortame* and *Commission v United Kingdom*[61] concerned conditions imposed by the United Kingdom in order for a fishing vessel to be registered as a British fishing vessel. The vessel's owner[62] and any charterer, manager, or operator were required to be a 'qualified person or company'. 'Qualified person' was defined as a British citizen resident and domiciled[63] in the United Kingdom, or a local authority in the United Kingdom. 'Qualified company' was defined as a company (a) both incorporated in and with its principal place of business in the United

---

[55] Para 19 and operative part.

[56] Para 4 of the Opinion, other than the final two sub-paras, is a precursor to paras 13 and 14 of the judgment.

[57] In the English text, for 'There is no danger' in the second sentence of the second full paragraph on 2379 read 'There is a danger'.

[58] Which means, given the need to allow for translation, that it must have been finalized very shortly after the hearing.

[59] *The Queen v The Secretary of State for Transport, ex p Factortame* [1991] ECR I–3905.

[60] [1991] ECR I–3533.

[61] See the case-note by Churchill, R R (1992) 29 CMLR 405.

[62] The provisions as to ownership were of some complexity; the gist is described here, and is sufficient for these purposes.

[63] In the specific English law meaning of living in a State with the intent to make it a fixed and permanent home.

Kingdom; (b) at least 75 per cent of whose shares were owned by qualified persons or companies and (c) at least 75 per cent of whose directors were qualified persons. In the *Factortame* case, the Court was asked to rule on inter alia the lawfulness of those requirements. In *Commission v United Kingdom*, the Commission brought proceedings under Article 169 of the Treaty for a declaration that, by imposing the nationality requirements, the United Kingdom had failed to fulfil its obligations under Articles 7, 52 and 221 of the Treaty.

First, the Court observed that the concept of establishment within the meaning of Article 52 *et seq* of the Treaty involved the actual pursuit of an economic activity through a fixed establishment in another Member State for an indefinite period. On that basis, the Court found that, where a fishing vessel constituted an instrument for pursuing an economic activity which involved a fixed establishment in the Member State concerned, the registration of that vessel could not be dissociated from the exercise of the freedom of establishment. Accordingly, the conditions laid down for registration must not form an obstacle to freedom of establishment.[64]

Second, the Court considered the stipulation that the shareholders and directors of a company be nationals of or resident and domiciled in a Member State before that company could own or charter a fishing vessel and hence pursue an economic activity which involved a fixed establishment in that State. It ruled, unsurprisingly, that the nationality condition was contrary to Article 52, which prohibited discrimination on grounds of nationality as regards the right of establishment.[65] It may be inferred that the Court accepted the Commission's argument that the requirement applicable to shareholders and directors of companies infringed Article 52 in two distinct ways: first, it deprived nationals of other Member States of their right to set up, and act as directors of, companies in the sea-fisheries sector in the United Kingdom; second, it restricted the possibility for companies of other Member States to pursue sea-fishing activities from the United Kingdom through agencies, branches or subsidiaries.[66]

The Court further ruled that the nationality requirement was contrary to Article 221, under which Member States must accord nationals of other Member States the same treatment as their own nationals as regards participation in the capital of companies or firms within the meaning of Article 58.[67]

With regard to the residence and domicile requirement, the Court ruled that it resulted in discrimination on grounds of nationality: the great majority of nationals of the Member State in question were resident and domiciled in that State and therefore met that requirement automatically, whereas nationals of other Member States would, in most cases, have to move their residence and domicile to that State

---

[64] Paras 20–3 of the judgment in the *Factortame* case and paras 21–4 of the judgment in *Commission v UK*.

[65] Paras 28–30 in the *Factortame* case and paras 29–31 in *Commission v UK*.

[66] See para 19 of the judgment in *Commission v UK*. Mischo AG explicitly endorses the Commission's submissions: see paras 29–33 of the Opinion.

[67] Para 31 in *Factortame* case and para 33 in *Commission v UK*.

in order to comply with the requirements. It was therefore also contrary to Article 52.[68]

With regard to the requirement that corporate owners of fishing vessels have their principal place of business in the United Kingdom, Advocate General Mischo[69] made the additional observation:

to require a company incorporated under the law of one Member State, which has its registered office, central administration or principal place of business in that Member State (within the meaning of Article 58)—or even in another Member State—to transfer its principal place of business to the Member State where a certain activity, such as fishing, is to be carried on, deprives that company of the possibility of exercising its right of establishment through the setting up of agencies, branches or subsidiaries as is expressly provided for in the second sentence of the first paragraph of Article 52.[70]

Case C–330/91 *The Queen v Inland Revenue Commissioners, ex p Commerzbank AG*[71]

Commerzbank AG, a company incorporated and with its registered office in Germany with a branch in the United Kingdom, had paid tax in the United Kingdom on interest received from companies in the United States to which it had granted loans. It subsequently sought repayment of the tax on the basis that the interest was exempt by virtue of the double-taxation treaty in force between the United States and the United Kingdom, which provided inter alia that interest paid by a United States company was taxable in the United Kingdom only when it was paid to a United Kingdom company or a company resident for tax purposes in the United Kingdom.[72] Since Commerzbank was not resident for tax purposes in the United Kingdom, the tax was refunded but the statutory interest (repayment supplement) additionally claimed by Commerzbank[73] was refused on the basis that it was available only to companies resident for tax purposes in the United Kingdom. Commerzbank sought judicial review of that refusal on the basis that it constituted a restriction of the right of establishment and indirect discrimination on grounds of nationality since the companies affected were for the most part foreign. The Divisional Court[74] referred a series of questions to the Court of Justice for a

---

[68] Para 32 in *Factortame* case.

[69] Who delivered a single Opinion in the two cases [1991] ECR I–3932.   [70] Para 50.

[71] See Williams, D, 'Freedom of Establishment and Double Taxation Agreements' (1994) 19 ELR 313; the case-note of Kornprobst, E [1994] Droit fiscal 571; and Campbell, A I L, 'Having Your Cake . . .?' [1994] JBL 191.

[72] Commerzbank had, after paying £4,222,234 tax, successfully challenged the Inland Revenue's interpretation of the relevant provision of the double-taxation treaty: *Inland Revenue Commissioners v Commerzbank* [1990] STC 285, Ch D. The dispute had arisen because the company was neither a US resident nor a UK resident. See Williams (n 71 above).

[73] Amounting to £5,199,258, and thus more than the total tax paid.

[74] *The Queen v Inland Revenue Commissioners, ex p Commerzbank AG* [1991] STC 271.

preliminary ruling, essentially asking whether the refusal of the supplement on the ground of non-residence was contrary to Articles 52 and 58.[75]

The Court restated (correcting the translation errors) the ruling in paragraph 18 of the judgment in *Commission v France* set out above[76] and added that the rules regarding equality of treatment forbade not only overt discrimination by reason of nationality or, in the case of a company, its seat, but all covert forms of discrimination which, by the application of other criteria of differentiation, led in fact to the same result.[77] The criterion of fiscal residence for the grant of repayment supplement on overpaid tax was liable to work more particularly to the disadvantage of companies having their seat in other Member States.[78]

The United Kingdom had argued that, far from suffering discrimination under its tax rules, non-resident companies in Commerzbank's situation enjoyed privileged treatment since they were exempt from tax normally payable by resident companies: they were treated differently with respect to the repayment supplement because they were in different situations for tax purposes. The Court, adopting Advocate General Darmon's approach, dismissed that argument, concentrating solely on the fact that, in circumstances where tax had been wrongly paid and subsequently repaid to the taxpayer, resident companies were entitled to the supplement and non-resident companies were denied it.[79]

Case C–1/93 *Halliburton Services v Staatssecretaris van Financiën*[80]

Netherlands land transfer tax was charged on the intra-group transfer by a German subsidiary to a Netherlands subsidiary of the assets of the Netherlands branch of the German subsidiary, including land in the Netherlands. The transfer was made in the context of a reorganization of the group whereby the Dutch part of the German company was to be transferred to a Netherlands company. There was a statutory exemption from the charge for transactions carried out 'as part of an internal reorganization of *naamloze vennootschappen* [public limited companies] and *besloten vennootschappen met beperkte aansprakelijkheid* [private limited companies]'. The tax authorities refused to apply the exemption on the ground that the transferor company was a German company. The Netherlands company, liable to pay the tax, appealed. A question was referred to the Court of Justice for a preliminary ruling,

---

[75] It may be noted that the impugned legislation was changed before the Court of Justice delivered its judgment; with effect from 1 September 1993 non-resident companies became entitled to the repayment supplement.

[76] Para 13 of the judgment in the *Commerzbank* case; for the relevant passage from *Commission v France*, see the text to n 30 above.

[77] Para 14, citing Case 152/73 *Sotgiu v Deutsche Bundespost* [1974] ECR 153.

[78] Para 15. See below, p 363, for a further argument raised on this point.

[79] Paras 16–19 of the judgment and paras 44–5 and 55–6 of the Opinion.

[80] See Keeling, E and Shipwright, A, 'Some Taxing Problems Concerning Non-Discrimination and the EC Treaty' (1995) 20 ELR 580, including a discussion of the implications of the judgment for the UK tax system.

asking essentially whether it was contrary to Articles 52 and 58 for relief from such a charge arising in the context of an intra-group reorganization to be available if the transferor is a company incorporated under the laws of the Member State concerned but not if it is an equivalent form of company incorporated under the laws of another Member State.

The Court disposed of the Netherlands Government's argument that the situation was purely internal since the person liable to pay the tax was the Netherlands company, stating that, since the payment of tax on the transaction made the conditions of sale more onerous, which affected the vendor, the transferor German company was in a distinctly less favourable position than if it had chosen to establish itself in the Netherlands by way of a subsidiary incorporated in the Netherlands rather than by way of a branch.[81] The Court ruled that, although the difference in treatment had only an indirect effect on the position of companies constituted under the law of other Member States, it constituted discrimination on grounds of nationality prohibited by Article 52.[82]

The Court thus did not directly address the question whether, and if so, how, the refusal to grant the exemption restricted the German company's freedom of establishment, appearing to assume that differential treatment of branches and agencies on the one hand and local subsidiaries on the other of necessity infringed Articles 52 and 58.[83] Advocate General Lenz considered this issue in more depth, dealing squarely with the argument of the Netherlands Government that neither the acquisition of the establishment by the transferor nor its operation was adversely affected.[84] He analysed the issue in two stages.

First, the Advocate General considered whether the disposal of assets representing the whole or part of the branch of a company with its seat in another Member State fell within the scope of freedom of establishment. He expressed the view that measures which made the disestablishment of a branch more onerous than that of a subsidiary would weigh with the foreign company when it made its initial choice of form of secondary establishment.[85] They could moreover discourage a company from giving up an existing branch in one Member State in order to set up a secondary establishment in another Member State, which would restrict its freedom of establishment; they may in addition operate as a disincentive to the partial surrender of the assets of a branch, and thereby affect the 'pursuit' of activities within the meaning of Article 52.[86]

Second, the Advocate General considered whether the contested rule affected the right of establishment. In his view, the refusal to grant tax relief was liable to affect the purchase price, and thus 'likely to hinder or render less attractive the exercise by Community nationals of the basic freedoms guaranteed by the Treaty'.[87] By analogy with the situation in the Segers case, where the discrimination was against

---

[81] Para 19.   [82] Paras 19 and 20.   [83] See paras 14–16.
[84] Paras 15–29.   [85] Paras 17–18.   [86] Para 20.
[87] Case C–19/92 Kraus v Land Baden-Württemberg [1993] ECR I–1663, para 32 of the judgment, quoted by Lenz AG in para 24 of the Opinion.

employees, the causal link through which the disadvantage affected the company concerned was irrelevant.[88] The referring court had assumed for the purposes of the question referred for a preliminary ruling that the transferor was a company from another Member State 'similar' to a public or private limited company incorporated under Netherlands law. Since the tax exemption was granted where the disposal was by a Netherlands limited company but not if the transferor was incorporated under the law of another Member State, the Advocate General concluded that the obstacle to freedom of establishment infringed Article 52: 'the conditions laid down for its own nationals by the law of the country where such establishment is effected' did not impose a comparable burden, with the result that discrimination was involved.[89]

The Netherlands Government had also sought to invoke the lack of harmonization as a defence. It pointed out that the tax exemption at issue was granted only if the companies concerned belonged to the same 'group', which presupposed that the companies involved had a certain structure. It argued that tax relief in the case of companies from other Member States could be granted only if the relevant legislative provisions were harmonized. Since as yet Community law provided no uniform definition of the term 'group', it was still a matter for the Member States.[90]

The Court did not address this argument. Advocate General Lenz, however, responded, albeit somewhat indirectly. He stated that the lack of Community legislation on the equivalence of like forms of companies in the Member States did not mean that in a situation such as that at issue the national authorities could refuse the tax relief sought: 'The practical effect of the prohibition of discrimination in Article 52 presupposes that in a case such as this they compare the legal form of the transferor company from another Member State with the forms of the national companies which qualify for exemption.'[91]

The Netherlands Government had further contended that the restriction of the exemption to companies constituted under national law was necessary because its tax authorities were unable to check whether the legal forms of entities constituted in other Member States were equivalent to its *naamlozen venootschappen* and *besloten venootschappen met beperkte aansprakelijkheid*. The Court rejected the argument, pointing out that the authorities could use the system of exchanging information envisaged by Directive (EEC) 77/799.[92]

Advocate General Lenz addressed this argument more fully, making the obvious point that Article 52 would be deprived of practical effect in a case such as *Halliburton* unless the authorities compared the legal form of the transferor company from another Member State with the forms of the national companies which qualified for exemption. He then considered the alleged problems pleaded in that

---

[88] Para 25.   [89] Paras 26–9.   [90] See the Opinion of Lenz AG, paras 32 and 34.
[91] Para 40.
[92] Council Directive (EEC) 77/799 concerning mutual assistance by the competent authorities of the Member States in the field of direct taxation [1977] OJ L336/15, as amended by Council Directives (EEC) 79/1070 [1979] OJ L331/8 and (EEC) 92/12 [1992] OJ L76/1.

case, and concluded from a review of the case-law concerning the comparison of professional qualifications that:

those principles imply that the host State cannot simply refer to 'difficulties' of verification if the exercise of the basic freedoms depends on its own provisions being compared with those of the State of origin. On the contrary, it is possible to propound the *rule* that it is *obliged* to undertake such verification and must accordingly accept the additional administrative costs involved.[93]

Case C–101/94 *Commission v Italy*[94]

The Commission sought a declaration that, by requiring dealers in transferable securities to be constituted in the form of a *società per azioni* (limited company)[95] with its registered office on Italian territory, Italy had infringed Articles 52 and 59 of the Treaty. With regard to Article 52, the Commission argued that the rule prevented dealers from other Member States from making use of certain forms of establishment, such as a branch or agency, and discriminated against them by obliging them to bear the expense of setting up a new company. The Italian Government did not deny these allegations, simply arguing that the difference in treatment was objectively justified since it was not possible to compare the conditions laid down by the Italian legislation regarding authorization, supervision and solvency of securities dealers with those laid down by the other Member States and dealers could not be supervised and effectively sanctioned unless they had their principal establishment in Italy.

The Court rejected Italy's defence, finding that it had not been shown that the requirement was the only means of achieving the legitimate aim of regulating the securities market: there were no insuperable difficulties in carrying out such a comparison. Under the second paragraph of Article 52, freedom of establishment was to be exercised under the conditions laid down by the law of the country of establishment for its own nationals. Where access to or the exercise of a specific activity was subject to such conditions, a national of another Member State who wished to exercise that activity must in principle comply with them. However, Article 52 prohibited any discrimination against nationals of other Member States resulting from national rules, prohibiting in particular rules liable to place nationals of other Member States in a less favourable situation than that of a national of the Member State of establishment in the same circumstances. The Court accordingly upheld the Commission's complaint of breach of Article 52.

Advocate General Lenz made the additional specific point that, although authorization was undoubtedly easier if the subject was established in the territory of the Member State, that element could also be fulfilled by a branch or agency, so that

[93] Para 45.
[94] See Andenas, M, 'Italian nationality requirement and Community law' (1996) 17 The Company Lawyer 219.
[95] Or *società in accomandita perazioni*, a corporate entity akin to a partnership limited by shares.

the requirement of a seat in the narrower sense (of registered office) was not in itself necessary.[96]

Case C–250/95 *Futura Participations SA and Singer v Administration des Contributions*[97]

Luxembourg law provided that resident taxpayers, including collective bodies, could deduct from their taxable income losses carried forward from previous years provided that they had kept 'proper accounts during the financial year in which the losses were incurred'. Companies incorporated abroad with a branch in Luxembourg were treated as non–resident taxpayers and taxed on income earned by that branch. If they did not keep separate accounts relating to their Luxembourg activities, they could determine the amount of their taxable income on the basis of an apportionment of their total income. Tax losses carried forward from previous years could however be deducted provided that they were economically related to income received locally and that accounts complying with Luxembourg rules were kept within Luxembourg. The Court was asked whether Article 52 precluded a Member State from making the carrying forward of previous losses by a non-resident taxpayer with a branch in that State subject to the conditions (a) that the losses must be economically related to the income earned by the taxpayer in that State and (b) that, during the financial year in which the losses were incurred, the taxpayer must have kept and held in that State, in respect of activities he carried on there, accounts complying with the relevant national rules.

The Court first considered the requirement of an economic link. It referred to previous decisions to the effect that, although direct taxation fell within the competence of the Member States, the latter must none the less exercise that competence consistently with Community law and therefore avoid any overt or covert discrimination on grounds of nationality.[98] In the present case, the Luxembourg law provided that all the income of resident taxpayers was taxable, the basis of assessment to tax not being limited to their Luxembourg activities. Consequently, although there were exemptions under which some or all of their income earned outside Luxembourg was not subject to tax in Luxembourg, the basis of assessment for resident taxpayers at any rate included profits and losses arising from their Luxembourg activities. On the other hand, for the purpose of calculating the basis of assessment for non-resident taxpayers, only profits and losses arising from their Luxembourg activities were taken into account. The Court did not consider that

---

[96] Para 57.
[97] See the case-note by Hatzopoulos, V (1998) 35 CMLR 493; Clayson, M, 'Futura Participations: Luxembourg Account-Keeping Requirement Unlawful' (1996–97) 2 EC Tax Journal 133; and 'European Court of Justice Releases Branches of EU Companies from Duplication of Bookkeeping Requirements' (1997) 25 Intertax 322.
[98] Case C–279/93 *Finanzamt Köln-Alstadt v Schumacker* [1995] ECR I–225, paras 21 and 26; Case C–80/94 *GHEJ Wielockx v Inspecteur der Directe Belastingen* [1995] ECR I–2493, para 16; and Case C–107/94 *Asscher v Staatsecretaris van Financiën* [1996] ECR I–3089, para 36.

such a system, which was in conformity with the fiscal principle of territoriality, entailed any discrimination, overt or covert, prohibited by the Treaty.[99]

The second condition was that, during the financial year in which the losses were incurred, the taxpayer must have kept, in the Member State in which tax was to be charged, accounts complying with the relevant national rules applicable during that year, relating to his activities in that State. The Court referred to Article 58 of the Treaty, which provides that, for the purposes of, inter alia, the rules on freedom of establishment, companies or firms are to be treated in the same way as natural persons who are nationals of a Member State. The condition meant in practice that, if a company or firm with a branch in a Member State different from that of its seat wished to carry forward any losses incurred by its branch, it had to keep, in addition to its own accounts complying with the tax accounting rules applicable in the Member State of its seat, separate accounts for its branch's activities complying with the tax accounting rules applicable in the State of the branch. Furthermore, those separate accounts had to be held, not at the company's seat, but in the State of its branch.[100]

The Court ruled that such a condition, which specifically affected companies or firms having their seat in another Member State, was in principle prohibited by Article 52 of the Treaty. It could only be otherwise if the measure pursued a legitimate aim compatible with the Treaty and were justified by pressing reasons of public interest. Even if that were so, it would still have to be such as to ensure achievement of the aim in question and not go beyond what was necessary for that purpose.[101]

The Court referred to the established principle that the effectiveness of fiscal supervision constituted an overriding requirement of general interest capable of justifying a restriction on the exercise of fundamental freedoms guaranteed by the Treaty.[102] A Member State may therefore apply measures enabling the amount of both the income taxable in that State and the losses which could be carried forward there to be ascertained clearly and precisely.[103] Provided that the taxpayer demonstrated, clearly and precisely, the amount of the losses concerned, the Luxembourg authorities could not refuse to allow him to carry them forward on the ground that in the year concerned he had not kept and not held in Luxembourg proper accounts relating to his activities in that State.[104]

The Court accordingly concluded that Article 52 of the Treaty did not preclude a Member State from making the carrying forward of previous losses by a non-resident taxpayer with a branch in its territory subject to the condition that the

---

[99] Paras 19–22.   [100] Paras 24–5.

[101] Para 26, citing Case C–55/94 *Gebhard v Consiglio dell'Ordine degli Avvocati e Procuratori di Milano* [1995] ECR I–4165, para 37 of the judgment; Case C–19/92 *Kraus v Land Baden–Württemberg* [1993] ECR I–1163, para 32; and Case C–415/93 *Union Royale Belge des Sociétés de Football Association and Others v Bosman and Others* [1995] ECR I–4921, para 104.

[102] See, for example, Case 120/78 *Rewe v Bundesmonopolverwaltung für Branntwein* [1979] ECR 649, para 8 of the judgment.

[103] Para 31.   [104] Para 39.

losses must be economically related to the income earned by the taxpayer in that State, provided that resident taxpayers did not receive more favourable treatment. Article 52 did however preclude a Member State from making the carrying forward of losses subject to the condition that, in the year in which they were incurred, the taxpayer must have kept and held in that State accounts relating to his activities carried on there which complied with the relevant national rules. The Member State concerned could however require the non-resident taxpayer to demonstrate clearly and precisely that the amount of the claimed losses corresponded, under its domestic rules governing the calculation of income and losses applicable in the financial year concerned, to the amount of the losses actually incurred in that State by the taxpayer.[105]

Case C–264/96 *ICI v Colmer*

ICI and Wellcome Foundation Ltd, companies resident in the United Kingdom, formed a consortium through which they owned 49 per cent and 51 per cent respectively of a holding company whose sole business was to hold shares in subsidiary trading companies, four of which (including CAH) were resident in the United Kingdom, six in other Member States and thirteen in third countries.

Legislation in the United Kingdom[106] permitted tax relief for losses and other items to be surrendered by a member of a group of companies and allowed to another company in the group. Group relief was also available inter alia where one of the companies concerned was a member of a consortium and the other was a subsidiary trading company of a holding company owned by the consortium. A holding company was defined as a company the business of which consisted wholly or mainly in holding shares in subsidiary trading companies. For all the above purposes 'company' was defined as a body corporate resident in the United Kingdom.

The United Kingdom Inland Revenue refused ICI's application to set losses incurred by CAH against its chargeable profits by way of consortium relief on the ground that, since the majority of the holding company's subsidiaries were not resident in the United Kingdom, it was not a holding company for the purposes of the relief. On ICI's challenge to that refusal, the House of Lords sought a preliminary ruling from the Court of Justice on, essentially, the question whether Article 52 of the Treaty precluded legislation of a Member State which, in the case of companies established in that State belonging to a consortium through which they controlled a holding company, made a particular form of tax relief subject to the requirement that the holding company's business consisted wholly or mainly in the holding of shares in subsidiaries established in the Member State concerned.

The Court first referred to its earlier rulings in *Commission v France* to the effect that, in the case of companies, it was their corporate seat in the sense of their registered office, central administration or principal place of business that served as the

---

[105] Para 43.   [106] Income and Corporation Taxes Act 1970, ss 258–64.

connecting factor with the legal system of a particular State, like nationality in the case of natural persons, and in the *Daily Mail* case[107] to the effect that Article 52 prohibited the Member State of origin from hindering the establishment in another Member State of a company incorporated under its legislation within the scope of Article 58.

The Court noted that the national legislation applied the test of the subsidiaries' seat to impose differential tax treatment of consortium companies established in the United Kingdom, limiting consortium relief to companies controlling, wholly or mainly, subsidiaries whose seats were in the national territory. It accordingly considered whether there was any justification for such inequality of treatment.

The Court rejected the United Kingdom Government's submission that the differential treatment was justified because of the risk of tax avoidance. It noted that the legislation was not specifically designed to counter wholly artificial arrangements set up to circumvent United Kingdom tax legislation, but applied generally to all situations in which the majority of a group's subsidiaries were established, for whatever reason, outside the United Kingdom; the establishment of a company outside the United Kingdom did not, however, necessarily entail tax avoidance, since that company would in any event be subject to the tax legislation of the State of establishment.

The United Kingdom Government had also submitted that the legislation further sought to prevent a reduction in revenue caused by the mere existence of non-resident subsidiaries, since the Inland Revenue could not tax profits made by subsidiaries located outside the United Kingdom in order to offset the revenue lost through the granting of relief on losses incurred by resident subsidiaries. The Court rejected that argument, stating that such diminution of tax revenue was not one of the grounds listed in Article 56 of the Treaty nor could it be regarded as a matter of overriding general interest which could justify unequal treatment. The Court distinguished its earlier decisions in *Bachmann v Belgium* and *Commission v Belgium*[108] on the ground that, in those cases, there was a direct link between the tax deductibility of contributions and the taxation of sums payable by insurers under old-age and life assurance policies, which link had to be maintained in order to preserve the cohesion of the tax system in question, whereas in the present case there was no such direct link between the consortium relief granted for losses incurred by a resident subsidiary and the taxation of profits made by non-resident subsidiaries.

The Court accordingly ruled that Article 52 precluded legislation of a Member State which, in the case of companies established in that State belonging to a consortium through which they controlled a holding company, by means of which they exercised their right to freedom of establishment in order to set up subsidiaries in other Member States, made a particular form of tax relief subject to the

---

[107] Case 81/87 *The Queen v HM Treasury and Commissioners of Inland Revenue, ex p Daily Mail and General Trust PLC* [1988] ECR 5483, para 16. See further pp 376–81 below.
[108] Case C–204/90 [1992] ECR I–249 and Case C–300/90 [1992] ECR I–305.

requirement that the holding company's business consisted wholly or mainly in the holding of shares in subsidiaries established in the Member State concerned. The Court noted however that the Treaty did not preclude domestic legislation under which tax relief was not granted to a resident consortium member where the business of the holding company owned by that consortium consisted wholly or mainly in holding shares in subsidiaries having their seat in non-member countries.

Seat, Residence and Nationality

In *Commission v France*, the Court focused on discrimination by reason of the location of a company's seat, which it assimilated to the nationality of a natural person. Once that link between seat and nationality had been made, the conclusion that discrimination by reference to seat was in principle unlawful was inevitable. In the words of Advocate General Jacobs in *Collins v Imtrat Handelsgesellschaft mbH*,[109] 'The prohibition of discrimination on grounds of nationality is the single most important principle of Community law. It is the leitmotiv of the EEC Treaty.'[110]

The Court in assimilating corporate seat to nationality in *Commission v France* had in mind the broad concept of seat in any of the three specific senses mentioned in Article 58. In the *Segers case*, the different treatment was by reference to the location of the company's registered office and its status as a company incorporated in the United Kingdom; in the *Halliburton* case, analogously, the different treatment was determined by whether the transferor was constituted as one of two types of Netherlands incorporated companies, and expressly described by the Court as discrimination on grounds of nationality.[111]

It may be noted that the Court in *Commission v France* also assimilated the location of a company's seat to the place of residence of a natural person: in the context of a case concerning allegedly unlawful tax legislation, that is perhaps the more appropriate analogy to make. It will be recalled that in the *France* case, the tax credit at issue was made available to natural persons habitually resident in France or companies with their seat there. The *Commerzbank* case took this further: the criterion at issue in that case was fiscal residence in accordance with national law, and the Court took the opportunity to bring within the net of unlawful restrictions covert discrimination by reference to fiscal residence, noting that:

although it applies independently of a company's seat,[112] the use of the criterion of fiscal residence within national territory . . . is liable to work more particularly to the disadvantage of companies having their seat in other Member States. Indeed, it is most often those companies which are resident for tax purposes outside the territory of the Member State in question.[113]

---

[109] Joined Cases C–92 and 326/92 [1993] ECR I–5145.
[110] Para 9 of the Opinion.   [111] Para 20 of the judgment.
[112] This is of course not so for most of the Member States, for whom the concept of seat is for all practical purposes indistinguishable from the former UK concept of fiscal residence, namely the locus of central management and control.
[113] Para 15 of the judgment.

That proposition begs an interesting question raised by the United Kingdom in its observations. The Government had argued that discrimination on grounds of nationality assumed that a measure principally affected nationals of other Member States. That rule must however be different in tax matters, where there would be no discrimination where a 'significant' number of national taxpayers were also affected: that exception had been recognized by the Court in its case-law on indirect taxation but should also apply to direct tax. The Government submitted that the legislation at issue affected numerous English companies who had their fiscal residence abroad.[114] Neither the Court nor the Advocate General focused on this argument. In the context of its argument that the companies which are refused the supplement are mainly foreign companies, Commerzbank, on the other hand, made the point that the companies affected by the rule were resident in another Member State and, since a number of Member States used the residence of companies as the criterion for determining their nationality, were also nationals of that State.[115] It is interesting to see how the same factual premiss can lead to mutually exclusive conclusions depending on whether it is considered from the perspective of the incorporation theory or the real seat theory.

The *Futura* and *ICI* cases similarly concerned different treatment by reference to fiscal residence. In the *Futura* case fiscal residence would in practice, given that Luxembourg adopts the real seat theory, coincide with the location of its seat. In *ICI v Colmer*, the Court assimilated residence to seat[116] without further discussion, thus blurring the distinction it had drawn in the *Commerzbank* case[117] between overt discrimination on the express basis of seat and covert discrimination on the basis of fiscal residence.

The *Factortame* case and *Commission v United Kingdom*, in so far as they concerned restrictions on companies' freedom of establishment, focused on a requirement that in a particular sector a business could be operated only by a company whose shareholders and directors were nationals and residents, thus restricting the right of companies incorporated in other Member States to establish themselves by way of any of the forms of secondary establishment.

Whether different treatment is based on nationality or residence has more than academic significance, since as will be seen it determines the possible justifications: overt discrimination by reference to nationality may be justified only on very narrow public-interest grounds laid down in the Treaty, whereas covert discrimination by reference to residence, although prima facie unlawful, may be justified on a wider category of grounds provided that the aim of the measure in question is an objective in line with the Treaty and that the measure is proportionate to that aim. Given the relevance of the distinction, it is particularly unfortunate that the Court has so clouded the issue in relation to companies. *Commission v France* is in part

---

[114] [1993] ECR I–4025.   [115] [1993] ECR I–4022.   [116] See paras 22 and 23.
[117] See pp 353–4 above.

expressed and frequently regarded[118] as a case of discrimination on the basis of nationality, although it may be more naturally considered to turn on residence and thus properly analysed, like the *Commerzbank* and *Futura* cases, as covert discrimination. The three cases of *Segers*, *Halliburton* and *Italy*, on the other hand, may less equivocally be analysed as examples of overt discrimination by reference to nationality, since in all those cases the impugned legislation distinguished according to whether a company was incorporated in the form of a national company. That interpretation is borne out by the fact that in all three cases, the possibility of a 'public policy' justification under Article 56 of the Treaty was considered (and discounted).[119]

The difficulties in arriving at a satisfactory analysis of the cases illustrate again the problems created by the Treaty's attempt to extrapolate to companies principles which apply comfortably to national persons and to dovetail two mutually exclusive theories of corporate nationality. It may none the less be concluded that any legislation which, in conferring a fiscal or other benefit liable to affect (even indirectly) the setting up of branches, agencies or subsidiaries or the taking up or pursuit of activities by a company within the meaning of Article 58, differentiates between national and foreign companies, whether on the basis of location of corporate seat, including registered office, or fiscal residence, or constitution under a particular system of law or in a particular national corporate form, will prima facie infringe Articles 52 and 58. It is also clear from *The Queen v HM Treasury and Commissioners of Inland Revenue, ex p Daily Mail and General Trust PLC*[120] that restrictions imposed by the State of origin on a company seeking to exercise its right of establishment in another Member State are equally contrary to Articles 52 and 58. Such restrictions include fiscal disincentives to the exercise by a company of its right of freedom of establishment by the setting up of subsidiaries in other Member States.[121] There remains the possibility of justification of the measure in question.

It may finally be noted that, in contrast to the case-law on individuals' freedom of establishment, the case-law on corporate freedom of establishment appears to have little evolved towards a restriction-based analysis, namely the principle which the Court has increasingly applied in the context of Articles 30 (free movement of goods) and 59 (freedom to provide services), and to a lesser extent in the context of Articles 48 (free movement of workers) and Article 52 in relation to individuals, to the effect that even non-discriminatory rules may fall within the Treaty pro-

---

[118] See, for example, Case C–112/91 *Werner v Finanzamt Aachen-Innenstadt* [1993] ECR I–429, in which the Court expressly distinguished *Commission v France* on the ground that it was a case of discrimination by reference to nationality as opposed to residence: para 15 of the judgment, and the *Commerzbank* case, paras 13 to 14, which strongly suggest the same construction by the Court.

[119] See the *Segers* case, para 17 of the judgment; the *Halliburton* case, para 51 of the Opinion of Lenz AG; and *Commission v Italy*, para 26 of the judgment.

[120] Case 81/87 [1988] ECR 5483, discussed in ch XVIII.

[121] *ICI v Colmer*, para 22. See also the Opinion of Tesauro AG, para 21 (where in keeping with tradition 'registered office' should read 'seat').

hibitions where they restrict freedom of movement. The Court however in the *Futura* case adopted this approach in relation to the requirement, applicable to both resident and non-resident taxpayers, that accounts complying with local law should be kept within the territory, ruling that, in so far as it applied to non-resident taxpayers, that requirement was contrary to Article 52.

Attempts to Justify Restrictions

Determining whether a particular case of different treatment accorded to foreign companies is overt discrimination by reason of nationality or covert discrimination by reason of fiscal residence is not merely an academic exercise: it also determines whether the different treatment may be justified and, if so, which justifications may validly be pleaded. In all the cases discussed, the Member State concerned sought to rely on various grounds to justify the difference in treatment based on corporate nationality or fiscal residence. Some of these defences are relevant not to determining whether the alleged discrimination is justifiable as a matter of Community law but to the issue whether the difference of treatment is in fact discriminatory. These will be considered first.

Is the different treatment discriminatory?

Objective difference in situations

In *Commission v France*, the French Government sought to justify the denial of the tax credit to branches and agencies on the basis that the difference was based on the distinction between 'residents' and 'non-residents', which is to be found in all legal systems and is internationally accepted.[122] Although that argument failed in that case (and in the *Commerzbank* case), it is important to note that different treatment of non-nationals or non-residents will not necessarily be unlawful *per se*: it is only discriminatory if they are in all material respects in the same position as the nationals or residents of the Member State concerned. That underlines the importance of making the correct comparison.

Although the Court in *Commission v France* left open the possibility that a distinction based on the location of a company's seat or the place of residence of a natural person may, under certain conditions, be justified in an area such as tax law, the argument could not work in that case: since French tax law did not distinguish between the forms of secondary establishment for the purpose of determining their income liable to corporation tax, different treatment in regard to the grant of an advantage related to taxation, such as the tax credits at issue, could not but be discriminatory.[123] In the *Futura* case, Advocate General Lenz expressly referred to that

---

[122] Para 17 of the judgment.
[123] See also the arguments of Mancini AG on this point, at 281–3 (note that 'relevant' in the left-hand column at 282 should read 'irrelevant').

passage in the judgment in *Commission v France* and applied it to the case before him:

No difference of treatment of Luxembourg companies and branches in the area of the taxation of profits is apparent in this case either. If the Luxembourg legislature treats them in the same way in respect of the taxation of profits, it cannot follow that they are in a different situation as regards an advantage such as the carrying forward of losses.[124]

The Court in *Commission v France* also dismissed an argument by the French Government that the refusal to grant the tax credit was justified since it was balanced out by certain advantages enjoyed by branches and agencies. The Court stated that, even if there were such advantages, they could not justify a breach of the obligation laid down in Article 52 to accord foreign companies the same treatment in regard to shareholders' tax credits as is accorded to French companies.[125]

Similarly in the *Commerzbank* case the Court focused specifically on the allegedly discriminatory rule and would not be distracted by arguments about offsetting advantages enjoyed by branches. The United Kingdom had argued that, far from suffering discrimination under its tax rules, non-resident companies in Commerzbank's situation enjoyed privileged treatment since by virtue of the Anglo-American double-taxation treaty they were exempt from tax on such income whereas resident companies would be liable to pay tax in such circumstances: in the Government's view, non-resident companies were treated differently with respect to the repayment supplement because they were in different situations for tax purposes. The Court, adopting Advocate General Darmon's approach, dismissed that argument, concentrating solely on the fact that, in circumstances where tax had been wrongly paid and subsequently repaid to the taxpayer, resident companies were entitled to the supplement and non-resident companies were denied it.[126]

The approach endorsed by the Court in these cases, therefore, is not to compare the tax situation of a non-resident with that of a resident as a whole, but rather to consider whether they are in the same situation with regard specifically to the impugned measure.

Discrimination is avoidable

In the three cases of *France*, *Commerzbank* and *Futura*, where, in each, different treatment of branches on the one hand and subsidiaries on the other was at issue, the Member State concerned sought to argue that the different treatment could have been avoided if the company seeking to establish itself had done so by way of a subsidiary rather than a branch. Since the essence of discrimination is different treatment applied to a particular situation, it is a truism that discrimination is avoidable by changing that situation. It can hardly be regarded as a justification, and unsurprisingly the Court has not accepted it, stating in *Commission v France*:

---

[124] Para 39. The Court did not specifically deal with this point.   [125] Para 21.
[126] Paras 16–19 of the judgment and paras 44–5 and 55–6 of the Opinion.

the fact that insurance companies whose [seat] is situated in another Member State are at liberty to establish themselves by setting up a subsidiary in order to have the benefit of the tax credit cannot justify different treatment. The second sentence of the first paragraph of Article 52 expressly leaves traders free to choose the appropriate legal form in which to pursue their activities in another Member State and that freedom of choice must not be limited by discriminatory tax provisions.[127]

Although Advocate General Darmon referred to this point in the *Commerzbank* case, stating that the fact that a bank could have set up a subsidiary rather than a branch could not justify an infringement of the right of establishment and citing the passage from *Commission v France* set out above, it is hard to see how the defence could have been sensibly raised in the *Commerzbank* case, since if Commerzbank had operated in the United Kingdom by way of a subsidiary tax resident there, that subsidiary would have been liable to pay tax on the interest, there would have been no right to repayment and the issue of repayment supplement would not have arisen.

In the case of *Futura*, the argument was dealt with briefly by Advocate General Lenz, who referred to the Court's statement in *Commission v France* and concluded that different tax rules affecting branches and subsidiaries would restrict freedom to choose between the various possible forms of establishment, which was not allowed under the case-law of the Court. The Court itself in that case did not expressly consider the point.

It should perhaps be emphasized that the Court's statement in *Commission v France* that traders should be free to choose the appropriate legal form of secondary establishment does not necessarily mean that branches, agencies and subsidiaries must be treated identically in all respects, simply that, as the Court made clear, discriminatory restrictions are not permitted.

Public interest grounds

Various grounds have been pleaded by Member States as justification for restrictions on companies' freedom of establishment. Where the restriction in question distinguishes by reference to nationality, the only valid grounds are those set out in Article 56 of the Treaty, which provides:

The provisions of this Chapter and measures taken in pursuance thereof shall not prejudice the applicability of provisions laid down by law, regulation or administrative action providing for special treatment for foreign nationals on grounds of public policy, public security or public health.

The Court briefly considered the Article 56 defence in three of the cases considered above.

In the *Segers* case, the Court noted that Article 56 allowed within certain limits special treatment for companies formed in accordance with the law of another

[127] Para 22 of the judgment.

Member State provided that that treatment was justified on grounds of public policy, public security or public health.[128] In that case, the social security association had sought to justify its refusal to grant sickness cover to Mr Segers on the basis of the need to combat possible abuse and to ensure the proper implementation of the national social security legislation, in particular to ensure that directors did not elect to form a company under foreign law solely in order to circumvent the restrictions provided for in the Netherlands legislation concerning the formation of private companies.[129] The Court, although conceding that the need to combat fraud may justify a difference of treatment in certain circumstances, ruled that the refusal to accord a sickness benefit to a director of a company formed in accordance with the law of another Member State could not constitute an appropriate measure in that respect.[130] That approach echoes Advocate General Darmon's view that the mere possibility of a fraudulent purpose in an operation of the same type could not justify a general restriction on the right of establishment of natural and legal persons.[131]

In *Commission v Italy*, the Government had argued that the requirement that securities dealers be constituted as a *società per azioni* with its registered office in Italy was justified in the interests of investor protection and market stability. The Court stated:

Even if the aims pursued by the Italian legislation may be regarded as aims of 'public policy' within the meaning of those provisions, it follows *a fortiori* from what has been said above that the obligations at issue are not indispensable for achieving those aims and thus cannot be regarded as justified from the point of view of those provisions.[132]

In *ICI v Colmer*, the Court noted somewhat elliptically that diminution of tax revenue was not one of the grounds listed in Article 56. The Court in making that statement was dismissing an argument adduced by the United Kingdom to the effect that the national legislation at issue sought to prevent a reduction in revenue which would arise where a group had non-resident subsidiaries, since the Inland Revenue could not tax profits made by subsidiaries located outside the United Kingdom in order to offset the revenue lost through the granting of relief on losses incurred by resident subsidiaries.[133]

In the absence of more helpful guidance by the Court as to the scope of the public interest defence in the case of companies' freedom of establishment, some assistance may be found by analogy with the principles developed by the Court in relation to the scope of the public interest exceptions in the Treaty to the freedom to provide services and freedom of movement for workers.[134]

---

[128] Para 17 of the judgment.   [129] Para 10.   [130] Para 17.
[131] Para 6 of the Opinion.   [132] Para 26.
[133] See para 25. See further para 14 of the Opinion of La Pergola AG in Case C–212/97 *Centros Ltd v Erhvervs- og Selskabsstyrelsen*, delivered on 16 July 1998.
[134] See in particular the Opinion of Warner AG in Case 30/77 *Regina v Bouchereau* [1977] ECR 1999, pp 2023–6, for a discussion of the concept of public policy.

First, the Court has stated that, since the particular circumstances justifying recourse to the concept of public policy may vary from one country to another and from one period to another, it is necessary to allow the competent national authorities an area of discretion.[135] That discretion however is similarly subject to control by the institutions of the Community.[136]

Second, the Court in considering the concept of public policy as a permitted ground of derogation from the principle of the freedom of movement for workers has stressed that the concept must be interpreted strictly.[137]

Third, the Court has made it clear that a Member State may not rely on the public policy exception to the principle of freedom of movement for workers to justify measures seeking to exclude nationals of other Member States on the basis of conduct which is not penalized to an equivalent extent, *mutatis mutandis*, when undertaken by its own nationals.[138]

Finally it may be noted that, in considering whether a Member State is entitled to plead that a measure is justified on public policy grounds, the Court has shown itself ready to override domestic legal categorization where it is not appropriate in the relevant Community law context.[139]

Where the impugned measure is applicable without distinction to nationals and non-nationals but discriminatory in effect, it may none the less be lawful if it is justified by imperative reasons of public interest and suitable and necessary for attaining the aim pursued (in other words, proportionate). In the cases discussed in this chapter, Member States have put forward various grounds in (unsuccessful) attempts to validate the measure. There is however a great deal of confusion—not always corrected by the Court—in this area. Measures which the Court has in some contexts appeared to treat as discriminatory, such as those at issue in *Commission v France* and in the *Halliburton* case, have been defended on the basis of grounds going beyond the public interest defences set out in Article 56. This confusion, like other clouded issues in this area, reflects the difficulty of transposing to companies principles developed in the context of individuals. Although the Court stated clearly in *Commission v France* that a company's seat connects it to a particular State in the same way as nationality in the case of individuals, it is more appropriate, particularly in a fiscal context, to assimilate the location of a company's seat rather to residence. The issue thus becomes one of covert rather than overt discrimination, with the broader panoply of possible justifications. Those which have been raised in this context are briefly discussed below.

[135] Case 41/74 *Van Duyn v Home Office* [1974] ECR 1337, para 18 of the judgment. See also Case 36/75 *Rutili v Minister for the Interior* [1975] ECR 1219, para 26.

[136] *Van Duyn v Home Office*, para 18 of the judgment. See also *Rutili v Minister for the Interior*, para 27 and Case 72/83 *Campus Oil Ltd v Minister for Industry and Energy* [1984] ECR 2727, para 32.

[137] *Van Duyn v Home Office*, para 18 of the judgment, and *Regina v Bouchereau*, para 35.

[138] Joined Cases 115 and 116/81 *Adoui and Cornuaille v Belgium* [1982] ECR 1665, para 8 of the judgment.

[139] Case 16/83 *Prantl* [1984] ECR 1299, para 33 of the judgment. See also the Opinion of Advocate General Slynn, p 1338.

Lack of harmonization

In *Commission v France*, the French Government argued that the differential treatment was due to and took account of the differences between national tax systems. Until harmonization of the relevant taxes, it argued that different measures were necessary. The Court summarily disposed of that argument.[140] Similarly, Advocate General Lenz gave short shrift to the argument that tax relief in the case of companies from other Member States could be granted only if the relevant legislative provisions were harmonized.[141] Thus, although pending harmonization a company's tax position continues to be governed by national law, delay on the part of the Community legislature does not suspend the Member States' obligation to apply their tax laws in a non-discriminatory way.[142]

As will be seen, in relation to restrictions on the right of primary establishment the lack of harmonization of laws relating to the retention of legal personality on the transfer of a company's seat has, in contrast, been accepted by the Court as relevant: see further below.

Risk of tax avoidance

In *Commission v France*, the French Government had also pleaded the danger of tax avoidance, arguing that if the legislation were abolished, foreign companies owning shares in French companies might allocate those shares to a branch or agency operating in France solely in order to benefit from the tax credit. The Court stated that the risk of tax avoidance could not be relied upon in this context.[143]

It must be borne in mind that what is at issue here is tax avoidance, namely the lawful exploitation of, for example, lacunae in fiscal legislation to the taxpayer's advantage, and not tax evasion,[144] which involves the contravention of fiscal legislation. Tax evasion is conceptually more akin to fraud than it is to tax avoidance, and a genuinely substantiated risk of tax evasion may more properly be considered to be a matter of public policy and fall within the Article 56 exception.

In *ICI v Colmer*, the United Kingdom Government sought to raise a justification of tax avoidance, arguing that the legislation at issue was designed to reduce the risk of tax avoidance arising from the possibility for members of a consortium to channel the charges of non-resident subsidiaries to a subsidiary resident in the United Kingdom and to have profits accrue to non-resident subsidiaries. The purpose of the legislation was accordingly, in the view of the Government, to prevent the creation of foreign subsidiaries from being used as a means of depriving the United Kingdom Treasury of taxable revenues.[145]

---

[140] See p 347 above.   [141] See p 356 above.
[142] Para 6 of the Opinion of Mancini AG in *Commission v France*.   [143] See p 347 above.
[144] Notwithstanding the use of the term in the English text of the first part of the judgment (294) in translation of the French '*évasion fiscale*'; the latter is a *faux ami*, and means tax avoidance, tax evasion being rendered in French by '*fraude fiscale*'.
[145] See para 25 of the judgment.

The Court dismissed this argument in very summary fashion in the following terms:

As regards the justification based on the risk of tax avoidance, suffice it to note that the legislation at issue in the main proceedings does not have the specific purpose of preventing wholly artificial arrangements, set up to circumvent United Kingdom tax legislation, from attracting tax benefits, but applies generally to all situations in which the majority of a group's subsidiaries are established, for whatever reason, outside the United Kingdom. However, the establishment of a company outside the United Kingdom does not, of itself, necessarily entail tax avoidance, since that company will in any event be subject to the tax legislation of the State of establishment.[146]

It is unfortunate that the Court did not take the opportunity to give some more useful guidance on the scope of tax avoidance as a justification. It would seem to be unnecessarily restrictive if only legislation which was wholly and exclusively designed to combat tax avoidance could fall within the scope of the justification.

Double-taxation treaties and reciprocity

Again in *Commission v France*, the Court had occasion to rule on this attempted defence. The French Government had argued that the different treatment could be resolved only by adding reciprocal provisions to the existing double-taxation conventions. Although the Court found that the conventions relied on were not in fact relevant, it took the opportunity to state:

The rights conferred by Article 52 of the Treaty are unconditional and a Member State cannot make respect for them subject to the contents of an agreement concluded with another Member State. In particular, that article does not permit those rights to be made subject to a condition of reciprocity imposed for the purpose of obtaining corresponding advantages in other Member States.[147]

In the *Commerzbank* case, the United Kingdom had sought to argue that the Anglo-American double-taxation convention removed any possibility of discrimination against non-resident companies since the latter were exempt from tax which only resident companies had to pay. Although this argument goes primarily to the issue of the correct comparison and the irrelevance of offsetting advantages (and as noted above failed in that context), Advocate General Darmon picked up the double-taxation treaty point, and explicitly extended the ruling of the Court in *Commission v France*, set out above, to the application of a double-taxation convention concluded between a non-member country and a Member State before accession to the Community.[148] It may be noted that the Anglo-American

---

[146] Para 26.

[147] Para 26. Double-taxation conventions have however been used to reach the same result as the Court reached in *Commission v France*: see n 30.

[148] Para 21. See further on the complex issue of double taxation treaties Farmer, P, 'EC Law and Direct Taxation—Some Thoughts on Recent Issues' (1995–96) 1 EC Tax Journal 91; Farmer, P, 'EC Law and National Rules on Direct Taxation: A Phoney War?' [1998] EC Tax Review 13; Hinnekens, L, 'Non-Discrimination in EC Income Tax Law: Painting in the Colours of a Chameleon-Like

double-taxation convention at issue in the *Commerzbank* case was concluded in 1946. In *Commission v France*, where several conventions were applicable, the Court did not consider the chronology; Advocate General Mancini assumed that they post-dated France's accession and invoked Article 234 of the Treaty.[149]

Finally, in the different context of securities market regulation, the Court noted in *Commission v Italy* that a Member State could not plead failure by another Member State to respect the principle of reciprocity to justify its own default.[150] It will be recalled that Italy's argument was in essence that it was not possible to compare the conditions laid down by the Italian legislation regarding authorization, supervision and solvency of securities dealers with those laid down by the other Member States.

Administrative difficulties

In the case of *Halliburton*, the Netherlands Government contended that the restriction of the exemption to companies constituted under national law was necessary because its tax authorities were unable to check whether the legal forms of entities constituted in other Member States were equivalent to its *naamlozen venootschappen* and *besloten venootschappen met beperkte aansprakelijkheid*. The Court rejected the argument, pointing out that the authorities could use the system of exchanging information envisaged by Directive (EEC) 77/799.[151]

Similarly in *Commission v Italy* the Court considered and rejected Italy's argument that dealers could not be supervised and effectively sanctioned unless they had their principal place of business in Italy. The Court noted in particular that, given that there were no convincing reasons why Italy could not require dealers based abroad who wished to operate by way of a branch or agency in Italy to agree to be subject to checks and guarantees and to provide certain information and documents, the requirement that dealers operate as a *società per azioni* with its registered office in Italy was not indispensable for achieving Italy's aims of transparency and stability of the securities markets and hence could not be regarded as justified from the point of view of the public policy exception in Article 56.[152]

Fiscal supervision

It had been argued in the *Futura* case that a national measure such as the condition that a non-resident taxpayer keep, in the Member State in which tax was to be

Principle' [1996] European Taxation 286; Vanistendael, F, 'The Limits to the New Community Tax Order' (1994) 31 CMLR 293; and Williams, D, 'Freedom of Establishment and Double Taxation Agreements' (1994) 19 ELR 313, 318. The latter comments on Darmon AG in the *Commerzbank* case: 'An inconvenient aspect of the Advocate General's argument is that it might completely undermine the European approach to the sanctity of tax agreements, even if it does so for the best of reasons.'

[149] See para 7 of the Opinion.   [150] Para 27.

[151] Cited in n 92 above. See pp 356–7 above for further discussion of this point, and for a critique of the Court's 'mantra-like' reference to the Mutual Assistance Directive as a solution, see Vermeend, W, 'The Court of Justice of the European Communities and direct taxes: "Est-ce que la justice est de ce monde"?' [1996] EC Tax Review 54, 55.

[152] Paras 21–6.

charged, accounts relating to his activities in that State which complied with the relevant national rules was essential in order for the amount of income taxable in that State to be ascertainable by the State's tax authorities. The Court ruled that the effectiveness of fiscal supervision constituted an overriding requirement of general interest capable of justifying a restriction on the exercise of fundamental freedoms guaranteed by the Treaty, and that a Member State could therefore apply measures enabling the amount of both the income taxable in that State and the losses which could be carried forward there to be ascertained clearly and precisely.[153] However, the Court again considered that the measures at issue went beyond what was necessary to attain the desired aim, namely to enable the amount of deductible losses carried forward to be ascertained: there were other ways by which the taxpayer could clearly and precisely demonstrate the amount of the losses concerned; moreover, under Directive (EEC) 77/799 the competent authorities of a Member State could always request the relevant information from the authorities of another Member State.[154]

In this context it may be noted that the justification of fiscal coherence[155] accepted by the Court in *Bachmann v Belgium*[156] and *Commission v Belgium*[157] has been marginalized by future case-law: see most recently *ICI v Colmer*.[158]

---

[153] Para 31.   [154] Paras 39–41.

[155] Sometimes, less accurately, rendered as 'cohesion', an over-literal translation of the French 'cohésion'. The concept has been graphically described by Knobbe-Keuk, B, as 'arcane' and 'slippery': 'Restrictions on the Fundamental Freedoms Enshrined in the EC Treaty by Discriminatory Tax Provisions—Ban and Justification' [1994] EC Tax Review 74, 81, 84.

[156] Case C–204/90 [1992] ECR I–249.   [157] Case C–300/90 [1992] ECR I–305.

[158] Cited in n 18; para 29 of the judgment.

XVIII

Primary Establishment and Mutual Recognition of Companies

A Right of Primary Establishment?

A natural person exercises his right of primary establishment under Article 52 by removing himself from one Member State and establishing himself in another. The equivalent procedure for a company consists in the removal of its seat from one Member State to another while retaining the links giving it corporate nationality of the first Member State, normally by virtue of the fact of incorporation and retention of registered office there.[1] For a number of reasons, it is rare in practice for a company to wish to do this. As indicated above, the State of incorporation may, because it applies the real seat theory of corporate nationality, require the dissolution and consequent loss of legal personality of a company wishing to relocate in such a way; the host State may similarly refuse to recognize the foreign company as a properly constituted corporate entity unless it is wound up and reconstituted as a local company. The effect of this refusal to recognize the corporate status of the company may be, as in Germany, that the shareholders incur personal liability for the company's debts, that the company will be treated for tax purposes as a partnership and taxed accordingly,[2] and that the company will be unable to enter into contracts, own property or bring legal proceedings in its own right.[3]

On any common sense view, so treating a foreign company restricts its right of establishment; certainly impediments on the right to contract, hold property and bring proceedings are explicitly recognized as such in the Council's General Programme for the abolition of restrictions on the freedom of establishment,[4] and

---

[1] An alternative procedure is envisaged by the draft Proposal for a 14th Directive on the transfer of the registered office or *de facto* head office of a company from one Member State to another with a change in the applicable law, issued by the Commission in 1997 (XV/6002/97). See further p 383 below.

[2] Subject to any applicable double-taxation treaty: see for further discussion Frommel, S N, 'The Real Seat Doctrine and Dual-Resident Companies under German Law: Another View' (1990) 30 European Taxation 267, responding to Ebenroth, C T and Daiber, C, 'Dual-Resident Companies Under German Law' (1990) 30 European Taxation 175.

[3] Put more colourfully, 'The carefully structured corporation turns into a formless group of co-owners, as Cinderella's harnessed steeds became scrambling, squeaking mice at the stroke of midnight': Conard, A F, 'Company Laws of the European Communities from an American Viewpoint' in Schmitthoff, C M (ed), *The Harmonisation of European Company Law* (1973).

[4] 18 December 1961, OJ Spec Ed IX, Resolutions of the Council and of the Representatives of the Member States, 7. The Court has stated that the General Programme 'provides useful guidance for the

Advocate General Darmon expressed the view in his Opinion in *The Queen v HM Treasury and Commissioners of Inland Revenue, ex p Daily Mail and General Trust PLC*[5] that the incorporation theory was 'more consistent with Community objectives in regard to establishment'.[6] At least before the judgment in the *Daily Mail* case, many commentators were of the view that the Treaty provisions on freedom of establishment implicitly required the host State to recognize a company incorporated in another Member State.[7] Understandably however few businessmen are likely to be willing to be test cases, particularly since there are attractive alternatives to primary establishment with all its uncertainties: setting up a foreign subsidiary or acquiring an existing company as a subsidiary, both rights unequivocally protected by the Treaty, are clearly safer alternatives; if even that is regarded as too burdensome or costly, a branch or agency may be used. It is therefore scarcely surprising that companies rarely seek to move their seat and that questions relating to companies' rights of primary establishment have so rarely come before the Court of Justice.[8]

There are however two cases in which those issues have been raised, although since the first, *Segers v Bedrijfsvereniging voor Bank- en Verzekeringswezen, Groothandel en Vrije Beroepen*, is normally—and it is submitted incorrectly—regarded as a case concerning secondary establishment, it has already been discussed. Both concerned an actual or proposed corporate structure involving a company which was incorporated and had its registered office in England while its real seat or central management and control was in or was sought to be transferred to the Netherlands. Since both the United Kingdom and the Netherlands apply the incorporation theory, the corporate decision-makers concerned ran no risk of encountering problems of recognition. In the *Daily Mail* case however they encountered a problem of another order, and the proceedings generated by the company's attempt to have that problem resolved in its favour led to the Court's ruling that the transfer of a company's central management and control does not fall within the right of establishment protected by the Treaty.

---

implementation of the relevant provisions of the Treaty' (Case 71/76 *Thieffry v Conseil de l'Ordre des Avocats à la Cour de Paris* [1977] ECR 765, para 14 of the judgment and Case 79/85 *Segers v Bedrijfsvereniging voor Bank- en Verzekeringswezen, Groothandel en Vrije Beroepen* [1986] ECR 2375, para 15).

[5] Case 81/87 [1988] ECR 5483. [6] Para 13.

[7] See to this effect Goldman, B, 'The Convention between the Member States of the European Economic Community on the Mutual Recognition of Companies and Legal Persons' (1968) 6 CMLR 104; Stein, E, *The Harmonization of European Company Laws* (1971); Boyle, A J, 'The Recognition of Companies in the EEC' in Goode, R M and Simmonds, K R (eds), *Commercial Operations in Europe* (1978); Timmermans, C W A, 'The Convention of 29 February 1968 on the Mutual Recognition of Companies and Firms' (1980) Netherlands International Law Review 357; Cerexhe, E, *Le droit européen—La libre circulation des personnes et des entreprises* (1982); Cath, I G F, 'Freedom of Establishment of Companies: a New Step Towards Completion of the Internal Market' (1986) 6 Yearbook of European Law 247; Burrows, F, *Free Movement in European Community Law* (1987). The Convention, which has not been ratified, is considered further below (see pp 384–6).

[8] Another reason for the paucity of case-law at the national level is that there is a latticework of bilateral conventions requiring recognition as between certain Member States subscribing to the real seat theory.

The *Daily Mail* case[9]

Daily Mail, an investment company incorporated under English law and with both its registered office and its central management and control (and hence under UK law its fiscal residence[10]) in the United Kingdom, wished to transfer its central management and control to the Netherlands. It was common ground that the principal reason for the proposed transfer was to enable it to realize in a tax-efficient manner certain holdings of shares. If it sold the shares while tax-resident in the United Kingdom it would be liable to United Kingdom capital gains tax[11] of over £13 million. If in contrast it transferred its fiscal residence to the Netherlands, it would no longer be liable to United Kingdom capital gains tax while incurring liability to Netherlands capital gains tax solely on any gain in the value of the shares since the transfer of residence. United Kingdom Treasury consent was required in order for a company resident for tax purposes in the United Kingdom to cease to be so resident. The Treasury proposed making such consent dependent on the company's first liquidating a substantial proportion of its portfolio, which would trigger the liability to capital gains tax designed to be eliminated by the proposed transfer. The company brought proceedings in the High Court essentially seeking a declaration that it was entitled under Article 52 either to transfer its residence to the Netherlands without the consent or in the alternative to receive unconditional consent. The High Court,[12] expressing doubt whether the relevant United Kingdom legislation should be allowed to prevent or fetter the voluntary movement of residence of a corporation which wished to take advantage of a better fiscal climate in another Member State, asked the Court in essence whether Articles 52 and 58 precluded a Member State from prohibiting a company from transferring its central management and control to another Member State where the proposed transfer would reduce the company's tax liability.[13]

The arguments of both the applicant and the United Kingdom (the only government to submit observations) focused on whether the right to leave was an

---

[9] See Schmitthoff, C M, 'Tax and Company Migration' [1988] Business Law Brief, December, 2–3, and case-note in [1988] JBL 454; van Thiel, S, 'Daily Mail Case—Tax Planning and the European Right of Establishment—A Setback' (1988) 28 European Taxation 357; Lever, J's case-note in (1989) 26 CMLR 327; Frommel, S N, 'EEC Companies and Migration: A Setback for Europe?' [1988] Intertax 409; Cath, I G F, 'Free Movement of Legal Persons' in *Free Movement of persons in Europe: Legal Problems and Experiences* (1993); Knobbe-Keuk, B, 'Restrictions on the Fundamental Freedoms Enshrined in the EC Treaty by Discriminatory Tax Provisions—Ban and Justification' [1994] EC Tax Review 74.

[10] At the time of the facts, this was by virtue of the locus of its central management and control. The law was subsequently changed so that a company is now treated as resident for tax purposes in the UK if it is incorporated there or has its central management and control there. See Gammie, M, 'UK Company Residence: The New Rules' [1988] Intertax 416.

[11] More correctly, corporation tax on capital gains.

[12] [1987] 2 CMLR 1; [1987] STC 157, DC.

[13] The court also asked whether Council Directive (EEC) 73/148 on the abolition of restrictions on movement and residence within the Community for nationals of Member States with regard to establishment and the provision of services [1973] OJ L172/14 conferred such a right of transfer. The Court ruled that the directive did not apply to legal persons.

essential component of the right of establishment and whether on the facts the proposed relocation of the company's central management and control would amount to genuine establishment in the host State. The Commission however considered the issue against the background of the different approaches of the Member States to the question of corporate mobility. In its view, where the transfer of central management and control was possible under national legislation, the right to transfer it to another Member State was protected by Article 52.

The Court's starting point was that the Treaty provisions guaranteeing freedom of establishment, although directed mainly at ensuring that foreign nationals and companies were treated in the host Member State in the same way as nationals of that State, 'also prohibit the Member State of origin from hindering the establishment in another Member State of . . . a company incorporated under its legislation . . . the rights guaranteed by Article 52 et seq. would be rendered meaningless if the Member State of origin could prohibit undertakings from leaving in order to establish themselves in another Member State'.[14]

The Court noted that the legislation at issue imposed no restrictions on the exercise by a company incorporated in the United Kingdom of its right of establishment by way of setting up branches, agencies or subsidiaries or by taking a lesser stake in another company incorporated in another Member State[15] or on the transfer of its business to a company incorporated in another Member State, if necessary after winding up and consequential settling of tax affairs;[16] the Court had already noted that the latter structure was permissible in all Member States.[17]

With regard to the transfer of its central management and control by a company retaining its legal personality and status as a United Kingdom company however the Court, like the Commission, considered the issue against the background of the fundamental differences within the Community on whether national laws permitted such a transaction, stating:

. . . it should be borne in mind that, unlike natural persons, companies are creatures of the law and, in the present state of Community law, creatures of national law. They exist only by virtue of the varying national legislation which determines their incorporation and functioning. As the Commission has emphasized, the legislation of the Member States varies widely in regard to both the factor providing a connection to the national territory required for the incorporation of a company and the question whether a company incorporated under the legislation of a Member State may subsequently modify that connecting factor. . . . The Treaty has taken account of that variety in national legislation. In defining, in Article 58, the companies which enjoy the right of establishment, the Treaty places on the same footing, as connecting factors, the registered office, central administration and principal place of business of a company.[18]

---

[14] Para 16 of the judgment.
[15] In which case Article 221 of the Treaty requires that the foreign shareholder be treated equally with national shareholders.
[16] Paras 17 and 18. [17] Para 14. [18] Paras 19–21.

The Court referred to the lack of any convention under Article 220 of the Treaty providing for the retention of legal personality in the event of cross-border transfer of a company's seat[19] and to the failure of any of the company law directives to address the issue[20] before concluding:

It must therefore be held that the Treaty regards the differences in national legislation concerning the required connecting factor and the question whether—and if so how—the registered office or real head office[21] of a company incorporated under national law may be transferred from one Member State to another as problems which are not resolved by the rules concerning the right of establishment but must be dealt with by future legislation or conventions.

Under those circumstances, Articles 52 and 58 of the Treaty cannot be interpreted as conferring on companies incorporated under the law of a Member State a right to transfer their central management and control and their central administration to another Member State while retaining their status as companies incorporated under the legislation of the first Member State.[22]

The Court's apparently bold statement early in the judgment that there is a right of primary establishment for companies[23] seems thus to be whittled down to nothing until the differences in national law have been smoothed out by legislation or convention: the Treaty right of an undertaking to leave a Member State in order to establish itself in another Member State, recognized by the Court in paragraph 16, has by paragraph 24 moved out of the scope of the Treaty. Although commentators are hostile to the Court's reformulation of the tax question into a conflict-of-laws matter, it is perhaps understandable. Even if the Court had not given an answer that was as explicit as that suggested by the Commission, a more neutral ruling that the impugned measure was prima facie contrary to Article 52 would have risked being seen as an implied endorsement by the Court of the incorporation theory at the expense of the real seat theory: it would in effect have protected from discrimination companies moving between States which applied the incorporation theory while failing to dismantle the impermeable barriers preventing companies from moving between States which applied the real seat theory. It may be however that that would have been preferable to the very narrow line in fact taken by the Court.[24] Article 220 of the Treaty imposes an obligation on Member

---

[19] Again mistranslated as 'registered office', despite the facts that Art 220 itself refers to 'in the event of transfer of [a company's] seat from one country to another' and that the *Daily Mail* case did not concern a transfer of registered office. Art 220 probably refers to both registered office and real seat: that is the implication of para 23 of the judgment in the *Daily Mail* case and appears to be the assumption of the Commission in framing the draft 14th Directive (see following note).

[20] A draft Proposal for a 14th Directive on the transfer of the registered office or *de facto* head office of a company from one Member State to another with a change in the applicable law was issued by the Commission in 1997 (XV/6002/97). See further p 383 below.

[21] In French, *siège réel*.   [22] Paras 23 and 24.   [23] Para 16; see text to n 14 above.

[24] The decision has been described as 'a set-back' (van Thiel (n 25 below) and Frommel, S N, 'EEC Companies and Migration: A Setback for Europe?' [1988] Intertax 409), 'totally wrong' (Schmitthoff, C M, 'Tax and Company Migration' [1988] Business Law Brief, December 2–3), 'regrettable' (Schmitthoff, ibid), and 'truly disappointing' (Frommel, ibid).

States, so far as is necessary, to enter into negotiations with each other with a view to securing for the benefit of their nationals the retention of legal personality in the event of transfer of their seat from one country to another. It is surely perverse that the Court in the *Daily Mail* case severely restricted companies' rights of primary establishment on the ground that no agreement under this head of Article 220 had been reached; moreover such reasoning appears to conflict directly with the fundamental principle in Community law that the failure of a Member State to fulfil its obligations under the Treaty cannot erode the directly applicable rights conferred by the Treaty on natural and legal persons.[25] It is ironic that lack of action under Article 220 was invoked by the Court in a case in which it was clearly not necessary for the Member States concerned, both of which recognized the retention of legal personality in the event of cross-border transfer of corporate seat.

The Court's reliance on the absence of harmonization of the rules relating to transfer of corporate seat may also be contrasted with its readiness in the context of secondary establishment to dismiss arguments based on the lack of harmonization: see for example *Commission v France*[26] and the *Halliburton* case.[27]

The approach of the Court may be contrasted with that of Darmon AG. The Advocate General first analysed the concept of establishment, stating that it was essentially an economic concept, implying a genuine economic link. He concluded that the transfer of the central management and control of a company, understood by reference to criteria which were economic rather than legal, was covered by the right of establishment where what was at issue was the genuine siting of[28] 'the economic centre of gravity of the undertaking'.[29]

The Advocate General then discussed the difficulties in laying down specific rules for determining whether, in a given case, a proposed transfer of central management and control constituted genuine establishment[30] and suggested a non-exhaustive list of factors to be taken into account in making such an assessment.[31] Where the proper conclusion to drawn from the circumstances was that the transfer of the central management genuinely constituted establishment, the Advocate General considered that the Member State of origin was not prevented from requiring the company to settle its fiscal position before the transfer.[32] He reached that conclusion in the light of the different consequences attached by Member States to such a transfer. As he pointed out, it was generally accepted (and was in fact implicitly confirmed by the Court in its judgment[33]) that the winding-up, and consequent settlement of its tax position, required by some Member States as a condition for the emigration of a company, was not contrary to Community law,[34]

---

[25] See further van Thiel, S, 'Daily Mail Case' (1988) 28 European Taxation 357, 363–4.

[26] See p 347 above.   [27] See p 356 above.

[28] '*dès lors qu'il s'agit de situer concrètement*', delphically translated in the ECR as 'in so far as it is necessary to determine in concrete terms'.

[29] Para 5, original footnotes omitted.   [30] Para 7.   [31] Para 8.   [32] Para 13.

[33] See paras 20–3.

[34] See for a criticism of this reasoning KPMG European Business Centre, Brussels, *Study on Transfer of the Head Office of a Company from One Member State to Another* (1993). It is argued that this approach

and it would be 'paradoxical if a Member State not requiring winding-up were to find itself placed by Community law in a less favourable fiscal position precisely because its legislation on companies was more consistent with Community objectives in regard to establishment'.[35]

Darmon AG thus proposed that the Court should rule that:

(1)   The transfer to another Member State of the central management of a company may constitute a form of exercise of the right of establishment, subject to the assessment by the national court of any elements of fact showing whether or not such a transfer reflects a genuine integration of the said company into the economic life of the host Member State;

(2)   Under Community law a Member State may not require a company wishing to establish itself in another Member State, by transferring its central management there, to obtain prior authorization for such transfer;

(3)   However, Community law does not prohibit a Member State from requiring a company established on its territory, upon establishing itself in another Member State by transferring its central management there, to settle its tax position in regard to the part of its assets affected by the transfer, the value of which is to be determined at the date of the transfer . . .

In this, and in contrast to the Court, he kept the issue within the confines of the questions as posed by the national court. It is submitted that a ruling along the lines of the Advocate General's suggested solution would have been preferable.

Where however the circumstances showed that the purpose of the proposed transfer was to circumvent national legislation, the Advocate General considered that Community law would offer no assistance.[36] In this context, he stated:

The fact that the essential activities of a company take place on the territory of a Member State other than that to which it intends to transfer its central management may not be ignored. Such circumstances may, in certain cases, constitute an indication that what is involved is not genuine establishment, in particular when the effect of the transfer of the central management is to cause the company to cease to be subject to legislation which would otherwise apply to it. I believe that that conclusion can be drawn from the judgments of the Court in Van Binsbergen[37] and Knoors.[38]

In Van Binsbergen v Bedrijfsvereniging Metaalnijverheid, the Court first formulated the principle that a Member State is entitled to take measures in order to prevent a

considers the question of freedom of establishment from the point of view only of the legislation of the State of arrival and not of the State of departure and thus fails to consider whether the fact that the company is dissolved is itself an obstacle to the freedom of establishment imposed by the State of departure: 15.

[35]   Paras 11 and 13.

[36]   Para 9. See however the Opinion of La Pergola AG in Case C–212/97 Centros Ltd v Erhvervs- og Selskagbsstyrelsen, delivered on 16 July 1998, where it appears to be argued that the principle invoked by Darmon AG can have no application in the context of the freedom of establishment of a company constituted in accordance with the law of a Member State: para 20.

[37]   Case 33/74 Van Binsbergen v Bedrijfsvereniging Metaalnijverheid [1974] ECR 1299.

[38]   Case 115/78 Knoors v Secretary of State for Economic Affairs [1979] ECR 399.

provider of services whose activity is entirely or principally directed towards its territory from exercising the freedom to provide services in order to avoid the legislation applicable in the State of destination. Similar principles were invoked by the Court in the context of the right of establishment in *Knoors v Secretary of State for Economic Affairs*, in which the Court stated that it was not possible to disregard the legitimate interest which a Member State may have in preventing certain of its nationals, by means of facilities created under the Treaty, from attempting wrongly to evade the application of their national legislation as regards training for a trade, and in the context of the free movement of goods in *Leclerc v Au Blé Vert*,[39] in which it stated that Article 30 would not invalidate a measure prima facie contrary to it where it was established that the goods in question had been exported for the sole purpose of re-importation in order to circumvent the measure. The principle was applied by the Court in *Vereniging Veronica Omroep Organisatie v Commissariat voor de Media*[40] and *TV10 SA v Commissariat voor de Media*.[41] It has moreover been endorsed by the Community legislature: the preamble to the Second Banking Directive[42] states that a Member State may refuse to license a credit institution where the circumstances show that the institution 'has opted for the legal system of one Member State for the purpose of evading the stricter standards in force in another Member State in which it intends to carry on or carries on the greater part of its activities' (see the 8th recital).

Possible application of the *Van Binsbergen* principle could resolve the concern of commentators that an unqualified ruling that a prohibition on transfer of a company's seat was contrary to Article 52 would lead to a flood of tax-motivated transfers. In any event, the response to such a ruling would be unlikely to be on the scale envisaged had the Court followed the Advocate General in endorsing a Member State's right to settle its tax position before transfer.[43]

Reconciling the cases of *Segers* and *Daily Mail*

Any attempt to derive coherent principles from these two cases is somewhat hampered by the Court's misconceived analysis in *Segers v Bedrijfsvereniging voor Banken Verzekeringswezen, Groothandel en Vrije Beroepen*.[44] Nonetheless, it is submitted that the two judgments are not, as has been suggested,[45] irreconcilable. It is clear

[39] Case 229/83 [1985] ECR I. [40] Case C–148/91 [1993] ECR I–487.

[41] Case C–23/93 [1994] ECR I–4795.

[42] 2nd Council Directive (EEC) 89/646 on the coordination of laws, regulations and administrative provisions relating to the taking up and pursuit of the business of credit institutions and amending Directive (EEC) 77/780 [1989] OJ L386/1.

[43] It may be noted that the UK changed its legislation in March 1988, before both the Opinion and the judgment, to this effect: the Finance Act 1988, s 105, deems a company ceasing to be UK resident to have disposed of and reacquired at their market value all its chargeable assets (with the exception of any UK branch assets remaining within the charge).

[44] Case 79/85 [1986] ECR 2375.

[45] See e g Frommel, S N, 'EEC Companies and Migration: A Setback for Europe?' [1988] Intertax 409 and Reindl, A, 'Companies in the European Community: Are the Conflict-of-Law Rules Ready for 1992?' (1990) 11 Michigan Journal of International Law 1270.

from the *Daily Mail* case that the question whether a company's seat, in the sense of any of the three connecting factors listed in Article 58, may be transferred from one Member State to another, and therefore whether the State of origin may in effect fetter a proposed transfer, cannot be answered by reference to the Treaty provisions on the freedom of establishment. Where, however, a company's seat has in fact been so transferred, as it was in the case of *Segers* where there was no tax issue and hence no requirement for authorization, it is clear from the *Segers* case that the host State cannot treat the company (including its employees) differently from companies incorporated under its national law where the difference is based on the company's form, the State where it was incorporated or the location of its registered office. It is therefore still the case that a national of a Member State may, like Mr Segers, 'take advantage of the flexibility of United Kingdom company law and . . . exploit the effect of the attraction, which in his view, an Anglo-Saxon designation has for his customers'[46] where the United Kingdom imposes no restriction on corporate exit.

The Commission's response

Whatever criticism may be levelled at the judgment in the *Daily Mail* case, it had the benefit of prompting a legislative initiative by the Commission, which in 1993 published a study on the transfer of a company's seat from one Member State to another.[47] The study focuses on the transfer of a company's head office—the place of its central management and control[48]—without the company's dissolution and is limited to considering whether Member States' rules of company and private international law should be harmonized so as to enable a company to transfer its *siège réel* to another Member State without dissolution.

After examining the academic and pragmatic arguments in favour of a harmonized framework for the transfer of a company's real seat, the study considers a number of practical problems which would need to be resolved by harmonization: namely protection of shareholders, unsecured and secured creditors, employees, debenture-holders and holders of securities other than shares, forum-shopping, tax and legal certainty (in particular, how to ensure a simple mechanism for recognizing when a company's real seat has in fact been transferred). It then discusses the option of providing for the transfer of a company's registered office and reviews the provisions of existing Community legislation governing analogous transfers in the context of the European Economic Interest Grouping,[49] the European

---

[46] Opinion of Darmon AG in the *Segers* case, para 6.

[47] *Study on Transfer of the Head Office of a Company from One Member State to Another*, carried out by KPMG European Business Centre, Brussels (1993). For a commentary see Bellingwout, J W, 'Company Migration in Motion: The KPMG Report 1993' in Wouters, J and Schneider, H (eds), *Current Issues of Cross-Border Establishment of Companies in the European Union* (1995).

[48] 'Head office' is stated to mean *siège réel*, defined as 'the place where the company has established its central management and control'. The study sometimes uses one term, sometimes the other.

[49] Council Reg (EEC) 2137/85 on the European Economic Interest Grouping (EEIG) [1985] OJ L199/1.

Company[50] and cross-border mergers.[51] The study concludes by proposing two possible solutions, reflecting first the incorporation doctrine and second the real seat doctrine without dissolution: Annexed to the study[52] are draft directives on the transfer of the real seat from one Member State to another Member State without dissolution (the company remaining subject to the law of the State of incorporation) and on the transfer of the registered office from one Member State to another Member State without dissolution (with change of applicable law).

The Commission has opted for a combination of the two approaches suggested in the study, and in 1997 issued a draft Proposal for a Fourteenth Directive on the transfer of the registered office or *de facto* head office of a company from one Member State to another with a change in applicable law.[53] In brief, this directive would require Member States to take all measures necessary to allow a company to transfer its registered office or *de facto* head office to another Member State without being wound up and reincorporated but with the law applicable to the company changing as from the date of registration of the transfer. 'Registered office' is defined as 'the place where the company is registered' and '*de facto* head office' (*siège réel* in the French version) as 'the place at which a company has its central administration and is registered'.

Detailed procedural requirements are laid down, which more or less and *mutatis mutandis* reflect those required by the Third Directive of a merger of public companies.[54] There is provision for the protection of minority shareholders and creditors. Significantly, a Member State would be permitted to refuse to receive a company seeking to transfer its registered office or *de facto* head office to its territory if the company's central administration was also not situated in that territory: real-seat Member States may thus continue to require a territorial nexus between registered office and real seat. The draft proposal is framed so as to require implementation by 1 January 2000. Whether it has a smooth legislative passage will depend largely on whether it proves possible to allay German fears that it may be used to permit German companies to avoid national laws on employee participation. Political agreement on the European Company Statute,[55] if forthcoming, may smooth the way for support for the Fourteenth Directive, regarded by the Commission as an essential part of the framework for corporate mobility it hopes to put in place in the near future.

---

[50] Amended Proposal for a Council Reg (EEC) on the Statute for a European Company COM (91) 174 final, 6 May 1991; [1991] OJ C176/1. See pp 399–404 below

[51] Proposal for a 10th Council Directive based on Art 54(3)(g) of the Treaty concerning cross-border mergers of public limited companies COM (84) 727 final, 8 January 1985; [1985] OJ C23/11.

[52] Although it should be noted that the study is expressed not to constitute an official position taken by the Commission. The draft directives are published in Wouters, J and Schneider, H (eds) *Current Issues of Cross-Border Establishment of Companies in the European Union* (1995).

[53] XV/6002/97. For a brief commentary, see Hughes, P and Dine, J, *EC Company Law* (1991) 3–16/2.

[54] See ch IV.   [55] See ch XIX.

Mutual Recognition of Companies

The above discussion on the freedom of establishment of companies would be incomplete without a brief mention of the associated issue of the mutual recognition of companies and the early unsuccessful Community attempt to resolve the problem by multilateral Convention within the framework of Article 220.

Article 220 provides:

Member States shall, so far as is necessary, enter into negotiations with each other with a view to securing for the benefit of their nationals:

. . .

—the mutual recognition of companies or firms within the meaning of the second paragraph of Article 58, the retention of legal personality in the event of transfer of their seat from one country to another . . .

As discussed above, the view that the freedom of establishment provisions of the Treaty implicitly require Member States to recognize companies incorporated in other Member States seeking to relocate to their territory, however compelling, can no longer be regarded as tenable since the Court's decision in the *Daily Mail* case. In any event, recognition may be at issue in a wider context than the right of establishment (and the associated right to provide services into another Member State): a company may, for example, wish to bring legal proceedings against a defendant in the Member State of the defendant, even though the company itself was neither established in nor providing services into that State; if that State failed to recognize the company as a legal entity, it would be unable to sue. It is perhaps for that reason that Article 220 is set in a wider context than the freedom of establishment (it is in Part Six of the Treaty, General and Final Provisions, whereas the right of establishment finds its place in Part Three, Community Policies).[56]

In 1968 the six original Member States, 'desirous of implementing the provisions of Article 220', signed the Convention on Mutual Recognition of Companies and Legal Persons.[57] It was never however ratified by the Netherlands and hence never came into force. For a period after it was signed there were continuing hopes that it would become law: thus for example a Protocol conferring jurisdiction on the European Court of Justice to give preliminary rulings on its interpretation[58] was signed on 3 June 1971, but similarly never came into force; and by Article 3(2) of the Acts concerning the conditions of accession the new Member States undertook

[56] The text of Art 220 was originally included in the chapter on establishment: see Cerexhe, E, *Le droit européen—La libre circulation des personnes et des entreprises* (1982), 338.

[57] The text may be found in [1968] Revue trimestrielle de droit européen 400; an English text is in [1969] EC Bull Supp 2 and an unofficial translation by Stein in Stein, E, *Harmonization of European Company Laws* (1971), 525.

[58] A Convention under Art 220 is not technically a Community act, but a Treaty between the Member States, hence Art 177 is not applicable. For a discussion of the background to and legal basis of the Convention, see Boyle, A J, 'The Recognition of Companies in the EEC' in Goode, R M and Simmonds, K R (eds), *Commercial Operations in Europe* (1978), 6–7.

to accede to, inter alia, the 1968 Convention and the Protocol and to enter into negotiations with the existing Member States in order to make any necessary amendments. Negotiations were even opened in 1979 but led to nothing.

Given that there appears to be no likelihood of the Convention's ever coming into force, a detailed analysis of its provisions would be out of place.[59] A brief outline is however of interest, if only to explain the reluctance of the Netherlands to ratify the Convention.

The Convention starts[60] by leaning firmly in the direction of the incorporation theory, requiring recognition as of right for companies formed in accordance with the law of a Contracting State and having their registered office within the territories to which it applies.[61] Articles 3 and 4 however, immediately undermine this by permitting Contracting States to opt out of the basic rule to some extent: they may declare[62] that they will not apply the Convention to companies whose real seat (defined as central administration) is outside those territories if they have no genuine link with the economy of one of the territories[63] and that they will apply such provisions of their national law as they consider mandatory[64] to companies whose real seat is in their territory, even though they were formed under the law of another Contracting State.[65] Even non-mandatory national laws may be applied to such companies if the company's constitution makes no reference to the law of its incorporation or if the company fails to prove that it has actually exercised its activity for a reasonable time in the Contracting State under whose law it was formed.

The effect of Articles 3 and 4[66] clearly undermines the apparent attempt in Article 1 to impose a uniform criterion, leading one commentator to describe the

---

[59] The Convention is described in some detail in Goldman, B, 'The Convention between the Member States of the European Economic Community on the Mutual Recognition of Companies and Legal Persons' (1968) 6 CMLR 104; Stein, E, *Harmonization of European Company Laws* (1971); Morse, G, 'Mutual Recognition of Companies in England and the EEC' [1972] JBL 195; Boyle (n 58 above); Timmermans, C W A, 'The Convention of 29 February 1968 on the Mutual Recognition of Companies and Firms' (1980) Netherlands International Law Review 357; Cerexhe (n 56 above); Wooldridge, F, *Company Law in the United Kingdom and the European Community: Its Harmonization and Unification* (1991); Santa Maria, A, *EC Commercial Law* (1996). For an entertaining summary, see Conard, A F, 'Company Laws of the European Communities from an American Viewpoint' in Schmitthoff, C M (ed), *The Harmonisation of European Company Law* (1973).

[60] Art 1.

[61] The European territories of the Contracting States, the French overseas departments and the French overseas territories: Art 12.

[62] By a formal declaration in accordance with Art 15.

[63] Art 3.

[64] 'Mandatory' and 'non-mandatory' are Stein's terminology: the official translation refers to 'essential' and 'suppletory' provisions. Goldman uses 'peremptory' and 'supplementary', Conard 'imperative' and 'suppletive', following the French text which refers to '*dispositions impératives*' and '*dispositions supplétives*'.

[65] Art 4, 1st para.

[66] The formula in Art 4 is described by Stein as having 'all the disadvantages of complexity and ambiguity that characterize a laborious compromise': *Harmonization of European Company Laws* (1971), 411. More temperately he comments that the effect of the provision 'indicates that the Convention does not achieve the fullness of uniform treatment which is a major, if not the paramount, objective of private international law': 412.

Convention as 'a typical, but extreme, example of Community fudge'[67] and another to state that it 'proclaims generous principles, which it perforates with crippling reservations.'[68] Admittedly Article 4 does not constitute a total derogation from the incorporation theory,[69] since the obligation under Article 1 to recognize a company incorporated in another Contracting State remains intact. The result is none the less to enable a State making such a declaration to impose its own laws and thus one company will become in effect subject to two systems of company law.

There are moreover valid criticisms of form as well as of substance: the terminology of 'genuine link with the economy' and 'mandatory provisions'[70] is frustratingly vague. Germany, France and Italy made declarations under Article 3, to meet concerns that they would otherwise be obliged by the Convention to recognize companies owned by interests in, and managed from, the United States, but incorporated in the Netherlands with no effective link with that State.[71] All the original six Contracting States except the Netherlands did so under Article 4. It appears[72] that the Netherlands was not prepared to make such a declaration, since it undermined to such an extent the incorporation theory current in that State. It did however have genuine concerns after the United Kingdom's accession that some companies incorporated in the United Kingdom were establishing offices in the Netherlands in circumstances indicating an intent to avoid mandatory provisions of Netherlands company law, and it wished to retain some remedy against such specific abuse. The public policy exception in the Convention was not wide enough to be of use in such circumstances, unlike the general public policy ground which, as a matter of private international law, would entitle the Netherlands to refuse to recognize companies so abusing its laws. It accordingly refused to ratify the Convention; as a result it has remained, and looks likely to remain, a dead letter.

---

[67] Clarke, M G, 'The Conflicts of Law Dimension' in *Corporate Law: The European Dimension* (1991), 164.

[68] Conard, A F, 'Company Laws of the European Communities from an American Viewpoint', in Schmitthoff, C M (ed), *The Harmonisation of European Company Law* (1973), 58.

[69] Timmermans, however, forcefully argues that Art 4 of the Convention is incompatible with Articles 52 and 58 of the Treaty, 'in that the application of the company law of the country of establishment would wreck the right to set up a principal establishment in that country': 'The Convention of 29 February 1968 on the Mutual Recognition of Companies and Firms' (1980) 27 Netherlands International Law Review 357.

[70] Stein (n 66 above) reports that the working group of governmental experts charged with drafting the Convention were unable to reach an understanding on the interpretation of mandatory provisions: 411.

[71] The same concerns by the same States led to the requirement in the General Programme to a link with the economy . . . before such a company could exercise any right to establish itself elsewhere in the Community: see ch XVI, pp 340–1 above.

[72] See generally Diephuis, J H, 'Recognition of Foreign Companies and Bodies Corporate' 27 (1980) Netherlands International Law Review 347, 355–6.

XIX

Overview of Miscellaneous Draft Legislation

This chapter considers briefly the various company law instruments which have not been adopted: the draft Fifth Directive on the structure of public companies, the draft Ninth Directive on Groups of Companies, the draft Tenth Directive on cross-border mergers, the draft Thirteenth Directive on takeovers, and the draft Regulation for a European Company Statute with its complementary draft Directive on employee participation. Of these, the European Company Statute and the linked directive look increasingly likely to be finalized in the near future; the draft Fifth Directive on the structure of public companies and the draft Ninth Directive on Groups of Companies seem unlikely to be revived; and the others fall somewhere in between these two stages of legislative life. The draft Fourteenth Directive on the cross-border transfer of a company's registered or head office is considered in outline in chapter XVIII.

The Draft Fifth Directive

The draft Fifth Directive on the structure of public limited companies and the powers and obligations of their organs had its origins in reports prepared for the Commission by Professors Houin and Würdinger, two of its special consultants on company law, in the late 1960s.[1] These led ultimately to the Commission's first Proposal for a fifth directive to coordinate the safeguards which, for the protection of the interests of members and others, are required by Member States of companies within the meaning of the second paragraph of Article 58 of the Treaty, as regards the structure of *sociétés anonymes* and the powers and obligations of their organs, submitted to the Council in 1972.[2]

---

[1] Houin, 'Rapport sur l'administration de la société par actions', 1ère partie Comm Doc 12.364/III/C/67–F and 2ème partie Comm Doc 317/III/C/68–F; Würdinger, 'Die Versammlung der Aktionäre', Comm Doc 14.653/III/C/67–D. For a full discussion of these reports see Stein, E, *Harmonization of European Company Laws* (1971) 331–46.

[2] COM (72) 887 final, 18 July 1972; [1972] JO C131/49; EC Bull Supp 10/72. For commentaries see Ficker, H C, 'The EEC Directives on Company Law Harmonisation' in Schmitthoff, C M, *The Harmonisation of European Company Law* (1971) 80–2; Temple Lang, J, 'The Fifth EEC Directive on the Harmonisation of Company Law; Some Comments from the Viewpoint of Irish and British Law on the EEC Draft for a Fifth Directive concerning Management Structure and Worker Participation' (1975) 12 CMLR 155 and 355; Conlon, T, 'Industrial Democracy and EEC Company Law: A Review of the Draft Fifth Directive' (1975) 24 ICLQ 348.

The Proposal sought to lay down mandatory rules for all public limited-liability companies as regards their internal structure and decision-making processes. The Proposal covered company structure, the management organ and supervisory organ, the general meeting, the adoption and audit of the annual accounts, and general provisions. Two highly controversial aspects of these rules were the mandatory creation of a two-tier board structure[3] consisting of a managing organ (which would manage and represent the company) and a supervisory organ (which would supervise the management organ) and mandatory provision for employees' representation on the supervisory board[4] for companies with a workforce greater than 500.[5] A further contentious aspect of the Proposal was the imposition of civil liability on members of the boards towards the company for all damage caused by wilful or negligent violation of the law or of the company's statutes; liability could not be excluded or limited and actions could be brought by minority shareholders.[6] The company's auditors were subject to similar liability.[7]

The Economic and Social Committee delivered its Opinion in April 1974,[8] noting (presumably at the initiative of the United Kingdom, which had acceded to the Community in the previous year and which was and is fiercely opposed to the introduction of a mandatory two-tier board system or any form of formal employee participation) that it realised that:

the introduction of the structure proposed by the Commission for all national sociétés anonymes would be attended with practical and psychological difficulties in some Member States; it therefore has its doubts whether such a radical coordination would be a responsible move at this juncture, especially in view of the new situation which has arisen since new Member States joined the Community . . .

The Committee accordingly proposed as a compromise that Member States with a unitary board system (such as the United Kingdom) should have the option of continuing with a single board structure if they wished.

In 1975 the Commission produced a Green Paper further exploring the issues of employee participation and board, summarizing the positions in the various Member States and exploring possible solutions.[9] The Economic and Social Committee issued a further Opinion specifically addressing the Green Paper,[10] reaffirming its commitment to the two-tier board as an option and suggesting that, in large companies which did not have employee representation on the board, a special body should be set up on which employees were represented. The Parliament took this paper into account when delivering its Opinion on the Proposal in May 1982,[11] in which it indicated inter alia that there was 'a need for

---

[3] Art 2, based on the structures in place in Germany and the Netherlands.
[4] By one of two alternative models, based respectively on the German and Dutch models.
[5] Art 4(2)(3).   [6] Arts 14 and 16.   [7] Art 62.   [8] [1974] OJ C109/9.
[9] *Employee Participation and the Decision Making Structure of Companies, in particular of 'Sociétés Anonymes', in the European Community*; EC Bull Supp 8/75. For a commentary see Däubler, W, 'The Employee Participation Directive—A Realistic Utopia?' (1977) 14 CMLR 457.
[10] [1979] OJ C94/2.   [11] [1982] OJ C149/17.

equivalent statutory provisions to implement employee participation in the Member States'. The Parliament approved the Proposal subject to numerous amendments. In order to take account of these various opinions, the Commission in August 1982 submitted to the Council an amended Proposal for a Fifth Directive founded on Article 54(3)(g) of the Treaty concerning the structure of public limited companies and the powers and obligations of their organs.[12]

The amended Proposal offered more flexibility as regards both board structure and employee participation. Member States were permitted to retain a unitary board system provided that they introduced a two-tier system so that companies would have a genuine choice as to which structure to adopt.[13] As for employee participation, four possible models were provided for companies with 1,000 or more employees:[14] (a) participation through employee representatives at board level; (b) participation in the appointment of supervisory board members through co-optation procedures (the board co-opts its own members but the employee representatives have the right of veto); (c) participation through representative bodies outside the board; or (d) participation through collective agreements analogous to one of the preceding models.

A further text was issued by the Commission in 1988 but never published.[15] It was followed by a published second amendment to the Proposal, submitted by the Commission in December 1990,[16] and a third amendment to the Proposal, submitted in November 1991.[17] Neither of those amendments tackled the thorny issues of board structure or employee participation.

When the Commission issued its communication on worker information and consultation in 1995,[18] it reported that the third amended Proposal was still before the Council. In 1996, the Commission asked Ernst & Young to consider the relevance of the draft Fifth Directive in the study it had commissioned on corporate governance.[19] In the consultation paper on company law which it circulated in 1997, based on the study,[20] the Commission indicated that no work was then under way on the Proposal.[21] It appears that the Proposal has now been abandoned. However, the Commission still hopes to deal with matters relating to corporate structure and governance. A company law forum is to be set up to address these

---

[12] COM (83) 185 final, 12 August 1983; [1983] OJ C240/2; EC Bull Supp 6/83. For commentaries see Murray, J, 'New Concepts in Corporate Law' and Tabachnik, E, 'Minimum Standards of Industrial Democracy' in *Corporate Law—The European Dimension* (1991); Welch, J, 'The Fifth Draft Directive— A False Dawn?' (1983) 8 ELR 83. For an interesting discussion of the political implications from a UK perspective, see Boyle, A J, 'Draft Fifth Directive: Implications for Directors' Duties, Board Structure and Employee Participation' (1992) 13 The Company Lawyer 6.

[13] Art 2(1).

[14] Art 4. The threshold of 1,000 could be lowered but not raised by Member States.

[15] The text is published in Dine, J and Hughes, P, *EC Company Law* (1991). For a commentary and outline see Du Plessis, J J and Dine, J, 'The Fate of the Draft Fifth Directive on Company Law: Accommodation Instead of Harmonisation' [1997] JBL 23.

[16] COM (90) 629 final, 13 December 1990; [1991] OJ C7/4.

[17] COM (91) 372 final, 20 November 1991; [1991] OJ C321/9.

[18] COM (95) 547 final, 14 November 1995.   [19] See further ch XX.

[20] See further ch XX.   [21] At p 7.

issues,[22] and this may well lead to a code of conduct or some other non-legislative document in the next few years.

The Draft Ninth Directive on Groups

The legal regulation of groups of companies varies strikingly between the Member States. In some States, the area is wholly ignored by legislation, and legal problems arising out of a group's existence, or intra-group relationships, are dealt with by the courts in a legislative vacuum.[23] Germany, by contrast, has a sophisticated codified law on groups of companies which seeks to protect both shareholders and creditors of groups of companies. The absence of any general Community legislation on groups is frequently lamented[24] as one of the major lacunae[25] in the harmonization programme, particularly in view of the fact that several of the adopted directives presuppose the existence of groups by regulating specific areas relevant to groups: see for example some of the capital maintenance provisions of the Second Directive,[26] the provisions of the Third Directive regulating mergers between parents and subsidiaries[27] and the Seventh Directive on consolidated accounts,[28] not to mention the draft Thirteenth Directive on takeovers.[29]

The idea of Community legislation regulating groups of companies, although it never developed into an adopted Proposal, has a long history. At an early stage the Commission had the benefit of reports prepared by Professor van Ommeslaghe on the legal treatment of groups[30] and by Professor Würdinger on groups and related and affiliated companies.[31] It subsequently appointed a working party of experts to survey existing legal provisions and prepare a first draft of a Proposal for a directive. In 1974 and 1975, the Commission issued its first drafts[32] of a Proposal for a Ninth

---

[22] See further ch XX.

[23] See further Lutter, M, 'The law of groups of companies in Europe' (1983) 1 Forum Internationale; Sugarman, S and Teubner, G (eds), *Regulating Corporate Groups in Europe* (1990) and Wymeersch, E (ed), *Groups of Companies in the EEC* (1993).

[24] See for general discussion of the issue Buxbaum, R M, Hertig, G, Hirsch, A and Hopt, K J (eds), *European Business Law* (1991) 227–65; Gleichmann, K, 'The Law of Corporate Groups in the European Community' in *Regulating Corporate Groups in Europe*, cited in n 23 above. The late Professor Gower was a particularly ardent advocate of Community legislation on groups, going so far as to state that 'to my way of thinking, the one thing that the EC ought to be concentrating on in the corporate field is doing something about groups. . . . something has got to be done about this, instead of bothering about piddling little things like harmonizing rules about the one-member private limited company': *European Business Law* 248–9.

[25] The other principal lacuna being the absence of harmonization of cross-border mergers and takeovers: see further below.

[26] See ch III.   [27] See ch IV.   [28] See ch VI.   [29] See below.

[30] Published in [1966] Revue pratique des sociétés 153.

[31] See Comm Docs 5875/XIV/C/2/68–F, 5928/XIV/C/68–F and 15524/XIV/70–E.

[32] Preliminary Draft of a Directive based on Article 54(3)(g) on Harmonization of the Law of Groups of Companies, Doc XI/328/74 (Part I) and Doc XV/593/75 (Part II). Part I contained amendments to other adopted or proposed directives and general definitions relating to groups of companies; Part II contained the substantive provisions.

Directive on links between undertakings and in particular on groups.[33] The Proposal has been described by one commentator[34] as the most radical of all the legislative proposals then included in the company law harmonization programme. The early drafts were widely circulated; they met with a reception which was at best lukewarm and at worst hostile.[35] The Commission subsequently revised the draft Proposal in 1977,[36] 1980[37] and 1984;[38] the texts of those revisions, regarded by the Commission as internal working documents, were not made public, although their gist can be divined from the writings of one or two authors who had access to the documents.[39] In brief, there were two broad themes to the draft Proposal, which would have applied only to subsidiaries which were public companies,[40] although the controlling company could have had any legal form. First, it would have required the dominant undertaking or the group as whole to accept liability for the obligations of the dependent undertaking. Second, transparency rules would have required disclosure of the relationship between the dominant and dependent undertakings, with remedies in certain circumstances for damage resulting from that relationship.

Since the 1984 version, no further work has been undertaken on the draft Proposal, which at least for the foreseeable future seems to have sunk without trace.

The Draft Tenth Directive on Cross-border Mergers

The draft Tenth Directive on cross-border mergers of public limited companies, which complements the Third Directive on domestic mergers of public limited

[33] The drafts were not formally published. There is a detailed commentary, including vigorous criticism, by Rodière, R, 'Réflexions sur les avant-projets d'une directive de la Commission des Communautés Européennes concernant les groupes de sociétés' [1977] Recueil Dalloz Sirey, vol 18, Chronique, 13.

[34] Schneebaum, S M, 'The Company Law Harmonization Program of the European Community' (1982) 14 Law and Policy in International Business 293, 317.

[35] See Engrácia Antunes, J, Liability of Corporate Groups (1994), n 205 p 286 for a list of responses.

[36] Proposal for a 9th Directive based on Article 54(3)(g) of the EEC Treaty on Links between Undertakings and, in particular, on Groups of Companies, Doc XI 215/77–E.

[37] Good commentaries include Schneebaum (n 34 above); Engrácia Antunes (n 36 above) 285–9 and Farmery, P, 'The EC Draft Proposal For a Ninth Company Law Directive on Groups: A Business Perspective' (1986) 7 Business Law Review 88.

[38] Proposal for a 9th Directive based on article 54(3)(g) of the EEC Treaty on Links between Undertakings and, in particular, on Groups of Companies, Doc III/1639/84–E. The German text is reprinted in 14 Zeitschrift für Unternehmens- und Gesellschaftsrecht 444 (1985), the French text in Commission Droit et Vie d'Affaires, Modes de rapprochement structurel des entreprises (1986) and a compilation of some of the provisions is published in Böhlhff, K and Budde, J, 'Company Groups—The EEC Proposal for a 9th Directive in the Light of the Legal Situation in the Federal Republic of Germany' (1984) Journal of Comparative Business & Capital Market Law 163. There is a good commentary by Immenga, U, in 'L'harmonisation de droit des groupes de sociétés. La proposition d'une directive de la Commission de la C.E.E.' (1986) 14 Giurisprudenza Commerciale 846, and a summary by Avgitidis, D K, in Groups of Companies: The Liability of the Parent Company for the Debts of its Subsidiary (1996) 262–9.

[39] See sources in the preceding notes together with further sources cited in Engrácia Antunes (n 35 above) 285–6, n 199.

[40] The draft was strongly influenced by the German legislation on groups, which is also limited to public companies.

companies,[41] started life as a draft Convention under Article 220 of the Treaty. Article 220 requires Member States, so far as is necessary, to enter into negotiations with each other with a view to securing for the benefit of their nationals a number of aims including the possibility of mergers between companies or firms governed by the laws of different countries. By 'mergers' is meant, not a takeover by the acquisition of shares as is common in the United Kingdom, but rather the absorption by one company of another by acquisition of its assets and liabilities in consideration of the issue of shares by the absorbing company to the shareholders of the absorbed company, followed by dissolution of the absorbed company.[42]

The preliminary draft of the Convention was prepared in 1967.[43] Even at that early stage, the German delegation was concerned to ensure that the scope of the Convention—namely the required link between a company and a Member State—was defined so as to obviate any risk of international mergers being used by companies as a method of avoiding German worker-participation laws.[44] In December 1972 a further draft of the Convention was adopted by the working group which had prepared and developed it under the aegis of Professor Goldman and submitted to the Council, the Commission and the permanent representatives of the Member States.[45] By 1980 further work on the draft Convention was abandoned because of the German position. The Commission decided to revive the Proposal as a directive and in 1985 submitted its Proposal for a Tenth Council Directive based on Article 54(3)(g) of the Treaty concerning cross-border mergers of public limited companies.[46]

The Economic and Social Committee delivered its Opinion in September 1985.[47] The European Parliament was consulted on the Proposal in January 1985 but more than a decade later had still not delivered its Opinion, thus effectively blocking progress on the directive. The controversial provision is Article 1(3) of the Proposal, included in an attempt to break the deadlock with Germany over worker participation. Article 1(3) permits Member States, pending subsequent coordination,[48] not to apply the provisions of the Tenth Directive where an undertaking (whether or not party to the merger) would as a result no longer meet the conditions required for employee representation in that undertaking's organs. The

[41] See ch IV.
[42] For further explanation of this type of transaction, to which the 3rd Directive equally applies, see ch IV.
[43] Comité des experts de l'article 220 alinéa 3 du Traité CEE, Droit des sociétés—Fusions internationales, Avant-projet de convention relatif à la fusion internationale de sociétés anonymes, Document de travail no 4, 16.082/IV/67–F. See Stein, E, *Harmonization of European Company Laws* (1971), 387–94.
[44] Stein, ibid, 387.
[45] See EC Bull Supp 13/73. For a commentary see Goldman, B, 'La fusion des sociétés et le projet de convention sur la fusion internationale des sociétés anonymes' [1981] Cahiers de droit européen 4.
[46] COM (84) 727 final, 8 January 1985; [1985] OJ C23/11; EC Bull Supp 3/85. For commentaries, see Farmery, P, 'Removing Legal Obstacles to Cross Border Mergers: EEC Proposal for a Tenth Directive', Business Law Review (Feb 1987) 35, and van Solinge, G, 'Corporate Law Aspects of Cross-Border Mergers' in Wouters, J and Schneider, H (eds), *Current Issues of Cross-Border Establishment of Companies in the European Union* (1995).
[47] [1985] OJ C303/27.   [48] By way of the proposed 5th Directive: see above.

remainder of the draft Tenth Directive incorporates by reference many of the provisions of the Third Directive on domestic mergers, with various amendments where necessary to cater for the international nature of the proposed transaction. Like the Third Directive, the draft Tenth Directive applies only to public companies. It should be noted that the Merger Directive[49] introduced common tax rules for, inter alia, cross-border mergers of this sort, designed to make such mergers tax neutral.

Political compromise on the European Company Statute,[50] if forthcoming, may well lubricate the negotiating process on the Tenth Directive, and it is presumably against this background that the Commission announced in 1997 that it would shortly be putting forward a fresh Proposal for a Tenth Directive. A further possibility would be to provide, as a preliminary stage, for cross-border mergers between companies below the threshold for mandatory employee participation.[51]

The Draft Thirteenth Directive on Takeovers

As indicated above, the draft Tenth Directive on cross-border mergers of public limited companies does not apply to takeovers by the acquisition of shares. Those transactions, much more common in the United Kingdom than mergers by absorption, were intended to be regulated by the Thirteenth Directive on takeovers. To borrow the definition suggested by the Commission:

A takeover bid is generally understood to mean an offer made to the holders of securities carrying voting rights in a company or convertible into securities carrying such rights . . . to acquire their securities for a consideration in cash or other securities, the purpose of the offer usually being to acquire control of the company or consolidate the offeror's existing control, and the offer being made conditional upon sufficient offerees accepting it to achieve the offeror's objectives.[52]

The seeds of the Thirteenth Directive were sown in the Commission's 1985 White Paper *Completing the Internal Market*[53] which stated:

There is a case . . . for making better use of certain procedures such as offers of shares to the public for reshaping the pattern of share ownership in enterprises, since the rules currently in force in this sphere vary a great deal from one country to another. Such operations should be made more attractive. This could be done by requiring minimum guarantees, particularly on the information to be given to those concerned, while it would be left to the Member

---

[49] Council Directive (EEC) 90/434 on the common system of taxation applicable to mergers, divisions, transfers of assets and exchanges of shares concerning companies from different Member States [1990] OJ L225/1.

[50] See below.

[51] Accepted for the purposes of the current proposal for a European Company Statute as 1,000 employees: see below.

[52] Explanatory Memorandum to the Proposal for a 13th Council Directive on Company Law, concerning takeover and other general bids COM (88) 823 final, 16 February 1989; [1989] OJ C64/8; EC Bull Supp 3/89.

[53] COM (85) 310 final, 14 June 1985.

State to devise procedures for monitoring such operations and to designate the authorities to which the powers of supervision were to be assigned. A proposal will be made in 1987 and the necessary decisions should be taken by 1989.[54]

The Commission's first Proposal for a Thirteenth Council Directive on Company Law concerning takeover and other general bids was eventually submitted to the Council in January 1989.[55] That Proposal covered bids relating to securities in public companies. Its provisions broadly reflected the United Kingdom's *City Code on Take-overs and Mergers*, the body of rules administered by the self-regulatory Panel on Takeovers and Mergers.[56] The Proposal laid down the principle of equal treatment of shareholders,[57] required Member States to set up a supervisory authority,[58] and imposed a series of obligations on the prospective bidder and the board of the target company broadly designed to ensure transparency. A prospective bidder was thus required to make public its intentions as soon as it decided to make a bid[59] and to draw up and publish an offer document with specified contents[60] including the period for accepting the offer which must be within specified limits.[61] The circumstances in which a bid, once made public, could be withdrawn, were restricted.[62] Where the bidder aimed to acquire up to a certain proportion[63] of the voting shares in a company it was required to bid for all the securities.[64] The offeror and any holder of 1 per cent or more of the voting shares in any company involved in the proposed takeover were required to keep the supervisory authority informed of all acquisitions by or on behalf of such persons.[65] The target company's board was required to report on the bid[66] and its powers were restricted so as to limit tactics for frustrating a forthcoming bid.[67] In addition, the Proposal required the target board to communicate to its workers' representatives the offer document, its own report and certain other documents.[68]

The Economic and Social Committee delivered its broadly positive Opinion on the Proposal in September 1989.[69] The Parliament approved the Proposal as substantially amended by it in January 1990.[70] The Commission issued an amended Proposal in September 1990[71] which took into account some of the Parliament's

---

[54] Para 139.

[55] COM (88) 823 final, 16 February 1989; [1989] OJ C64/8; EC Bull Supp 3/89. For commentaries on the 1989 proposal see Buijs, D C, 'The next step in European Community Harmonisation of Company Law: Regulation of Public Bids' (1989) 2 Leiden Journal of International Law 107 and Greenbaum, J P, 'Tender Offers in the European Community; The Playing Field Shrinks' (1989) 22 Vanderbilt Journal of Transnational Law 923.

[56] See further on the UK system Sealy, L S, 'The Draft Thirteenth EC Directive on Take-overs' in Andenas, M and Kenyon-Slade, S (eds), *EC Financial Market Regulation and Company Law* (1993) and Cann, J W A, 'Consideration of the Proposed Takeover Directive in the Light of the United Kingdom Experience of Takeover Regulation' in Kleyn, J D (ed), *Conference on Mergers & Acquisitions* (1991).

[57] Art 3.   [58] Art 6.   [59] Art 7.   [60] Arts 10 and 11.

[61] Art 12: the period must be between four and ten weeks from publication of the offer document.
[62] Art 13.   [63] Which Member States could not fix at more than 33.33%.
[64] Art 4.   [65] Art 17.   [66] Art 14.   [67] Art 8.   [68] Art 19.
[69] [1989] OJ C298/56.   [70] [1990] OJ C38/41.
[71] COM (90) 416 final, 10 September 1990; [1990] OJ C240/7. Good commentaries on the amended Proposal include Depser, I, 'Amended EC Proposal for a 13th Council Directive on Company

suggested amendments as well as modifications suggested by Member States and the Economic and Social Committee. The principal amendments were (a) the scope of the Proposal was narrowed from public companies to listed companies;[72] (b) a series of guiding principles was laid down for the supervisory authority (all target company shareholders in the same position were to be treated equally and have sufficient time and information to reach a properly informed decision, the target board was to act in the interests of all shareholders and could not frustrate a bid, false markets were not to be created in the securities of any company involved in or concerned by the bid, and target companies were not to be hindered in the conduct of their affairs beyond a reasonable time by the bid);[73] (c) the board of the target company could call an extraordinary general meeting during the offer period;[74] and (d) the offer document must include information as to any future indebtedness of the offeror or the target company resulting from financing the bid[75] and as to any proposed restructuring of the target company.[76]

The Proposal and the amended Proposal both met with much criticism.[77] The United Kingdom in particular was extremely hostile. Although the Proposals both echoed to a large extent the principles and approach of the non-statutory *City Code*, the suggestion that the rules governing takeovers should be given the force of law was anathema to the City, where the Takeover Panel prides itself on the speed and flexibility with which it is able to give rulings on issues arising in the course of a bid and its ability to reconsider and adapt the rules it administers in the light of constantly changing techniques and practices.[78] Although the Panel's rulings are subject to judicial review, the courts have discouraged tactical litigation, generally accepting the Panel's interpretation and application of the *City Code* and intervening only in exceptional circumstances.[79] It was felt that the structure envisaged by the proposed directive would lead to frequent recourse to the courts by parties to a bid—as happens in the United States and Australia where the regulatory framework is statutory—thus delaying the progress of a bid with commercially undesirable consequences.[80] Further aspects of the Proposals which led to discord

Law concerning Takeover and other General Bids' [1991] International Business Lawyer 483; Sealy, L S, 'The Draft Thirteenth EC Directive on Take-overs' and Kenyon-Slade, S and Andenas, M, 'The Proposed Thirteenth Directive on Take-overs: Unravelling the United Kingdom's Self-Regulatory Success?' in Andenas, M and Kenyon-Slade, S (eds), *EC Financial Market Regulation and Company Law* (1993); Cann, J W A, 'Consideration of the Proposed Takeover Directive in the Light of the United Kingdom Experience of Takeover Regulation' in Kleyn, J D (ed), *Conference on Mergers & Acquisitions* (1991); Bentley, P, 'Public Takeover Bids' in *Corporate Law: The European Dimension* (1991); Wouters, J, 'Towards a Level Playing Field for Takeovers in the European Community? An Analysis of the Proposed Thirteenth Directive in light of American Experiences' (1993) 30 CMLR 267.

[72] Art 1(1).   [73] Art 6a.   [74] Art 8(2).   [75] Art 10(1)(ga).
[76] Art 10(1)(l).   [77] See generally sources cited in n 71.

[78] The Economic and Social Committee, which delivered its Opinion on the amended Proposal in February 1991: [1991] OJ C102/49, similarly regretted that the Proposal did not take more account of the desirability of flexibility and a framework of general principles.

[79] *R v Panel on Take-overs and Mergers, ex p Datafin plc* [1987] QB 815, CA.

[80] See in particular the discussions by Kenyon-Slade and Andenas, Sealy and Cann, and for a discussion of the position in the US Wouters, all cited in n 71.

among the Member States were the principle of a mandatory bid when a bidder wanted to acquire more than one-third of a company and the provision protecting workers' rights.

In June 1991 negotiations on the directive were suspended. In 1992 the directive was included in the Edinburgh Council list of directives which were to be revised in accordance with the principle of subsidiarity adopted earlier that year in the Maastricht Treaty.[81] The following year the Commission carried out extensive consultation with a view to relaunching the initiative, the responses to which indicated that most Member States favoured a framework directive which would enable them to retain their structures and traditions. In February 1996 the Commission submitted a fresh Proposal for a Thirteenth European Parliament and Council Directive on company law concerning takeover bids.[82] This Proposal was a much streamlined version of the earlier documents; rather than imposing detailed requirements, the Proposal sought to ensure that shareholders of listed companies in Member States enjoyed equivalent safeguards on a change of control and to provide minimum guidelines for the conduct and transparency of takeover bids. To that end the Proposal laid down 'a framework consisting of certain common principles and a limited number of general requirements which Member States will be required to implement through more detailed rules according to their national systems and their cultural contexts'.[83]

The 1996 Proposal required Member States to ensure that the rules or other arrangements made pursuant to the directive respected the principles laid down in the 1990 amended Proposal.[84] Member States no longer had to require a mandatory bid where a person held a specified percentage of the voting shares in a company provided that 'rules or other mechanisms or arrangements are in force which . . . offer other appropriate and at least equivalent means in order to protect the minority shareholders of that company'.[85] Otherwise most of the themes of the 1989/90 Proposals remained (designation of supervisory authority,[86] requirement for disclosure of decision to bid,[87] preparation and publication of offer document[88] and other relevant information[89] and obligations of the target company's board[90]), but couched in terms of directions to Member States to make the necessary provision rather than in terms of detailed prescriptive rules. Workers' rights were no longer addressed, a point which was regretted by the Economic and Social Committee which delivered its Opinion[91] in July 1996, approving the Proposal subject to specific suggested amendments.[92]

---

[81] See Art 3b of the Treaty.
[82] COM (95) 655 final, 7 February 1996; [1996] OJ C162/5.   [83] 4th recital in the preamble.
[84] Art 6; see text to n 73.   [85] Art 3(1).   [86] Art 4.   [87] Art 6(1).
[88] Art 6(2)(3).   [89] Arts 6(4) and 7(2).   [90] Art 8.
[91] Since the Proposal was an entirely fresh instrument, the legislative process had to be started again and hence the Economic and Social Committee and the Parliament were consulted again. See further n 97.
[92] [1996] OJ C295/1.

Of particular interest to the United Kingdom was the attempt to preserve the extra-judicial status of Takeover Panel proceedings. Article 4(5) of the 1996 Proposal provides:

This Directive does not affect the power which courts may have in a Member State to decline to hear legal proceedings and to decide whether or not such proceedings affect the outcome of the bid provided that an injured party enjoys adequate remedies, whether through an appeals procedure operated by the supervisory authority or through the right to take proceedings before the courts to claim compensation.

This provision did not however wholly succeed in allaying the United Kingdom's fears, particularly expressed by the Takeover Panel which in 1996 launched a public campaign against the Proposal. It was considered that there was still scope for tactical litigation and the consequential risk of unacceptable delay in the course of a bid. If takeover regulation were governed by a directive rather than, as present, a code with no legal status, rulings could be sought from the Court of Justice on questions arising out of the implementing provisions: the delay in obtaining such rulings would effectively stop many bids. The Panel's fears were endorsed by the House of Lords Select Committee on the European Communities,[93] which recommended that the directive should not be adopted. The leitmotiv of the critics was that any gain by way of harmonization and improvement in the regulatory systems of other Member States would be outweighed by the risk of damage to the United Kingdom system, widely accepted as being entirely adequate. Moreover the Proposal has many lacunae: there were, for example, no definitions of essential terms such as 'control', 'offer' and 'concert party'[94] and the directive would do little to remove real barriers to takeovers (such as different levels of capitalization in national markets, domestic company law provisions permitting concentration of voting power, cross-shareholdings, bearer shares and proxies given to individuals).

The Netherlands also opposed the 1996 Proposal. In the Netherlands target companies enjoy a number of defensive tactics for frustrating a hostile bid, as a result of which there has never been a successful hostile bid.[95] Other Member States were ambivalent about the Proposal, partly because there is relatively little takeover activity compared to the City and partly because many Member States introduced some form of takeover regulation along the lines suggested in the

---

[93] 13th Report (Session 1995–96, HL Paper 100). Many of the organizations submitting evidence to the Committee were similarly hostile to the Proposal, although some accepted that there was a need for Community action to create a level playing field and one or two (notably the Financial Law Panel and the Institute of Chartered Accountants) doubted that the directive if adopted would have the negative effect feared.

[94] See ch XV for a discussion of concert parties.

[95] See further Slagter, W J, 'Takeovers and the Draft 13th EC–Directive' in Wymeersch, E (ed), *Further Perspectives in Financial Integration in Europe* (1994) and Schwartz, C, 'The Draft 13th EC Directive Concerning Take-over and other General Bids and its Influence on the Dutch System of Company Law' in De Witte, B and Forder, C (eds), *The common law of Europe and the future of legal education* (1992).

1989/90 Proposals and reflected in streamlined form in the 1996 Proposal.[96] The United Kingdom mustered support against the proposed directive and in favour of a non-legislative recommendation from Germany and Sweden, as well as the Netherlands, all of which also have a functioning non-statutory system of takeover regulation. France, Spain and Italy however were concerned to see employee protection provisions reinstated in the directive, and their views were accepted by the Legal Affairs and Citizens' Rights Committee of the European Parliament. In June 1997 the Parliament approved the 1996 Proposal subject to its suggested amendments.[97] Those amendments included a clearer definition of 'offeror' and of the remedies available to an injured party and controversial requirements that the target company board consult employee representatives before finalizing its report on the bid and that the board's duty to act in the interests of the company as a whole include safeguarding jobs, as well as the introduction of more general provisions for informing and consulting employees.

In November 1997 the Takeover Panel took up arms again. Having obtained an opinion from leading counsel[98] that the directive failed to satisfy the principles of subsidiarity (in that takeover regulation can be effectively dealt with at national level) and proportionality and was accordingly unlawful, the Panel's director general, Alistair Defriez, called on the Commission to abandon the Proposal altogether or replace it with a non-binding recommendation or voluntary code. Mario Monti, the single market commissioner, sought to allay the Panel's fears in a reply sent as the Commission submitted its amended Proposal,[99] which did not incorporate the Parliament's two particularly controversial amendments[100] but included requirements that employees be informed as soon as a bid has been made public[101] and that the offer document be communicated to them.[102] Moreover the general principle requiring target boards to act in the interests of the company has been expanded to make it clear that those interests include employment.[103] The article on dispute resolution has also been redrafted, now reading:

This Directive does not affect the power of Member States to designate the judicial or other authorities responsible for dealing with disputes and for deciding on irregularities committed during the bid procedure, provided that an injured party enjoys appropriate and adequate

---

[96] By 1997 all Member States except Luxembourg and Austria had systems for regulating takeovers, and those two States planned to introduce systems in the near future. For the reactions of the Netherlands, Germany, Italy and Sweden to the 1996 proposal, see Wymeersch, E (ed), 'The Proposal for a 13th Company Law Directive on Takeovers: A Multi-Jurisdiction Survey Part 1' (1996) 3 European Financial Services Law 301. For reactions from Finland and Belgium, see the second part of the survey (1997) 4 European Financial Services Law 2.

[97] [1997] OJ C222/20. The 1995 Proposal, the 1990 and 1991 amended proposals for the 5th Directive and the proposed directive complementing the European Company Statute were the first company law instruments required to follow the post-Maastricht co-decision procedure, which gives the Parliament much greater influence over legislation than the previous procedure: see Art 189b of the Treaty.

[98] David Vaughan QC.

[99] COM (97) 565 final, 10 November 1997; [1997] OJ C378/10.

[100] See previous paragraph.   [101] Art 6(1).   [102] Art 6(2).   [103] Art 5(c).

remedies to defend its interests and, where appropriate, obtain compensation for any loss suffered.[104]

The Commission explained in its Explanatory Memorandum that 'the question as to what extent these authorities may deal with a dispute during the bid procedure and whether the bid procedure should be halted is thus left to Member States' discretion'. Whether the amended Proposal will be regarded by the United Kingdom as meeting its concerns remains to be seen.[105] It may be that the principal issues of statutory regulation and judicial remedies will now be accepted as satisfactorily resolved[106] but doubts as to the employee protection provisions may be expected to surface instead.

The European Company[107]

Of all the outstanding Proposals for company law instruments, the European Company goes back the furthest: the idea was first mooted forty years ago in 1959 by Professor Sanders in an inaugural lecture at the Rotterdam School of Economics.[108] Six years later the Commission, prompted by the French Government, set up a working group of experts chaired by Professor Sanders to prepare a draft Statute for a uniform type of limited company which could be used throughout the Community without being subject to national law. Straddling frontiers, the European Company would enable a business to operate across borders without the administrative burdens involved in setting up and running subsidiaries, all of which typically remain subject to domestic law. The draft was completed by the end of the following year and served as the basis for the Commission's first Proposal, issued in 1970.[109]

---

[104] Art 4(5).

[105] The Takeover Panel reiterated its opposition to the proposed directive in its 1998 annual report. For an interesting general discussion of the UK's reactions to the proposal see Andenas, M, 'Company Law Reform in the UK and European Harmonisation' in Rider, B A K (ed), *The Corporate Dimension* (1998) 303, 307–13.

[106] For a spirited defence of the Proposal and a well-argued refutation of the UK's arguments centring on these two issues, see Andenas, M, 'European Take-over Regulation and the City Code' (1996) 17 The Company Lawyer 150 and Dine, J, 'The Framework Thirteenth Directive on Takeovers—the Protection of Shareholders and the Basis of Judicial Review of the Panel' in Rider, B A K and Andenas, M (eds), *Developments in European Company Law* (1997).

[107] A useful discussion of the European Company Statute and the background to it, together with several relevant texts, may be found in Dine, J and Hughes, P, *EC Company Law* (1991), ch 3.

[108] Sanders, P, 'Towards a European Company?' Published also in French [1960] Le droit européen 9, German [1960] Aussenwirtschaftsdienst des Betriebsberaters 1, and Italian [1959] Rivista delle Società 1163. The Dutch, English, French, German and Italian texts are collected in Sanders, P, *European Stock Corporation* (1969). For a commentary see Thompson, D, 'The Project for a Commercial Company of European Type' (1961) 10 ICLQ 851. Suggestions for a similar proposal had also been put forward earlier in 1959 at the 57th Congress of French Notaries in Tours.

[109] COM (70) 600 final, 24 June 1970; [1970] JO C124; EC Bull Supp 8/70. For further discussion of the early history leading up to the 1970 proposal see Stein, E, *Harmonization of European Company Laws* (1971) and the sources listed at 424–6, n 267; Thompson, D, 'The Creation of a European Company' (1968) 17 ICLQ 181 and *The Proposal for a European Company* (1969); Sanders, P, 'The

The Proposal[110] was for a Statute to be enacted by way of a regulation based on Article 235 of the Treaty,[111] in contrast to the Sanders draft which had proposed an international convention. The draft regulation would permit a European Company (or Societas Europea, abbreviated to SE, the linguistically neutral term preferred by Professor Sanders) to be formed by public companies from different Member States by way of either a merger between such companies or forming a holding company or joint subsidiaries. The draft Statute was a daunting and ambitious instrument comprising 284 Articles; it sought to regulate all aspects of the European Company, dealing with constitution, capital, organs, employee representation, accounts and audit, groups of companies,[112] amendment of statutes, dissolution and liquidation, transformation into a national company, fusion, and tax. The draft sowed the seeds of its ultimate destruction in the requirement that the company have a two-tier board, executive and supervisory. The supervisory board was to 'exercise permanent control over the management of the company by the executive board';[113] it also had power to advise the executive board on any matters of importance to the company, either on request or of its own initiative,[114] although it was not to intervene directly in the management of the company.[115] Between one-third and one-half of the members of the supervisory board were to be employees' representatives, with the balance appointed by the general meeting.[116]

In 1972 the Economic and Social Committee delivered a broadly favourable Opinion on the 1970 Proposal.[117] The Parliament was also generally supportive, subject to numerous suggested amendments. In 1975 the Commission submitted to the Council an amended Proposal, incorporating many of the Parliament's suggestions including an amendment to the composition of the supervisory board which would consist of one-third shareholders' representatives, one-third employees' representatives and one-third members co-opted by both groups and representing general interests.[118] The amended Proposal was even more complex than

European Company' [1968] JBL 184; Storm, P, 'Statute of a Societas Europea' (1967) 5 CMLR 265; Gordon, M W, 'European Community Company Law', 544–7, in Folsom, R H, Lake, R B and Nanda, V P, *European Community Law after 1992* (1993).

110 For commentaries on the 1970 Proposal see Coleman, R, 'The Fifth Directive and the European Company Statute' [1971] Bulletin of Comparative Labour Relations 247; Ficker, H C, 'A Project for a European Corporation' [1970] JBL 159 and 'The Proposal Statute of a European Corporation' [1971] JBL 167; Sanders, P, 'The European Company on its Way' (1971) 8 CMLR 29 and 'Structure and Progress of the European Company' in Schmitthoff, C M (ed), *The Harmonisation of European Company Law* (1973); Mann, F A, 'The European Company' (1970) 19 ICLQ 468; Hood, J B, 'The European Company Proposal' (1973) 22 ICLQ 434;.

111 See Introduction, p 2.

112 Relevant because two of the means of creating an SE (formation of a holding company or a subsidiary) automatically result in the creation of a group of companies.

113 Art 73(1).   114 Art 73(2).   115 Art 73(3).   116 Art 137.

117 [1972] JO C131.

118 COM (75) 150 final, 19 March 1975; EC Bull Supp 4/75. For commentaries see Sanders, P, 'The European Company' (1976) 6 Georgia Journal of International and Comparative Law 367 and Zec, C E, 'The "Societas Europea"—a European Company—and United States Corporation Laws: a Comparison' [1977] Comparative Law Yearbook 285.

the original Proposal. The Council appointed an ad hoc working party which between 1976 and 1982 worked its way through the first reading of the Proposal. It proved impossible to reach a consensus on such issues as the rules governing groups of companies and the tax provisions, as well as the two-tier board structure and workers' representation. Discussions were eventually suspended in 1982 when completion was made conditional on 'seeing Commission proposals for harmonisation of Member States' legislation of groups of companies.'[119]

In the late 1980s the Commission relaunched the Proposal, issuing first a memorandum on the Societas Europea[120] and shortly thereafter a fresh Proposal for a Council Regulation on the Statute for a European company.[121] The 1989 Proposal abandoned the earlier models of the mandatory two-tier board and employee representation discussed above. Instead, it provided for either a two-tier (management and supervisory) or a one-tier (administrative) board system;[122] employee representation was to be dealt with in a separate directive complementing the Statute for a European company with regard to the involvement of employees in the European company, a Proposal for which was submitted by the Commission to the Council on the same day as the fresh Proposal for the European Company Statute.[123] The proposed directive describes itself as 'an indissociable complement'[124] and 'an essential supplement'[125] to the regulation, the preamble to which states that the directive forms 'an indissociable complement to this Regulation and must be applied concomitantly'.[126]

The proposed directive provided that employee participation was to be determined in accordance with one of the following models:[127] (a) appointment of between one-third and half of the members of the supervisory or administrative board by the company's employees or their representatives or, subject to veto by the employees' representatives or the shareholders in general meeting, co-opted by the board;[128] (b) representation of employees by a separate body, whose composition was to be laid down in the statutes in consultation with the representatives of the employees of the founder companies;[129] or (c) establishment of another model by agreement between the management and administrative boards of the founder companies and the representatives of the employees of those companies.[130] The

---

[119] See Memorandum from the Commission to Parliament, the Council and the two sides of industry, 'Internal Market and Industrial Cooperation—Statute for the European Company—Internal Market White Paper, point 137' COM (88) 320 final, 15 July 1977; EC Bull Supp 3/88.

[120] Cited in n 119 above.

[121] [1989] OJ C263/41; COM (89) 268 final, 25 August 1989; EC Bull Supp 3/88. For an interesting discussion of the background to the 1989 Proposal, see Gordon, M W, 'European Community Company Law' in Folsom, R H, Lake, R B and Nanda, V P (eds), *European Community Law After 1992* (1993), 547–52. For commentaries on the 1989 Proposal, see Gordon, M W, ibid; Wooldridge, F, *Company Law in the United Kingdom and in the European Community: Its Harmonization and Unification* (1991); Murray, J, 'New Concepts in Corporate Law' in Corporate Law: The European Dimension (1991). The UK House of Lords reported on the 1989 Proposal in its 19th Report (Session 1989–90, HL Paper 71).

[122] Art 61.   [123] COM (89) 268 final, 25 August 1989; [1989] OJ C263/69.
[124] 6th recital in the preamble.   [125] Art 1.   [126] 19th recital in the preamble.
[127] Art 3(1).   [128] Art 4.   [129] Art 5.   [130] Art 6.

choice of model was to be determined by agreement between the founder companies' boards and the representatives of their employees provided for by the laws and practices of the Member States; in default of agreement, the choice was to be for the boards.[131]

Further changes since the earlier Proposals included the dropping of provisions seeking to regulate groups (the 1989 Proposal simply referred to certain provisions of the law of the State where the SE had its registered office and the legal system governing the controlling undertaking[132]) and the abandonment of the ambitious attempt to provide a tax framework for the SE's operations (the 1989 Proposal contained only one fiscal provision, relating to the taxation of permanent establishments of an SE[133]). These changes, together with the slimming down of the provisions on accounts and audit made possible by reference to the Fourth, Seventh and Eighth Directives which had been adopted since the earlier Proposals, and the increasing use of references to national law to govern certain issues, resulted in a shorter document: 137 Articles, together with a further thirteen in the complementary worker participation directive.

More fundamentally, the legal basis for the proposed regulation changed from Article 235, which requires unanimity in the Council, to Article 100a, which provides for the adoption by qualified majority in accordance with the cooperation procedure[134] of 'measures for the approximation of the provisions laid down by law, regulation or administrative action in Member States which have as their object the establishment and functioning of the internal market'. It has been argued that, since the European Company is a new entity, a regulation for its statute cannot be a measure for the approximation of national law. Since Article 100a cannot be used for measures relating to the rights and interests of employed persons,[135] the complementary directive is based on Article 54 of the Treaty, which concerns measures for the attainment of freedom of establishment: the choice of Article 54 for a directive concerning the participation of employees in a supra-national entity also seems anomalous.

After delivery of the Opinions of the Parliament[136] and the Economic and Social Committee,[137] the Commission issued an amended Proposal in May 1991.[138] This extended the circumstances in which an SE could be formed to include the conversion of a public limited company with a subsidiary or branch in a Member State

---

[131] Art 3(1).   [132] Art 114.   [133] Art 133.

[134] Which gives the Parliament an enhanced role: see Art 189b of the Treaty.

[135] Art 100a(2). Nor can it be used for fiscal provisions, although the 1989 Proposal contains a tax Article.

[136] [1991] OJ C48/72.   [137] [1990] OJ C124/40.

[138] COM (91) 174 final, 6 May 1991; [1991] OJ C176/1. Commentaries include Wehlau, A, 'The Societas Europea: A Critique of the Commission's 1991 Amended Proposal' (1992) 29 CMLR 473; Israel, S, 'The European Company Statute—"SE"' in Wymeersch, E (ed), *Further Perspectives in Financial Integration in Europe* (1994); Dine, J, 'The European Economic Interest Grouping and the European Company Statute: New Models for Company Law Harmonisation' in Andenas, M and Kenyon-Slade, S (eds), *EC Financial Market Regulation and Company Law* (1993); and Dine, J and Hughes, P, *EC Company Law* (1991), ch 3.

other than that of its central administration.[139] For some years thereafter the Proposal stalled as a result of disagreement at a political level, mainly centring on the complementary worker participation provisions: Germany in particular considered that the legislation should contain mandatory provisions so as to prevent German companies from choosing to form an SE solely in order to avoid national provisions, while other Member States, including the United Kingdom, considered the Proposals excessive.[140] In November 1995 the Commission sent a communication to the Council presenting several options for forms of worker participation in inter alia the management of the SE.[141] A year later, the Commission established a high level group, chaired by Viscount Davignon, to seek a solution to the deadlock. While the Davignon group was deliberating, the Commission was no doubt encouraged by the fact that a majority of the respondents to its consultation paper on company law[142] (Member States, academics and organizations representative of economic interest groups) expressed hope that the European Company Statute would be adopted rapidly, in order to enable companies to take full advantage of the potential of the single market.[143]

The Davignon group reported in May 1997,[144] proposing that, in respect of each European company, the management and the employees should seek to reach an agreement on a system of worker participation, failing which, default 'reference rules' would come into play. In addition, the group proposed that one-fifth of the members of the administrative or supervisory board should be employees' representatives, with a minimum of two members. The reaction of the Commission and Member States, including Germany and the United Kingdom, was initially favourable and negotiations within the Council were resumed in June 1997. However the United Kingdom soon resumed its former stance, finding the proposed default rules for worker participation unacceptable.

Negotiations in the Council continued for another year, enmired in particular in the content of the default provisions, the correct legal basis for the regulation, whether an existing company should be permitted to convert into an SE, and a requirement in the Proposal that the SE's head office be in the same State as its registered office. There was however broad agreement that, in addition to the Davignon principles of free negotiation and default rules, in each case there should be a Special Negotiating Body made up of employee representatives and management in accordance with specified geographical and proportional criteria and that

---

[139] Arts 2(3) and 37a.

[140] The UK also has concerns about the protection of creditors in the event of an SE transferring its head office from one Member State to another.

[141] Communication on worker information and consultation, COM (95) 547 final, 14 November 1995.

[142] Circulated in February 1997: see further ch XX.

[143] *Analysis of Replies to Commission Consultation Paper on Company Law* (XV/6013/97), point 1(a).

[144] The text of the report may be found in Dine, J and Hughes, P, *EC Company Law* (1991) (which, since the work is loose-leaf, is up-to-date to 1998), A3.77–A3.126.

employees' rights to information and consultation should broadly reflect those laid down in the Works Council Directive.[145]

In April 1998 the United Kingdom, in a last-ditch bid to secure agreement on the regulation during its Presidency of the Council, put forward a further compromise on worker participation. It proposed inter alia that, where an SE was formed by merger of existing companies, the employee participation rights applying to employees of the merging companies should continue to apply to the SE, except where two-thirds of the employees decide otherwise, and that in other situations there should be no obligation to introduce worker participation to the SE subject to agreement to the contrary within the Special Negotiating Body. This compromise was substantially accepted,[146] although other areas remained contentious. Finally however, the Proposal stalled once again. In view of its forthcoming parliamentary elections in September 1998 and the politically explosive nature of any concession on employees' participation, Germany requested that consideration of the Proposal be postponed for a few months. Moreover two stumbling blocks remained, namely the voting rules within the Special Negotiating Body (France, Spain and Italy objected to the proposal whereby one-third of the employees could in effect insist on importing participation provisions from another Member State) and the question whether an SE may be constituted by transformation of an existing company (Ireland, supported by Italy, Spain, the United Kingdom and Greece, objecting to the proposed dropping of that possibility).

Whether the European Company Statute will be adopted remains to be seen. For a brief window, the requisite but elusive political will seemed to be there. If it is adopted, the compromise as to worker participation which that will necessarily represent may well pave the way for a resumption of negotiations on the draft Tenth Directive, also deadlocked as a result of German fears that its employee participation legislation will be undermined by the structures put in place by the directive.

---

[145] Council Directive (EC) 94/45 on the establishment of a European Works Council or a procedure in Community-scale undertakings and Community-scale groups of undertakings for the purposes of informing and consulting employees [1994] OJ L254/64.

[146] The Economic and Social Committee, which issued an Opinion on the proposed compromise, also broadly endorsed it subject to certain suggestions: [1998] OJ C129/3.

XX

Conclusion and Outlook

Much of this book has been devoted to tracing the development and adoption of the company law and securities directives proposed by the Commission in the last thirty years. After a steady stream of important legislation in the 1970s and 1980s, the harmonization programme seemed to stagnate for a decade.[1] The preceding chapter has outlined some of the reasons for this decline in legislative activity and shown how the Commission's more recent approach, coupled with a revival of political enthusiasm for particular areas of company law harmonization, has breathed fresh life into certain ailing and aged Proposals. This conclusion reviews the Commission's current initiatives in relation to company law harmonization, from which the contours of the likely future action at Community level can be clearly discerned.

The Commission had an active year on the company law front in 1997, starting with consultation and concluding with a conference. The final stage of the process will be a communication outlining the legislative steps which it intends to pursue in the near future. The results of the consultation and conference are considered below, after a brief outline of the study commissioned as a starting-point for the consultation.

The Ernst & Young study

Before it began its formal consultation process, the Commission commissioned a study on corporate governance under the responsibility of Ernst & Young, with a view to determining whether harmonization of national laws on the structure of public companies would be desirable and in particular whether the draft Fifth Directive was legally and economically relevant.[2] Lawyers and economists from all Member States participated in the study, which started with an overview of corporate governance regulation across the Community. The study concluded that there was need for simplification and adaptation in relation to administration and management, internal and external supervision, shareholders' rights and obligations, voting rights and the principle of proportionality between voting rights and subscribed capital, the protection of minority shareholders and the liability of

---

[1] See ch I for a discussion of the evolution of company law harmonization in the Community and an evaluation of the harmonization programme.

[2] *The Simplification of the Operating Regulations for Public Limited Companies in the European Union* (1996).

directors towards third parties. It suggested means of implementing its recommendations and considered the extent to which the stalled Proposal for a Fifth Directive[3] met the needs which it had identified.

Of particular interest are the four essential lessons, set out below, which Ernst & Young, responsible for the study, believe may be drawn from it.[4]

Corporate mobility

Forty years after the Treaty of Rome was signed, free movement of companies is still not a reality: in particular, they cannot change their seat, merge across borders or convert into a company of another Member State. The study identified employee participation and dual management as the fundamental stumbling blocks. It pointed out that, because of size thresholds for employee participation, those issues concerned fewer than 1 per cent of European companies. Progress could be made in the significant sector of companies falling below those thresholds.

The need for objective criteria for corporate governance regulation

The study proposed two criteria for the imposition of corporate governance structures on a company, namely the number of shareholders and the size of the undertaking. It stressed that the approach followed by several company law directives, namely subjecting companies to specific rules by virtue of their corporate form alone (usually regulating public companies), was unsatisfactory and not in line with economic reality: patterns of public versus private company operation varied widely between Member States, with Germany, for example, having a mere 3,000 public companies whereas Spain had 250,000.

Information

It was noted that there were significant differences in the quality of access to commercial information, that presentation of information was not harmonized and that there was in general insufficient recourse to modern communication techniques. The study considered that all three areas called for progress.

Awareness of harmonization

In compiling the study it was observed that much of the domestic legislation implementing the adopted company law directives made no reference to its European origins. This could have negative consequences. Lawyers in one Member State may, for example, have no idea that certain national laws have a counterpart throughout the Community. Moreover, greater awareness of successfully adopted and implemented directives would help counterbalance awareness of stalled Proposals and improve the image of Community company law.[5]

---

[3] See ch XIX.
[4] See *Acts of the Conference on Company Law and the Single Market* (1997), 11–13.
[5] This point is of particular relevance to the UK: see pp 410–11 below.

The consultation exercise

In February 1997 the Commission began a process of consultation of Member States and interested parties with a view to helping it draw up a work programme for company law to meet real needs.[6] In December 1997 it published an analysis of the replies it had received to its consultation paper.[7] Two conflicting themes could be identified: on the one hand, many respondents felt that, without a cross-border corporate structure, cross-border mergers and cross-border transfer of seat, much work remained; on the other hand, there was a view that, like Penelope, the Commission should start unweaving the legislation it had patiently woven over the last thirty years,[8] liberating companies by deregulating, simplifying and applying the principle of subsidiarity. The latter camp was, however, in the minority. The broad consensus was as follows.

Corporate mobility

An overwhelming majority of respondents were in favour of the establishment of a Community legal framework guaranteeing genuine free movement of companies throughout the Community which would in particular permit cross-border mergers and the cross-border transfer of seat without any change of legal personality, provided that such transfers, like mergers,[9] could be fiscally neutral.

Simplification

Apart from the Accounts Directives, the subject of a separate exercise,[10] the main areas where a need for simplification at Community level was perceived were the provisions on disclosure in the First Directive and certain provisions in the Second Directive dealing with capital.

Corporate governance

There was consultation on a number of separate points relating to corporate governance. The overall conclusion was that, given the extreme diversity of national rules and practices, much of this sphere should be left to the Member States. There were however specific areas where Community action would be helpful.

(1) A majority of respondents favoured Community-wide definitions of common principles of corporate governance for large companies and of the criteria for such companies, although it was felt that the detailed rules should be left to the

---

[6] *Commission Consultation Paper on Company Law.*

[7] *Analysis of Replies to Commission Consultation Paper on Company Law* (XV/6013/97).

[8] Blanquet, F, 'Analysis Of The Responses Received On The Questionnaire' in *Acts of the Conference on Company Law and the Single Market* (1997) 15–23.

[9] Council Directive (EEC) 90/434 on the common system of taxation applicable to mergers, divisions, transfers of assets, and exchanges of shares concerning companies from different Member States [1990] OJ L225/1.

[10] See ch V.

Member States. An overwhelming majority opposed board representation of minority shareholders, although it was accepted that in 'open' companies (companies with widely held shares) holders of 5 per cent or 10 per cent of the capital should have certain rights, namely to convene a general meeting, to form associations to defend their interests and to be bought out in certain circumstances. Conversely, in certain circumstances majority shareholders should have the right to buy out specified minorities. In both cases there was consensus that there should be Community legislation.

(2)   There was a general view that the setting up of committees to monitor management in large companies should not be regulated by law.

(3)   There was broad acceptance of the principle that voting rights should be in proportion to the capital subscribed. A majority favoured the abolition of shares with multiple voting rights and of ceilings on voting rights; the abolition of non-voting shares however was opposed. Simplification of the exercise of voting rights so as to encourage participation in general meetings also received strong support.

(4)   The majority expressed themselves satisfied with national laws on management liability, but there was support for the idea of defining the apportionment of liability between individual directors and the company.

(5)   Finally, there was strong support for relaxing corporate governance rules for small and closely held companies.

Information

The Commission's suggestion of a single standardized multilingual document for the provision of information in commercial registers was widely welcomed.

Forum

Finally, a large majority supported the idea of a company law forum, where company law issues could be debated with a view to better preparation of further Community initiatives.

The conference

The results of the consultation exercise were further debated at a two-day conference on company law and the single market organized by the Commission in December 1997.[11] Discussion focused in particular on the Commission's three priority proposals for corporate mobility, namely the European Company Statute, the draft Tenth Directive on cross-border mergers and the draft Proposal for a Fourteenth Directive on the cross-border transfer of seat[12] without a change of legal personality.

With regard to corporate governance, the Commission accepted that any general Community-wide regulation of many of the issues raised would be precluded

---

[11] See *Acts of the Conference on Company Law and the Single Market* (1997).
[12] Registered office or *de facto* head office.

by the principle of subsidiarity. It none the less encouraged discussion of whether it was possible to define groups of companies for which a degree of harmonization of corporate governance practices was desirable and, if so, what form the harmonization should take. Other possible candidates for Community legislation in this area included the principle of 'one share one vote' and certain rights *vis-à-vis* minority shareholders.

Finally, the conference addressed the implications of modern communication techniques and in particular how they could improve access to company information.

The conclusions drawn by the Director-General of DG XV, Mr John Mogg, from the proceedings at the conference confirmed the Commission's view that the Proposals for the European Company Statute, the Tenth Directive on cross-border mergers, the Thirteenth Directive on takeovers and the Fourteenth Directive on cross-border transfers of seat,[13] notwithstanding the great age of the first two, were more relevant today than ever before. As the single market becomes an economic reality, partitions arising from company law structures increasingly seem anomalous and the need for progress on the outstanding instruments becomes increasingly pressing. Further areas where work will be needed in the near future include complementary legislation regulating the tax treatment of the European company and the tax consequences of a transfer of seat.

No specific plans were announced for the simplification of company law directives already adopted, although the Commission indicated that it was open to reasoned suggestions.

Finally, it was announced that a company law forum would be set up to address in particular, and it was hoped with the support of industry, the issues of corporate governance which the consultation exercise had suggested could benefit from Community legislation and the question of applying modern communication methods to company law areas.

Auditors

In the context of corporate governance, the Commission in summing up the conference referred to its Green Paper, published in 1996,[14] which has since been followed by its Communication on the statutory audit in the European Union: the way forward.[15] The communication expresses the Commission's concerns that the lack of a harmonized view of the role and liability of auditors has a negative impact on audit quality and hence on confidence in audited accounts. That could become an obstacle in current international negotiations with a view to improving the access of European companies to international capital markets, since European

[13] Registered office or *de facto* head office.
[14] *The Role, the Position and the Liability of the Statutory Auditor within the European Union* [1996] OJ C321/1.
[15] [1998] OJ C143/12.

company accounts will not be accepted on those markets unless they have been audited in accordance with internationally accepted standards.

The Communication proposes setting up a Committee on auditing, composed of government experts nominated by Member States together with representatives of national auditing standards boards and the accounting profession. The Committee's most urgent task will be to review international auditing standards in a Community context. Improvements in quality control in the auditing field, which currently vary widely between Member States, are also needed. Discussion will in addition focus on the scope for strengthening the position of the auditor within the corporate structure, for example by way of audit committees. The Commission indicates that it will examine in more detail the issue of auditors' liability with a view to judging whether legislation is necessary. Finally, the Commission will review the effectiveness for auditors of the General Directive on Mutual Recognition[16] and in the light of that consider the feasibility of a sectoral directive on freedom to provide services.

Assessment

It remains to be seen whether the Commission's enthusiastic forecasts of forth-coming agreement on the critical legislative foundations of genuine cross-border corporate mobility, namely the European Company Statute and the draft Tenth, Thirteenth and Fourteenth Directives, are realized. If so, the basic framework of a truly European company law laboriously constructed over three decades will be completed. There will remain additional elements required to complete the struc-ture: alignment of the Community requirements for consolidated accounts with international accounting standards is becoming increasingly imperative; certain issues of corporate governance could usefully by addressed at a Community level; and some action is needed on coordinating national laws on auditors' liability and other aspects of auditing relevant to audit quality generally. The Commission is clearly keen to consult with experts and practitioners wherever possible in these areas, so that it may be hoped that the next round of specific company law initia-tives will reflect economic realities and be welcomed by industry.

Company law in the United Kingdom

In the United Kingdom, much of the companies and securities legislation enacted since our accession to the Community, including the Companies Acts 1980, 1981 and 1989, implements Community legislation. The result is that the bulk of the national legislation on ultra vires, pre-incorporation contracts, maintenance and

---

[16] Council Directive (EEC) 89/48 on a general system for the recognition of higher-education diplomas awarded on completion of professional education and training of at least three years' duration [1989] OJ L19/16.

alteration of capital, annual and consolidated accounts, qualification of auditors, Stock Exchange listing conditions and public offers of listed and unlisted securities, acquisitions and disposals of major shareholdings, and insider dealing derives from Community Directives. The impact of these directives 'is such that no company lawyer can operate without a secure knowledge of the Community dimension'.[17] Company lawyers in the United Kingdom frequently give the impression, however, of a Nelson-like blindness to European influences, perfectly illustrating the point made by Ernst & Young in their study that awareness of Community company law may focus disproportionately on negative aspects.

A particularly striking recent example may be found in the consultation paper on company law, *Modern Company Law for a Competitive Economy*, issued by the Department of Trade and Industry in March 1998 to launch a 'thorough and wide-ranging review of our core company law'. The document opens with the statement: 'Our current framework of company law is essentially constructed on foundations which were put in place by the Victorians in the middle of the last century'. The final paragraph of the final substantive chapter states: 'A number of EC directives have an impact on company law; and the review will of course take these into account'.[18] Before that, apart from a brief reference to the Companies Act 1989 having implemented the Seventh Directive, there are only two references to EC company law, both negative: implementation of the directives is stated to have left national legislation 'in a worse state than at any time this century'[19] and the Second Directive is cited for its blocking effect on any amendment to certain domestic provisions on capital maintenance.[20]

The decision of the Court of Justice in *Marleasing v La Comercial Internacional de Alimentación*[21]—described by the British judge at the Court, David Edward, as 'a case of particular significance for British company lawyers who are used to looking at the Companies Acts without regard to the underlying Community directives'[22]—illustrates the principle that, in interpreting the provisions of national law implementing the company law directives, national courts are required to do so, as far as possible, in the light of the wording and the purpose of the directive in order to achieve the result pursued by the latter.[23] Company law practitioners cannot afford to ignore the Community foundations of their national legislation.

Conclusion

It has been stated that 'the European effort to harmonize corporate laws seems . . . to be a process in search of a justification'.[24] A review of the harmonization

---

[17] Weatherill, S and Beaumont, P, *EC Law* (1995), 601. [18] Para 6.7.
[19] Para 2.6. [20] Para 3.2. [21] Case C–106/89 [1990] ECR I–4135.
[22] 'Corporations and the Court' in *Corporate Law—The European Dimension* (1991) 149, 155.
[23] Para 8.
[24] Charny, D, 'Competition among Jurisdictions in Formulating Corporate Law Rules: An American Perspective on the "Race to the Bottom" in the European Communities' (1991) 32 Harvard International Law Journal 423, 424.

programme in the light of the Commission's recent consultation suggests that on the contrary the achievements have been not only many but necessary and largely appreciated. The current outstanding instruments are keenly awaited and industry is enthusiastic about cooperating with the Commission to focus legislative attention where it is next needed. The next few years should prove to be among the most interesting in the brief history of company law harmonization: the essential political will seems to be present for adopting legislation of major significance for the single market and thus paving the way for the next stage.

Bibliography

Articles and contributions to books

(Articles and contributions dealing with specific cases and legislation are listed in the footnotes to the relevant chapter;   the following items are of more general interest)

Andenas, M, 'Company Law Reform in the UK and European Harmonisation' in Rider, B. A. K. (ed), *The Corporate Dimension* (1998)

Ault, H. J., 'Harmonization of Company Law in the European Economic Community' (1968) 20 Hastings Law Journal 77

Baltic, C. V., 'The Next Step in Insider Trading Regulation: International Cooperative Efforts in the Global Securities Market' (1991–2) 23 Law & Policy in International Business 167

Benoit-Moury, A, 'Droit Européen des sociétés et interprétations des juridictions communautaires' [1993] Revue de droit international et de droit comparé 105

Boyle, A. J., 'The Recognition of Companies in the EEC' in Goode, RM and Simmonds, KR (eds) *Commercial Operations in Europe* (1978)

Brazier, G, 'The Problem with Securities Law' [1994] NLJ 469

Cath, I. G. F., 'Freedom of Establishment of Companies: a New Step Towards Completion of the Internal Market' (1986) 6 Yearbook of European Law 247

Cath, I. G. F., 'Free Movement of Legal Persons' in *Free Movement of Persons in Europe: Legal Problems and Experiences* (1993)

Charny, D, 'Competition among Jurisdictions in Formulating Corporate Law Rules: An American Perspective on the "Race to the Bottom" in the European Communities' (1991) 32 Harvard International Law Journal 423

Clarke, M. G., 'The Conflicts of Law Dimension' in *Corporate Law - The European Dimension* (1991)

Diephuis, J. H., 'Recognition of Foreign Companies and Bodies Corporate' [1980] Netherlands International Law Review 347

Dine, J, 'The Harmonization of Company Law in the European Community' (1989) 9 Yearbook of European Law 93

Dine, J, 'The Community Company Law Harmonisation Programme' (1989) 14 ELR 322

Edward, D, 'Establishment and Services: An Analysis of the Insurance Cases' (1987) 12 ELR 231

Edward, D, 'Corporations and the Court' in *Corporate Law - The European Dimension* (1991)

Emlyn Davies, J. A., 'Company Law and the Common Market: The First Step' in *An Introduction to the Law of the European Economic Community* (1972)

Ficker, H. C., 'The EEC Directives on Company Law Harmonisation' in Schmitthoff, CM (ed), *The Harmonisation of European Company Law* (1973)

Fitchew, G, 'The European Dimension in Company Law' (1992) 13 The Company Lawyer 5

Frommel, S. N., 'The Real Seat Doctrine and Dual-Resident Companies under German Law: Another View' [1990] European Taxation 267

Gaillard, E and Pingel, I, 'Les opérations d'initiés dans la Communauté économique européenne' (1990) 26 Revue trimestrielle de droit européen 329

Gammie, M, 'UK Company Residence: The New Rules' [1988] Intertax 416

Garzaniti, L, 'Single Market-Making: EC Regulation of Securities Markets' (1993) 14 The Company Lawyer 43

Gleichmann, K, 'The Law of Corporate Groups in the European Community' in Sugarman, S and Teubner, G (eds) *Regulating Corporate Groups in Europe* (1990)

Goldman, B, 'The Convention between the Member States of the European Economic Community on the Mutual Recognition of Companies and Legal Persons' (1968) 6 CML Rev 104

Gordon, M. W., 'European Community Law' in Folsom, RH, Lake, RB and Nanda, VP (eds), *European Community Law after 1992* (1993)

Gower, L. C. B., '"Big Bang" and City Regulation' (1988) 51 MLR 1

Großfeld, B and Erlinghagen, S, 'European Company and Economic Law' in De Witte, B and Forder, C (eds) *The Common law of Europe and the Future of Legal Education* (1992)

Houin, R, 'Le régime juridique des sociétés dans la Communauté Economique Européenne' [1965] Revue trimestrielle de droit européen 11

Hurst, J. E., 'Harmonization of Company Law in EEC' (1974) 2 Legal Issues of European Integration 63

Keeling, E and Shipwright, A, 'Some Taxing Problems Concerning Non-Discrimination and the EC Treaty' (1995) 20 ELR 580

Knobbe-Keuk, B, 'Restrictions on the Fundamental Freedoms Enshrined in the EC Treaty by Discriminatory Tax Provisions - Ban and Justification' [1994] EC Tax Review 74

Latty, E. R., 'Pseudo-Foreign Corporations' (1955) 65 Yale Law Journal 137

Lee, R, 'Should There Be a European Securities Commission? A Framework for Analysis' (1992) 3 European Business Law Review 102

Leleux, P, 'Corporation Law in the United States and in the EEC' (1967) 5 CML Rev 133

Lempereur, C, 'Myth and Reality in the European Harmonization Process' in Wymeersch, E (ed), *Further Perspectives in Financial Integration in Europe* (1994)

Loussouarn, Y, 'Le droit d'établissement des sociétés' (1990) 26 Revue trimestrielle de droit européen 229

Lutter, M, 'The law of groups of companies in Europe' (1983) 1 Forum Internationale

Lyons, T, 'Discrimination Against Individuals and Enterprises on Grounds of

Nationality: Direct Taxation and the Court of Justice' (1995–96) 1 EC Tax Journal 27

Morse, G, 'Mutual Recognition of Companies in England and the EEC' [1992] JBL 195

Murray, J, 'New Concepts in Corporate Law' in *Corporate Law - The European Dimension* (1991)

Niessen, H, 'Aims, Objectives and Achievements of The Company Law Harmonization Programme' (1984) 7 Journal of the Irish Society for European Law 1

Nobes, C. W., 'The Harmonisation of Company Law Relating to the Published Accounts of Companies' (1980) 5 ELR 38

Olivier, H, 'Perspectives du contrôle légal des comptes dans la communauté européenne' (1989) 66 Revue de droit international et de droit comparé 209

Pennington, R. R., 'Company Law in the EEC' (1972) 1 Anglo-American Law Review 187

Pennington, R. R., 'Prospectuses for Securities Offered to the Public' (1983) 4 The Company Lawyer 151

Prentice, D. D., 'Some Reflections on the Harmonisation of Company Law: An English Perspective' in De Witte, B and Forder, C (eds), *The Common law of Europe and the Future of Legal Education* (1992)

Proctor, C, 'Share Capital and the Euro – Redenominating Shares' [April 1998] Practical Law for Companies 17

Raaijmakers, M. J. G. C., 'Which Way With Company Law Harmonization?' in Wymeersch, E (ed), *Further Perspectives in Financial Integration in Europe* (1994)

Reid, D and Ballheimer, A, 'The Legal Framework of the Securities Industry in the European Community under the 1992 Programme' (1991) 29 Columbia Journal of Transnational Law 103

Reindl, A, 'Companies in the European Community: Are the Conflict-of-Law Rules Ready for 1992?' (1990) 11 Michigan Journal of International Law 1270

Rodière, R, 'L'harmonisation des législations européennes dans le cadre de la C.E.E.' [1965] Revue trimestrielle de droit européen 336

Sanders, P, 'Review of Recent Literature on Corporation Law' (1966) 4 CML Rev 113

Schmitthoff, C. M., 'New Concepts in Company Law' [1973] JBL 312

Schmitthoff, C. M., 'The Success of the Harmonisation of European Company Law' (1976) 1 ELR 100

Schmitthoff, C. M., 'Company and Commercial Law in Europe' in Cheng, C-J (ed), *Clive M Schmitthoff's Select Essays on International Trade Law* (1988)

Schmitthoff, C. M., 'The European Prospectus' in *Recht und Wirtschaft in Geschichte und Gegenwart: Festschrift für Johannes Bärmann zum 70. Geburtstag* (1975)

Schneebaum, S. M., 'The Company Law Harmonization Program of the European Community' (1982) 14 Law & Policy in International Business 293

Scholten, Y, 'Company Law in Europe' (1967) 4 CML Rev 377

Suckow, S, 'The European Prospectus' (1975) 23 AJCL 50

Timmermans, C. W. A., 'The Convention of 29 February 1968 on the Mutual Recognition of Companies and Firms' (1980) Netherlands International Law Review 357

Tridimas, T, 'The Case-Law of the European Court of Justice on Corporate Entities' (1993) 13 Yearbook of European Law 348

Tridimas, T, 'Insider Trading: European Harmonisation and National Law Reform' (1991) 40 ICLQ 919

Tunc, A, 'A French lawyer looks at British company law' (1985) 45 MLR 1

Van der Tas, LG, 'European Accounting Harmonization: Achievements, Prospects and Tax Implications' [1992] Intertax 178

Van Hulle, K, 'The EEC Accounting Directives in Perspective: Problems of Harmonization' (1981) 18 CML Rev 121

Van Ommeslaghe, P, 'La Première Directive du Conseil du 9 mars 1968 en Matière de Sociétés' [1969] Cahiers de droit européen 495

Van Raad, K, 'The Impact of the EC Treaty's Fundamental Freedoms Provisions on EU Member States' Taxation in Border-crossing Situations - Current State of Affairs' [1995] EC Tax Review 190

Vermeend, W, 'The Court of Justice of the European Communities and direct taxes: "Est-ce que la justice est de ce monde?"' [1996] EC Tax Review 54

Warren, M. G., 'Global Harmonization of Securities Laws: the Achievement of the European Communities' (1990) 31 Harvard International Law Journal 185

Warren, M. G., 'The Common Market Prospectus' (1989) 26 CML Rev 687

Welch, J, 'The English Private Company - A Crisis of Classification' [1974] JBL 277

Welch, J, 'The Harmonisation of Company Laws in the EEC' in Panebianco, M (ed) Europa Comunitaria e America Latina (1983)

Werlauff, E, 'The Development of Community Company Law' (1992) 17 ELR 207

Willott, B, 'EC Capital Markets' in Corporate Law - The European Dimension (1991)

Wolff, G, 'The Commission's Programme for Company Law Harmonisation: The Winding Road to a Uniform Company Law?' in Andenas, M, and Kenyon-Slade, S, (eds) EC Financial Market Regulation and Company Law (1993)

Wolff, S, 'Securities Regulation' in Folsom, RH, Lake, RB and Nanda, VP (eds) European Community Law after 1992 (1993)

Wooldridge, F, 'The Harmonization of Company Law: The First and Second Directives of the Council of Ministers of the European Economic Community' [1978] Acta Juridica 327

Wooldridge, F, 'The Definition of a Group of Companies in European Law' [1982] JBL 272

Wooldridge, F, 'Some Recent Community Legislation in the Field of Securities Law' (1985) 10 ELR 3

Wouters, J, 'EC Harmonisation of National Rules Concerning Securities Offering,

Stock Exchange Listing and Investment Services: An Overview' (1993) 4 European Business Law Review 199

Wouters, J, 'The Case-Law of the European Court of Justice on Direct Taxes: Variations upon a Theme' (1994) 1 Maastricht Journal of European and Comparative Law 179

Wymeersch, E, 'The Regulation of Insider Dealing within the European Community' in *Insider Dealing: Papers from the I.C.E.L. Conference October 1990* (1990)

Wymeersch, E, 'L'action de la Communauté européenne dans le domaine des valeurs mobilières' (1988) 3 Revue de droit des affaires internationales 365

Wymeersch, E, 'From Harmonization to Integration in the European Securities Markets' (1981) 3 Journal of Comparative Corporate Law and Securities Regulation 1

Books

Andenas, M, and Kenyon-Slade, S (eds) *EC Financial Market Regulation and Company Law* (1993)

Argitidis, D. K., *Groups of Companies: The Liability of the Parent Company for the Debts of its Subsidiary* (1996)

Bergmans, B, *Inside Information and Securities Trading* (1991)

Burrows, F, *Free Movement in European Community Law* (1987)

Buttaro, L and Patroni Griffi, A (eds) *La Seconda Direttiva CEE in Materia Societaria* (1984)

Butterworths' *Compendium of EC Company Law* (1990)

Buxbaum, R. M. and Hopt, K. J., *Legal Harmonization and the Business Enterprise* (1988)

Buxbaum, R. M., Hertig, G, Hirsch, A and Hopt, K. J., *European Business Law* (1991)

Buxbaum, R. M., Hertig, G, Hirsch, A and Hopt, K. J., *European Economic and Business Law* (1996)

Cerexhe, E, *Le droit européen - La libre circulation des personnes et des entreprises* (1982)

Corporate Law - The European Dimension (1991)

Davies, P. L., *Gower's Principles of Modern Company Law* (6th edn, 1997)

De Kluiver, H.-J., and Van Gerven, W (eds) *The European Private Company?* (1995)

De Witte, B and Forder, C (eds) *The Common Law of Europe and the Future of Legal Education* (1992)

Dorresteijn, A, Kuiper, I, Morse, G, *European Corporate Law* (1994)

Engrácia Antunes, J, *Liability of Corporate Groups* (1994)

European Commission, *Acts of the Conference on Company Law and the Single Market*

Farmer, P and Lyal, R, *EC Tax Law* (1994)

Goode, R. M. and Simmonds, K. R. (eds) *Commercial Operations in Europe* (1978)

Gower, L. C. B., *Gower's Principles of Modern Company Law* (4th edn, 1979)

Gower, L. C. B., *Gower's Principles of Modern Company Law* (5th edn, 1992)

Hannigan, B, *Insider Dealing* (2nd edn, 1994)

Hughes, P and Dine, J, *EC Company Law* (1991)

Hopt, K. J. and Wymeersch, E (eds) *European Company and Financial Law* (1994)

Hopt, K. J. and Wymeersch, E (eds) *European Insider Dealing* (1991)

Izquierdo, M, *Los Mercados de Valores en la CEE* (1992)

Karayanni, F. A., *Les sociétés d'une seule personne dans le droit des états membres de la Communauté européenne* (1992)

KPMG European Business Centre, Brussels, *Study on Transfer of the Head Office of a Company from One Member State to Another* (1993)

Pennington, R. R. and Wooldridge, F, *Company Law in the European Communities* (1982)

Rider, B, *Insider Trading* (1983)

Rider, B and Ashe, R. M., *Insider Crime* (1993)

Rider, B and Ffrench, H. L., *The Regulation of Insider Trading* (1979)

Romano Orlando, P, *Borse Valori e Interpenetrazione dei Mercati Nella Comunità Europea* (1984)

Santa Maria, A, *EC Commercial Law* (1996)

Schmitthoff, C. M, (ed) *The Harmonisation of European Company Law* (1973)

Smit, H and Herzog, P. E., *The Law of the European Economic Community - A Commentary on the EEC Treaty* (1979)

Steil, B, *Illusions of Liberalization: Securities Regulation in Japan and the EC* (1995)

Stein, E, *Harmonization of European Company Laws* (1971)

Sugarman, S and Teubner, G, *Regulating Corporate Groups in Europe* (1990)

Suter, J, *The Regulation of Insider Dealing in Britain* (1989)

Terra, B and Wattel, P, *European Tax Law* (2nd edn, 1997)

Wachter, B, Van Hulle, K, Landau, W, Schaafsma, J and Raaijmakers, M, *Harmonization of company and securities law—The European and American approach* (1989)

Walmsley K, (ed) *Butterworths Company Law Handbook* (11th edn, 1997)

Weatherill, S, and Beaumont, P, *EC Law—The essential guide to the legal workings of the European Community* (2nd edn, 1995)

Werlauff, E, *EC Company Law: The common denominator for business undertakings in 12 states* (1993)

Wooldridge, F, *Company Law in the United Kingdom and the European Community* (1991)

Wouters, J, and Schneider, H (eds) *Current Issues of Cross-Border Establishment of Companies in the European Union* (1995)

Wymeersch, E (ed) *Groups of Companies in the EEC* (1993)

Wymeersch, E (ed) *Further Perspectives in Financial Integration in Europe* (1994)

Recent articles not referred to in the text

Arden, Mary, 'True and fair view: a European perspective' (1997) 6 The European Accounting Review 675

Blanaid, C, 'The Draft 13th Directive and Employees—an Irish Law Perspective' (1998) 9 European Business Law Review 311

Caprasse, J.-N. and Setareh, S, 'Dèminor Corporate Governance Survey—A poll among 110 European institutional investors—A study on 248 European corporations from 9 countries' (1998) 9 European Business Law Review 326

Drury, R, 'The Prospects for a European Close Company' (1998) 9 European Business Law Review 24

Macgregor, L and Villiers, C, 'Independence of Auditors' (1998) 9 European Business Law Review 318

Noack, U, 'Modern Communications Methods and Company Law' (1998) 9 European Business Law Review 100

Shrimpton, C, 'The Financial Services Authority' [October 1998] Practical Law for Companies 14

Van Hulle, K, 'Communication from the Commission on the Statutory Audit in the European Union: the way forward' (1998) 9 European Business Law Review 298

Viandier, A, 'Free Movement and Mobility of Companies' (1998) 9 European Business Law Review 301

Watkins, O, 'The Proposals for Regulatory Reform of Financial Services in the United Kingdom' (1998) 9 European Business Law Review 107

Werlauff, E, 'Common European Company Law: Status 1998 (1)—Equal treatment of domicile under company law and related concepts' (1998) 9 European Business Law Review 169

Werlauff, E, 'Common European Company Law: Status 1998 (2)—The Background to Harmonisation, Disclosure, Capital etc' (1998) 9 European Business Law Review 210

Werlauff, E, 'Common European Company Law: Status 1998 (3)—Group, Company Structure, New Company Forms etc' (1998) 9 European Business Law Review 274

Wooldridge, F, 'Liability of members of German *Vorstand* (executive board)' [1998] Journal of the Society for Advanced Legal Studies 27

Index